Cambridge Mentalization-Based Treatment (MBT)

A complete and practical guide that offers a concise overview of mentalization-based treatment (MBT) and its application in different situations and with different groups of patients to help improve the treatment of mental health disorders. Featuring an introduction to mentalizing and the evidence base to support it, followed by an explanation of the principles of MBT and the basic clinical model in individual and group psychotherapy. Individual chapters offer extensive clinical illustrations of the treatment of patients with depression, psychosis, trauma, eating disorders, and borderline, antisocial, narcissistic, and avoidant personality disorders. The final section of the book outlines the application of mentalizing and MBT in different populations (children, adolescents, families, and couples) and in different settings (the professional community, schools, parental and foster care, and emergency care settings).

Part of the Cambridge Guides to the Psychological Therapies series, offering all the latest scientifically rigorous and practical information on the full range of key, evidence-based psychological interventions for clinicians.

Anthony Bateman is Consultant to the Anna Freud Centre, London, Visiting Professor at University College London, and Honorary Professor in Psychotherapy at the University of Copenhagen, Denmark.

Peter Fonagy is Director of the Division of Psychology and Language Sciences at University College London, Chief Executive of the Anna Freud Centre, London, and National Clinical Advisor on Children and Young People's Mental Health for NHS England.

Chloe Campbell is Deputy Director of the Psychoanalysis Unit at University College London. She is series co-editor of the Anna Freud Centre/Routledge Best Practice Series.

Patrick Luyten is Professor of Clinical Psychology at the Faculty of Psychology and Educational Sciences, University of Leuven, Belgium, and Professor of

Psychodynamic Psychology at the Research Department of Clinical, Educational, and Health Psychology, University College London.

Martin Debbané is Professor of Clinical Psychology at the Faculty of Psychology and Educational Sciences at the University of Geneva, Switzerland, and Professor of Psychopathology at the Research Department of Clinical, Educational, and Health Psychology, University College London.

Cambridge Guides to the Psychological Therapies

Series Editor

Patricia Graham
Consultant Clinical Psychologist, NHS Lanarkshire, UK

The go-to resource for up-to-date, scientifically rigorous, and practical information on key, evidence-based psychological interventions.

This series of clinical handbooks provides clear and concise guides to understanding and delivering therapy, and offers clinicians a handy reference for matching a specific therapy to a particular patient. Each book follows a consistent style, with chapters on theory, technique, indications, and efficacy, so that healthcare professionals can move seamlessly between different volumes to learn about various therapies in a consistent, familiar, and trusted format. The books also provide guidance on relevant adaptations for each therapy, such as for children, adolescents, and older people, as well as different methods of delivery, such as group interventions and digital therapy.

Books available in the series

Cambridge Guide to Cognitive Behavioural Therapy (CBT)
Jessica Davies, Kenneth Laidlaw and Paul Salkovskis

Cambridge Guide to Cognitive Behavioral Analysis System of Psychotherapy (CBASP)
Massimo Tarsia, Todd Favorite and James McCullough Jr.

Cambridge Guide to Dialectical Behaviour Therapy (DBT)
Jim Lyng, Christine Dunkley, Janet Feigenbaum, Amy Gaglia and Michaela Swales

Cambridge Guide to Interpersonal Psychotherapy (IPT)
Laura Dietz, Fiona Duffy and Patricia Graham

Cambridge Guide to Mentalization-Based Treatment (MBT)
Anthony Bateman, Peter Fonagy, Chloe Campbell, Patrick Luyten and Martin Debbané

Cambridge Guide to Psychodynamic Psychotherapy
Adam Polnay, Rhiannon Pugh, Victoria Barker, David Bell, Allan Beveridge, Adam Burley, Allyson Lumsden, C. Susan Mizen and Lauren Wilson

Cambridge Guide to Schema Therapy
Robert N. Brockman, Susan Simpson, Christopher Hayes, Remco van der Wijngaart and Matthew Smout

"This book brilliantly brings together, in accessible language, the research and clinical wisdom that have accumulated over the past 20 years in mentalization-based theory and practice. It definitively establishes mentalization-based treatment as the transdiagnostic treatment it is. Requiring no prior exposure to mentalization-based therapy, this must-read guide provides clinicians with essential tools that can be immediately implemented. Read it! It will be worth it!"

Carla Sharp, John and Rebecca Moores Professor, Associate Dean for Faculty and Research, CLASS Department of Psychology, University of Houston

"Cambridge Guide to Mentalization-Based Treatment (MBT) is destined to become a seminal guide. The authors have invested decades in examining how mental processing influences our well-being and share their brilliant clarity of thought regarding mentalizing theory and relevant research. They further provide rich, detailed, and practical accounts of the guiding principles of MBT and describe potent interventions that can harness mentalizing capacities and improve treatment across a range of clinical problems. This book illustrates important ideas that will be relevant to psychotherapists at all levels who are working to improve their clinical practice."

Shelley McMain, Senior Scientist, Centre for Addiction and Mental Health (CAMH) Director, Psychotherapy Division, Department of Psychiatry, University of Toronto

"Must-read book for anyone practicing MBT. The guide is a mind meld of brilliant clinical, scientific, and conceptual brains, clearly showing that MBT is not a "guru therapy" but democratic, full of life and kicking! Having collected the experiences of 30 years of training MBT, this guide is highly didactic with numerous detailed individual and group case descriptions giving insights into the magic potion of how to strengthen mentalizing in very diverse mental problems and clinical settings. MBT follows recommendations of modern psychotherapy research by including all common factors and still provides a convincing narrative for the clinician in terms of disorder conceptualization, goals, tasks, and change theory. With this guide MBT proves that it has become a stand-alone transdiagnostic treatment, with a strong theoretical and empirical underpinnings and—most important for clinicians—very clear and concrete directions for users."

Svenja Taubner, Professor for Psychosocial Prevention, Medical Faculty Director, Institute for Psychosocial Prevention, University of Heidelberg

"The charm of MBT is the balance between clear hypotheses and one's own critical ability to constantly question them. Thus, MBT is a psychotherapy factory in the best sense: creative, inspiring, and interface-compatible; for clinical practitioners oriented toward scientific evidence and for researchers oriented toward clinical implementation. This book is a catalyst that will greatly advance both the practice and theory of psychotherapy."

Martin Bohus, Prof. em. Psychosomatic Medicine and Psychotherapy, Heidelberg University; Central Institute of Mental Health, Mannheim, Germany

Cambridge Guide to Mentalization-Based Treatment (MBT)

Anthony Bateman
University College London and Anna Freud Centre, London

Peter Fonagy
University College London and Anna Freud Centre, London

Chloe Campbell
University College London and Anna Freud Centre, London

Patrick Luyten
University of Leuven and University College London

Martin Debbané
University of Geneva and University College London

Shaftesbury Road, Cambridge CB2 8EA, United Kingdom

One Liberty Plaza, 20th Floor, New York, NY 10006, USA

477 Williamstown Road, Port Melbourne, VIC 3207, Australia

314–321, 3rd Floor, Plot 3, Splendor Forum, Jasola District Centre, New Delhi – 110025, India

103 Penang Road, #05–06/07, Visioncrest Commercial, Singapore 238467

Cambridge University Press is part of Cambridge University Press & Assessment, a department of the University of Cambridge.

We share the University's mission to contribute to society through the pursuit of education, learning and research at the highest international levels of excellence.

www.cambridge.org
Information on this title: www.cambridge.org/9781108816274

DOI: 10.1017/9781108896054

First published 2023

Library of Congress Cataloging-in-Publication Data.
A Cataloging-in-Publication data record for this book is available from the Library of Congress

ISBN 978-1-108-81627-4 Paperback

Contents

Preface ix
A Note from the Series Editor xiii
Acknowledgments xiv

Part I Overview of the Model

1 **A History of Mentalizing and Mentalization-Based Treatment** 1

2 **The Supporting Theory of Mentalization-Based Treatment** 4

Part II The Mentalization-Based Treatment Model in Practice

3 **What Is Mentalization-Based Treatment?** 43

4 **The Clinical Process of Mentalization-Based Treatment: A Step-by-Step Guide** 52

5 **MBT Group (MBT-G)** 136

Part III Application and Adaptations for Mental Health Presentations

6 **Narcissistic Personality Disorder** 155

7 **Antisocial Personality Disorder** 174

8 **Avoidant Personality Disorder** 203

9 **Depression** 230

10 **Psychosis** 253

11 **Trauma** 277

12 **Eating Disorders** 298

Part IV Application of Mentalization-Based Treatment in Different Populations and in Different Settings

13 **Working with Children** 319

14 **Working with Adolescents** 328

15 **Working with Families** 340

16 **Working with Couples** 347

17 **Mentalizing in Other Settings** 353

18 **Mentalizing and Emergency Care** 364

Index 388

Preface

Justifying another clinical guide to the practice of mentalization-based treatment (MBT) caused considerable discussion and reflection between us: "*Surely this has all been covered well enough over the past two decades?*"; "*Is there anything new to say?*"; "*Are there enough theoretical, research, and clinical changes to warrant a new book?.*" Manifestly, our decision to write this book testifies to our conclusion that enough has changed over the past few years both in the theoretical framework underpinning MBT and in its delivery in clinical practice to justify another book. This is a multi-author book rather than a collection of independent chapters by experts. Our aim has been to write a coherent manuscript from beginning to end that summarizes all the varied strands and applications of mentalizing theory without becoming repetitive. In summarizing the new material, we attempt to describe the theory of mentalizing and the clinical interventions applied in a range of mental health problems and contexts in a way that is accessible to the interested reader who has little prior knowledge of the theory and its practical applications. Clinicians need a framework that they can carry with them to inform their interventions along with clinical examples of how to transform that framework into effective clinical practice. This is the aim of this book—to be an MBT starter pack!

Recognition of the importance of effective mentalizing as a higher-order mental processing system that underpins social processes and individual resilience has stimulated ever more research about its developmental origins and its centrality—or otherwise—in mental health problems. This in turn has led MBT, a general model of intervention organized to enhance an individual's mentalizing, to become more refined in terms of how to help people rebuild their ability to mentalize in challenging interpersonal and social environments. We never considered our initial iterations of the clinical model to be the final say on how to facilitate robust mentalizing, and we continue to develop our transdiagnostic approach to helping individuals to build resilience in their relationships and social interactions. Indeed, outcome research suggests that although MBT is effective across a range of symptomatic domains, many patients continue to show problems with social adaptation and personal life satisfaction. Too many of them fail to reach their full potential in satisfying relationships and life achievements, both at the end of treatment and in the long term. We feel that we have made progress in broadening the ambitions of our treatment approach, but clearly there is much further to go in developing the effectiveness of MBT. To some extent this book summarizes where we have got to.

We have attempted to make the focus of the book the clinician struggling with a patient of greater acuity and complexity than they might have encountered before. The mentalizing model of mental disorder conceptualizes mental health problems as developmental, certainly emerging from different routes (genetic, individual historical, cultural, societal, environmental, both internal and external, and so on), but ultimately narrowing through a single funnel of the uniquely human capacity to think socially—that is, to mentalize. Problems of mentalizing can occur for different reasons, and the manifestation of these problems will obviously reflect individual attributes and histories, as well as the social context within which the individual lives. There is great clinical merit to the developmental psychopathology concept of equifinality.

The causes may be complex and multifarious, yet the intervention that addresses an important common mediator creates a pragmatic therapeutic opportunity. We are not, in this book or elsewhere, attempting to reduce the multiple forms of mental disorder to a single cause. Yet the high rate of so-called comorbidity of mental disorders calls for us to try to identify common factors that may be involved in many disorders, which can offer a transdiagnostic approach to remediation. This book views mentalizing as one such common factor. Mentalizing allows the clinician to create a therapeutic framework that supports them, when confronted with a confusing range of presentations in a single patient, to offer both generic and problem-specific interventions. We are not sure whether in MBT we have got the balance right between generic and specific—both are needed for sure. Our overarching conceptualization that enduring mental health problems reflect a lack of capacity to adapt to the social world and the unproductive resistance to change despite the information available to the individual rests on the concept of epistemic trust—that is, the ability of the human mind to be open or closed to social influence. Epistemic vigilance may be a natural state, but hypervigilance points to a state of "hearing but not listening," and therefore failing to internalize social knowledge offered by others. Mentalizing may be a key to generating epistemic trust and dissolving the epistemic dysfunction that characterizes the persistence of mental disorder. If this is so, it might explain why enhancing mentalizing helps in such a transdiagnostic way and has been studied as an intervention for a wide range of mental health problems. Improved social understanding not only corrects unforced errors of social cognition in relation to self and others, but it also opens the person to new understandings, garnered from the therapy room in the first instance, but then, beyond that, from the attachment partnerships—family relationships, work, and community relations—to which all of us are exposed. These constantly and consistently influence our understanding of ourselves and others, keeping us on the interpersonal straight and narrow. This understanding is relatively new, but it has increased our confidence in advocating a generalist approach to psychological therapy that is relatively easy to adopt and enhances—or rather draws on—many existing models of psychological intervention. We are fond of saying that there is little that is new in MBT, and that it draws on psychological principles that are simply part of our evolutionary heritage. Yet it is the fundamental truth of this statement that has encouraged us to produce yet another book representing a further attempt to find the correct balance between the general and the specific for clinicians and for those who benefit from this most remarkable of mechanisms of human processes of interpersonal healing—psychotherapy.

In Part I of this book (Chapters 1 and 2) we cover the history of mentalizing and MBT, outline some of the basic developmental processes that contribute to robust mentalizing, summarize the outcome research, and consider what makes things go wrong during childhood and adolescence. In Part II (Chapters 3–5) the key clinical principles that are followed in MBT are set out. We hope that throughout this book we have used enough everyday language to cut through the jargon for clinicians coming fresh to the mentalizing world to lay the foundations of clinical practice. We chart the progress of Sarah, who has borderline personality disorder (BPD)—the mental health problem on which our therapeutic approach initially focused—by describing the implementation of MBT for BPD in a stepwise fashion. The principles underpinning MBT (Chapter 3) and all the different stages of the core model are illustrated as they are used in clinical practice in her individual (Chapter 4) and group (Chapter 5) sessions. Sarah is a "prototype"—that is, she is a fictionalized composite of someone with a diagnosis of BPD, rather than a real patient.

Although we use the categories of borderline, antisocial, narcissistic, and avoidant personality disorder, and so on, in this book to delineate different mental health presentations, this is done primarily to link with earlier literature. Throughout, we emphasize that the mentalizing approach follows a dimensional system and transcends the issue of categorization. MBT requires a clinician to assess an individual's personality in terms of the dimensional domains of mentalizing, rather than to establish the presence or absence of specific descriptive characteristics that make up a "category" of diagnosis. The details of the (im)balance of dimensional mentalizing components that may be creating disruption to the patient's social experience are at the center of a personalized evaluation; the patient's formulation avoids categories and is organized around process and function. We hope that this personalized approach is clear throughout the chapters. Sarah has a range of experiences and behaviors that create problems for her and others, and yet—like so many of our patients—she is trying hard to manage her emotions and reactivity to others and is motivated to change. Targeting mentalizing requires the clinician to see things from Sarah's perspective and to respond to them compassionately so that she experiences the clinician as seeing her as she sees herself. This generates epistemic trust (trust in the knowledge that the therapist conveys) within the patient–therapist relationship, which we see as a requirement if the change we observe is to become enduring and Sarah is to take advantage of the opportunities in her life. Sarah is depicted as a typical MBT patient—she is moderately responsive to treatment.

Groups are an essential part of MBT. The aim of the group is to support learning about oneself with and through others, and some specific interventions that differentiate MBT groups from other group treatments are outlined in Chapter 5. Sarah starts in the group and gradually begins to participate and learn about herself through others—a process that gradually leads to increasingly robust and effective mentalizing. Learning about oneself through others in a group is the main format used in MBT for antisocial personality disorder (MBT-ASPD) (described in Chapter 7), which, along with other adaptations of MBT, is covered in Part III (Chapters 6–12). In these chapters, the way in which treatments diverge from the original model for BPD are discussed as they apply to other personality difficulties. In adapting the model for different disorders, clinicians follow the principles at the heart of MBT, define and formulate the mentalizing problems of the person in front of them rather than define their "disorder," and tailor their interventions accordingly. Again, although we use the categories of personality disorder, this is only to link the reader to the area of discussion. The MBT clinician is rarely concerned with "disorders" and "diagnosis," but instead tries to ensure that the person behind the "personality function" is assessed in terms of the dimensional domains of mentalizing. Through the lens of interpersonal understanding that the mentalizing perspective offers, we see people thinking, feeling, wishing, and desiring, rather than simply as mental disorders or personality disorders. The observation and gentle enhancement of mentalizing is at the center of everything that the MBT clinician does. To some extent, the labels of the different types of disorders are translated into different commonly observed patterns in the way that we as individuals think and feel about ourselves and other people, which to a greater or lesser extent characterizes all of our patients (and, dare we say, all of us). So, the clinician implementing MBT for narcissistic aspects of personality functioning (MBT-NPD) (Chapter 6), for antisocial aspects (MBT-ASPD) (Chapter 7), or for avoidant, anxiety-dominated features of social function (MBT-AvPD) (Chapter 8) follows the same core principles (Chapter 3) and the pattern of interventions outlined in MBT-BPD (Chapter 4), but tweaks the MBT format and process of intervention according to the mentalizing formulation of the individual. We see no binary distinction between the more stable and slower-changing aspects of functioning usually encapsulated by the description "personality disorder" and the more specifically described and arguably episodic mental disorders. Both involve characteristic failures of mentalizing, offering therapeutic opportunities for MBT, which are discussed in the chapters that come next. The approach to the treatment of mental-state disorders such as depression (Chapter 9) and psychosis (Chapter 10) further confirms our transdiagnostic approach. Each chapter outlines a mentalizing framework and formulation of the problem areas, and then describes the interventions that naturally arise from these constructions of the patient's mental function.

In Chapter 11, MBT for individuals who have experienced trauma is discussed, and an MBT-trauma focused (MBT-TF) intervention approach is described. In its original iteration for BPD, MBT took into account the fact that most patients had a considerable history of attachment trauma. Working on the sequelae of these experiences was incorporated into the model. Data suggest that to some extent this generic clinical approach to the effects of trauma on the patient worked—those who had experienced identifiable trauma had treatment outcomes that were no worse than those who did not report a history of trauma. Nevertheless, it is apparent that some symptoms of complex trauma may need special attention. Again, the first step requires reframing trauma from a mentalizing perspective. Understanding the relationship between mentalizing and trauma is detailed in the first part of Chapter 11. Based on the four mentalizing themes of trauma—being alone, mental isolation and avoidance, shame, and epistemic vigilance—the MBT therapeutic approach (MBT-TF) is then discussed. Unusually for an approach to complex trauma, MBT-TF is delivered in a group format on the basis that the patients may be able to share with and learn more from others whom they see as having had the same experiences as them. Individual sessions may be added to support the patients in the group. Chapter 12, the final chapter of Part III, covers eating disorders, which are seen in MBT as conditions arising in the context of developmentally determined mentalizing problems, genetic predispositions, attachment, and childhood and adolescent adversity. We argue that the range of symptoms associated with eating disorders may share the function of being different attempts at social self-regulation. This is important. The focus of MBT for eating disorders is then not so much on body weight and shape, for example, but on dysfunctional relationships and social anxieties, and the mentalizing problems that maintain the disorders.

The chapters that make up Part IV consider the use of mentalizing as a framework for working with children (Chapter 13), adolescents (Chapter 14), families (Chapter 15), and couples (Chapter 16), and in a range of contexts (Chapter 17). Finally, Chapter 18 discusses the organization of a service using mentalizing to inform the overall assessment and care of those who present in crisis situations in emergency settings.

Anthony Bateman
Peter Fonagy
Chloe Campbell
Patrick Luyten
Martin Debbané

A Note from the Series Editor

I remember when I first met Sarah Marsh, Editor at Cambridge University Press - it seems like a lifetime ago now. We met at a café in central Edinburgh in June 2017 to discuss an idea that she had to create a series of books focussed on evidenced based Psychological Therapies. The idea was simple – the books would be attractive to a trainee and simultaneously to an expert clinician. We wanted to enable readers to conceptualise a psychological difficulty using different theoretical models of understanding, but not become overwhelmed by the volume of information. We saw the need for a series of books that could be easily read and yet would examine complex concepts in a manageable way.

So, when Sarah asked me if I would become the Series Editor, I couldn't say no. What we could never have predicted back then, when making early plans for the series, was that we would soon face a global pandemic. There were days when we didn't even know whether we could leave our house or if our children could go to school - the world effectively stopped. Yet through all the chaos, uncertainty and fear, I saw the determination and successes of those around me shine through. I was in awe of the resilience of my own son, Patrick, who lived his adolescence in 'lock-down'. I watch him now and the young man he has become – he walks tall with a quiet confidence. I am so proud as he and his friends laugh together and now enjoy what most of had previously taken for granted: their freedom at university. In a similar way, I watched the many authors of these books, most of whom are busy and tired clinicians, continue to dedicate their precious time to this venture – an incredible achievement through a most challenging time. They each welcomed me into their academic, clinical and theoretical worlds, from all over the globe. They have all been an honour to work with. I would personally like to thank every contributor and author of this series for their hard work, determination and humour even in the darkest of days. Despite all of the unknowns and the chaos, they kept going and achieved something wonderful.

I would like to thank Sarah, and Kim Ingram at Cambridge, for giving me the opportunity to be Series Editor. I have loved every minute of it; it has been a longer journey than we anticipated but an amazing one and for that I am incredibly grateful. Sarah and Kim are my friends now – we have literally lived through a global pandemic together. It has been my absolute pleasure to work together and in collaboration with Cambridge University Press.

Patricia Graham, Series Editor
Consultant Clinical Psychologist, NHS Lanarkshire, UK

Acknowledgments

This book would not be complete without thanking all those around us who have put up with us over many years and given us ideas that we can take as our own, when they are in fact theirs and should be attributed as such. To them we apologize and we hope that our integration of their ideas into the mentalizing framework has done them a modicum of justice. We thank the series editor, Patricia Graham, for encouraging us to write this book, and the publishers for waiting patiently for a manuscript that was "nearly finished" for a considerable period of time. Finally, the support provided by colleagues at the Anna Freud Centre and the Research Department of Clinical, Educational and Health Psychology at University College London with clarifying, editing, and finalizing the manuscript was second to none—thank you.

Part I Overview of the Model

Chapter 1

A History of Mentalizing and Mentalization-Based Treatment

Introduction

How does a person come to intuitively know that a certain look from their partner means they have had a tough day at work? How can best friends have entire dialogues with each other without completing a single sentence? For millennia, philosophers have thought about how the mind works, and twentieth-century playwrights, novelists, singers, and poets have told stories about what it is like to be inside someone else's mind. More recently, psychologists have used experimental methods to deepen our understanding of how our minds work. But in our everyday life we are all philosophers of the mind—almost all of us devote substantial amounts of our "headspace" to wondering what is going on in other people's heads, and tracking our own thoughts or feelings. There are several terms that have been used to cover this territory of thinking about thoughts—mental-state inference, Theory of Mind, intentional stance, reflective functioning, and mentalizing—all of which signify the ability to represent something beyond, behind, or simply different from physical objects, moving bodies, and expressive faces. We have increasingly come to realize that such "mind-wondering" is pretty central to social interaction, culture, and morality—and, while we are at it, to politics, religion, and technology. In the world of mentalization-based treatment (MBT) we have focused on the concept as a way of making sense of mental health difficulties, and used it to shape a new form of psychotherapeutic treatment.

We all know what mental states are—they encompass intentions, beliefs, pretense, irony, and knowledge; the German philosopher Franz Brentano identified that what they have in common is *being about something* [1]. The other thing about such mental states is that they require qualification, such as "I believe that. . . ." They need this note of caution because thoughts lack physical substance and are invisible to others—but, of course, despite being intangible, they can have very real consequences through their power to direct action. Human beliefs are determinants of behavior with massive observable consequences; for that reason, they are of far greater significance than the physical world from which they emerge and with which they have only a loose relationship. To give an example, the last European victim to be burned at the stake for witchcraft was a woman in the Polish city of Reszel, in 1810. Three years earlier, there had been a fire in the city for which no cause could be found. A woman—who for years had been suspected of witchcraft—was accused and tortured, and although she did not admit to the offense, she was declared guilty and sentenced to be burned at the stake. The case went through every level of the Prussian court, even reaching the king, but the sentence was upheld and the execution was carried out. There are many more dramatic examples of the horrendous impact that false beliefs can have, and human history stands as testament to the gravity of the consequences of mentalizing when it goes wrong. This book describes how MBT seeks to harness what we know about the human mind's sometimes troubled fascination with the content of other human minds, in order to help to improve the treatment of mental health disorders. We shall start in Part I (this chapter and Chapter 2) by giving some background on mentalizing, the ideas that are behind it, and the evidence base to support it. The bulk of the rest of this book is quite practical—we aim to give a concise overview of MBT and how it is applied in different situations and with different groups of patients. But first we shall give a theoretical overview.

"Theory of Mind" was a term first used half a century ago to refer to the capacity of people to anticipate the actions of a protagonist acting on a false belief (looking for an object that was, unknown to them, displaced). As the Theory of Mind industry took off, a wide range of experimental designs and philosophical conceptualizations began to be squeezed into this shallow suitcase of "having a Theory of Mind" (e.g., Daniel Dennett's concept of "taking an intentional stance") [2]. Because Theory of Mind mixed the concept with an experimental design, and risked reifying such a multifaceted and abstract activity, another term—mentalizing—was independently proposed by two psychologists from dramatically different traditions. Uta Frith introduced the term in presenting a cognitive account of autism [3]. Peter Fonagy launched it from a psychoanalytic perspective when thinking about the interpersonal difficulties experienced by patients with a diagnosis of borderline personality disorder (BPD)—in particular, the clinical experience of working with someone for whom thinking about the content of other people's minds was so aversive and frightening that in certain situations it became impossible [4].

In the meantime, Anthony Bateman and Peter Fonagy—as peers and colleagues in clinical training and practice—found themselves increasingly aware of and concerned by the ineffectiveness of help that was currently available to individuals with a diagnosis of BPD within the UK's National Health Service. Reviews of treatments in the 1990s, at the time when MBT was developed, indicated that 97% of patients with BPD who presented for treatment in the USA received outpatient care from an average of six therapists. An analysis of outcomes measured 2 to 3 years after treatment suggested that this treatment was at best only marginally effective (see [5]), and that most patients failed to improve or even deteriorated—suggesting that the psychosocial treatments being provided actually impeded patients' capacity to recover. In Michael Stone's classic follow-up of patients, a recovery rate of 66% was only achieved after 20 years [6]. A rethink about treatment approaches was required, and MBT was developed for the treatment of BPD in the 1990s to meet some of this need. Perhaps because MBT emerged as a response to this gap in the clinical options available, it has always been an unashamedly pragmatic approach. Although its origins are in psychodynamic psychotherapy, it quite openly cherry-picks whatever techniques are available from other models that enhance robust mentalizing, and it studiously avoids interventions that have the potential to undermine mentalizing, in order to minimize potential harmful effects of therapy.

MBT is primarily informed by the idea that mentalizing is a complicated task that we all wrestle with quite a lot of the time and which, as with most complex skills, it is easy to do badly, often regardless of how hard we try. Some feelings are complex and hard to pin down—for example, who can say that they completely understand love? Talking of which, intense emotions often disrupt mentalizing (for more on this, see Chapter 2), even though understanding feelings is one of the primary tasks of mentalizing.

Mentalizing is made even more difficult by the fact that people often do not want to reveal their mental state, and so the evidence that we have about what they are really thinking may be very much less than what we need. Often we make assumptions—sometimes wild ones—about what people are thinking. We sometimes presume mental states as potential explanations of behavior, and use this theory as an explanation for others' reaction to us (e.g., "*I have heard them explaining their work far better in the past; they must have been quite anxious—you know, perhaps they were feeling intimidated by having to explain what they're doing to us*"). This kind of reasoning can be quite simple, but as situations become more complex and more players are involved, these lines of thinking become more elaborate (e.g., what does A think I think about B, and how does B understand A's relationship with C?). We offer these examples of how easy it is to mentalize inaccurately to suggest that humility in relation to mind reading has to be the order of the day. In fact, perhaps the clearest indicator of poor mentalizing is excessive certainty when faced with such complexities.

Concluding Remarks

In summary, it seems that we are saying something quite contradictory—that mentalizing is quite an ordinary and everyday process (we all do it, all of the time, and we all know that we do it even if we have never thought of ourselves as "mentalizers" before), and yet it is also multifaceted, liable to go awry, and sometimes needs careful attention. This is part of the paradox of human consciousness—its nature and complexities form one of the great unsolved mysteries of philosophy and science, but most of the time we use it to plan ahead or mull over why our neighbor is being so annoying as we try to navigate within our social world. In Chapter 2 we shall explain more about what mentalizing is and why thinking about it can be so helpful for understanding psychopathology, beginning with the different facets—or *dimensions*—of mentalizing, and how we tend to act and think when mentalizing goes "offline."

References

1. Brentano F. *Psychology from an Empirical Standpoint.* London, UK: Routledge, 1973/1874.
2. Dennett D. *The Intentional Stance.* Cambridge, MA: MIT Press, 1987.
3. Frith U. *Autism: Explaining the Enigma.* Oxford, UK: Blackwell, 1989.
4. Fonagy P. On tolerating mental states: theory of mind in borderline patients. *Bull Anna Freud Centre* 1989; **12**: 91–115.
5. Lieb K, Zanarini MC, Schmahl C et al. Borderline personality disorder. *Lancet* 2004; **364**: 453–61.
6. Stone MH. *The Fate of Borderline Patients: Successful Outcome and Psychiatric Practice.* New York, NY: The Guilford Press, 1990.

The Supporting Theory of Mentalization-Based Treatment

Introduction

Given that mentalizing is, as we have described in Chapter 1, rather difficult and prone to going wrong, and that it can cause us considerable psychological distress when it does go wrong, why do we do it so much? Humans are a social species and, in order to support our survival, natural selection has provided us with the tools necessary to interact with and manage the hugely complex terrain of our social world. Understanding the thoughts, intentions, and mental states of our fellow humans is the key to the creation of human societies and our attainment of dominance over other species on our planet. We constantly infer thoughts, feelings, and beliefs in the minds of other people, and much of our mental life is spent engaging with the task of processing social information [1]. Many writers and researchers believe that the evolutionary advantages of living in relatively large social groups were made by possible by humans developing the capacities to interpret, explain, and predict each other's behavior, and using these capacities to share and accumulate experiences, to plan and collaborate, and to attain joint goals that they would not have been able to achieve as individuals or as members of smaller groups [2–4]. There are excellent neuroscientific experimental studies which provide ample evidence that mentalizing, as indicated by the activation (or inhibition) of the network of neurons involved in Theory of Mind, is critical for evaluating the morality of others (including those who are harmful), for predicting how competitors will behave, and for learning from those who have special information about a shared environment (e.g., stock markets) [5].

We have argued that vulnerability to mental health disorders is the flipside of the advantages that mentalizing brings [6]. On the basis of data from epidemiological studies, only one in five people will go through life without experiencing a diagnosable mental health condition [7]. Looking at such prevalence figures from the perspective of natural selection, it is clear that whatever the neural systems are that underpin mental disorder, they must have other functions that are critical for survival. A defining feature of mental disorder is the experience of "wild imagination," and we consider that mentalizing difficulties—the tendency to get caught up in unhelpful ways of imagining what is going on both for ourselves and for other people—are the price we as a species pay for the immense benefits of the human imagination [6].

The Non-Mentalizing Modes

Mentalizing is a complicated and multifaceted process. We have pinpointed three *non-mentalizing modes*, which describe different states of mind that are encountered when mentalizing is ineffective, to help clinicians to understand and recognize when a client's mentalizing is poor. These modes are called *psychic equivalence*, *teleological mode*, and *pretend mode*.

Psychic Equivalence

Psychic equivalence is a way of thinking that involves assuming that what you are thinking is what everyone else is thinking, is obviously true, and is the same as external reality. Mental is equivalent to physical. An example of psychic equivalence in a young child can be seen in their feelings of fear about being alone in the dark at bedtime translating into a genuine terror that there is a monster under the bed, or that the unpalatable cabbage they are being encouraged to eat is poisonous. An adult in a state of psychic equivalence, if feeling angry and upset, may assume that others around them are hostile and angry too—potentially generating a destructive interpersonal cycle in which the other person *does* become hostile in response to the first person's behaviors, which were prompted by their assumptions.

Teleological Mode

In teleological mode, only the behavioral outcomes of mental states are taken seriously. Mental states themselves lose their significance. Again, if we think about this in terms of the pre-mentalizing states of young children, we can see the teleological mode in the ways that toddlers behave—actions speak louder than words, affection is accompanied by gifts, kisses, or hugs, and "badly behaved" toys are physically punished. In adulthood, this mode may manifest in an individual requiring physical or sexual contact from others in order to escape their feeling of being unlovable or worthless, or it may play out in a tendency toward violence or self-harm when feeling overwhelmed or angry.

Pretend Mode

In pretend mode, there is a lack of appropriate connection between one's thoughts about mental states and external reality. The concept of pretend mode was based on observation of the ways in which young children enjoy using and enacting mental states in play, but only when they can clearly separate the game from physical reality. When an adult breaks the pretense by clumsily joining in from the real world, the game is spoiled. In adults, pretend mode can appear as *pseudomentalizing*, which is important to recognize in clinical work—it can involve what seems to be rather elaborate mentalizing, with plenty of discussion and apparent thought about mental states, but in rather aimless, contradictory, or meaningless ways. Many of us have been in meetings where possible points of action are endlessly discussed, but with a sinking background feeling that there will be little real progress.

We shall refer back to these three modes in our discussions of clinical work, as we encounter different clinical scenarios and expressions of mentalizing breakdown. It is also important to bear in mind that these different modes can overlap and be observed at the same time. It is not uncommon, for example, for the distress generated in a state of psychic equivalence, because a thought is experienced as real without the moderation of psychological status, to spill over into teleological mode. For example, the thought "*I feel terrible; obviously everybody hates me and I am a bad person*" may trigger and converge with the thought, in teleological mode, "*I need to hurt myself to deal with how hateful I feel.*"

The Mentalizing Dimensions

To help us understand the *how* and *why* of the ways in which mentalizing and non-mentalizing can take these different forms, we need to appreciate that mentalizing draws on several different kinds of social-cognitive activities, underpinned by different neurobiological processes. We have categorized these into four mentalizing *dimensions* (which are sometimes called *polarities*, as they are not dimensional in the everyday sense):

- automatic/controlled
- self/other
- cognitive/affective
- internal/external.

We all move backward and forward along these dimensions in response to changes in our environment and adjustments in what we are thinking. At times, for example, we might be focused on our own mental states, while at other moments we might be more caught up in what we think is in the minds of other people. We often find that individuals who are experiencing emotional distress or behavioral difficulties tend to be more "stuck" at one pole of one or more of the dimensions. We shall briefly explain these dimensions here, but we shall also refer to them in our account of clinical processes, to illustrate how thinking about them can help us in our work.

Automatic/Controlled Mentalizing

Most of the time, we mentalize in a fairly automatic way—we do not stop to think very explicitly or reflectively about what is going on. In fact, when someone is excessively controlled in their mentalizing, the interpersonal experience can feel rather like hard work and unspontaneous. To return to the example given at the beginning of Chapter 1, when we meet a partner, flatmate, or friend after work we respond to their demeanor in quite an immediate, unreflective way. But on registering that they look unhappy, worried, or preoccupied, we may slow things down a little and start to think in a more conscious and controlled way about what might be going on for them—was there a particular problem at work that has been bothering them, and how should we best respond to their upset in a helpful or sympathetic manner? In that moment, we are moving along this dimension of mentalizing, from automatic to controlled, in response to the demands of the situation.

Self/Other Mentalizing

Traditionally, Theory of Mind has focused on the way in which we think about the mental states of others. Mentalizing theory—and here it reflects some of its origins in psychoanalysis—assumes that the ability to understand our own mental states cannot be taken for granted either. Even though we tend to have a lot more information about our own states (e.g., our physical sensations, our internal narrative voice, an understanding of what the limits of our knowledge are) than about those of other people, we are still vulnerable to substantial biases and significant errors when making judgments about the reasons for our actions [8–10], or we may not want to admit to ourselves the real reasons for our behavior.

Effective mentalizing requires us to be aware of someone else's mental states as being distinct from our own. But because we are such a socially driven species, the mentalizing of self and other often interfere with each other—for example, the mere awareness of the presence of another perspective slows down thinking [11]. Indeed, there is evidence that overlapping neural networks are activated when reflecting on the self or others [12]. This neural correspondence reflects the way our own mental experiences (thoughts, feelings, and memories) can create a template for understanding someone else [13,14], just as the effort to understand others' thoughts, feelings, and reflections about us (which we call personal second-order mentalizing) might clarify and elaborate our own sense of ourselves [15–17].

From a clinical perspective, an individual who tends to be more stuck at the "other" pole of the self/other dimension might be more vulnerable to being overwhelmed by the emotions of others, and to being swept up by another's perspective. This can leave them vulnerable to contagious emotional storms and also, in some cases, to exploitation, as they allow the mental states of another person to dominate them. In contrast, some individuals who have a strong capacity to mentalize others but who lack emotional empathy (see this chapter: Cognitive/Affective Mentalizing) can have a tendency to misuse or exploit others. Meanwhile, an excessive focus on self-mentalizing can deprive an individual of access to the regulating effects of other people's perspectives, and reduces their social connectedness.

Cognitive/Affective Mentalizing

This mentalizing dimension covers, at the cognitive pole, the capacity to identify, label, and invoke reasoning about mental states in oneself or in others. The opposite pole, affective mentalizing, is concerned with the *feeling* of what is going on—again in oneself or in others. If an individual is stuck at the affective end, without the labeling and contextualizing of emotions that cognition provides, they may experience overwhelming dysregulated emotions, which come to dominate their behavior. The lack of balance and the absence of contextualizing of feelings can lead to catastrophizing. Cognition adds reflection and questioning to mentalizing, whereas the domination of emotion leads to an unnatural lack of hesitancy and to a particular certainty about ideas that emotional conviction can add to beliefs. Domination by affect potentially makes anything that is thought feel as if it is real, and leads to an intolerance of alternative ways of seeing things. We are equally familiar with the constraint that accompanies being stuck at the cognitive pole. In this state, an individual can describe feelings in the absence of these emotions actually being experienced. Such an intellectual understanding can serve as helpful protection against being overwhelmed by emotions; however, in the absence of the experience of feeling it can feel disconnected from reality, becoming a form of pretend mode functioning (discussed earlier in this chapter), and it can lack genuine empathy.

Internal/External Mentalizing

The internal/external dimension refers to the possibility of inferring someone's mental states from external cues, such as their facial expressions, as opposed to thinking about what is going on for them on the basis of what we imagine about their internal state—that is, what we imagine that they know, think, or believe. An exclusively external orientation can make a person hypervigilant, constantly looking for external evidence and judging by appearance. If evidence for attitudes and other internal states has to come from the outside, there will be a corresponding lack of conviction about one's own intuitions and an excessive need to seek external reassurance. Similarly, we might, for example, find it difficult sometimes to recognize how anxious we are feeling until we notice how much we are fidgeting. An excessive external focus can lead to a neglect of the internal, and the absence of a way of generating a model for how one feels can lead to overwhelming feelings of "not knowing" and even emptiness. This vacuum can drive the individual toward seeking intense experiences to fill the gap. Excessive focus on external states can also cause an individual to be highly reactive to other people's physical actions and behaviors, even if these actions are not directed at them. This is because the individual is unable to anchor their response in a coherent understanding of the other person's mental state, which would require contextualizing and creating hypotheses about the reasons for the other person's actions. Meanwhile, an excessive focus on internal states can lead to unwarranted inferences and complicated suppositions about another's state of mind without a sufficient anchor in external reality—that is, a tendency toward the pretend mode that we described earlier in this chapter.

We hope that this description of the four dimensions captures some common mentalizing difficulties. Good or effective mentalizing assumes that there is flexible "movement" between the poles of each dimension, achieving a balance between them in processing mental representations. Depending on the context and subject, ineffective mentalizing can look quite different. We all have different strengths and weakness according to where we tend to land on each mentalizing dimension. Although we often (probably unhelpfully!) talk of "breakdowns" or "failures" in mentalizing, as if mentalizing is a single process that simply stops, these breakdowns can appear in different ways, depending on how the individual is functioning across the different dimensions.

Developmental Aspects of Mentalizing: Child/Adolescent/Adult

Mentalizing is a developmental achievement, and the full repertoire of mentalizing skills emerges over the course of childhood and adolescence. There are two reasons why it is helpful to understand how mentalizing develops. The first reason is that, when we are working with children and adolescents, it is useful to know what level of mental-state understanding we can expect from them, and what signs there might be of problems in the development of their individual functioning. The second reason why it is useful to understand the unfurling of ever more complex mentalizing skills across development is that, from the perspective of developmental psychopathology, it helps us to make sense of a patient's vulnerabilities and how these affect their functioning.

The non-mentalizing modes, discussed earlier in this chapter, were partly inspired by careful observations of how children operate—recognizing the literality of the toddler's horror of "poisonous" cabbage, or understanding the precursor of pretend mode in young children's play. Indeed, in some of our earlier work we described these modes as *pre*-mentalizing rather than *non*-mentalizing modes. Moving forward through development from toddlers to adolescents, our growing understanding of the heightened and unstable experience of mentalizing in adolescence helps to explain why this life stage is a period of particular vulnerability in terms of the emergence of mental health difficulties.

Bertram Malle has provided a helpful summary of the developmental emergence of mentalizing in what he describes as the "tree of social cognition" [18]. At the base of the "tree," in the first 6 months of life, infants show capacities that are shared with non-human primates, such as differentiating between biological and non-biological agents. They develop a special interest in reading faces, and can detect that biological agents have goals, in contrast to movement by objects that is not goal directed. By the end of the first year, they can follow another person's gaze (i.e., they show an interest in the direction of other people's attention), they socially reference with others (e.g., they might look at a caregiver as if to ask "*Should I be frightened of this stranger or new object?*"), and, critically, they can engage in shared social attention—they enjoy the feeling of looking at things together. After another 6 months, infants are able to detect intent behind an action and can mimic others, usually to establish social links. Between the second and third years of life, a capacity for genuine empathy emerges, along with deliberate imitation and the capacity to infer wishes and desires. During the third and fourth years, children start inferring knowledge (which can be tested in the well-known false-belief test of Theory of Mind) and start to show self-knowledge and self-awareness. Non-human primates can also make inferences about what others want, but the evidence for their ability to infer false beliefs is debated and, if this ability is present, it is certainly not robust.

From middle childhood onward, the child develops an ever-increasing sophistication in ascribing mental states to others. Arguably, this ability continues to improve gradually right through to young adulthood. For example, by the age of 7–9 years, children master third- and fourth-order false beliefs (e.g., "*If you think that I think that you think …*" [19]), and develop increasingly complex explanations of actions [20]. At the top of the "tree" is explaining action in terms of the stable characteristics of an agent (so-called trait inference). This capacity reflects how the child has come to view the world as being occupied by people with different behavioral tendencies, based on a sense of "what so-and-so is like," and therefore, by sampling another person's actions, we can create a general picture of them that will help us to predict their behavior in a new situation. Of course, infants do this implicitly (behaviorally) via non-mentalizing processes from the earliest days of attachment to their caregivers, but at this point attachment moves to the level of representation and is experienced in terms of the anticipated mental states of attachment figures.

A defining feature of adolescence is the increased importance of social relationships, marked by an increase in social sensitivity [21]. There is evidence that adolescents are more likely to report bad mood and anxiety following an experience of rejection [22], and that they expect less favorable positive feedback from their peers [23]. The network of brain regions involved in mentalizing (especially the medial prefrontal cortex) is more responsive to social rejection in adolescents than in adults [24], perhaps as a result of greater functional connectivity between the regions of the mentalizing network [25].

This brief review of the development of mentalizing across childhood and adolescence has highlighted two things. The first is that mentalizing capacities are based on the emergence of multiple interlinked components, with explicit, content-led mental state ascriptions—what we think of as fully fledged mentalizing—developing quite late. A second repeated theme concerns the role of the relationship between the self and the other in the emergence of these capacities. The abilities that we describe may be conceptualized in purely cognitive terms, but the content of mental-state attributions, especially in the early years when a child is totally dependent on their caregivers, can be of the utmost seriousness, implying the availability of food, protection, and warmth, or indeed the opposite—risk, danger, and death. Self-awareness and self-regulation play a critical role in differentiating and modifying numerous mentalizing capacities, thus providing important functions that make social living possible, and this self-awareness and self-regulation is supported by the relationships and social environment that construct the sense of self. In the next section we shall describe the interpersonal nature of these developmental processes in more detail.

The Impact of the Environment on the Emergence of Mentalizing

How do we acquire our understanding of mind across development? Findings from neuroscience research show that the ability to mentalize is a prewired evolutionary adaptation—the process of acquiring increased social cognition, described in the preceding section, is a normative developmental trajectory. However, the achievement of full and robust mentalizing is dependent on environmental input. There are good reasons for this—in the same way that we are prewired for language acquisition, but not for the acquisition of any particular language, we need to be open to learning a different "language" for thinking and talking about mental states. We learn to understand mental states from how others around us frame them. Infants and young children have wants and feelings, and caregivers "read" their behaviors—their need for food, or assistance, or comfort—and offer evidence of intuitive understanding through actions or verbal responses [26]. Carers are predisposed to guess, with typical utterances such as "*You are tired, you have had enough of this game*" or "*Oh, it was the shiny silver foil that you were after!*" Different cultures vary in the interpretations that they give to a child's behavioral reactions [27], and even within the same culture caregivers will not give the same labels to expressions of supposed internal states. However it is expressed, toddlers rapidly acquire internal-state language from those around them. They like to explore and often talk confidently about others' feelings, preferences, desires, and perceptions, allowing rich communication within families that includes increased empathy but also, for example, teasing [28]. The constant asking of questions by young children—the notoriously persistent "why" questions—is, we argue, partly about obtaining information, but more fundamentally about reveling in the process of joint attention on a shared object. The more children hear mental-state words and are exposed to mentalizing talk, the more their ability to successfully interpret false-belief tasks is likely to improve [28,29]. Some families engage in a lot of mental-state talk, and their children's ability to mentalize is advanced, whereas others do much less—parents' self-reported use of elaborated mentalizing conversation appears to predict higher scores on tasks that assess Theory of Mind [30].

A young child develops a sense of their own mind, and then of other people's minds, through early experiences of having how they are feeling being accurately recognized, mirrored, and responded to by a caregiver. These interpretations of and responses to what is going on for children help them to build a sense of who they are and to develop a sense of agency—that is, the ability to carry an idea of themselves as an active presence in the world, whose experiences matter, are of interest to those around them, and can make things happen. The caregiver's responses that reflect back to the child what they are feeling are called "secondary representations." It is as a result of having adults around us to decipher and delineate "who we are" for us that we can develop a coherent sense of self (sometimes called self-representation); in that sense selfhood, rather than being all about individuality, is an intrinsically social construct. Individuals who have not had the benefit of such secondary representations may have a diminished or less coherent self-representation (see this chapter: The Alien Self); these may include individuals who have been exposed to such responsive care but, for a complex range of possible reasons, have not been able to benefit from it.

There is plenty of evidence of the importance of being mentalized for a child's development. The significance of parental mentalizing was first revealed in a large empirical study exploring parents' capacity for reflective functioning, which found that a parent's ability to think about and understand their childhood relationship to their own parents, measured during pregnancy, strongly predicted their infant's attachment security [31]. A follow-up study found that antenatal parental mentalizing continued to be a predictor of the child's reflective functioning 17 years later, when the children had grown into young adults [32]. Since this initial research, there has been a great deal of work on the effects of caregivers' mentalizing on outcomes for their children. In the area of child attachment outcomes, a meta-analysis by Zeegers et al. examined the relationships between parental mentalizing, parental sensitivity, and infant attachment outcomes. This meta-analysis found that both mentalizing and sensitivity had significant direct effects on infant–parent attachment after controlling for the effects of each other, which suggests that parental mentalizing is directly related to infant–parent attachment security [33].

As well as evidence for the impact of parental mentalizing on attachment security, there is also a growing body of evidence which indicates that better parental mentalizing fosters mentalizing in children [34] and in adolescents [35,36]. Whereas associations between parental mentalizing and infant attachment typically represent small effect sizes (defined as Cohen's $d = 0.20$), the association between parental and infant mentalizing is typically stronger, representing medium to large effect sizes (Cohen's $d = 0.50–0.80$). For instance, Rosso and Airaldi found a particularly strong association between mothers' ability to mentalize negative and mixed-ambivalent mental states, but not positive mental states, and the corresponding ability in their adolescent children ($r = 0.40–0.50$) [35]. Findings such as these suggest that the capacity of caregivers to reflect on difficult and affect-charged mental states is particularly important in the context of the transmission of mentalizing between generations, from parents to their children.

Studies on mentalizing and adversity during childhood have provided some of the strongest evidence for the potential role of caregivers' mentalizing capacities in the development of their children's mentalizing capacity. Early adversity and complex trauma (i.e., negative experiences in early life involving neglect or abuse, typically within an attachment/caregiving context) in particular have been shown to have the potential to severely impair mentalizing. This impairment is apparent in strongly biased mentalizing, hypersensitivity to the mental states of others, and a defensive inhibition of mentalizing, or a combination of these features (for reviews, see Borelli et al. [37] and Luyten and Fonagy [38]). At the same time, there is increasing evidence that high levels of caregivers' reflective functioning, particularly reflective functioning with regard to their own traumatic experiences (see Chapter 11), may be an important buffer in the relationship between early adversity and child outcomes (reviewed in Borelli et al. [37]). For instance, higher trauma-related reflective functioning in parents with a history of sexual abuse and neglect has been shown to be related to lower risk of infant attachment disorganization [39], and to a substantially lower risk of exposure to childhood sexual abuse in their own infants [37]. These findings are of particular clinical interest as they suggest the value of both prevention and intervention work, making use of mentalizing, with vulnerable parents. Finally, mentalizing difficulties reported in childhood are associated with social-emotional and cognitive problems, such as difficulties in emotion regulation and interpersonal problems, internalizing and externalizing problems, and difficulties in attentional control, effortful control, and academic achievement (for reviews, see Fonagy and Luyten [40–42]).

Whereas our earlier work tended to heavily emphasize the role of attachment in supporting or inhibiting the development of mentalizing [43,44], more recently our views have evolved into a more comprehensive set of considerations about the role of family members, peers, and broader sociocultural factors, such as socioeconomic deprivation, social isolation, and school climate, in the development of mentalizing [45,46]. In keeping with this view, there is growing evidence for mentalization-based treatment (MBT)-related interventions that focus on the family and the broader social context that surrounds an individual. Several studies have provided evidence of the effectiveness of MBT in various groups, such as substance-abusing mothers and their infants [47], fostered and adopted children [48], mothers living in underserved poor urban communities with children at high risk of maltreatment [49,50], individuals supporting a family member with borderline personality disorder (BPD) [51], and school-based prevention and intervention programs [52]. These types of family and "system-level" interventions might be most effective in addressing the problems that non-mentalizing social environments (e.g., neighborhoods with high levels of crime and violence, or schools with a culture of bullying) tend to generate, by creating a mentalizing climate as a counterweight against competitive, hostile, and aggressive wishes and tendencies. We are of the view that the social network around an individual serves to support the recovery of mentalizing when it is inevitably lost in the course of the daily difficulties encountered in life—the "micro-traumas" to which we are all continuously exposed. Connecting to others at moments of stress affords powerful protection against these problems because it ensures some balanced mentalizing, and thus resilience, in relation to the experience [53,54]. We consider that creating a mentalizing climate around the individual or family is particularly important for children and young people, and for providing support to their families/carers (for further discussion of mentalizing-based interventions that aim to do this, see Chapters 15 and 17). An important additional aspect of this view is that it acknowledges the need to provide a supportive mentalizing system around mental health professionals, given the many internal and external pressures and anxieties that they face in their work.

The Alien Self

The idea of the alien self is something we use in MBT to capture the experience of individuals who, in a high state of stress or distress, find their sense of self to be so frightened/frightening and incoherent that an "alien self" steps in. As we shall see in Chapters 14 and 18, the alien self has been particularly useful in understanding some cases of suicidality, serious acts of self-harm, interpersonal aggression/violence, and other mental health crises. When we speak of the alien self, we mean that disturbances in core self, sensory, and cognitive psychological processes lead the individual to experience various forms of loss in their personal agency. Their experience, which could be related to bodily, cognitive, or affective (dys)control, is of a "not-me," and there is a failure to integrate the experience of self coherently—essentially, parts of selfhood, experienced in the here and now, are alienated. We consider this representation to originate from the internalization of an insensitive or overwhelming caregiver, as a consequence of the child's exposure to failed mirroring by the caregiver. By "mirroring," we mean interactions where the caregiver recognizes the infant's mental states and is able to reflect those states back to the infant in a "marked," or regulated, way which shows that they understand and empathize with the infant's feelings but are not overwhelmed by them. Later in development, hostile or abusive caregiving is managed by the activation of a split-off part of the self-representation—the alien self—which presents the child with the possibility of obtaining a degree of control over an uncontrollable social environment by identifying with the aggressor (the abusive caregiver) using this alien self; the individual then becomes host to a torturing figure within the self-structure. In a sense, alien self-representations can help individuals to cope with disturbances of the self; the emergence of the alien self is an attempt at an emergency rescue from the intense emotional experiences that the individual is unable to manage or regulate. Although this defensive process affords something of a sense of temporary control, it also causes an acute experience of fragmentation and a feeling of being tortured from within. The alien self is a threat to psychological integrity, and can often lead to behaviors such as self-harm and suicide attempts that are linked to the affective pressure coming from the alien self-experience. Importantly, psychological contact with alien self-representations may also lead to dissociation, which is a hallmark of a mental process coming in as an attempt to protect psychological self-integrity. The importance of the alien self in clinical work is considered further in Chapters 10 and 12.

As we described in the previous section, the sense of self, and the ongoing coherence of the sense of self, is partly constructed on the basis of the secondary representations of who we are that are communicated to us, in the first instance, by our caregivers in early life. An individual who has missed out on sufficiently benign, coherent, or accurate secondary representations, or who has difficulty in recognizing and internalizing these secondary representations (possibly because of a lack of exposure to such representations), may be particularly vulnerable to developing a fragmented self-structure (i.e., an alien self), which is then called upon in response to a chaotic or empty sense of self-experience. The latter is sometimes called a "black hole" by individuals with BPD, who unsurprisingly find it terrifying, as it threatens their very existence.

Attachment and MBT

MBT is strongly shaped by attachment theory—the idea that the development of mentalizing emerges in the context of attachment relationships has always been central to our thinking, and evidence from research supports the view that there is a "loose coupling" between attachment, emotional sensitivity, and parental mentalizing capacities [55]. In MBT work, a patient's attachment experiences and representations will play a key part in the therapist's understanding of the challenges that the patient faces when thinking about other people's mental states. However, in the practice of MBT, it is also vital that the therapist understands the impact of attachment arousal in the here and now of treatment, and how the experience of such strong emotions can hinder effective mentalizing.

Brain-imaging studies have shown that the activation of the attachment system inhibits the neural systems that support mentalizing [56–58]. Trauma can activate the attachment system, and attachment trauma may cause chronic hyperactivation. This explains how some patients may be able to mentalize when they are under little or no stress; however, arousal related to attachment may cause a collapse of mentalizing at moments of stress in individuals who are prone to this form of hyperactivation. This has important implications for clinical work. Any intervention that calls for reflection—for example, by asking the patient to clarify or elaborate on a thought—is by its very nature asking the patient to engage in controlled mentalizing. If the topic that the patient is being asked to reflect on triggers arousal related to attachment, it may be very difficult for them to engage in such reflective activity. This may be one of the reasons why, historically, dynamic therapy for BPD was often found to be ineffective—traditional psychotherapeutic methods trigger the attachment system, both through the nature of the relationship between therapist and patient and through the subject matter that is explored in therapy. In effect, the patient is being asked to carry out a potentially impossible task—to think about mental states in a regulated way while being placed under circumstances that make such reflection almost impossible.

For all that MBT is about mentalizing, the work of MBT should not involve a relentless onslaught of reflective mentalizing on the part of the therapist. A patient who is in a state of high emotion, whose attachment system is ringing alarm bells, and whose mentalizing has gone "offline" should not be met with further demands to mentalize—these will either be ignored or be experienced as insensitive and unhelpful. Rather, the appropriate response from the therapist is recognition and validation of the patient's feelings at that moment. The reasons for this will unfold in the next sections of this chapter, in which we shall explain how the capacity for shared attention and thinking together is made possible by a sense of personal recognition. First, we shall explain how our clinical experiences directed our thinking in this regard.

Borderline Personality Disorder and MBT

As we mentioned in Chapter 1, MBT was first developed as a response to an acute awareness of how few patients with a diagnosis of BPD were receiving the therapeutic help and support that they needed. MBT was deliberately built on the awareness that a form of treatment was required that (a) really addressed the clinical needs and real-life experiences and difficulties endured by these patients, and (b) was sufficiently usable for a broad range of mental health workers to implement reliably without undergoing years of intensive training.

Given how much thinking about BPD has influenced the development of MBT, we believe it will be useful to give an overview of the nature of the difficulties associated with BPD, to help the reader to understand some key elements of the general mentalizing approach and the rationale for this approach. One of the most common features of BPD is emotional dysregulation, which involves a hypersensitivity to emotional stimuli that can spark intense and unstable emotional responses. Individuals with BPD may struggle to find coping strategies that help to reduce their distress, and the emotional dysregulation is often coupled with impulsive symptoms such as self-injurious behavior (including impulsive self-harming behaviors), cognitive disturbances (including dissociation), and interpersonal problems. Individuals with BPD often experience intense anguish, and they are 50 times as likely to attempt suicide as members of the general population [59].

Stress-related dissociation is common in individuals with BPD [60], and can affect the sense of identity, episodic memory, perception, and consciousness [61]. Disruptions of such fundamental social-cognitive processes can be understood as defensive (i.e., self-protective) in nature, by which we mean they are adaptations to stressful internal experiences that function to limit the impact of these experiences on the person (or their body, as in derealization or emotional numbing). We see the symptoms of BPD as understandable mental adjustments made by the individual to cope with what would otherwise be overwhelming subjective experiences of stress or distress [62]. Sometimes the impulsivity observed in BPD plays out as impulsive aggression [63,64]. Aggression shares with emotional dysregulation an association with high levels of stress and distress [65], but also features a lack of consideration for the mental state of the person toward whom the anger is directed [66]. A range of negative behaviors, such as aggressive outbursts, binge eating, risky sexual behavior, substance abuse, or suddenly ending a relationship, can be triggered in negative emotional contexts where the individual perceives these actions as uncontrollable and inevitable reactions to an impossible (social) situation [67,68].

Interpersonal disturbances are widely thought to be central in the work of helping people with BPD. There is strong evidence that individuals with BPD have difficulty in developing trust in others, a heightened sensitivity to social exclusion and rejection, and lengthy histories of conflicted unstable relationships with unresolved conflict about separating [69,70]. Often the histories of individuals who present for treatment amply explain their reluctance to place trust in social relationships [71,72]. Whether interpersonal disturbances should be regarded as attempts to manage earlier developmental problems (e.g., as in transference-focused psychotherapy) or as caused by other difficulties (as conceptualized in dialectical behavior therapy) remains a source of controversy, but from the pragmatic standpoint of a clinician, both the emotions themselves and their impact on relationships need to be tackled.

Mentalizing and BPD

A growing literature suggests that mentalizing difficulties are an intrinsic aspect of BPD and may drive the interpersonal disturbance, affect dysregulation, and impulsivity that are characteristically shown by individuals with this diagnosis. The mentalizing difficulties found in people with BPD can cover all four of the mentalizing dimensions (which were outlined in detail earlier in this chapter).

In relation to automatic/controlled mentalizing, the dysregulation and impulsivity associated with BPD reflect a tendency toward automatic mentalizing. In what was perhaps the first demonstration of the failure of reflective mentalizing in BPD, Fonagy et al. showed a dramatically reduced ability of BPD patients to reflect on their own and others' mental states in the context of attachment relationships [73]; this deficit in reflective functioning has been shown to be reversible by psychotherapy [74]. The findings on reflective functioning have been replicated by two relatively large studies [75,76] and confirmed in a recent meta-analysis [77].

A number of studies have shown that BPD patients show mentalizing impairments when tested with the Movie for the Assessment of Social Cognition (MASC), which is currently probably the best validated and most reliable measure of this mentalizing domain [78–80]. The MASC is a video-based test of mentalizing that requires participants to recognize the mental states of characters as they interact in an everyday-life scenario involving relationships. The misinterpretation of interpersonal situations because of a limited reflective capacity may generate extreme or inappropriate emotions in social interactions [81], particularly if there is also an overemphasis on externally oriented social cognition.

The self/other mentalizing dimension can often appear in BPD as an excessive focus on the mental states of others. Within the MBT model, knowledge of self and knowledge of other are complementary but interdependent. We learn about ourselves from others, and this self-knowledge helps us to place ourselves in another's shoes. We would expect mentalizing problems to manifest as a reduction in self-knowledge and unstable self-representations. Another area of mentalizing the self is its role in generating a sense of ownership over one's own actions. Several studies suggest that the experience of agency may be reduced in people with BPD relative to those without BPD [82–84]. There is emerging evidence of difficulties with self–other differentiation in BPD [85], with, for example, observations of greater proneness to the Rubber Hand Illusion [82,86], and confusion in identifying the self from graded morphed self-images [87]. Several investigations have shown that people with BPD are more likely to recognize negative than positive self-attributes, suggesting distortions in their self-concept toward greater negativity [88–91]. However, these studies gave a less clear picture in relation to the structural complexity of the self-concept. One study of adolescents and young adults reported that patients with BPD endorsed a greater number of attributes as being self-related, indicating a more diffuse sense of self [88], whereas another study of adults did not mirror this observation [90]. The differences in the findings of these studies could reflect the tendency of adolescents with emerging BPD to hypermentalize, which is likely to decrease with age [92]. In line with the greater prominence of the self in BPD, memory studies suggest that individuals with BPD have enhanced recall of self-relevant social events uninfluenced by emotional valence [93]. A "mind-wandering" paradigm suggested that self-related thoughts fluctuate more, and are more extreme, in individuals with BPD [91].

The evidence in relation to the internal/external dimension of mentalizing in BPD is mixed. Accuracy of emotion recognition appears to be reduced for static facial stimuli in individuals with BPD in some studies [94,95], but not in others [96–98]. Similarly, whereas some studies reported that patients with BPD take longer than individuals without BPD to decode faces with emotional expressions [98], other studies did not find this difference [99,100], and a meta-analysis confirmed the absence of a reliably identifiable deficit in the speed of emotional face processing in people with BPD [101]. There are also mixed findings regarding facial reactivity to brief emotion-induction videos. One study reported reduced reactivity in individuals with BPD (effect size = −0.67) [102], whereas another found reduced reactivity only to positive emotions, and also reported that BPD patients displayed more negative and mixed facial emotions in response to social exclusion than individuals without BPD [103]. There is evidence that facial mimicry is enhanced in BPD. In a task in which participants' facial muscle activity in response to dynamic facial expressions was recorded, BPD patients showed enhanced responses to angry, sad, and disgusted facial expressions, and attenuated responses to happy and surprised faces [104]. This finding suggests a specific rather than general hypersensitivity to the emotional state of others, expressed by exaggerated responses to negative social signals and attenuated responses to positive signals. Some studies have also identified a strong negative attribution bias, with BPD patients attending more quickly to negative faces and spending more time looking at them [105].

A large number of studies have explored mental-state discrimination in BPD. Most of these studies reported a medium-sized effect across a large number of measures. The most prominent of these measures is the Reading the Mind in the Eyes test, which has yielded both the largest reported advantage for mind reading [106,107] and the greatest deficits in those with BPD [108,109]. A meta-analysis by Hanegraaf et al. revealed a substantial and significant heterogeneity between the studies ($Q = 151.55$, $p < 0.0001$) [101]. However, this comprehensive meta-analysis provides extensive and robust evidence that people with BPD tend to be poorer at mental-state discrimination than people from other clinical populations, including those with other personality disorders (cluster C, avoidant, and narcissistic personality disorders) and those with major depression. Obviously this adds empirical support to the MBT approach and justifies our focus on mentalizing in our therapeutic work with patients with a diagnosis of BPD. BPD tends to be associated with difficulties in both selecting and displaying optimal social signals during interpersonal interactions, through facial expressions, language, and caregiver–infant behavior, and when interpreting the social signals of others.

Not surprisingly, given that the diagnostic criteria for BPD include rejection sensitivity, in experimental studies of social exclusion it has been found that individuals with this diagnosis report more severe experiences of ostracism than control participants without BPD; in fact, BPD patients are more likely to report feelings of exclusion even in conditions of social inclusion (e.g., [110]). There is evidence that rejection sensitivity is mediated by social-cognitive factors (tolerance of ambiguity, effortful control) and attachment-related factors (attachment anxiety, feeling of belonging, self-criticism) [111,112]. In the meta-analysis by Hanegraaf et al., BPD patients were also found to tend to feel more excluded than individuals with social anxiety disorder, major depressive disorder, or non-suicidal self-injury [101]. A failure of mentalizing combined with the expectation of negative outcomes from social interactions leaves individuals with BPD vulnerable to misinterpreting such interactions as instances of rejection.

Widening the Lens: Mentalizing in Psychopathology

We hope the description of the mentalizing challenges that individuals with BPD have to face has helped to provide a good sense of the rationale for the MBT approach. We shall now explain how and why this thinking can also inform the psychological treatment of other mental health disorders, ranging from other personality disorders to anxiety and depression, and to psychosis. This widening application of MBT is based on the view that mentalizing difficulties are common to many forms of mental health problems.

There is a lively and growing body of research around what is called the *general psychopathology factor*, or "*p factor*," in mental disorder. This is the idea that it might be more useful to understand the many overlapping mental health diagnoses that exist as sharing a common vulnerability factor, which then interacts with individual circumstances and genetic tendencies to manifest as a particular set of symptoms. To give quite a crude example, adolescent boys on the whole are statistically more likely to show externalizing symptoms, such as conduct disorder, whereas adolescent girls are more likely to develop internalizing symptoms, such as anxiety or depression. What is more, an adolescent boy with conduct disorder may well go on to experience depression and anxiety as an adult, with or without continuing conduct problems. So, across different populations, or across one individual's life course, there will be a range of experiences and behaviors that appear quite different in terms of both outward behavior and emotional experience, but, according to the thinking around the p factor, the underpinning vulnerability that leads to all of these different symptoms remains the same—it is just that they play out differently for different people as a result of a combination of their different social circumstances and genetic factors. There are various reasons for giving credence to this idea—for example, how do we make sense of the numerous concurrent and often overlapping difficulties that people experience? Findings from behavioral genetics and molecular biology are also consistent with the argument that there is a common underlying factor. Studies of families and twins tend to show that genetic risk is not specific to particular disorders, but is largely a transdiagnostic vulnerability factor [113–116]. Similarly, a genome study of 17 mental disorders with over one million participants found that, in terms of genomic markers, the mental disorders shared common variance risks [117].

The argument for the possibility that a single common factor underpins vulnerability also arises from population studies that use bifactor modeling of symptoms and diagnoses. Bifactor modeling involves exploring a possible general factor that a broad range of different variables—in this case symptoms and diagnoses—may share in common. Work in this area has found that psychiatric disorders are more convincingly explained if a general psychopathology factor is assumed to exist alongside clusters of symptoms (internalizing, externalizing, and psychosis) and individual mental disorders—for example, schizophrenia, generalized anxiety disorder, and depression [118–120]. Numerous studies with samples of children, adolescents, and adults indicate that the p factor appears to capture an underlying propensity for any kind of psychopathology as indicated through the apparent symptoms [121–123].

The emphasis on the p factor leaves us with the question of what this factor actually is, other than a useful statistical construct. Many studies suggest that all mental disorders involve a dysfunction of just one or two parts of the brain—the prefrontal cortex and perhaps the limbic regions [124,125]. There may be, and indeed there are very likely to be, many other areas of the brain that place an individual at risk of having a mental disorder. In fact, it is increasingly likely that it is not so much the structure of particular parts of the brain but the connections between different areas that cause these problems [126]. So general psychopathology, or the p factor, or perhaps most accurately the risk of mental disorder, at the level of the brain, may be to do with irregular connectivity in the cortex of the brain. This hypothesis is consistent with the growing consensus that psychopathology is best seen as a dysfunction of brain networks rather than of localized brain regions [127]. A study in which high-quality resting-state brain scans were obtained in 6593 children aged 9–10 years found that a high p factor was associated with reduced connectivity within the default mode network (DMN), and increased connectivity between the DMN and multiple control networks [128]. The DMN is active when the mind is not engaged in any specific cognitive task—that is, when a person is "mind-wandering". The DMN overlaps with and extends beyond the network of brain regions involved in mentalizing. One study showed that a set of tasks concerned with social cognition (i.e., reasoning about the mental states of other persons) activates the DMN [129]. The DMN is activated in thought processes such as daydreaming, imagining the perspectives of others, imagining the future, and recalling autobiographical memories [130], and is generally considered to subserve mentalizing. In other words, vulnerability to psychopathology, as measured by a high p factor, is associated with anomalies in connectivity in the neural network that is implicated in mentalizing processes.

Neuroscience research has consistently implicated two related major domains of functioning across most mental health disorders. The first is emotional dysregulation. Poorly managed emotions interfere with purposeful activity [131]. People who regulate their emotions well have an accurate idea about the risks of a given situation that triggered emotion, and can direct their attention to what they need to do to cope with it, use their attention to focus but also to distract themselves if focusing is unlikely to help, and reassess the risks as the results of their actions unfold [132]. Emotional dysregulation has been shown to be a feature of almost every psychiatric diagnostic condition [133]. Researchers believe that a weakness in emotion regulation can amplify emotional experience that is going on in the background, cause distortions in the way children see and experience social situations, and lead to intense emotional reactions just because the person is anticipating and experiencing an intense feeling. It can generate inappropriate feelings and lead to sometimes dramatic actions to avoid unpleasant intense emotion.

The second general domain that is consistently associated with mental disorder is executive function [134]. Executive function is the capacity to control thought and generally direct information in the appropriate direction relevant to any specific task; it includes self-regulation, decision making, sequencing of actions, planning, prioritizing, and navigating new tasks [135]. These cognitive processes are deemed to be essential for healthy functioning. The quality of executive function is thought to affect the p factor. Individuals with a high p factor score, signifying what we might term *high persistent psychological distress*, are oversensitive to difficult social interactions, and they find it hard to reliably interpret the reasons for others' actions and put out of their mind potentially upsetting memories of experiences. This state leaves them vulnerable to emotional storms.

To return to the role of mentalizing, we can see that because mentalizing supports executive function and affect regulation, both emotional dysregulation and poor executive function—the two areas reliably associated with psychopathology—are associated with poor mentalizing. We do not know where cause and effect lie in relation to mentalizing here; from a pragmatic clinical perspective, whether mentalizing problems are the consequence or the cause of emotional dysregulation and failures in executive function may be something of a "chicken-and-egg" question. The issue, clinically, is that all of these processes are closely linked to one another. The restoration of the capacity to think about mental states, both in oneself and in others, may be critical to making affect regulation and more protective executive function possible; this provides the rationale for the application of MBT approaches to a range of mental health disorders. In the next section, we shall set out why we consider mentalizing to have such great significance for healthy functioning.

Mentalizing, Social Learning, and Epistemic Trust

We have defined *epistemic trust*, which is a key part of mentalizing theory, as "trust in the authenticity and personal relevance of interpersonally transmitted knowledge about how the social environment works and how best to navigate it" (Fonagy et al. [136], p. 177). We have argued that mentalizing has a specific function in enabling individuals to take a position in relation to having epistemic trust in others—something that is vital if they are to benefit fully from opportunities to learn from others about the world in general and the social world, including themselves, in particular. We suggest that this is one of the reasons why disruptions in mentalizing appear to be so detrimental to social functioning [6] and so closely linked to vulnerability to any long-term mental disorder, and why they appear to be associated with the p factor [128]. To survive in the socially complex networks that humans inhabit, we have to be able to learn from other people [137]. In learning the skills that we need to survive, we observe and listen to experts, we avoid punishments and gain rewards by imitating others, we make complex strategic decisions after taking others' experience and views into account, and throughout all of this we learn about ourselves through social interactions. Learning efficiently from others is a central part of human existence. The transmission of information from parents to children, as well as between peers, constitutes a core mechanism of adaptive cultural learning, but can also cause maladaptive behaviors, such as antisocial actions, exaggerated avoidance, and anxiety [138].

The development of mentalizing is intricately related to epistemic trust and openness to social learning—that is, the ability to learn from others by trying to understand what they have to teach us. Human infants quickly learn to infer a model's goal and copy successful (but not failed) actions, but non-human primates acquire this capacity earlier than humans. Humans take a slightly different approach to learning. By the age of 3, children start showing what is called over-imitation, by which we mean that young children readily learn and copy behaviors that are unnecessarily complicated and do not seem to have a more functional purpose, if they seem to be the "right" way of doing things (a simple example would be learning to eat with a spoon rather than the faster and more efficient method of using one's hands) [139]. For a period, young children are prone to unselectively and unreflectively copy the behavior and acquire the beliefs of the majority of people with whom they interact [140], and will copy a person's failed as well as successful attempts to complete a task [141]—something that non-human primates have not been observed to do [142]. The reasons for this are that what the child is learning when, for example, they learn to use a spoon is complex. They are not only learning how to break up food and transport it to their mouth [143]. In fact, most small children find it easier to use their hands to eat—but learning to use a spoon correctly is one tiny example of the huge ocean of cultural and social knowledge that infants are born into. Trusting the demonstration by reliable elders that spoons are the correct way to eat, and copying how to use them, is an example of the small steps the young child starts to make in learning to navigate the world. Relatively inefficient routines are frequently socially transmitted as part of the cultural knowledge shared by members of a child's community [142]. Acquiring such routines is therefore an important developmental task that allows children to become members of their cultural group. The term "over-imitation" does not signify that children imitate knowledgeable adults when they should not. Rather, the tendency to over-imitate actions that are cognitively opaque is a cultural learning strategy, presumably identified through natural selection, based on the assumption that learning to do things that one does not fully understand is beneficial because they are culturally relevant, despite their opacity to the learner [144]. Preschool children's detailed mimicking of new behaviors may represent an openness to learning novel skills, unusual social norms, and rituals, and thus to affiliating with members of their community [145]. Over-imitating declines as mentalizing emerges, but it remains part of culture and of how humans learn, because a comprehensive understanding of causation is beyond humans even in relation to the physical world. The predisposition to over-imitate is sustained into adulthood [146], and is enhanced by the social context [147,148].

This account of social learning is relevant to our thinking about mentalizing and MBT because we suggest that learning and trusting others so that we can learn from them—that is, epistemic trust—is enabled by mentalizing. We have said elsewhere, "If I feel that I am understood, I will be disposed to learn from the person who understood me, who I feel is a trustworthy potential collaborator. This will include learning about myself but also learning about others and about the world I live in" (Fonagy et al. [6], p. 7). The outcome of this process is what we have called an *epistemic match*. This sounds like quite a simple proposition, but there are several mentalizing stages involved in this process. It requires the listener to (a) have a coherent enough sense of self to be able to recognize the match in the first place, (b) recognize the image of themselves that the communicator is describing to them (in a situation where the communicator is somehow expressing their own perception of the listener), and (c) judge the similarity or difference between their own self-perception and how the communicator is describing them. In addition, the process requires the communicator to have mentalized the listener well enough to have a good understanding of them. Thus epistemic trust as a social process depends on mentalizing on the part of both the listener and the communicator.

When co-mentalizing as occurs in an epistemic match is achieved, a particular subjective experience of social cognition is generated, which has been labelled the "*we-mode*." The we-mode is a mental state that describes an interpersonal experience of being enjoined with someone else, where intentional states are shared with a common purpose [149,150]. The we-mode triggers trust, which in turn triggers the potential for learning from the trusted source. The task of restoring mentalizing in MBT is thus undertaken to (re)open the possibility of experiencing the we-mode and an epistemic match that is crucial for enabling the social learning that underlies social functioning. In addition, there is a relational aspect to the we-mode, which generates the feelings of both agency and belonging that arise from a sense of "jointness," or the epistemic connectedness that shared intentionality creates. It is important to note that the we-mode is not some kind of merging of minds. The self, with its full sense of agency, remains important; in fact, in the absence of a robust self that temporarily subverts itself for a joint purpose, access to the we-mode may be only illusory and achieved by self-distortion. The we-mode is not an abdication of the awareness of separate mental states, nor is it some sort of psychic fusion. Rather, it involves holding in mind the idea that others are separate "agents or persons just as real as oneself" (Tomasello [151], p. 56), with whom we momentarily share a view of the world, an ambition, a plan, or an understanding that supersedes our individual perspective. Indeed, the benefits of the we-mode accrue from separate minds joining together to focus on a shared object; joint attention brings new knowledge and perspectives that a single mind cannot [4]. We shall describe in more detail in the next sections how disruptions in epistemic trust and in experiencing the we-mode are implicated in the development of psychopathology.

Trust in BPD

Mistrust as a Core Feature of BPD

An investigation of core dysfunctional beliefs in 288 individuals with a diagnosis of personality disorder found that the item that best distinguished individuals with a diagnosis of BPD from those with other personality disorders on the 126-item

Personality Belief Questionnaire was "I cannot trust other people"[152]. Another study comparing patients with BPD, patients with mood disorder, and control participants without a mental health diagnosis used a different self-rated instrument, the Trust Scenario Questionnaire, which taps into interpersonal trust between one person and another, and reported that patients with BPD scored significantly lower than either of the other groups [153]. These robust findings justify both a behavioral and a developmental focus on issues of trust in BPD, as well as consideration of the implications for other social and emotional aspects of the disorder.

Given that mistrust is such a key feature of BPD, it is hardly surprising that individuals with this disorder rate faces they do not know as less trustworthy and take longer to make these ratings [154], as well as identifying less trustworthiness and approachability in faces [155]. A more recent study replicated the untrustworthiness bias among BPD patients, who showed more biased trustworthiness and less ability to discriminate facial expressions than a matched control group [156]. The BPD group also exhibited slower reaction times when appraising ambiguous trustworthiness compared with the controls. Furthermore, the neural activation of BPD patients during trustworthiness ratings, assessed using functional magnetic resonance imaging, evidenced less activity in the anterior insula and lateral prefrontal cortex compared with the controls. This decrease in activity was proportional to the degree of trustworthiness bias and impaired discriminability demonstrated by both the BPD patients and the controls.

Development of Epistemic Mistrust

We suggest that one of the consequences of childhood adversity is that it can lead to the establishment of *epistemic mistrust*—that is, the misattribution of intentions and the assumption of malevolent motives behind another person's actions. Campbell and colleagues recently published a study of a self-report trait measure of epistemic trust that distinguishes three dimensions—epistemic trust, mistrust, and credulity (an indication of lack of discernment) [157]. The study found that mistrust and heightened credulity characterize individuals with histories of childhood adversity. We suggest that, for these individuals, attachment trauma following neglect in childhood generates a general background expectation of an imminent rupture of communication between them (as either listeners or communicators) and others in any social exchange. When an individual has a history of being repeatedly exposed to the communication of unreliable or ill-intentioned information, they may learn to reject these communications [158,159]. Orme et al. observed BPD symptoms from admission to treatment and to discharge in a sample of adolescents, and reported a significant negative correlation between BPD symptoms at admission and participants' self-reported trust in their parents [160]. The findings support the assumption that lower levels of trust in their parents may lead to an individual developing stable and rigid dysfunctional beliefs, and untrusting dispositions toward others in general, during adolescence and adulthood.

The social context of neuro-economic tasks, which tend to quantify interpersonal trust in monetary terms, seems to affect the performance of BPD patients. A study contrasted the performance of patients with major depressive disorder or BPD in two contexts—social interaction and playing against a computer [161]. BPD patients behaved more inconsistently, showing volatile and unpredictable reactions, but only in the condition involving social interactions. When exposed to social situations, those with

BPD showed a proneness to perceive counterparts as threatening, and this perception activated untrusting behaviors with trustees. Social interactions trigger the mentalizing system and bring forth expectations of interpersonal behaviors about the counterpart, which might explain the BPD patients' inconsistent behaviors in this study.

Ebert et al. followed up findings related to a potential mediating role of the neuropeptide oxytocin [162], where abnormalities have been linked to lower interpersonal trust [163]. BPD patients and controls were randomly assigned to receive oxytocin or a placebo, and were then invited to play a trust game. In this game there is an investor with a fixed number of points (say, 20), who is asked to give whatever number of points they would like to a trustee, who will look after the points for them. The trustee automatically triples the number and then has to decide how many points to give back to the investor. So if the investor gives 10 points, the trustee then has 30 points to play with and may, for example, give back half, leaving the investor with 10 points remaining from the start of the game and a further 15 points, while the trustee now has 15 points. Another round then takes place. A lot of mentalizing is required in this game. Intentions and causes that underlie lending/giving behavior between partners are given meaning and determine the interactional attitudes in the next round—one person's behavior (how many points they give) has an effect on the other's mind, which subsequently determines their behavior, and so on. This study found no correlation between childhood trauma scores and trust behavior in the control group of people without BPD, whether they had been given oxytocin or the placebo. The BPD patients who had a history of childhood neglect showed more limited trusting behavior and gave less money to the trustee, but only in the oxytocin condition, which activated interpersonal relational experience. It seems that increased oxytocin levels reduce trusting behaviors in BPD patients with a history of early parental neglect. These patterns of findings make sense if we assume that oxytocin generally acts to make social stimuli more salient [164], which may have a negative impact on individuals with a history of social adversity.

These findings and assumptions about the developmental roots of the high level of mistrust in individuals with BPD can be linked to their rejection sensitivity. The experience of being rejected could explain their tendency to mistrust. There is evidence from a study of a non-clinical population that there is a negative correlation between the facial appraisal of trust from unfamiliar faces and BPD features, which is explained by rejection sensitivity [165]. Rejection sensitivity, particularly its emotional aspect (anxiety and anger) [111, 112], is likely to have a role in mediating the relationship between mistrust and BPD [166].

The triggering of emotional arousal would be expected to decrease interpersonal trust. Masland and Hooley studied groups of non-clinical adults with higher or lower numbers of BPD descriptive symptoms who rated the trustworthiness of unfamiliar faces after completing an affective priming paradigm in which they looked at negative, neutral, or positive images [167]. Participants with higher numbers of BPD symptoms made less trusting appraisals. The negative priming images had a greater impact on the high-BPD group than on the low-BPD group, which suggests that the influence of negative emotional states on trust appraisal performance is stronger in individuals with more BPD symptoms.

One study investigated interpersonal trust in romantic relationships involving individuals with BPD compared with that in romantic relationships involving controls [168]. The authors asked heterosexual couples in which the women had been diagnosed with

BPD, and control couples with no psychiatric history, to discuss three topics: neutral (favorite films), personal (personal fears), and relationship-threatening (possible reasons for separation from their partner). After each discussion, the participants rated their partner's trustworthiness. The authors expected a lower appraisal of the partner's trustworthiness in the BPD couples than the control couples, especially after the relationship-threatening discussions. Women with BPD expressed lower trust toward their partner following the personal or relationship-threatening discussions but not the neutral discussions. These findings fit with the assumption that emotional arousal has a negative impact on mentalizing in individuals with BPD [169].

Mentalizing and Social Rejection

Social rejection, when repeated and severe, is implicated in the development of almost all psychiatric disorders [170]. Unusual reactivity and vulnerability to social rejection is used as a criterion in the diagnosis of social anxiety disorder, major depression, BPD, avoidant personality disorder, premenstrual dysphoric disorder, bulimia nervosa, body dysmorphic disorder, acute suicidal ideation, and substance/alcohol use disorders, although the specific behavioral, affective, and neural responses to rejection may differ among these disorders [71]. Social rejection or acceptance is directly linked to self-perception, which is dependent on mentalizing and is at the core of many mood, anxiety, and personality disorders.

Feeling rejected interacts with mentalizing. If we know that someone who appears to be deliberately ignoring us is actually unusually shy, we can rethink why they are avoiding eye contact with us and feel less rejected by them, because rejection normally has something to do with how we think the other person might be thinking and feeling about us. Over-interpreting reactions that are actually neutral as distant, cold, or uninterested might lead us to ask "*Why don't they like me?*" Many instances of rejection are linked to how another's thoughts, feelings, or intentions are perceived.

Social rejection has been investigated in the exclusion condition of the Cyberball paradigm (a virtual ball-toss game), which consistently elicits feelings of social distress. Here, rejection consists of participants observing that they are not being passed a virtual ball that is being passed by two avatars belonging to presumed players who are strangers to the participant. The intensity of the experience of social rejection is such that Eisenberger and Lieberman have suggested that the social signaling system may have piggybacked on to the neural system involved in perceiving physical pain (the dorsal anterior cingulate cortex and anterior insula) [171, 172]. The affective pain signal indicates the grave risk of broken social bonds that could compromise access to shared resources, support, and beneficial social relationships.

Sahi and Eisenberger have suggested that the neural underpinnings of social rejection entail the activation of the mentalizing neural network [173], based on findings that the dorsomedial and ventromedial prefrontal cortex and precuneus are generally active in the exclusion phase of Cyberball and other rejection paradigms [174]. They also argue that the development of self-conscious emotions and fear of social rejection emerge in early childhood, associated with increased mentalizing competence and maturation of mentalizing networks. The characteristic hypermentalizing of adolescents may account for their heightened sensitivity to social rejection rooted in greater responsiveness of the mentalizing network at this age. Neural responses to peer acceptance and rejection in socially anxious early adolescents are greater than those in older adolescents [175] or in adults [176]. Although Sahi and Eisenberger [173] make a case for mentalizing anomalies mediating the abnormal reactions to social rejection of patients with schizophrenia [177] and individuals with autism [178], it is not conclusive.

There is better evidence to support the existence of mentalizing anomalies in individuals with a diagnosis of BPD who respond atypically to social rejection. A significant number of studies have linked rejection sensitivity to BPD (e.g., [179–181]). A large meta-analysis of 28 Cyberball studies confirmed a robust disposition of individuals with BPD to expect rejection [182]. Individuals diagnosed with BPD perceived that they received fewer ball tosses compared with the control groups in both the exclusion condition (when they did not receive the ball as often as others) and inclusion condition (when they received the ball more often) of Cyberball. They also showed more overall negative affectivity after exposures to rejection, and an even larger effect following social inclusion. Notably, the reaction to social inclusion in a situation where participants had been excluded distinguished individuals with BPD from typical controls. Mentalizing theory would understand this effect as part of an inability to overcome a pervasive pre-existing bias toward rejection underpinning hypervigilance about the intentions of others, and an inability to mentalize a change in attitude in the context of acceptance. Evidence consistent with this hypothesis includes the findings that individuals with BPD were impaired in processing positive social feedback but integrated negative feedback better than controls [183], experienced reduced positive emotions such as pride and happiness after reading self-relevant appreciative sentences [184], and changed their social expectations in response to negative, but not positive, social feedback [185]. These observations are critical from a clinical perspective, where the therapist often waits in vain for a positive reaction from the patient in response to their unconditional acceptance and interventions aimed at increasing therapeutic inclusion, only to encounter the resentment and even deeper suspicion that arises from the patient's confusion in the face of the experience of being accepted.

Trauma and Mentalizing

The mentalizing model originated from understanding of the psychological consequences of trauma (see also Chapter 11), with the assumption that one possible outcome of childhood adversity was a limited capacity for mentalizing, driven by anxiety. A child's fear of understanding the mental states of an individual who poses a genuine threat to them is understandable, and generalization of this fear to other minds might be expected [186]. Considerable evidence has accumulated to suggest that limitations in mentalizing are commonly associated with the experience of trauma, particularly post-traumatic stress disorder. Differences in mentalizing have been demonstrated in tests of emotional intelligence [187], tests of empathy and compassion [188,189], and tests developed specifically to measure cognitive mentalizing, such as the Faux Pas test and the Strange Stories task [190,191]. Our theoretical approach predicts a bias against internal cues to mental states (mental-state understanding) but a potential hypersensitivity to external indicators of mental states (observations) to balance the defensive avoidance of "looking behind" the external. In line with this prediction, patients with a history of trauma appear to show no or only small deficits in emotion-recognition tests [192–194].

Our assumption in relation to childhood trauma is rooted in the psychoanalytic history of MBT, but a rare aspect of this history is shared by modern psychiatry. Anna Freud and

Dorothy Burlingham, who observed children's responses to the bombing of London during the Second World War, noted that the objective danger a child was in appeared to be less predictive of a phobic reaction than the mother's level of anxiety [195]. Their observations antedated the substantial interest in the vicarious learning of children in the context of social referencing [196,197] and other related, particularly facially transmitted, ways of deriving emotional information about risk and danger [198–200].

In our developmental approach to trauma, we have suggested that adversity becomes traumatic when it is compounded by the sense that one's mind is alone. Normally, an accessible other mind provides the social referencing that enables one to frame a frightening and otherwise overwhelming experience [186]. Recent experimental studies have provided strong support for this view. A study of conditioning found that vicarious safety learning (when participants watch a calm-looking demonstrator modeling safety) leads to better attenuation of a conditioned threat response than traditional direct safety learning training when a model is not present [201]. This observation suggests that the mind is programmed to be attuned to socially accessible agents so as to judge the threat response through the availability of another person, such as an attachment figure.

Three Communication Systems

In drawing out some of the clinical implications of the theory we have covered so far in this chapter, we have developed the idea that there are three "communication systems" which are associated with effective therapeutic help [202]. These communication systems do not just apply to MBT; rather, we suggest that any form of meaningful psychotherapeutic help tends to involve the communication, internalization, and (re-)application of new forms of learning about oneself, and about oneself in relation to other people.

Communication System 1: The Teaching and Learning of Content

All different therapeutic schools activate the first communication system when the clinician conveys to the patient a model for understanding the mind that feels relevant to the patient and makes them feel recognized and understood. The experience of being recognized as an independent agent in this way reduces the patient's epistemic vigilance and begins to prime them to become open to social learning. The clinician's capacity to mentalize the patient is crucial to this system, as it requires the clinician to apply and communicate their therapeutic model in a way that is experienced as meaningful by the patient, creating an epistemic match. The initial stages of MBT, particularly the MBT-Introductory group (see Chapter 4), attest to the importance of this communication system, and the ability of the clinician to make mentalizing relevant to how patients think about themselves and others is key to engagement in treatment. This is the beginning of patients rethinking themselves and seeing themselves in a different light.

Communication System 2: The Re-Emergence of Mentalizing

When the patient is once again open to social communication in contexts that had previously been blighted by epistemic disruption, they show increased interest in the clinician's mind and use of thoughts and feelings, which stimulates and strengthens the patient's capacity for mentalizing: "*How does this person see me as they do?*" The not-knowing stance of the clinician, with assiduous focus on the patient's experience, kick-starts this process. The emergence of mentalizing in the patient leads to a "virtuous circle" in which curiosity about mental states and social learning through greater epistemic openness support each other within the therapeutic relationship.

Communication System 3: Applying Social Learning in the Wider Environment

Being mentalized by another person frees the patient from their state of temporary or long-term social isolation, and (re-)activates their capacity to learn. This frees the patient to grow in the context of relationships outside therapy. This view implies that it is not just the content and techniques of the therapy, or the insight acquired in the course of treatment, that are key to its success; perhaps primarily it is the patient's capacity for social learning and thinking about mental states that improves their functioning as they become able to "use" their environment in a different way. A further implication is, of course, that there may be a need to intervene at the level of the patient's social environment when necessary or appropriate.

Although we have described the three communication systems as forming a neat, numerically linear sequence, in fact—particularly for patients who are receiving fairly lengthy treatment—the process is rather less linear and straightforward. There are inevitable disruptions, ruptures, and work on repair across treatment, which may involve the activation of different communication systems, or the overlapping activation of more than one system at once. An example may involve a patient receiving a knock-back in a close personal relationship outside therapy, which creates feelings of intense distress and triggers the emergence of one or more of the non-mentalizing modes described earlier in this chapter. In such a state of mind, the patient may regard anything that the clinician says as meaningless, useless, or provocative; communication breaks down and any expectation that the patient will take in or apply social learning is likely to fail. In this situation, the clinician needs to go back to the first communication system, in which the patient's state of mind is understood and recognized, and their capacity for thinking and learning is gently reinstated.

Summary of Empirical Research on MBT

In 2020, a Cochrane Review identified MBT as one of two therapies (the other being dialectical behavior therapy) with a reasonable evidence base for the treatment of BPD [203]. A meta-analysis that included 33 randomized controlled trials (RCTs) of specialized psychotherapies for BPD compared with non-specialized psychotherapies for adult patients diagnosed with BPD supported the efficacy of MBT in patients with BPD [204]. Another meta-analysis of psychological treatments for BPD, which covered 87 studies, found that MBT (along with schema therapy and reduced dialectical behavior therapy) was associated with higher than average effect sizes compared with treatment as usual (TAU), which was associated with lower than average effect sizes [205]. A review of RCTs found that MBT for BPD tended to be associated with medium to large or very large effect sizes on a range of outcome measures, including BPD symptoms, educational attainment, and interpersonal functioning [206]. A systematic review similarly concluded that MBT is associated with significant improvements in BPD symptom severity, comorbid symptom severity, and quality of life [207].

Bateman and Fonagy tested the effectiveness of MBT as a treatment for BPD in a series of RCTs. A day-hospital program of MBT was investigated in outcome studies culminating in an 8-year follow-up study—the longest follow-up of treatment for BPD conducted to date [208]. Compared with TAU, MBT achieved decreases in suicide attempts, emergency-room visits, inpatient admissions, medication and outpatient treatment use, and impulsivity. Far fewer patients in the MBT group than in the TAU group met the criteria for BPD at follow-up (13% versus 87%). Patients in the MBT group also showed greater improvements in interpersonal and occupational functioning.

An intensive outpatient MBT program was found to be more effective than structured clinical management for BPD at the end of the 18-month treatment period [209], particularly for patients with more than two personality disorder diagnoses [210]. Compared with TAU, the outpatient MBT treatment resulted in lower rates of suicidal behavior and non-suicidal self-injury, and fewer hospitalizations. The primary outcome measure of 6-month periods free of suicidal behaviors, severe self-injurious behaviors, and hospitalization showed improvements from 0% to 43% in the structured clinical management group and 73% in the MBT group. In addition, the MBT group showed improved social adjustment and reduced depression, symptom distress, and interpersonal distress [209]. An 8-year follow-up of this study found that, of the 73% of the sample who agreed to participate, a significantly higher proportion of patients in the MBT group (74%, compared with 51% in the structured clinical management control group) still met the primary criteria for recovery [211]. Finally, an RCT of MBT for comorbid BPD and antisocial personality disorder found that MBT was effective in reducing symptoms such as hostility, paranoia, anger, and frequency of self-injurious behavior and suicide attempts, and achieved improvements in negative mood, general psychiatric symptoms, interpersonal problems, and social adjustment [212].

An RCT in Denmark that investigated the efficacy of MBT compared with a less intensive manualized supportive group therapy in patients with BPD found that MBT achieved better results in terms of clinician-rated Global Assessment of Functioning [213]. These results were sustained 18 months later [214]. In a second study in Denmark, patients who were treated with partial hospitalization followed by group MBT showed significant improvements after treatment (average duration 2 years) on a range of measures, including Global Assessment of Functioning, hospitalizations, and vocational status, with further improvements at 2-year follow-up [215]. A multi-site RCT in the Netherlands that compared day-hospital MBT with specialist TAU in patients with BPD found that both forms of treatment were effective, although the MBT program was associated with higher patient acceptability, indicated by significantly lower early dropout (9% for MBT versus 34% for TAU) [216].

Another study in the Netherlands investigated the effectiveness of an 18-month manualized program of MBT in 45 patients with severe BPD [217]. Patients showed significant positive changes in symptom distress, social and interpersonal functioning, and personality pathology and functioning, and effect sizes were moderate to large; however, it should be noted that this study did not use a control group. A naturalistic longitudinal study in Norway that compared psychodynamic group-based treatment and MBT found that greater clinical severity of BPD was associated with poorer outcomes in the group-based treatment, whereas it had no significant effect on treatment outcome in the MBT group [218]. This observation supports Bateman and Fonagy's finding that MBT may be particularly indicated for patients with more severe BPD [210].

An RCT compared a form of MBT for eating disorders and specialist supportive clinical management for patients with eating disorders and symptoms of BPD. This study had a high dropout rate, with only 15 of the 68 participants who were eligible for randomization (22%) completing the 18-month follow-up, making the results difficult to interpret. However, MBT was associated with a greater reduction in patients' concerns about body shape and weight as assessed by the Eating Disorder Examination [219].

In an RCT of MBT for adolescents (MBT-A) (see also Chapter 14), 80 adolescents who presented to mental health services and had engaged in self-harm in the preceding month were randomized to MBT or TAU; 97% were diagnosed with depression, and 73% met the criteria for BPD. At the end of 12 months of treatment, MBT-A was found to be more successful than TAU in reducing self-harm and symptoms of depression. On the basis of self-report, the recovery rate was 44% for MBT-A and 17% for TAU, whereas on the basis of interview assessment the recovery rates were 57% and 32%, respectively. There was also a greater reduction in depressive symptoms and BPD diagnoses and traits in the MBT-A group. Both groups showed significant reductions in self-harm and risk-taking behavior, based on Risk-Taking and Self-Harm Inventory scores, following both a linear and a quadratic pattern. The group × time interaction term was also significant for both self-harm and risk taking, indicating that the linear decrease was significantly greater for the MBT-A group on both variables. At 12 months, self-harm scores were significantly lower for the MBT-A group [220]. However, a recent Cochrane Review of treatments for self-harm in adolescents has suggested that more evidence for effectiveness is needed for MBT-A [221].

An uncontrolled pilot study in Denmark of 34 female adolescents with BPD who participated in 12 months of structured mentalization-based group therapy found that of the 25 adolescents who completed the study, 23 displayed improvements in BPD symptoms, depression, self-harm, peer and parent attachment, mentalizing, and general psychopathology. Enhanced trust in peers and parents in combination with improved mentalizing capacity was associated with a greater reduction in borderline symptoms, pointing to a candidate mechanism for the efficacy of the treatment [222]. On the basis of this pilot study, an RCT was developed to compare group MBT with TAU (which involved individual supportive care) for 112 adolescents with BPD in an outpatient setting; this study found that both treatments had similar effectiveness. The authors suggest that group MBT might be better indicated as an early-stage intervention, and that a group MBT program also including individual sessions should be tested [223]. Finally, a naturalistic multi-informant study of MBT in 118 adolescent inpatients with personality pathology symptoms found that the participants improved on general and personality pathology measures, and in terms of health-related and generic quality of life. These improvements were clinically important as well as statistically significant, particularly in internalizing domains [224].

Concluding Remarks

In Part II of this book we shall discuss the translation of this developmental, evidence-based theory into clinical practice. To summarize, the central question is how to help patients to generate robust and effective mentalizing that will be conducive to constructive personal and social functioning in their life. Better mentalizing, particularly when attachment processes are activated, fuels epistemic learning within the social world and allows personal change over time. MBT is designed to stimulate this pathway of change, and is organized as a coherent set of interventions that are systematically applied over time to help the patient to learn about and practice mentalizing skills in their everyday life, while taking into account how attachment anxiety and other stressors can undermine the stability and effective use of mentalizing.

References

1. Meyer ML, Davachi L, Ochsner KN, Lieberman MD. Evidence that default network connectivity during rest consolidates social information. *Cereb Cortex* 2019; **29**: 1910–20.
2. Bloom P. Religion is natural. *Dev Sci* 2007; **10**: 147–51.
3. Dunbar RI, Shultz S. Evolution in the social brain. *Science* 2007; **317**: 1344–7.
4. Tomasello M. *Becoming Human: A Theory of Ontogeny*. Cambridge, MA: The Belknap Press of Harvard University Press, 2019.
5. Park BK, Kim M, Young L. An examination of accurate versus "biased" mentalizing in moral economic decision-making. In: Gilead M, Ochsner K, eds. *The Neural Basis of Mentalizing*. Cham, Switzerland: Springer, 2021; 537–53.
6. Fonagy P, Campbell C, Constantinou M et al. Culture and psychopathology: an attempt at reconsidering the role of social learning. *Dev Psychopathol* 2022; **34**: 1205–20.
7. Schaefer JD, Caspi A, Belsky DW et al. Enduring mental health: prevalence and prediction. *J Abnorm Psychol* 2017; **126**: 212–24.
8. Nisbett RE, Ross L. *Human Interface: Strategies and Shortcomings of Social Judgment*. Englewood Cliffs, NJ: Prentice-Hall, 1980.
9. Nisbett RE, Wilson TD. Telling more than we can know: verbal reports on mental processes. *Psychol Rev* 1977; **84**: 231–59.
10. Johansson P, Hall L, Sikstrom S, Olsson A. Failure to detect mismatches between intention and outcome in a simple decision task. *Science* 2005; **310**: 116–9.
11. Samson D, Apperly IA, Braithwaite JJ et al. Seeing it their way: evidence for rapid and involuntary computation of what other people see. *J Exp Psychol Hum Percept Perform* 2010; **36**: 1255–66.
12. Beeney JE, Hallquist MN, Ellison WD, Levy KN. Self-other disturbance in borderline personality disorder: neural, self-report, and performance-based evidence. *Personal Disord* 2016; **7**: 28–39.
13. Bradford EE, Jentzsch I, Gomez JC. From self to social cognition: Theory of Mind mechanisms and their relation to Executive Functioning. *Cognition* 2015; **138**: 21–34.
14. Gordon RM. Simulation, predictive coding, and the shared world. In: Gilead M, Ochsner K, eds. *The Neural Basis of Mentalizing*. Cham, Switzerland: Springer, 2021; 237–56.
15. Cooley CH. *Human Nature and the Social Order*, revised ed. New York, NY: Shocken Books, 1964/1902.
16. Mead GH. *Mind, Self, and Society*. Chicago, IL: University of Chicago Press, 1934.
17. Fonagy P, Gergely G, Jurist E, Target M. Developmental issues in normal adolescence and adolescent breakdown. In: *Affect Regulation, Mentalization, and the Development of the Self*. New York, NY: Other Press LLC, 2002; 317–40.
18. Malle BF. The tree of social cognition: hierarchically organized capacities of mentalizing. In: Gilead M, Ochsner K, eds. *The Neural Basis of Mentalizing*. Cham, Switzerland: Springer, 2021; 337–70.
19. Osterhaus C, Koerber S, Sodian B. Scaling of advanced Theory-of-Mind tasks. *Child Dev* 2016; **87**: 1971–91.

20. Atance CM, Metcalf JL, Martin-Ordas G, Walker CL. Young children's causal explanations are biased by post-action associative information. *Dev Psychol* 2014; **50**: 2675–85.

21. Somerville LH. Special issue on the teenage brain: Sensitivity to social evaluation. *Curr Dir Psychol Sci* 2013; **22**: 121–7.

22. Sebastian C, Viding E, Williams KD, Blakemore SJ. Social brain development and the affective consequences of ostracism in adolescence. *Brain Cogn* 2010; **72**: 134–45.

23. Moor BG, Guroglu B, Op de Macks ZA et al. Social exclusion and punishment of excluders: neural correlates and developmental trajectories. *Neuroimage* 2012; **59**: 708–17.

24. Sebastian CL, Tan GC, Roiser JP et al. Developmental influences on the neural bases of responses to social rejection: implications of social neuroscience for education. *Neuroimage* 2011; **57**: 686–94.

25. Burnett S, Blakemore SJ. Functional connectivity during a social emotion task in adolescents and in adults. *Eur J Neurosci* 2009; **29**: 1294–301.

26. de Villiers JG. The role(s) of language in theory of mind. In: Gilead M, Ochsner K, eds. *The Neural Basis of Mentalizing*. Cham, Switzerland: Springer, 2021; 423–48.

27. Aival-Naveh E, Rothschild-Yakar L, Kurman J. Keeping culture in mind: a systematic review and initial conceptualization of mentalizing from a cross-cultural perspective. *Clin Psychol: Sci Pract* 2019; **26**: e12300.

28. Dunn J, Brophy M. Communication relationships and individual differences in children's understanding of mind. In: Astington JW, Baird JA, eds. *Why Languages Matter for Theory of Mind*. New York, NY: Oxford University Press, 2005; 50–69.

29. Meins E, Fernyhough C, Arnott B et al. Mind-mindedness and theory of mind: mediating roles of language and perspectival symbolic play. *Child Dev* 2013; **84**: 1777–90.

30. Ebert S, Peterson C, Slaughter V, Weinert S. Links among parents' mental state language, family socioeconomic status, and preschoolers' theory of mind development. *Cogn Dev* 2017; **44**: 32–48.

31. Fonagy P, Steele M, Moran GS et al. Measuring the ghost in the nursery: a summary of the main findings of the Anna Freud Centre/University College London parent-child study. *Bull Anna Freud Centre* 1991; **14**: 115–31.

32. Steele H, Perez A, Segal F, Steele M. Maternal Adult Attachment Interview (AAI) collected during pregnancy predicts reflective functioning in AAIs from their first-born children 17 years later. *Int J Dev Sci* 2016; **10**: 117–24.

33. Zeegers MAJ, Colonnesi C, Stams GJM, Meins E. Mind matters: a meta-analysis on parental mentalization and sensitivity as predictors of infant-parent attachment. *Psychol Bull* 2017; **143**: 1245–72.

34. Meins E, Fernyhough C, Wainwright R et al. Maternal mind-mindedness and attachment security as predictors of theory of mind understanding. *Child Dev* 2002; **73**: 1715–26.

35. Rosso AM, Airaldi C. Intergenerational transmission of reflective functioning. *Front Psychol* 2016; **7**: 1903.

36. Rosso AM, Viterbori P, Scopesi AM. Are maternal reflective functioning and attachment security associated with preadolescent mentalization? *Front Psychol* 2015; **6**: 1134.

37. Borelli JL, Cohen C, Pettit C et al. Maternal and child sexual abuse history: an intergenerational exploration of children's adjustment and maternal trauma-reflective functioning. *Front Psychol* 2019; **10**: 1062.

38. Luyten P, Fonagy P. Mentalizing and trauma. In: Bateman A, Fonagy P, eds. *Handbook of Mentalizing in Mental Health Practice*, 2nd ed. Washington, DC: American Psychiatric Publishing, 2019; 79–99.

39. Berthelot N, Ensink K, Bernazzani O et al. Intergenerational transmission of attachment in abused and neglected mothers: the role of trauma-specific reflective functioning. *Infant Ment Health J* 2015; **36**: 200–12.

40. Fonagy P, Luyten P. A multilevel perspective on the development of borderline personality disorder. In: Cicchetti D, ed. *Developmental Psychopathology. Vol. 3: Maladaptation and Psychopathology*, 3rd ed. New York, NY: John Wiley & Sons, 2016; 726–92.

41. Fonagy P, Luyten P. Conduct problems in youth and the RDoC approach: a developmental, evolutionary-based view. *Clin Psychol Rev* 2018; **64**: 57–76.

42. Luyten P, Fonagy P. The stress–reward–mentalizing model of depression: an integrative developmental cascade approach to child and adolescent depressive disorder based on the Research Domain Criteria (RDoC) approach. *Clin Psychol Rev* 2018; **64**: 87–98.

43. Fonagy P. Attachment and borderline personality disorder. *J Am Psychoanal Assoc* 2000; **48**: 1129–46.

44. Fonagy P, Steele M, Steele H et al. The capacity for understanding mental states: the reflective self in parent and child and its significance for security of attachment. *Infant Ment Health J* 1991; **12**: 201–18.

45. Fonagy P, Luyten P, Allison E, Campbell C. What we have changed our minds about: Part 1. Borderline personality disorder as a limitation of resilience. *Borderline Personal Disord Emot Dysregul* 2017; **4**: 11.

46. Fonagy P, Luyten P, Allison E, Campbell C. What we have changed our minds about: Part 2. Borderline personality disorder, epistemic trust and the developmental significance of social communication. *Borderline Personal Disord Emot Dysregul* 2017; **4**: 9.

47. Suchman NE, DeCoste C, Borelli JL, McMahon TJ. Does improvement in maternal attachment representations predict greater maternal sensitivity, child attachment security and lower rates of relapse to substance use? A second test of Mothering from the Inside Out treatment mechanisms. *J Subst Abuse Treat* 2018; **85**: 21–30.

48. Redfern S, Wood S, Lassri D et al. The Reflective Fostering Programme: background and development of a new approach. *Adopt Foster* 2018; **42**: 234–48.

49. Slade A, Holland ML, Ordway MR et al. *Minding the Baby*®: enhancing parental reflective functioning and infant attachment in an attachment-based, interdisciplinary home visiting program. *Dev Psychopathol* 2020; **32**: 123–37.

50. Byrne G, Sleed M, Midgley N et al. Lighthouse Parenting Programme: description and pilot evaluation of mentalization-based treatment to address child maltreatment. *Clin Child Psychol Psychiatry* 2019; **24**: 680–93.

51. Bateman A, Fonagy P. A randomized controlled trial of a mentalization-based intervention (MBT-FACTS) for families of people with borderline personality disorder. *Personal Disord* 2019; **10**: 70–79.

52. Fonagy P, Twemlow SW, Vernberg EM et al. A cluster randomized controlled trial of child-focused psychiatric consultation and a school systems-focused intervention to reduce aggression. *J Child Psychol Psychiatry* 2009; **50**: 607–16.

53. Fonagy P, Allison E, Campbell C. Mentalizing, resilience, and epistemic trust. In: Bateman A, Fonagy P, eds. *Handbook of Mentalizing in Mental Health Practice*, 2nd ed. Washington, DC: American Psychiatric Association Publishing, 2019; 63–77.

54. Fonagy P, Steele M, Steele H et al. The Emanuel Miller Memorial Lecture 1992. The theory and practice of resilience. *J Child Psychol Psychiatry* 1994; 35: 231–57.

55. Luyten P, Campbell C, Allison E, Fonagy P. The mentalizing approach to psychopathology: state of the art and future directions. *Annu Rev Clin Psychol* 2020; **16**: 297–325.

56. Bartels A, Zeki S. The neural correlates of maternal and romantic love. *Neuroimage* 2004; **21**: 1155–66.

57. Zeki S, Romaya JP. Neural correlates of hate. *PLoS One* 2008; **3**: e3556.

58. Nolte T, Bolling DZ, Hudac CM et al. Brain mechanisms underlying the impact of attachment-related stress on social cognition. *Front Hum Neurosci* 2013; **7**: 816.

59. Pompili M, Girardi P, Ruberto A, Tatarelli R. Suicide in borderline personality disorder: a meta-analysis. *Nord J Psychiatry* 2005; **59**: 319–24.

60. Korzekwa MI, Dell PF, Links PS et al. Dissociation in borderline personality disorder: a detailed look. *J Trauma Dissociation* 2009; **10**: 346–67.

61. Miller CE, Townsend ML, Grenyer BFS. Understanding chronic feelings of emptiness in borderline personality disorder: a qualitative study. *Borderline Personal Disord Emot Dysregul* 2021; **8**: 24.

62. Vermetten E, Spiegel D. Trauma and dissociation: implications for borderline personality disorder. *Curr Psychiatry Rep* 2014; **16**: 434.

63. Ende G, Cackowski S, Van Eijk J et al. Impulsivity and aggression in female BPD and ADHD patients: association with ACC glutamate and GABA concentrations. *Neuropsychopharmacology* 2016; **41**: 410–18.

64. Sebastian A, Jung P, Krause-Utz A et al. Frontal dysfunctions of impulse control – a systematic review in borderline personality disorder and attention-deficit/hyperactivity disorder. *Front Hum Neurosci* 2014; **8**: 698.

65. Krause-Utz A, Keibel-Mauchnik J, Ebner-Priemer U et al. Classical conditioning in borderline personality disorder: an fMRI study. *Eur Arch Psychiatry Clin Neurosci* 2016; **266**: 291–305.

66. Bateman A, Bolton R, Fonagy P. Antisocial personality disorder: a mentalizing framework. *Focus* 2013; **11**: 178–86.

67. Cackowski S, Reitz AC, Ende G et al. Impact of stress on different components of impulsivity in borderline personality disorder. *Psychol Med* 2014; **44**: 3329–40.

68. Jacob GA, Zvonik K, Kamphausen S et al. Emotional modulation of motor response inhibition in women with borderline personality disorder: an fMRI study. *J Psychiatry Neurosci* 2013; **38**: 164–72.

69. Lis S, Bohus M. Social interaction in borderline personality disorder. *Curr Psychiatry Rep* 2013; **15**: 338.

70. King-Casas B, Sharp C, Lomax-Bream L et al. The rupture and repair of cooperation in borderline personality disorder. *Science* 2008; **321**: 806–10.

71. Reinhard MA, Dewald-Kaufmann J, Wustenberg T et al. The vicious circle of social exclusion and psychopathology: a systematic review of experimental ostracism research in psychiatric disorders. *Eur Arch Psychiatry Clin Neurosci* 2020; **270**: 521–32.

72. Jowett S, Karatzias T, Albert I. Multiple and interpersonal trauma are risk factors for both post-traumatic stress disorder and borderline personality disorder: a systematic review on the traumatic backgrounds and clinical characteristics of comorbid post-traumatic stress disorder/borderline personality disorder groups versus single-disorder groups. *Psychol Psychother* 2020; **93**: 621–38.

73. Fonagy P, Leigh T, Steele M et al. The relation of attachment status, psychiatric classification, and response to psychotherapy. *J Consult Clin Psychol* 1996; **64**: 22–31.

74. Levy KN, Meehan KB, Kelly KM et al. Change in attachment patterns and reflective function in a randomized control trial of transference-focused psychotherapy for borderline personality disorder. *J Consult Clin Psychol* 2006; **74**: 1027–40.

75. Fischer-Kern M, Schuster P, Kapusta ND et al. The relationship between personality organization, reflective functioning, and psychiatric classification

in borderline personality disorder. *Psychoanal Psychol* 2010; **27**: 395–409.

76. Gullestad FS, Johansen MS, Høglend P et al. Mentalization as a moderator of treatment effects: findings from a randomized clinical trial for personality disorders. *Psychother Res* 2013; **23**: 674–89.
77. Bora E. A meta-analysis of theory of mind and 'mentalization' in borderline personality disorder: a true neuro-social-cognitive or meta-social-cognitive impairment? *Psychol Med* 2021; **51**: 2541–51.
78. Preissler S, Dziobek I, Ritter K et al. Social cognition in borderline personality disorder: evidence for disturbed recognition of the emotions, thoughts, and intentions of others. *Front Behav Neurosci* 2010; **4**: 182.
79. Ritter K, Dziobek I, Preissler S et al. Lack of empathy in patients with narcissistic personality disorder. *Psychiatry Res* 2011; **187**: 241–7.
80. Sharp C, Pane H, Ha C et al. Theory of mind and emotion regulation difficulties in adolescents with borderline traits. *J Am Acad Child Adolesc Psychiatry* 2011; **50**: 563–73.
81. Dziobek I, Preissler S, Grozdanovic Z et al. Neuronal correlates of altered empathy and social cognition in borderline personality disorder. *Neuroimage* 2011; **57**: 539–48.
82. Bekrater-Bodmann R, Chung BY, Foell J et al. Body plasticity in borderline personality disorder: a link to dissociation. *Compr Psychiatry* 2016; **69**: 36–44.
83. Pavony MT, Lenzenweger MF. Somatosensory processing and borderline personality disorder features: a signal detection analysis of proprioception and exteroceptive sensitivity. *J Personal Disord* 2013; **27**: 208–21.
84. Pavony MT, Lenzenweger MF. Somatosensory processing and borderline personality disorder: pain perception and a signal detection analysis of proprioception and exteroceptive sensitivity. *Personal Disord* 2014; **5**: 164–71.
85. De Meulemeester C, Lowyck B, Luyten P. The role of impairments in self-other distinction in borderline personality disorder: a narrative review of recent evidence. *Neurosci Biobehav Rev* 2021; **127**: 242–54.
86. Neustadter ES, Fineberg SK, Leavitt J et al. Induced illusory body ownership in borderline personality disorder. *Neurosci Conscious* 2019; **2019**: niz017.
87. De Meulemeester C, Lowyck B, Panagiotopoulou E et al. Self–other distinction and borderline personality disorder features: evidence for egocentric and altercentric bias in a self–other facial morphing task. *Personal Disord* 2021; **12**: 377–88.
88. Auerbach RP, Tarlow N, Bondy E et al. Electrocortical reactivity during self-referential processing in female youth with borderline personality disorder. *Biol Psychiatry Cogn Neurosci Neuroimaging* 2016; **1**: 335–44.
89. Beeney JE, Stepp SD, Hallquist MN et al. Attachment and social cognition in borderline personality disorder: specificity in relation to antisocial and avoidant personality disorders. *Personal Disord* 2015; **6**: 207–15.
90. Vater A, Schroder-Abe M, Weissgerber S et al. Self-concept structure and borderline personality disorder: evidence for negative compartmentalization. *J Behav Ther Exp Psychiatry* 2015; **46**: 50–58.
91. Kanske P, Schulze L, Dziobek I et al. The wandering mind in borderline personality disorder: instability in self- and other-related thoughts. *Psychiatry Res* 2016; **242**: 302–10.
92. Sharp C, Ha C, Carbone C et al. Hypermentalizing in adolescent inpatients: treatment effects and association with borderline traits. *J Personal Disord* 2013; **27**: 3–18.
93. Winter D, Koplin K, Schmahl C et al. Evaluation and memory of social events in borderline personality disorder: effects

of valence and self-referential context. *Psychiatry Res* 2016; **240**: 19–25.

94. Ritzl A, Csukly G, Balazs K, Egerhazi A. Facial emotion recognition deficits and alexithymia in borderline, narcissistic, and histrionic personality disorders. *Psychiatry Res* 2018; **270**: 154–9.
95. Lowyck B, Luyten P, Vanwalleghem D et al. What's in a face? Mentalizing in borderline personality disorder based on dynamically changing facial expressions. *Personal Disord* 2016; **7**: 72–9.
96. Bertsch K, Krauch M, Stopfer K et al. Interpersonal threat sensitivity in borderline personality disorder: an eye-tracking study. *J Pers Disord* 2017; **31**: 647–70.
97. Fenske S, Lis S, Liebke L et al. Emotion recognition in borderline personality disorder: effects of emotional information on negative bias. *Borderline Personal Disord Emot Dysregul* 2015; **2**: 10.
98. Bertsch K, Gamer M, Schmidt B et al. Oxytocin and reduction of social threat hypersensitivity in women with borderline personality disorder. *Am J Psychiatry* 2013; **170**: 1169–77.
99. Kobeleva X, Seidel EM, Kohler C et al. Dissociation of explicit and implicit measures of the behavioral inhibition and activation system in borderline personality disorder. *Psychiatry Res* 2014; **218**: 134–42.
100. Dyck M, Habel U, Slodczyk J et al. Negative bias in fast emotion discrimination in borderline personality disorder. *Psychol Med* 2009; **39**: 855–64.
101. Hanegraaf L, van Baal S, Hohwy J, Verdejo-Garcia A. A systematic review and meta-analysis of 'Systems for Social Processes' in borderline personality and substance use disorders. *Neurosci Biobehav Rev* 2021; **127**: 572–92.
102. Renneberg B, Heyn K, Gebhard R, Bachmann S. Facial expression of emotions in borderline personality disorder and depression. *J Behav Ther Exp Psychiatry* 2005; **36**: 183–96.
103. Staebler K, Renneberg B, Stopsack M et al. Facial emotional expression in reaction to social exclusion in borderline personality disorder. *Psychol Med* 2011; **41**: 1929–38.
104. Matzke B, Herpertz SC, Berger C et al. Facial reactions during emotion recognition in borderline personality disorder: a facial electromyography study. *Psychopathology* 2014; **47**: 101–10.
105. Schulze L, Schmahl C, Niedtfeld I. Neural correlates of disturbed emotion processing in borderline personality disorder: a multimodal meta-analysis. *Biol Psychiatry* 2016; **79**: 97–106.
106. Fertuck EA, Jekal A, Song I et al. Enhanced 'Reading the Mind in the Eyes' in borderline personality disorder compared to healthy controls. *Psychol Med* 2009; **39**: 1979–88.
107. Frick C, Lang S, Kotchoubey B et al. Hypersensitivity in borderline personality disorder during mindreading. *PLoS One* 2012; **7**: e41650.
108. Berenson KR, Dochat C, Martin CG et al. Identification of mental states and interpersonal functioning in borderline personality disorder. *Personal Disord* 2018; **9**: 172–81.
109. Anupama V, Bhola P, Thirthalli J, Mehta UM. Pattern of social cognition deficits in individuals with borderline personality disorder. *Asian J Psychiatr* 2018; **33**: 105–12.
110. Brown RC, Plener PL, Groen G et al. Differential neural processing of social exclusion and inclusion in adolescents with non-suicidal self-injury and young adults with borderline personality disorder. *Front Psychiatry* 2017; **8**: 267.
111. Sato M, Fonagy P, Luyten P. Rejection sensitivity and borderline personality disorder features: a mediation model of effortful control and intolerance of ambiguity. *Psychiatry Res* 2018; **269**: 50–55.
112. Sato M, Fonagy P, Luyten P. Rejection sensitivity and borderline personality disorder features: the mediating roles of attachment anxiety, need to belong, and self-criticism. *J Pers Disord* 2020; **34**: 273–88.

113. Franic S, Dolan CV, Borsboom D et al. Three-and-a-half-factor model? The genetic and environmental structure of the CBCL/6-18 internalizing grouping. *Behav Genet* 2014; **44**: 254–68.

114. Lahey BB, Van Hulle CA, Singh AL et al. Higher-order genetic and environmental structure of prevalent forms of child and adolescent psychopathology. *Arch Gen Psychiatry* 2011; **68**: 181–9.

115. Pettersson E, Anckarsater H, Gillberg C, Lichtenstein P. Different neurodevelopmental symptoms have a common genetic etiology. *J Child Psychol Psychiatry* 2013; **54**: 1356–65.

116. Pettersson E, Larsson H, Lichtenstein P. Common psychiatric disorders share the same genetic origin: a multivariate sibling study of the Swedish population. *Mol Psychiatry* 2016; **21**: 717–21.

117. Anttila V, Bulik-Sullivan B, Finucane HK et al. Analysis of shared heritability in common disorders of the brain. *Science* 2018; **360**: eaap8757.

118. Caspi A, Moffitt TE. All for one and one for all: mental disorders in one dimension. *Am J Psychiatry* 2018; **175**: 831–44.

119. Caspi A, Houts RM, Belsky DW et al. The p factor: one general psychopathology factor in the structure of psychiatric disorders? *Clin Psychol Sci* 2014; **2**: 119–37.

120. Lahey BB, Applegate B, Hakes JK et al. Is there a general factor of prevalent psychopathology during adulthood? *J Abnorm Psychol* 2012; **121**: 971–7.

121. Lahey BB, Krueger RF, Rathouz PJ et al. Validity and utility of the general factor of psychopathology. *World Psychiatry* 2017; **16**: 142–4.

122. Smith GT, Atkinson EA, Davis HA et al. The general factor of psychopathology. *Annu Rev Clin Psychol* 2020; **16**: 75–98.

123. Patalay P, Fonagy P, Deighton J et al. A general psychopathology factor in early adolescence. *Br J Psychiatry* 2015; **207**: 15–22.

124. Macdonald AN, Goines KB, Novacek DM, Walker EF. Prefrontal mechanisms of comorbidity from a transdiagnostic and ontogenic perspective. *Dev Psychopathol* 2016; **28**: 1147–75.

125. Wise T, Radua J, Via E et al. Common and distinct patterns of grey-matter volume alteration in major depression and bipolar disorder: evidence from voxel-based meta-analysis. *Mol Psychiatry* 2017; **22**: 1455–63.

126. Hinton KE, Lahey BB, Villalta-Gil V et al. White matter microstructure correlates of general and specific second-order factors of psychopathology. *Neuroimage Clin* 2019; **22**: 101705.

127. Protzner AB, An S, Jirsa V. Network modulation in neuropsychiatric disorders using the virtual brain. In: Diwadkar VA, Eickhoff SB, eds. *Brain Network Dysfunction in Neuropsychiatric Illness.* Cham, Switzerland: Springer Nature Switzerland AG, 2021; 153–70.

128. Sripada C, Angstadt M, Taxali A et al. Widespread attenuating changes in brain connectivity associated with the general factor of psychopathology in 9- and 10-year olds. *Transl Psychiatry* 2021; **11**: 575.

129. Jack AI, Dawson AJ, Begany KL et al. fMRI reveals reciprocal inhibition between social and physical cognitive domains. *Neuroimage* 2013; **66**: 385–401.

130. Ekhtiari H, Paulus M. Preface: Neuroscience for addiction medicine: from prevention to rehabilitation. *Prog Brain Res* 2016; **224**: xxv–xxvi.

131. Beauchaine TP. Future directions in emotion dysregulation and youth psychopathology. *J Clin Child Adolesc Psychol* 2015; **44**: 875–96.

132. Gross JJ. Emotion regulation: conceptual and empirical foundations. In: Gross JJ, ed. *Handbook of Emotion Regulation*, 2nd ed. New York, NY: The Guilford Press, 2014; 3–20.

133. Beauchaine TP, Cicchetti D. Emotion dysregulation and emerging psychopathology: a transdiagnostic, transdisciplinary perspective. *Dev Psychopathol* 2019; **31**: 799–804.

134. McTeague LM, Huemer J, Carreon DM et al. Identification of common neural circuit disruptions in cognitive control across psychiatric disorders. *Am J Psychiatry* 2017; **174**: 676–85.

135. Banich MT. Executive function: the search for an integrated account. *Curr Dir Psychol Sci* 2009; **18**: 89–94.

136. Fonagy P, Campbell C, Bateman A. Mentalizing, attachment, and epistemic trust in group therapy. *Int J Group Psychother* 2017; **67**: 176–201.

137. Masten CL, Morelli SA, Eisenberger NI. An fMRI investigation of empathy for 'social pain' and subsequent prosocial behavior. *Neuroimage* 2011; **55**: 381–8.

138. Espinosa L, Golkar A, Olsson A. Mentalizing in value-based vicarious learning. In: Gilead M, Ochsner K, eds. *The Neural Basis of Mentalizing*. Cham, Switzerland: Springer, 2021; 517–36.

139. Hoehl S, Keupp S, Schleihauf H et al. 'Over-imitation': a review and appraisal of a decade of research. *Dev Rev* 2019; **51**: 90–108.

140. Lyons DE, Damrosch DH, Lin JK et al. The scope and limits of overimitation in the transmission of artefact culture. *Philos Trans R Soc Lond B Biol Sci* 2011; **366**: 1158–67.

141. Huang C-T, Heyes C, Charman T. Preschoolers' behavioural reenactment of "failed attempts": the roles of intention-reading, emulation and mimicry. *Cogn Dev* 2006; **21**: 36–45.

142. Clay Z, Tennie C. Is overimitation a uniquely human phenomenon? Insights from human children as compared to bonobos. *Child Dev* 2018; **89**: 1535–44.

143. Gergely G, Csibra G. Sylvia's recipe: human culture, imitation, and pedagogy. In: Enfield NJ, Levinson SC, eds. *Roots of Human Sociality: Culture, Cognition, and Human Interaction*. London: Berg Press, 2006; 229–55.

144. Altınok N, Hernik M, Király I, Gergely G. Acquiring sub-efficient and efficient variants of novel means by integrating information from multiple social models in preschoolers. *J Exp Child Psychol* 2020; **195**: 104847.

145. Nielsen M. The social glue of cumulative culture and ritual behavior. *Child Dev Perspect* 2018; **12**: 264.

146. Flynn E, Smith K. Investigating the mechanisms of cultural acquisition. *Soc Psychol* 2012; **43**: 185–95.

147. Gruber T, Deschenaux A, Frick A, Clement F. Group membership influences more social identification than social learning or overimitation in children. *Child Dev* 2019; **90**: 728–45.

148. Marsh LE, Ropar D, Hamilton AFC. Are you watching me? The role of audience and object novelty in overimitation. *J Exp Child Psychol* 2019; **180**: 123–30.

149. Gallotti M, Frith CD. Social cognition in the we-mode. *Trends Cogn Sci* 2013; **17**: 160–65.

150. Higgins J. Cognising with others in the we-mode: a defence of 'first-person plural' social cognition. *Rev Philos Psychol* 2020; **12**: 803–24.

151. Tomasello M. *A Natural History of Human Morality*. Cambridge, MA: Harvard University Press, 2016.

152. Butler AC, Brown GK, Beck AT, Grisham JR. Assessment of dysfunctional beliefs in borderline personality disorder. *Behav Res Ther* 2002; **40**: 1231–40.

153. Botsford J, Schulze L, Bohlander J, Renneberg B. Interpersonal trust: development and validation of a self-report inventory and clinical application in patients with borderline personality disorder. *J Pers Disord* 2021; **35**: 447–68.

154. Fertuck EA, Grinband J, Stanley B. Facial trust appraisal negatively biased in borderline personality disorder. *Psychiatry Res* 2013; **207**: 195–202.

155. Nicol K, Pope M, Sprengelmeyer R et al. Social judgement in borderline personality disorder. *PLoS One* 2013; **8**: e73440.

156. Fertuck EA, Grinband J, Mann JJ et al. Trustworthiness appraisal deficits in borderline personality disorder are associated with prefrontal cortex, not

amygdala, impairment. *Neuroimage Clin* 2019; **21**: 101616.

157. Campbell C, Tanzer M, Saunders R et al. Development and validation of a self-report measure of epistemic trust. *PLoS One* 2021; **16**: e0250264.
158. Mascaro O, Sperber D. The moral, epistemic, and mindreading components of children's vigilance towards deception. *Cognition* 2009; **112**: 367–80.
159. Fonagy P, Luyten P, Allison E. Epistemic petrification and the restoration of epistemic trust: a new conceptualization of borderline personality disorder and its psychosocial treatment. *J Pers Disord* 2015; **29**: 575–609.
160. Orme W, Bowersox L, Vanwoerden S et al. The relation between epistemic trust and borderline pathology in an adolescent inpatient sample. *Borderline Personal Disord Emot Dysregul* 2019; **6**: 13.
161. Preuss N, Brandle LS, Hager OM et al. Inconsistency and social decision making in patients with Borderline Personality Disorder. *Psychiatry Res* 2016; **243**: 115–22.
162. Ebert A, Kolb M, Heller J et al. Modulation of interpersonal trust in borderline personality disorder by intranasal oxytocin and childhood trauma. *Soc Neurosci* 2013; **8**: 305–13.
163. Theodoridou A, Rowe AC, Penton-Voak IS, Rogers PJ. Oxytocin and social perception: oxytocin increases perceived facial trustworthiness and attractiveness. *Horm Behav* 2009; **56**: 128–32.
164. Shamay-Tsoory SG, Abu-Akel A. The social salience hypothesis of oxytocin. *Biol Psychiatry* 2016; **79**: 194–202.
165. Miano A, Fertuck EA, Arntz A, Stanley B. Rejection sensitivity is a mediator between borderline personality disorder features and facial trust appraisal. *J Pers Disord* 2013; **27**: 442–56.
166. Preti E, Casini E, Richetin J et al. Cognitive and emotional components of rejection sensitivity: independent contributions to adolescent self- and interpersonal functioning. *Assessment* 2020; **27**: 1230–41.
167. Masland SR, Hooley JM. When trust does not come easily: negative emotional information unduly influences trustworthiness appraisals for individuals with borderline personality features. *J Pers Disord* 2020; **34**: 394–409.
168. Miano A, Fertuck EA, Roepke S, Dziobek I. Romantic relationship dysfunction in borderline personality disorder—a naturalistic approach to trustworthiness perception. *Personal Disord* 2017; **8**: 281–6.
169. Fonagy P, Luyten P. A developmental, mentalization-based approach to the understanding and treatment of borderline personality disorder. *Dev Psychopathol* 2009; **21**: 1355–81.
170. Hsu DT, Jarcho JM. "Next up for psychiatry: rejection sensitivity and the social brain." *Neuropsychopharmacology* 2021; **46**: 239–40.
171. Eisenberger NI, Lieberman MD. Why rejection hurts: a common neural alarm system for physical and social pain. *Trends Cogn Sci* 2004; **8**: 294–300.
172. Eisenberger NI. The pain of social disconnection: examining the shared neural underpinnings of physical and social pain. *Nat Rev Neurosci* 2012; **13**: 421–34.
173. Sahi RS, Eisenberger NI. Why don't you like me? The role of the mentalizing network in social rejection. In: Gilead M, Ochsner K, eds. *The Neural Basis of Mentalizing.* Cham, Switzerland: Springer, 2021; 613–28.
174. Vijayakumar N, Cheng TW, Pfeifer JH. Neural correlates of social exclusion across ages: a coordinate-based meta-analysis of functional MRI studies. *Neuroimage* 2017; **153**: 359–68.
175. Smith AR, Nelson EE, Kircanski K et al. Social anxiety and age are associated with neural response to social evaluation during adolescence. *Dev Cogn Neurosci* 2020; **42**: 100768.
176. Jarcho JM, Tanofsky-Kraff M, Nelson EE et al. Neural activation during anticipated peer evaluation and laboratory meal intake in overweight girls with and

without loss of control eating. *Neuroimage* 2015; **108**: 343–53.

177. Gradin VB, Waiter G, Kumar P et al. Abnormal neural responses to social exclusion in schizophrenia. *PLoS One* 2012; 7: e42608.

178. Sebastian C, Blakemore SJ, Charman T. Reactions to ostracism in adolescents with autism spectrum conditions. *J Autism Dev Disord* 2009; **39**: 1122–30.

179. Feldman S, Downey G. Rejection sensitivity as a mediator of the impact of childhood exposure to family violence on adult attachment behavior. *Dev Psychopathol* 1994; **6**: 231–47.

180. Gao S, Assink M, Cipriani A, Lin K. Associations between rejection sensitivity and mental health outcomes: a meta-analytic review. *Clin Psychol Rev* 2017; **57**: 59–74.

181. Zhang W, Hu N, Ding X, Li J. The relationship between rejection sensitivity and borderline personality features: a meta-analysis. *Adv Psychol Sci* 2021; **29**: 1179–94.

182. Cavicchioli M, Maffei C. Rejection sensitivity in borderline personality disorder and the cognitive-affective personality system: a meta-analytic review. *Personal Disord* 2020; **11**: 1–12.

183. Korn CW, La Rosee L, Heekeren HR, Roepke S. Social feedback processing in borderline personality disorder. *Psychol Med* 2016; **46**: 575–87.

184. Reichenberger J, Eibl JJ, Pfaltz MC et al. Don't praise me, don't chase me: emotional reactivity to positive and negative social-evaluative videos in patients with borderline personality disorder. *J Pers Disord* 2017; **31**: 75–89.

185. Liebke L, Koppe G, Bungert M et al. Difficulties with being socially accepted: an experimental study in borderline personality disorder. *J Abnorm Psychol* 2018; **127**: 670–82.

186. Allen JG, Fonagy P, Bateman AW. The role of mentalizing in treating attachment trauma. In: Vermetten E, Lanius R, eds. *The Hidden Epidemic: The Impact of Early Life Trauma on Health and Disease*. New York, NY: Cambridge University Press, 2010; 247–56.

187. Janke K, Driessen M, Behnia B et al. Emotional intelligence in patients with posttraumatic stress disorder, borderline personality disorder and healthy controls. *Psychiatry Res* 2018; **264**: 290–96.

188. Palgi S, Klein E, Shamay-Tsoory SG. Oxytocin improves compassion toward women among patients with PTSD. *Psychoneuroendocrinology* 2016; **64**: 143–9.

189. Mazza M, Tempesta D, Pino MC et al. Neural activity related to cognitive and emotional empathy in post-traumatic stress disorder. *Behav Brain Res* 2015; **282**: 37–45.

190. Nietlisbach G, Maercker A, Rossler W, Haker H. Are empathic abilities impaired in posttraumatic stress disorder? *Psychol Rep* 2010; **106**: 832–44.

191. Mazza M, Giusti L, Albanese A et al. Social cognition disorders in military police officers affected by posttraumatic stress disorder after the attack of An-Nasiriyah in Iraq 2006. *Psychiatry Res* 2012; **198**: 248–52.

192. Nazarov A, Frewen P, Oremus C et al. Comprehension of affective prosody in women with post-traumatic stress disorder related to childhood abuse. *Acta Psychiatr Scand* 2015; **131**: 342–9.

193. Passardi S, Peyk P, Rufer M et al. Impaired recognition of positive emotions in individuals with posttraumatic stress disorder, cumulative traumatic exposure, and dissociation. *Psychother Psychosom* 2018; **87**: 118–20.

194. Bell CJ, Colhoun HC, Frampton CM et al. Earthquake brain: altered recognition and misclassification of facial expressions are related to trauma exposure but not posttraumatic stress disorder. *Front Psychiatry* 2017; **8**: 278.

195. Freud A, Burlingham DT. *The Writings of Anna Freud. Vol. 3. Infants Without Families: Reports on the Hampstead Nurseries, 1939-1945*. New York, NY: International Universities Press, 1973.

196. Klinnert MD, Campos JJ, Sorce JF et al. Emotions as behavior regulations: social referencing in infancy. In: Plutchhik R, Kellerman H, eds. *Emotion: Theory, Research, and Experience*. New York, NY: Academic Press, 1983; 57–86.

197. Sorce JF, Emde RN, Campos J, Klinnert MD. Maternal emotional signaling: its effect on the visual cliff behavior of 1-year-olds. *Dev Psychol* 1985; **21**: 195–200.

198. Askew C, Field AP. Vicarious learning and the development of fears in childhood. *Behav Res Ther* 2007; **45**: 2616–27.

199. Debiec J, Olsson A. Social fear learning: from animal models to human function. *Trends Cogn Sci* 2017; **21**: 546–55.

200. Olsson A, Knapska E, Lindstrom B. The neural and computational systems of social learning. *Nat Rev Neurosci* 2020; **21**: 197–212.

201. Golkar A, Haaker J, Selbing I, Olsson A. Neural signals of vicarious extinction learning. *Soc Cogn Affect Neurosci* 2016; **11**: 1541–9.

202. Bateman A, Campbell C, Luyten P, Fonagy P. A mentalization-based approach to common factors in the treatment of borderline personality disorder. *Curr Opin Psychol* 2018; **21**: 44–9.

203. Storebø OJ, Stoffers-Winterling JM, Völlm BA et al. Psychological therapies for people with borderline personality disorder. *Cochrane Database Syst Rev* 2020; 5: CD012955.

204. Cristea IA, Gentili C, Cotet CD et al. Efficacy of psychotherapies for borderline personality disorder: a systematic review and meta-analysis. *JAMA Psychiatry* 2017; **74**: 319–28.

205. Rameckers SA, Verhoef REJ, Grasman R et al. Effectiveness of psychological treatments for borderline personality disorder and predictors of treatment outcomes: a multivariate multilevel meta-analysis of data from all design types. *J Clin Med* 2021; **10**: 5622.

206. Volkert J, Hauschild S, Taubner S. Mentalization-based treatment for personality disorders: efficacy, effectiveness, and new developments. *Curr Psychiatry Rep* 2019; **21**: 25.

207. Vogt KS, Norman P. Is mentalization-based therapy effective in treating the symptoms of borderline personality disorder? A systematic review. *Psychol Psychother* 2019; **92**: 441–64.

208. Bateman A, Fonagy P. 8-year follow-up of patients treated for borderline personality disorder: mentalization-based treatment versus treatment as usual. *Am J Psychiatry* 2008; **165**: 631–8.

209. Bateman A, Fonagy P. Randomized controlled trial of outpatient mentalization-based treatment versus structured clinical management for borderline personality disorder. *Am J Psychiatry* 2009; **166**: 1355–64.

210. Bateman A, Fonagy P. Impact of clinical severity on outcomes of mentalisation-based treatment for borderline personality disorder. *Br J Psychiatry* 2013; **203**: 221–7.

211. Bateman A, Constantinou MP, Fonagy P, Holzer S. Eight-year prospective follow-up of mentalization-based treatment versus structured clinical management for people with borderline personality disorder. *Personal Disord* 2021; **12**: 291–9.

212. Bateman A, O'Connell J, Lorenzini N et al. A randomised controlled trial of mentalization-based treatment versus structured clinical management for patients with comorbid borderline personality disorder and antisocial personality disorder. *BMC Psychiatry* 2016; **16**: 304.

213. Jørgensen CR, Freund C, Boye R et al. Outcome of mentalization-based and supportive psychotherapy in patients with borderline personality disorder: a randomized trial. *Acta Psychiatr Scand* 2013; **127**: 305–17.

214. Jørgensen CR, Bøye R, Andersen D et al. Eighteen months post-treatment naturalistic follow-up study of mentalization-based therapy and supportive group treatment of borderline personality disorder: clinical

outcomes and functioning. *Nord Psychol* 2014; **66**: 254–73.

215. Petersen B, Toft J, Christensen NB et al. A 2-year follow-up of mentalization-oriented group therapy following day hospital treatment for patients with personality disorders. *Personal Ment Health* 2010; **4**: 294–301.

216. Laurenssen EMP, Luyten P, Kikkert MJ et al. Day hospital mentalization-based treatment v. specialist treatment as usual in patients with borderline personality disorder: randomized controlled trial. *Psychol Med* 2018; **48**: 2522–9.

217. Bales D, Bateman A. Partial hospitalization settings. In: Bateman A, Fonagy P, eds. *Handbook of Mentalizing in Mental Health Practice.* Arlington, VA: American Psychiatric Publishing, 2012; 197–226.

218. Kvarstein EH, Pedersen G, Folmo E et al. Mentalization-based treatment or psychodynamic treatment programmes for patients with borderline personality disorder – the impact of clinical severity. *Psychol Psychother* 2019; **92**: 91–111.

219. Robinson P, Hellier J, Barrett B et al. The NOURISHED randomised controlled trial comparing mentalisation-based treatment for eating disorders (MBT-ED) with specialist supportive clinical management (SSCM-ED) for patients with eating disorders and symptoms of borderline personality disorder. *Trials* 2016; **17**: 549.

220. Rossouw TI, Fonagy P. Mentalization-based treatment for self-harm in adolescents: a randomized controlled trial. *J Am Acad Child Adolesc Psychiatry* 2012; **51**: 1304–13.

221. Witt KG, Hetrick SE, Rajaram G et al. Interventions for self-harm in children and adolescents. *Cochrane Database Syst Rev* 2021; **3**: CD013667.

222. Bo S, Sharp C, Beck E et al. First empirical evaluation of outcomes for mentalization-based group therapy for adolescents with BPD. *Personal Disord* 2017; **8**: 396–401.

223. Beck E, Bo S, Jorgensen MS et al. Mentalization-based treatment in groups for adolescents with borderline personality disorder: a randomized controlled trial. *J Child Psychol Psychiatry* 2020; **61**: 594–604.

224. Jørgensen MS, Storebø OJ, Bo S et al. Mentalization-based treatment in groups for adolescents with borderline personality disorder: 3- and 12-month follow-up of a randomized controlled trial. *Eur Child Adolesc Psychiatry* 2021; **30**: 699–710.

Chapter 3

What Is Mentalization-Based Treatment?

Introduction

The appreciation of the difference between your own experience of your mind and someone's else perspective on what they think is going on for you is a key focus of mentalization-based treatment (MBT) work. The integration of your current experience of mind with an alternative view—for example, that presented by the clinician in the course of therapy—is the foundation of a process of change. The capacity to understand behavior in terms of the associated mental states in self and other—the capacity to mentalize—is essential for the achievement of this integration of perspectives. Although most people without major psychological problems are in a relatively strong position to make productive use of an alternative point of view presented by a therapist, those individuals who make ineffective use of their own and others' understanding of mind are unlikely to benefit from traditional (particularly insight-oriented) psychological therapies. In Chapter 2 we reviewed evidence that individuals with borderline personality disorder (BPD) appear to have an impoverished model of their own and others' minds. However, our understanding of ineffective mentalizing in these individuals is not that there is a permanent deficit, but rather that, in some individuals, genetic risk combined with unsupportive early experiences, including neglect and trauma, may create vulnerability to a loss of mentalizing in conditions of high emotion, especially those associated with interpersonal interactions and attachment activation. Individuals with this vulnerability then exhibit schematic, rigid, and sometimes extreme ideas about their own and others' states of mind, which make them vulnerable to powerful emotional storms and apparently impulsive actions, and can create profound problems in behavioral regulation, including affect regulation. The weaker an individual's sense of their own subjectivity, the more difficult it is for them to compare the validity of their own perceptions of the way their mind works with that presented by a "mind expert"—that is, a therapist or other clinician. When they are presented with a coherent and most likely accurate view of mental function in the course of psychotherapy, they are unable to compare the picture offered to them with their own self-generated model; this means that all too often they either accept the therapist's alternative perspectives uncritically, or reject them out of hand. All of this implies that "everyday" psychological interventions, whether psychodynamic or cognitive, need to be modified in order to be helpful for patients with BPD. Recognizing this need was, and remains, central to our thinking behind the development and delivery of MBT, which is summarized in the rest of this chapter. More detail about the model can be found in earlier publications [1,2].

The primary objective of MBT is recovery of the capacity to mentalize in the context of attachment relationships. Patients with BPD are sensitive in interpersonal contexts, and particularly vulnerable to deterioration of mental-state awareness in relationships when their poorly organized attachment system is stimulated—as attachment is triggered, mentalizing becomes vulnerable. Combine that with psychotherapy, which is inherently relational, and there is a potentially toxic mix. Consequently, MBT is defined by a constellation of interventions that promote mentalizing, and active avoidance of interventions that might cause harm by undermining mentalizing. The MBT clinician negotiates a potentially stormy passage, balancing attachment stimulation and relational exploration with supporting mentalizing strength. If these two aspects are not balanced so that they work together rather than against each other, patients with BPD will struggle to develop the capacity to function effectively in interpersonal relationships—the lack of which is at the core of their difficulties. Treatment can be effective only if it is able to enhance the patient's mentalizing capacities without generating too many negative (iatrogenic) effects by emotionally overstimulating their attachment system.

Managing the level of arousal in the consulting room is the clinician's responsibility. The patient–clinician relationship needs careful attention if a positive therapeutic alliance is to develop without encouraging overdependence or ambivalent attachment. As a guide, interventions that focus on more complex aspects of the relationship—a necessity if the detail and understanding of mind states are to be explored—should be used only when the patient's attachment system is not overstimulated. If things start to go wrong—for example, if the patient becomes increasingly aroused and disturbed—the clinician should retrace the interaction, openly asking if they, the clinician, have been responsible for making an error or whether there is some other cause of the problem that has arisen. Offering alternative perspectives is crucial, but allowing the patient to reject them is equally important, while at the same time ensuring that all perspectives are explored before any are discounted. The clinician who feels able to reconsider their own perspectives—their mind having been changed by the patient's mind—will foster mentalizing.

To summarize the psychotherapy paradox in MBT, any treatment for BPD needs to stimulate attachment to the clinician while asking the patient to reflect on, evaluate the accuracy of, and potentially modify beliefs concerning their own mind states and those of others. Effective treatment entails balancing these components against a background of gradually increasing complexity without inducing serious side effects. To do this, the MBT clinician needs to follow a series of principles.

MBT as a Principle-Driven Intervention

In any treatment, there is intrinsic value in the clinician's powerful commitment to the patient's subjectivity. At the core of the clinical practice of MBT is a consistent focus on the patient's subjective reality, and a consistent effort by the clinician to convey that they are working to grasp the world from the patient's perspective. To maintain this focus, clinicians implement MBT by following a series of principles within a structured intervention process. These principles are summarized in Box 3.1.

Box 3.1 Principles of MBT.

Emotions and Mentalizing

- Manage anxiety and titrate attachment anxiety.
- Balance mentalizing: follow affective mentalizing if mentalizing is stable, otherwise use contrary moves.
- Activate relational process: work with deactivation and hyperactivation of mental/attachment systems.

Responsiveness of Clinician

- Roll with the patient's and your own reactivity and reaction.
- Empathic validation is the initial intervention: a contingent and marked response to the patient's mental state is recommended as the first step in sessions.
- Move from a dominant theme to a subdominant affective theme (often relational interaction).

Mentalizing Focus: Do's and Don'ts

- Do monitor current mentalizing—process versus content.
- Don't join in with low mentalizing—for example, don't respond to the patient as if they are mentalizing by elaborating content currently processed in low mentalizing, but reinstate mentalizing first.
- Don't take over the patient's mentalizing—for example, don't meet their low mentalizing with your high mentalizing, or mentalize their low mentalizing.
- Don't assume that the patient's mind works like your mind.

Manage Anxiety

The first principle that MBT clinicians follow in treatment is to maintain anxiety within a range that encourages rather than inhibits or unbalances any of the dimensions of mentalizing. Mentalizing and anxiety interact, and there is a particularly strong interrelationship between attachment anxiety and the quality of mentalizing. Mentalizing improves initially with increasing anxiety, until a tipping point is reached beyond which the chance of effective mentalizing decreases rapidly, leaving anxiety untethered and likely to trigger a fight-or-flight response. Patients with BPD can reach this tipping point particularly quickly and in a wide range of circumstances, albeit primarily in circumstances that present interpersonal and social challenges. Escalating anxiety in sessions, whatever the reason for it, is treated with great care to ensure that the patient's mentalizing is supported rather than undermined. The converse situation—that of insufficient anxiety—is also a danger for the clinician, as the patient's attachment/mentalizing system will not be productively stimulated, leading to the disengaged patient failing to learn how to manage feelings, maintain mentalizing in relationships, and bring about change. Some patients, such as those with more antisocial characteristics, down-regulate or deactivate attachment anxiety to maintain their mentalizing, but at considerable cost to others and themselves. For these individuals, mentalizing becomes restricted, for example, by the excessive use of cognitive mentalizing and limited activation of affective mentalizing. Cognitive rigidity ensues, generating the cold, calm appearance of the person with antisocial personality disorder and psychopathic traits (see Chapter 7), who uses excessive cognitive mentalizing that is not balanced by either access to self-affective states or the subjective experience of others, which might have enabled them to empathize emotionally with them. For mentalizing to flourish in social and personal interactions, attachment and anxiety are both necessary, but need to be kept within a manageable range—not too much and not too little.

Balance Mentalizing

The second principle is to focus on the balance of the poles of mentalizing across all of its dimensions so as to maintain flexibility and adaptability. In clinical interactions this is done through the use of *contrary moves*, which trigger the patient's mind states back and forth between the poles of the four dimensions of automatic/controlled, self/other, cognitive/affective, and internal/external mentalizing (see Chapter 2), particularly in the context of attachment anxiety. Patients with personality disorders appear to over- and underuse some of the poles in a way that is often characteristic of their particular disorder. For example, patients with BPD, when anxious, show difficulty in separating experiences of self and other, so the task is to help them to develop a separateness and distinction between what they feel themselves to be and how they experience themselves as seen by others. In contrast, patients with narcissistic personality disorder may over-inflate their self-experience and derogate the experiences of others. So with these individuals the task is to use contrary moves to rekindle the underused pole of regard for others, or to puncture gently (with careful concurrent empathic validation) the inflated interest in the self-valuation pole.

Activate Relational Process

The third principle is to develop mentalizing of self and other into more complex conversations about what is happening within the therapeutic relationship. This begins with ensuring that the mentalizing of both self and other experience is activated. The mental states and affective experiences of both patient and clinician need to be differentiated and, when possible, processed together in the we-mode. This can be accomplished by moving from a dominant theme within the session, say the more conscious content, to a subdominant theme, say that of an underlying dynamic process between patient and clinician, such as both the clinician and the patient "treading on eggshells" as the content is being discussed, for fear of triggering too strong an emotional reaction in either or both of them (see the discussion of affect focus, later in this chapter). We-ness, or the "we-mode," is a perspective that transcends what occurs within the separate selves of "you" and "me" to represent what is occurring for the relational unit of "us" (see Chapter 2). Higher levels of relational mentalizing go beyond individuality. Effective social collaboration is partly dependent on groups of individuals seeing their actions as being directed in pursuit of a shared goal (i.e., as a "we"). When individuals share their minds in a collective mode of cognition, they create a "joint mind." So, in the clinical interaction, we-ness is distinct from either the patient's or the clinician's individual perspectives on self and other. As an inherently relational representation, it is a state which is actively developed and promoted in MBT in a number of ways that follow a path to relational work, including:

1. joint formulation and a collaborative stance
2. personal mentalizing profile
3. working explicitly not only with the mind states of the patient but also with those of the clinician
4. prioritizing empathic validation

5. focus on the alliance, its ruptures, and joint intentionality
6. encouragement of self-disclosure in relation to the clinician's own interpersonal strategies.

The MBT clinician openly presents their thoughts and feelings and their counter-relational responses to the patient, clarifying that neither person in the therapeutic interaction has a monopoly on valid views of reality, and that both must accept that each side experiences interpersonal interactions only impressionistically. As a part of relational mentalizing, the patient is asked to mentalize the clinician just as the clinician is required to mentalize the patient. A sense of we-ness emerges as the clinician and patient engage in the shared task of mentalizing both self and other, but it is recognized as a momentary state of awareness of mutual understanding, which is nevertheless critical in determining the value and quality of the communication between them. In MBT groups (see Chapter 5), a sense of we-ness is additionally generated as the participants define the values of "our" group at the outset, and then revisit and reformulate the group project around those values at regular intervals.

Process Versus Content

The fourth principle is for clinicians to be careful not to over-elaborate poorly mentalized content or reinforce ineffective mentalizing processes. The easiest way for the clinician to think about differentiating process and content is by considering the "how" versus the "what" and "why" of thoughts and feelings. How a thought or feeling is processed first needs to be taken into account. Taking unmentalized content at face value will not engage the patient's mentalizing and stimulate their curiosity. In addition, it is all too easy to start persuading a patient, for example, that their self-criticism is incorrect or lacking in evidence, or to argue with their subjective experience of rejection by pointing out their social sensitivity. Interventions that either confirm or oppose the patient's unmentalized content join with them in a non-mentalizing process by validating it as a pure reality or by arguing with it, leaving the patient feeling misunderstood. The overarching aim is to change "how" the experience is processed and to restore effective mentalizing. The MBT clinician therefore steers a middle course between confirming and debating content until effective empathic validation of some aspect of the content can be delivered. Only then can a mentalizing process be triggered. At this point, "what" the experience is about can be explored and then given credible meaning to the individual—this is the "why."

Empathic Validation of the Impact of Experience

The move from content (in low-mentalizing mode) to a focus on process follows the fifth principle, which is that the clinician initially intervenes using contingent and marked responses of *empathic emotional validation* [3]. Humans are sensitive to the existence of contingencies between their behavior and environmental events, and are equally sensitive to their own mental-state intention and the mental response from others. We contend that contingency detection, as an aspect of interpersonal interaction, is crucially involved in progressively developing the awareness of affective states through identifying one's own reaction in the contingent response of the other. More specifically, the clinician's contingent reflections of the patient's expressive displays while struggling to mentalize play a central causal role in the development of emotional self-awareness and control in the patient; this is a central aspect of mentalizing, but it requires scaffolding and support in people with personality disorders. Importantly, empathic validation of the patient by the clinician does not require the clinician to agree with what the patient is saying (as we have outlined earlier); rather, it means showing awareness of the impact that the thoughts and feelings may have on the subjective state of the person they are working with. So the clinician operates within a framework of empathic validation of the patient's experience as the foundation for all other interventions. The facilitation of a sense of we-ness is organized around first seeing things jointly from the patient's perspective.

Focus on the Mentalizing Process: How Mental States are Processed

The clinician needs to ensure that the therapeutic process remains a joint creation by patient and clinician. At the same time, it is essential that the clinician:

1. recognizes ineffective, low-level mentalizing
2. does not take over mentalizing for the patient
3. does not try to mentalize non-mentalizing discourse
4. does not engage in vacuous superficial mentalizing.

None of these edicts is easy to follow—all too often clinicians are "tricked" by their inborn reactions into thinking that pretend mode (see Chapter 2) reflects psychological insight when in fact it is a subtle form of hypermentalizing, in which one's own and/or others' motives and mental states are described in elaborate detail, but with little or no grounding in reality. Clinicians also have robust mentalizing capacities and are well trained in psychological understanding, making it easy and tempting for them to take over a patient's struggle to explore problems by suggesting constructive solutions to their concerns; it is natural to support and to offer help and provide alternative perspectives and solutions for the patient's challenges. But once the clinician starts down these paths, although their own mentalizing processes may be ably demonstrated, the patient's capacities—their "mentalizing muscles"—will not be strengthened without the exercise that they need. Therefore the clinician needs to desist from doing the mentalizing for the patient, and instead work consistently to trigger the patient's mentalizing and then help them to maintain it.

Democracy, Equity, and Collaboration

The patient and clinician decide what to work on together, they are equal partners in the work, and they collaborate to build increasingly salient personal narratives and understandings. Openness to different perspectives is at the heart of mentalizing, along with humility and being ordinarily human and without arrogance. In terms of mental states, the patient and clinician are equal—neither person has a more valid experience of interactions and their associated mental processes than the other, and both have the capacity to misinterpret experiences. Understanding mental states should be a joint and collaborative process. If patients perceive themselves as "inferior" or lower in a hierarchy, this will inhibit their capacity to think for themselves and predispose them to simply accept the clinician's formulations. Power asymmetry is antithetical to thinking genuinely jointly and collaboratively, and to learning about oneself from and through others. To learn from the clinician in a manner that enables personal change, the patient has to feel that the clinician's mind is approachable, accessible, and agreeable. At a dynamic level, equality of mind states and the requirement to consider each other's mind state is a two-way process. The clinician is necessarily focused on the mind of the patient, and the patient needs to be equally interested in the mind of the clinician ("*Why does the clinician say that?*"; "*Where does he get that idea from?*"; "*What does it mean about me?*"). For the patient to be able to do this, epistemic trust has to be created, which will take time. So, inevitably, the direction of flow of mental-state interest is often one-way at the start of treatment, with the patient being rightly concerned about their own mind states. But it is important to remember that the directional imbalance can be in both directions, with the patient being overly concerned about the mind of the clinician or, at times, the clinician being preoccupied with themselves for personal or other reasons. Even in these situations the subjective experiences of both parties have equal merit and require equally serious scrutiny.

A word about democracy—or, perhaps better, equity. We have already considered the importance of power differentials in the ordinary therapeutic setting, and explained that feeling like the weaker (i.e., help-seeking) person in an interpersonal dialogue is destructive to mentalizing, probably because a sense of inferiority is almost inevitably accompanied by shame, which leads to withdrawal. Openness and a willingness on the part of the clinician to disclose some of their mentalizing processes is part of appropriate "levelling up" of the patient, through the clinician accounting for, and being accountable for, their own thoughts and feelings. Another aspect of "democratization" in MBT is when the clinician thinks of the person coming to see them as a *conversational partner* rather than a patient or a client (as these labels carry a tone of supplication). Important in this regard is the clinician's declaration of their own vulnerability to ineffective mentalizing and their open acceptance of it when it happens in sessions—which it inevitably will.

The MBT clinician explicitly shares their mind states with the patient when this is relevant to the process of treatment, just as the patient does. This allows the interactional aspects of subjective experience to be considered. Sharing becomes particularly important when the interaction between the patient and clinician interferes with the work of therapy, or when the clinician loses their own capacity for mentalizing. The patient may—often unwittingly—be intimidating or touch on latent fears in the clinician, inducing anxiety in the clinician, who then cannot think clearly. It is important that the patient is made aware of any interference in the clinician's ability to think, as this will not only prevent the delivery of effective help, but may also confuse the patient who is suddenly facing an ineffective clinician. Sharing the interactional experience from the clinician's point of view allows the patient to consider the effects they may have on others, as well as enabling the clinician to stabilize their own mind through the activation of better mentalizing by putting their thoughts and feelings into words. At other times, the clinician's mind may go blank, or they may be uncertain how to respond to the patient; this is a common reaction to ineffective mentalizing by the patient. In these situations, the MBT clinician should not worry, but should simply share their state of mind: "*You know, I am not sure what to say about that. You have stumped me there. Help me think about it. You were saying . . . .*"

The mind of the MBT clinician is therefore ideally a benign "open book" to be considered by the patient. We learn about ourselves through others; if others close their mind to us, we shall learn less. Just to be clear, this should not be seen as permission for the clinician to talk about their own life problems to the patient! It is a reminder to the clinician to be open in reaction to their experience of the patient. But note the qualification: *benign* means open, courteous, generous, kind, and sensitive; it does not mean brutal, critical, haughty, frosty, or uncharitable.

Authenticity and the "Not-Knowing" Stance

You don't really know about mental states, because they are subjective and can never be fully knowable. However, you do know about BPD as a heterogeneous set of problems and psychological processes and other facts and figures that you have learned over the years. The "not-knowing" stance is an authentic attitude of curiosity about what is going on in someone's mind—how thoughts and feelings can feel part of us and sometimes be something that seems alien and imposed on us, almost with a life of their own. They can be overwhelming. In MBT the focus on mental states is about getting to know them, taming them, and managing them so that they serve our interactions and life constructively.

The not-knowing stance comes from an interpersonal perspective. It considers the reciprocity of mental states and is rooted in the idea that minds can change minds. The clinician's attitude toward their own mind is the same as their attitude toward the patient's mind. They are tentative in the way that they comment on their own constructions, and avoid regarding their own mental states as privileged. The not-knowing stance includes mental playfulness, and uses imagination and humor to facilitate the joint project of understanding the complexity of minds. Thoughts and feelings are serious because they can change the world (they generate action), but they are also transitory, which gives them a provisional quality of flexibility and transformation. Above all, the not-knowing stance is the most effective avenue for exploring problems hand in hand, or better still mind in mind, so that no one has to go into the dark and dangerous places of their mind alone. When done skilfully, it promotes the we-mode of shared intentionality.

On the other hand, when the not-knowing stance is used clumsily it can seem to a patient like being inundated with questions—an interrogation—rather than talking with someone who is present as a conversational partner. This can happen if the clinician defaults to consistently asking "why" questions. Patients, like most of us, do not know "why" most of the time, so these are usually pointless questions. We know that "why" questions demand the activation of the mentalizing network, whereas "how" questions do not. So if the patient's mentalizing is less than optimal, "why" questions are likely to be pointless in any case. If you find yourself falling into an interrogatory trap, think about how you would talk to a friend with the same problem. You would not ask "why" they are feeling sad, "why" they think their child is being difficult, or "why" their partner has decided to leave them. You would ask them to elaborate on what has happened and what they thought and felt about it. You are more likely to talk with some astonishment and genuine curiosity about what happened and what it has been like for them. This will get you back to a not-knowing stance.

Thus the MBT clinician differentiates between taking a fact-finding stance, a Socratic questioning (open but focused cognitively) stance, and an exploratory, not-knowing stance. All three methods of questioning might be used in any session, but once exploration is required the not-knowing attitude needs to be in the forefront of the dialogue, with interactive discussion, in order to establish trust.

Concluding Remarks

This chapter has outlined the principles that an MBT clinician follows in their clinical interactions with patients. The clinician uses these principles to underpin all other MBT interventions so as to maximize their effectiveness. To this extent, when followed, the principles create an interactional process in which mentalizing between the patient and the clinician can flourish. Only then can robust mentalizing in the patient—the primary aim of MBT—be established. The form of clinical problems during treatment is specific to the individual patient, so having clear principles to follow allows the clinician to maintain their own mentalizing in the face of uncertainty. This is especially important in the treatment of patients with severe metacognitive disorganization, such as those with BPD (see Chapters 4 and 5), who can all too easily create metacognitive disorganization in the clinician. When the clinician is in doubt, they should model regaining their own mentalizing ("*I need a moment to get my mind back; I am not sure what I think here. Can we wait a minute?*"), return to the formulation agreed with the patient (described in Chapter 4), use an empathically validating stance, and restart the exploration of problems with a clear focus on the mentalizing process.

References

1. Bateman A, Fonagy P. *Mentalization-Based Treatment for Personality Disorders: A Practical Guide*. Oxford, UK: Oxford University Press, 2016.

2. Bateman A, Fonagy P, eds. *Handbook of Mentalizing in Mental Health Practice*, 2nd ed. Washington, DC: American Psychiatric Association Publishing, 2019.

3. Gergely G, Watson JS. The social biofeedback theory of parental affect-mirroring: the development of emotional self-awareness and self-control in infancy. *Int J Psychoanal* 1996; 77: 1181–212.

Chapter 4

The Clinical Process of Mentalization-Based Treatment

A Step-by-Step Guide

Introduction

A brief summary of mentalization-based treatment (MBT) as a structured and integrated treatment delivered over time is provided in Box 4.1. MBT requires a team approach of combined individual and group psychotherapy offered together over a period of 12–18 months. MBT groups (MBT-G) are discussed in Chapter 5. More recently, MBT has also been offered as either individual therapy or group therapy alone, but at the time of writing the outcomes from using only a single mode of implementation are unclear, as there have been no dismantling studies comparing these different modes of delivery.

Box 4.1 Summary of MBT.

MBT is a structured treatment that can be implemented in a range of settings. It integrates individual and group psychotherapy, targeting suicidality and self-harm, emotional processing, and relational instability through a focus on improving the capacity for mentalizing and improving social learning through the development of increasing epistemic trust. Treatment usually lasts for 12–18 months.

Initial Phase

- Psychoeducation (MBT-Introductory Group).
- Collaboratively developed formulation.
- Formation of a treatment alliance based on understanding of the patient's specific long-term attachment processes.
- Safety planning.
- Identification of mentalizing vulnerabilities, particularly in relation to high-risk behaviors, and establishing the contexts that trigger ineffective modes of mentalizing.

Treatment Phase

General Strategies

- Stabilization of high-risk behaviors.
- Supportive, empathic validation to enable mentalizing.
- Clarification and elaboration to create a foundation for basic mentalizing that entails affect identification and contextualization.
- Interpersonal focus that enables an exploration of alternative perspectives.
- Repairing alliance ruptures.

Box 4.1 *(cont.)*

Specific Strategies

- Using mentalizing to manage impulsivity.
- Building stable mentalizing processes in attachment relationships through activation of relational constructs in both group and individual therapy; linking learned therapy experience to daily social and personal life with a focus on social exclusion/inclusion and personal rejection sensitivity; increasing self and other reflective capacity when under stress.
- Re-establishing mentalizing when ineffective mentalizing is triggered.
- Trauma-focused personal narrative work.

Final Phase

- Experience of ending treatment for patient and clinician, and review of treatment.
- Specific focus on BPD processes (e.g., fears of abandonment).
- Generalization of stable mentalizing and learned social understanding.
- Mentalizing skills to maintain self-care.

As shown in Box 4.1, MBT can be divided into phases, with each phase being subdivided into specific clinical tasks. Each phase is underpinned by the *patient as a partner*, and more specifically as a *conversational partner*, who becomes equally expert in understanding their own mentalizing and using the MBT framework as a structure for understanding their problems and how to address them. Remember that "knowing about" mind states is not the exclusive preserve of the clinician. Different perspectives are equally valid, because our representations of thoughts and feelings have impressionistic origins and each has to be given, as far as possible, impartial consideration without prejudgment or prejudice.

Throughout this chapter we shall refer to the case of Sarah, a young woman who has prototypical features of borderline personality disorder (BPD). The clinical example that follows is used to illustrate the process of MBT implementation, which consists of five main clinical components:

1. assessment
2. formulation
3. psychoeducation
4. exploration of identified problems using general and specific strategies to build the patient's mentalizing
5. finishing.

Clinical Example: Information about Sarah

Sarah is 28 years old. She has had problems with drug addiction. She used cocaine and cannabis for a number of years, but she has now been clear of all drugs for over 6 months. Her current complaint is that she cannot bear to be alone. She separated from a long-term partner around 1 year ago. They have a son who is now aged 5, and she has joint custody of him with her partner. She feels "normal" when she is looking after her son, but when she is on her own in her flat she becomes anxious and needs to see people. Consequently, she goes out frequently because, in her own words, "*I am desperate to be with other people.*"

There is some indication of relationship problems: her previous partner was controlling and at times violent. Sarah did not believe that she was in danger and so she continued the relationship until 1 year ago, when her partner left her. She is now in a relationship with another man whom she thinks is devoted to her. She recognizes that she causes problems in this relationship by constantly asking for reassurance. She constantly asks him if he loves her, and frequently asks about his previous girlfriends and how they compare to her.

She shows some mood fluctuations, and has in the past engaged in self-harm. She is not currently at risk in terms of suicidal impulses, but she took an overdose of drugs 2 years ago, because she wanted to die.

When the clinician first saw Sarah, she presented as someone able to talk about herself and she seemed a likeable person. She has rapidly shifting mood states, which seem to be dependent on environmental triggers. She feels good when she is with other people and bad when she is alone.

Initial Phase

Assessment

A general assessment of psychological resilience and mental health problems is undertaken for all patients who request psychological treatment. Having established that a psychotherapeutic approach to the patient's problems is the most appropriate method, an assessment is made of the patient's suitability for MBT. This creates a series of clinical dilemmas for the clinician, as there is limited evidence on which to base a decision to recommend MBT rather than other evidence-based interventions. There are no established patient characteristics (e.g., dependency), BPD features (e.g., the predominance of interpersonal problems over impulsivity), or psychiatric symptoms (e.g., high levels of anxiety) which suggest that a patient will specifically benefit from MBT. Furthermore, there is no evidence to suggest that MBT is actively harmful for some types of patients and should therefore be avoided. Research trials of MBT, in contrast to trials of other treatments for BPD, have kept exclusion criteria to a minimum; patients with co-occurring conditions that might be expected to interfere with good outcomes, such as antisocial personality disorder (ASPD) and complex post-traumatic stress disorder, have always been included [1]. MBT was more effective than the comparator (standard) treatment for these patients with co-occurring conditions, so such clinical characteristics should not be a reason to exclude patients from being offered MBT [2,3]. This should not be taken to mean that these patients' treatments would have been less effective had their comorbid conditions been specifically attended to. The limited research evidence available suggests that MBT may be particularly helpful for patients with more severe personality disorder, measured as the number of personality disorder diagnoses at the start of treatment. Patients with more than two personality disorder diagnoses did less well with the comparator treatment than with MBT [2,3].

Clinical consensus suggests that certain patients present difficulties with regard to treatment. Patients with restrictive eating disorders and low body mass index may require a focus on diet and eating habits to achieve weight gain, which needs additional clinical intervention (MBT for patients with eating disorders is discussed in Chapter 12). Substance abuse disorder, particularly alcohol dependence, interferes substantially with a patient's organizational abilities; these patients may find it difficult to attend sessions regularly and to reflect meaningfully on their mental processes. Patients with avoidant personality disorder (discussed in Chapter 8) may feel distinctly uncomfortable in MBT groups for people with emotional dysregulation, which have a primary focus on interpersonal interaction, emotional regulation, and impulsivity (MBT groups are described in Chapter 5); the clinician may wish to consider a more tailored mentalizing intervention for patients who are highly avoidant. However, long-term follow-up studies of MBT have shown little evidence of poorer outcomes associated with these comorbid conditions [4].

Assessment of Mentalizing Profile

The adaptability and flexibility of the four primary dimensions of mentalizing (which are described in Chapter 2) are assessed in the first phase of MBT, and this assessment forms a central part of the formulation. In making the assessment, the clinician takes into account that temporary imbalances and loss of flexibility in mentalizing dimensions are normative. Controlled or well-regulated mentalizing involves rapid movement between the poles of each dimension in a self-correcting way, with the poles balancing each other just as they help the person to balance their position within their social world. Concern should arise only when mentalizing becomes fixed, rigid, and inflexible, with one of the poles of any dimension being over- or under-used or regularly applied out of context.

Clinical Example: Sarah (continued)

Sarah is unable to be alone at home, but can feel comfortable when she is there with her son. The clinician explores this issue with Sarah, who says that she feels "Yuk" when sitting at home alone, and becomes restless and feels compelled to go out. Asking her to give further descriptors of "Yuk" elicits only vague and undifferentiated bodily/mental experience; despite probing questions, she is unable to describe the feelings or even specific triggers in detail, or link them to other experiences that may be similar. She gets into a painful state that she has to try to avoid. All of this suggests that Sarah has difficulties accessing a differentiated internal psychological (mental) self. Her subjective experience of herself in terms of her thoughts and feelings is not well anchored in previous experiences that would give her continuity, coherence, and a differentiated inner experience. Her state of mind seems "untethered" and subject to the anxieties associated with the black hole of emptiness described by so many patients with BPD. The clinician notes "self" experience as a major problem for Sarah.

Recognizing and understanding feelings of emptiness in people with BPD is hard for clinicians because it is such an alien state to them, and yet it is essential for the clinician to be able to identify these feelings and empathize with the existential threat that they pose to the patient. There is limited information in the literature to guide the clinician, but Miller et al. have summarized the views of expert clinicians in their description of the chronic feelings of emptiness, numbness, and disconnection reported by patients with BPD in interviews [5]. Importantly, the expression of emptiness by the patient should alert the clinician to look for other evidence of risk, as the state of mind is intensely painful, and suicide may emerge as an apparent solution.

If there is a problem at one pole of a dimension of mentalizing, there will be a problem at the other pole, usually associated with excessive, inappropriate utilization.

Clinical Example: Sarah (continued)

As the MBT clinician has noted that Sarah has difficulties with self-experience, he now explores Sarah's ability to represent "others"—that is, others thinking about her and how she sees them representing herself. Can she represent others' mental states as distinct from her own? She talks about her current partner and how she worries whether he loves her as much as she loves him, as she "needs to be with him." When asked to contrast her need to be with him and her feeling of love for him and his love for her, she answers *"Aren't they all the same thing?"* Gentle probing failed to lead to elaboration. This suggests that Sarah can find it hard to discriminate between her different feelings when they are intense, and to use their variability to inform her evaluation and experience of her relationship (at least with her partner). In addition, exploring her persistent questioning of her boyfriend's love for her suggests that she has a need to be reassured by constant statements or actions which demonstrate that his love for her is ongoing. This suggests that her ability to create and access both a stable representation of herself as worthy of affection, and a picture of a boyfriend loving her, is highly vulnerable to collapse. The MBT clinician makes a note to focus on this aspect of the self/other mentalizing dimension.

It is helpful to check whether Sarah's difficulty with creating stable self/other representations is particular to the emotional and loving aspects of her relationships. She may be able to read her boyfriend's mind well in other contexts—for example, when he is concerned about how he is doing at work. So the clinician needs to explore an example of the couple interacting constructively and, if appropriate, identify some of Sarah's stronger capacities for reading others' mental states. This adds positive elements to the formulation and allows a contrast with the difficulties associated with their relationship that arise when attachment processes are the most active.

Cognitive/affective processing is assessed next.

Clinical Example: Sarah (continued)

Sarah is temperamentally anxious and her emotions are easily activated in interpersonal interactions, particularly those that are more intimate. But, again, the clinician notes that she describes herself as stable and not overly emotional when she is with her son. However, other situations can lead her to become so anxious that her thoughts become uncontrolled, and she feels frightened and needs other people to help her to calibrate her internal states and to stop her from overreacting—*"I am lost, I am just feeling so frightened, it's horrible, I don't know what to do. What do you think I should do?"* This is a natural response to anxiety, but the problem for Sarah is that her anxiety is not soothed by any response or, if it is, this is only momentary and she has to seek further reassurance. This suggests that her cognitive/affective mentalizing poles are out of balance. She struggles to make use of cognitive mentalizing to help to regulate her emotions effectively. She experiences considerable confusion (metacognitive disorganization) in the context of high arousal, and she becomes unable to process emotions through the combination of emotion-regulation strategies that people generally use: recognition of physical/bodily experience and assigning the appropriate causal attributions to it; identifying the source of anxiety, the context, and an appropriate action to take; and tethering the experience to similar previous experiences. The clinician makes a note of a cognitive/affective imbalance with domination of affective processing.

Next, the clinician considers the patient's reliance on automatic and controlled mentalizing, which can be thought of as "fast" and "slow" thinking. In Chapter 2 we explained that automatic mentalizing is rapid and serviceable for most types of everyday interaction. Problems arise when there is overuse of automatic process. Assumptions are made that are not reflected on, modified, and questioned when expectations based on them fail to connect with observed reality (e.g., they fail to elicit a desired response); they may be treated as accurate despite obvious incompatibilities with evidence from observable reality.

Clinical Example: Sarah (continued)

Sarah assumes that others will not like her. She is highly sensitive to rejection and even to very small slights. She is aware of this but unable to stop herself reacting, and easily becomes demanding and angry when she feels unwanted. This is very marked with her partner, but is also notable with others (friends, colleagues, and even people she does not know well). Sarah relies on automatic mentalizing and shows very limited activation of controlled mentalizing, with which she could ask herself, for example, *"What is it that he is doing that makes me feel unwanted? What is making me feel rejected at the moment?"* The MBT clinician makes a note for the formulation. The clinician also notes that when Sarah tries to reflect, prompted by her friends or partner, her efforts are disappointing in their outcome. She misreads people and creates implausible personal narratives.

Momentary self-reflection is the hallmark of mentalizing that is well regulated or controlled. Patients who are stuck at the automatic mentalizing pole sail on with their assumptions, oblivious of contradiction or challenge, and rarely pause until they hit an immovable reality (e.g., loss of their job or relationship, a physical attack, or an instance of immense humiliation). Meanwhile, the caring observer (e.g., a loved one, the clinician, or another person who is in the role of conversational partner with the patient) becomes increasingly perplexed, annoyed, deeply concerned, helpless, and frustrated, with an overwhelming experience of "*I want to help but I don't know what you are talking about.*" Communication has become disrupted because the patient has ceased to take their conversational partner's mind into consideration—they project into the conversational partner their own narrative, creating a mismatch. As the discourse progresses over time, there is a clash between the patient's self-experience and their conversational partner's understanding of the patient's reality, which is based on the conversational partner's mental model of what they expect the patient's mind contains. So there are two mismatching expectations—the model that the patient is generating of their conversational partner, and the conversational partner's expectation of the patient's mind, based on their shared reality as it seems from their own perspective. The clinician notes that in the course of intense emotion there is typically a collapse into social confusion.

Finally, the clinician assesses the external/internal mentalizing poles. The use of external mentalizing without an adequate link to the internal mentalizing process creates excessive reliance on observable phenomena to understand mental states. This typically applies to the mental states of others, but can also involve being overly influenced by external factors when making judgments about internal self-states—that is, the person relies more on "out there" than "in here" to understand what they are experiencing. Commonly, there is some degree of assumed synchronicity between a person's facial expression, eye movement, body posture, and tone of voice and their internal state of mind, so we safely assume a continuity between someone's words, their bodily expression, and their underlying mental state. Of course, the reality is that context and the capacity to reason within it matter more than the expressions themselves. So whenever we over-rely on external appearance for understanding the mental states of others without reasoning from the context and reflecting that our impressions may not match our understanding, which is based on what else we can expect of the conversational partner's internal state, we will be easily misled and jump to inaccurate conclusions. To give an example from the clinician's perspective (as the clinician, like anyone, will use an external focus and link it to automatic mentalizing), suppose that a patient like Sarah tells us something with a little hesitancy in their voice, and their eyes flicker as their gaze moves slightly away. This immediately generates in us a sense of doubt about the truth of what they are telling us. So we question them further to make sure that we are not developing an interaction based on a falsehood that would interfere with our relationship and how we understand the problems being addressed. The likelihood that we are accurate in this specific situation is to some extent a matter of chance, but this does not stop us from believing in our intuition, as we have prior experience of similar interactions. However, on gaining more information, we correct and clarify our assumptions.

In the case of Sarah, it is obvious that she is not an accomplished liar, and to some extent she reveals her vulnerabilities to others all too easily. Therefore asking her about what is behind her apparent discomfort shows us that we were wrong in our assumption about the content and meaning of her discomfort, and we modify our understanding. But Sarah is not so flexible and adaptive in her assumptions linked to external mentalizing. When Sarah relies on external mentalizing, this can trigger automatic, poorly regulated thinking in relation to predominant themes in her personal narrative, which often relate to rejection: "*I am rejected once again. It took him over 3 minutes to respond to my WhatsApp message.*" She is unable to reflect on her immediate assumptions when she is with someone, and to correct these assumptions using further information from memory or by moving to controlled mentalizing. When she is with her partner, she relies predominantly on her external focus, which continually triggers immediate and powerful assumptions that are not modified and corrected by being checked out and calibrated within the interaction. She lives the experience rather than grounding it in reality.

Clinical Example: Sarah (continued)

The priority that Sarah gives to observable physical reality is hardly surprising, given her lack of confidence about her representations of mind. The clinician notices her tendency to focus on detail that seems to the clinician to be marginal in importance. Sarah is highly superstitious and assigns significance to particular configurations of events that seem improbable: the time it takes for the bus to arrive indicates whether the day is going to be good or bad; the episodes of the soap she follows on television accurately reflect her future. On one occasion when she is not greeted by the clinic's receptionist she assumes that the clinic has taken a decision to ban her from attending as she is clearly not suitable for MBT. The clinician notes that she is biased toward observable reality and fails to check her judgments about internal reality.

Non-Mentalizing Modes/Ineffective Mentalizing

The MBT clinician is trained to be sensitive to indicators that mentalizing is vulnerable to breakdown, and makes a considerable effort to identify when a patient shows signs of its imminent collapse. The general indication is an effort by the patient to stabilize their mental processes by using the "three-legged stool" of psychic equivalence, teleological mode, and pretend mode. These are the modes of functioning that strike the clinician most clearly when the patient's dimensions of mentalizing are fixed in an imbalanced position. Box 4.2 provides a reminder of what these ungainly terms mean, and lists some more accessible terms that could be used to explain the non-mentalizing modes to patients.

Box 4.2 Quick reference for non-mentalizing/ineffective mentalizing.

Psychic equivalence: things are as I see them and no one can tell me different; thoughts are facts; images are reality.

- Inside-Out Mind.
- Boom Brain.
- Blow-up time.
- Know and Now time.

Teleological mode: you are what you do; I am what my actions tell me.

- Outside-In Mind.
- Action Person.
- Doing time.
- Action not words.

Pretend mode: I am in my own world going round and round and it is unaffected by anyone; I understand the complexity of others and myself; I ruminate and get nowhere in particular.

- Bubble time.
- Talking the talk but not walking the walk.
- Bullshit mode.

Non-mentalizing modes are adaptive to the extent that they "save the day" when disaster would otherwise result due to extreme disorganization of thoughts and feelings. Psychic equivalence supports an unerring belief in one's own perspective and an apparent inability or unwillingness to represent and consider others' perspectives. It is quickly identified from a reliance on shallow schematic representations of oneself and others (e.g., victim/victimizer), and rigidity of self-experience, which can be both painful and immutable.

Sarah shows enough vulnerabilities in her use of the dimensions of mentalizing for her mind states to stabilize in non-mentalizing modes. Her default low-mentalizing modes can be identified during the assessment.

Clinical example: Sarah (continued)

Sarah feels unloved and unwanted, which in psychic equivalence is experienced as a current and definite reality rather than an anxious thought. In addition, she is compelled to act on undifferentiated feeling states; this means that the emotions she has when she is alone, for example, undermine her mentalizing, resulting in behaviors that can reinstate mental stability. In the past she has taken drugs and self-harmed; these days she goes out to bars instead. Exploring this pathway, the MBT clinician elicits that Sarah feels better about herself as soon as she gets changed and leaves her flat. When she enters a bar, she is exhilarated and excited, and when a man looks at her she knows someone cares about her.

When Sarah feels compelled to go out in this way, it seems that a teleological mode (or "Outside-In" mode) has been activated, in which changes in the physical world can cause powerful changes in her mental state, particularly her experience of herself. Ultimately, her noticing someone (a man) noticing her can make her feel real, that she matters, and, as it turns out, that she is "loved." Although what happens in the physical world is generally highly informative and, in conjunction with other mentalistic information, may well suggest the thoughts and motives of others, it is the unique reliance on teleological thinking that is of concern to the clinician working with Sarah. The clinician notes that, in this case, Sarah's adaptation to rely on environmental change and a specific risky (albeit predictable) environment leads Sarah to be quite compulsive in her behaviors, which at times place her at risk of serious harm. The MBT clinician discusses Sarah's teleological adaptation to the terrible empty feelings that she reports experiencing when she is alone in her flat, so that it can become a focus of joint work in treatment.

Alongside teleological mode, there may be some indications that Sarah uses pretend mode, which is also of concern to the clinician.

Clinical example: Sarah (continued)

Sarah is insistent that "everything is perfect," "just fine," when she is with her son. Of course, the clinician will have the welfare of her son in mind throughout treatment. The clinician will question and perhaps even express doubt about the claimed calm of their relationship, and probe to see whether Sarah can talk about her son as a person with his own character and not primarily discuss their relationship in transactional terms. Pretend-mode thinking tends to be characterized by a blandness of description ("He is fine," "He is a good boy") with little elaboration or link to additional mental-state-imbued personal narrative. Dialogue about Sarah's son tends to come to an unexpected stop or go around in circles—*"No, I do not worry about him, I am quite lucky, because he is such a good boy."* Further probing elicits a restatement rather than an elaboration.

It is important to identify pretend mode if it is activated when Sarah is talking about her relationship with her son, as her ability to support her son's development over time requires her to be able to mentalize him as a person with his own very real needs and wishes, which will be in conflict with hers at times. The MBT clinician is reminded of Winnicott's description of how a "false self" can be created in a child [6]. Being able to represent her son as a person with an independent mind is essential if both he and the mother–child relationship are to thrive.

Attachment Processes

MBT clinicians identify the dominant attachment processes that are most frequently deployed by their patients. Awareness of interpersonal relationships and their impact on patients' lives is a core focus of MBT both as a medium of change—as mentalizing is the material of interpersonal relationships—and also as a target for improvement. Given that evidence shows that attachment relationships are one of the common sources of difficulties, they invariably become a priority for intervention, but not without qualification. In the assessment process, the MBT clinician initiates an exploration of the details of the patient's current and past relationships in an effort to identify recurring patterns. They use a template of common attachment styles that are identified in people with BPD. Research has shown that the most commonly adopted styles are insecure-avoidant and insecure-ambivalent (also known as anxious-preoccupied). Furthermore, in a proportion of BPD patients, both of these forms of insecure attachment style are present and interact to create disorganized attachment, which is characterized by chaotic and unstable interpersonal interactions [7] (see Box 4.3).

Box 4.3 Common attachment patterns in people with BPD.

Anxious-Avoidant

- Fear intimacy.
- Lack confidence.
- Try not to express emotions to others.
- Turn on people who try to get close to them.
- Are unable to manage themselves and so are constantly in contact with others.

Examples

"I am uncomfortable getting close to others."

"I want emotionally close relationships, but I find it difficult to trust others completely or depend on them."

"I worry that I will be hurt if I allow myself to become too close to others."

"I don't do things like Valentine's Day or family Christmas."

Anxious-Ambivalent

- Over-involved and may be demanding in relationships.
- Seek reassurance and confirmation of their worth, while at the same time being suspicious, vigilant, or frankly distrustful of others.

Examples

"I want to be really close to others, but I often find that others are reluctant to get as close as I would like."

"I am uncomfortable being without close relationships, but I sometimes worry that others don't value me as much as I value them."

"Does my partner really love me?"

Few patients with BPD will describe relationships that reflect a secure attachment style. It is possible, due to the limitations of the available assessment instruments, that patients whose personality function is dominated by psychopathic and narcissistic traits may appear to be secure in their attachments. In these instances, the clinician will have other indications that this is an anomaly, given the range of other problems presented by the patient. Having said that, it is unwise to simply impose the insecure-disorganized attachment style on anyone with a BPD diagnosis and assume that all of the patient's current relationships are dysfunctional. Some patients arrive with strong and secure relationships that they are fighting to maintain, although their efforts are compromised by the emotional and behavioral problems they bring to their interactions. The supportive nature of these relationships can be literally life-saving.

Clinical example: Sarah (continued)

Sarah shows evidence of an anxious-ambivalent attachment style—she desperately reaches out to people but remains disequilibrated (very anxious, and inaccessible to reassurance) even when she has achieved proximity to an attachment figure. Her interactional pattern of making high demands on others but remaining quite dissatisfied with the support that she receives is understandably causing problems with her current partner, who gets angry and frustrated with her. There is evidence that the same relationship style led her to feel trapped in her earlier relationship with the father of her child. She was unable to leave him despite his violence toward her. She was dominated by him, constantly felt she was doing something wrong, and ended up apologizing for herself. It was only after they had separated that she realized she had been a victim of his abuse. When the clinician raised the issue of possible repetition, she recognized the problem. However, she was of the view that she was not in danger. This opinion was shared by the local social services' Child in Need team, which supported the view that Sarah's son should continue to be looked after by both of his biological parents. In the MBT assessment, Sarah's decision not to return to her previous relationship was considered a "moment of mentalizing interest" because she became able to assert her own wishes—a positive feature indicating resilience and the ability to access a stable view of what she wanted and did not want.

Formulation

The information elicited during assessment is organized into a *formulation*—a written account of the patient's problems that attempts to bring coherence to the patient's life narrative using a mentalizing framework for understanding relationships, emotional turmoil, impulsivity, and other difficulties [8]. In general, the conflict between the patient's presenting problems and their life goals and values is highlighted in the formulation to provide motivation for the therapy. For example, a patient might place a high value on supportive relationships, which conflicts with their lack of self-control and impulsive actions. Importantly, the initial focus for treatment and areas of mentalizing strength and resilience are identified. The aim of the formulation is twofold. First, it establishes structure, coherence, and organization for the therapy, which is as important for the clinician as it is for the patient when struggling against a background of psychic equivalence, pretend mode, and teleological constructions. Second, it establishes a collaborative approach in drawing together a shared understanding that is both meaningful and respectful of the patient's point of view, including their priorities, concerns, motives for change, and moral, ethical, and social values. It is therefore essential that the formulation is negotiated and agreed with the patient.

The clinician:

1. writes a first draft of the working formulation in a language that is meaningful to the patient, linking the most important presenting problems to the mentalizing difficulties that have been identified
2. explains it to the patient and discusses it, modeling mentalizing through collaboration
3. asks the patient to consider the working formulation and to rewrite it, with support, where necessary

4. finally agrees the focus for the current psychotherapy sessions as a collaborative clinical agreement.

Box 4.4 provides a summary template as an aide-memoire for clinicians to use when developing a joint formulation. It includes a number of headings that the clinician bears in mind when establishing an agreed clinical formulation. It is not necessary to follow the exact content, and the domains of the formulation listed should be used flexibly. These are:

1. summary of values and problems
2. general vulnerability factors
3. resilience factors
4. mentalizing vulnerabilities—dimensional profile
5. use of low-mentalizing modes and their triggers
6. attachment style(s)
7. treatment goals
8. anticipated difficulties in group and individual treatment.

Box 4.4 Summary of formulation.

The formulation needs to be made in collaboration with the patient, using their words, and should be aimed at their mentalizing level. It should not be technical or intellectual, and should use ordinary language. The formulation should be revisited, made more complete, and revised at clear points within the treatment.

Overall Formulation

- Developmental summary/family background/traumatic or difficult consequences (3–4 sentences).
- Triggering situations for loss of mentalizing (1 sentence):
  - In what situations do your interpersonal difficulties occur?
  - What situations do you struggle with most?
- View of self at the time (1 sentence):
  - How do you see yourself at this moment?
- Experience of other at the time/adult relational pattern (1 sentence):
  - What do you think is in the mind of the other and how does that affect you?
- Dominant affect/most difficult emotions (1 sentence):
  - What feelings are present in that moment?
- Ways of coping/reaction, including self-harm and destructive behavior (1 sentence):
  - These are likely to fit with non-mentalizing.
- Strengths (1 sentence):
  - Despite these difficulties, what have you managed to achieve?

General Vulnerability Factors

- Past experiences.
- Present social, financial, and relational circumstances.

Box 4.4 *(cont.)*

Resilience

Example(s) of effective personal change and overcoming adversity (two main illustrations with emphasis on the use of mentalizing of self to increase self-confidence and self-esteem).

Mentalizing Vulnerabilities and Low-Mentalizing Modes

- Summary of mentalizing profile/key mentalizing vulnerabilities.
- Should be written in ordinary language.
- Needs to be relevant to key non-mentalizing modes:
  - psychic equivalence
  - pretend mode
  - teleological mode.
- Should have relevance to mentalizing dimensions and indicate when there is imbalance between:
  - automatic/controlled mentalizing
  - self/other
  - internal/external
  - affect/cognition.

Attachment Styles

Patterns of relationships, with examples. Keep in mind for exploration (but there is no need to "categorize"):

- anxious-ambivalent
- anxious-avoidant
- disorganized.

Agreed Treatment Goals

Given the understanding that has been outlined, we agreed the following goals for psychological treatment:

- regarding yourself and ways in which you act
- regarding your relationships with other people
- regarding making changes in your life and changing or increasing activities.

These goals will relate to the examples that you may bring into the group, and it would be useful to consider how other people's examples link with the areas you would like help with.

Anticipated Difficulties in Group and Individual Treatment

This also includes ending treatment and what the desired mentalizing changes and behaviors would be.

Sarah's working formulation, which includes examples of flexibility in the summary headings outlined earlier and in Box 4.4, is shown in the following clinical example and summarized as a diagram in Figure 4.1.

Clinical Example: Formulation Discussed with Sarah

We have talked about a lot of things and I will summarize those aspects that we have identified as really important for you to focus on in MBT. I have put these down as our initial "aims" to be agreed.

Strengths

You have shown personal strength in very difficult circumstances over a long time—right from the start things were really frightening in your childhood, and you had to grow up too quickly and look after yourself. Unsurprisingly, this was hard for you, and as a teenager you used drugs to ease some of the pain. But later you managed to stop misusing them—well done you! You also managed to use your strength to stop cutting yourself even though it is still tempting.

A final impressive decision was to stick to your decision to leave Jack's father despite him trying to persuade you to return. You held on to what you wanted then rather than give in to him, which had been your tendency. We need to identify those times when you decide what is best for you compared with those times when you decide on things because someone else wants you to.

> **Aim**: Let us work out what gives you this strength and build on it.

One more recent aspect has been your ability to work things out with Jack's father about your shared care for Jack.

Who Am I and What Do I Want?

You often have problems working out what you think and what you feel. This is really difficult when you are on your own in your flat and also when you are with your boyfriend. In these situations, you have feelings that are intense and take you over. You found it difficult to name those feelings but you know they make you "get out" and "do things."

Sometimes, mostly when you feel bad about yourself, you try to work out what is going on in other people's minds and be whatever they want you to be—just like with Jack's dad. It makes you feel better, but then you start resenting them.

> **Aim:** Knowing and naming what I feel and think about myself.

Action Person and Outside-In Mind

On your own you feel "Yuk" and want to get out to be with people as you feel better then, as long as people show that they like you. This has led to you putting yourself at risk of harm. So, looking at what triggers Action Person and Outside-In Mind is one of the first things to think about in therapy.

> **Aim**: Action Person and Outside-In Mind: what brings them on and how can this be prevented?

Know and Now Mind

When you are with people you can become convinced that they don't like you. This is really powerful with your boyfriend, and you quickly become convinced that he does not love you even though he has said he does. You get so anxious that you keep asking him about it but cannot be reassured. This is when you are in Know and Now Mind. It is so real that you cannot think of anything else.

Know and Now Mind makes you more "needy" and then action becomes necessary, like seeing him straightaway. He needs to show you he loves you. This is how Know and Now Mind works.

Know and Now Mind comes on when you feel criticized. We need to watch out for how sensitive you can be and check it out when it happens in therapy, perhaps most easily in the individual sessions we talked about, but also in the group, too.

> **Aim**: Learn when Know and Now Mind is functioning and get out of it. It is best to be alert to when it is just starting if possible.

Relationships

You mentioned that you try to please your current partner. There was a similar situation with Jack's father for a long time. You worried that you were not pleasing him enough and that you were always doing something wrong—being "clingy." We talked about "anxious-ambivalent attachment," and you will discuss this more in the first phase of MBT in the introductory group.

Perhaps this style of relationships links with not knowing who you are. It will be important to look at it in the group therapy when you are with other people, to see if you have the same pattern with others there—will you try to be liked, for example, or find it hard to stand up for yourself?

The good relationship you have with your son is important, and you have said that you "know you are a good mother." We need to build on that. You also told us that Jack's social support worker is concerned that you can go into your own world a bit when you are with him. We called that "Bubble Mode."

> **Aim**: Build on the effective aspects of your relationships. Understand what creates the problem interactions in relationships.

MBT

We talked about how some of these feelings and behaviors might come up in therapy. For example, you might even worry that you aren't doing well enough in therapy or that you have displeased your therapist. Naturally you will go into Action Person/Outside-In Mind if this happens, and will want to see your therapist quickly to be reassured. So we need to work out what happens if you worry too much between sessions and get into this state of mind.

Aims at the Beginning

We can list the aims I have suggested here if we agree them, and I have organized a cycle of problems for us to use so that we can consider what sends your mind into Outside-In Mind and Inside-Out Mind. When that happens, things start to go wrong for you.

We still have to decide how to measure if we are achieving our aims and things are getting better for you.

The manner of creating and delivering the formulation enhances the patient's mentalizing by generating a shared mental process with a joint goal embodied in the "collaborative clinical agreement." This "we-mode" process ("we-mode" is described in more detail in Chapter 2) entails two minds focusing on a shared object—in this case, the

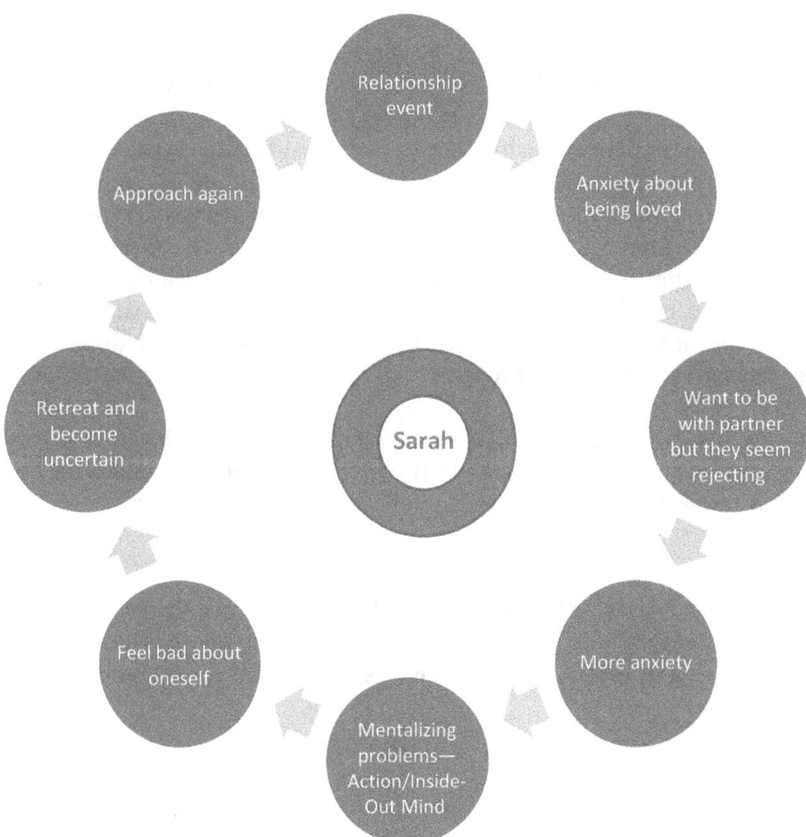

Fig. 4.1 Sarah's cycle of problems.

task of defining the best focus for treatment using a shared conceptual framework for scaffolding the patient's problems in the context of their overarching values and ambitions in life. This process is the first step toward stimulating an experience of we-mode functioning, which remains the organizing principle of the intervention.

The process of developing the formulation is made easier because part of the process involves establishing the tentative nature of mentalizing—both the clinician and the patient know that neither of them has to get the formulation "right." There can be no fixed formulation in MBT, as the treatment is inherently dynamic; all mentalizing leads to fresh understandings and changes of perspective, which drive reformulation of the collaborative agreement. The formulation is labeled a "working formulation" to highlight the fact that it is open to revision. In MBT, the formulation following assessment is a starting point rather than a fixed map of the terrain to be covered, which is as yet unexplored. What is set is the length and intensity of the treatment. The working formulation can identify questions to be answered but should avoid pre-defining solutions.

The formulation does not require a sophisticated psychological understanding on the part of the clinician about the complex determinants of mental health problems. As we have said in Part I of this book, mentalizing is rooted in everyday experiences, and the (relatively sophisticated) understanding that all human beings use to interpret individual and social action. Adopting an expert stance would, in any case, break a defining principle of MBT (see Chapter 3) that asks the clinician not to take over mentalizing for the patient and not to use their ability to mentalize to compensate for the challenges experienced by the patient, and thereby risk creating a relationship of dependence. However, the alert reader will note that the delivery of a formulation, however collaboratively this is approached, breaks this principle to some extent. Our defense for allowing the principle to be breached at this point is based not on the content of the formulation but on the process engendered in its formation and delivery. The formulation is presented as a shared approach to a complex puzzle that needs to be put together piece by piece, refined, and improved in joint exploration, rather than as a statement of certainty about motivation and cause. The terrain to be explored will look different as each peak is reached, to reveal further heights! MBT is not about scaling the summit; rather, it is about going for a hike in the mountainous terrain of the mind. In practical terms, this means that the MBT clinician is asked, jointly with the patient (who is seen as a conversational partner in this regard), to revisit the working formulation on a 3-monthly basis at the very minimum, or when indicated by events such as:

- repeated crises
- new challenges and problems that were not evident at the time of assessment
- resources to be taken advantage of that were not known about previously (e.g., a new relationship)
- a new understanding of determinants that changes the current formulation
- lack of progression.

Sarah's working formulation mentions a number of areas of concern, which were discussed with her. In particular, the clinician and Sarah contrasted the tension between her values of wanting a stronger and more stable relationship with her partner and her son, and her going out to bars and engaging in risky behavior that might undermine "living" those values. An agreement was made that Sarah would try to inhibit her "action" response to loneliness, and attempt to accept it as something of interest that could be addressed in other ways. In the first section of the formulation some of her strengths are outlined, which include her ability to stop using self-harming and her ability to stand up to the father of her child and assert herself. These positive changes need exploring not only to strengthen them but also to understand how they came about and how Sarah might harness them further. The second section of the formulation summarizes the difficulties that Sarah has in identifying and constructively deploying her subjective self-states, along with her struggle to maintain a coherent self-representation over time. She is not sure who she is or what she wants. The target in treatment is to harness, develop, and stabilize the "self" pole of the self/other dimension of mentalizing. Sarah's "other" mentalizing pole is overactive, as indicated by her constantly trying to work out the mind states of others as they apply to her, which she is unable to do, as indeed it is hard for anyone to do on any long-term basis. Therefore the self/other mentalizing dimension becomes a focus for Sarah's treatment, and is placed in the current aims so that both she and the clinician are alert to how it will play out in treatment. The next sections summarize some of the low-mentalizing modes, namely psychic equivalence and teleological mode (here termed Know and Now Mind or Inside-Out Mind, and Action Person or Outside-In Mind, respectively, when relevant), that are activated when Sarah is under stress. The purpose of identifying and naming these mind states is so that Sarah becomes aware of them and both she and the MBT clinician can "name and note" them as they occur, and then explore what triggered them in the moment. Finally, there is a summary of her attachment strategies as understood at the beginning of treatment. Further details will emerge in treatment, and these can be added to the formulation over time.

Psychoeducation: MBT-Introductory Group

MBT-Introductory group (MBT-I)* introduces the framework of MBT to the patient. Alongside this, it has a number of wider aims:

1. to inform/educate patients about mentalizing and personality disorder and associated areas of knowledge
2. to prepare patients for long-term treatment
3. to increase patients' motivation
4. to elicit more detail about patients' mentalizing capacities
5. to confirm the initial assessment and diagnosis.

In summary, the primary purpose of MBT-I is to ensure that patients entering treatment do so with a reasonable understanding of the process they are engaging in, that they are aware of the focus of treatment, and that they appreciate the expectations placed on them as well as the expectations they can have about treatment. Patients with BPD are offered 10–12 MBT-I initial sessions in a weekly group with others. All the patients start at the same time and have to attend a minimum of two out of the first three group sessions in order to continue in the rest of the program. This condition is imposed on the basis that failure to attend the initial sessions, which cover the topics of mentalizing and non-mentalizing, leads to problems in learning about the topics covered in the later sessions. However, patients who do not attend these early sessions are not discharged but are offered a place in the next available new group. Patients who remain in the group need to attend 75% of the subsequent sessions in order to move on to MBT-G (the structure of MBT-G is discussed in Chapter 5). People with ASPD are offered 6–8 sessions; recommended adaptations to the core modules of MBT-I to make them more appropriate for working with people with ASPD are discussed in Chapter 7 (see also [9]). The total number and order of sessions are not essential factors for the goals of MBT-I to be achieved; imparting knowledge, increasing understanding and motivation through empowerment, and developing a therapeutic alliance with clarity about the patient's problems are more important.

At the end of MBT-I, all patients have a meeting with a senior member of the clinical team to review their experience of MBT-I and plan further treatment.

Format of MBT-I

MBT-I is organized as group psychoeducation with a maximum of 10 patients in a group. The sessions are organized over 12 weeks, and each session lasts for 1.5 hours. Some modules contain a lot of content and can extend over two sessions if necessary. In the course of the sessions, some patients may realize that MBT is not for them, and the clinician does not expect that all patients will fit into the treatment model outlined in MBT-I. The treatment model needs to be relevant to the patient's difficulties. If it becomes apparent that MBT might not be right for the patient, the clinician and patient review treatment and consider alternatives if appropriate.

---

* A detailed manual for MBT-I is available at www.annafreud.org/media/14626/mbt-i-for-internet.pdf

Session Structure

Each group session follows a similar sequence:

1. welcome to patients
2. summary of the previous session's material
3. feedback from the previous session's homework
4. introduction to a new topic
5. discussion relating the topic to the participants' symptoms and personal lives
6. final summary and discussion of homework.

The sessions are built on the following principles.

- Exercises are arranged in a sequence, progressing from emotionally "distant" scenarios to some that are more personalized.
- Discussions are related to participants' personal experience only when the group has developed a cohesive atmosphere and some trust has been established between participants.
- New exercises and illustrations are encouraged if they increase the psychoeducational understanding of the topic.
- Homework is voluntary and generally requires the participants to increase their focus on their mind states.
- Over the course of the sessions, participants build up a "directory" of indicators of non-mentalizing (e.g., use of particular words, certainty of opinion).

Each topic is accompanied by a handout and a worksheet. The topics include mentalizing and personality disorder, ineffective mentalizing, emotions and how to manage them, attachment, and treatment expectations.

Role of Group Leader

The group leader, a clinician, remains "in charge" of the group throughout each session and across all 12 sessions, and takes an active role in structuring the group. The term "in charge" is used here not to suggest that the group leader is autocratic, but rather to imply that they manage the group carefully to ensure that each topic is covered adequately and discussed in enough detail to make certain that patients are aware of the relevance of the topic. The group leader often makes use of a whiteboard and/or flip chart to highlight key points or note down contributions from participants in the course of discussions. Crucially, the group leader models a mentalizing stance throughout any discussion, while maintaining an expert stance in terms of knowledge about mentalizing and personality disorder. This balance is important. A mentalizing or "not-knowing" stance can become confused with a lack of knowledge or understanding. However, nothing could be further from the truth. The application of our knowledge to inform our own mental states and to stimulate thought in others is the essence of mentalizing. The group leader models the mentalizing stance by demonstrating that their knowledge, although that of an expert, can be extended, clarified, and enriched by the contributions of the group members. Critically, the group leader's mind can be changed by the minds of others; the participants' understanding of and ideas about a given topic under discussion feed back to the discussion itself. Hence there is an emphasis on the group leader stimulating discussion among the group members. Maintaining a balance between providing information to the group members and learning from their perspectives is a key skill for group leaders. The group leader should be careful not to be too "lecturing" in the sessions, as this tends to encourage passivity in the group members. The leader needs to generate some group process even though the group is task oriented. The process engendered should be related to the topic of the group so that there can be a seamless return to task.

There is a certain amount of material that must be covered in each session, and the group leader needs to follow the manual closely. Experience has shown that it is easy to digress and get lost, which impedes the completion of the program. It is also important that learning takes place through the participants' own activities, although the group leader maintains a psychoeducational perspective. The group leader uses examples given by the patients to illustrate points related to the topic under discussion.

Treatment Phase: Structure of Individual MBT Sessions

Empathic Validation, Clarification, and Elaboration of Experience

The MBT clinician follows a stepwise intervention process in each session [10]. Of course these steps have to be implemented skillfully and should not be followed slavishly. Often the patient and clinician will follow a different pathway, dictated by the clinical material presented or the state of mind of the patient. In principle, the first step is to identify with the patient what is currently troubling them and to explore the problems within the context of the working formulation. This is the empathic exploratory phase of the session, which leads to *empathic emotional validation* of the patient's experiences both as they are remembered and as they are experienced in the present as the story is told and reflected on during the session. Empathic validation has three main components (see Chapter 3):

1. showing the patient that their emotions at the time and in the current moment are recognized and resonated with
2. empathizing with the basic emotion more than the social emotion, which is often a secondary emotion—the basic emotion is the driver of existence
3. identifying and also recognizing the effect that the emotional experience is having on the patient.

The clinician explores the initial narrative using a not-knowing stance to try to expand the perspectives on the story and to gauge the focus for further work in the session. Gradually a theme linked to the current formulation is likely to emerge. If it does not, the clinician can ask how the subject matter links to the formulation and, if this remains unclear, consider rewriting part of the working formulation making use of the new material.

Clinical Example: Sarah (continued)

Sarah began her session by telling the clinician that she had been sitting on her own at home and was trying to "busy" herself. But in the end she had had to go out. She explained that it had been no good and that she had failed again (*showing the self-judgment and self-criticism Sarah is prone to*).

Clinician: Let's not jump to such quick judgment without working out what happened. (*An attempt to stop Sarah immediately going into non-mentalizing mode in which she has a fixed view of herself.*)

Tell me more about sitting on your own. Put yourself back there and get me to where you were in your thoughts and your feelings at the time. (*Clinician using a not-knowing stance, trying to explore the "there and then" from the "here and now," and stopping Sarah falling into the experience of the "there and then in the here and now" during the telling of the story.*)

Sarah: I cannot describe it. My insides are churning and I want to walk around. It is horrible and then I think that no one wants to see me and then that my boyfriend doesn't love me. I tried to phone him but he didn't pick up. So I just thought he knew it was me and so he didn't answer. Then I knew I wanted to go out. And that makes me feel better and a bit calmer. (*Uncertainty of self-experience and psychic equivalence with teleological mode. Note that although Sarah says "calmer," she means that the excitement of risk taking has the paradoxical effect of calming her.*)

Clinician: What about this churning—where is it in you and what do you make of it? (*Asking Sarah to mentalize her bodily experience to see if she can move toward embodied mentalizing.*)

Sarah: It is my stomach and it means that I am frightened but I don't know what about.

Clinician: Hmm. That is pretty dreadful, to have such a strong physical feeling that you can't escape from and not know what it is about and it doesn't even seem to link with anything that is happening. Let's think about that. (*Empathy with a small effort at clarification highlighting the inescapability and the namelessness of the dread. Much is communicated here by the way the words are spoken rather than purely by the content.*)

Sarah: It just always makes me walk around and I don't know what is in my head or what I want to do. I just know that going out gets rid of it and makes me better. To be honest, you made me feel it a bit just now.

Clinician: So the churning and anxiety has nothing up here (*clinician points to his head*). As you put yourself there now, what are you thinking? How does it feel?

Sarah: I want to get up and walk out. You don't think I am trying hard enough. (*Sudden reactivity, perhaps activated by the bodily experience, experienced for real in psychic equivalence—"there and then" moving into the "here and now."*)

Clinician: Really? Where has that come from? I am not aware of thinking that (*clinician reports directly what is in his mind*). In fact, I was thinking that you are trying so hard (*rewarding in order to down-regulate the self-questioning*). So it seems to bring up harsh and unpleasant thoughts that you think others have about you when you are on your own and you end up confused about how you feel and what you think. It doesn't surprise me that you then need to get out and see someone who can show you that you are a person worth seeing (*an empathically based clarification*).

Sarah: I just want to get someone to love me. I have always wanted to be loved and I was looking at pictures of me with my father yesterday and things have never been normal. All I want is to have a happy and loving family and nothing has ever been like that. I tried everything to stay with Jack's father even when he was violent. I just wanted things to be normal with a mum and dad and baby. But it is never going to be like that, is it? I can't have anything that is normal. Even now every day I think John (*her partner*) is going to leave me. With Jack's father I did everything to make him feel good so that he would want me—but that's all messed up, isn't it?

CLINICIAN: What makes you say it is messed up?

SARAH: Well—I was doing things that he wanted me to do and not what I wanted to do and I don't know why as, when I think about it, he was using me most of the time. That is what is messed up. I am just some kind of nutter that people exploit.

CLINICIAN: What concerns me is your sense that you know now that you didn't want to do some of the things you did for him or put up with his treatment of you, but then you didn't realize that. What was happening then? (*Clinician trying to place time between then and now to encourage more reflective, less affective mentalizing about the event.)*

SARAH: It was that stuff we talked about. The things he made me do. (*Sarah relays a sexually traumatic memory associated with Jack's father. Feeling sexually traumatized and feeling exploited but helpless left her feeling "horrid." This is not the first time that these experiences are referred to, but there is slightly greater clarity. At the end, her mentalizing fades and she seems confused.*) I don't know who I am or what I want. How do I work that out when I am in the situation?

CLINICIAN: That's something *we* have to work out so that you are more sure of yourself. (*Clinician aims to share responsibility with Sarah and stress that she is not alone when she remembers traumatic experiences from her past. Then he moves back or rewinds to where the narrative was more coherent and mentalizing was more evident.*) You tried really hard to have a happy family and you wished for it so much that you even did things that you now think you didn't really want to do. And at the moment you feel you will never have that sense of being together and relaxed —and that hopelessness is horrible. Perhaps we can work out now what you really think and feel about things with John, as you mention you might be starting to do things for him that you are not sure you really want to do, and you really don't want to feel the horrid feelings of being exploited. (*Empathic validation to anchor the discussion and join together with Sarah.*)

The clinician is now using an empathic validating summary to focus the session on an aspect of the formulation, namely Sarah's ability to access a robust, albeit subjective, experience of a sense of self that is distinct from how others tell her she is. Can she "know" this enough to be more assertive and not necessarily acquiesce to others' demands?

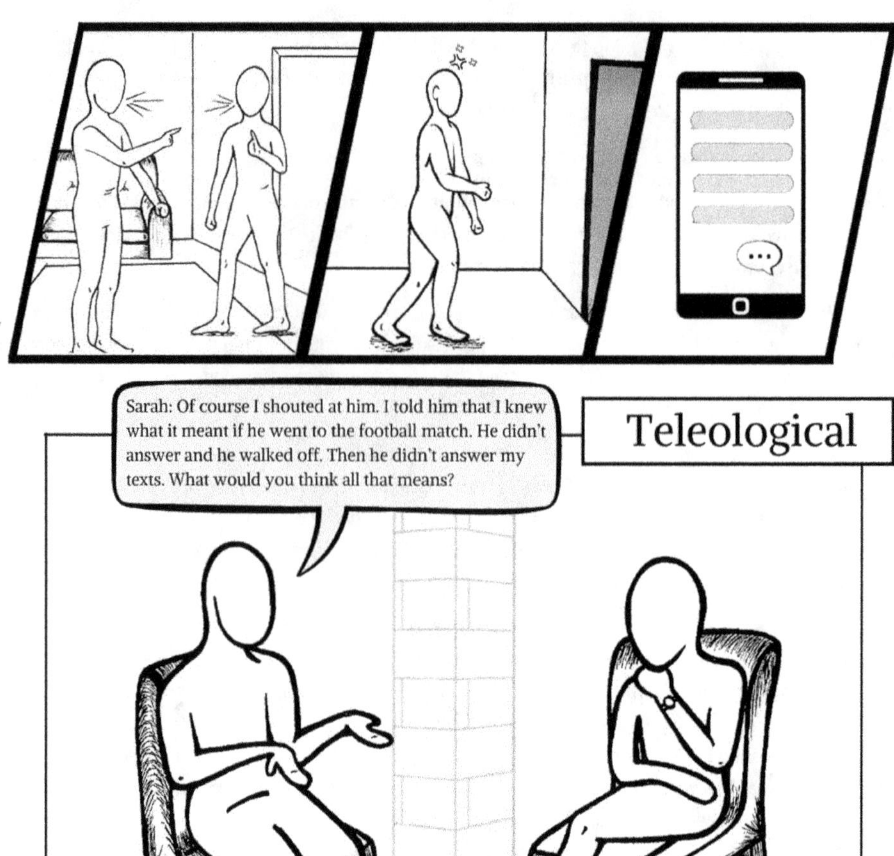
Sarah: Of course I shouted at him. I told him that I knew what it meant if he went to the football match. He didn't answer and he walked off. Then he didn't answer my texts. What would you think all that means?
Teleological

Sarah: He doesn't care about me. Never has. When he got back I refused to come out of the bedroom.
Clinician: His actions spoke louder than words. What did it mean to you?

Sarah: See, you don't even care!! You just want to be somewhere else.
Clinician: Whoops, sorry. Another action by me. I can see what you mean. I just want to see how much time we have left to unpack all this in our session.

The clinician, having named and noted the potential for action mode, now tries to insert reflectiveness about the assumed relationship between Sarah's partner's action and her internal experience while remaining neutral about its accuracy and empathic about her negative personalized interpretation. Once achieved, Sarah can monitor her tendency to express herself through action between sessions. The clinician can also use the moment in the session of looking at his watch and how that leads to an immediate assumption about his motive.

Not-Knowing and Managing the Mentalizing Process

The not-knowing stance of the MBT clinician is an active stance aimed at promoting the exploration of mental states in relation to actions and events. The clinician seeks to support the patient to take a step back and consider what lies behind their actions and inner experiences. The stance creates a tension (an implicit pressure) for the patient to be reflective rather than reactive.

This is a double-edged sword. On the one hand, reflection is a necessary mental process in everyday life, as all people need to monitor themselves as they express their current feelings and thoughts. On the other hand, a patient can feel under too much pressure and forced to think about things that they either cannot easily understand or do not want to talk about because they trigger intense and painful feelings. Therefore the stance has to be implemented skilfully and sensitively, taking into account the patient's current mentalizing capacities and remembering the aim—to create a range of perspectives "on the fly" to stop the patient becoming fixed in a single viewpoint and open up the possibility of them seeing something for what it is rather than what it seems to be.

The not-knowing stance is a method used to stimulate being imaginative, able to contemplate alternatives and to use one's imagination in a balanced way that is neither untethered from reality and shifting into pretend mode, nor too closely bound to physical facts, which liberates the person from psychic equivalence. Not knowing can help to achieve this balance, and enables mentalizing to be managed well. MBT clinicians have to "not know" (or "un-know") mental states, to resist being presumptive but not be indifferent to finding them out (i.e., to show genuine curiosity). In life, people who are experienced as genuinely supportive are curious about things, constantly learning and asking questions, rarely drawing premature conclusions, and frequently leaving things open rather than seeking closure. Wisdom is admirable but is helpful only in tiny doses. End points are not the goal; rather, the journey, and what might be discovered along the route, is. To put it bluntly, MBT is not an insight-oriented approach where the clinician provides a model-motivated "interpretation" of the patient's experience and behavior. It is an approach of collaborative discovery where the clinician's role is merely to scaffold the recovery of mentalizing. This may involve less glamour than other orientations in which the interpersonal scenario of patient and clinician is apparently "discovered" but closer scrutiny shows it to have been preordained by texts representing accumulated clinical experience. MBT is respectful of and not skeptical in relation to such clinical generalizations. It finds a balance between the risk of undermining personal agency by providing solutions, and the benefit to the patient from those understandings, and favors the un-knowing option, particularly with patients at the more severe end of the spectrum of BPD.

The scaffolding of MBT is developed in MBT-I, and Sarah has attended this group for 10 sessions. In the MBT-I group, the clinician illustrates the not-knowing stance. One possible way of doing this is as follows.

Clinical Example: Learning about the Not-Knowing Stance

The clinician is holding what appears to be a book.

Clinician: I am going to ask a silly question. What am I holding?

The clinician has to deal with some blank faces as the patients worry that this is such a silly question with an obvious answer that it might be a trick. They are of course right to some extent.

Clinician: I told you it was a silly question. But bear with me please—what am I holding?

Patients: A book.

Clinician: What makes you say it is a book?

Patients: It is obviously a book.

Clinician: What characteristics does it have?

The members of the group describe the shape of the book, the spine with a title on it, the front with a picture, a title, and an author's name, and a number of other features.

Clinician: What sort of book? Is it a crime novel, a children's book, a romantic novel?

Patients: Don't know. The title and picture look like a romantic novel.

Clinician: What is it about the picture?

And so the discussion goes on until the clinician or one of the patients suggests reading the book to find out.

Clinician: Exactly. We will have to read it to find out. So let's have a look inside.

The clinician opens the book, revealing that it is a box of chocolates disguised as a book.

Clinician: So, looking at something more carefully shows it is not what it first seemed. Presupposition about minds is even more obvious than it is with books. We do not perceive thoughts—we hypothesize about them. And we are often wrong. Being wrong is fine. Convincing yourself that you could not possibly be wrong is the risky attitude. The therapy you are about to undertake is all about being less certain and more doubtful than you are used to being. And take my word for it, that will help! I am absolutely certain. (*The irony and self-mocking used here are deliberate in MBT. They turn out to encourage mentalizing.*)

The process of discovery is the essence of the not-knowing stance; when applied to understanding self-states, the mental states of others, and social interactions, it stimulates mentalizing. Assumptions no longer dictate reality but create curiosity and exploration, without which we are misled and unable to learn. This is the stance that the MBT clinician has to model for the patient, who so often has closed down their curiosity and interest in other people and their minds as the results have led to incomprehension and, at times, horror.

Sarah needs to be able to differentiate her feelings, locate them in context, and link them to other experiences to give them substance, meaning, and continuity. She experiences her inner world quite passively, especially when she is alone. She needs to develop a sense of being able to manage it actively. The first part of helping her to generate a sense of mental agency and autonomy is to notice her current states and then name them. Altering her reliance on reflection through others and the "people-pleasing" interactions that this generates can be addressed only by her developing increased awareness of her inner states and greater confidence about asserting her own wishes.

Contrary Moves

Mentalizing flexibility is stimulated by the clinician's attention to the dimensions of mentalizing as the patient reports and reflects on their personal narratives. In Sarah's case, the self/other dimension is one of those obviously out of balance, caused by a lack of self/other differentiation. Her ability to represent others' thinking about her in a way that soothes her and informs constructive interaction is unstable. She loses her sense of being loved and as a result she uses most of her mind power to monitor others' mental states, asking them to reassure her so that she can rebuild a transitory experience of "feeling loved." As her attention turns to others, she inevitably neglects her inner world and abandons what should be her privileged position regarding her own self-experiences. The MBT clinician may focus on generating a sense of agency, but at the same time has to increase the adaptive flexibility of the self/other dimension. To achieve this, the clinician engages in *contrary moves*, encouraging Sarah to elaborate her self-experience when her attention is exclusively focused on other minds, and, equally, encouraging a deeper awareness of the other when her superficial and unhelpful depictions of the other suggest that she is replacing detailed mind-reading with a projection of the self, creating a "needed" rather than realistic image of the other. In essence, although she is apparently focused on the other, she is in fact stuck supporting a vulnerable self, which is felt to be at risk of disintegration. Of course, when Sarah is being supported in building a felt sense of agency, the clinician may focus on either the self or the other pole for considerable periods, as the aim is to achieve improved self/other differentiation by stimulating flexibility. In MBT, becoming comfortable with moving across all of the mentalizing dimensions is the key. Good mentalizing involves using the dimensions fluently to ensure optimal adaptation to each social context.

Clinical Example: Sarah (continued)

Sarah: I keep asking my boyfriend what he thinks of me. To be frank, he is a bit fed up with it. But I can't stop myself. I become uncertain that he cares about me. I convince myself he does, but then I start having these terrible doubts. I try to work out whether he does or not by watching carefully how he does things and whether he does things for me. Like last night he was cooking and I said that I don't like chilies much. He said he would only put in a few then. So I counted how many he was putting in. Why? It's so stupid.

Here, Sarah is anxious to sustain self-coherence and her mentalizing comes under the sway of the Outside-In Mind/teleological mode. She is focused on her partner's mental state, but—unable to achieve a clear representation from looking beyond—she has defaulted to external behavioral indications. On reflection during the session, she recognizes that this was not entirely sensible.

Clinician: So where are you in this? You were able to tell him about your dislike of chilies. That's great—you so often hold back on making your preferences clear. (*Here the clinician identifies and reinforces helpful mentalizing.*) But somehow you lost having a feeling for what he felt about you—otherwise why judge him in terms of the number of chilies? You kind of lose sight of him and start to worry about his feelings for you, but how does that worry leave you feeling about you? (*Here the clinician tries to encourage flexibility by switching the focus on to the self—a contrary move.*)

Sarah: I don't know what mine are except I know I really like being with him.

Clinician: What tells you that? (*Here the clinician is recapturing the not-knowing stance, trying to help Sarah to elaborate and strengthen her "felt" self.*)

Sarah: I just feel good when I am with him. I feel I can relax. It is just that that feeling can disappear so quickly.

Clinician: Now you have made me curious. Tell me what you think about when you reach that sense of relaxation. What are your thoughts about yourself when the feeling good is there? (*Again, the clinician does not assume he knows. In a way he could take it for granted that feeling relaxed is good and is filled with general positivity about the self. But the not-knowing stance demands that further elaboration of the self-state is provided.*)

The clinician has moved Sarah subtly from her preoccupation with her boyfriend's state of mind to deeper scrutiny of her own changing thoughts about herself. He keeps her working on her own thoughts and feelings about herself and then engages in the opposite movement, asking her about her boyfriend's mind states in relation to hers.

Sarah: It just switches into what it was like with Jack's father. I am not good enough for him. I was not good enough for my father. I am not good enough for anyone.

Clinician: Do you think you could share this kind of thinking with John? What do you think he would make of it? Could he give a response that was more reassuring than counting the number of chilies?

Practice makes perfect, so the MBT clinician keeps engaging in this rebalancing procedure, pushing the patient between the poles of mentalizing on each dimension. Sarah's tendency to polarize is not resolved at any point, but movement seems to get easier—among other things, she begins to anticipate the clinician's line of questioning. She notices the contrary moves. Could it be that she is developing an image of the clinician's mind?

Intervention using contrary moves to "oil" all of the other dimensions is necessary if fully flexible mentalizing is to be established. The patient who overuses cognitive processing is coaxed to pay attention to and trust more in their feelings. But when emotional processes predominate, questioning then focuses on the beliefs and expectations that drive these feelings, and the patient is pushed to increase the recruitment of cognition to help to manage the emotions.

Clinical Example: Sarah (continued)

Sarah: I am very good with Jack. I make all his favorite foods and make sure that he is clean and tidy when he goes to school. I know that if other people start to think that I am not looking after him properly they will tell the Child in Need team and they will start suggesting that his father looks after him more. (*Cognitive/external determining action; not thinking beyond.*)

Clinician: Oh, that is so worrying. (*Starting with supportive empathy.*) But tell me, what does it feel like to be a mother who is being observed all the time? (*Question relating to emotion with focus on the self.*)

Sarah: I don't mind, as I show them that he is being well looked after. (*Sarah's realistic anxiety about her son being taken away makes movement away from the observed, cognitive other quite hard.*)

Clinician: I see. And how do you feel inside when you see that Jack is clean and tidy? (*The clinician is making a second attempt to shift to emotional self-focus.*)

Sarah: I feel proud. I am a proper mum. I don't leave Jack dirty and neglected like I was.

Clinician: Ah. So you feel proud. That is quite something. (*The clinician is not missing an opportunity to be reinforcing and to show the value in mentalizing.*) And is that proud just of yourself, or also of him?

Sarah: Well, I feel proud of myself as I can get him to dress properly and look good. But when I look at him, I think maybe he will feel better about himself than I am feeling about how I am.

Clinician: That is important. We don't often talk about what Jack thinks. What about him? How do you think he thinks and feels about having Sarah as his mum? (*The clinician is moving to new mentalizing other territory, trying to achieve a balance between cognition and affect.*)

The clinician persists in his efforts to get Sarah to use her emotional experiences to think about her relationship with her son, concerned that she thinks that receiving physical attention is all that is required for his healthy development. Her history of deep deprivation tells the clinician that this could become a problem. Sarah has great difficulty in reaching the part of herself that experienced neglect—she finds it hard to recall what she thought and what she felt when she was a child exposed to neglect and adversity. She finds it easier to think of childcare in cognitive and externally readily verifiable terms of "eating well" and "being clean." Yet if she does not take a deeper, more mentalizing interest in her relationship with Jack, he will suffer in terms of constructing his own sense of mental self, adding to the cycles of generational traumatization that we see clinically every day. To prevent this, and being implicitly aware of (mentalizing) the Child in Need team, the clinician aims to free Sarah from the constraints of her teleological thinking, which has been enabling her to care for Jack physically but, when dominant, has prevented her from giving due attention to emotional states and their contribution to his development and the beneficial unfolding of the mother–child relationship.

Thus, in MBT, a patient who relies on excessively externally focused mentalizing is stimulated to consider the internal experience of others and themselves.

Clinical Example: Sarah (continued)

Sarah: So you think that I am not doing very well here and I should be better by now.

Clinician: Whoa! Where has that come from? Can you get me to how you have come to that? I am not aware that I thought that at all! (*Stopping and exploring and insisting on controlled mentalizing to appraise the assumption.*)

Sarah: Well, when I was talking then you crossed your arms, which looks to me like you are fed up.

Clinician: I am sorry I did that. I was not aware of doing it at all and I forgot momentarily just how sensitive you are to the meaning of small gestures. You just have to bear with us insensitive folk. Next time could you warn me when I am doing something like that and then we can stop and you can help me to reflect on why I might have done it.

Sarah might or might not be accurate. She is using her well-attuned and superbly sensitive external mentalizing to fully inform her understanding about the clinician's mental state. The clinician should not challenge here. Rather, he encourages slowing the process down and checking it out. This way, the issue does not focus on a question about whether Sarah's assumption is correct or incorrect. It is about whether she can *stop and explore* before continuing headlong into well-primed negativity.

Intervening in Low Mentalizing

In any session the clinician is likely to encounter problems with the "how" of the patient's attempts to process and communicate their personal narrative. In patients with severe personality disorder, low mentalizing often starts as soon as they become emotional while recounting their experiences. For example, the clinician may note that arousal brings with it a higher than typical level of the individual being certain and insistent about the accuracy of their perspective. This is characteristic of "Inside-Out Mind"—psychic equivalence. How is this managed?

The MBT clinician listens sensitively throughout a session for low mentalizing. This means listening not just to the content of the patient's story but also to how they tell their story. The clinician resists trying to reframe or interpret the content, which is the natural reaction. Their intervention aims to rekindle effective mentalizing rather than to give low mentalizing meaning. Without such an intervention, low mentalizing leads to increasing distress for patients. Their mental pain comes to feel increasingly real. They fail to reorganize and incorporate earlier experiences in a way that is useful for achieving change. Even distant events start to have the power of current reality, and traumatic memories can take over.

There are two barriers to intervention. The first is that the event itself is experienced in low-mentalizing mode and as a result is not fully available for reflection and change. The second is that the current state of low mentalizing prevents fruitful exploration of other issues during the session. Therefore the clinician retreats in order to advance—first taking steps to recover the patient's mentalizing, and then revisiting the incident/narrative for learning purposes. In summary, this involves four steps.

1. Avoid joining with current low mentalizing.
2. Use the MBT Loop (see this chapter: What is an MBT Loop?) to rekindle mentalizing.
3. Revisit the low-mentalized incident in the narrative.
4. Reclaim the narrative within effective mentalizing.

Avoiding Joining with Low Mentalizing

Remember that in low mentalizing the mind is fixed and rigid and not in a state of conflict. Paradoxically, this is true even if what is being narrated simultaneously holds diametrically opposing views. In low mentalizing, alternative perspectives are not available, and therefore it is counterproductive for the clinician to enter into the inconsistency. Intervention at the level of counterarguments does not match the patient's mind state, which is not about debate but rather about a painful and fixed totality. Effective intervention is difficult because low mentalizing, when painful for the patient, leads to empathic distress and low mentalizing in the clinician. It becomes challenging for the clinician to avoid joining with low mentalizing (agreeing or disagreeing) and to maintain therapeutic equipoise and engage initially with the patient using empathic validation about their experience. The temptation is to advance counterarguments or to reassure them that their interpretation of their experience is partial or even incorrect. Yet if the clinician just passively goes along with and accepts the low mentalizing without question, the patient can interpret this as confirming their experience and as colluding with their possibly erroneous construction of their own or others' attitudes and motivations. To prevent this situation from arising, the MBT clinician starts an MBT Loop.

What is an MBT Loop?

An MBT Loop is a three-step maneuver. First, the patient and clinician *notice and name* the low-mentalizing mode. This will have been discussed in the MBT-I phase; Sarah is aware of her "Action Mind," "Outside-In Mind," and "Know and Now Mind," and is also to some extent aware of her "Bubble Mode" with her son.

Second, the clinician curiously *explores the content* of the low mentalizing, slowly and sensitively moving away from detailed direct examination to broader exploration of the topic, which is more likely to re-establish reflection. Empathy is used extensively in this context for the purpose of emotion regulation.

Third, once the patient has achieved self-regulation and a sense of agency, the content and context of the narrative that appears to have triggered the low mentalizing can be re-explored. *Memory work* is used to increase the capacity for mentalizing by enhancing episodic memory with enriched contextual cues to achieve a broader vantage point of the event and the experience that it generated. The memory work achieves a transformation of the episode from a singular, impenetrable, and toxic mental experience into a mentalizing memory narrative with links to other mental experiences explicating the context of the experience and stimulating improved metacognitive organization.

Clinical Example: Sarah (continued)

Sarah tells the clinician that the Child in Need care support worker was being difficult during her last visit to check up on Sarah and her son; the support worker "told" Sarah that she was not a good mother.

Clinician: How disappointing! You are trying so hard. (*Empathy is being used to regulate emotion.*) How did she come to that idea?

Sarah: She asked about whether I cook nutritious food for him, as she said he looked thin. Of course I do, and he is not thin anyway. I cook things that he likes, and I said to her "What am I supposed to cook?" We had an argument, as she said that I had to cook things that were good for him and not just give him things that he liked. I asked her if she had any children herself and she would not answer. Who does she think she is to tell me what to do? I'm fed up with her.

Clinician: You were pretty direct with her then, and you *are* doing your best with Jack. I can see that you reacted strongly. Sounds like your relationship with her took a turn for the worse? (*An attempt at slowly and gently broadening.*)

Sarah: She doesn't like me and has now taken against me and she will write a horrible report. (*The first attempt at broadening was clearly unsuccessful.*)

Clinician: That is a terrible worry for you and feels unfair as you think she is quite wrong about what she was saying. What was your relationship with her like before this week? (*A second attempt at slight expansion and diversion away from the current problem, moving to a broader discussion about their relationship.*)

Sarah: That's it! It was all just such a shock. She could be helpful about some things. She had some really good ideas about how to encourage him to get up for school. She didn't criticize me before.

Clinician: So what about this criticism? Was that what you were reacting to? Or was there something else in it?

Sarah: I felt she was against me and she had no idea and was not recognizing how hard I tried. Before she seemed to see that I tried really hard and made a lot of effort. I have made a lot of effort to get Jack to eat, which is why I offer him things he likes. I do make sure that it is nutritious. I don't just give him chips. (*Sarah is now a little more reflective.*)

Clinician: So, looking back, she seems to have missed on this occasion how much you try.

Now the clinician and Sarah are going to consider whether Sarah was over-reactive or over-sensitive, or whether she was understandably angry about the support worker's lack of sensitivity and their failure to see all of Sarah's efforts in feeding her son.

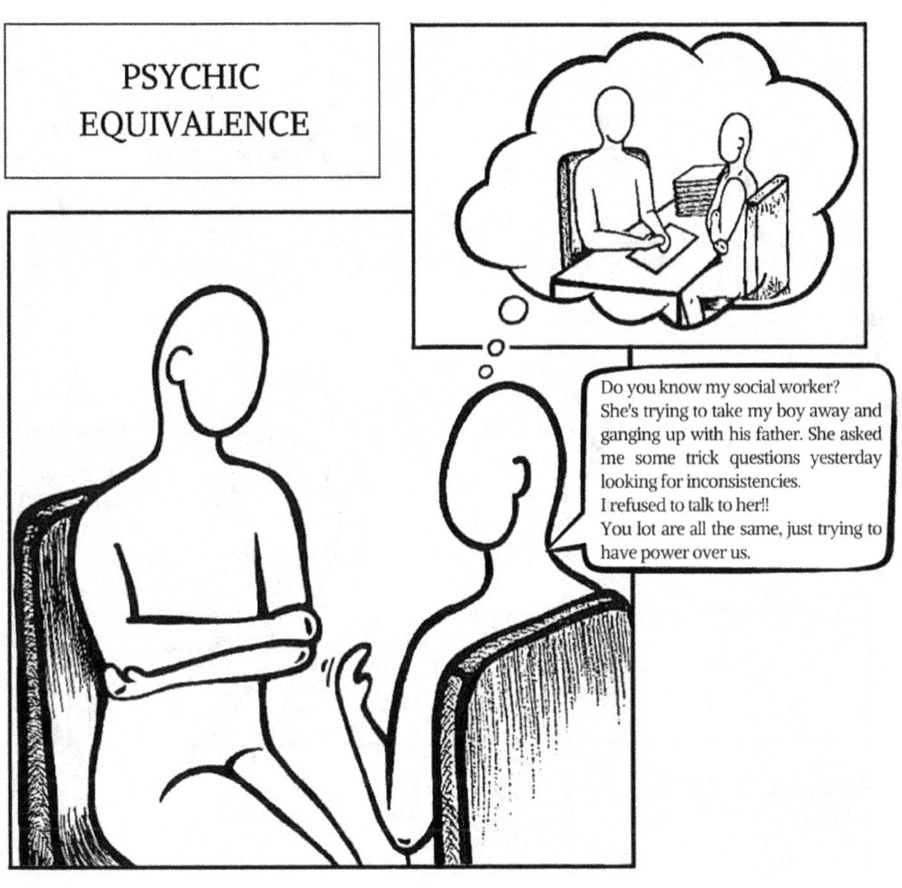

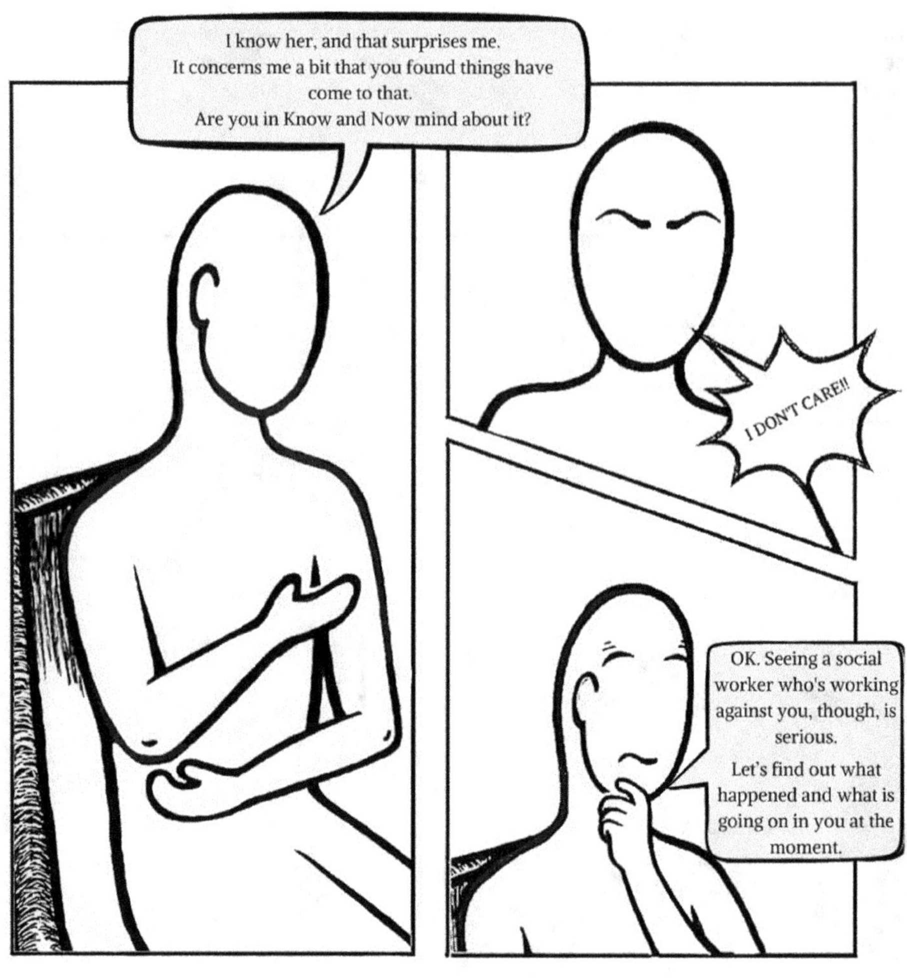
I know her, and that surprises me.
It concerns me a bit that you found things have come to that.
Are you in Know and Now mind about it?
I DON'T CARE!!
OK. Seeing a social worker who's working against you, though, is serious.
Let's find out what happened and what is going on in you at the moment.

She had been told by his father that I had been out drinking
and she asked me questions to see if I would report the same
thing. She wants to show that I don't tell her the truth or
write in her report that I have an alcohol problem.
Well I don't.

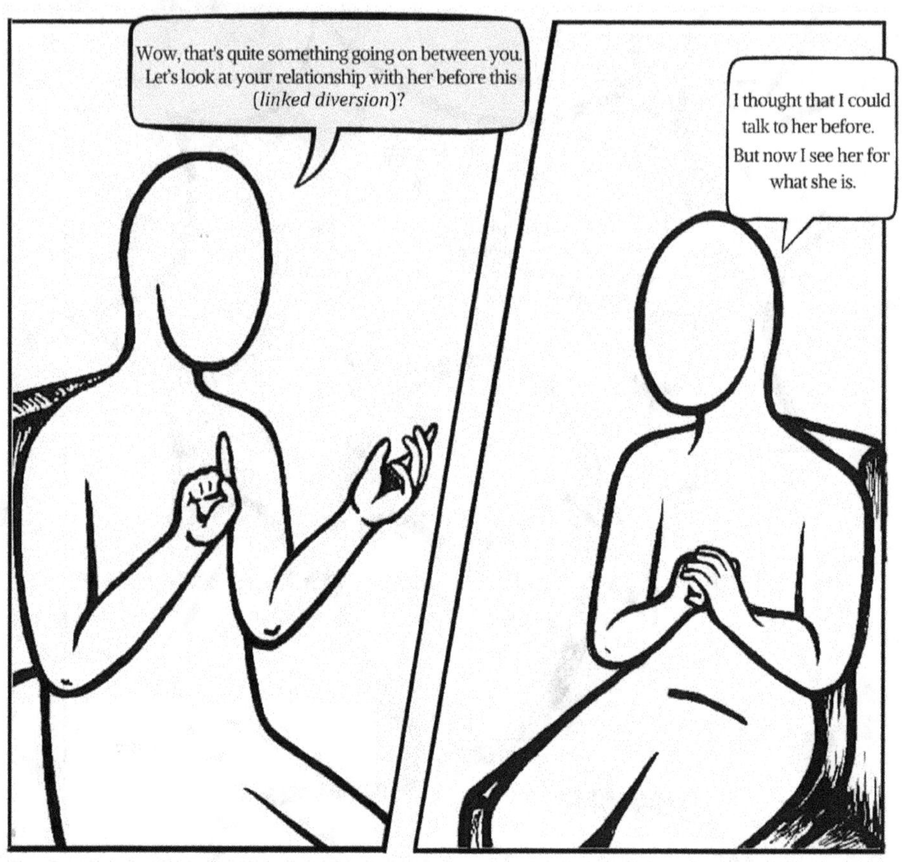
Wow, that's quite something going on between you. Let's look at your relationship with her before this (*linked diversion*)?
I thought that I could talk to her before. But now I see her for what she is.

The clinician continues to explore their earlier relationship before revisiting the Know and Now mind incident.

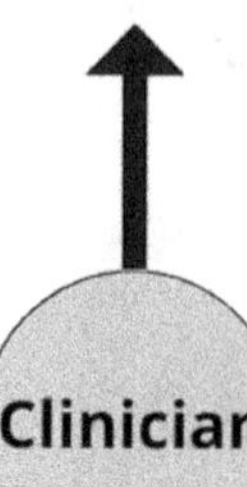

Pretend Mode

The onset of pretend mode in clinical sessions is an ominous sign, as it ossifies the interaction and prevents change. In clinical practice, a patient may be functioning in pretend mode when (a) they use excessive rationalization and intellectualization, (b) their narrative feels hard to follow, (c) comments about others, the patient, or the therapy are bland, "canned," and predictable, (d) there is a felt disconnection in the dialogue between patient and clinician, or (e) explanations of symptoms and personal relationships seem trite, repetitive, and even take a textbook form. Attributing complex motives to others without evidence and/or the use of labyrinthine reasoning for motives without strong links to reality, leaving the listener perplexed about how these can be justified—a state of hypermentalizing in which there is over-recruitment of cognitive processing with limited affectively informed experience—describes this state well. It has also been referred to as "bullshit mode," as in "*No, surely not—are you are bullshitting me?*", said with a compassionate twinkle in the eye. Identifying and labeling it—naming and noting—serves to bring the patient's attention to it and expresses the clinician's concern that smoke and mirrors/"talking the talk but not walking the walk" may be happening in the session. Pretend mode can be perspective specific, and so a patient can move in and out of pretend mode function while they talk about the same issue.

The inevitable result of pretend mode embedded in the patient's mental function is for the clinician to experience a sense of being not quite present or in the same room as the patient. They find it difficult to engage meaningfully, and the interaction does not feel subjectively personal. There is a disconnection between patient and clinician, which grows as the clinician struggles to be able to follow the convoluted inferences of the patient's understanding of others' motives. The recursive quality of mentalizing of course lends itself well to pretend mode thinking—"*She just thinks that I am concerned that people think I am X. Well, I will tell you that's just plain wrong!*" (wrong that they think you are X, that you think you are X, that you are concerned about being X, that she thinks people think something they do not think, that anyone can think of you and X in the same sentence . . .).

Patients in pretend mode are aiming to achieve some kind of balance, talking to themselves and not to the clinician, although the clinician is needed to maintain the pretense of communication (hence the term "pretend"). The clinician's mind state has an illusory link to the patient's mind state (another way in which it is pretend). It is an uncomfortable position for the clinician, so what can they do? There are several approaches that they can take.

1. Probe and name and note if possible.
2. Increase immediate relational anxiety.
3. Challenge the patient with counterfactuals.
4. Challenge the patient sensitively or more directly with therapeutic "ambush."

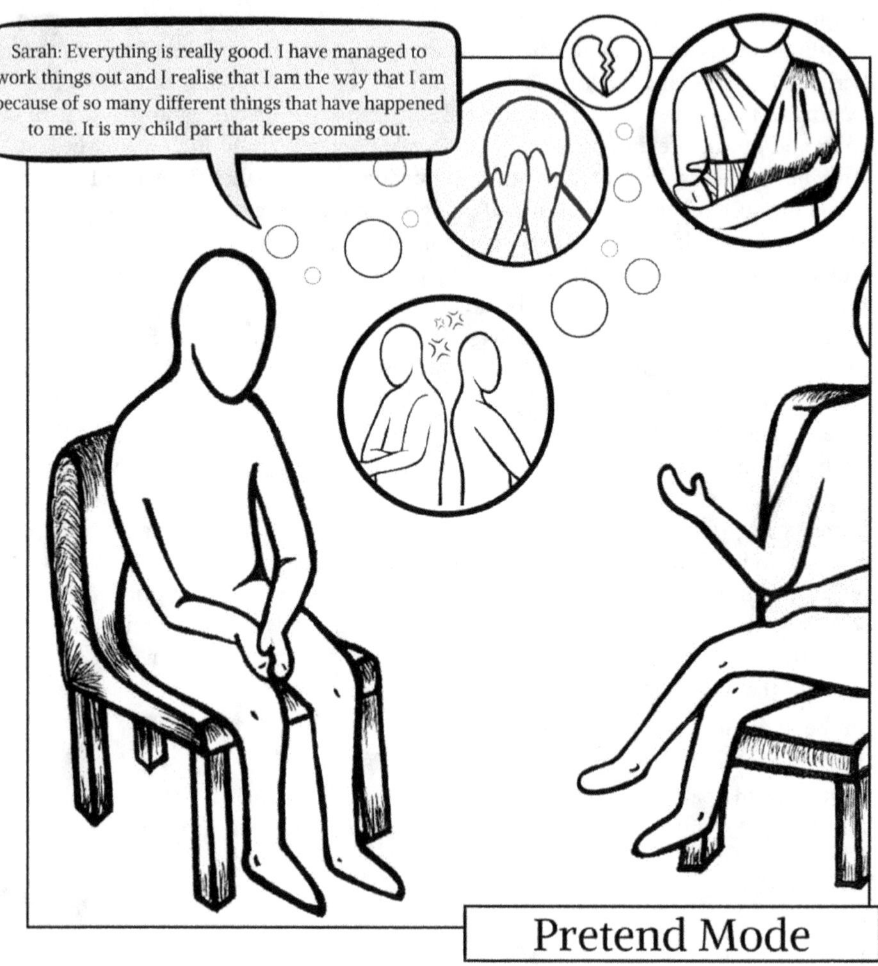
Sarah: Everything is really good. I have managed to work things out and I realise that I am the way that I am because of so many different things that have happened to me. It is my child part that keeps coming out.
Pretend Mode

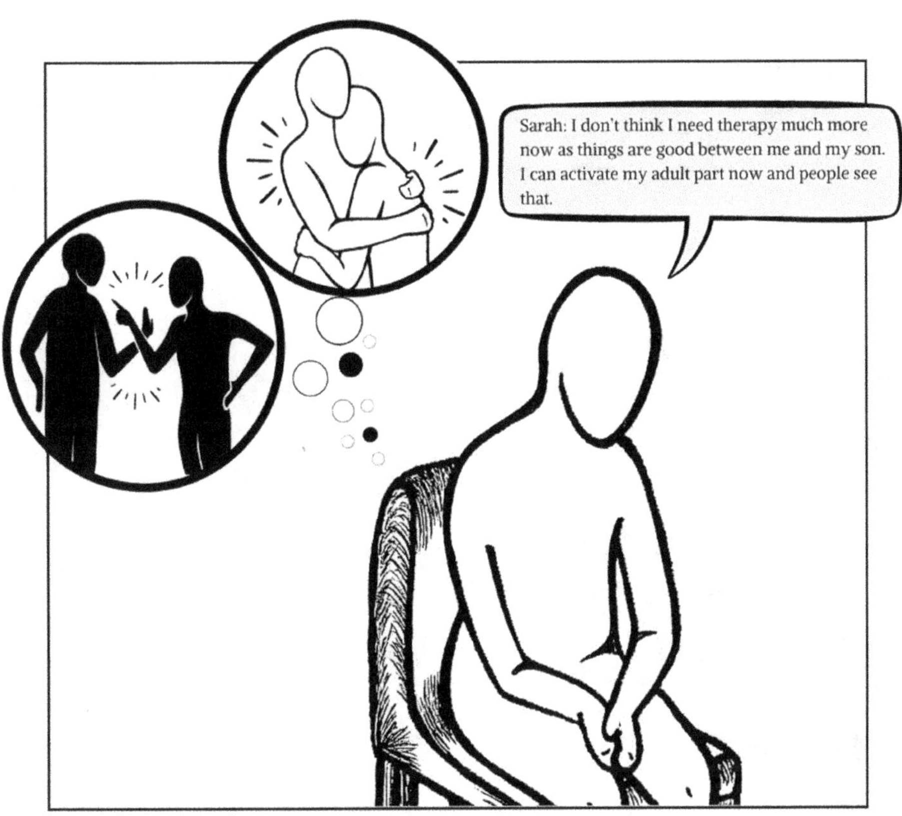

Sarah carries on talking with increasing detail about her understanding of herself and her relationship with her son.

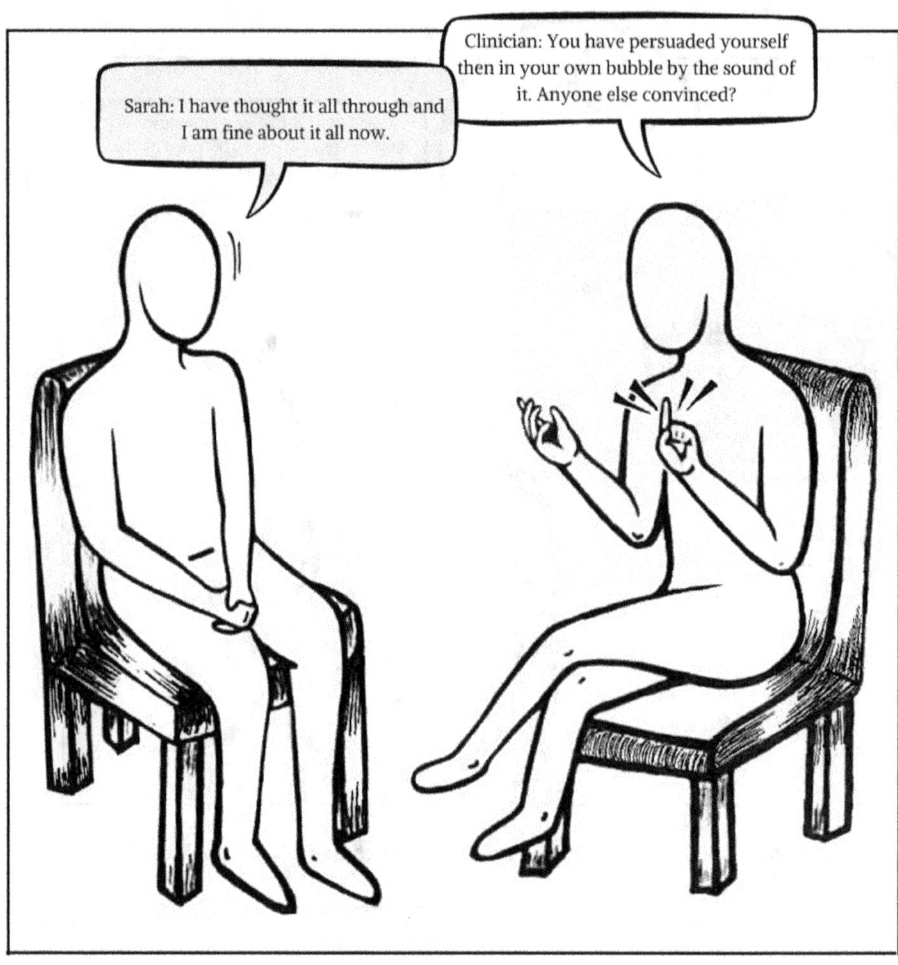
Sarah: I have thought it all through and I am fine about it all now.
Clinician: You have persuaded yourself then in your own bubble by the sound of it. Anyone else convinced?

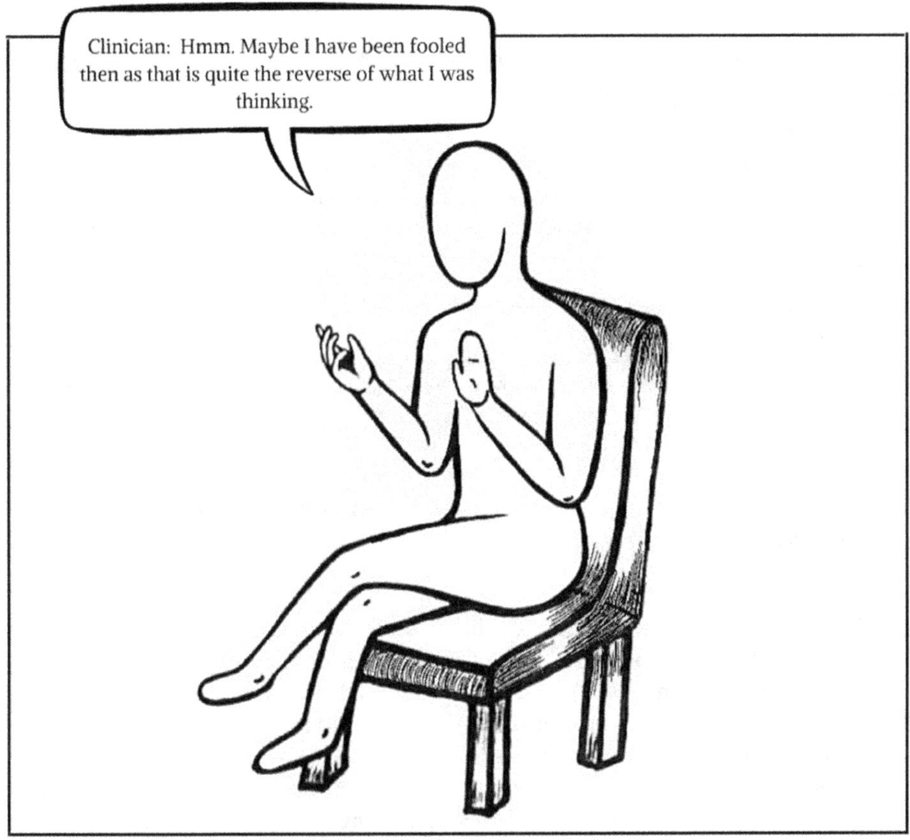

The clinician tries to activate Sarah into having an interest in his mind. Sarah is talking to herself. Intervention summary—Name and Note pretend mode, increase focus on current interactive relationship to trigger clinician becoming "alive" in patient's mind, challenge unrestrained imagination about self and others

Importantly, the clinician needs to recognize pretend mode, refrain from joining with it (which is difficult when the content appears insightful and meaningful in terms of treatment), and get themselves "back in the room," feeling real, agentive, and in mental contact with the patient. Initially, perhaps the clinician probes and asks penetrating questions about the content of the patient's narrative, not to express doubt but to make clear that they are a real part of the conversation, and the clinician also comments on the qualities associated with the presentation (e.g., "*You seem rather flat as you tell me about that*"). The aim is to say something that is striking—that serves to shatter the illusion of a monologue masquerading as a conversation.

Clinical Example: Sarah (continued)

Sarah is talking about her relationship with her son, Jack. The clinician thinks her story about him is being relayed in pretend mode.

Sarah: You know that Jack is like his father. But like with his father he is just about appearances. (*A helpful warning from Sarah.*) I look after Jack well and I think I have done well with him. If I don't check, if I look away, then it goes pear-shaped. He is dressed well for school, he does all his homework, the school is pleased with him. None of that is him. It's me via him. Know what I mean?

Clinician: It is great that the school is pleased with him. Tell me how you get him to do his homework. That is quite something.

Sarah: Oh, I make him sit down and tell him he has to be a good boy for his mum, otherwise she will be upset. He doesn't want to upset me.

Clinician: How not?

Sarah: A boy doesn't want to upset his mother, does he? Jack wants to look after his mother. I say that to him and he agrees.

This conversation has a detached quality. The current probing from the clinician does not make any discernible difference so, after further probing, the clinician moves to the second level of trying to dismantle pretend mode, which involves making the interaction more relationally focused on the current moment. Pretend-mode function is sensitive to current relational affective experience, as there is a momentary immediacy of minds and the isolation of the patient's mind processes is no longer able to maintain a level of "quarantine" that is decoupled from representing other minds. Pressure is placed on the patient to consider the mind state of the clinician. This can involve making counterintuitive or "what if?" interventions to surprise the patient; these are additional interventions that undermine pretend mode and can make the patient more alert and less self-contained.

Clinical Example: Sarah (continued)

Clinician: Hmm. But what does a good mother who wants to look after Jack look like?

Sarah: What do you mean? (*Sarah is suddenly alert.*)

Clinician: Well, a good boy looks after his mother, and I was wondering what a good mother who looks after her son looks like.

Sarah: I am a good mother.

Clinician: I know that, and I was thinking about how you work that out and if it would be good for us to think about it. From my point of view, I realized that I am not so sure about what makes a good boy and what makes a good mother. I realize that I am putting a bit of pressure on here and you will worry about what I think about you being a good mother.

Sarah: What do you think?

Now the interaction has become more immediate, and at last there are two people in the room. The patient and the clinician now monitor the levels of anxiety carefully. Anxiety is inevitably engendered when the bubble of pretend mode is popped and the patient becomes more aware of their own engagement in "pretend" therapy and telling "pretend" stories to themselves. It is essential that the use of pretend mode is reduced, as its self-serving nature fails to engender change. Pretend mode keeps things the same and does not fuel change and development. Therefore if the initial maneuvers do not work, the clinician has to consider challenging more directly—a kind of therapeutic ambush or surprise. This intervention works best if it is communicated in a tone of light-hearted mischief, and even better if it has some shared humor within it. The principle is that the intervention by the clinician is unexpected and surprises the mind of the patient; it is outside the normal therapeutic dialogue.

Clinical Example: Sarah (continued)

When Sarah was in pretend mode, the clinician looked out of the window while thinking about how to intervene.

Sarah: Don't look out of the window when I am talking. Listen to me.

Clinician: Oh yes, of course. Sorry. I was trying to think. I am looking out using my eyes and I listen with my ears. I can multi-task, you know. Do you know why?

Sarah: (*with some surprise at the question*) No, I don't.

Clinician: Because I am a man. We can do that sort of thing.

Sarah: Hmm.

Clinician: But seriously, as I am a man I can only do it for a short time. At the moment I am trying to listen and think, which is where my multi-tasking is not working. I really want to think about this as it is so important.

Sarah was not quite sure whether to be angry or to laugh at the sudden change of interaction, and it gave time for the clinician to present his state of mind, which Sarah could no longer ignore. Both conversational partners were then established in the room.

Clinicians understandably worry about using this type of mischievous or direct challenge to the flow of a session, and indeed it can be a high-risk intervention, albeit with the major advantage of kick-starting the patient's mind or tripping it up with surprise. The clinician has to be in emotional equipoise, and this intervention cannot be used out of frustration or anger with a patient. It is effective only if the patient experiences it within the context of a robust therapeutic alliance, and as arising from a compassionate cognitive empathic perspective.

Mentalizing an Affective Narrative: Creating a Compassionate Story

Patients with BPD commonly discuss and process their personal narratives in low-mentalizing mode. The task of treatment is to transform the narrative to create a mentalized version. Mentalizing adds coherence, nuance, accuracy, and continuity to a narrative by placing the experience in a personal context, enabling learning and

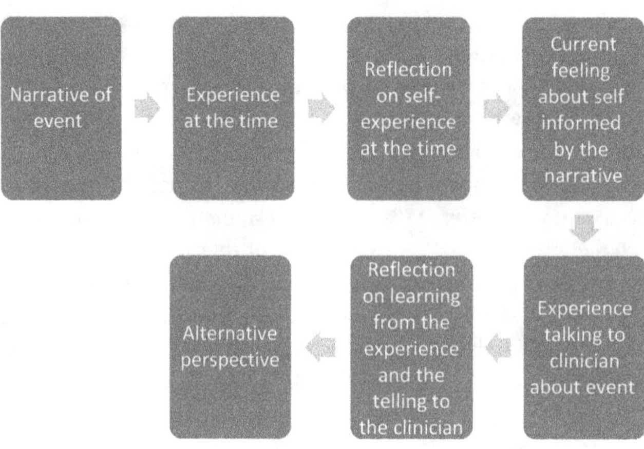

Fig. 4.2 Mentalizing the affective narrative (content).

constructive action. This is the point at which the clinician considers the content of mental states in detail—the "what" and the "why" mentioned in Chapter 3. Once severely low mentalizing has been addressed in the session using the interventions described in the previous section of this chapter, the MBT clinician is able to focus constructively on the content of the patient's narrative. Understanding the meaning of events—making links with present anxieties when talking about events from the past, and linking and placing current problems in a historical narrative—generates a sense of continuity and coherence that is essential for building psychological health and resilience. The process of making connections between events and the psychological experience that surrounds them is "metatherapeutic," by which we mean that it builds the competence and capacity ("mentalizing muscle") necessary for managing routine social experience. This model is depicted in Figure 4.2.

To create a mentalized narrative, the patient is initially asked to tell their story and to describe their experience and their affect at the time.

Clinical Example: Sarah (continued)

Sarah: When I was with my boyfriend yesterday, I kept asking him if he loved me more than his last girlfriend. He told me he did but I was not sure he really meant it.

Clinician: Tell me what made you have doubts.

Sarah: Just the way he was. It was like he didn't seem to be listening to me some of the time. Mind you, he was watching TV. He was watching his [football] team playing.

Clinician: What was it like not being listened to?

Sarah: I felt that I was less important than his football.

The clinician and Sarah chuckle and both say "Probably were!" (*A moment of we-mode occurs as both clinician and patient access a shared experience looking at the mind state of Sarah's boyfriend. Shared humor can be a potent source of we-mode function.*)

Clinician: Something in it caused you trouble, though. Can you describe how it felt?

This promotes a vantage point from which Sarah can consider herself as a person to be thought about, as a mental image constructed in the mental quiet of now, allowing calm reflection. Building on this mental distance, the clinician asks the patient to consider their emotions in the "there and then" and to scrutinize them, examining their strength and considering their complexity—simple feelings, mixed feelings, ambivalent feelings, conflicting feelings, multiple feelings, secondary feelings (feelings about feelings), primary feelings (anger), and social emotions (guilt, shame). Elaborating the detail of feelings can bring greater clarity to the patient about their emotional reactions and responses, and can initiate a move toward self-identification of the cause of their feelings (distress or excitement). In the process, a way of acquiring control over emotions is achieved, along with the opportunity for patients to know themselves and their natural reactions better. Elaborating on emotions enables elaboration of the interpersonal contexts that gave rise to them. Mentalizing entails adopting metacognitive positions—for example, it requires us to take into account our current state and how current experience can color recollections. Being aware of the potential for such distortion strengthens the accuracy of self-reflection. Therefore the clinician intervenes to ask the patient to describe both how they feel now about their experience earlier, and how their affective experience of telling the story impacted them. All of these maneuvers serve to increase the stability of mentalizing.

Clinical Example: Sarah (continued)

Clinician: As you are talking about this, what comes into your mind about yourself and your boyfriend?

Sarah: I start to worry that I am asking him things that are really my anxiety and he just does not know what I am talking about.

Clinician: What is the anxiety that makes you ask him what he thinks and feels about you so much of the time? As you imagine yourself, what was going on inside you?

Sarah: It is like I am when I am sitting on my own at home. I start to go into a haze that feels awful and I don't know what I am thinking or feeling. I have to get him to say something about me to clear the haze.

Clinician: Gosh. What is this haze that comes over you when you are alone?

Sarah: I shouldn't be like that, should I? When I talk about it now it makes me think I am pathetic and should sort myself out.

When exploring narratives with the patient's self as a mental image constructed during the session, one frequent problem is that patients, assuming the projected perspective of the clinician, become judgmental about themselves, as Sarah has just done. This is not surprising given what we know about the predominance of negative constructions in BPD. Self-imagery in these contexts entails little self-understanding, which is part of the limitations of mentalizing that MBT aims to address. Given the patient's lack of understanding of affects and personal compassion, the clinician's role is to regenerate a more positive self-affective state by enhancing the patient's capacity for self-understanding. The absence of compassion in relation to the self will often trigger intense negative feelings that threaten mentalizing. It is therefore important for the clinician to be alert to this possibility, and to intervene immediately to block the patient from following their self-condemnation. The clinician should counteract it by enhancing mentalizing that generates self-compassion.

Clinical Example: Sarah (continued)

CLINICIAN: Hang on a minute. You jump to judgment so quickly. You were saying that you can go into a haze, which is painful and unpleasant. So if you are scared of that, of course you need him to get you out of it, whether he is watching the match or not. But let's go back to see what this haze is and where it is coming from, and if you can get yourself out of it without help.

If the clinician does not interject at these points of self-judgment, the patient may fall into fixed and persistent self-criticism that triggers low mentalizing. Even if the response appears more positive, the clinician is advised to continue to explore the patient's past and current experience in the interpersonal context of the story before moving to a general appraisal of what the story means to them. Personal meaning making is best done when the whole event has been underpinned with mentalizing, so that there is coherence, continuity, and self-compassion within the narrative. Once this has been achieved, the clinician works toward placing their exploration in the context in which it is being discussed; the patient is asked to consider the emotional experience as they tell their narrative to the clinician in an attempt to stimulate some we-mode functioning and to consider how current emotions can color experiences. When the patient adopts a third-person perspective on themselves this primes questions about the onlooker's (i.e., the clinician's) reaction to or attitude toward what the patient is reporting about their life. Social emotions such as shame or a sense of failure relative to some vague imagined norm might be triggered, or, more positively, perhaps pride in managing something that hitherto was problematic. These feelings, which will reflect to some extent the state of the current relationship between the patient and the clinician, are critical as a basis for establishing *relational mentalizing* (see this chapter: Relational Mentalizing). Exploration adds to the complexity and potentially intensifies arousal, risking the loss of effective mentalizing, but the risk is worth taking in relation to the benefit of gaining improved understanding of how problematic emotions are processed with others.

In general, mentalizing personal narratives enhances mentalizing competence, initiates a focus on alternative perspectives, generates opportunities to enhance self-compassion, and counterbalances the predisposition toward negativity.

Clinical Example: Sarah (continued)

The clinician notices that Sarah keeps on glancing at him. From the formulation the clinician is aware of the need to be alert to an external mentalizing focus, so he immediately asks about the mental state behind the glances, making no assumptions about what state of mind they indicate.

CLINICIAN: I am noticing some quick looks at me—what's going on in there?

Sarah: I keep thinking you think I am an idiot and just being stupid, or that you think I am just hopeless.

Clinician: Where is that coming from? I am not sure what you mean. Certainly I was not aware that I was thinking that about you. I was thinking how you seemed to be putting yourself down again and how quickly you do that. And this is not when you are in a haze!

Sarah: But I think I am. I am not really sure what I am saying. I have to look at you to tell me what I am saying is right. I see myself going into a haze when I feel that I am not anyone really and not sure about myself.

Clinician: That's really helpful, Sarah. (*The clinician is quick to reinforce mentalizing.*) What makes you not so sure about yourself at the moment?

Sarah is now beginning to link her experience with her boyfriend and her experiences in the present moment with greater continuity. Effective mentalizing enables her to simultaneously be observed and be part of both of these experiences, able to step back from them and observe herself observing. She can identify that the discussion of the events during her session triggered her brief episode of "haze" experience, this time with the clinician rather than with her partner. The clinician's task now is to keep Sarah's reflective mentalizing active in order to consider the link between her loss of a subjective self, which has created a painful existential crisis (the haze), and her need to find a teleological solution to her crisis through action (getting her boyfriend to show her that she is a person by telling her that he loves her).

This stepwise process of stimulating mentalizing, discussed here as a therapeutic intervention, is actually no more than what might happen in everyday life. Most of us hold on to our feelings until we can tell someone we trust about them. We cannot fully reflect on experience without considering it in the presence of someone else. As we tell our trusted friend about an experience, we monitor (a) the emerging picture of our experience at the time, (b) our current experience in reflecting on the experience, and (c) our experience of our trusted friend's picture of the event and our reactions to it. These are interdependent concurrent processes, which effective mentalizing affords. The generation of perspective on self-experience is in many instances only possible through the availability of a trusted other whose reaction enables this process of calibrating internal experience. The disruption of interpersonal trust deprives individuals like Sarah of a naturally occurring but essential system that we perhaps all need for processing emotionally challenging social experience. We have described this process for infants as "marked mirroring" as they acquire an understanding of emotional experience (see Chapter 2). Beyond infancy, marked mirroring is also part of the social process of deepening self-consciousness and self-understanding. It is the vital gift that social support provides for individuals. The manner of this mirroring helps us to integrate our emotional response into a more comprehensive picture of ourselves in which we recognize our feelings for what they are. It also helps to calibrate the intensity of our reaction. Was our reaction "normal"—that is, how one might expect a person to respond—or was it exaggerated? The friend helps us to reconsider our reaction so that we learn more about our sensitivities. In the telling we change and even deepen our relationship with the friend who sees things that we did not see. We learn about ourselves.

Elephants in the Room

During social interactions our automatic mentalizing "antennae" are constantly alert, mostly monitoring our reciprocal communications quietly and beneath the surface. They immediately alert us when we experience inconsistencies—for example, when someone says that they are in a particular mood but in fact seem to be communicating a different internal state. We then switch to controlled mentalizing and ask a question: "*You say you are 'fine' but you come across as rather miserable. Are you sure you are OK?*" A firm rebuff tends to make us step back and we continue on the basis that we can do no more for the moment. However, it means that the continuing conversation, discussion, and exploration are now distorted, as some of the interaction is now excluded from shared subjective experience. There is a proscribed subtext while we concentrate on the dominant narrative.

We all have our working theories about ourselves, and our own ways of presenting them. We call them *personal narratives* or our *imagined self*—a model of who we feel that we are at any given moment, and why we feel that we are the way we are, based on the evidence arising from our subjective experience. These narratives tend to shape the way in which we mentalize ourselves and how we tell people about ourselves—they are a way of making sense of our actions. For most of us, at any given moment there is one predominant working theory—that is, the most obvious, straightforward way of describing ourselves. This is what the patient commonly presents in any therapy session. But we also have more *subdominant* narratives; these are the understandings of ourselves that are more nuanced or complex, and that are hidden from the normal shorthand we might use to describe ourselves. The dominant narrative is in the foreground, but there may be a range of other narratives behind it.

Sarah has a dominant narrative: "*I need to be admired and liked, and to achieve that I need to meet all the expectations you have of me.*" The clinician senses that this is true, but also realizes that there is a subdominant narrative of Sarah being tired of working so hard to try to please people all the time. This subdominant narrative will be active but not expressed openly. Unspoken between clinician and patient, the conflict between Sarah's wish to please and her frustration with this role is like an "elephant in the room"—nobody explicitly acknowledges that it is there even though it increasingly interferes with the interaction. The mutual recognition of these subdominant narratives is a particularly potent way of establishing epistemic trust in therapy, because it brings with it a shared we-mode interaction. Therefore the MBT clinician makes the "elephant" recognizable by moving the automatic/controlled dimension of mentalizing slightly in the direction of controlled mentalizing, usually by identifying a disjunction within the therapy process with the aim of making this a subject for scrutiny.

Clinical Example: Sarah (continued)

Clinician: I have noticed just how hard you work to make sure you meet all the expectations that the people around you have; you know, in your shoes I would just get exhausted trying to meet every expectation anyone might have of me.

Sarah: You think I should not do it? Do you think this is interfering with my therapy? Do you want me to stop doing it?

CLINICIAN: That is what I am getting at—my sense is that you are checking me all the time to see if you are getting the therapy right, and I am saying enough already, what about what Sarah needs? Isn't Sarah tired worrying about what everyone else wants all the time? So I am doing the opposite, trying to get you to work out what is right for you while you are busy worrying about me. Maybe we need to think about the possibility that sometimes we find ourselves pushing and pulling in opposite directions a bit.

In MBT the intervention of identifying the elephant in the room is known as *exploring the affect focus*. It is affective because before the subdominant narrative is identified and named, it generates an emotional experience, a feeling state in the room, rather than a clear idea; it is focused because it points to the need to specifically target a current and shared relational space. It is not solely about the patient's internal state, as there is reciprocity in developing the elephant. The clinician and the patient unwittingly create elephants that loom larger and larger in the room as therapy continues. Identifying an interactive elephant is important as, if it remains subdominant without being expressed, it potentially becomes corrosive by constricting self/other mentalizing, which then cannot be harnessed to develop a more nuanced understanding of ourselves and our interactions. Compassionately verbalizing the elephant increases epistemic trust by allowing the patient to "feel felt," it stimulates explicit mentalizing of the current relational processes activated in therapy, and it provides an entry point for exploration of the patient's attachment and relational dynamics. But elephants, although big, may be surprisingly hard to find when you are looking for one.

Relational Mentalizing

BPD is a relational and attachment disorder. MBT identifies and explores the different attachment strategies and their activation in many aspects of the patient's life. The relational mentalizing focus has three main components:

1. explicit identification and formulation of the patient's attachment strategy during assessment
2. MBT-I group—psychoeducational input about attachment processes, and personalizing attachment (e.g., understanding current relationships using the lens of attachment)
3. recognition and exploration of the complexity of relationship dynamics in individual and group psychotherapy.

Often, this process has to be built over time. In earlier iterations of MBT, identification by the clinician early in treatment of historical patterns of relationships in the patient's life and links between these and the way in which the therapeutic relationship unfolds were called "transference tracers"—that is, interventions to indicate the relevance of looking at the relationship between patient and clinician in order to understand the patient's problems in more detail. To a large extent, this process of setting a framework for the exploration of relationships is now incorporated into the psychoeducation about attachment in the MBT-I group (i.e., step 2 in the three-point list).

Relational mentalizing follows the principle of democracy in MBT and is the quintessential intervention for activating the we-mode. The interaction between patient and clinician is jointly created, and exploration of both contributions without prejudice is the key process. Remember that facilitation of mentalizing is a journey, not a destination.

1. No particular understanding from a historical or current experience is necessary.
2. There is little room for causal interpretation of experience.
3. The answers to the "why" questions are sparse.
4. There is more room for the "how" and the "what" of interactional process.

All of this is in contrast to the reliance on "genetic," past–present transference interpretation of traditional psychodynamic therapy as a primary intervention [11].

We identify a series of steps to be followed when mentalizing the relationship in MBT. First, the clinician has to be sure that the patient has a mentalizing capacity that is able to differentiate between mental states of self and other and can contrast them without excessive diffusion, muddling what is in the clinician's mind and what is the patient's mind. Complex interventions such as those related to detail of the patient–clinician interaction require the patient to be thoughtful and reflective if they are to further the joint project of nuancing relational understanding constructively. An ineffectively mentalizing patient rigidly holds on to understandings and is unlikely to draw on the richness and nuance of past experience. Ineffective mentalizing is not a productive basis for imagining different perspectives and actively comparing them with alternatives that may be distinct in complex and subtle ways. Therefore the first step will always be to check the current capacity for mentalizing—in both the clinician and the patient—and, linked to this, the level of anxiety. A robust we-mode can develop only in the context of stable representation of the participating minds, which are then joined to consider something else together as one mind, which in this case is their relationship—the relationship that was created to focus on the shared task of understanding the patient's personal relationships in everyday life.

The next step is for the clinician to validate the feelings expressed by the patient about the relationship, and to explore those feelings. The danger of the genetic approach to the relationship (i.e., linking current events to past events and the feelings and beliefs that they have generated) is that it might unintentionally and implicitly invalidate the patient's current experience. Moving attention from present salient determinants to putative past ones can feel like disinclination to face up to the challenges of the present. In MBT, the clinician spends considerable time using the not-knowing stance, exploring and clarifying what the patient says they are experiencing.

Clinical Example: Sarah (continued)

The clinician told Sarah that he needed to rearrange her next appointment as he was going to be away at their usual time the following week. Sarah said that they could sort it out at the end of the session. However, at the end of the session the clinician forgot to rearrange the appointment, but he remembered a few minutes later. So he ran to the hospital gate and caught up with Sarah. As he called out to her she turned and said "Nearly forgot, did you?" He apologized, and they rearranged the next session. They discussed this event during the next session.

Sarah: I thought that therapy had ended last week as it was obvious you did not want me.

Clinician: I am so sorry that I forgot to fix a time at the end of the session. I am not sure what happened. What did you take from it?

Sarah: It confirmed what I already knew. That this is just another place where I am not wanted. If you had wanted to carry on seeing me, you would have remembered.

Clinician: It is quite a thing, isn't it, when something so important doesn't happen and we could have been left with a real problem of being in touch to rearrange. I can quite see that. Where are you now with those feelings?

Sarah: Well, I think that you felt guilty and that was why you ran after me, and that you thought you should not have been like that so were trying to make up for it by catching me at the gate.

Clinician: You are right in a way. I felt a bit anxious, too, as it is not like me and I am not sure what happened.

Sarah: You were out of breath.

Clinician: When I caught up with you, you made a comment that sounded as if *you* had remembered but somehow did not feel able to remind me.

Sarah: Yes, I did. I thought "He does not want me so I won't remind him. I just won't go back. When he phones, I won't answer." That's what I thought. "He doesn't care so it doesn't matter to him that he doesn't know what has happened to me."

Clinician: So it was kind of a test and I failed spectacularly. I walked into it.

Sarah: I am not sure, but I couldn't tell you.

Clinician: So at the moment we are both here thinking about being wanted or not. My forgetfulness has set it all off as it showed that I was not looking after you with enough care.

Sarah: I don't want to be here sitting with someone who doesn't want me here. It makes it hard to think about anything else really. Do you feel guilty about it?

Clinician: It was me that forgot and I am still not sure why I only remembered after the end of the session. So I do, a bit.

Sarah: Only a bit?

Clinician: What is it like for you sitting here with a therapist who feels "a bit" guilty?

Sarah: I quite like it (*hiding a smile*).

Clinician: It seems there is a tiny pleasure in imagining a guilty therapist?

Sarah: Not sure.

Clinician: You smiled as you said that and I thought maybe there is a tiny compensation in being able to watch me suffer a little when you feel I was quite cruel to you.

Sarah: Yes, I do. That is why I was finding it a bit funny I suppose. I like the idea that you should suffer a bit. You would not know where I was or what I was doing. I knew you would have to worry about me a bit. It would be your fault. I couldn't remind you. To be honest, I was a bit disappointed that you caught up with me at the hospital gate. But at least you had to run as I was walking quite fast.

As a result of this exploration, with some validation and sharing of responsibility for the problem, the third step will be generated. As the events that created the feelings in the relationship are identified, and the behaviors to which the thoughts or feelings are tied are made explicit, sometimes in painful detail, the contribution of the clinician to these feelings and thoughts will become apparent. It takes two hands to make a clapping sound. The unpacking of the clinician's experience and the modeling of ownership for actions and the mental states driving those actions is the journey to recovery on which patient and clinician join. Equity is key—for there to be progress, the clinician needs to accept their contribution to the patient's experience. The core element of intersubjectivity is mutual recognition. Sarah gradually becomes able to recognize the clinician's subjectivity, developing the capacity for attunement and tolerance of difference. Here she is struggling to separate from the subverting of her needs to those of the clinician. This is a fight for recognition in which the outcome is an embryonic ability to recognize another person's subjectivity at the same time as retaining awareness of her own. Her journey of differentiation is not just separation, but the continual breakdown and repair of mutuality in the world beyond the self. Her sense of the clinician comes and goes, as does her awareness of "I-mode." The ability to hold on to both simultaneously is challenging but also increasingly accessible as the session moves on. For Sarah, the breakdown and reconstruction of the interpersonal world is an endless experience of aggression and the generation of a shared *sense of being with* the clinician.

We now know that even infant attachment relationships are driven by interaction structures with characteristic *patterns of mutual regulation*, which the infant comes to remember and expect. Patterns of mutual regulation between mother and infant in the early months of life illustrating matching and derailed exchanges, based on microanalyses of film and videotape, demonstrate a dynamic process of *reciprocal adjustments*. The irreducible unit of a dyadic system of what is represented is an emergent dyadic phenomenon that cannot be described on the basis of either partner alone. We distinguish this from the non-productive complementarity characteristic of situations that were common earlier in the therapy, when the clinician and the patient were locked into a relationship in which each assumed a role in a predictable well-choreographed dance, each nudging the other to perform what they themselves needed (i.e., Sarah needing a figure who rejects her, and the clinician needing the patient to enact her sense of helplessness and frustration).

The patient's experience of their interaction with the clinician is likely to be based on a partially accurate perception of the interaction, even if only a small component of it. It is often the case that the clinician has been drawn into the relationship and acted in some way that is consistent with the patient's perception of them. It may be easy to attribute this to the patient, but to do so would be misleading. In order to create the mutual awareness of the we-mode, it is often better for the clinician to share with the patient their contribution to the patient's experience as an inexplicable, involuntary action for which they accept responsibility, rather than identifying it as caused by—or, worse still, the imaginings of or a distortion by—the patient. The clinician does this with Sarah by suggesting that forgetting to reschedule her appointment was his responsibility and it is currently unexplained. To do this well requires authenticity. Drawing attention to the clinician's contribution may be particularly significant in that it demonstrates to the patient that it is possible to accept responsibility for involuntary acts, and that such acts do not invalidate the general attitude the clinician is trying to convey. Only after this consideration of the clinician's contribution can distortions be explored.

The capacity to maintain internal awareness—to sustain the tension of keeping one's own mental perspective while simultaneously representing and being attuned to that of someone else—forms the basis of what we call the we-mode. This is the coordinating function of genuine mentalizing. The sustained tension of difference in perspectives helps to create an intersubjective co-creation; the MBT clinician offers an alternative to the asymmetric complementarity of knower and known, giver and given to. The experience of the adoption of common purpose is critical. The we-mode is achieved when the clinician–patient unit is the shared object of experience and is evaluated principally from the perspective of the likely success of therapy experienced as a *collaborative* activity. Clinically, the concept of a co-created intersubjective joint intentionality helps to elucidate stepping beyond the complementarity in impasses and enactments, and suggests how recognition is restored through mutual surrender by the patient and clinician of what we call the I-mode for the we-mode. This is the essence of MBT—and perhaps of every psychotherapy.

The we-mode is an entry point and not the end of the process. It makes the fourth step possible, which is collaboration in arriving at an alternative perspective. Mentalizing alternative perspectives about the patient–clinician relationship must be done in the same spirit of mutual involvement as any other form of mentalizing. The metaphor that we often use in training is that the clinician should imagine sitting side by side with the patient, rather than opposite them. The patient and the clinician sit together, looking at the patient's thoughts and feelings and, where possible, both adopting an inquisitive stance in relation to them. Using these insights, the clinician works to present a fresh view, and the final step is to carefully monitor the patient's reaction as well as the clinician's own response.

Clinical Example: Sarah (continued)

Clinician: Get me to how you knew you could not just remind me directly by saying "*What about my appointment for next week?*"

Sarah: It has something to do with me accepting that I feel so not wanted and not being allowed to demand attention for myself.

Clinician: Allowed?

Sarah: Yes. I think people don't want me when I am here. It is when I am *not* here that they think about me and worry about me, and realize that they quite liked me.

Clinician: Gosh! You have to be absent to be liked? That's hard!

Sarah: I never told you, but I used to want to be in a film that people would watch. They would have to concentrate on me, to think about me, and would have to leave themselves out of it so all their attention was on me. If you had forgotten and I had not answered my phone I would imagine you thinking about me and wanting me to be here.

Clinician: Oh I see, if you were not there then I would not have the real you but this image of a person who is missing who does not have to do anything because she is just an image.

Sarah: I can't bear seeing disappointment on people's faces when I feel I am letting them down.

Clinician: It seems to me that you do so much to avoid the situation of having to face the possibility of people being disappointed with you.

Sarah: When I see that I just want to die. I couldn't risk asking you for my appointment in case you looked disappointed that you would not have your own time without me.

The clinician and Sarah are now beginning to work out an alternative perspective that is centered around elaborating the wider meaning of the experience of the clinician forgetting to rearrange the session. It is complex and nuanced, it is deeply relational, and it is clearly to do with the ineffectively mentalized experience of interpreting the clinician's reaction. Whatever the childhood or other determinants of Sarah's inability to ask for an appointment, the conversation between her and the clinician is fully engaging both of their capacities to mentalize.

We suggest that these steps are taken in sequence, and we talk about *mentalizing the relationship* or *relational mentalizing* to distinguish the process from *interpretation*, which is an effective method of providing patients with insight. Relational mentalizing is a shorthand term for encouraging the patient and the clinician to think about the relationship they are in at the current moment (i.e., the patient–clinician relationship). The aim of this is to focus the patient's attention on another mind—that of the clinician—and to assist the patient in (a) engaging with the thoughts and feelings of the clinician in a mutual process that enables them to contrast their own perception of themselves with how they are perceived by another, and (b) elaborating within the context of relationships the personal meaning of what has happened. This requires the we-mode to be active: "the two of us are trying to work out what happened here and what it means."

Although the clinician might point to similarities in patterns of relationships within the therapy, in the patient's childhood, or currently outside the therapy, the aim of doing so is *not* to provide the patient with an explanation (insight) that they might be able to use to control their behavior. Far more simply, these similarities are raised as just a puzzling phenomenon that requires thought and contemplation, as part of the general inquisitive stance that aims to facilitate the recovery of mentalizing within affective relational states, which is the overall aim of treatment.

It is assumed that in successful interventions the patient and the clinician are working simultaneously at an implicit relational level to create increasingly collaborative forms of dialogue. This includes careful attention to the particular state of the other's intersubjective experience, open acceptance of a broad range of emotional experiences, active scaffolding to more inclusive levels of dialogue, and engaged struggle and intersubjective negotiation through periods when the other's mind is changing and new ways of relating are needed. Here MBT takes a leap away from content-bound understanding of specific relational experience to understanding that "the medium is the message"—that is, engaging in the process of understanding may be the common factor across the almost innumerable theoretical positions that therapeutic approaches can take.

Counter-Relational Mentalizing

Mentalizing the relationship cannot be discussed without briefly considering the counter-relationship. Counter-relational mentalizing by definition links to the clinician's self-awareness, and often relies on the affective components of mentalizing. It also links to the principle of mental democracy described in Chapter 3. We contrast counter-relational responsiveness with "being ordinary." Some clinicians tend to default to a state of self-reference in which they consider most of what they experience in therapy as being relevant to the patient. This default mode needs to be resisted, and clinicians need to be mindful of the fact that their own mental states might unduly color their understanding of the patient's mental states, and that they tend to equate these without adequate foundation. In an earlier publication, we suggested that clinicians must "quarantine" their feelings (Allen et al. [12], p. 47). How this "quarantining" is achieved informs the technical approach in MBT to counter-relational mentalizing, defined as those experiences (both affective and cognitive) that the clinician has in sessions that might further develop an understanding of mental processes.

All aspects of therapeutic activity are determined in part by the clinician's personal psychology. The traditional approaches to counteracting undue influence—by which clinicians reduce their own subjective biases by being modest, remaining open to surprise, seeing themselves as students who learn from their patients, and focusing on the patient's inner psychic reality—are valuable up to a point, but even in combination they are not sufficient. MBT rejects the notion of objectivity in a therapeutic setting, and demands humility from the clinician to accept the inevitable subjectivity of technique. It should be unnecessary for MBT clinicians to attempt *not* to be passionately (and irrationally) involved in their everyday clinical work. In any case, it is hopeless to ask clinicians to do this. Counter-relational experience, expressed verbally by the clinician as part of the democratic process of equality of mental-state scrutiny, is an important aspect of MBT, but when such an experience is expressed it must be marked as an aspect of the clinician's state of mind. It is not attributed to the patient, even though it may well be a reaction to the patient.

In difficult situations when there is a need to express counter-responses that are complex, we suggest the following simple procedure.

1. Anticipate the reaction of the patient.
2. Express your recognition that they might feel in a particular way regarding what you are about to say.
3. Express it with sensitivity.
4. Monitor the patient's reaction carefully.

Clinical Example: Sarah (continued)

Clinician: I would like to bring up something that is quite difficult for me but I think is important for the therapy. I worry that you will think I am saying something about you being a bad mother, and I do not mean to do that. I wanted to bring up my worry that you look after Jack's physical needs very well but that you can suddenly become very emotional and lose your temper with him. When I try to bring it up you change the subject, and I realize that I am becoming a bit impatient with you about it, as I think that it may be important.

Sarah: I don't really want to talk about that sort of thing. The social support worker asks me about it all the time and she thinks I am a bad mother.

Clinician: Yes, I appreciate that it can sound like that when any of us bring it up, but it interferes somewhat with working on your care for him. Perhaps both of us need to talk about our impatience! What about yours with Jack?

COUNTER-RESPONSIVENESS
You know I can't be with people. I just can't. I remember I used to want to be in films. In a film people look at you and feel for you, empathize with you and imagine what it would be like to be you. They pay attention to you.

People who are watching me would understand me. That is what I wanted.

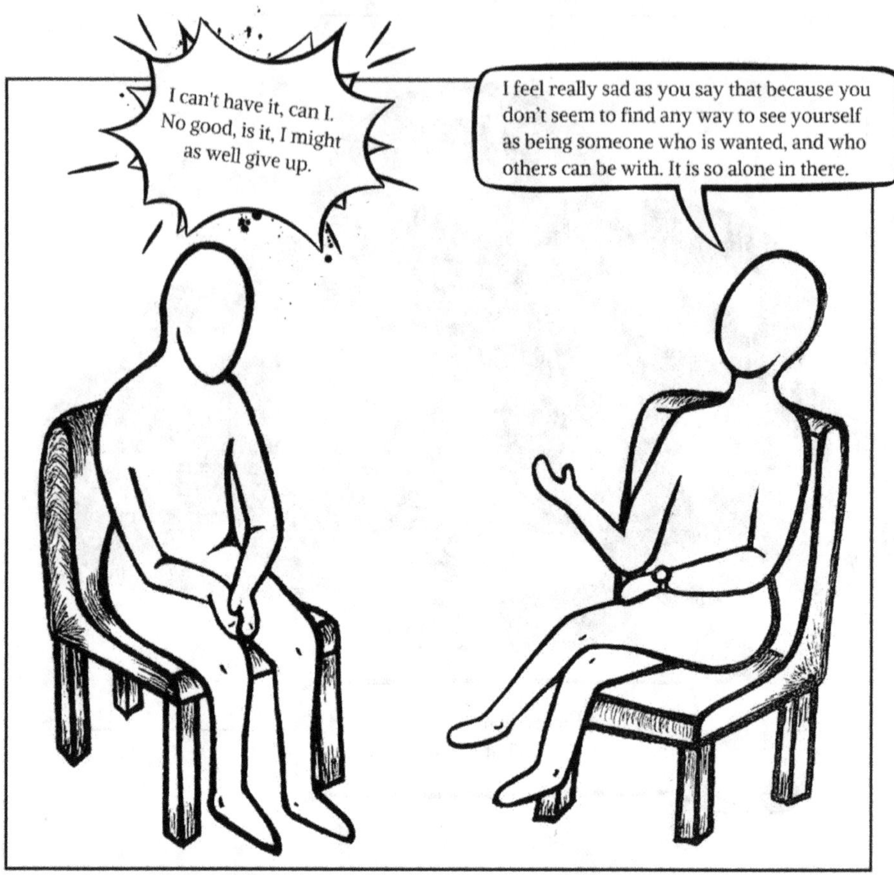

Presenting counter-responsiveness is not simply reporting how the clinician feels. It is presenting the feeling of the clinician in relation to the patient's inner experience.

Clinical Example: Stanley

Expressing more problematic responses to patients requires skill and sensitivity. Here is an example involving another client, Stanley, who is intimidating and who triggers anxiety in the clinician:

CLINICIAN: (*when the patient seems calm*) Stanley, I have to talk about our meetings and what happens in them. I don't mean to be critical of how you behave, but when you sit forward and shout at me I become quite anxious. When I am like that I cannot listen carefully and think properly. I don't know what I do to make you do that. Can we review what happens? The main thought I have is that perhaps you have a sense that I don't understand something.

Counter-relational experience can be intensely felt during treatment of people with a diagnosis of personality disorder, with clinicians struggling with sometimes strong feelings of rage, hatred, hurt, anxiety, and helplessness. Patients seem able to identify clinicians' sensitive spots and sometimes will even focus on them as they try to control their own emotional processes during a session. As previously mentioned, the task of the clinician is to let the patient know that what they do and say evokes a state of mind in the clinician and, similarly, that what the clinician does and says stimulates mental processes in the patient. Patients need to consider in their own mind the effects that they have on others' minds, rather than ignore those effects or maintain that they are of no consequence. It is the task of the clinician to ensure that this work is done as part of exercising recognition of others' mental states and increasing the capacity for empathy with others. To do this work it is essential that the clinician is supported in maintaining their own mentalizing and in recognizing and reflecting on counter-relational feelings and their origins. Supervision is an integral part of achieving this.

MBT Supervision

Supervision is integral to the effective delivery of MBT.* Clinicians need support from expert supervisors for a range of reasons (see Box 4.5), and supervisors need to keep these all in mind and work with an MBT team to decide which areas need the most focus at any particular time. This section of this chapter will be mostly concerned with the importance of the clinical aspects of supervision. However, it is important to bear in mind that clinicians work within a system and a service pathway, so supervisors need to take into account the milieu and the levels of mentalizing within the organization in which their supervisees are working.

Box 4.5 Supervision tasks.

- Implementation of an MBT service within an organization.
- Development of clinical structures and materials that support the delivery of MBT.
- Ensuring that mentalizing theory links to clinical practice.
- Supporting the learning and refining of clinical skills.
- Maintaining mentalizing of the supervisee clinician(s).

Implementation and Clinical Structures

Implementation of MBT needs to fit well with an organization, and the organization needs to fit with and support the delivery of MBT. Organizations need to have a clear strategy of developing treatment pathways for people with personality disorder; an MBT team that leads the development of a treatment pathway within a wider mental health system may be responsible for ensuring that the service is organized to fit well with the overall service, so as to maximize the effective and efficient delivery of treatment in an arrangement that offers patients rapid access to assessment. The supervisor supports all of these tasks and helps to create a functioning MBT team with members who have

* Full details of MBT supervision can be found in *A Quality Manual for MBT* (www.annafreud.org/media/1217/a-quality-manual-for-mbt-edited-april-23rd-2014-2.pdf)

defined roles, with a range of MBT skills—perhaps some new trainees and some at experienced practitioner level. A within-team peer-support process is encouraged along with an overall team approach as part of the basis for implementation.

The evidence suggests that patient outcomes are maximized if MBT is delivered within an organization that supports the MBT program, and by a mentalizing team composed of staff who are able to model the process in their service milieu, particularly in the way *all* of the staff interact with patients, from the receptionist to the lead clinicians to the managers [13]. A supervisor acts as a sounding board and advisor to ensure that the staff work together, forming a mentalizing team who show respect for each other. To some extent, a supervisor anticipates the difficulties of implementation and helps the MBT leads and supervisees to think through the effects that the context in which MBT is being implemented might have on them as well as on their patients.

The supervision system as part of a wider MBT system is not modeled on an expert coming in from "outside." The supervisor may be a skilled practitioner who is a senior member of the treatment team, or a member of another MBT team working in a different treatment program. The former allows the integration of all aspects of treatment within the team, whereas the latter facilitates new ideas and promotes cross-fertilization.

Supervisor Materials for MBT Supervision

A wide range of materials can be used in supervision. Supervisors should have access to manuals, chapters, and research on MBT, and these materials should be made available for supervisees, to inform discussions on implementation and clinical practice. Planning of MBT supervision sessions is essential, with supervision perhaps taking the form of a time-limited course with supervision meetings covering topics agreed in advance, each with reading material and a requirement for supervisees to present clinical material related to the topic in question. This format is used for new trainees who are developing practitioner-level skills. Essential topics that should be covered over an 18-month period of supervision are listed in Box 4.6.

Box 4.6 Essential topics for supervisees who are starting to deliver individual and group MBT.

- Assessment and formulation.
- Not-knowing stance.
- Starting therapy.
- Mentalizing the counter-relationship—initial sessions.
- Recognizing ineffective mentalizing.
- Intervention for pretend mode.
- Intervention for psychic equivalence.
- Intervention for teleological mode.
- Mentalizing process—managing arousal, contrary moves, parking.
- Mentalizing process—acknowledging positive mentalizing.
- Affect focus—clarification, affect identification, mentalizing functional analysis of an event.
- Affect focus—"elephant in the room," group interventions.
- Mentalizing the relationship.
- Mentalizing the counter-relationship in group sessions.

Ensuring That Mentalizing Theory Is Linked to Clinical Practice

Joining theory to clinical practice fosters an increasingly coherent model in the mind of clinicians, and allows them to make decisions according to clear principles during psychotherapy sessions, which by their nature are infinitely variable. Separation of the ideas of theoreticians, the findings from academic research, and clinical practice bedevils psychological interventions in general, with clinicians often wondering what an idea embedded in empirical research—for example, about social interaction—means in terms of how they might change their practice. MBT is, and hopefully always will be, a joint endeavor between those working in empirical research and those engaged in delivering treatments to patients. A crucial part of these links is the work of a supervisor, making reading an important part of supervision and encouraging discussion about the clinical ramifications of new ideas. For example, if it is correct that epistemic trust (see Chapter 2) is the door that needs to be opened for change to occur, how does contemporary MBT practice concentrate on the opening of this door? Are some current interventions uniquely capable of doing so? Are there any interventions that could be used more, or any that can be used less? The supervisor becomes the conductor of discussion, stimulating debate and ideas about the translation of research into practice, rather than acting as an expert who delivers answers.

Supporting the Learning and Refining of Clinical Skills

The supervisor can use a variety of methods to support the development and skillful delivery of MBT interventions.

First, they can model the playful, not-knowing stance used in MBT during interactions within supervision as a method to explore the supervisee's clinical work, seeing it from the supervisee's perspective of their own experience as well as elaborating their understanding of the patient's experience. This process demonstrates that the clinical difficulties are explored from the perspective of the supervisee, which, along with an emphasis on the positive aspects of the supervisee's work, serves as an ostensive cue system that opens up a channel of trust between supervisor and supervisee. This is necessary before more complex problems, such as counter-relational responses, can be addressed.

Second, once mutual trust has been established between the supervisor and supervisee, video recordings of clinical sessions can become the focus for supervision. Actual clinical moments in treatment are used as a trigger for discussing what intervention to use and how best to deliver it.

Third, role play can be used to practice some of the clinical difficulties encountered in the supervisee's work—with the supervisor playing the role of the clinician, and the supervisee playing the part of the patient. This not only demonstrates the delivery of interventions but also allows the supervisee to subjectively feel the impact of the intervention, which may give them a sense of the patient's experience.

Fourth, the supervisor can use the development and review of formulations as a means of working directly with the supervisee on their clinical reflections on treatment and practicing how they might share them with the patient. Developing them together (rather than the supervisor assessing the supervisee's creation) generates joint attention by the supervisor and supervisee on a central component of MBT, and also models a mentalizing approach.

Finally, the supervisee needs to be supported in using their counter-relationship with the patient. The supervisor may need to recognize and carefully highlight the clinician's sensitivities, particularly when these interfere with the treatment process. All clinicians have strengths and weaknesses, and supervision is the place for these to be discussed, at least to the extent that they can be addressed in relation to the treatment of a particular patient. Some clinicians are more skillful with certain patients and less so with others, who activate their mentalizing weak spots. Being able to recognize one's own interpersonal strengths and mentalizing weak spots is essential in order to avoid inadvertently causing harm to patients (e.g., by engaging with them in a way that is dominated by the clinician's own imbalances in mentalizing). A critical patient might trigger defensive self-protection in some clinicians more readily than in others; if that self-protection takes the form of retaliation from which the clinician cannot easily recover, the therapeutic relationship will become increasingly problematic. Clinicians' characteristics can interfere with outcomes in psychotherapy with patients with personality problems. Some patient–clinician interactions cause considerable problems, which will need to be addressed in supervision. For example, patients with ASPD tend to elicit in the clinician feelings of being criticized and mistreated, whereas when working with patients with BPD the clinician's counter-responsiveness often includes feelings of helpless inadequacy, or of one's mind being overwhelmed, disorganized, and unable to think. The opposite may also occur, with the clinician feeling "special" and becoming over-involved [14]. In these and other circumstances in which the patient–clinician interaction interferes with the effective delivery of treatment, the management of the clinician's problematic responsiveness has to be the subject of supervision. The focus is, of course, on maintaining the mentalizing of the clinician.

Maintaining the Mentalizing of the Clinician

Clinicians have been found to have significantly more negative responses toward patients with BPD and to experience them as less responsive and more withdrawn than patients with major depressive disorder [15]. When this is combined with the hostility and/or high dependency that clinicians experience as being directed toward them in the context of suicide attempts and self-harm (see this chapter: Adaptations of the MBT Model: The "At-Risk" Patient), and their anxiety about feeling responsible for keeping the patient alive, clinicians can feel useless, undermined, and persistently anxious. These feelings inevitably lead to a rapid loss of mentalizing within sessions. Non-mentalizing in either the clinician or the patient leads to non-mentalizing in the other—which is, of course, the complete opposite of the primary aim of MBT. If this situation is arising in sessions, the clinician and their supervisor need to work to address the problem.

Working in supervision on the counter-relational response of the clinician is part of the support required to help clinicians to maintain their own mentalizing to the extent that they can reflect on themselves and the patient during a session; this helps them to escape from being trapped in a maladaptive process that is preventing change. This aspect of supervision is discussed in Chapter 8 in the context of work with patients with avoidant personality disorder, during which boredom may become a problem. Self-reflection by clinicians—seeing themselves in the context of the treatment process—results in them feeling more confident and less likely to be reactive and defensive when under fire. They will be able to see their inappropriate responsiveness and use it to inform treatment, instead of covering it up or, worse still, engaging in an interaction that is harmful to the patient. The supervisor is both part of a support system around the clinician, and part of a wider MBT system that protects the implementation of MBT at patient level. The supervisor also has a comparable ring of protection through regular discussions about their supervisory work with other supervisors as part of their own continuing professional development.

Supervision is a skill in itself—it cannot be assumed that someone will automatically become a supervisor in MBT simply because they have been practicing as a clinician for a certain period of time and have seen a particular number of patients in treatment. More important are the supervisory skills of an individual and their ability to impart knowledge and to stimulate a mentalizing process within supervision itself. A relaxed, facilitative, and generous interpersonal style and a flexibility of mind that is consistent with being an accomplished MBT practitioner may be the most important characteristics of a good supervisor.

Adaptations of the MBT Model: The "At-Risk" Patient

This section outlines how the MBT clinician intervenes to help patients to reduce risky behaviors such as suicide attempts, self-harm, and violence, all of which can imperil treatment as well as the patient's and clinician's physical safety. The guidelines apply in the following circumstances:

1. at the beginning of treatment, when assessing a patient who has a history of suicide and self-harm or violent behaviors
2. after a suicide attempt, serious self-harm, or an act of violence has occurred
3. when the patient threatens an imminent suicide attempt or self-harm or violence
4. if suicidal ideation is persistent
5. if other recurrent self-destructive action or risk-taking behavior occurs that threatens life or treatment.

Any self-destructive event must be taken seriously, even if at first sight it seems to be of limited risk to the patient or others. Right from the start it is important that the clinician is alert to factors that suggest a change in risk, and that they monitor their own reactions to risk (see Box 4.7).

Box 4.7 Warning signs of a change in risk.

Warning signs include:

- an increase in statements and thoughts about suicide
- anxiety and depressive symptoms
- uncontrolled emotion
- sleeplessness
- a change in alcohol or drug use
- recent loss events, including failure of treatment or discharge from support due to breaking of a contract
- social withdrawal
- interpersonal conflict in close relationships
- planning a method of suicide and "tying up" personal matters.

Box 4.7 *(cont.)*

Clinical Top Tips

- Beware of low mentalizing in the clinician, and becoming "inoculated" against taking risk seriously, often due to its regularity (e.g., frequent self-harm becomes "acceptable," small overdoses become "another one of those actions").
- Beware of compassion fatigue, in which the clinician stops caring.

Understanding Suicide Attempts, Self-Harm, and Violence: A Summary

The clinician needs to keep in mind a mentalizing framework to scaffold their work with people who are a risk to themselves or others. This topic is also discussed in Chapter 18. Recognizing that suicide attempts and other actions result from a cascade of mental collapse is key. The generic MBT intervention process applies to all self-destructive and violent behaviors and other harmful risk-taking actions, such as drug or alcohol misuse (in the rest of this chapter we shall refer to these collectively as "actions"). The mentalizing understanding of these actions is summarized in Figure 4.3.

Even verbalizing "I am suicidal" or "I have thoughts about killing myself" indicates that a *mental escape procedure* has been activated. A subsequent action itself means that the escape procedure has been ineffective and the state of mind has become increasingly painful and threatening to self-coherence and self-existence. Actions such as suicide attempts, self-harm, and violence are the result of a disorganized and painful mind state. They are an end product

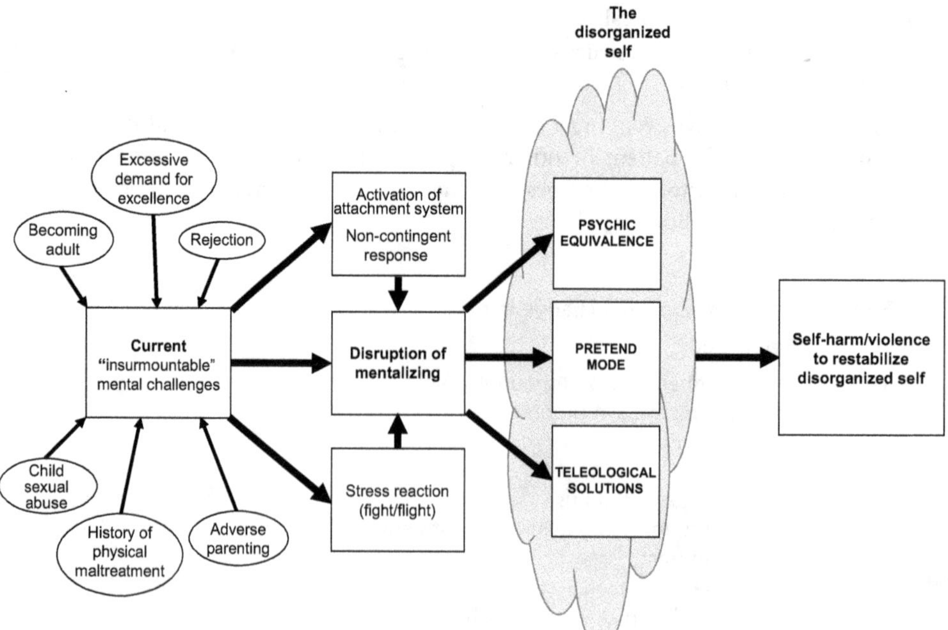

Fig. 4.3 Understanding how loss of mentalizing can lead to high-risk behavior.

rather than the problem that is creating pain. It is far too easy for clinicians to become focused on the thoughts or actions themselves because they are anxious and frightened about the level of risk. This results in a failure to explore the mental circumstances and interpersonal contexts that lead to the patient's self-destructive thoughts.

Pathway to Destructive Action

Earlier vulnerabilities, whether genetic or environmental—and of course most usually both—sensitize an individual to current stressors, which are experienced as insurmountable problems to which the patient has limited resilience. Stress reactions, anxieties, and painful mental states automatically trigger the attachment system, which in turn activates a range of responses, including seeking proximity to an attachment figure. The patient will try to get support from a partner, friends, or (mental) healthcare services, only to find that their experience of the response they receive lacks adequate contingency and fails to decrease their desperation. Further panic ensues as this "mismatch" represents a further threat—that of isolation. With increased emotional arousal, mentalizing is disrupted, leading to experiences being processed ineffectively—either being exaggerated and intensified through psychic equivalence, or being denied and split off through pretend mode. This makes any affective and cognitive experience increasingly acute and painful because the mind loses the capacity to differentiate reality from inner experience. Doubt is lost and certainty of belief dominates. Only action can then change mental processing, and teleological solutions are required.

Teleological Mode/Outside-In Mind and Actions

A patient who experiences a failure of effective mentalizing and falls into the teleological mode fails to believe claims made by others about their own subjective states—for example, that they are concerned about the patient. The patient finds the articulated mental states of others credible only if they are accompanied by action: "*I know you care if I live or die if you act in relation to my risky behaviors.*" To this extent, during threats of self-harm and suicide a patient may be stabilized through the action of the clinician—for example, the clinician might express care by visiting the patient at home, contacting a crisis system on their behalf, or offering to see the patient more often while the risk is high. In these circumstances the interaction between the patient and the clinician might become organized around threats of suicide or self-harm that lock the patient, clinician, and service together in an endless cycle of action and reciprocal action, which manages the immediate risk but fails to change the underlying problem that has led to the threat. This is not a conscious, manipulative interaction on the part of these patients. It is a system for survival that follows from their loss of mentalizing and the acute need for stabilization of their sense of self through action, generating teleological experience (creating observable outcomes) for themselves and socially.

Function of Self-Harm

Narrative reviews of published studies have highlighted that affect regulation is the most frequently reported function of non-suicidal self-harm, followed by self-punishment and interpersonal influence (i.e., communicating distress, influencing others, and/or seeking support). Intrapersonal functions such as emotion regulation, avoidance of aversive affect, or self-punishment may therefore have to be explored with all patients. In addition, commentators discuss the disturbance to the sense of self (e.g., dissociation) that is frequent in people who harm themselves, and the stabilizing effects of action on the sense of self. The concept of the alien self (which is elaborated in Chapters 2, 14, and 18) is useful for understanding this in more detail.

Cutting, burning, or otherwise injuring oneself reduces anxiety, prevents dissociation, and clarifies mental states. From the MBT clinical perspective, the purported function identified by the patient's narrative description is not central. We assume a final common pathway—the loss of mentalizing function. The aim of interventions is to ensure that mentalizing is stabilized both acutely and in the long term.

Clinical Intervention Process

Clinically, in MBT there is a series of interventions to be made when addressing self-harm, suicide attempts, and other associated self-destructive or socially destructive behaviors. These are outlined in Box 4.8.

Box 4.8 Summary of the clinical intervention process for high-risk events.

1. Establish shared responsibility (agreement).
2. Identify the level of current risk—safety planning (fact finding).
3. Rewind from the current event back in time to a point when the patient's mental experience of self-destructive thinking was absent. (Rewind in time and reflect on what was then from the perspective of what is now, and prevent the patient from falling into non-mentalizing modes.)
4. Explore the context and mental experience of wellness/wholeness/absence of threat when the threat of self-harm is absent (exploration of positive and manageable mind states).
5. Micro-slice toward the mental-state changes that lead to thoughts/feelings about self-harm (mentalizing functional analysis).
   a. Focus on affect and contextualizing emotions.
   b. Manage mind states.
   c. Identify the core domain of the problem—interpersonal and affective.
   d. Establish a dominant theme.
   e. Respect the subdominant theme.
6. Identify strategies for managing mental turmoil using focus and a not-knowing stance (generating patient autonomy/agency).
7. If required, use the "elephant in the room" (described earlier in this chapter) to identify relational factors that interfere with effective exploration of self-harm events (working with the "we-mode"/"us" process).

Here we shall provide an illustrative clinical example of the intervention process with Sarah, going through the intervention step by step.

Clinical Example: Sarah (continued)

Sarah was admitted to the psychiatric ward because she was thought to be at risk after the child protection team had expressed concerns about her ability to care emotionally for her son. At the time of admission she was not actively suicidal, but had fleeting suicidal thoughts. The following day she cut her wrist. She was taken to the emergency department to have her wounds sutured.

The interviewing clinician elicited the following story. Early in the evening on the day after her admission to the psychiatric ward, Sarah approached the nurses' station saying that she needed to talk to someone. The nurse responded in a friendly way, pointing out that she was currently doing the medication round but that as soon as she had finished she would come straight to Sarah's room. Sarah responded angrily, saying "I need to talk to someone now, not later." The nurse, now somewhat testily, reiterated her offer to come to Sarah's room a little later, and again pointed out that she was currently occupied with another task. Sarah, now clearly furious, stomped out and returned to her room. Shortly afterwards, she smashed a cup and cut her wrist while screaming "I want to die."

Establishing Shared Responsibility

The clinician cannot assume full responsibility for a patient's actions. In the initial phase of MBT, an agreement defining the extent of the clinician's responsibility and the patient's responsibility is documented in the crisis plan.

Clinical Example: Possible Response from the Clinician

You and I have to work on reducing and stopping this dangerous behavior. We need to agree that whenever you have suicidal thoughts—and certainly if you do try to harm yourself—we look at it in detail, however painful that might be. We cannot ignore it as it will be difficult to work together on your problems with the danger of death hanging over us both. Can we talk about this for a moment so that we both have some understanding of each other's views? Then we can work on what happens and who does what if you get into a dangerous state of mind.

The joint agreement of immediate clinical aims early in treatment will need to specify reducing self-harm and suicide attempts and any other destructive behaviors that are likely to interfere with treatment.

Identifying the Level of Current Risk: Safety Planning

All MBT clinicians who are treating people with BPD are expected to be familiar with safety planning and risk assessment [16]. Certainly it is necessary to establish the facts about self-destructive actions. Question the patient about events that occurred before, during, and after the action, remembering that:

- many serious suicide attempts and instances of self-harm by patients with BPD occur in the context of interpersonal conflicts and emotional turmoil
- negative interpersonal events predict non-suicidal self-injury.

Some of the factors that need to be considered are summarized in Box 4.9.

Box 4.9 **Enquiries about self-harm and other problematic actions.**

This is a process of fact finding.

Before the Event

- Were there obvious interpersonal or other precipitants, such as an argument with the patient's partner?

Box 4.9 *(cont.)*

- Where were they? Had they gone to a remote place?
- Was the action planned or impulsive? Many acts by people with BPD are impulsive, occurring without obvious pre-planning or worry about the consequences. However, on careful exploration there are indicators, which were imperceptible to the patient at the time, that can be used in the future as early warning signs of self-harm or other destructive actions.
- Had the patient been stockpiling tablets?
- Did the patient organize their affairs and write a suicide note? In this case there was some pre-planning, indicating a more serious wish to die.
- Were there other factors that reduced personal control, such as use of alcohol or drugs?

The Event Itself

- What was the lethality of the event and what method of self-harm was involved?
- Was it violent toward the self (e.g., hanging, self-stabbing)?
- Was the patient alone, or did the event occur in the context of a row with a partner/family member?
- Did the patient think that their self-harm would kill them?
- What did they do straight after the self-harm?

Following the Event

- Did the patient call anyone? How did they get help? Who found them?
- How did they feel when help arrived?
- How does the patient feel about the attempt now? Do they regret it? Do they wish that it had worked?
- Does the patient still feel suicidal?
- What is the patient's current mood? Are they depressed?
- If the patient was to go home today, have purposeful daily activities covering the following week been agreed, including who the patient might meet with?

Clinical Top Tip

Identifying the current level of risk requires "fact finding." There is no need to take a not-knowing stance about mental states for this part of the process—you are interested in the facts rather than the mental states.

Clinical Example: Sarah (continued)

The immediate interpersonal precipitant of Sarah's action was her interaction with the nurse. She had asked to talk and, in her view, been rebuffed. She stated that the nurse did not want to listen to her: *"If she had, I would have talked to her."* The MBT clinician recognizes this as a teleological understanding of mind states. A person's willingness to listen is only experienced as credible if it is accompanied by fairly immediate action. Sarah experienced the second rebuff as a rejection, interpreting the nurse's slight impatience as "hostile," "'stigmatizing," and "an attack." At this point, Sarah could not process her accumulated painful mental states (her original urgent need for assistance with down-regulation, her frustration, her sense of rejection, feeling picked on and being attacked, and the overwhelming righteous indignation of victimhood) and she panicked. She returned to her room. She denied even thinking about self-harm before and had not planned anything. Her next action was impulsive—on seeing the teacup in the room she smashed it and stabbed the shard into her hand and cut her wrist. She did not call for help, and had shut her door when she returned to her room. After cutting herself she did indicate that there was a problem by shouting that she wanted to die. The clinician assesses this narrative as showing impulsivity and strong interpersonal components—for example, in the proximal interaction with the nurse. The risk was judged to be low to moderate because no pre-planning was evident. There is ongoing risk related to impulsivity with interpersonal triggers unless Sarah's sensitivities to rejection in interpersonal situations are addressed and her mentalizing becomes more stable in the identified circumstances.

Importantly, the MBT clinician now has hints from the fact-finding process about what went wrong. Sarah is in distress, she feels afraid and unsafe, she feels unable to regulate these feelings internally, and this triggers her attachment system and proximity seeking. She reaches out to the nurse as someone with whom she may be able to down-regulate herself. Not only is the nurse's response non-contingent, but also her refusal to immediately attend to Sarah's need is unacceptable. She needs help *now* and not after the nurse has finished giving out the medication. Her mind is in teleological mode, and any response other than obvious action that comprehensively meets her need will not signal relief. This results in increased anxiety, which hyperactivates her attachment processes. Sarah becomes more demanding, and when her need is further frustrated she tries to shut her mind down by leaving the interpersonal interaction. Attachment has failed in its primary purpose of eliciting a reciprocal response of caregiving that might soothe and alleviate Sarah's fear. The second, more demanding, request comes from a different place—one of angry hurt and deep frustration. Sarah nudges the nurse into a familiar complementary role of irritated denial of access. Her own role is feeling the victim of stigma and of incompetence, now filled to the brim with righteous grief. Intense feelings trigger further intense feelings. Her head feels as if it will burst. She escapes from the painful encounter only to be left alone with overwhelmingly intense feelings and confusing ideas. She does not want to die, she does not even want to hurt herself—she just wants it all to stop. The cup acquires perceptual salience. She smashes it against the wall but that dramatic act upsets her even more. She grabs the sharpest piece she can find and uses it to cut into her hand and wrist. She does not really know why she did that. The cry "*I want to die*" is something of an afterthought. But the act of shouting and cutting achieved its function. She feels a little calmer.

Rewinding from the Current Event in Time: Focusing on Mental States before the Event

Having gathered all the details of the event, the clinician "rewinds" to a time when the patient was able to identify their internal states and manage their emotions (managing mentalizing process). The most common error is for the clinician not to rewind far enough back in time and to get stuck on the immediate precipitant(s), which in this case appears at first sight to be the interaction with the nurse. However, by the time Sarah decided to go and speak to the nurse it is likely that her mentalizing was already compromised.

This MBT intervention seeks the point of vulnerability for the patient in terms of when their anxiety starts to undermine their mentalizing. This can be identified only by finding a point when their mentalizing was still stable and then tracing forward to a point at which it is apparent to the patient that their mentalizing is becoming vulnerable, but which is well before their mind enters the uncontrollable cascade of ineffective mentalizing that will inevitably result in action. The aim of this "detective work" is to work with the patient on finding solutions or workarounds to this process.

In this example, as always, there are various time points to which the clinician can rewind. It is not essential to get the right time point every time, as it is easy to rewind further if questioning reveals that the patient was in a state of poor mentalizing at the time that the clinician is focusing on. It is important for the clinician to remember that they are exploring the patient's *past* mental states from the perspective of *current* mentalizing.

Clinical Example: Sarah (continued)

Clinician: Tell me what you wanted to talk to the nurse about.

Sarah: It doesn't matter now. That was then. It has gone. I needed to talk then and not now *(dismissive and defensive).*

Clinician: Yes, I understand that, but it was very important then, so perhaps it can tell us something about what you sometimes need help thinking about. *(The clinician is maintaining the focus.)*

Sarah: All I wanted to know was if my son's dad was bringing him to visit as I had not heard from him. I knew he was supposed to be visiting, but he usually rings me and he had not contacted me and I thought he might have talked to the nurses. Of course, you know he wants to take my son away from me because I am supposed to be insane.

The clinician has taken Sarah back to what was in her mind when she felt the urge to talk to the nurse. However, her answer suggests that her mentalizing was lowered at the time. The immediacy and tone of her response now suggest that her mentalizing is possibly reduced *currently*—she explains her desire to talk to the nurse as seeking information and believes, perhaps with good reason, that her former partner "*wants to take my son away from me.*" So it is obvious that the visit has complexity and significance beyond a mere hospital visit. The clinician is not surprised that the threat of her son being taken away from her could have powerful effects on Sarah's mentalizing, and obviously this will need to be talked about in some detail if she is to be protected from similar experiences in the future.

Clinical Example: Possible Alternative Responses from the Clinician

Tell me what you were thinking about in relation to your son's father not being in touch with you. I can imagine it would have got you quite worried given what is going on between the two of you in relation to custody issues. (*The clinician rewinds to focus on a more general component of the problem.*)

How had the day been before you started to think like this about your son and his father? (*The clinician rewinds to a point at which Sarah might have been calm and thoughtful.*)

How have things been recently between you and your son's father, before you came into hospital? (*The clinician starts an MBT Loop by rewinding to focus on the overall relationship with Sarah's son's father.*)

In general, we suggest that the clinician should rewind to a point when the patient was calm and functioning.

Exploring the Context and Mental Experience of Wellness/Wholeness/Absence of Threat

Once the patient's level of arousal has been lowered and they are able to access earlier stable mental states, the clinician starts to explore the troubling context and linked mental content. For example, if the rewind in time has focused around Sarah's current relationship with her son's father, the clinician can begin to explore this relationship: "*What is your relationship with him like at the moment?*"

At this point, the clinician starts by asking about times when the relationship was going relatively well, rather than focusing on the acute negative and highly problematic interaction. To establish stable mentalizing, the clinician affirms the possibility of a positive relational process and validates Sarah's role in maintaining the relationship. As she defaults to talking about the problems, he then gently keeps her focused initially on relatively neutral aspects of the current relationship by asking factual questions and preventing the conversation from immediately deteriorating into a panicked and confused tirade about her son being taken into care or her losing custody. As is inevitable, notwithstanding the clinician's care, genuine worries about problems with the coordination of shared care with the father are emerging. The clinician takes a not-knowing stance at this point, stimulating Sarah to reflect on the details of interactions, all the time trying to enhance her mentalizing. Listening to the narrative, the clinician cuts across non-mentalizing generalizations, moralistic reasoning filled with "shoulds" and "oughts," black-and-white thinking, automatic thoughts, and ungrounded assumptions, steers her away from unjustified inferences based on appearances, and introduces cognition to accompany intense affect, all the while discussing his thoughts and feelings but ignoring her own reactions, her feelings about her son, and her anxieties about losing custody. In other words, the clinician uses what he knows about the polarized nature of mentalizing to create a narrative that is balanced across the dimensions, to ensure that mentalizing is retained even though such an intensely emotional issue is being discussed. The clinician encourages openness and flexibility while also persistently refusing to let Sarah off the topic that triggered the collapse of mentalizing and her episode of self-harm. When she claims that it is no longer relevant, he suggests that nevertheless, just as a favor to him, they should spend another few minutes talking about it.

Micro-slicing Toward the Mental-State Changes that Lead to Thoughts/Feelings of Self-Harm (Mentalizing Functional Analysis)

The mentalizing functional analysis is concerned with the patient's changing state of mind and its interdependent interaction with external circumstances. This is not simply a discussion about environmental sensitivities and triggers [17]. It is a discussion about changes in subjective experience as an event unfolds. The clinician takes the process seriously and controls the speed of exploration—the slower and more detailed the better. Let us imagine that we are the supervisors of Sarah's clinician, who would like to work through the events that led to the episode of self-harm.

Clinical Example: MBT Advice to Guide Sarah's Clinician for the Session Following the Episode

Take Sarah back to what was in her mind before she even thought about whether her son and his father were coming to visit. What was in her mind when she began thinking about the visit? Was she looking forward to them coming, albeit concerned about the visit, given her concerns about the father's long-term motives, or was she anxious, and if so, about what? Try to get an impression of what happened to her thoughts and feelings as she approached the point when she felt she needed to ask for support. Try to make a judgment—is her thinking muddled, excessively fixed and certain, judgmental, or black-and-white? What was the moment in her thinking when the quality turned from reasoned and reasonable to dominated by affect and hard to understand? You are trying to follow experiences associated with the lowering of mentalizing, a reduction in the ability to integrate feelings and cognitions, and an inability to maintain a barrier between what is just a thought and what is physical reality. Identify the dominant and subdominant ("elephant in the room") emotions that contribute to this. It can be helpful to establish the mode(s) of mind states that is brought forward when mentalizing generates too much anxiety. Is it psychic equivalence, teleological mode, pretend mode, or a combination of two or more of these modes? What is the emotional impact of ineffective mentalizing? Does it help to re-equilibrate emotion and solidify Sarah's sense of self? Or (more likely) does it add to her troubles by generating even more emotion and confusing her thinking about who she is and what she hopes for?

Keep going back and forth in time. Establish some early points at which Sarah was still in control, and focus more intently around these points. Might she have questioned her own experience at that time? How might she have managed her anxiety better? Can you help her with some pointers if this kind of situation were to happen again? Don't forget that it is the process that is helpful here, not the point at which you arrive. Next time it will be different, but you hope that what she learns is the way you encouraged her to observe her thoughts, even if the specific thoughts will be about something completely different next time. Do not get hung up on small and subtle differences in feelings and attitudes, or about consistency or inconsistency with what you heard on other occasions. Follow the patient's words for emotion and make certain that you know what experiences those words refer to. Make sure that the discourse you are having is about thoughts and feelings and that they feel real to you (i.e., not pretend) at all times.

Focusing on Affect and Contextualizing Emotions

Emotions interfere with decision making based on mentalizing, and thus interfere with effective responsiveness to stressful situations. In people with BPD, this can have tragic consequences. It is necessary for the clinician to attend to the emotional state that the patient experiences as their thoughts become increasingly self-destructive. Is it anger or is it a reaction to something that is more complex, such as being misunderstood or feeling uncared for? Is it helplessness and disappointment after trying so hard to improve a relationship? As discussed earlier in this chapter, being able to label and organize feelings is part of basic mentalizing. It is important to validate the patient's initial attempt to label their feelings and try to focus on them while looking for misunderstandings in communication and interference with effective responses. The clinician should not become side-tracked by emotions that are reactions to responses from others arising from the patient's attempt to communicate their distress.

It is important to identify the initial feelings in the trajectory to the loss of mentalizing, because later feelings tend to be reactive to the initial states. Although later feelings may be felt more strongly due to the loss of ability to mentalize them, they are often less central to the patient's triggering sensitivities.

The clinician manages the conversation by expanding the frame within which emotional states are explored, following the pathway outlined earlier (see this chapter: Mentalizing an Affective Narrative: Creating a Compassionate Story).

Managing Mind States

Most patients in treatment will have gained some understanding of mind states from completing the MBT-I phase. Sarah needs to become sensitive to her changing mind states, and in particular to be aware of the emergence of psychic equivalence and teleological mode, both of which become common during the onset of self-harming thoughts and behaviors. As we described earlier, it is important to locate the beginnings of psychic equivalence and the context in which the patient begins to realize that their thoughts are becoming rigid and certain. For many patients, it is possible to label these mind states and help them to rewind themselves once they realize that they are experiencing them. Once psychic equivalence has been recognized by the patient, label it—for example, as "Boom Brain Time," "Inside-Out Mind," "Know and Now Mind," or some other shorthand term. When teleological mode is recognized, label it too—for example, as "Action Mind" or "Outside-In Mind." This may help the patient to become more sensitive to the onset of these states and to take steps to stop them before they become overwhelming.

Identifying the Core Domain of the Problem: Interpersonal and Affective

As we mentioned earlier, evidence shows that many suicide attempts and self-harm episodes in people with BPD occur in interpersonal contexts, against a background of high emotion. Negative interpersonal events predict self-harm. It is not an easy task to differentiate dysfunctions of interpersonal interaction from problems with emotion regulation, as both tend to occur in an interpersonal context and they exacerbate each other. High emotion distorts the way in which a person reads social meaning and how they understand others' mind states, resulting in interpersonal discord and confusion. Interpersonal discord in turn stimulates problematic intrapersonal emotions and misperceptions of others' motives. Nevertheless, the MBT clinician uses a not-knowing stance to explore the interaction between interpersonal function and emotion dysregulation, trying (but never successfully) to identify which is the "chicken" and which is the "egg," and which came first. Why does the clinician do this? Again we emphasize that it is not the destination but the journey that matters. Exploring both of these domains strengthens metacognitive capacity. From an MBT perspective, the difficulty lies in translating this exploratory journey into practical therapeutic action. The most common error is to assume that the problem is related solely to a dysfunction of managing emotion, and then logically following this by trying to implement emotional management strategies apart from the interpersonal context in which emotional dysregulation occurs. If decontextualized from the patient's interpersonal sensitivities, emotional regulation will not achieve improved quality of life. Interpersonal vulnerabilities enable the exploration of relational and attachment processes that are central to the problems of people with BPD, and that trigger emotional dysregulation. It is likely that for individuals with BPD, biological (e.g., genetic) factors and the social environment make such triggering more frequent and more severe, but addressing the response without looking at the antecedent is likely to have a very limited impact.

Establishing a Dominant Theme

Clinical Example: Sarah (continued)

Sarah experiences tensions in her relationship with the father of her son, which have an impact on her relationship with her son and perhaps also disrupt (or at least create complications in) her relationships with others, including the child protection team. In the review of the self-harm narrative, an interactional problem emerges with the nurse whom Sarah approached for support. All of these interpersonal contexts trigger attachment strategies, which are embedded in the way that Sarah habitually reacts to interpersonal stress. The clinician explores all of the relationships to see whether there are obvious overlaps in what Sarah appears to be sensitive to. It turns out that Sarah felt "overlooked," "ignored," and "not listened to" by people in all of these contexts. No one had been thoughtful enough to discuss the hospital visit with her, the child protection team was expressing concerns but failing to recognize her increasing efforts to look after her son, and the nurse did not recognize her distress and "ignored" her request to talk. This allowed the dominant theme for exploration to be about her vulnerability to people leaving her out of any interaction. Sarah quickly felt pushed aside, and her sensitivity to rejection meant that she reacted strongly to defend her sense of self. Reacting when in teleological mode leads to insistence and a demanding presentation that people feel unable to appreciate—hence the conflict with the nurse, who certainly could not see that, at that moment, validation of Sarah's anxiety was a matter of life and death for her. When rebuffed, Sarah could not understand the nurse's motivation; rather, she felt so confused that she withdrew, but at that point she could only retain a subjective sense of self-existence through self-harm.

The clinician modifies the formulation, having identified a pattern that substantiates and clarifies the interactional cycle. Both clinician and patient then focus on aspects of the cycle as a dominant theme of their sessions.

Respecting the Subdominant Theme

There are always subdominant themes and subdominant emotions that need to be identified and respected in any exploration of problems. This was discussed earlier (see this chapter: Elephants in the Room). Subdominant emotions are often those that are on the periphery of the basic dominant emotion. Subdominant themes are part of a wider integration of information—for example, "*I am hurt* (dominant emotion) *and constantly feel hurt by others, but within all of this is a* (subdominant) *sense that I want to be close to others but I feel I fail.*" The clinician tries to work with both the dominant theme and the subdominant process implicated in the self-harm/suicidal event.

Identifying Strategies for Tolerating and Managing Mental Turmoil Using the Not-Knowing Stance

In MBT, clinicians do not know how the patient "should" have reacted or "could" have reacted differently to the personal and emotional stressors. However, they are aware that suicidal thoughts, suicidal acts, non-suicidal self-injury, and other destructive actions represent a failure of psychological resilience when managing stress. The clinician considers how the patient might react differently to stress, but continues to show concern that the issue is how sensitivities and vulnerabilities are managed. The patient is reactive rather than proactive, so finding solutions to the reactivity is expedient. The aim in MBT is to increase early awareness of mental stress and for the patient to become sensitive to and able to proactively reduce (down-regulate) their level of anxiety using an improved understanding of the mental states and functions.

If the patient asks "*What should I have done?*" then the MBT clinician responds with the answer "*That is a great question. I don't know, so let's look at that. What sorts of things come to your mind?*" If the patient is unable to say much, the clinician can stimulate the conversation: "*What about standing back from it and having time to think about it rather than dropping straight into Boom Brain? Could you ask yourself a question, for example, as it is happening, and if so what sort of question?*"

The clinician does not give specific solutions but supports the patient to consider alternative perspectives. Encouraging patients to be compassionate toward themselves rather than self-condemning is important. This can help them to find active ways of retrieving balance when their mind stops functioning. The clinician models coping, but is never a "super-competent" model. The principle of equity dictates that the clinician admits to the same need for self-compassion in relation to their own mentalizing failures.

Other Useful MBT Principles for Addressing Risky Behavior

Throughout the focus on self-harm, it is important that the clinician continues to follow the principles that underpin MBT (see Chapter 3).

- Maintain a not-knowing stance when exploring themes.
- See things from the patient's perspective.
- Validate the patient's emotional discomfort using marked and contingent responsiveness.
- Join with mentalizing; do not join with non-mentalizing.
- Use affect focus and clinician counter-responsiveness to identify the effects of suicidality and other risk behaviors on therapy.
- Do not take over the patient's mentalizing by telling them what is in their mind or what they feel.
- Avoid using your high mentalizing to manage the patient's low mentalizing.

What To Do if the Patient Does Not Want to Talk about Suicide Attempts and Self-Harm Events

There are occasions when patients will not want to talk about self-destructive acts. In this case the clinician can do a number of things while remembering the imperative to avoid becoming coercive (see Figure 4.4).

1. Reconsider the contract made at the beginning of treatment in which addressing self-harm has been agreed if it was part of the patient's symptoms and behaviors associated with BPD. The contract needs to be discussed.
2. Address the *difficulty* of talking about the action rather than talking about the circumstances of the event itself, recognizing that talking can cause the patient to feel

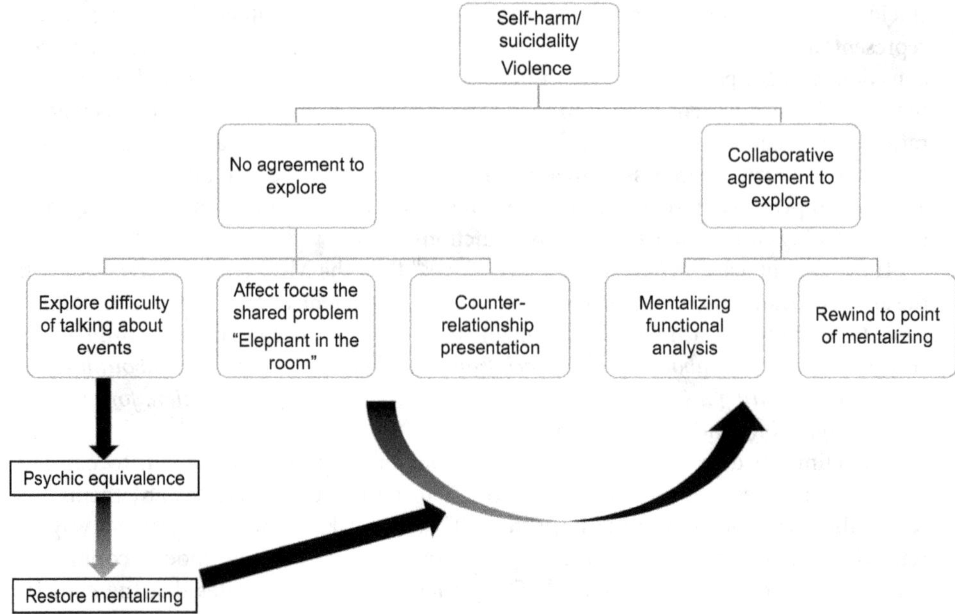

Fig. 4.4 Intervention algorithm for exploration of impulsive behavior.

shame, and that they might even begin to relive the events in psychic equivalence. The patient and the clinician then need to manage their anxiety levels carefully.

3. Use an affect focus (the "elephant in the room") to identify the difficulty manifested between the patient and the clinician as a result of not talking about the action. This leaves the clinician worrying about the patient's level of risk and unable to concentrate on the topics the patient talks about, while the patient is sensitized to the clinician wanting to raise the question of self-harm; this will distort the interaction between them. This "elephant in the room" can be identified and discussed. As a result, the immediate toxicity of talking about the act of self-harm may be reduced.
4. Explore the consequences of the action and question the effectiveness of the behavior even if the outcome was apparently positive in terms of the "real" world—for example, the patient felt better after self-harming. Self-destructive behavior is an ineffective way to manage emotional distress within certain interpersonal contexts.

Clinical Example: Further Example of Mentalizing Functional Analysis

Sarah's boyfriend announced that he and his friends were heading off to a football match. This was despite his and Sarah's earlier agreement that they were going to visit friends together. He said that he had been offered a ticket to the match and he wanted to take up the opportunity. Soon after he had left with his friends, Sarah cut herself. Her experience of being alone and his choice of others over her produced an unbearable stress that in turn led to a breakdown in mentalizing. The initial announcement by the boyfriend is an attachment loss—a loss of anticipated physical and emotional "togetherness." Initially, Sarah felt that his choosing to go to the football match rather than join her and her friends meant that he did not love her. Although this is understandable, the problem was not the thought, but the fact that the thought began to take on all the characteristics of reality due to her vulnerability to ineffective mentalizing—in this instance, psychic equivalence. Her thought became a fact with certainty, and her boyfriend's absence was additional proof that he did not love her. Further development of this idea led her to more rigid schematic thinking in which she "knew" he was really out on a date with someone else. This inevitably produced more intolerable feelings, which she could no longer manage. Her only option, or rather the only possibility she could think of, was to cut herself. This self-destructive act made her relax, but unfortunately it also produced feelings of shame. When her boyfriend returned, he became angry when he noticed her bandaged wrist. This perpetuated Sarah's cycle of self-criticism.

By working through these patterns of rapidly changing mental states in a wide range of circumstances the patient gradually learns that feelings do not simply spontaneously arise. Rather, they are created by interactions with others, and personal interpretation is a part of those interactions. Understanding and representing the process as it is happening through the mentalizing functional analysis allows mentalizing to be maintained and the consequences of mentalizing failure to be explored and reflected on.

The emphasis needs to be on feeling states as part of an overall mental state, and not solely on cognitive states or antecedent triggers. Thus the mentalizing functional analysis is more about how the context interacts with the feelings and mental state of the patient ("*What was going on in your mind at the time?*"). It has components of (a) metacognition, (b) first-order mentalizing (*what I think X thinks or feels*), (c) personal second-order mentalizing (*what X thinks I am thinking and feeling*), and (d) vicarious mentalizing (*what Y can teach me about what X is thinking*). In particular, the clinician looks out for communication difficulties and oversensitivity, which lead to difficulties in managing feelings of rejection, abandonment, and humiliation, or, conversely, powerful feelings of love, desire, and need, which lead to a flood of affect overwhelming the mind and destabilizing the patient's subjective experience of self. Remember that, within the context of a collapse of mentalizing, patients with BPD experience feelings at the level of psychic equivalence. Thus "feeling bad" becomes "I am bad." The clinician's interventions must reflect a sense that they understand this and are not underestimating the power of the patient's experience.

The conscious determinants of the self-harm are explored initially, without trying to second-guess more complex psychological reasons. During this exploration, the patient's explanation should be questioned if it is schematic and formulaic, because these are non-mentalizing phenomena that will prevent the development of a more robust mental buffer to future emotional experiences that might result in self-harm. The patient's action (e.g., self-harm, suicide attempt) should not be interpreted in terms of their personal history, the putative unconscious motivations, or their possible manipulative intent in the "heat of the moment"—this will alienate the patient. Only later will the clinician be able to build up evidence for underlying vulnerabilities and sensitivities of which the patient is only vaguely aware, whether these are unconscious determinants or current events to which they are sensitized by their past.

Clinical Example: Sarah's Reaction to Feeling Abandoned

Sarah talked about an episode of self-harm the previous day, glossing over what had happened and insisting that it was unimportant.

Clinician: Tell me a bit more about what happened.

Sarah: There is nothing more to say really. I cut myself.

Clinician: Let's go back and tell me when you first began to feel something was wrong. (*The clinician rewinds the focus to an earlier time point.*)

Sarah: I don't know really.

Clinician: Bear with me—can you remember what you felt, for example yesterday or even before then? (*The clinician is trying to identify a context or a time when the patient was aware of feeling OK.*)

Sarah: No. I was OK yesterday and I think it was when I got home in the evening. I arranged to see two of my friends and we went for a drink as I said, and it was only when I got home after that I began to feel miserable.

Clinician: So you were aware that you were miserable at that point. It sounds like something might have occurred during the evening. Tell me about the evening, starting with how you felt before you went out.

The session continued in this way, with the clinician insisting on exploring the detail of the miserable affect along with the positive enjoyment of being with her friends. It turned out that Sarah had felt abandoned (a feeling that she experienced before the misery) by her two friends when they had gone off to the toilet together and left her alone for what she felt was an excessive length of time.

Sarah: I felt so hurt (*a further affect complicating the internal state of the patient at that time*) that I nearly cut myself then with my knife, but I scratched myself with my fingernails to get a bit of blood out instead. Then I got the idea that I should just get up and go so that when they came back they would not know where I was. (*The motive of revenge appears to have been stimulated by the severe scratching. Only with a mentalizing mind can the patient have feelings of revenge, which require self and other representation, and hence her revenge fantasy occurs after she has scratched herself.*) But just as I was about to leave they came back.

Clinician: And?

Sarah: I didn't say anything at all. What's the point? They had already spent ages together.

Clinician: Drawing blood is a strong reaction to them being in the toilet for a long time. What were you thinking and what was the hurt about? (*The clinician is trying to focus on the strength of the reaction—the problem is not so much the feeling of being left alone when Sarah's friends go off to the toilet, but rather the reaction to the feeling, which is excessive and inappropriate, and is probably based on an experience of psychic equivalence.*)

Sarah: They always exclude me. (*The use of words like "always" that have a totality and absolute component commonly implies non-mentalizing.*)

Clinician: So you felt excluded and hurt, and didn't know what to do about how you felt (*empathic and validating statement*). Scratching yourself made you a bit clearer, and I can understand how you could become momentarily vengeful to get back at them, although you then became miserable later. I guess that you felt that cutting was the only way you could make things feel better at that point.

The clinician is focusing on the affective relief produced by cutting, and is also hinting at a stabilizing effect of the action—it brings back the patient's mind at the point at which it was lost. Cutting and other actions are ways of reinstating a mentalizing mind. However, there is a danger here of the clinician overstating their own understanding and going beyond the patient's mentalizing capacity.

Sarah: It always clears how I feel and then I can get on with things again. I was OK with them until we left the pub and I was able to watch TV for a time.

Clinician: But you cut yourself again.

Sarah: Soon after I got home, I felt awful again and so really wanted to do it that time. I used a razor.

Clinician: Can you say what was going on then?

Sarah: Don't know.

Here Sarah is struggling to reflect more on what led her to self-harm. The clinician can empathize with this at this point:

Clinician: It's difficult to grasp what it was like then, especially if things are OK now (*empathic statement*).

Sarah: I can't remember. I was just alone. I went to bed after that.

Clinician: Tell me more about the awful feeling before you used your razor.

Sarah: I just felt that the evening had been ruined and that every time I try to enjoy myself something goes wrong. I was then on my own again.

Clinician: In this case what has gone wrong is that you felt excited about seeing your friends and then were more sensitive to being left out. This seems to have returned when you were alone at home and you didn't know how to manage it. We need to go back to consider how you manage your feelings of being left out.

Sarah: Hmm.

At this point the clinician decides that Sarah does not feel able to reflect more on what has been happening, and so the conversation moves on to other topics. However, later in the session the clinician assesses that Sarah is mentalizing more robustly, at a time when she is talking about her sensitivity to being let down. Therefore he brings her back to the experiences that led to her episode of self-harm, bringing her attention to the need to be alert to such experiences so that she can begin to manage the emotions either by redirecting them or by using interpersonal interaction more constructively to reduce her urge to self-harm.

Summary: Working with At-Risk Patients

Targeting risky behaviors in MBT requires a concentrated focus by the clinician and the patient on the mentalizing vulnerabilities that lead to the patient's dangerous actions. This may require the clinician to put compassionate pressure on the patient to explore the events in painful detail, as they naturally may avoid mental states associated with the distress that is elicited during the discussion. A treatment impasse will result if the clinician is in a constant state of anxiety about the patient's safety. Therefore the matter has to be addressed, and working with high-risk events is another example of how the MBT clinician may have to impose their own needs on the clinical process, while of course taking into account the patient's sensitivities.

Concluding Remarks

Clinicians who maintain the structure of MBT and follow the principles outlined at the beginning of this chapter will have a good chance of engaging patients in treatment. Dropout from treatment is low in MBT. Sarah, whose case we have followed throughout this chapter, engaged with treatment and was willing to join an MBT group. Chapter 5 describes her entry into the group.

References

1. Smits ML, Luyten P, Feenstra DJ et al. Trauma and outcomes of mentalization-based therapy for individuals with borderline personality disorder. *Am J Psychother* 2022; **75**: 12–20.
2. Bateman A, Fonagy P. Impact of clinical severity on outcomes of mentalisation-based treatment for borderline personality disorder. *Br J Psychiatry* 2013; **203**: 221–7.
3. Smits ML, Feenstra DJ, Eeren HV et al. Day hospital versus intensive out-patient mentalisation-based treatment for borderline personality disorder: multicentre randomised clinical trial. *Br J Psychiatry* 2020; **216**: 79–84.
4. Bateman A, Constantinou MP, Fonagy P, Holzer S. Eight-year prospective follow-up of mentalization-based treatment versus structured clinical management for people with borderline personality disorder. *Personal Disord* 2021; **12**: 291–9.
5. Miller CE, Townsend ML, Grenyer BFS. Understanding chronic feelings of emptiness in borderline personality disorder: a qualitative study. *Borderline Personal Disord Emot Dysregul* 2021; **8**: 24.
6. Winnicott DW. Ego distortion in terms of true and false self. In: *The Maturational Process and the Facilitating Environment.* New York, NY: International Universities Press, 1965; 140–52.
7. Smith M, South S. Romantic attachment style and borderline personality pathology: a meta-analysis. *Clin Psychol Rev* 2020; **75**: 101781.
8. Grove P, Smith E. A framework for MBT formulations: the narrative formulation and MBT passport. *J Contemp Psychother* 2022: 52: 199–206.
9. Bateman A, Fonagy P. *Mentalization-Based Treatment for Personality Disorders: A Practical Guide.* Oxford, UK: Oxford University Press, 2016.
10. Bateman A, Unruh B, Fonagy P. Individual therapy techniques. In: Bateman A, Fonagy P, eds. *Handbook of Mentalizing in Mental Health Practice,* 2nd ed. Washington, DC: American Psychiatric Association Publishing, 2019; 103–15.
11. Bateman A, Fonagy P. The use of transference in dynamic psychotherapy. *Am J Psychiatry* 2007; **164**: 680.
12. Allen JG, Fonagy P, Bateman AW. *Mentalizing in Clinical Practice.* Washington, DC: American Psychiatric Publishing, 2008.
13. Bales DL, Verheul R, Hutsebaut J. Barriers and facilitators to the implementation of mentalization-based treatment (MBT) for borderline personality disorder. *Personal Ment Health* 2017; **11**: 118–31.
14. Colli A, Tanzilli A, Dimaggio G, Lingiardi V. Patient personality and therapist

response: an empirical investigation. *Am J Psychiatry* 2014; **171**: 102–8.

15. Bourke ME, Grenyer BF. Psychotherapists' response to borderline personality disorder: a core conflictual relationship theme analysis. *Psychother Res* 2010; **20**: 680–91.

16. Bales D, Bateman A. Partial hospitalization settings. In: Bateman A, Fonagy P, eds. *Handbook of Mentalizing in Mental Health Practice*. Arlington, VA: American Psychiatric Publishing, 2012; 197–226.

17. Kjolbe M, Bateman A. Outpatient settings. In: Bateman A, Fonagy P, eds. *Handbook of Mentalizing in Mental Health Practice*. Arlington, VA: American Psychiatric Publishing, 2012; 227–45.

MBT Group (MBT-G)

Introduction

Mentalization-based treatment (MBT) is offered as a group intervention, known as mentalization-based treatment group therapy (MBT-G), for adults and adolescents. This chapter will summarize some key elements of MBT-G. More detail can be found elsewhere [1,2].

Offering MBT-G requires the clinician to consider how to use the group process to facilitate mentalizing without triggering too much anxiety in the patients. This is less of a problem in the introductory phase of MBT (MBT-I; see Chapter 4), in which every group session is organized around a topic and task. In this early phase the patients are learning about the model and trying to apply the framework to themselves rather than being asked to express their concerns about themselves to others and to "learn" about themselves from seeing themselves as others see them. MBT-I is the first part of engendering the "we-mode" (see Chapter 2) in patients; the group members are thinking together about a topic, beginning to apply the knowledge to themselves, and expressing their thoughts about the topic to others. However, when the group becomes organized around each patient expressing their personal problems to the others and learning from them, and focusing on their more immediate interactions with each other, attachment anxiety is stimulated, potentially leading to panic or avoidance. To address the potential harmful effects of intense attachment anxiety, the clinician follows the MBT principles outlined in Chapters 3 and 4, and structures the group process. The clinician holds authority within the group by "stage-managing" the process of the group, somewhat less than normally occurs in a psychoeducation group but more than is usual in a fully process-oriented group.

Structure of the Group

MBT-G is organized in a way that provides the best chance of engaging patients and ensuring that the process of mentalizing themselves and others becomes the primary focus. The structure is discussed in detail elsewhere [1–3]. The steps to follow in each group session follow a trajectory as summarized in Figure 5.1.

To a large extent, group participants are trained into the structure and function of any group by the clinicians who are facilitating the group, and MBT-G clinicians have authority in the group to set out the structures of the group and what is expected from the participants. This is more than simply outlining practicalities, although of course that is important to set the "macro-culture" of the group. Many of these practical aspects, particularly at the outset, are determined by the method of treatment—for example, rules about timing and frequency, seating arrangements (e.g., in a circle or "classroom" style),

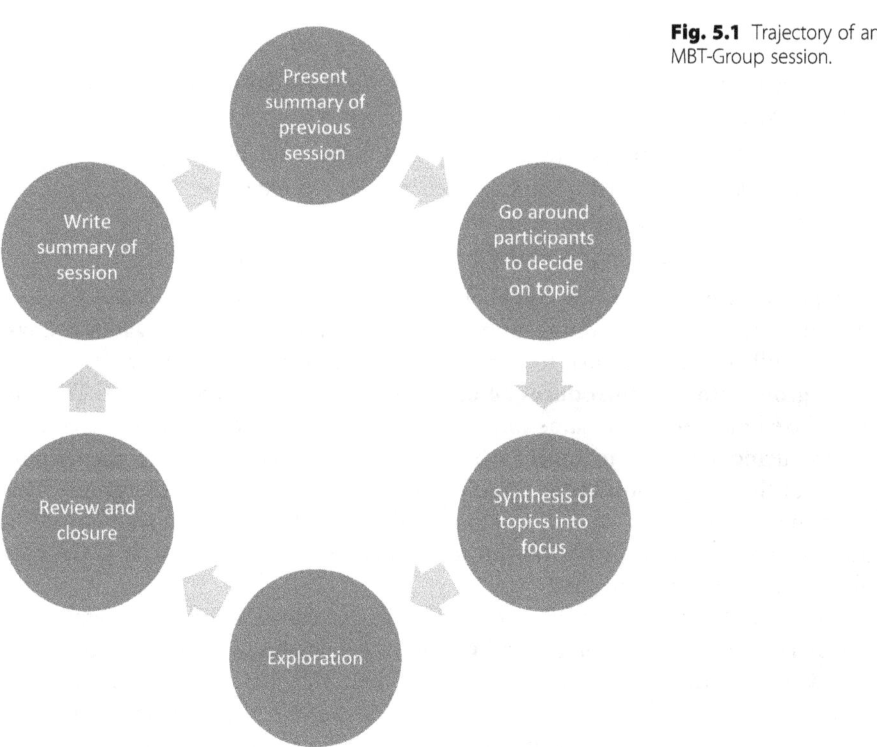

Fig. 5.1 Trajectory of an MBT-Group session.

and constraints on communication outside the group. It is the "micro-culture" within this that sets the atmosphere and specific social culture of the group, and is of distinct importance in MBT-G. Any group starts to develop its own micro-culture, based on agreed mores or traditions, but in MBT-G these are systematically developed through the initial exploration and agreement of values. As a group develops, there will be other more complex and subtle aspects of the group's culture, which will be more unique to the group—for example, the "climate" of the group, the position of authority figures, attitudes of deference or otherwise to the group leader(s), and ways of managing interruptions and emotional outbursts. The experience of being part of, being challenged by, and contributing to the culture of this group is a fundamental aspect of MBT, because it introduces and regulates the experience of making a cultural contribution.

The main components that the new clinician has to master in order to generate a mentalizing culture within the group include how to introduce new patients into the group and help them get started, and encouraging interpersonal mentalizing among group members so that all of the discussion is not routed through talking only to the clinician. Central to mentalizing is the principle that all participants are equal in terms of learning from each other; the clinician and patients are all equally unable to know the mental experience of others, although of course the clinician is often more skilled at taking a not-knowing stance in order to explore this. Many patients will feel better understood by their peers in the group than by the clinician, so an important task for the clinician is to get the patients to talk to each other.

We shall now follow Sarah, the patient whose individual treatment we covered in Chapter 4, as she starts in the group.

Starting in an MBT Group

Engaging a new patient in an MBT group follows a structured process that is orchestrated by the MBT clinician. This comprises:

- preparation of the existing group members and the new member
- relational passport presentation from the current group members
- relational passport presentation from the new member
- introduction and re-evaluation of the group values and culture.

MBT groups are open to new members when a place becomes available. Current members transmit the group culture to new members in a number of organized ways; the cultural milieu is not assumed to transfer and be absorbed passively.

1. The group clinician introduces all of the members to the new patient. They do this in a relaxed manner, in the same way as they would do in an everyday social context when introducing someone to others who did not know them, perhaps mentioning something to the new person about each individual as they go round the group. This introduction by the clinician allows them to say a little about themselves and their role in the group before the group members introduce themselves in turn (which is the next step, described in step 2 of this list).

Depending on the cohesion of the group, the clinician can also decide to present how they experience themselves as being seen by each of the patients in the group. So, having introduced themselves and said something about their role and their personality (e.g., "*I tend to interrupt quite a lot and sometimes can say too much*"), they characterize the way others see them in terms of a dynamic process (e.g., "*Stan tends to be somewhat suspicious of me as I experience it, and I contribute to that by wondering if you, Stan, are saying exactly what you mean,*" "*Layla listens to what I say very carefully and makes me anxious occasionally as I feel that you, Layla, remember in incredible detail what I have said before and then show me where I am going wrong or am inconsistent*"). The aim here is to model an ability to characterize dynamic interactions in the group, both between the group members and between the group members and the clinician(s) (some MBT groups have more than one clinician). After the clinician's introduction, each group member is then asked to undertake the same exercise and introduce themselves to the new participant.

2. Personal introductions prepared in the group the week before are delivered, going round each person in turn. All of the patients revisit their current formulation and are asked to use it as the basis of their personal introduction. The current group members "rehearse" their welcome to a new patient the week before their arrival in the group. Rehearsal involves the patients revisiting their own formulations, including their relational problems when they started in the group, and discussing what they have learned during their time in the group. They are also asked to explore how they see themselves now and, as outlined earlier for the clinician, how they think others in the group see them. Similarly, new patients are coached in introducing themselves to the group in an individual meeting before their entry into the group. In this initial meeting, the patient and the group clinician use the formulation already developed in the assessment sessions (as described in Chapter 4). The assessment and formulation stage may have been completed by another member of the MBT team, and if this is the case a handover of the clinical material from the assessor to the group clinician is necessary. This is done in a tripartite meeting—of both clinicians and the patient—in which the assessor introduces the patient to the group clinician. The assessor may stay only for the introduction, so that the patient and the group clinician can use the session to get to know each other and write a *relational passport.* This is the document that all patients present to the group on joining. In effect it is their own summary of why they are attending the group, with an emphasis on their relational difficulties. This process ensures that all patients in the group remain focused on the primary purpose of the group, which is to explore mentalizing in the context of relationships.

Clinical Example: Preparation of the Group for Entry of a New Patient

The clinician has informed the group that Sarah is joining them the following week. He sets up the "rehearsal" of welcoming her.

CLINICIAN: Sarah starts next week, so we need to work out how we are going to make her welcome. In MBT groups we like to revisit why we came and what things have been like in the group for us, so we can tell Sarah about ourselves next week and help her feel relaxed about talking about herself. I have brought everyone's early relational passport with me on these cards just as a reminder (*he hands them out*). So let's talk about ourselves and consider how we were at the start and whether we have changed. It helps to consider how we think we are seen by others in the group as well. I would like everyone to write down some headlines about themselves on the cards and to use those to introduce yourselves to Sarah next week. (*Some clinicians may ask the patients to write down a few key points about these questions before they present what they think to the group.*)

JOHN: When I came to this group I thought that I did not like people much and I was called avoidant by the person who saw me. I thought that was rude really. I didn't think this was right, although I knew that I kept away from people who annoyed me. This was most people, and I didn't bother to listen to them. I think that now I listen more carefully to people and try to think about what they say. So I think I am better at being with people, and my partner says I am a nicer person.

CLINICIAN: How do you think you are seen in the group? It will be good for all of us to let Sarah know how we are viewed in the group as well as how we see ourselves.

JOHN: That is for others to say, how they view me. But I think I am seen as a bit argumentative, when really I am just trying to work things out for myself.

CORA: Yes. You are a bit argumentative, but I didn't realize that you were mostly trying to work things out yourself.

CLINICIAN: Let's discuss that for a moment. Tell us, Cora, what comes to your mind now John says that is what he is doing when he appears argumentative?

The following week, Sarah attends the group for the first time.

Clinical Example: The First Group Session with a New Patient

CLINICIAN: Welcome to Sarah. Sarah, we always start the same way in the group. I will summarize what happened last week as a reminder, and then we are all going to introduce ourselves.

After the summary, the clinician orchestrates the introductions, starting with themselves.

CLINICIAN: When I started in the group I was anxious a lot of the time about making the group useful to people. I still worry about that, as some of you don't always come and I often want to ask what can be done to make it more useful. I am the sort of person who has the urge to tell people what to do, so I have to stop myself sometimes. I can talk too much as well, so I am happy for people to tell me to shut up when I am talking too much. I think people see me as too controlling and there is some tension about that, especially between me and Cora. Over time I have felt accepted by everyone, though, and listened to, so I look forward to the group each week.

The group members then introduce themselves using the personal "headlines" that they developed the week before. It is anticipated that Sarah will be naturally anxious about introducing herself, so the clinician offers support. Sarah, too, uses her relational passport as the basis of her introduction.

CLINICIAN: Sarah, now it's your turn to say a little about yourself if you can.

SARAH: I am here because I want to save my relationship at the moment. I get very emotional and insecure so I pester people all the time and ask them what they think of me. I want to be liked, and coming in here frightens me. So I won't say anything in the group today and will listen if that is OK.

CLINICIAN: Thanks, Sarah. If you have some thoughts about what is being talked about then please do say, even though you feel a bit anxious. I will ask all the others not to bite!

3. The group atmosphere and values are then discussed. For example, do the participants find the group facilitating, supportive, considerate, or more tense and troubled? Is the current focus on relationships in their lives, or about managing emotions, or about impulsivity, or all of the above? Are the values that were agreed at the beginning of the group (e.g., respect, tolerance, acceptance of alternative perspectives and views) being adhered to, and do they need further discussion?

For each proposed value, the group members discuss three specific questions, all of which facilitate mentalizing in the group.

1. Is this value important to *me*, or do other people think that it is important and that I *should* see it as important?
2. If we agree that it is important, how will we decide whether it is being followed? For example, what are the indicators of intolerance/tolerance, or of unfairness/fairness?
3. Does this joint value play a role in my life at the present time?

Clinical Example: Group Values

CLINICIAN: Let's now look again at the values we talk about so that Sarah knows about them and how we implement them. Sarah, we all agree the values we follow in the group and try to keep to them as best we can. The first one we have is "respect." Cora, would you like to say something about that, as it is one that you are very keen on?

CORA: Do I have to?

Clinician: Yes!

Cora: Well, the others have to help me. Basically, Sarah, we have to listen to each other and care for each other. Really it is like we think about the effects we are having on each other, but they have to think about what effect they have on us, so it is shared out.

John: It has something to do with agreeing with each other.

Clinician: Can you say more about what you mean, John? (*The clinician's view is that agreeing with someone is not a necessary component of respect.*)

John: Well, if you agree with something someone says it means you respect the person. I feel respected when someone agrees with me.

Clinician: What about when someone disagrees with you?

Reflection then takes place about how respect is shown and experienced in the group, including the clinician's question about whether agreement is necessary or unnecessary, until a shared understanding between all of the members is achieved. In this group, the following points were agreed and written up on the board as a "Values Sheet."

- Use kind or polite words, even when you are upset.
- Use manners like sharing, waiting your turn, and giving positive regard to others.
- Ask questions of others with genuine interest in the answer.
- Accept difference, or at least use kind words when disagreeing.
- Be careful not to damage places or things or threaten others.

The list of agreed values on the Values Sheet can be emailed to all of the participants or printed out for them after the session.

Stimulating Interpersonal Mentalizing

A key concern for clinicians is how to promote mentalizing between participants. The interventions described in Chapter 4 are also all part of the clinician's activity in a group, and the clinician has to have the skill to re-establish mentalizing in the face of non-mentalizing. In groups, low mentalizing in one patient will trigger low mentalizing in others, and disrupting this interactive process requires sensitivity and skill on the part of the clinician. Interventions such as diversion, de-escalation, siding with vulnerable patients, and triangulation are used by the clinician when low group mentalizing is emerging. Siding is an important intervention for managing interpersonal anxiety between participants and for preventing the escalation of a tense situation. Taking the example of an interaction in which one patient is critical of another, who reacts by falling silent, the clinician becomes the advocate for the vulnerable patient in responding to the critical patient. The clinician responds on behalf of the person who seems to be the most vulnerable: "*That sounded a bit harsh. Where did that come from?*" Once the tension has been released and the event can be thought about, the clinician can return to a not-knowing stance that is more equidistant from both patients' mental states.

Another factor in the group reduces learning about oneself from others. Too often the conversational partnership is between each patient and the clinician rather than where it should be—between the patients themselves. The clinician needs either to be an active but equal participant or to fade into the background and simply act as a catalyst for the mentalizing process. They cannot be a "central distribution office" for all discussion. This collaborative and democratic process can be promoted by the following approaches:

1. education and discussion about the purpose of the group
2. allocation of protagonists to start discussion of an identified problem
3. using the not-knowing stance and triangulation
4. role play and exercises.

Purpose of the Group

The patients have already been socialized into the model through the MBT-I group and so they already have some understanding of the purpose of the group. Nevertheless, the purpose requires further explanation whenever a new patient joins the group, or if the group loses direction, the purpose seems to have been lost, and a return to "factory settings" is required. In this situation, the purpose of the group is explained in everyday language, making it relevant to the patients' everyday concerns.

Asking other patients to explain the purpose of the group to a newcomer is fine, but the clinician also needs to be clear in their mind about the purpose of the group. So in this clinical example the clinician outlines the purpose of the group to Sarah.

Clinical Example: Outlining the Purpose of the Group

Clinician: Sarah, this group is about learning about ourselves by talking to others. To do so, we have to open ourselves up and let people know about our often more private struggles. This is why we have just discussed the values we are using to work together. Being compassionate to each other and kind is essential if we are going to talk openly and feel safe to do so. What we have to do is listen carefully to each other and "see how others see us," especially if that clashes with how we see ourselves. We also have to do the same for others in the group and be open about how we see them, even if this might sound critical at times. So it is a practice ground really for managing our relationships out there in the real world. We need to take what we learn here and apply it out there and see what happens—do things work better or worse, do we feel better about ourselves, can we stand up for ourselves when we need to, and so on. So one thing that is there in your passport (*pointing to Sarah's card, which she used as an aide-memoire to introduce herself to the group*) is your worry about whether you are liked, so no doubt that will be in your mind already in relation to everyone here. When it is in your mind, perhaps you can let us know so that we can all join in to work out where it is coming from in real time.

Allocation of Protagonists of the Discussion

After providing a summary of the last group session and going round all of the participants asking if they have problems to discuss, the clinician works with the group to bring their problems together. The aim of synthesizing problems is to stimulate "we-mode" in the group and make a focus that is shared through overlapping but different aspects of a problem. For example, one patient may have difficulty with their partner, whereas another is having trouble negotiating with an employer; for both patients this is likely to involve a focus on the ability to interact with others constructively. Alternatively, one patient may be concerned about being liked when with others, whereas another has no concerns about being with others or being liked or disliked by them; here the contrast between opposites can be used to explore the issue of being with others and anxieties about being liked or disliked. The clinician merely appoints the obvious protagonists to start the conversation and asks the others to contribute as things come into their mind: "*Why don't Sarah and John start off and we will join in as things go along. So why not tell each other about yourselves in this regard and perhaps give us a recent example.*"

Clinical Example: Mentalizing the Narrative Between Group Members

Sarah describes a recent interaction with her current partner in which he became frustrated when she kept on asking him if he loved her and what she was like compared with his previous girlfriend.

John: You shouldn't even think about that. He would not be with you if he didn't want to be.

Sarah: I realize that, but you see I keep thinking about it and can't stop myself asking him. I believe him but then I don't and I have to ask again.

John: You like people too much, that is your problem. Most of us here don't like people so much, so it's easier.

Clinician: I like people, or at least I like being with people. So I hope that you are not counting me in the most of us!

Cora: You have to. But Sarah, what are you like when you are on your own? Do you need to be with him for some reason?

Sarah: I don't know. I am not good on my own and I have talked about that before. When I am on my own I feel "yuk" and have to go out. I don't know what it is.

The interaction can now go on between Sarah and John, and the other patients are asked to engage with the work. The task of the clinician is to maintain the focus so that the group addresses Sarah and John's issues, which can be summarized as dependent versus avoidant.

Clinician: Let's keep this in mind, then—we are discussing whether we need people, enjoy being with people, or are avoidant of people. I think we can all relate to something in that!

Triangulation Leading to a "Four-or-More-Way" Interaction

The MBT clinician uses triangulation to facilitate interaction between participants that gradually creates the potential for "we-mode" or collective mentalizing (see Chapter 2). The aim is to increase the patients' experience of learning within a collective mentalizing process. Collective mentalizing stimulates feelings of belonging, of no longer being alone, or of being part of something more than oneself. Many patients lack this experience; its absence is particularly poignant for people with BPD. Others, such as those diagnosed with narcissistic personality disorder or antisocial personality disorder (discussed in more detail in Chapters 6 and 7, respectively), find it hard to generate socially constructive collective mentalizing, and live within collective distrust; a positive experience of collective mentalizing can be transformative for them. In collective mentalizing we tend to be influenced by others, which may of course be a bad thing in some contexts, but in this intervention it is encouraged so that no single perspective is allowed to dominate; rather, a process of developing a shared perspective is given priority. Taking the perspective of others and understanding their minds, adjusting the interaction gradually to a mutual understanding, and then creating a shared reality are the key elements. Together, these processes form robust affiliative and trusting relational bonds, which are at the core of social cohesion but are so often lacking for patients in MBT.

Engendering these processes can be viewed as a stepwise procedure, but of course when the intervention is used skillfully there will be no obvious structure and only a natural human interactive process.

1. **Create a situation in which two patients are interacting and focusing on a problem.** This emerges naturally after the clinician has appointed the two main protagonists to start the discussion.
2. **Involve a third person to act as the commentator and questioner on the problem in focus.** This is the initial triangulation. This person is not encouraged to talk about their own problems at this point, but is tasked with supporting the elaboration of the problem areas under scrutiny by the protagonists, using a not-knowing stance.
3. **Other patients may also be included in the discussion of the problem in focus**—this creates a "four-or-more-way" interaction.
4. **Once the problem has been elaborated, the whole group then talks together** about what they have learned from the two patients who were the initial protagonists of the discussion; this is the final phase of collective mentalizing. What do they take for themselves, individually? What can we (as a group) get out of this together and then take home to use in our life outside treatment?

The initial step helps the two protagonists to begin to develop alternative perspectives about their problem area, seeing it from a new angle and in more detail. The third person is then introduced and guided by the clinician to take a not-knowing stance (in which they have been trained during the MBT-I group), and is prevented from giving the protagonists advice or telling them what to do. The aim of the fourth and final step is to stimulate learning in the other patients who have observed the process and listened to the discussion. In order to achieve a shared understanding, it is necessary to attune one's own view toward another's views with the overarching goal of affiliative motivation toward this person. Although patients with personality disorders commonly appear to lack this motivation, there is no doubt that it is not far beneath the surface, pushing to get out. The evidence indicates that from infancy onward individuals need to share their inner states (beliefs, goals, thoughts, and feelings) and build a shared mind (or common goal), but trauma and persistent distrust in the world get in the way. Therefore triangulation and "four-or-more-way" interaction become a primary goal in MBT-G. There is nothing like rehearsal and repetition for learning, and so repeating these four steps of triangulation and four-or-more-way interaction envelops the exploration of problems in MBT-G.

Clinical Example: Triangulation

Clinician: Perhaps if Stanley and Sarah start and you, John, ask them questions as they go along. We will then chip in to try to follow from your points of view. Afterwards we will have a brainstorm about what we have learned for ourselves.

Sarah: Stanley, you go first.

Stanley: OK. I had an argument with my girlfriend and she is now frightened to come home. I told her that I have calmed down but she does not believe me.

Sarah: What happened?

Stanley describes a brutal argument he had with his partner as she was going out with a friend and he did not want her to.

Sarah: She shouldn't have gone then, if you felt so strongly about it.

Clinician: Hang on. That is a comment on her, Sarah, and we are trying to work out what has been going on in Stanley's mind.

Sarah: Oh, OK then. What was so important, why didn't you want her to?

Stanley: I think she was only going out because I didn't want her to and she knew that.

Sarah: What is the difficulty for you that she wants to?

Stanley: We are a couple and she should ask me.

John: Is that how you are together—you in charge of what she does?

Stanley: Yes, our relationship works like that.

Cora: For whom? (*Adding a slightly challenging four-way intervention without any prompting from the clinician.*)

After some further discussion, the clinician moves the discussion to the final step.

Clinician: Let's all talk together about what we are learning from this about how we manage our own relationships.

Cora: It makes me think about how much I try to control what happens in a relationship. Stanley likes to be in control and I can see that I quite like to have that, too. I'm not sure why though. I suppose it is because I get anxious that my partner doesn't like me or something or might meet someone else. Not very confident, I suppose.

Stanley: Yes, that is right for me, although I am confident. I just think she might meet someone else and prefer them.

Cora: What is it about you that she doesn't like, then?

Sarah: Do you ask her all the time if she loves you? That is what I do, as you know. I always think my boyfriend likes other people more than me.

The group has returned to the triangulation four-or-more-way interaction, which is perfect for further exploration, and the clinician now only needs to monitor the conversation, checking that it is in "mentalizing mode" and that interactions do not trigger low mentalizing. However, the clinician will eventually return to the final step of the intervention, ensuring that there is discussion about what the group as a whole has learned from each individual perspective.

Role Play and Exercises

MBT is permissive in terms of interventions as long as they are in the service of stimulating mentalizing and increasing mental flexibility within social and personal relationships. In running MBT-G, the clinician constantly follows the principal aim of stimulating a mentalizing culture. Although role plays and exercises are a vehicle for explicit mentalizing process and observational examples, the purpose of using them in MBT-G is to instill over time an implicit, intuitive understanding of internal states that supports the creation of a mentalizing group and facilitates personal mentalizing in social interactions. The patients then have a chance of repositioning themselves in their own social worlds outside the group. There is a constant tension in MBT between the clinician teaching without being a teacher and generating a culture for patients to learn without being "told" and "educated." Patients do not want to feel that they are in a classroom, and yet there has to be a route to embedding intuitive understanding in mental function. This is in part achieved by incorporating explicit understanding and learning into implicit processing. In MBT we assume that in any successful social interaction the balance between implicit and explicit processing is optimal, so rehearsing this effectively in the group on a regular basis is warranted. To achieve this aim, occasional role plays are especially useful in MBT-G. Above all, when they work well, they encourage perspective taking within an atmosphere of playfulness (see [4]).

Many MBT groups have two clinicians, and it is instructive for patients if the clinicians are the main players in mini role plays. This is a technique commonly used in the MBT-I group to emphasize some key points—for example, for illustrating poor mentalizing or how to take a not-knowing stance. In MBT-G, mini role plays are less frequent but can nevertheless be useful. The clinician can perhaps invert the roles and "become" the patient while one of the members of the group becomes the clinician. This inverted role play can be started by the clinician stating: "*Imagine that I am you, Sarah, and you are me. I am telling you how I feel, and you, as the therapist, will respond to what I am saying.*" This technique makes use of the curated temporary loss of self-mentalizing; the real patient is now someone else (the clinician), and is freed from their own concerns about how the other person's views affect and challenge their self-perception. Patients become the other person momentarily, forgetting themselves. Working in this way allows individuals to assume a meta-perspective, freeing them from themselves to look at themselves. At the same time, the other patients who are observing can also reflect on what they have observed (step 4 of the triangulation process described earlier), with the clinician returning to their own role and asking them to report on what they have observed and learned for themselves from the role play.

Role plays can also be used to explore problematic interchanges between patients, or between the clinician and patients. Here the clinician manages the mentalizing process (see Chapter 4) and presses the pause button, rewinds the discussion if possible, and initially addresses non-mentalizing modes. Once calm has been restored and mentalizing is stable in most of the participants, a role play can be established that replays the argument, but with the patients who are involved changing chairs and "being" the other person. This exercise usually proves challenging, and the patients may refuse to take part. In this situation it is best to manage the low mentalizing at the time and then revisit the interpersonal problem later, perhaps in a subsequent group session. Therefore the clinician:

1. names and notes the interaction and the main protagonists
2. summarizes the problem at the end of the session
3. re-presents the problem in the next group session.

However, if the current level of mentalizing in the participants and the atmosphere and the overall culture of the group allows, the clinician can suggest that they "replay" the argument, but with interchanged roles following the procedures for triangulation and four-or-more-way interaction. The protagonists are asked to change seats and to "be" the other person, with each having to use the attitude and precise words that the other had delivered previously, which had triggered the problem. If possible, it is best for each person to say aloud what they think was going on in the mind of the person they are role playing before the incident: "*John, you are now Stanley. Can you talk as Stanley before this happened, saying aloud what is going on in your mind? How were you, Stanley, before this happened* (the clinician looks at John, who is playing Stanley)*? What sort of things were you thinking about?*" This encourages everyone in the group to consider personal mental context as having a significant influence on an individual's current sensitivity and reactivity to others in the group.

Closure

A short period of time for closure of each group session, around 10–15 minutes, is recommended. This is a phase of consolidation of what has been learned in the session and how it can be translated usefully into everyday life, what themes were relevant to social relationships, what remains unaddressed, and how the group will take any issues forward. The outcome of this discussion forms the main body of the summary of the session that is written by the clinician ready for the following week's session.

Clinical Example: Closure of the Group Session

Clinician: So, let's think about all the things we have talked about today. What comes across to me is the uncertainty we all have about who is in control of a relationship and how that can interfere with what we want.

Sarah: Yes, I feel completely out of control of all my relationships except with my son. His father is a nightmare, and I worry all the time that he will report me so I try not to be difficult with him; my current partner is really nice but I nag at him about how much he loves me and I am so dependent it frightens me.

Stanley: I am in control but I have to listen to you all because it is messing up my relationship and my girlfriend doesn't need to be frightened of me. Maybe I will try to say sorry to her.

Clinician: Yes, see how that goes. You have to really mean it, though. Is there something in all our discussion about whether we value ourselves as well? Stanley, you talked about feeling small when your girlfriend did what she wanted and went out. I am not sure we have got to the bottom of that. Can you have a think about it and we can bring it back next week?

There was further discussion about whether men were naturally in charge of any relationship. There were indications that the group members were organizing this discussion in pretend mode, with generalization to society and the patients concluding that this imbalance was normal in a relationship, as men were stronger than women. Sarah in particular seemed to defer to this view: *"I think that is right and I feel better when it is like that."* This discussion, elaborated in pretend mode, was challenged by the clinician:

Clinician: Hang on. That is very convenient. So we don't have to concern ourselves with the issue, I suppose? We have just been considering how you, Stanley, feel weak and that is the problem. Sarah, we also discussed your insecurity within yourself and difficulty in knowing what you want as the main issue. So let's not get away from how much we are contributing to the balance, or lack of it, in our relationships. I am going to write it down for next week: *"Who am I when I am with someone else?"* We can start there.

The clinician is now beginning to note the theme of "vulnerable self," and he writes this up on the Values Sheet. Sarah has a fragile experience of herself, especially when she is with others. Stanley has a more self-serving view of himself as the most important player in any relationship. Cora is more secure in her self-experience. Later, the other patients in the group will be asked to consider themselves in the light of this theme, as in step 4 of triangulation.

Virtual and Digital Health: Online MBT

There is increasing interest in the delivery of MBT through telehealth (i.e., online). Although this might seem straightforward for individual sessions, it is more problematic for groups. In this section we shall discuss some aspects of group and individual work that are relevant to translating MBT from a face-to-face treatment to a clinician-led online format.

The time-honored method of delivering psychological treatments has remained more or less unchanged since the inception of psychotherapy. In group or individual therapy, patients attend a consulting room at a particular time and meet a clinician face to face. MBT is no exception to this arrangement. Sitting in a circle as a group, or at a slight angle to each other in individual sessions, the patient(s) and clinician create a physical setting that is insulated as far as possible from the distractions of external reality, to create conditions in which to explore the patient's internal states of mind, engage in exercises, or practice skills in order to reduce their distress and improve their mental health. The setting establishes an almost "virtual reality," created by the clinician and the patient(s), in which they have a shared world in which physical reality symbolizes the mental reality of "we-mode" functioning (see Chapter 2). Unsurprisingly, this cosy model has come under scrutiny, challenged by the development of new technologies and factors such as infection control in the earlier phases of the COVID-19 pandemic, when social isolation of the population was mandated by governments around the world, and face-to-face meetings were limited. More significant are the changing styles of social interaction, which are making virtual interaction the "new normal." Young people in particular may communicate more through text chat and social networking sites than they do in person; others may inhabit their own fantasy worlds in cyberspace, living parallel lives as different characters; computer games become more real than the "real world," which is experienced as alien and uncomfortable. The conventional boundaries and channels of communication between the internal world and the external world are blurred. Virtual worlds sometimes feel safer and more manageable than daily reality. As a consequence of all these changes, MBT is also now offered remotely. Remote interventions were already being used in "traditional" MBT at times of crisis, via telephone, email, or text messages, but the whole treatment program can be conducted online with nearly all of the sessions taking place remotely.

The move to online treatment has some immediate advantages in terms of patient access, which is no longer limited by geographical distance and problems with travel. Many patients prefer the easy access offered by online treatment, and anecdotal evidence suggests that attendance rates for online MBT groups are higher than those for in-person groups. Patients can join from home and can be provided with secure links to access the treatment sessions, and, if they prefer, they can remain relatively anonymous. However, some patients may not have access to a computer or smartphone or an adequate internet connection, limiting their opportunity to take part in sessions. Providers of online psychological treatments (and indeed all telehealth services) need to offer practical ways to address these problems so that online/remote treatment is accessible and practicable for everyone. Psychological vulnerability may also influence the uptake of online treatments. Vulnerable participants may find it difficult to engage with digital content; for these patients, it may be helpful to provide some initial face-to-face sessions that offer preparatory support and information. Patients with BPD are often relationship/treatment seeking [5] and want human contact, so they may prefer face-to-face meetings and refuse online treatment, although in the authors' current experience this is rare.

Once the practical considerations have been addressed, the question arises of how, if at all, the format of delivery influences the delivery of interventions that facilitate the development of robust mentalizing. Here we provide a few suggestions about transferring face-to-face MBT to a remotely delivered program. This format of treatment will be the subject of future research.

Assessment and Formulation

Some MBT clinicians prefer to complete the assessment and formulation stage of MBT face to face. The clinician who completes the assessment phase is the primary clinician for the patient's subsequent treatment. Initial face-to-face meetings allow all practical concerns to be addressed, as well as the development of a more personal relationship between the patient and the clinician so that they have a physically embodied subjective experience of each other. The "feel" of having another person in the room can help the development of a therapeutic alliance and support the collaborative construction of a personalized MBT formulation. Necessarily, the patient and clinician discuss problems and anxieties about treatment, and "rehearse" the beginning of the group sessions that the patient will join. In practical terms, the patient can also be given a tutorial on negotiating the platform on which online materials are stored (e.g., the materials for MBT-I; see Chapter 4), and treatment will be offered.

Qualitative feedback suggests that crisis planning is also better done in person. Clinicians use considerable subjective experience in their assessment of risk—for example, taking into account their own level of anxiety about a patient's suicidality—and this feels more substantial and accessible to them in face-to-face meetings.

MBT-I Online

The online MBT-I group is run by two clinicians and follows the same structure as the in-person group (see Chapter 4). In the first session, the patients introduce themselves and present some of their relational passport (described earlier in this chapter), which has been rehearsed with the assessing clinician in the initial assessment phase. Before this somewhat exposing beginning, an "icebreaker" is used (as will be described shortly) with discussion about the problems that come with meeting online. Group principles are agreed and decisions taken about whether participants will have their cameras on or off, how to manage any patients who feel unable to look at themselves on screen (the patient can be advised to use the Hide Self View option if this is available, or to place a sticky note on their laptop screen to cover their image, which some patients find useful), and how to leave the group if this becomes necessary (the patient can interrupt with their hand raised or put a message in the chat saying "I need to move to a breakout room"; the clinician then moves the patient to another virtual room and joins them to assess the situation).

Patients are given access to the material for each group session in advance of the session, and are encouraged to read it ahead of time so that they are in a position to question the clinician about the material as it is discussed. Exercises in online MBT-I are used in the same way as in face-to-face sessions. The clinician can use a range of features and tools to make things easier for the patients during online sessions.

- Use icebreakers for the group, such as "animal masks" (the avatars and virtual masks that are features of some online platforms, e.g., Zoom). The clinician and each of the patients choose a mask and put it on. Led by the clinician, the patients have to say what they think each person's choice of mask says about the person. The patient then talks about why they have chosen the mask.
- Divide the group into two breakout rooms, each with a clinician. The groups discuss the topic of the session and then each group reports back to the main room about their discussion.
- Share the clinician's screen for showing materials and for creating them (e.g., a list of the agreed group values) in the course of the group session.
- Show the patients some aspects of the room in which the clinician is sitting, and explain their origins and meaning. Ask the patients to choose one or two objects in their room that they feel able to talk about.
- Use breakout rooms to take a participant out of the main group if they become anxious or at risk. One clinician goes with that patient to talk to them privately while the other clinician continues with the group.
- Use the chat facility to allow patients to note down their thoughts while others are talking; some patients may be hesitant to interrupt and assert themselves verbally, and find using the chat easier.
- Online materials can be made available for the patients week by week, as well as some guided self-help content.
- Online video/tasks related to topics, such as film clips or role plays, can be used.

MBT-G Online

Once the practicalities have been worked out, the initial sessions focus on how mentalizing each other "on screen" can be enhanced. In groups, mentalizing of others occurs more reliably if all of the participants can be seen on a single screen. In those groups that use a structured discussion of problems after going around the participants at the beginning of the group, or those that give patients a particular task (for an example of this type of work with patients with trauma, see Chapter 11), the clinicians spotlight themselves and the person who is presenting their problem for discussion; the others become the viewers and can gain more detailed information about the person's mental state from their facial expression and body posture. Patients are asked to be as expressive as they can when talking online, because it can be much harder for the other participants to read facial expressions and eye movements on screen than in person.

Early in the formation of the group, practicing mentalizing others' inner states interactively using exaggerated facial expressions (e.g., happy/sad/angry faces) can help to ease anxieties—for example, the clinician playfully makes a face and the patients have to say what emotion is being expressed. A range of exercises will already have been used in MBT-I, and these can be repeated as role plays between the clinicians to illustrate the importance of looking at each other online—for example, one clinician makes a sad face and the other clinician has to take a not-knowing stance as they explore the underlying mental states.

In the exploratory phase of MBT groups, clinicians need to maintain the interest of all participants and be especially sensitive to frustrations arising from the online format. A patient who has continual problems with their computer or internet connection may dominate a group, dropping in and out and causing interruptions and irritation to the rest of the group. A patient who is at risk may suddenly leave the group, causing anxiety in the clinician and perhaps in other patients who might demand that the clinician "does something." In such situations it is best to have a pre-arranged plan of action agreed with all patients about what will happen—for example, the clinician will contact the patient at the end of the group, and the patient agrees to answer a telephone call.

Exercises between all of the participants may be used more often. For example, when working on the values of the group or thinking about a particular patient's problem, the group can be divided into two using random allocation of participants, with each group then being placed, with one of the clinicians, in a separate breakout room to discuss the problem.

In the previous clinical example in this chapter, Sarah recognizes that she has an issue with being out of control in her relationships, and Stanley is aware that he has an issue with over-control. Let us explore how this issue might be tackled in the next session, which is taking place online.

Clinical Example: Mentalizing Exercise

Clinician: Let's do more work on this issue about control in relationships. Perhaps each of us needs to consider whether we are under- or over-controlling in our relationships, like Sarah and Stanley have done. Then we can think together with Sarah about managing her feeling of being out of control.

Clinician: (*turning to Stanley*) Stanley, we can do the same later with you about having too much control.

Clinician: We will divide into two groups and go to different rooms. I will be in one and my colleague will be in the other, and we can see what we can come up with. Sarah, you join one of the groups and you can change halfway through, just as we normally do, if you like.

Clinician: So, think about ourselves first and then how we might manage our relationships when we feel out of control. Remember, we are not trying to come up with practical advice for Sarah. We want to think about ourselves in terms of being under- or over-controlled and then think about how that helps us understand the struggle Sarah is having.

After the discussions in the breakout rooms, the two subgroups then report back to each other. This process facilitates interaction and discussion between members, with the aim of engendering "we-mode" function within the whole group. The subgroups engage in a shared activity, talking together about a problem that is not theirs. In effect they are sharing their thoughts, feelings, and impressions with a subgroup of a social system (the whole group), collaborating and then repositioning themselves back into the whole group, which subsequently collaborates to join up the subgroup experiences and embed them within the larger group. This creates a perspective that is similar to but not the same as the point of view of either of the subgroups, and hopefully is one around which all of the participants can organize to support Sarah.

In all MBT groups the clinician(s) and patients review the themes of the session and reflect on what has been discussed and learned toward the end of each weekly session. This forms the basis of the summary to be presented at the start of the next session. In online treatment, the summary is routinely emailed to all of the participants before being recorded in the patients' notes. The aims of emailing the summary are to encourage further reflection by the patients on the material discussed, to establish continuity of the digital format between group sessions, and to maintain transparency about the clinician's thoughts and impressions about the group process. An emailed summary can also be used after face-to-face group sessions to maintain continuity between sessions and encourage self-reflection, and many MBT clinicians now do this.

MBT Individual Therapy Online

Individual sessions online are to some extent less complex than group sessions and require only limited alteration. Some patients, perhaps those with avoidant attachment strategies, become more comfortable and find it easier to talk online than when meeting in person. In contrast, those who are anxious and ambivalent can find online sessions more difficult, and cannot easily use the relationship with the clinician to soothe their anxieties. The MBT clinician has to appraise the patient's level of anxiety carefully and use the digital interface to create a more comfortable interaction. To do this, the clinician identifies early in treatment the "elephant in the room" (see Chapter 4) that is created by the online format, and immediately tries to characterize it by verbalizing the anxieties that interfere with the patient–clinician relationship. As with all "elephants," the clinician's own anxieties are also specified. Clinicians may find working online more problematic than working face to face and feel uncomfortable themselves: "*I find it difficult to see myself all the time as well, especially when I think I look so old. What is it like for you looking at yourself? How shall we address this?*"

Using anxieties and problems related to the virtual format to share experiences supports relational mentalizing and the creation of a "virtual we-mode." The clinician and the patient talk together about the limitations of the format and how meeting online is not the same as meeting in person: "*What do you feel is missing? What seems easier?*" Taking a not-knowing stance to address these concerns makes relational mentalizing more of a natural conversation and less subjectively intense than in person. Nevertheless, the dangers that accompany relational mentalizing, such as triggering pretend mode, are as relevant during online sessions as they are in face-to-face interactions. Clinicians need to take care not to attribute things to the patient's psychological problems when they are really to do with the interface and, conversely, not to put things down to the online format when they are in fact relevant to the patient's problems. Those patients who have problems connecting online on a regular basis may be those who would also find it difficult to arrive on time for meetings in person, and this problem needs sensitive exploration. Others may have a limited understanding of computer/smartphone function and become frustrated as they experience a sense of alienation and cannot get the help they need. Rather than working immediately on their alienation, it might be best initially to give them some coaching sessions on the platform that is being used for the therapy sessions.

Concluding Remarks

The MBT group is a practice ground for mentalizing with others. The clinician is an integral part of the group and an active participant, who has authority for managing the group but without being authoritarian. In keeping with the principles of MBT, there is a level of equality between patients and clinicians in terms of sharing mental states, and so the clinician is *in* the group rather than on the edge commenting *on* the group. Taking a not-knowing stance to stimulate exploration and using organized interactions between participants encourages all of the group members to play a part. Clinician-led exercises may be used to facilitate this, and when working online these are particularly important for embedding the active participation of all group members as part of the group culture. The importance of generating group values that are carried forward by the group over time cannot be overstated. Learning from others in constructive social interactions requires a level of epistemic trust between people that can only be engendered if there is a shared culture created by everyone who takes part.

References

1. Karterud S. *Mentalization-Based Group Therapy (MBT-G): A Theoretical, Clinical, and Research Manual.* Oxford, UK: Oxford University Press, 2015.
2. Bateman A, Kongerslev M, Hansen SB. Group therapy for adults and adolescents. In: Bateman A, Fonagy P, eds. *Handbook of Mentalizing in Mental Health Practice*, 2nd ed. Washington, DC: American Psychiatric Association Publishing, 2019; 117–33.
3. Bateman A, Fonagy P. *Mentalization-Based Treatment for Personality Disorders: A Practical Guide.* Oxford, UK: Oxford University Press, 2016.
4. Asen E, Fonagy P. *Mentalization-Based Treatment with Families.* New York, NY: The Guilford Press, 2021.
5. Tyrer P, Mitchard S, Methuen C, Ranger M. Treatment rejecting and treatment seeking personality disorders: Type R and Type S. *J Pers Disord* 2003; **17**: 263–8.

Part III

Application and Adaptations for Mental Health Presentations

Chapter 6

Narcissistic Personality Disorder

Introduction

Clinicians have become increasingly interested in narcissistic personality functioning (NPF). Perhaps this is just as well given the earlier threats from the DSM and ICD-11 work groups on personality disorder to remove narcissistic personality disorder (NPD) from categorical classifications due to the lack of research into the condition [1,2]. Taking a mentalizing approach transcends the issue of category, as it requires the clinician to assess personality in terms of the dimensional domains of mentalizing, rather than to establish the presence or absence of specific descriptive characteristics. The details of the (im)balance of dimensional components that may be creating disruption to the patient's social experience form the center of a more personalized evaluation. Our general preference is to avoid labeling where possible and to refer to process and action. Therefore, in this chapter, for much of the time we refer to NPF, narcissistic functioning, or simply narcissism, rather than NPD. However, being somewhat inconsistent, we also refer to mentalization-based treatment (MBT) for NPD (MBT-NPD) to indicate that treating patients with high levels of narcissism requires modification of the original MBT protocol, which was developed to treat patients with borderline personality disorder (BPD).

In many ways the mentalizing approach aligns with a common-sense approach often found in everyday life, where people describe a range of attributes of narcissism when talking about people they know. Individuals are described in characteristic ways—for example, "*full of themselves,*" "*only thinks of himself,*" "*she thinks that she is better than everyone else,*" "*He is a show-off, bumptious.*" The emphasis is on the person's heightened self-regard and self-image—for example, "*They are all self, self, self, with no consideration of others.*" There is perhaps excess focus on feeling and looking good, in order to impress and be admired by others. Then there are those who show different aspects of narcissism, described as "*somewhat too perfectionistic*" or "*too meticulous*"—they spend an excessive amount of time working on getting something "right," being over-particular, and trying to meet mysterious unachievable standards, only to collapse in a heap and become unable to function when they fail. There is an essential flaw to all this self-obsession, which becomes apparent when extreme sensitivity to criticism (real or perceived) leads to reactivity and defensiveness because it activates the threat of humiliation. Even violence can be used to manage this risk.

The disparate aspects of everyday narcissism have one thing in common—they all relate to self-esteem and its management. Mentalizing is the manager of self-esteem. In short, healthy narcissism is the internal management of self-regard and public image through effective mentalizing. If psychic equivalence, pretend mode, or teleological thinking (described in Chapter 2) start to emerge in relation to how understanding action is experienced in self and other, the potential for distorted self-evaluation increases. To manage self-regard and public image well, we need not only a stable self-experience but also an ability to use external factors and relationships appropriately to augment our self-esteem while simultaneously reducing threats that might diminish our positive sense of ourselves. Ineffective mentalizing undermines these processes. Managing the social environment in a manipulative teleological mode undermines social relationships. Interpreting comments or actions by others excessively concretely, in psychic equivalence, makes the person vulnerable to feeling criticized and devalued. By contrast, detaching from social experience in pretend mode can exaggerate self-worth and may increase the risk of grandiosity. Effective mentalizing addresses the reactions of others with curiosity, does not accept an initial reaction in either the other or the self as real and definitive but as momentary and liable to change, and, most importantly, is always cautious in relation to black-and-white thinking, and addresses even positive evaluations with humility and judicious balance. When ineffective mentalizing dominates, these healthy narcissistic processes are compromised, the balance of effective mentalizing is disrupted by over- or underuse of a particular aspect, and natural self-protective narcissism begins to interfere with intimate relationships with others and distorts social interactions. In the next section (Assessment and Formulation) we shall describe how this can happen.

Before doing this, we wish to inject a little cautious (mentalizing) humility. We recognize that MBT is following a long line of therapies and therapists that have tackled this issue, perhaps better and more effectively than how we suggest here. Our aim is not to try to rival alternative approaches to supporting individuals who find themselves struggling with low self-worth or exaggerated self-importance. It is merely to place a selection of ideas and techniques presented by many brilliant clinical minds in the context of an MBT formulation and treatment. Along with many who offer such support, we also believe that when implementing the mentalizing model in clinical practice it is useful to think about grandiose and vulnerable narcissism, also known as thick- and thin-skinned narcissism, respectively. The characteristics of the grandiose type have been well described in the literature, and are summarized in Box 6.1.

Box 6.1 Characteristics of individuals with grandiose narcissism.

- Have an exaggerated sense of self-importance.
- Have a sense of entitlement and require constant, excessive admiration.
- Believe that they are superior and can only associate with equally special people (e.g., need to be treated by the head of the clinic).
- Expect to be recognized as superior even without obvious achievements.
- Exaggerate their achievements and talents.
- Are preoccupied with fantasies about success, power, brilliance, beauty, or the perfect partner.
- Monopolize conversations and belittle people whom they perceive as inferior or a threat.
- Expect special favors and unquestioning compliance with their expectations/opinions.
- Take advantage of others to get what they want.
- Lack empathy.
- Are envious of others and believe that others envy them.
- Behave in an arrogant or haughty manner, coming across as conceited, boastful, and pretentious.

Many authors believe that these characteristics serve to cover profound feelings of insecurity and shame and to keep at bay a pervasive sense of inadequacy. Whatever the merits of this view, the excessive self-regard can become habit forming, "structured into the personality," with little hint of the turbulent waters beneath. Other patients show a mix of characteristics and are not stable in either their grandiosity or their vulnerability. Some patients are persistently fragile—this is the person whose experience is dominated by vulnerable narcissistic function, who may be almost unrelentingly shy, avoidant, needy, hypervigilant, and sensitive to others' regard, and whose fragile self-esteem needs continual top-ups of admiration from others. In all of these presentations the MBT clinician will readily find the hallmarks of inadequate mentalizing. Social interactions become dangerous if psychic equivalence dominates, and comments that are possible to interpret as criticism are immediately represented as permanent and as unchangeable as physical reality. It is hardly surprising that hypersensitivity is the consequence. By the same token, in psychic equivalence, imagining oneself to possess exceptional capabilities is as good as actually having them. This impression can, of course, be bolstered by teleological thinking and organizing those around the individual to act toward them in a way that confirms their imagined exceptional talent. Pretend mode removes the tethering that physical reality normally imposes on thoughts and feelings about what others are actually experiencing, which means that claims can be made about being loved, admired, and appreciated without the usual requisite evidence for this in others' behavior.

Although this presentation is not hard to understand or interpret in terms of inadequate mentalizing, it creates challenges for the direct application of the techniques that we have considered thus far in this book. The complexity of the presentation creates a range of difficulties for the clinician, necessitating some modifications to the MBT clinical model, which are the subject of this chapter. However, the most important point to make is that the backbone of the MBT structure remains the same—assessment of mentalizing, formulation in terms of long-term problems in mentalizing, socializing the patient to the MBT model, an intervention process that aims to repair ineffective mentalizing, and ending the process in the way that is most likely to ensure long-term change.

Assessment and Formulation

Unsurprisingly, assessment of self-function and other representation take priority, although all of the other components of MBT assessment and formulation are also required (see Chapter 4). The compassionate and non-judgmental stance of MBT is an absolute requirement during assessment of narcissistic functioning. Enquiry is framed throughout to give credibility to the patient's explanations, to avoid challenging their narrative. Imagine how humiliating it is for individuals with high ideals and an over-valued idea of themselves to ask for help, or for those who feel particularly vulnerable and require admiration from others to feel misunderstood and unwanted by the very person they are coming to for help. A reaction to the shame experienced with the intensity of psychic equivalence is likely to blow therapy out of the water by activating the protective armor of the narcissism, with the clinician being accused of incompetence, inadequacy, and not being up to the job. Such explosive criticism can easily lead to formal complaints, a demand to see someone more senior and experienced, and similar time-consuming outcomes, all of which can be avoided with adequate clinician sensitivity and understanding of the complications of predominantly ineffective mentalizing.

When appraising the patient, the clinician is explicit about the aims of the assessment—that is, to develop a detailed mentalizing profile and evaluate how this impacts on the patient's life. In early iterations of mentalizing theory there were attempts to contrast the developmental origins of narcissistic and borderline function. It was suggested that in both conditions there had been a developmental insult arising from an imbalance in contingent marked mirroring from the caregiver. Vulnerability to borderline functioning arose from the caregiver providing congruent but unmarked mirroring, leading to an unstable self. In contrast, in narcissistic functioning the opposite was true, with the caregiver providing marked but incongruent mirroring, leading to a "not-me"/false self-structure [3]. If only life and development were so simple!

Yet the developmental perspective is a reminder that during assessment the clinician needs to explore the patient's social activity in order to understand whether their subjective experience is that others are providing adequately marked and contingent responses to their inner states of mind. In NPF we are more likely to find a person who is persistently at odds with what they experience as being reflected of them in interpersonal contexts. Non-contingent or incongruent reflection, which feels like a poor match to their subjective experience, will leave a person feeling that although the response might be about them, it does not fully or accurately reflect their subjective (emotional) self. In the absence of this match they are left feeling non-validated and, if their self-esteem is particularly low, invalidated. The incongruence or mismatch therefore engenders emptiness and a lack of recognition of "true" feeling states, which is a hallmark of vulnerable narcissistic function. It also leads to isolation and loneliness in the socially interactive world.

This mismatch is experienced even if the reflection from others is positive. The essential part is the mismatch of inner state in the timing, valence, or intensity of reflection from others. Non-contingent parental overvaluation in place of a more nuanced evaluation of self may have the same effect. The child is seen as superior to others, more talented, special, and having the right to feel entitled. However, this is the parental belief about the child and not necessarily the child's constitutional self-experience, where the grounded sense of self is located. Therefore the feeling self remains unseen and an alien self develops (see Chapter 2) based on an overvalued but inaccurately mirrored self-experience, which can become dominant and more firmly established than the constitutional self.

Self and Other Mentalizing

The process of getting the patient to elaborate their self-experience can be difficult. It is not an easy task for patients to describe how they see themselves. This is an assessment of "I-mode" mentalizing. A direct question such as "*What sort of person are you?*" or "*How would you describe yourself to others?*" may work, but requires adequate metacognitive capacity to be meaningful. Adding examples of personality characteristics can help: "*Are you a confident person or reticent when with others?*" followed by "*Can you give an example?*" Alternatively, the clinician can use a personality descriptor word chart with a range of descriptors to be indicated by the patient, or the patient can be asked to complete a structured questionnaire to focus the discussion. For some patients, asking them to describe how others see them can be even more perplexing. This is an assessment of "me-mode" (self-as-object) mentalizing. Listen carefully for a sense that other people fail to appreciate them or to see them as they see themselves. If this elaboration creates disquiet, frustration, and anger rather than curiosity, self-reflection, and perhaps self-deprecating acceptance—"*what it is to live a life being unappreciated!*"—the clinician should consider underlying narcissistic functioning.

Context of Narcissistic Activation

Appraising the vulnerabilities of a patient to the activation of narcissistic processes requires exploration of the circumstances in which they expect to be valued by others only to find that people do not respond in the anticipated manner. Such triggers are commonly relational, so the clinician asks specifically about different social and relational contexts and is alert to how ineffective mentalizing contributes to feelings of disappointment.

Clinical Examples: Relational Activation of Narcissism

You were really quite sensitive to them and noticed how they did not seem to be appreciating how much you had done and how well you had done it. Tell me more about that. Can you explain what it was in their reaction that made you realize that they didn't appreciate your efforts? (*Relational activation.*)

You spend a lot of time fighting injustice and you often seem to see this going on even when the person directly affected has not noticed. You say you want to show up the exploiters for what they really are and show them that what they are doing is wrong. It is clearly important, but can you tell me a little about how you see your role in this? (*Relational and vicarious mentalizing; inflating self-esteem through superiority to others.*)

It really deeply upsets you when you see someone being taken advantage of and they do not react. It is great that you are able to take up so many causes for other people, but how does it affect you? (*Relational; automatic mentalizing with self-experience overlapping with other experience.*)

You tell me that not managing something even though you know that it was really difficult can nag and nag at you and you start feeling that you're a failure. Let's explore the expectations you have about yourself a little. (*Vulnerable narcissism activated by self-expectation and out of line with reality.*)

Other triggers generated by ineffective mentalizing may be related to the "how" of everyday interaction—for example, perceived criticism from others, arguments, being left out of decision making, or being ignored by people of importance at work or in social situations are interpreted as disparaging and harmful to the self. Details of the style of interaction may be necessary in order to get a sense of where the patient's mentalizing is ineffective. The clinician needs to probe about conflict and sensitive reactions.

Sometimes the problems in interactions are more subtle. In smooth everyday interactions, conversations move along easily, with the participants' dialogue being automatically aligned with each other. Gaps between turns are only milliseconds in duration, as each respondent predicts the completion of what the other is saying, often with an accuracy that is astonishing. They do so by mentalizing based on monitoring physical cues such as body movement, gestures, or tone of voice—the external focus of mentalizing—which allows them not to be solely reliant on content, but to be sensitive to flow and modulation. We automatically mentalize and, integrating with content, predict when the person is coming to the end of what they are saying, while balancing our focus on the other with the preparation of our own content. This smooth reciprocal process may be disrupted in NPF, as it may be in other personality disorders. In this mode, the individual is hypersensitive to others' interruptions and questions, yet fails to self-monitor, and expects others to listen to them constantly, ignoring cues and giving little time for the other person to interject. They may be hypersensitive to external cues, resulting in them reacting too quickly and before the other person has had their say. The final common pathway of ineffective mentalizing is the absence of reciprocity and the loss of the "dance" of a smooth interaction in communication. The clinician should look out for this in the interactive dialogue during the assessment phase, along with the sudden activation of dismissive strategies to manage the immediate interaction—for example, "*I am already aware of that,*" "*There is nothing new in what you are saying,*" "*I haven't come here to listen to some cod psychology,*" or "*This is rubbish.*"

Focus on Interactive Style in Grandiose/Thick-Skinned Narcissistic Function

Clinical Examples: Addressing Interactive Style

Hmm. You are certainly good at picking out the mistakes in what I say. Maybe you are right and I am wrong there, but help me a little—take me through how we got here.

It comes across that you are very certain about your views when talking with me and others. But let's take this last issue. Help me understand how you are so sure about this.

Would you say you were a person who enjoyed a good argument? Tell me about the argument you had with your friend? It sounds like it was quite engaging for both of you.

Do you often get into conflict at work/home/social events? Let's talk about the last time it happened.

What happens when there is tension between you and others? Are you able to carry on with other things? Are there times when you become rather preoccupied with it?

Or, more challengingly:

Wow, you are quick to pick up the weaknesses in someone's argument. Can you see their strengths at times?

Narcissistic Expectation and Disappointment

Collapse in narcissistic function is potentially extremely painful, and patients may seek treatment because they realize that their relationships are not working. An overwhelming sense of personal despair breaks in if they are unable to shore up their self-esteem by, for example, blaming someone else for their failure, or dismissing others summarily. The mental collapse can be sudden and dramatic, like that of Richard Cory in Edward Arlington Robinson's poem, who was looked up to by all and was "*admirably schooled in every grace*" and "*thought that he was everything, To make us wish that we were in his place*" [4]. He went home one night and "*put a bullet through his head.*" He was not what he seemed to be, and was a "me" as others saw him but had no central "I."

"Me" refers to the self-as-object, the self as defined by others' depictions, or rather these depictions are seen and felt but experienced "as if" they were the self—the "I" [5].

By definition the "me" is context dependent—it is, after all, a function of the immediate social environment, which is far from immutable to change, making self-experiences that originate from within the "me" inherently unstable. Like other approaches, MBT distinguishes the "me" from the "I," with the latter ideally being a coherent representation that results from the accumulated integration and synthesis of sensory information pertaining to the person through mentalizing. Over time this generates an embodied sense of personhood with continuous and stable contact with the surrounding world. Under optimal combinations of nature and nurture the "I" is coherent, robust, and stable. Of course a dominant "me"—a context-dependent self-experience—can certainly obscure and may eclipse "I" experiences. In circumstances that compromise the integration of the "I" (e.g., genetic vulnerability, adversity, deprivation), the "me" becomes the primary determinant of self-experience, leaving the individual, as in the case of Richard Cory, alone and suddenly encountering the emptiness of their existence.

Why is this distinction clinically important to bear in mind in relation to narcissistic function? The lesson for assessment and ongoing treatment in this context is that sudden changes in risk may not be preceded by the obvious warning signs that are more typical in people with BPD, who may become more and more emotionally dysregulated and demanding as their "I" is increasingly experienced as fragmented. In narcissistic function, the "I" can go from 100 to zero with shocking immediacy with (perceived) changes in interpersonal context.

The MBT clinician needs to get a picture of the patient's need for relationships, as much as the avoidance of them, by exploring examples from the patient's life of when personal expectations are met and when they are not met. This may expose the chinks and vulnerabilities in the armor of narcissistic function; it is the patient who needs to decide whether these are fault lines that need to be repaired. It is not easy for anyone to recognize their own weaknesses, so the vulnerabilities are best characterized as "exceptional sensitivities" so that the focus does not undermine the patient's self-esteem. Individuals who present with vulnerable thin-skinned narcissistic function, even more than most, may engage better and are more likely to open an epistemic channel for learning when feeling empathically validated than when directly challenged. In contrast, empathic validation in thick-skinned, grandiose narcissistic function will have little effect because the individual is impervious to others, having created a bubble of self-importance that isolates them. Individuals in that state experience little need of others' affective understanding of their mental states, and may themselves have over-recruited their cognitive processing systems in order to buttress their self-esteem independent of their immediate social context.

Elaborating Self-Expectation and Self-Devaluation in Thin-Skinned Narcissism

Thin-skinned narcissists require mental scaffolding and support. There are many ways to do this, and again the MBT clinician tries to address the style and process along with the content—"the how with the what."

Clinical Examples: "The How with the What"

You seem to be putting yourself down a little at the moment. What sort of expectations do you have about yourself in this context? Where do you think these come from?

When you told me that story you sounded like you believed you should have done better. Tell me of a time when you have done things as well as you had hoped.

You sound quite pleased with how they responded. Were you expecting that? Did it affect how you felt about yourself?

Wow! They seemed to have appreciated you. How has that affected you?

You have really sensitive antennae for how people say things, and especially if what they are saying is about you. It is quite hard picking up things so quickly. But perhaps you are not as sure as you appear to be, because you then seem to go over and over things in your mind working them out. Can you describe to me what happens and how your certainty turns to doubt?

Narcissism and Attachment Strategies

In keeping with the generic MBT model, the clinician explores the overarching attachment strategies that are commonly activated in the patient's relationships. In contrast to BPD, in which there is a hyperactivation of attachment processes, individuals with predominantly narcissistic function may disregard "chat about relationships" and actively derogate previous attachment experiences, for example, with their parents: "*My mother was a nobody. It is amazing that so many people turned up at her funeral;*" "*My father never managed to complete anything properly and I soon outgrew his ability to support me.*" Hypoactivation of attachment makes it difficult for the clinician to engage compassionately in a therapeutic and empathic manner, just as it does for others in the patient's life. Individuals with narcissistic function do not appear to wish to share their inner states with others, including the clinician. Self-reliance is given priority over need and dependence. Dismissive and secondary avoidant attachment processes, which are often activated in response to criticism or lack of appreciation, are commonly associated with narcissistic function, and this becomes apparent as relationships are explored. There may be elements of disorganization, too, with the patient presenting opposing states of mind about a relationship within a short time in the discourse. Lapses in reflective monitoring result in the contradictions passing unnoticed. Questioning by the clinician about the coherence of the narrative may lead the patient to become irritable, and perhaps even to say "*You have not been listening. What I said was . . .*" to justify their inconsistency. More reflective patients might take more responsibility and say "*Did I really? I wonder why I said that then if I did,*" but then slip into pretend mode: "*Perhaps my mind was on a different phase in the relationship I am describing.*"

Further evidence for dismissing strategies as part of narcissistic function (see also Box 6.2) may surface as relationships are elaborated and interactions are scrutinized in the sessions with the patient.

Box 6.2 What to look out for in dismissive attachment strategies.

- Denial of dependency and diminishing a need for help—the patient suggests that they need a few sessions *"just to clarify things."*
- Black-and-white thinking—derogation of some relationships and idealization of others.
- Overemphasis on personal strengths and achievements.
- Lack of coherence in descriptions of a relationship without elaboration: *"She was my closest friend;" "I could not talk to her."*

Box 6.2 *(cont.)*

- Dismissal of the clinician's perspectives that are not congruent with the patient's own perspectives.
- Direct diminishing of the clinician: *"Are you a professor? I have waited all this time to see you and what I get is this garbage. Is this it? A professor? You must be joking."*

Outcome of Assessment Process

In keeping with the core model (see Chapter 4) all of the information is integrated into an MBT formulation, which is written as a personalized and non-judgmental summary of the patient's mentalizing profile, their use of ineffective mentalizing modes, and descriptions of both problematic and effective relational processes. Most importantly, the clinician and the patient jointly agree the aims of treatment in some detail, and establish agreed priorities.

Clinical Example: James

James is 27 years old and currently unemployed, having been dismissed by his most recent employer for insulting and threatening behavior toward his line manager, who had suggested that a particular piece of work was inadequate and needed revision.

He presented complaining that he felt let down by others and that he did not *"suffer fools, like his boss, gladly,"* and it was this that had got him into trouble. He had read about MBT and thought he would explore the possibility of it being useful to him.

He started the assessment interview by asking the clinician about his qualifications, level of training, and expertise. The clinician was completely open about his training and expertise. James listened carefully and eventually responded by saying *"Well, I will reserve judgment for the time being."*

Clinician: So, get me up to speed about yourself.

James: I am aware that I am going to be difficult to help and that I need an expert rather than a beginner as I already have extensive understanding of psychology, both my own and others'.

Clinician: Yes, so tell me about your psychology as you have come to understand it, so I can get up to speed with how you see yourself.

The clinician places himself in a position of being educated in order to remain non-threatening. James's conceit may cover an easily awakened vulnerability, as suggested by his reaction to criticism from his employer. The initial assessment is not the time to confront established NPF. It is the time to evaluate mentalizing vulnerabilities and the balance of the patient's thin-skinned vulnerabilities and their thick-skinned armor.

James: Well, it all begins with my upbringing and my schooling.

James continued with an extensive report about his parental relationships and his adolescent friendships, which were all described as unimportant to him. The clinician's responses were exploratory, using the not-knowing stance of MBT, but framed to give credibility to James's explanations in order not to challenge his narrative. Establishing an alliance is the most important initial step if shared aims are to be established, and the essential element of this is that the patient experiences the clinician as attempting to see things from their point of view.

Clinician: So one challenge for us is to work out how you are going to manage others who do not have your abilities yet you have to work with them. I will note that down so that we can come back to it.

Clinician: What about how you get on with people in your social circle and people who you are particularly close to?

James: How long have you got? This is a complex and interesting story.

Clinician: We can take our time and always come back to it in our next meeting.

Again the clinician is being supportive and interested, and is making sure that he does not in any way diminish James's viewpoint about himself and his life.

After the next session, the clinician informed James that he was going to write something down to make sure that they were both building the same picture about treatment.

Clinician: I think the time has come when we need to write something down to see if we are both on the same page about the work that we have to do. I will have the first go at this so that you can think about it and let me know where I am getting it right and where I am going wrong. I will follow the MBT format so that you can decide if MBT is the right way forward for you.

The following week the clinician went through the clinical summary following the MBT format. He outlined James's complex story very briefly, and some of his vulnerabilities and achievements. Here the sections of the formulation related to James's use of the dimensions of mentalizing are reported, along with the focus on his relationship style and the problems that might arise in therapy.

Clinical Example: Extracts from James's Formulation

Mentalizing

Self and Other Experience

You have told me about how you see yourself and your ability to see things or understand them more quickly than others, and to some extent that is also the case with your psychological understanding. You are very sensitive to how others see you, and quite attentive to how they treat you. In particular you gave me a lot of examples of instances when people do not respect you enough. When you notice this, and you are quite alert to it, it can make you angry quite quickly. This happened at work recently. You blame them for what happened, and we discussed how you manage this sort of misunderstanding. We agreed that whatever the cause, the situation where others see you differently from how you see yourself was painful, and you wanted to be able to manage these situations better than simply getting angry about it.

Perhaps, in our work, we can focus on your sensitivity to others not appearing to see you as you see yourself. So, first, we can consider your own self-experience. I might therefore ask you a lot more about your reality and how mismatches occur between your sense of yourself and others' impression of you—why people can read you wrong—and also check out how you see people and if there are times when you also do not see what they present to you and about you so clearly. All of this will help us to help you cope with the differences between how you see yourself and how others tend to see you.

Cognitive and Affective Function

You are unusually well read about psychology and philosophy given that these are not your professions, and you are able to focus clearly on working out problems. We agreed that it was more difficult for you to think and talk about how you feel in almost all situations, and I suggested that you tended to ignore feelings, dismissing them as weak and unnecessary.

Perhaps, in our work together, we need to make sure that you are as good at identifying your own and others' feelings as you are at analyzing problems. So perhaps whenever we are talking about "content" we will also talk about your subjective feeling alongside that. What are you *aware of*, rather than what you *think*?

Automatic and Controlled Processing

We agreed that you found situations where you were not feeling in control as challenging. You listen carefully wherever you are and whoever you are with for comments that may be referring to you, and you work hard to work out what the relationship implications of these comments are. Although you are incredibly thoughtful about this, all the thinking makes it hard for you to relax into the interaction. Working things out can stop you being spontaneous, although you value that very much, too. You pointed out that when you are with me you have a constant monitoring in your own mind of whether I am saying something that indicates that I appreciate you or am criticizing you. I suggested in passing that this was hypermentalizing—overdoing the thinking. You found this idea interesting but you were not sure what to do with it.

In our work together, both of us will have to watch out for too much thinking and not enough living when being with others.

You spend a lot of time thinking about yourself and focusing on your own experience, and you deservedly enjoy the sense that you are important in your professional world. It is less helpful, though, when you become preoccupied with how others see you.

In our work together, there will be a tension about how much we focus on your own world and how much we consider others' worlds as different from yours. These differences can bring about a tension in you that leads to you becoming angry and reactive. Although you feel that is inevitable, we can both see that it would be better to find alternative ways of managing.

Finally, we worked out that your brain can go into overdrive and become rather "tram-like" and fixed along a specific line—*"people don't appreciate me"* and *"how is it that I become caught up with so many f***-wits?"* were a couple of examples. I suggested that this was "tram-crash" mode, as calling it "psychic equivalence mode" is unnecessarily jargonistic.

In our work together, when you are in tram-crash mode you understandably take action to avoid the crash. We need to find out in much more detail what leads to tram-crash mode if it is to be avoided.

Relationships

You talked openly about your preference for relationships in which are you are in charge. Your most recent relationship was with Amanda, whom you found hard to cope with; she often disagreed with you in front of others, which felt unacceptable. You decided that she was not for you, and you ended the relationship by phoning her and telling her that you were ending it and had decided not to see her again. When she tried to contact you to discuss it, you "ghosted" her.

This might be difficult for our therapy. I might disagree with you in the course of therapy, and that may lead you to want to end the relationship with me, too. As you have already said that you are monitoring me to see if I'm up to the job, the two of us seeing things differently might make things a little tense at times. Potentially you may decide that I am too stupid and it was not worth your while seeing me. It would be a shame if you were to simply phone me one day and say you are finishing. I am not asking you to commit to the full year of sessions, but perhaps we could have a pre-therapy agreement that if that happens we should have two sessions to review what has occurred. I would very much like to have that agreement at the outset.

Session Focus and Intervention in Narcissistic Personality Functioning

Modest changes to the basic MBT model described for treating patients with BPD are recommended in MBT-NPD/NPF. In patients with BPD there is a considerable focus on managing emotional dysregulation and hyperactivation of the attachment system and instability of self-function. In meeting grandiose narcissistic function in MBT there is more focus on establishing an alliance, probing the rigidity of self-structure and the formulaic representation of others in relation to self, and exploration of the denigration of attachment relationships. With patients with more vulnerable narcissism there has to be a considerable focus on the self-affirming needs of the relationship, with frequent empathic validation. The danger in this situation is of embedding dependency and interminable treatment. This can be guarded against by time-limited treatment and a gradual move from empathic–supportive interventions to challenge and a relational focus.

Whatever the mixture of narcissistic function, MBT promotes a safety-first ("do no harm") approach and the avoidance of iatrogenic interventions (for an outline of the interventions in MBT-NPD, see Box 6.3). MBT-NPD retains the usual MBT focus on strengthening mental-state representations, in this case largely focused on the mental states that underpin the self-representations and, later, self-as-object representations. The principle is to work on establishing clarity about the utility and strength of patients' "I-mode" function first, being empathically validating about their experience of themselves without challenge. Essentially this is a metacognitive, self-reflective process that is focused on generating increased coherence of the "I." Once the therapeutic alliance is robust, "me-mode"—which is a combination of first-order mentalizing of others and personal second-order representation systems that address the "how others see me" question—becomes the focus of the treatment. How the patient experiences being seen by others is key to both types of NPF, and the effective mentalizing of the other lies at the basis of this capacity, which may not be fully addressed without some challenge being introduced. This is followed by attempts to establish more detailed work in the "we-mode"—that is, relational mentalizing.

Box 6.3 Summary of MBT-NPD.

Assessment and Formulation

- Self and other mentalizing—detailed, and focused on self-image and self-esteem.
- Exploring the context of narcissistic activation.
- Narcissistic expectations and disappointments.
- Narcissistic attachment strategies.

Box 6.3 *(cont.)*

Intervention: From "I-Mode" to "Me-Mode" to "We-Mode"

Vulnerable Narcissism

- Empathic validation of and support for "I-mode."
- Affect focus (subdominant theme)—the patient's fears and clinician's anxieties are used as a step to focus on "me-mode" and "we-mode."
- Relational mentalizing—identification of anxious dependency.
- Counter-relational mentalizing—managing over-supportive/protective responses.
- Challenge—beware of this in the context of fragile "I."

Grandiose/Thick-Skinned Narcissism

- Empathic validation of "I-mode" but less support than in vulnerable narcissism.
- Affective narratives to target "me-mode."
- Affect focus—the patient's rigidity and conceit, and how these interfere with therapeutic work.
- Relational mentalizing—identification of dismissive attachment strategies.
- Counter-relational mentalizing—managing problematic responses by explicit identification and discussion.
- Challenge—sudden, robust, playful, and direct.

Supporting Narcissism to Establish an Alliance

The tone of James's formulation is highly supportive, and the wording of the formulation endeavors to take the constructive aspects of his self-aggrandizement by suggesting work on how he manages a world that is somewhat inferior to him. It is important that the clinician finds the aspects of the patient's self-appraisal that are accurate so that there is an authenticity to seeing things from the patient's perspective. It may be possible to build a therapeutic alliance by agreeing the working alliance, but the relational alliance can only come about if the patient experiences the clinician as being alongside them rather than imposing upon them. Therefore empathic validation is a key intervention in MBT-NPD. Self-exploration is necessary before any attempt is made to get the patient to meaningfully consider others' mind states in any mode other than psychic equivalence (assuming knowing). This can be problematic for the clinician, who may wish to ask questions about *why the patient thinks others behaved as they did*, only to find that the patient has no curiosity or interest in this (as they are convinced that they know). In addition, the clinician may find it hard to like a person with strong narcissistic characteristics and might even quite quickly become antagonistic to them, seeing them as insufferable and arrogant. Working with such dynamic responses too early in therapy will fracture a fragile alliance. The use of counter-relational responsiveness is therefore a more dominant feature later in treatment (see this chapter: Counter-Relational Mentalizing).

Probing Self-Structure and Relational Affect

Exploration of an experiential self is highlighted in the collaborative clinical agreement with James, who has already accepted that there will be reflection on his self-related feelings and beliefs. The most straightforward way to focus on this issue is to take a single episode in which there has been a clear mismatch between James's experience of himself and how others have treated him, building a detailed picture, identifying the differences, and reflecting on the affect and impressions of the interaction in its wider context.

Clinical Example: Exploration of an Experiential Self

The clinician and James decide to take the most recent "event," which had resulted in the loss of his job. Initially the discussion is about his experience during the event itself. This then needs to be extended to how he feels about himself now.

James: My intelligence is sharp and that is the main thing that set me apart from the people at work. They were stupid. I was useful to them until they realized that I was beyond them. They didn't like it as it showed them up for what they are.

Clinician: What are they?

James: Muppets.

Clinician: What was it like for you working with a bunch of muppets, and how do you feel about it now?

James: Vindicated. It makes me feel it is time for me to move on.

Clinician: Vindicated? In what way?

James: That I was better than them but they didn't realize it.

Clinician: As you say that now, is there an emotion that comes alive?

James: Well, I am obviously angry about the way they reacted, as there was nothing wrong with my work and they told me off in front of everyone in the office.

Now the clinician needs to work more doggedly on the affective experience of James at this point. He is describing a point of vulnerability.

Clinician: Is it important that this was done in front of other people?

James: Oh yes. If you want to say something to someone that is personal, you shouldn't do it in front of other people.

Clinician: What do you make of that?

James: It was to humiliate me. That was why I walked out.

Clinician: Wow, that is painful. Is that what you felt?

James: Absolutely. Wouldn't you?

The clinician now needs to hold the focus and grab James's sudden contact with his sense of shame and humiliation, which made him withdraw and strengthened his rigid and defensive (but ultimately unsustainable) belief in his superiority. The experience of unmentalized shame (experienced with the intensity that psychic equivalence brings) forced James's withdrawal from genuine interaction with others, which might otherwise have moderated his fragile exaggerated view of himself. Enhancing mentalizing and empathy in relation to the sense of undeserved humiliation is as far as the clinician is willing to go at this stage. The experience may be a driver of James's overt narcissistic presentation, but of course simply exposing it could be a humiliation in itself in the moment. This is why the MBT clinician immediately reverts to an empathic position.

Clinician: Yes, I would. Especially when they see you as the exact opposite to how you are. Managing the sense of being exposed like that is so hard.

James: I can still see their silly blaming contemptuous faces staring at me. I couldn't bear it. I just walked out.

Clinician: How did walking out make you feel?

James: Better, but then I couldn't go back in. I didn't know what to do, so I just left.

Toward the end of this session, the clinician and the patient summarize what has been learned and develop the formulation further as the exploration has led to better understanding of the struggle that James faces: *"I think what we are learning here is that when you are faced with people judging you negatively you naturally feel hurt and angry. But the pain of it is increased if you feel exposed in front of others. You then metaphorically and physically 'walk out.' Of course, then you are on your own and you are thrown on to that incredible self-sufficiency of yours. That is great, but while you left their blaming contempt behind, you are also left with the image of their faces, which perhaps makes it harder to feel good about yourself. How well the self-sufficiency works in relation to that is something we need to keep in mind as we talk more about all this."* This helps to focus future sessions.

Relational Mentalizing: From "I-Mode" to "Me-Mode" to "We-Mode"

In terms of changes in the intervention over time, exploration of the dynamics of the patient's relationships in their life at present and in therapy itself can bear fruit only once the patient feels that they are respected and validated by the clinician. Therefore the structure followed by the clinician in any session at any point in MBT-NPD continues to follow the stepwise procedure of empathic validation and managing the mentalizing process first. Only when self-mentalizing metacognition is stable does the clinician consider working on the patient's relationships and how they function in the patient's life.

Importantly in narcissistic functioning, though, working on stabilizing "I-mode" within the therapeutic encounter—primarily seeing things from the patient's perspective—is a necessary first step in treatment. Empathic adoption of the patient's perspective by the clinician helps to clarify and reinforce their understanding of the world in terms of mental states, even if this entails significant distortion. Next, the vulnerabilities and difficulties of "me-mode" functioning—how I see others seeing me (how I am seen by others)—becomes the subject of sensitive enquiry. The effectively mentalized personal second-order representation entails seeing oneself through the eyes of others, which obviously carries risks and dangers. Once this work has traction there can be a move to a relational focus of "we-mode"—the joining together of mental states of self and other, in this instance related to the self, in the spirit of joint intentionality. This entails the clinician and the patient seeing the same whole person (not just selected parts of the same person); self-understanding and the understanding of another fully coincide around the person, with the shared intention of the clinician assisting the patient with the issue or issues that they are jointly focusing on. Therefore the treatment trajectory over time in MBT-NPD is as follows:

1. early sessions—focus on stabilizing "I-mode"
2. middle sessions—emphasis on "me-mode," which fades into "we-mode"
3. later sessions—consolidation and generalization of "we-mode."

Of course this schematic approach is just that—schematic. In practice, the clinician and the patient will move between all three areas of exploration and focus. However, remembering that the sessions at the beginning are focused on the metacognitive "I-mode," and that this is followed by work on the self-as-object "me-mode," eventually alighting on the jointly experienced "we-mode," grounds the clinician in their tasks. In the "we-mode," the clinician and the patient can jointly attend to personal narratives while acknowledging that they may have different perspectives of equal validity alongside a joint vision of an aspect of internal experience to which both are witnesses.

A complication that can arise in NPF is "pretend we-mode." For some patients, particularly individuals with dependent traits, the joining of minds in the "we-mode" is appealing and may feel as if it is helping to reinforce a somewhat incoherent sense of self ("I-mode"). The clinician needs to be aware that some individuals with marked NPF are at times prone to depict themselves in the image of the person with whom they are talking. In social psychology this is described as the *chameleon effect*; this effect, which is likely to be non-conscious, entails a mimicry of lines of thinking, values, expressions, and even postures, mannerisms, and facial expressions to match those of the conversational partner. In these instances the "I-mode" is in a sense masquerading as "we-mode," such that the patient's behavior passively and unintentionally changes to match that of the clinician. The motivation behind this kind of mimicry is likely to be a wish to be liked, as the "we-mode" comes with affiliative properties (we tend to like people who are like us). Just like pretend mentalizing, "pretend we-mode" may be difficult for a clinician to spot. Individuals with NPF can be minutely and intuitively attuned to the way the clinician responds to them, and constantly adapt their own behavior to create an impression of near-perfect identity. On the whole, masquerading traits are seen by the clinician as largely positive and even useful, and can be mistaken for epistemic trust. However, the price the patient pays is that the increased stability of the "I-mode" is illusory. Real "we-mode" does not involve some mystical fusion of minds and perspectives—rather, its power rests on the fact that it is harnessing different perspectives on the same issue, and it is dependent on being able to hold on to an awareness of that difference in perspective, to gain the benefits of different people's points of view. Illusory "we-mode," on the other hand, is often characterized by an attempt to be entirely in agreement on the issue at hand, and a disavowal of different perspectives.

Patients' vulnerabilities are often more apparent when they are with others. Interactional mismatches, lack of reciprocity, and inadequate respect all lead to a hardening of the armored self, reinforcement of narcissistic structures, and a retreat from others. The clinician opposes this withdrawal whenever possible by highlighting it when it occurs in the patient's life (based on the patient's description of events) and when it happens in sessions. The work is to support the patient to be more involved and flexible in relationships. The patient's experience of the relationship with the clinician can be used for this purpose if there is adequate epistemic trust (with the patient perceiving that the meaning of their personal narrative is being mentalized by the clinician). Alongside the focus on the clinician–patient interaction, it is helpful if one or more of the patient's relationships outside therapy has been carefully explored and has changed from relational hypoactivation and epistemic dismissal to activation of need and epistemic vigilance or, better still, has moved toward epistemic trust, with the patient feeling that there are others in the world who are like-minded and likable, and who like them. These relationships can be explored safely and the patient can be asked to contrast their mind states with those of others whom they appreciate may have different perspectives. MBT is concerned not so much with the "why" of the relationships at this point as with "how" they are used and "how" they function—are they one-sided or do they have a mutuality that permits patients to learn more about themselves and to become compassionate about others' experiences?

Counter-Relational Mentalizing

Counter-relational mentalizing needs careful management and particular focus during the treatment of patients with marked narcissistic function. The patient's dismissive strategies and imperious attitude, and their apparent lack of compassion for and vulnerability to others, can become "tiresome." The clinician needs to remain grounded and in contact with the patient's vulnerabilities ("*see through the noise and seek the pain*"). Remaining "with" the patient's perspective is essential, albeit at times nigh on impossible; challenging the rigidity of their mental structure from the motive of compassion is necessary, although it can easily be taken over by challenging from the motive of irritation. Rigorous implementation of the not-knowing stance helps with these difficult counter-responses, but it is the use of the affect focus and presentation of clinician counter-responsiveness that places pressure on the patient to become more self-reflective about the dynamics of their relationships.

Affect Focus (the "Elephant in the Room") and Narcissism

The characteristic relational dynamic set up between the clinician and the patient with narcissistic function has to be identified, lived, and explored. As we outlined in Chapter 4, the affect focus is the emotionally salient interactional dynamic between patient and clinician that is currently being expressed in some way but may not be verbalized. The dynamic is part of a subdominant theme that often interferes with treatment and may be implicitly/automatically processed, remaining at a non-conscious level. It is an "elephant in the room." The task in MBT is twofold:

1. to move the subdominant interactional theme from the automatic to the more explicit
2. to explore the dynamic from a point of equity—where participants are part of a system in which they contribute equally to an interactional process.

To achieve this, the clinician openly identifies some of the dynamic processes as they become aware of them happening. A major part of this intervention may draw on the clinician's counter-relational experience, which may be the initial indicator of an unexpressed emotionally salient process that is relevant to the patient's narcissism. For example, the clinician might notice that everything they say is dismissed and not reflected on, even though the tone of the patient's responses sounds reasonable: "*No, I don't think that is right,*" "*I don't think this is relevant,*" "*Perhaps I need to explain this more.*" The clinician feels unappreciated and eventually irritated, as is illustrated by the next clinical example ("James's elephant").

The elephant can be significant in terms of clinical safety and management of risk. The patient may disavow their risk, but the clinician subjectively experiences a worry—for example, about suicidality—that becomes increasingly insistent as time goes on. It is incumbent on the clinician to bring this up and for its significance to be explored: "*You sound very confident about how you would manage such a disappointment. From my perspective I worry a little more than you seem to. You are sensitive to others' criticism. It worries me that when I ask you more about it you push me away. I would hate to miss something important here."*

Clinical Example: James's Elephant

The elephants in James's treatment were quite problematic. The clinician's frustration and reaction to his arrogance emerged early in treatment. At one point in treatment, James placed his feet on the low table between him and the clinician. Making himself comfortable, he asked the clinician *"to try a bit harder to help me understand myself. Most of the things here so far have been unsurprising to me. It has mostly come from me. I need more than this from you to change."* The clinician has to consider not only their own counter-responsive feeling but also the interaction of which it is part. At first, his counter-response needs to be "quarantined" while its source is defined.

Clinician: You are right, I think, about needing more. I can see that things are not changing at the moment. It looks a bit like we are back to that part of our agreement in which there was a question about how you manage people who do not have your abilities. So perhaps we can think about how you manage me a bit better at those times when I misunderstand things about you.

James: I was only wanting to be honest about it. I thought that was what I was supposed to be. I have been coming for nearly four months and I don't think I have learned very much from you yet.

Clinician: Yes. I too was thinking about the problem you and I have. To me, we seem to pull in different directions. I push and pull us around how sensitive you can be to other people, and you push the other way telling me I am off the point about this. What about an honest discussion around that?

James: Fine by me. You start. I will listen and then you have to listen to me.

Clinician: Well, as soon as I start to bring up your difficulties with others you seem to me to close off and I feel that you have made up your mind. I feel you make me out to be wrong before I even get started.

James: Well, it's not quite like . . .

Clinician: Hang on a minute, because that is exactly what I mean—I am only just getting started and we agreed that you are listening at the moment . . . But perhaps that is it really—we just don't listen enough to each other with an openness that means we take each other seriously.

The clinician is now trying to define the detail of the "elephant" and bring it into plain sight. The aim is to increase the recognition that "not listening to each other" is a subdominant dynamic process which is interfering with therapeutic work and the establishment of epistemic trust. But epistemic trust has to be present if listening is to be useful as a tool for personal learning and reflection. Currently, James is not listening to the clinician, and the clinician is finding it increasingly hard to listen to James. The first step is to define this problem, note it, and jointly identify "not listening" whenever it occurs—whether it is James's experience of the clinician, or the clinician's experience of James.

Challenge in the context of vulnerable narcissistic function needs to be undertaken quite sensitively, even tentatively, to avoid triggering shame and intensifying a sense of failure in the patient, which will compromise mentalizing. In grandiose narcissism, the challenge should also be sensitively done and carefully timed but it can be less tentative. Challenge should be avoided when the clinician feels intense annoyance, and should be deployed only when compassion for the patient dominates. When the therapeutic alliance is robust, challenge may be more forceful and insistent: "*I really cannot get my mind around the fact that all my attempts to understand your difficulties are a 'waste of space.' You and I need to decide what makes you come to see someone who you regard as so useless.*" This is a high-risk maneuver but it has a chance of freeing up the therapeutic relationship and triggering a moment of reflection in the patient. The clinician needs to hold the line while at the same time showing an attitude of wanting to sort out the problem rather than throwing in the towel and ending the treatment.

Concluding Remarks

In MBT-NPD/NPF, detailed assessment of the self/other dimension of mentalizing is required, and getting authentic "buy-in" from the patient about change is a necessary precondition for therapy. The focus of treatment changes over time, from exploring the rigidity and vulnerabilities of the "I-mode" of self to establishing more reflection and curiosity about the "me-mode," or "how others see me." A robust sense of self is essential for joint or relational mentalizing of the "we-mode" of shared mental states, so that joint attention can be given to personal narratives while acknowledging that the patient and the clinician may have different perspectives—both of which have equal validity. If this point of safe sharing of mental processes with those of others has been arrived at with a level of stability, the patient's narcissism will have been modulated enough to allow mutuality and a sense of belonging, which are the very foundations of social mentalizing and friendship making—a positive outcome indeed.

References

1. Skodol AE, Bender DS, Morey LC et al. Personality disorder types proposed for DSM-5. *J Pers Disord* 2011; **25**: 136–69.
2. Tyrer P, Crawford M, Mulder R et al. The rationale for the reclassification of personality disorder in the 11th revision of the International Classification of Diseases (ICD-11). *Personal Ment Health* 2011; **5**: 246–59.
3. Fonagy P, Gergely G, Jurist E, Target M. *Affect Regulation, Mentalization, and the Development of the Self.* New York, NY: Other Press LLC, 2002.
4. Robinson EA. *Robinson: Poems.* Donaldson S, ed. New York, NY: Everyman's Library, 2007 (originally published 1897); 33.
5. James W. *Principles of Psychology.* New York, NY: Henry Holt, 1890.

Antisocial Personality Disorder

Introduction

There is considerable overlap between the psychological profile of antisocial personality disorder (ASPD), narcissistic personality functioning (NPF), and borderline personality disorder (BPD) [1,2]. It is well known in clinical practice that many patients show characteristics of all three disorders. People with ASPD have high levels of NPF, and many individuals with BPD have high levels of antisocial traits, serving as a reminder that the categorical approach to personality disorder is not quite fit for purpose. The failure of categorization is not, however, an argument against having some general principles that help to distinguish between clinical presentations, because these presentations indicate that different forms of therapeutic intervention are required for the patient's needs to be met effectively. Thus in this chapter we shall use the term ASPD (and refer to patient and clinician, although the attitude we promote is one of equality), but we refer to ASPD not as a diagnostic entity but rather as an indicator of individuals who have a shared set of problems, which mentalization-based treatment (MBT) can address with a particular set of interventions, which we shall describe as MBT-ASPD. Importantly, individuals diagnosed with ASPD, who are more commonly male, show a persistent failure to manifest generalized prosocial behavior and to engage in constructive social collaboration; this leads to repeated conflict with society, formation of distrustful friendships, and problematic intimate relationships.

The Long- and Short-Term Aims of MBT with ASPD

Changing Identity and Achieving Desistance

As we discussed in Chapter 2, what is relevant for good outcomes from MBT is that social communications containing information relevant to the individual's ability to function in social collaborative contexts are useful as a resource for the individual to learn from. This information about how to work in the social world is then available to be used in more complex social environments, even against a background of stress and in non-mentalizing environments. Thinking about how to communicate is particularly relevant to working with people with ASPD, as they can be so distrustful of others that they fail to see the personal relevance of communication that in others might prompt changes in a person's identity, tastes, values, or preferences. They often find it harder to recognize positive opportunities and pathways for change, as they are stuck in a pattern of survival in what may be—and what they certainly experience as—a hostile world, which they manage through threat and violence. In this context, it is unsurprising that they find it hard to change. Desistance from violence itself, as demanded by criminal justice systems (and often used as a primary outcome in studies of treatment), is experienced by them as defeat. But the process that moves us all toward desistance is the relevant factor.

The process is actually about change in the perceived relevance of information to the self—a cognitive transformation from perceiving the world as a hostile place from which nothing can be learned, to perceiving it as a place from which learning becomes possible. Desistance occurs through the recognition, normally through others, of the negative attributes of a criminal identity and the gradual enhancement of the patient's subdominant prosocial identity. An offender's identity changes as a function of receiving new information that they consider relevant to them and generalizable to other settings, and therefore to be stored for future activation through modification of self-structures. Only then can we talk of the person as having, in a metaphorical sense, "broken with the past." A new self is progressively formed. New information, once it has been absorbed and integrated into relevant self-schemas, means that views of the world are altered and things that once mattered now do not (or they matter much less), and things that did not matter before now do (or they matter slightly more). Importantly, this process of change, driven by increasingly stable mentalizing, has compelled us to pay far more attention to the social context of our patients and the ongoing relationships that dominate the lives of offenders, and to directly address issues of trust and mistrust in the context of these relationships.

Therefore in ASPD the primary emphasis of change is not so much on the clinical setting and the recovery of mentalizing capacity, but rather on enabling changed social relationships between the individual with ASPD and the people around them. The work is to support the patient in becoming more open to information and knowledge from others that they previously were disinclined to accept as pertinent to them (i.e., *relevant*), and enabling them to apply this information to settings beyond the one in which it was encountered (i.e., *generalizable*) and integrate it with and modify existing knowledge structures (i.e., *memorable*). As epistemic trust (see Chapter 3) increases, the individual gradually becomes better integrated into the social network around them. This leads to increased learning opportunities for permanently modifying self-narratives, and this in turn leads to a reduction in the frequency with which violence-instigating social strategies are used at times of stress and distress.

In summary, change—that is, desistance from violence—depends on a combination of three critical influences:

1. the enhancement of mentalizing, which brings about
2. a reduction in antisocial behavior (e.g., violence) through enhanced concern with the experience of others and improved social connections characterized by epistemic trust, which in turn enables
3. prosocial agents to exercise influence on the individual's personal narrative, leading to persistence of change.

The starting point for generating this process is carefully curated group treatment with an emphasis on mentalizing, engagement in treatment and facilitation of trust in others, practicing "live" prosocial interactions, and generalizing the learning from these interactions to the individual's personal social context.

Mentalizing and Violence

This book has persistently emphasized that the starting point in MBT for the clinician involves mapping the mentalizing problems of the patient and defining the contexts in which their mentalizing is vulnerable, with a particular focus on social and interpersonal sensitivity when attachment strategies are activated. It is at these times that the patient's mind is vulnerable to the dominance of the low-mentalizing modes—psychic equivalence, teleological mode, and pretend mode (see Chapter 2). A rapid, attachment-dependent movement between these different modes of experiencing the self and the world is characteristic of BPD, but is modified by the co-occurrence of violence in ASPD. People with ASPD interpret the world according to teleological understanding ("doing" mode) for much of the time, and work on the basis that action is the only way to make people understand something, or to ensure that a threat to the self is neutralized. We suggest that this process maintains stability through the rigidity of the externalization of the alien self (see Chapter 2). This presents serious problems for the clinician who is working with the patient. The rigidity of the system has to be challenged, and yet the challenge might induce violence [3,4].

In ASPD the alien self is firmly and rigidly externalized. A partner may be portrayed as mindless and dependent, and therefore needing to be told what to do; a social system may be portrayed as authoritarian and threatening subjugation. Threats to these schematic representational structures—for example, a partner demanding an "unacceptable" level of independence—create a mismatch with expectation, leading to attachment anxiety. This triggers the inhibition of mentalizing, which in turn leads to fears of inability to control internal states and the threat of the return of the alien self. It is important for the clinician to remember key processes that can destabilize a carefully crafted system which is stabilizing an alien self. These are:

- threats to self-esteem
- threats to self-identity
- activation of shame.

Threats to self-esteem trigger violence in individuals whose self-esteem is not rooted in reality because they exaggerate their self-worth (narcissism; see also Chapter 6) and risk being seen differently by others. People with ASPD tend, at a superficial level, to inflate their self-esteem, demanding respect from others, controlling the people around them, and creating an atmosphere of fear. To a large extent this is adaptive within their social milieu, and to do anything different would open them up to personal danger. However, they throw the baby out with the bathwater. Their distrust of others is wholesale, and no information from the social world is available to them to learn from. Change requires them to notice glimmers of prosociality and maximize them to develop constructive, cooperative relationships. Many individuals with ASPD try to do this—they continually try to protect their relationships with their partner and children, only to find that these are disrupted by external threats that challenge their position and identity (e.g., as a father or head of the household). Loss of status is devastating, as the alien self returns and reveals internal states that threaten to overwhelm them. Experience becomes more firmly rooted in psychic equivalence, which adds intensity and reality to the situation of (perceived) loss of status, leading to a need to "sort things out." The problem is seen not as mental but as arising from the physical world, and so, in teleological mode, the person takes physical action. Access to emotions such as guilt, love for others, and fear for a physical self—which can prevent many of us from engaging in violent behavior—is not available, and the loss of mentalizing, along with the reduced ability of individuals with ASPD to experience such feelings, prevents the mobilization of such inhibitory mechanisms. For example, fear for the survival of a physical self is absent, and the ordinary dangers associated with violence are discounted. The onset of pretend mode means that the risk of being caught is "unreal," and an illusory sense of safety and lack of reality prevails. The internal state no longer links with external reality: "*It happened like in the movies,*" "*It didn't seem real.*"

The regulation of shame is a key factor in this process [5]. The return of the alien self induces feelings of shame, which are experienced in the reality of psychic equivalence, and so attempts to control the source, which is seen as "out there"—external to the self—are inevitable. Aggression toward the source of danger is not limited to non-physical aggression (e.g., shouting), as this would require awareness of the mental state of the other, which is lost when mentalizing breaks down. Retaining an ability to imagine someone else as a human being with a separate mind inhibits violence. It is the loss of mentalizing that allows a physical attack, as the other person becomes no more than a body or a physical threat. So it is to the subject of violence that we now turn in order to understand in more detail this final element of a complex picture.

The common path to violence is via momentary inhibition of the capacity for mentalizing. As we mentioned earlier, mentalizing protects against engaging in violence. Some individuals fail to desist from violence throughout childhood and adolescence, and appear to be constitutionally poor at using external mentalizing processes to accurately recognize the underlying mental states of others through their facial expressions or tone of voice. These individuals are commonly described as "callous and unemotional" or considered to be "psychopaths" who are unaffected by others' responses. For most of us, eliciting a painful state in others activates concern and leads to a change in our behavior. However, this does not occur in these individuals. It is likely that their nascent capacities for mentalizing were eroded by cruel and traumatic experiences in early life, or by an attachment figure who had persistent thoughts, attitudes, and responses that created considerable anxiety in the child, as a result of which these individuals avoid thinking about any subjective experience of others. Therefore in MBT it is important to retain an awareness of the possibility that violence may be rooted in the disorganization of the attachment system. A child may display an apparent callousness that is actually rooted in anxiety about attachment relationships, and not simply constitutional. They are not really callous and unemotional, but terrified and striving for a more reliable attachment that they never seem to be able to create. A harsh early childhood signals greater future need for interpersonal violence as a means of expressing underlying mental states. Violence becomes the currency for expression of the self and the management of relationships. In support of this model, studies have demonstrated that the association between childhood maltreatment and externalizing problems is probably mediated by inadequate interpersonal understanding (social competences) and limited behavioral flexibility in response to environmental demands (ego resiliency) [6].

We argue that patients whose aggression was high in early childhood and continued into adolescence and early adulthood are likely to have had attachment experiences that failed to establish both a robust yet flexible sense of self-agency and a stable experience of the other as a psychological entity [7]. There is an interplay between psychological defenses, neurobiological development, and shifts in brain activity during post-traumatic states that leads to compromise of mentalizing activity. The shift in the balance of cortical control locks the person with a history of childhood maltreatment into a mode of mental functioning associated with:

- an inability to employ alternative representations of the situation (i.e., functioning at the level of primary rather than secondary representations)
- difficulties in explicating the state of mind (meta-representation) of the person whom they face
- a predisposition to use modes of mental functioning associated with states of dissociative detachment, where their own actions are experienced as unreal or as having no realistic implications.

These issues must all be addressed in treatment.

Preparation for the MBT Group for Patients with ASPD

To achieve the aims of learning from others, learning about oneself through others, and creating a different experience of self, unencumbered by the previously fragile but heavily protected rigid self, the MBT group for patients with ASPD (MBT-ASPD-G) attempts to create a social environment with core values that are agreed between all the participants, and sensitively constructs interactions that promote reflection between participants. As such, there are some specific areas of MBT for patients with ASPD that need special attention in clinical practice [8,9]. These include:

- the format of treatment
- engagement: addressing equality versus hierarchy; discussion of personal values
- formulation: collaboration without stimulating threats to self-esteem (humiliation)
- reflection on personal agency
- identification by patients of emotion in self and others
- empathic concern for and interest in others
- elaboration and management of shame as a destabilizer of self-function
- considering aggression and violence as a catastrophic loss of mentalizing
- moving from hierarchical relationships to collaborative "we-mode" functioning.

Format of Treatment

Individual sessions are offered initially for assessment and engagement. Once the formulation has been agreed, the patient is offered MBT-ASPD-G. Individual sessions are offered only if requested by the patient and for specific purposes, which may include:

- change in the risk to self and/or others
- escalation of problem areas (e.g., drug/alcohol use); co-occurring conditions (e.g., depression); lying; excessive externalization
- non-attendance at group sessions and requiring support to remain in the group
- exploration of sensitive personal material
- work on symptoms of post-traumatic stress disorder
- discussion and agreement about reports to be written by the clinician (e.g., in relation to child custody decisions or court proceedings)
- reformulation.

MBT-ASPD centers around group work. In keeping with the mentalizing principle that an individual is more likely to listen to and learn from others whom they see as the same as them, everyone in the group has ASPD, and most will have had repeated brushes with the criminal justice system and feel abandoned by, and to a measure excluded from, society. From a mentalizing perspective, we assume that if people feel mentalized—that is, they experience that their concerns and emotional states have been accurately and compassionately reflected on from their perspective by another person, whom they see as similar to themselves—this may allow them to experience a sense of belonging and engagement in social processes that support mentalizing and also reduce their mental and social isolation and sense of epistemic injustice. Recovering mentalizing serves to reduce their background experience of social danger, which easily provokes violence, and improves their level of empathy, which has hitherto been lacking and has further enabled aggressive or violent antisocial acts. Recovering mentalizing also reinstates interpersonal connections and opens a channel for social learning, facilitating change in how they see themselves and how they interact with others.

Engagement in Treatment

Individuals with ASPD are very often highly sensitive about being seen as people who have mental health problems. In psychic equivalence (Inside-Out) and teleological mode (Outside-In) thinking, they see others as causing them problems. They don't even like the term "mentalizing," hearing only the "mental" part (as in "*You must be mental!*").

Engagement starts with the referrer, who needs to frame the referral carefully, making the reason for it relevant to the individual. The patients who readily agree to referral (MBT-ASPD is not offered as part of court-ordered mandatory treatment plans) may be those who feel depressed and want help. A common situation is that they are concerned about being portrayed as dangerous by a former partner or an organization such as social services, housing services, or the child protection team, and this portrayal is damaging for their lives. They may be described by authorities as a "bad influence" who should not, for example, be allowed access to their children, and their history of violence is used as evidence to support the credibility of a harsh decision. Few of us would portray ourselves as a bad influence, and being seen by others in a way that they do not see themselves leaves individuals with ASPD feeling misunderstood and further alienated from society and a social system with which they do not engage fully. As far as their teleological thinking is concerned, their actions have been a reasonable response to others' failure.

At the initial interview, "treatment" is usually far from the patient's mind; at the forefront is garnering support in their argument with authorities, for example, to get social support restored or to improve the access they have to their children. Only if they experience MBT as a route to achieving their personal goal will they attend "therapy"—which for most, at this point, is a "pretend" therapy. Changing pretend therapy into engaged personal therapy is the challenging function of the initial sessions. The difficulties in engaging patients with ASPD are distinct from those involved in the engagement of patients with BPD and some other categories of personality disorder, where patients commonly seek treatment for themselves and actively try to engage with their aim of improving a state of distress and anticipating feeling better in a supportive relationship.

Process of Engagement in Treatment: Summary

The key features of the MBT approach to the engagement of individuals with ASPD are as follows.

- Accept the person's stated practical aim.
  - *Do not* try to establish your own psychological and behavioral aims—for example, to support them in stabilizing mentalizing in the face of everyday stresses, to reduce violence and aggression, or to support prosocial behavior.

- As far as possible, the MBT clinician attempts to be open-minded, affirms the patient's motivation for wanting to join the group, and monitors the development of the therapeutic alliance to slowly present behavioral and psychological aims.

- Be ordinarily human and use a not-knowing stance. Do not make any assumptions or judgments.
- Empathically validate the patient's feeling of alienation and exclusion; recognize the annoying and distressing nature of being misunderstood by others.
- Collaboratively develop the content and focus relevant to the patient in the help being offered (which should *not* be identified as "treatment").
- Include an expert by experience who has completed treatment in the MBT-ASPD program to aid engagement (experts by experience are described later in this chapter).

Clinical Example: Bryan

Bryan, who is 24 years old, was referred because of his persistent threats of violence. His history of previous violence included attacking his partner and threatening her brother during an argument about access to their two children, aged 4 and 6 years. His partner had taken out a court injunction to stop him visiting the family home because of his threats. He was currently living with his father and mother in what was described as a home "full of threat," with his father constantly belittling him as a "pathetic specimen of a man."

In his account of his earlier life, Bryan stressed that his father had been involved in a criminal gang and was the enforcer for collection of "protection" money. If people did not pay their protection money, threats were issued. The consequences of non-payment included physical punishment. He was included in his father's money-collecting circuit from the age of 8, and by 12 years of age had become an expert in "kneecapping" using a crowbar. He reported that he had stopped all of this activity when he left prison two years ago, and refused to join his father in any criminal activity. His main occupation was going to the gym and weight training.

At the initial assessment he said he was present only because he needed a report to say that he was safe to see his children. This led to the following conversation:

Clinician: Let's talk about that. What are we to write in the report? Perhaps tell me about your children first and what they are like.

Bryan: They are my children.

Clinician: Yes. I was wanting to get a picture of what they are like and then perhaps how you are as well. Tell me about Jimmy, who is now 6 years old.

To some extent this initial approach has links with the MBT Loop (see Chapter 4) used by MBT clinicians to address low mentalizing. The aim of the initial interview is to turn around the mental telescope and change a narrow, circumscribed view or demand into a wider perspective (i.e., "zoom out") before bringing back specific concerns into focus for more consideration (i.e., "zoom in"). Therefore, as the content of the report is discussed in detail, the clinician sensitively moves back and forth from the exploration of the patient's understanding of his children (e.g., why it is important for them to see him) to how he sees himself as a father (e.g., why it is important for him to see the children more often). This movement has the potential to generate exploration and stimulate some self–self and self–other reflection. How are the children described? Are they people with character and personality (reflective mentalizing) or people whom it is the patient's "right to see as the father" (low-mentalizing description and demand)? In this case, the patient's response was a low-mentalizing response and had no elements personal to his son. Therefore the clinician presses the patient to consider how he sees his children as individuals with their own needs and attributes.

Eventually, the clinician can consider how the patient is seen by others ("me-mode" or personalized other–self mentalizing). His partner and her brother have banned him from the home, and he rails against this. To address the idea of "how I am seen by others," it is best to start by finding out what the patient thinks about another person, before asking how the other person sees them.

Clinical Example: Bryan (continued)

Clinician: How would you describe your partner when you were with her—not so much as you see her now, but when you were together with her and your children?

Bryan: She has changed. She was always very jumpy and sometimes would attack me, but the social services don't care about that, do they? I only hit her when she had attacked me. But before we had children she could be really nice and did things for me when I asked, and she visited me in prison.

Clinician: Tell me more about her jumpiness.

After some exploration of this description of Bryan's former partner, the clinician conversationally moves to how she might have seen him.

Clinician: How did she see you before things began to break down?

Formulation and Addressing Equality Versus Hierarchy

Bryan described a relationship with his partner that oscillated between her being dutiful and biddable, which he liked, and her being jumpy and aggressive toward him, which he did not like. He agreed that he managed this by being threatening and controlling to some extent, and that his partner often complained about him being a "control freak." Toward the end of the meeting, it was possible to identify that he felt comfortable when he was "the boss," but uncomfortable when the people he was with "did their own thing." The clinician at this point attempted to mentalize the developing relationship between himself and Bryan: "*You know, when you say that, I realize that when you came to this session you were the boss and rightly so, telling me that you wanted the report and that I had to provide it. What is it like now that we have agreed to wait a bit before it is done?*"

This relationship dynamic, variously described in the initial meetings as "Boss/Servant," "Demand/Compliance," "Control/Controlled," and "Superior/Inferior," was outlined in the written summary of the meeting that the clinician made with Bryan toward the end of the session. Bryan's pleasure at being seen as a "boss" suggested that his self-esteem is increased by such an image of himself. Therefore the clinician made a mental note to support rather than challenge this image in the service of generating an alliance early in treatment.

Jointly writing the summary of the meetings and giving patients open access to all written information is an essential element of equality, and is necessary to reduce the patient's level of distrust in the assessment and treatment process.

Clinical Example: Written Summary/Formulation for Bryan

We have discussed the way that people see you and your concern that this is wrong and based on your previous behaviors. You want us to work to write a report that supports your access to your children. I have said that I don't know whether any report will do that until you and I have worked on how that might happen—on who and what has to change. I realize that this is uncomfortable for you at the moment, as it challenges that Boss/Servant thing when you feel in control. We know that you are angry at times in relation to this. This comes from experiencing people as not respecting you and not taking you seriously, or doing things without discussing them with you. You feel good about yourself when people respect you and see you as someone to look up to, so we need to be aware of that. When you are not taken seriously you react, as you are excluded and people aren't listening to your point of view. This happened with your partner and led to you asserting yourself, which she and her brother called threats. We also agreed that at times, when you get angry, you are "in your own world."

You are coming into the group to meet others who have similar concerns in their lives, and you will use this summary to introduce yourself. The important part is that you expect people to listen to you and respect you, and you will find that the others have the same expectations. So we will ask you to tell them about your current situation when you start. In the meantime we will have some sessions together about how the group works.

One value we have agreed about our meetings is openness/transparency—we will discuss everything that comes to mind, and there will be no contact with the Child Protection Team or your probation officer without your knowledge.

This straightforward summary is the first part of the formulation, written with the aim of easing Bryan into the group and ensuring that the focus of the work is on his relationships and emotional reactivity. Additional elements related to the mentalizing dimensional profile are added during individual sessions before starting the group. Patient entry into the group follows the same procedure as that described in Chapter 5.

Discussion of Values before Joining the Group

The clinician explores the patient's values before they join the group by asking a number of questions about personal topics. For example:

1. *Do other people think that there are some things that should be important to you, such as not getting angry so easily, taking time before you feel in control, being less quick to boil over into violence, having loving relationships, or being employed? Are any of these things important to you, even if you think people are judging you unfairly?*" The patient has to consider the focus of treatment to be meaningful to them *personally*. It is not possible to engage people with ASPD in treatment if they feel that the focus is important to society but not to them.
2. *Is this "value"' still important if nobody knows about it and if nobody would judge you?* This question is used to ensure that the person is motivated by a wish to be different, rather than by external pressure to conform.
3. *Is it important to you even though it might not play a role in your current life?*

Exploration around these questions enables the clinician and the patient to address personally important concerns as well as to generate longer-term aims. In the end, the clinician and patient consider together how the patient would like to be, rather than how they are. Gradually they build a focus for treatment and jointly identify goals. These goals should have a broader focus than preventing aggression/violence, which is seen as an end product of a cascade of problems, rather than the focus for therapeutic work, which must be the mentalizing problems that lie behind the actions. Patients with ASPD often complain that they are seen as "angry people" and sent to anger management classes, which merely serve to make them feel stereotyped and misunderstood.

Other strategies for engaging and retaining patients in MBT groups include:

- actively calling the participants following missed sessions
- texting all of the participants on the day of the group or the day beforehand, whichever is agreed with the patients, to encourage them to attend
- providing refreshments for them before the group session starts
- having a flexible policy regarding non-attendance; fostering curiosity and understanding about the reasons why patients might not be willing or able to attend, rather than adhering to a more rigid procedure of discharging them after a certain number of missed sessions
- maintaining participants' trust by establishing clear and transparent guidance in relation to confidentiality
- using individual sessions to address issues that are impeding attendance at the group, which may relate to negative feelings and attitudes toward other group participants.

MBT-ASPD-G

MBT-I for MBT-ASPD-G

The initial group work in MBT-ASPD-G is psychoeducational. The patient learns about the mentalizing framework that will be followed during treatment. Central themes of the forthcoming work are discussed in MBT-Introductory Group (MBT-I) sessions, which follow the same structure as that used for patients with BPD (see Chapter 4).

In MBT-ASPD, the content of the MBT-I sessions is modified to some extent. The discussion about mentalizing, emotions, attachment, and relationships is very similar, but the clinician uses examples that are relevant to the patients. In addition, an extra module is included that links violence and other antisocial behavior to loss of mentalizing.

Mentalizing Modules

In the mentalizing modules, the clinician seeks to get the patients to:

1. consider their self-esteem and the basis on which they appraise it ("I-mode")
2. appraise the level of concern about others and what they think and feel ("me-mode")
3. identify how others see them ("personalized me-mode")
4. recognize when they "lose their mind," and in what way—Boom Time/Know and Now/Inside-Out (psychic equivalence), Action Man/Doing Time/Inside-Out (teleological mode), or Bubble Mode (pretend mode)
5. identify "we-mode" function—safety in intimacy and sharing.

Emotions Module

In the emotions module, discussion about shame as an emotion is necessary. There is some emphasis on aggression, too, but this is considered as a basic emotion required for survival; it is presented as a secondary response to environmental frustrations rather than a trait characteristic that is untreatable. The clinician uses everyday examples of situations that can trigger all of us to be angry, and explains how anger can be activated when shame is emerging—what happens when we are laughed at or criticized in front of others and feel humiliated, or when we are forced/coerced to do something against our wishes, so that we feel diminished, or when we make someone else do something against their wishes and later realize that we were cruel. At this point it can be helpful to ask the group members to begin to think about their own values and whether there are examples from their lives when they did not meet their personal standard.

Attachment Module

In the attachment module the relational patterns of each group participant are identified, without judgment or comment. These relational patterns will already have been discussed with each participant in their formulation. The aim here is to pick out the patterns and to note them as something that will be explored in treatment from the point of view of their helpful and harmful consequences. Which relationships are supportive and why is this so? Which are unhelpful and go against the person's long-term wishes? What creates the problem?

Violence Module

The violence module provides a brief outline of the ways in which interpersonal violence can be thought about—that is, "emotional explosion" versus "plotting and planning." The patients are asked if they can categorize their own actions and give examples of them. They are asked not to judge themselves and not to judge anyone else in the telling of personal examples. Most examples will be related to emotional violence, so the clinician draws out the detail of the cascade toward non-mentalizing, identifying the participants' experience of themselves, their experience of others' motives, and what feelings that experience provokes in them that they find unacceptable and unbearable. Violence is the outcome of a loss of mentalizing, and some of the information that we outlined at the beginning of this chapter is discussed in this module.

One way of focusing and personalizing some of the discussion is to use the Overt Aggression Scale Modified (OAS-M) [10] in the group, as this requires each patient to think about their verbal, physical, and self-aggression as well as their propensity to damage property.

Finally, an agreement is made that whenever violence or unconstructive social interaction occurs it should become a topic of discussion in the group. Is desisting from violence as the primary solution to their problems a value that they can sign up to? If not, why not? If so, why? The first question does not have to be answered affirmatively for the person to continue in the group. It aims to stimulate reflection among group members about the effects of antisocial behavior on their lives and what might change or be lost by them increasing their prosocial behaviors.

Meeting an Expert by Experience

Experts by experience—patients who have completed MBT-ASPD treatment—are employed within normal clinical confidentiality contracts to provide information and to discuss the program with new patients. The expert by experience sits in MBT-ASPD-G sessions and contributes to the discussions, often helping to clarify the focus for the sessions. This arrangement is in keeping with the mentalizing principle that new patients are more likely to accept information from and listen to those who they know have had similar experiences to themselves. In this context, epistemic vigilance is lowered and learning is increased. Experts by experience tend to be more direct toward patients than clinicians are—for example, telling new patients that they "*have to work on themselves*" or asking them "*Do you want to turn your life around?*" They emphasize that motivation has to come from within and that "*it is no good looking to everyone else to do things for you.*" Nevertheless, they are also aware of the difficulties faced by new patients, as they themselves often struggled for many years to turn their lives around.

There may be some side effects of the work of experts by experience to watch out for. Some experts by experience can be overly strict and censorious, or excessively directive—for example, one insisted that all members of the group should leave their mobile phones in a bucket when they came into the room, and told them that they were there to interact and think about themselves together, away from the world outside! This is taken into account in the brief training program that the experts by experience complete before they begin their work.

Other experts by experience can become over-involved, sharing their phone numbers or even visiting patients at home. To guard against these problems, it is important that the expert by experience is a fully incorporated member of the MBT clinical team and not simply an add-on. They come to team meetings once a week and are paid to do so. At these meetings patients are discussed, with the perspective of the expert by experience being given the same weight as the opinions of the rest of the team. This working relationship between experts by experience and clinicians requires attention from the treating team. Creating a place for the expert by experience in the team and generating an atmosphere of equality and mutual respect may have beneficial effects on the way that the team works, and in turn on how the group functions. Experts by experience are often more sensitive to the mental struggle of patients than the MBT clinicians are, and so they have the task of helping the clinicians to understand their patients better. They have to bridge the gap between the mental processing of the clinicians and that of the patients, nudging the group toward "we-mode" functioning in which all of the participants consider a problem from separate but overlapping perspectives, which is a complex task.

Structure of the Group and Focus on Self-Agency in the Group

MBT-ASPD-G follows the standard MBT-G framework (see Chapter 5), but with greater emphasis on the generation of agreed values and additional structure.

Agreed Values

The agreed values, such as openness, tolerance, and respect, are best written on a whiteboard or flip chart in the group room. Any individual value that is agreed between a patient and clinician in the assessment phase is included in the list of values for the group once it has been discussed by the group. The list serves as a reminder to group members and clinicians alike of what has been agreed, and may be referred to during the group when the "rules" are broken or when it is apparent that they are being adhered to in a prosocial way. The aim of establishing agreed values in an explicit way and of referring to them during the group is for those values to become gradually embedded in automatic mentalizing processes within the group, creating the potential for a prosocial culture. Whenever a value is broken, this is called out by a group member, the expert by experience, or the clinician, and the group is asked to revisit the value and to discuss it again on the basis that breaking agreed values is an antisocial attitude that needs to be addressed. The key is learning from, rather than reacting to, an infringement of the joint agreement.

Self-Agency

Self-agency sounds promisingly self-explanatory as a statement about an individual's capacity to act as a free agent and to exercise their free will. Yet it is curiously complex to target and enhance by clinical intervention. The clinician and patient need to follow a framework. In essence, self-agency has two main mentalizing elements. First, there is the ability to conceive of one's self in the moment on the basis of a coherent personal narrative that is normative and provides a sense of personhood even when under threat. Second, there is a time distinction in which there is a psychological connection established between a past self, activated through the retrieval of positive and negative memories holding personal values and experience, and a future self, which shares and elaborates that past. Bringing the two together allows the individual to become a "doer" within their current context, and so create an ongoing future and a life worth living that is continuous with the past. Thus it is inevitable that improving mentalizing will increase self-agency due to continuity between self in the past, self in the present, and self in the future. Working on this triad of content of self-mentalizing allows shared reflection on the complexity of relationships partly because having a more robust self-agency reduces defensiveness and self-protection through dismissal of others.

How the exploration of the present, past, and future self in relationships takes place in the group is discussed with the patients before they enter the group.

I-Mode to Me-Mode

The group participants are asked to organize around "I-mode" to "me-mode" and initially from present to past and past to present in any discussion of their personal experiences and events: "*If this is me now, where did 'I' come from? If this was me then, what does it mean for me now?*" There is an interplay between autobiographical and semantic memory processes.

This is followed by asking all of the other participants to talk together about their experience of what they have heard and what it means for them, not solely what it makes them think about the person who was presenting. After this, the discussion moves back to the presenter, who considers whether or not the "me-mode" interaction has changed their "I-mode" reflection and, if so, in what way.

Clinical Example: Bryan (continued)

Clinician: Bryan, what we are going to ask you to do is to take some of your problem areas and openly talk about them from your point of view (*I-mode*). The others in the group are asked not to judge or give advice about what you or anyone else should have done, but just to ask you questions that help you to elaborate and express the feelings associated with what you are talking about, what was difficult for you to navigate in terms of how you felt, what you were struggling with, and how you feel about it all now. So, for example, if you are discussing your problems with your partner, they will ask you what it is that she was saying or doing that made you react, what that brought up in you and how you expressed it, and what you think she was seeing in you. Everyone will then be asked to reflect on what your story means to them, and you are asked to listen to see if this brings up other things about you and your story.

Recognition of and Reaction to Others' Emotional States

People with ASPD make excessive use of automatic assumptions about others' mental states, and are slow to switch to controlled mentalizing in order to understand others' motives and their underlying emotions. They have a reduced ability to recognize facial and vocal cues and the associated underlying emotions in others; this includes recognition not only of negative emotions, such as anger, fear, disgust, and sadness, but also of positive emotions, such as surprise and happiness. As a result, others' responses may be a puzzle to them. In addition, they are often concerned that others may express something outwardly but that this is "fake" and inconsistent with what they feel inside. In effect they are distrustful of others' emotional expression. They are especially suspicious of people who seem helpful and inclusive, as this challenges their schematic and automatic representations of the world—for example, someone may appear pleasant but this covers a malign and exploitative state of mind. These patients' level of epistemic mistrust is high, and so they are wary even of pleasantness and expressions of trustworthiness. Differentiating between congruent and incongruent inner and outer expression requires practice in everyday life. Enhancing this process starts in the group, using the group interaction as a training ground for social discourse that uses the automatic/controlled mentalizing dimension in the service of recognizing emotional states in others and confirming what states of mind lie behind them.

Clinical Example: Bryan (continued)

Clinician: Let me give you an example—as I say this to you, you look a little puzzled and rather suspicious. But that is my reading of your mind as I observe your face and how you are looking at me. It makes me feel uncertain about what I am saying. I may be quite wrong, and so I will ask you—are you a bit suspicious of what I am suggesting we do in the group, and, if so, what makes you so suspicious?

Bryan: I can't see the point of it.

Clinician: Ah, so is my assumption about your reaction correct?

Bryan: Not really.

Clinician: So tell me what is behind your expression. What was in your mind?

Bryan: I don't know, but all this makes me think I don't want to be told that I have to ask people in the group what they are feeling.

Clinician: Can you get hold of what is uncomfortable about that?

Bryan: Not sure.

Clinician: Well, the main reason we focus on it is that all of us often make assumptions about each other's feelings and motives that turn out to be inaccurate, like you have found that the authorities have got you wrong. Right? (*Bryan nods.*) We make these immediate judgments about each other all the time. The authorities judged you to have a harmful state of mind, and based this on how you behaved, but you think they got that wrong. In this group, we practice how good we can be at reading each other and how accurate we can become. Often we get it wrong. That is how we learn about our blind spots, which are often fueled by how we feel in the moment, while at the same time practicing how to ask what is beyond our immediate guess.

Bryan: Hmm. OK.

Working with Shame as a Problematic Emotion

Shame is a multifaceted, complex emotion that involves disgust, anger, and anxiety and is often associated with behavior changes, such as withdrawal and avoidance of others. Shame has a "self" and an "other" component, with a negative experience of oneself, perhaps for not meeting one's internal standards, allied with a belief that others will see and judge the experience equally negatively and want to punish us severely. Shame elicits a concern about social rejection and a wish to distance oneself from the perceived trigger, whether this is interpersonal (something being seen by someone) or mental (something being thought or imagined). There may be a fine balance between internal and external shame, or it may be excessively weighted to one side or the other. Internal shame focuses on self-experience, and individuals become preoccupied with their own negative evaluation of themselves. This is less common in ASPD than external shame, in which individuals are more concerned with how they are seen by others. Worrying that they might be diminished in the eyes of others, they become preoccupied with changing others' minds, either by behaving differently themselves or, more often, by coercively demanding that the other person sees them differently—hence the sudden anger toward an individual who elicits feelings of shame in them. It is all too easy for a clinician to become judgmental about a patient's actions and in doing so trigger a shame reaction of anger and/or avoidance in the patient, who may then behave in a threatening manner or leave the session. In MBT-ASPD-G, patients can activate shame in each other, and the clinician has to be constantly aware of potential shame reactions, which may create explosive interactions and require immediate de-escalation (de-escalation of problematic or threatening interactions is described later in this chapter).

In patients with ASPD, shame may be persistent yet unrecognized by the individual, who is more concerned with deactivating relationships and avoiding emotion altogether than they are with managing their shame more constructively. Shame is not the same as guilt, which by definition is vestigial in people with ASPD. Guilt requires a recognition of having done something wrong, and it leads to efforts to right the wrong, often driven by empathy for the person who has been wronged and the wish to repair the social rupture. Persistent shame shows itself by the individual becoming excessively sensitive to others' states of mind and inferring all sorts of negative evaluations by others because of overuse of the external dimension of mentalizing.

There are several things that the clinician can do to make shame a more accessible theme and less of an "elephant in the room."

1. **Identify and normalize shame as an everyday human emotion**—that is, name it and note it—in the MBT-I meetings. Use everyday examples: "*Sometimes when someone sees us unable to do something that we think we should be able to do we become angry with them and force them to try, hoping that they will fail, too.*"
2. **Explore examples in the MBT-I modules and in MBT-ASPD-G sessions** when a patient reports that they have a negative self-evaluation.
3. **Ask other patients in the group what they think of a participant who is describing something about himself.** Their response is more often compassionate than condemning.
4. **Maintain the non-judgmental, not-knowing stance of MBT** when exploring potential shame, and use an empathic "we-mode" focus: "*Something flashed across your mind there, I think. Sometimes we can feel badly about ourselves in circumstances like this. How were you feeling about yourself when you were talking about that?*" The tone of the clinician's intervention and their body language are important here, as the patient will be overfocused on non-verbal cues. The "we" component must be authentic, and for this to be the case the clinician needs to identify with the shame to some extent.
5. **Explore prototypical shame events if the patient can manage this, and identify their mental approach and reaction to it.** Do they want to change their reaction, live with it, or hide it as best as they can? If change is important, how can that occur? Perhaps they need to be able to express the shame to others while simultaneously maintaining self-compassion rather than activating self-criticism. Recognizing how compassionate another person can be toward them and realizing how condemning they are toward themselves can be a game changer.

Future Self

Identifying how patients see themselves in the future and what they now want to change in themselves is an important discussion to have in the initial formulation and then in the group. The group discusses the topic together as part of the discussion of values: "*Where do we see ourselves in the future? What do we want to get out of our lives? What sort of social and personal roles do we have, and how would we like them to change?*" Patients may be overambitious about themselves or have impractical ideas, and the main aim in the group is for them to consider how comfortable they feel about themselves and their reactions to others in relationships. For example, it is more in keeping with the aims of MBT-ASPD-G to seek a personal future as a more demonstrably loving person as opposed to an unloving and unlovable person, or as someone who can be assertive but not aggressive.

Pretend Mode

MBT-ASPD-G sessions often begin with a discussion between participants that is couched in pseudo-philosophical-political language about how awful the system is, and how no one can be trusted. The discussion is in the context of a jointly held belief system that lacks connection to reality. In essence, this is pretend mode. However, contrary to the principle of always addressing pretend mode as soon as it is present, the clinician leaves the conversation until there is a natural lull, only then starting the session by linking back to the previous week. This opening can be considered as "chat mode," and it serves the useful purpose of bringing a sense of unity to the group. However, pretend mode that arises during the group session needs to be addressed in the normal way.

Working with Anger as a Problematic Emotion

Clinical Example: Anger as a Problematic Emotion

"I asked the barman for a drink very politely. He ignored me and carried on standing there and did not even look at me. I asked him again politely. When he ignored me again, I picked up the glasses on the bar and threw them at the mirror behind him. You cannot allow yourself to be treated like that."

This story contains within it many of the features associated with antisocial violence. The violence is as sudden as it is unexpected, and arises in the context of an interpersonal threat to self-esteem, with the narrator being, in their view, diminished, unseen, and disrespected. When treating people with ASPD, it is important that the clinician sees behind the act of aggression and does not become distracted by it. It is all too easy to focus on the drama and miss the psychological pain behind the action. As a rule of thumb, the clinician should assume until it is proven otherwise that the internal states most feared by people with ASPD are threats to self-esteem. As we have already discussed, people with ASPD inflate their self-esteem by demanding respect from others, controlling those around them, and even creating an atmosphere of fear. This maintains pride, prestige, and status—there is evidence in the world around them of their status, and people's behavior toward them matches their self-appraisal. Loss of status is devastating if experienced in psychic equivalence, as a new reality of a weak and diminished self emerges, revealing disavowed shameful internal states that threaten to overwhelm the person. Therefore any threat of loss of status becomes firmly rooted as a dangerous reality that has to be dealt with by physical force. A momentary inability to mentalize—to see behind the threat to what is in the mind of the person who is apparently threatening them—means that they have no way of keeping out a rapidly falling self-esteem and loss of position.

Clinical intervention in the group when exploring events follows the MBT affect trajectory (see Chapter 4) with a specific focus on the events leading up to the violence. Just as a patient who has engaged in self-harm is asked to review the events and the mental states associated with the act (see Chapter 4), so the patient who is violent is asked to consider in the group the events and mental states surrounding the violence. The group members are asked to:

1. explore the feelings and experiences of the narrator as the situation developed at the time
2. ask about the narrator's reflection on what was happening at the time, looking back at the event
3. enquire about the narrator's experience in the group while they are telling the story
4. consider their own reactions to the story and what they can learn from it.

Common Clinical Problems in MBT-ASPD-G

This section outlines some common clinical problems associated with treating patients with ASPD.

Recruitment to a Cause

Patients with ASPD recruit each other to their "cause." A cause is often related to how unfairly an organization or individual has treated them—for example, unfairness in the social benefits they receive, or failure of the probation service to provide effective help. The discussion between participants focuses on the failures and defects of the people within the organization. In talking about their problem, the narrator gradually recruits other members of the group to their cause and, in doing so, the group members organize themselves in support of the "victimized" group member and demand that the group leaders get something done about the problem.

Recruitment to a cause is a common pathway to pretend mode within the group. A single perspective emerges—unsurprisingly that of the protagonist, who now has widespread justification for their grudge—and all are agreed that someone else needs to do something. The task of the clinician is to halt this spiral into pretend mode by actively managing the group process.

Clinical Examples: Recruitment to a Cause

Example 1

A patient discussed how the local authority housing department had not dealt with his application for a flat in the way that he wanted. He had asked whether a medical officer had assessed his application. He was told that a senior housing manager had seen the application and that it was not being sent to the medical officer because this was deemed unnecessary. At this point the patient told the housing officer that they were not doing their job properly and threatened them, telling them he was coming to the department to "sort them out."

In response, another patient said that the housing department never did its job properly and the people there were only interested in themselves. He agreed that they needed "sorting out." Gradually this exchange developed into a discussion between all the members of the group about how people in the housing department were incompetent and useless. Many examples were given. Finally, the group turned to the clinicians leading the group, who were told that they needed to write to the housing department to get something done about it all.

Example 2

A patient reported that he had stabbed someone, not fatally, but to "wound and warn." He had allowed his flat to be used for meetings of a local gang, of which his nephew was a senior member. He told them that he wanted them to leave as it was late. The gang leader had been using some drugs and responded by saying that they would leave when he was ready and when he wanted to. In response, the patient gave him a 10-minute warning and then a 5-minute warning. When the leader did not appear to be leaving, the patient went to the kitchen, picked up a kitchen knife and, after a further brief warning, stabbed him in the arm. The gang leader ran off as the patient chased him, and the other gang members left quickly. On hearing the patient's story, the group immediately began to justify this action as being appropriate and proportionate to the disrespect.

Taking the second clinical example, the clinicians who were leading the group thought that this incident needed careful exploration due to the apparent risk, but when they tried to do this the other participants quickly pointed out that the stabbing had been an appropriate reaction to the circumstances. They referred to the fact that the patient had given warnings: "*That is fair. You give a warning and if they don't take any notice they have it coming to them,*" "*See, he gave three warnings. That is more than enough. Only one should be necessary.*" They pointed out that "*You can't allow younger people to take advantage of your generosity,*" "*They start getting the wrong idea about you and think you are soft,*" and "*People like that only understand that sort of lesson.*" The participants concluded that this reaction was the only sensible way to manage the situation, and that the clinicians would understand this if they were living in the same circumstances.

What Can the Clinician Do?

1. Empathize with the patients' experience—for example, of being ignored, disrespected, or taken advantage of—while remaining neutral about the points they are making: "*No one likes to be taken advantage of. If you ask someone politely to do something it is problematic if they challenge that request; no one likes their authority to be questioned. What was so difficult for you about this time?*"
2. Manage the mentalizing process—once the story has unfolded, rewind and explore the story with particular emphasis on the patient's experience during the event, and link this to their current experience in the telling of the story. *Does the feeling now have the same urgency and threat? Can they reappraise what was happening? What have they learned from it?* Ask other patients to identify and consider the feelings of the narrator during the event, and then ask them to describe their experience of listening to the story. The participants will identify with the narrator, and this may allow exploration of everyone's sensitivity to shame or humiliation or the experience of being controlled by another, which threatens their narcissistic grandiosity.

   In placing the action in an emotional context, the aim is to move the focus from behavioral actions, which are so admired by the participants, to an integrated cognitive/affective mental understanding of what has happened, and to place it in an interpersonal context—that is, to widen the field of scrutiny. For example, the discussion about the stabbing should not only be about the potential humiliation but also be about the challenge to authority. The focus moves from stabbing as an appropriate response in the circumstances: "*You know, sometimes when people don't do as we ask we feel challenged by it and need to make sure we don't lose our position in the eyes of others. If you look back now, was anything like that going on for you?*"
3. Question their insistence that the eventual action was the only appropriate response. People with ASPD believe that others will only "get the message" when it is delivered in teleological mode, and they themselves only understand others' mental states according to their action: "*The reason the housing manager did not pass the application to the medical officer was because she wanted to prevent me being rehoused*" or "*Stabbing him was the correct and reasonable response because it worked—the other person left the flat as I had told him to.*" The clinician needs to challenge the group to consider non-teleological solutions to the problem—for example, "*Write to the housing manager, copied to the medical officer, with the expert by experience's help,*" "*Mention that the patient could call the gang leader's big brother (or someone whom he respects and is concerned about) who is the patient's friend and ask this person to 'talk to him' over the phone and let him know that he has to leave, otherwise he will get into trouble.*"

In summary:

1. Listen to the story and allow other patients to identify with it.
2. Rewind and attempt to re-explore the narrative from the perspective of the emotional states of the narrator.
3. Encourage other participants to identify the complexity of the emotions of the narrator.
4. Generalize the experience when possible to focus on underlying or subdominant components, which commonly include potential humiliation and relational threat.
5. Identify ways to manage the underlying threat to self-esteem differently.

Defiance

People with ASPD are "rebels" when faced with rules, and oppositional to perceived or actual authority. This may have much merit, of course, and can be understandable in the context of their life experience, but there is a tendency for them to see clinicians as being in authority and a part of the "establishment," and therefore makers of rules. These beliefs and assumptions will interfere with patients' engagement and treatment, just as their high levels of epistemic mistrust infuse all of their relationships with suspicion. The dynamic between patients and the clinician is immediately competitive, and it is all too easy for a contrary attitude to be activated in the clinician. When this happens, the patient digs in.

For example, during the assessment the clinician may ask the individual to consider reducing their acts of aggression. However, the patient may not have this aim. The more the clinician tries to enforce the aim and insist on it as an area for change, the more defiant the person with ASPD is likely to become, arguing, for instance, that it is the world that needs to change rather than them. The patient may be fearful of change for many reasons, not least of which is that their relationship with the world is organized around maintaining a sense of personal safety and inviolability. Change is experienced as submission, loss of face, and an experience of shame; the clinician will evoke such feelings by challenging the patient directly. Therefore clinicians should avoid any insistence on their own perspective initially, and determinedly use a not-knowing stance to elaborate the patient's experience.

What Can the Clinician Do?

1. Ensure that an oppositional dynamic is not triggered. This is achieved by using the MBT Loop (see Chapter 4), with the clinician maintaining their mentalizing and inhibiting their counter-responsiveness.
2. Present their own view for the participant to consider once the participant's perspective has been identified, explored, and validated in part.

Clinical Example: Addressing Defiance

A patient was complaining about being forced by the job center to seek work.

> **Patient:** I am being hounded by the job center to go to work. They phone me all the time and insist I attend the job center on a daily basis. I am not going back to work. It is harassment.

Without commenting on the perceived harassment by the job center, the clinician sensitively moved the conversation on to how the patient appraised his own ability to work.

Clinician: What do you think about going back to work?

Patient: I want to, and I don't like the idea that I cannot earn money for myself. But I am not ready yet.

Clinician: In what way?

Patient: Just not ready.

Clinician: (*in the context of their mutual understanding of the patient's anxiety*) That sounds to me like your anxiety speaking.

Patient: Well, I haven't worked for a long time, so it's not surprising.

Clinician: Sounds like they don't see that. How do they see you, do you think?

Patient: As a sponger, but I'm not.

Clinician: So you are living with a feeling of not meeting your own standards at the moment and you are naturally concerned about a new pattern in your life. But it is terrible to be seen as a sponger by others when this is really not what is happening.

Patient: What do you think?

Clinician: I apologize if it sounds like I am suggesting you do go back to work, but I am thinking about another aspect of all this along with working with your anxiety. I thought that working might be one way of improving your sense of personal achievement and making you feel better about yourself. Is it worth us working on how you might begin to feel you are achieving something?

3. Validate the patient's perspective, but with a twist. In MBT terms, this is a subtle challenge (see Chapter 4) that does not go as far as being oppositional. The aim is to give a slightly different vantage point on the same situation, looking at it from a perspective that the patient has not considered: "*Working is a pain most of the time. I agree. But it is often how we use our talents and feel good about ourselves and gain confidence. Do you feel good about yourself generally at the moment?*"
4. Use an affect focus (see Chapter 4) about the interaction that the patient has engaged in, taking some responsibility for it: "*We seem to be getting into something here, where the more I ask about working and what might be stopping you, the more you oppose it. Do you have a sense of that? Maybe I am taking a position here that I should not be taking. It might be better for us to consider if this sort of interaction is something that repeats itself.*"

Escalating Threats: Patient to Patient

Participants may threaten each other in the group or even outside the group on WhatsApp, Facebook, or other social media sites. Of course this is unacceptable. Verbal threats and physical violence are proscribed for all participants in the agreement made at the beginning of the group. Nevertheless, aggression between group members, or between them and the clinicians (discussed later), may occur. Aggression between the group members is often related to misinterpretation of what someone says or automatic assumptions about the other person based on their facial expression or tone of voice. Threats between patients stimulate anxiety and fear in the clinician, and undermine their mentalizing. In this situation the key task is for the clinician to retain their mentalizing and intervene rapidly.

As soon as the clinician senses rising tension between patients it is important to intervene. De-escalating impending aggression early on is the key to successful resolution. Initially the aggression is usually verbal but, as the participants often point out, the time lapse between verbal and physical aggression can be very small.

What Can the Clinician Do?

1. Use any de-escalating technique that you think might be useful! Keep calm verbally and physically, and maintain a relatively neutral facial expression with natural eye contact. Do not stare at the patient, lean forward, or clench your fists. Maintain a physical distance if the patient is not seated, and do not touch them.

Clinical Example: Response to Physical Contact

A member of staff came out of a room to ask two patients who were talking loudly in the corridor to keep quiet. In doing so, he unthinkingly touched one of them on the shoulder. The patient stopped and turned on the member of staff: *"What did you touch me for? Don't you dare touch me. Who the f*** do you think you are?"*

Physical contact with a patient in low-mentalizing mode is likely to be experienced as an intrusion and dangerous to the continuity of bodily and mental self, and consequently perceived as an attack that has to be responded to.

Keep talking and suggest that the group returns to an earlier subject when mentalizing was present. If necessary, engage in a "broken-record" repetition of what you would like to do—rewind and re-consider.

2. The MBT clinician has to maintain a balance between taking authority to manage the group and their role in stimulating an interactive mentalizing process. Escalating threats between participants suggest that mentalizing has collapsed. This is the point at which the clinician should take authority (as distinct from becoming authoritarian, which would be an escalating approach).

Clinical Example: Roger and Steve

Roger: Come over here and say that.

Steve: You don't want me to come over there to say it. You really don't. You are a piss artist.

Clinician: Thank you. We are not here to call each other names. Steve, thanks for the apology, and Roger, thanks for accepting the apology. Let's now go back to where we were when we were talking about how we work out if someone is trustworthy.

Steve: I haven't given an apology.

Clinician: No, I gave it for you, and thanks for that. Going back, as I said . . .

Here the clinician is trying to manage the situation by reducing the aggression quickly, keeping some control over the interaction. It may be possible to revisit the problem between the two participants later. People with ASPD can tend to bear grudges and are unlikely to forgive in a meaningful way. Occasionally, the clinician will be told that they have sorted it out between themselves. This is an indicator to ask how this was done and if they could talk about it as an illustration of how to work out conflict without aggression.

3. If Steve leaves the group in the context of this altercation with Roger, one of the clinicians (if two clinicians are running the group) may go out to talk to him while the remaining clinician works to calm down the atmosphere in the group and talks to Roger. It is not necessarily optimal to persuade Steve to return to the group. It may be better that he goes home now and returns next week. But if Steve calms down, the clinician can go back into the group to find out if it is safe for him to return. He can then report back to Steve and negotiate a quick safety agreement between all of the participants and between Steve and Roger.

Clinical Example: Roger and Steve (continued)

Clinician 1 (*to Steve*): OK. I will go back in to see if things are safe for everyone and check out if Roger is calmer too.

Clinician 1 (*on coming back into the group*): I have been talking to Steve and he is OK now. If things are calmer here, shall I ask him to come back in and then we can go back to thinking about what has been happening? But I need to know it is safe and that we are not going to start an argument again. Roger, what do you think?

Roger: I don't care.

Clinician 2: Roger, do you think you can now manage not to get into an argument with Steve and we can think more about what was going on?

The two clinicians then take a decision. The principle to follow is for each clinician to support a different protagonist in the interaction (an approach known as siding; see Chapter 5), and it is for the clinicians to take authority over the decision on reconvening the group.

4. It may become necessary to ask both patients to leave a group. In this case, do not ask them to leave at the same time. Suggest that it would be better if they both left. One clinician then takes out one of the patients and has a brief conversation with them to try to maintain an alliance and to de-escalate the situation. The remaining clinician in the group does the same with the other person, and then asks them to leave after a suitable interval.

Escalating Threats: Patient to Clinician

To some extent threats to the safety of the clinician are more significant to the immediate continuation of the group. Clinicians will not be able to maintain their own mentalizing in the context of persistent threats toward them or even toward their families. Maintaining mentalizing in the clinician is a top priority for an MBT group. Therefore the principle is for the clinician to maintain or reinstate their own mentalizing in the context of a personal threat.

What Can the Clinician Do?

Above all, the clinician needs to ensure their own personal safety. If it is not clear that they are safe they should stop the group session and seek support from other staff. Assuming that their personal safety is not under threat, the clinician has a number of options.

1. De-escalate the situation as described in the section on patient-to-patient threats.
2. Apologize for their difficulty in thinking when under threat. The clinician needs to find a way to say this without becoming submissive—for example, "*It is really difficult for me to think about how to help when I feel under threat*" or "*It will make it hard for me to continue to try to help if I cannot feel safe in developing our work together about your problems.*"
3. If the threat is not severe but is related more to a hierarchical relationship between patient and clinician, this needs to be identified as an affect focus that is interfering with treatment.

Idealization of the Patients Themselves as a Group

Patients with ASPD rapidly identify with each other early in treatment, seeing their own personal qualities and problems as shared between them. This may be the first time that many of them have sat down with others who share similar problems, and they find it reassuring to be able to identify with other individuals. This is all to the good. But it soon becomes group pretend mode with groupthink.

Rapidly, perhaps too rapidly, the patients begin to think that they understand each other well. When the clinicians start to question a patient, other patients answer for that person and suggest that the clinicians do not understand the patient in the way that the group members understand each other. The clinicians are excluded from the patients' idealization of themselves as a group. The patients may even arrange something outside the group, framed as mutual support. If the clinicians try to challenge this, they are seen as interfering and as failing to understand how the group members can give each other mutual support: "*No one else helps us so we have to help each other.*" This is a time when giving practical advice to each other becomes the norm. However, teleology does not help to recover mentalizing.

What Can the Clinician Do?

1. Initially, it may be best to accept the cohesion and unity that idealization of themselves as a group brings. Let the pretend mode run for a time at the beginning of the group.
2. Validate the patients' experience of sharing their problems, the sense of belonging that this experience brings, and how valuable this is, especially when one does not have the experience of mutuality very often.
3. Move from validation to suggest that this unity is excellent because it gives the background that they all need to explore differences in perspectives, which is really helpful.
4. Consider challenging the whole group process (for a discussion of challenge, see Chapter 4). This will entail counterintuitive comments, clarification of the circularity and superficiality of the discussion, and mischief making—perhaps with some

cynicism, as, for example, in the context of a discussion about how all of the people they meet in organizations are unhelpful and "stupid:" "*It is amazing how all of us come across so many useless and hopeless people in our daily lives. We seem to all attract them somehow.*"

5. Work on the general advice that group members often give to each other in this context to make it more personal—for example, "*I have had that problem. You should do . . . .*" Here the clinician must attempt to extract a mentalizing process from the advice: "*What is it about Mark that makes you think that your solution might fit him?*" Explore aspects of the solution that helped the individual, and what it is about their suggestion that makes them think it is useful for the other person. Ask the other person to consider it in detail.

Emotional Expression: Self

Earlier in this chapter we suggested that people with ASPD have problems expressing affective components of their own internal states, particularly within interpersonal contexts. Identifying their feelings—especially those associated with vulnerability, such as shame and humiliation—and expressing them within the current interpersonal context is not something that patients will do naturally in the group. However, there is one exception to this—group members will express forcibly how tense they are or how "close to the edge" and explosive they feel. They will also express anger and issue threats. This is less often related to the interpersonal context in the group, and more likely to be an expression of their baseline state or a feeling about the organizations they discuss together, such as the police, the housing department, or the benefits office.

The aim in the group is to encourage patients to identify their current feeling in the group rather than to express their bitterness about external organizations, and to increase their recognition of the way that context influences this. So, for example, an experience of the clinicians listening to them and taking their problems seriously can be calming, whereas a sense of being ignored can be arousing.

People with ASPD may also have a limited recognition of the complexity of feelings, with basic emotions being colored by social emotions. This is covered in the MBT-I sessions, and it may be necessary to remind patients about this. Aggression as part of survival may be covering fear of humiliation, for example, or related to a fear of losing agency or that someone else is trying to control them.

Finally, expression of emotion by one participant allows the exploration of early recognition of that state by others in the group. The clinician combines emotional expression by an individual with a discussion of the recognition of this state by others.

What Can the Clinician Do?

1. Ensure that the participants are reminded of the information about emotions that was given in the MBT-I sessions.
2. Specifically work on identifying affects in the group: "*How do you feel now?*" If the patient is unable to label the emotion, ask them to describe their state as best they can, from their bodily feeling to their general level of tension.
3. Explore possible reasons for the feeling if it is identified: "*What makes you feel like that? Is this related to a particular interpersonal context?*"
5. Move on to ask other patients to describe what feeling the first patient is having and how they reach that conclusion. What evidence do they use? Is it based on their

sensitivity to the person's bodily and emotional expression, or is it more to do with identifying with the content of the discussion and related to how they themselves would feel in similar circumstances?

6. Finally, close the circle by asking the patients what feelings they have after having listened to the first patient, and what it brings up in their minds about themselves.

Emotional Expression: Recognition in Others

The inner emotional state of a person may or may not be recognized by other members of the group, but it is useful to remember that people with ASPD may be cognitively aware of the states of others but they do not empathize with the effect that feeling state has on the other person. At times they misuse their understanding of someone else's underlying state.

Clinical Example: Misuse of Understanding of Another Person's Emotional State

A patient described how difficult it was for him to identify how he felt. The clinician realized that asking the patient to say how he was feeling made this person feel exposed and embarrassed in front of the other members of the group. So the clinician, empathizing with the patient being in the spotlight and how difficult that was for him, sensitively changed the subject. Almost immediately, one of the other patients said *"Don't change the topic so quickly. I think Gary needs to say how he feels. How do you feel? Come on, tell us."* It became apparent that this person wanted the embarrassed patient to feel more and more uncomfortable, while he himself felt increasingly dominant and in control.

In this situation, the clinician tries to rebalance the mentalizing process by asking the individual who is tormenting the other person to start describing his *own* inner state. This is another example of "siding." The clinician becomes psychologically protective of the vulnerable person by moving the focus away from them, in this case toward the "attacker," who is made more uncomfortable by being asked what *his* current feeling is.

What Can the Clinician Do?

1. Work with the group members to see whether they identified how another participant was or is feeling. If not, why not? Is it because the feeling was or is not being expressed, or is it because they were not alert to the person's feeling? For example, they may not have noticed that one of the group members was distressed, yet the clinicians were aware of this due to the patient's demeanor and facial expression.
2. Explore the external mentalizing focus and how it increases understanding of how someone else feels but at the same time can create confusion unless we test out our assumptions.
3. Work with a specific example in the group of how a patient feels and whether it was apparent to the rest of the group.

Moving from an External Mentalizing Focus to an Internal Focus On Other Minds

Relying on external cues—such as facial expression, eye movements, and body posture—to indicate the motives of others is a normal process and it underpins many daily interactions. People with ASPD are usually quite sensitive to external cues, particularly if these are related to the way someone looks at them; "the look" is a universal trigger for aggression and violence, and yet they can rarely explain what it actually looks like to them. Reasoning with such ill-defined cues presents a problem: "*What is 'the look'? What does 'the look' mean about what someone thinks and feels?*" Expressions are well recognized when they occur, but cannot be meaningfully described. Sensitivity to external cues does not translate into interest in the internal emotional states of the other or into curiosity about the other's underlying motives. People with ASPD often assume that others' motives are malign unless proven otherwise, and react accordingly to counter the threat, regardless of the expressions of affect that they encounter. The clinician needs to help these patients to pause, stop this automatic type of thinking, and take a genuine interest in other people's internal states after having identified an external cue.

What Can the Clinician Do?

1. In group work, ask the patients to practice questioning someone in the group about their internal states: "*Tell me what makes you shout like that.*" Insist that the patients listen to that person's answers.
2. Take an interaction in the group and focus on elements of the interpersonal understanding.

Clinical Example: Understanding Other People's Internal States

One patient was saying how angry he was about a child protection social worker, raising his voice as he told the story of her alleged incompetence. When he paused in his diatribe, the clinician asked him to stop so that the group could explore their understanding of his current feelings and the basis for their understanding. The group said that he was obviously angry, because he was shouting. The clinician said that he could see that, but he thought that this person also felt aggrieved that he was being misunderstood by the social worker, and that in addition he now felt powerless to change anything. The clinician then asked the patient to appraise the accuracy of this understanding of his feelings.

3. Generate a process that supports the participants in appraising feeling states and recognizing underlying motives as more complex than the binary "for me or against me" understanding to which people with ASPD so often subscribe.

Paranoid Reactions

Paranoid reactions might occur in the group. These may result in escalating threats (described earlier), which are themselves often triggered by misunderstandings, sensitivity, and frank paranoid interpretations of something that is said, or by inappropriate reliance on an external mentalizing focus and associated assumptions about others' motives. Occasionally, a patient may react explosively to something that the clinician or one of the other participants says, and in this case the interventions suggested for de-escalating threats are recommended. However, the reaction may be primarily mental rather than physical, with the patient responding verbally, albeit expressing considerable anxiety.

Clinical Example: Paranoid Reactions

In a discussion about feelings, the clinician suggested that it might be useful for the group to consider how they begin to recognize that they are becoming angry.

***James** (reacting suddenly)*: You are trying to control us. You are trying to take us over. I am not doing this. You only want to find out how our minds work so that you can take over.

Clinician: I am so sorry, James. Can you tell me what I was saying or doing that makes you think that?

James: You just ask us to tell you what happens in our minds so that you can control what we think.

Clinician: Please can you describe how I do that? I don't want to do that at all. So I need to be sure that I don't keep making you feel that, as I can see that any of us would feel uncomfortable in circumstances like that and not want to let anyone know how we feel.

James: Why would you want to know what makes me angry? It is just so that you can deliberately make me angry whenever you want to.

What Can the Clinician Do?

1. Try to understand the patient's perspective. Suggest that the motive was not to control the patient, as the clinician has explained in the previous clinical example, but that you would like to try to see what it was that made the patient see it like that: "*Help me see how you took that from what I said. Do you know other people who try to do that? Can you remember when someone else tried to get control over you?*"
2. Explore patient-to-patient motives and reactions. Do they all have the same experience of the clinician's motivation? "*Is this something that others can relate to?*"
3. Try to find something that you can validate within the reaction. James had had some difficult experiences with his father, who asked him questions merely in order to find an opportunity to punish him: "*Does it make sense to others as well that if you have a father like James remembers his father, you end up being suspicious when anyone tries to ask you questions about yourself?*"
4. In opening up the discussion to the group and asking the participants if they had a similar understanding of the other's/clinician's motive (which is part of the MBT Loop; see Chapter 4), the clinician moves toward the likely driver of the paranoid reaction—the fear of helplessness and shame. Beware of humiliating the patient while doing this. Being reminded of one's powerlessness is certainly humiliating. The middle of a paranoid attack may not be the best time to try to explore underlying shame if it is part of the driver of the reaction. This exploration can be done only when the patients are calmer and more reflective, and can look back at themselves. Nevertheless, by picturing it in their own mind, the clinician can empathize with the fact that they would feel extremely vulnerable when answering questions about activities in the knowledge that this could lead to unpredictable punishment. The clinician can even express admiration of how well and courageously James had coped with a brutalizing parent.

Concluding Remarks

MBT is modified for the treatment of people with ASPD, but the core processes and interventions of the model are retained. The effectiveness of the approach is currently under investigation in a randomized controlled trial, following the principle that all mentalization-based treatment approaches should be subjected to rigorous assessment [11, 12]. The current indications are that treatment has beneficial effects, and that MBT-ASPD-G can be implemented successfully within a mental health service. Integration with the criminal justice system is necessary in order to disrupt a default of antisocial behavior being criminalized and leading to punishment, which serves only to further embed the individual's experience of alienation and social isolation, and prevents a personal attitudinal change through learning prosocial behavior from the social world.

References

1. Sharp C, Wright AG, Fowler JC et al. The structure of personality pathology: both general ('g') and specific ('s') factors? *J Abnorm Psychol* 2015; **124**: 387–98.
2. Wright AG, Hopwood CJ, Skodol AE, Morey LC. Longitudinal validation of general and specific structural features of personality pathology. *J Abnorm Psychol* 2016; **125**: 1120–34.
3. Bateman A, Bolton R, Fonagy P. Antisocial personality disorder: a mentalizing framework. *Focus* 2013; **11**: 178–86.
4. Bateman A, Fonagy P. Comorbid antisocial and borderline personality disorders: mentalization-based treatment. *J Clin Psychol* 2008; **64**: 181–94.
5. Gilligan J. *Violence: Reflections on Our Deadliest Epidemic.* London, UK: Jessica Kingsley Publishers, 2000.
6. Kim J, Cicchetti D. Longitudinal pathways linking child maltreatment, emotion regulation, peer relations, and psychopathology. *J Child Psychol Psychiatry* 2010; **51**: 706–16.
7. Sharp C, Vanwoerden S, Van Baardewijk Y et al. Callous-unemotional traits are associated with deficits in recognizing complex emotions in preadolescent children. *J Personal Disord* 2015; **29**: 347–59.
8. Bateman A, Fonagy P. *Mentalization-Based Treatment for Personality Disorders: A Practical Guide.* Oxford, UK: Oxford University Press, 2016.
9. Bateman A, Motz A, Yakeley J. Antisocial personality disorder in community and prison settings. In: Bateman A, Fonagy P, eds. *Handbook of Mentalizing in Mental Health Practice*, 2nd ed. Washington, DC: American Psychiatric Association Publishing, 2019; 335–49.
10. Coccaro EF. The Overt Aggression Scale Modified (OAS-M) for clinical trials targeting impulsive aggression and intermittent explosive disorder: validity, reliability, and correlates. *J Psychiatr Res* 2020; **124**: 50–57.
11. Fonagy P, Yakeley J, Gardner T et al. Mentalization for Offending Adult Males (MOAM): study protocol for a randomized controlled trial to evaluate mentalization-based treatment for antisocial personality disorder in male offenders on community probation. *Trials* 2020; **21**: 1001.
12. Bateman A, O'Connell J, Lorenzini N et al. A randomised controlled trial of mentalization-based treatment versus structured clinical management for patients with comorbid borderline personality disorder and antisocial personality disorder. *BMC Psychiatry* 2016; **16**: 304.

Part III

Application and Adaptations for Mental Health Presentations

Chapter 8

Avoidant Personality Disorder

Introduction

Avoidant personality disorder (AvPD) presents a special challenge to most clinicians. This is not simply because there is a paucity of research concerning this group, in stark contrast to the considerable body of research on borderline personality disorder (BPD)—nor is it due to the lack of a compelling theoretical framework that would support the formulation of an individual presenting with AvPD, or to the lack of structured evidence-based interventions for individuals who are obviously experiencing very substantial distress. The reason for the challenge is that the subjective experiences of people with AvPD are hard to articulate collaboratively, which often leaves the clinician in the dark about such basic questions as what "avoidance" or even "improvement" means for the patient. The usual clinical strategies of mentalization-based treatment (MBT) also fall short in the face of rudimentary descriptions of inner experiences and meager sense making.

The Diagnosis of AvPD

The dimensional classification of severity of self- and other personality functioning and the specification of personality trait domains as described in the alternative model in Section III of DSM-5 [1] and in ICD-11 [2] are far better suited to the MBT approach in general. This is without doubt the case for AvPD in clinical practice. However, the description of AvPD in DSM-IV as "a pervasive pattern of social inhibition, feelings of inadequacy, and hypersensitivity to negative evaluation" (American Psychiatric Association [3], p. 672) remains helpful in providing a clinical description, even if it is simplified for the sake of efficient communication. This and some other clinical descriptions in the literature [4–7] are summarized in Box 8.1.

Box 8.1 Descriptive characteristics of AvPD with some features that may differentiate it from other personality disorders.

- Pervasive pattern of social inhibition.
- Feelings of inadequacy.
- Hypersensitivity to negative evaluation.
- Reduced ability to experience pleasure.
- Hypersensitivity to psychic pain.
- Shyness and reticence, leading to a life with few rewards and much suffering.
- Reluctance to initiate social relationships (individuals with schizoid personality disorder do not want social relationships).

Box 8.1 *(cont.)*

- Intense feelings of internalized shame and a desire to actively avoid relationships despite feeling a need to belong.
- Fear of rejection or humiliation, which may result in the person appearing unassertive (individuals with dependent personality disorder may be more fearful of abandonment, show an inability to cope in isolation, and initiate and cling to relationships in which they feel accepted).

These descriptors highlight the phobic nature of AvPD and point to potential overlaps with social anxiety disorder (SAD), which is also characterized by fears of becoming embarrassed or of feeling inadequate as well as minimizing aspects related to low self-esteem and hypersensitivity to rejection. Some authors believe that there are qualitative differences between SAD and AvPD. From an interpersonal perspective, SAD, social phobia, and AvPD are defined by a marked tendency toward social avoidance and non-assertiveness [8]. Qualitative differences, if any, are likely to be subtle and relate to how the person manages this interpersonal challenge psychologically and physically [9]. The more intense concern about self-esteem, identity, and relational functioning, as well as reduced ability to experience enjoyment, may differentiate AvPD from SAD [10].

MBT largely sidesteps these diagnostic issues by seeking a single final common developmental pathway of vulnerability for a range of severe disorders that may nevertheless be addressed using a family of interventions based on a core model that requires technical modification to meet the needs of different clinical presentations. Thus the challenge for MBT formulations related to a specific diagnosis such as AvPD is twofold:

1. to identify a general failure in the domain of mentalizing that links the presentation to the "family" of difficulties that can be appropriately managed by MBT techniques
2. to define the presence of a specific configuration or pattern of mentalizing anomalies that directly link to the described phenomenology and current evidence base for AvPD, to allow individual formulations with sufficient detail to focus and guide the way in which treatment is undertaken.

Establishing the Key Concerns of Patients with AvPD

The characteristic difficulty associated with AvPD is an expectation that others will not be available, and therefore it makes sense to suppress emotions and individual needs in order to avoid negative outcomes, including the disapproval of others [11]. The intense concerns of people with AvPD are about self-esteem, identity, and relational functioning, and these individuals also find it difficult to experience enjoyment.

The Experience of AvPD

The complexity of the experience of AvPD mirrors some of the so-called "push-me-pull-you" dynamics of BPD, with intensely ambivalent attachment organization—on the one hand fearing and on the other hand longing for connection, while at the same time also intensely desiring solitude. It is confusing for both the patient and the clinician that someone can wish to fit in and be part of a community, and to establish meaningful connections to people around them, while at the same time expressing a powerful need for the freedom and restoration that being alone and even isolated provides for them.

Most threatening of all are the feelings and judgments of others, their reasons and drivers, and their possible objectives and aspirations. Proximity to others, although desirable, quickly becomes unhelpful, as people with AvPD feel increasingly vulnerable when intimacy increases—the possibility of getting closer increases the risk of being "found out" or "exposed" in some way.

Isolation is not a good solution for most individuals with a diagnosis of AvPD. Being by themselves leaves them alone with their painful subjective experiences and intense negative feelings about themselves, with a real danger of being crushed and drowned by untethered ideas and emotions spinning around in their mind. Some of these ideas are excruciating doubts about themselves, and deep uncertainties concerning their own accomplishments, attitudes, plans, perceptions, beliefs, feelings, wishes, intentions, and opinions—in fact any aspect that could be ascribed to the self.

As with individuals with narcissistic personality disorder (NPD) (see Chapter 6) and antisocial personality disorder (see Chapter 7), avoiding "loss of face"—that is, humiliation—is critically important for people with a diagnosis of AvPD. Patients may be reluctant to reveal the full extent of the distress that they experience because they benefit more than most from preserving an outward semblance of normality and appearing in the same way that others appear to them—calm, secure, competent, assured, and on. For these individuals, it is particularly important not to attract attention, stand out, or be noticed, because this enables them to avoid the crushing judgments that they can experience from any kind of reaction from others. Social withdrawal occurs when the strategy of "merging into the crowd" fails—in brief, avoidance is not related to wanting to avoid contact with others, but rather to wanting to avoid what can be felt as the inevitable reaction of others.

Because the level of distress engendered by these thoughts and ideas is substantial (comparable to that experienced by individuals with BPD), patients with AvPD are often quite self-absorbed, both studiously dissecting *and* trying to completely ignore their experiences. However, inadequate social exposure means that their capacity to make informed normative judgments about individual behaviors and cooperative social behaviors is quite limited. This leads to a sense of uncertainty about their place in the everyday world, and contributes to a sense of ontological insecurity. They present as somewhat alienated from their own experience, and give an impression that they understand little about their wishes, their agency, and, more generally, their subjectivity. For the clinician, this can make attempts to obtain information about the internal experiences of patients with AvPD deeply frustrating.

Often the best route into subjectivity may be via the physical world that surrounds the patient, as it provides a welcome refuge from painful and unproductive self-scrutiny. Enquiring into activities that give relief (e.g., nature walks, pets, art, music) may be a way of exploring interpersonal relationships when direct questioning might yield too little valuable information.

Clinical Example: Jane

In a matter-of-fact way, Jane, who is 24 years old, described her current feelings of being alone in the world and never really being with people even when they were there. She had always felt different from others, and could remember this experience from childhood. Even in primary school she often found herself looking at others playing and thinking that they seemed to have learned something that she had not. She felt different and tried to stay in the background as much as possible. She found the transition to secondary school difficult, and she remembered being confused and stressed by the change, as she had to learn new information and adapt to an unfamiliar environment. She was seen as different by others, but she managed to avoid being bullied as she was able to join in with a small group of peers. She was intelligent and managed her higher exams, but decided not to go to university and instead to stay at home with her parents. She got a job in the tax office, monitoring the information on tax returns and looking for anomalies which suggested that investigation into the tax return was needed. Her social life was limited to a few contacts from school. However, even now she still reported feeling isolated when she was with them, and feeling different and alone. She presented a rather forlorn figure and spent considerable time on her own. In the family home her experience had always been that her parents lived quietly themselves and generally disregarded her attempts to talk about herself, just as they had always done in her view: *"There was no one there to take care of me, to talk to, to ask about things or to help me begin to understand things I didn't understand."*

She wanted to know if there was something wrong with her or whether she was autistic. Careful assessment showed that this was not the case and that her problems were characterized more by fear of rejection and feelings of personal inadequacy and difference from others. This led to her extensive avoidance of social interaction, and particularly of friendship and closeness. It was this that she was concerned about. She wanted to have relationships.

The Experience of the Assessment

It is quite easy for the assessment interview with a patient who has a likely diagnosis of AvPD to turn into a relatively meaningless question-and-answer session. The questions are searching but the answers are shallow and feel superficial, lacking the rich and vivid descriptions of the patient's life that the clinician expects. Frequently the patient responds with "*I don't know*" or confirms the clinician's suggestion but gives the clinician the impression that they could equally well have confirmed the opposite of what was being suggested. The average clinician's training equips them to allow richly verbalized accounts to be articulated without hindrance, just giving gentle direction to keep the focus on the phenomenon in question. However, interviews with individuals with AvPD will not meet expectations that a detailed, in-depth account of phenomena will be obtained. In the face of the limitations of the information obtained the clinician is likely to feel inadequate, somewhat impatient, or even irritated, perhaps covering for a sense of shame they may feel in relation to the sparseness of the account they have been able to elicit. This is both inappropriate and deeply unhelpful. The sparseness is the message. What the clinical assessment reveals is the patient's experience conveyed according to their best ability, and within this general presentation two distinct forms of mentalizing are frequently discernible—a hypomentalizing form and a hypermentalizing form.

Hypomentalizing Form

In the hypomentalizing form, the message is the absence of content and is to be found in the blandness of what is actually being conveyed. The patient truly does not know what to tell the clinician. Here the issue to be explored is what it is like for the patient to be asked questions and not to know the answers—not knowing what to say or not understanding what others want from them, not understanding what the other person has said, and so on: "*What is it like to see me and be asked all these questions? What effect does it have on you that I ask things that you don't know how to answer?*" The not-knowing stance used in MBT to elicit the patient's internal experience is essential, but at the same time the clinician is almost forced to start filling in the patient's internal world with what they expect to find, as they find so little. Such impatience, whether implicit or explicit, feeds into the hypersensitivity to criticism with which these individuals come to the consultation, and it can (and frequently does) lead to the breakdown of the potential for a therapeutic dialogue.

Hypermentalizing Form

With other patients, the same configuration of overall problems can manifest in a different manner, characterized by hypermentalizing. The patient, well practiced in the long silences and painful communication failures which are a feature of question-and-answer sessions when these involve attempts to get them to elaborate their personal experience, offers an obliging and friendly narrative discourse in which they address very serious topics in the most superficial ways. MBT refers to this as an aspect of pretend mode, where the clinician is invited to engage in what is an imaginary discourse between an imagined person and their therapist. The patient finds it relatively easy to enter into this dialogue because it does not feel to them as if it is about them. Patients engage in this to reduce the embarrassment of the process of conversation, and are probably motivated by a wish to be liked; they prioritize trying to make the clinician feel comfortable despite being very uncomfortable themselves and being fully aware of the limitations of the process in which they are engaging. Challenge, a recommended intervention for fixed pretend mode in MBT (see Chapter 4), is in this context both counterproductive and unfair. Progress is more likely to be made if the clinician expresses gratitude to the patient for their efforts to create such a productive atmosphere, and shows empathy for them undertaking all the work and feeling that they have received little in return. Getting to the difficulty these patients have in talking about their experiences in the way that they sometimes hear others being able to do is the important end point of the assessment, and creates a desirable focus for the intervention.

Clinical Example: Jane (continued)

Jane talked about herself and her family in detail. In particular, she was aware that her brother was different from her. He had left home and was living with his girlfriend. He had been the one person she had tried to talk to, but he used to tell her that she was "weird" and "should stop worrying." This was how she thought other people saw her, and that they were seeing something that she did not see about herself.

Clinician: You talk about yourself very well. As you tell me this can you say what it makes you feel?

Jane: It is OK.

Clinician: Has it helped at all to tell your story?

Jane: Yes.

Clinician: In what sort of way?

Jane: It is helpful.

The story that Jane told was processed in hypermentalizing pretend mode. It was coherent and she had worked out what was happening for herself. But the few questions asked by the clinician suggest that the story is not tethered to experience and emotion. There is a disconnect between Jane's cognitive and affective processing. Her answers are brief and will eventually frustrate her and the clinician, pushing both of them toward a low-mentalizing interaction. The clinician's mind will go blank. This is where the importance of the MBT formulation comes to the fore. It can be used as the reference point when treatment becomes stuck.

The Experience of the Treatment

When initiating a treatment process, the relational problems identified in the assessment phase will return to a great extent, and the core processes of MBT have to be considered, namely:

1. a mentalizing understanding of the limitations of the therapeutic encounter
2. the attachment strategies of the patient
3. the characteristic mentalizing impairments with which they struggle.

Limitations

Just as the assessment might be taxing, the treatment can be equally challenging because, compared with the average therapy, the psychological content brought by the patient offers only sparse material to work with. This can affect even an experienced MBT clinician, challenging their ability to generate mentalizing by the usual strategies of the not-knowing stance, clarification, elaboration, affect narrative work, and relational mentalizing. One general aspect that may be helpful at the outset concerns the clinician's counter-response, which was mentioned earlier. Ineffective mentalizing gives rise to more ineffective mentalizing—it is contagious, and clinicians can "catch" it from their patients. There is a readily recognizable phenomenon of *secondary avoidance* that can occur in the course of treatment of individuals with AvPD. Clinicians who are unable to penetrate the barriers erected by the patient may be tempted to collude with the patient, either by implicitly accepting that the barriers are insurmountable, using various rationales (e.g., the patient is too vulnerable, their social context is genuinely hostile), or by engaging with the patient's pretend-mode thinking and working with them to elaborate what are fundamentally avoidant strategies. Whereas the impulsivity of patients with BPD rarely permits such an inappropriate blunting of therapeutic zeal, the lack of "drama" in the course of treatment of AvPD patients sometimes allows the clinician to be inappropriately complacent about the patient's underlying pain, and to forget that underneath the pretend sense of coping there is likely to be distress that is every bit as profound as it is—albeit in a more obvious way—in more "dramatic" patients.

Attachment Strategies in AvPD

Attachment anxiety, particularly intense fear of abandonment, is an important characteristic of patients with AvPD, who show high levels of both attachment anxiety and attachment avoidance, consistent with a fearful attachment style [12,13]. In an avoidant attachment style the other is characterized negatively, whereas an anxious attachment style is linked to negative representations of a self in need of support from others; the combination of anxiety and avoidance offers no solace in either proximity seeking or avoidance. As the previous chapters have shown, this combination of attachment strategies is by no means unique to individuals with AvPD, and is shared by those with BPD and NPD, and perhaps all those with high levels of symptoms of mental disturbance (see Chapter 2). However, as Simonsen and Euler have pointed out, although the configuration of attachment strategies may overlap, the psychopathology of patients with AvPD necessitates consideration of the social-status system in which their attachment relationships are embedded [14]. Patients with AvPD may fear separation, but in many cases—and in a similar way to individuals with NPD—they may also be focused on issues of autonomy and relational power dynamics.

An important aspect of the attachment strategies of patients with AvPD is the immense—almost life-and-death—power that can be given to the attachment figure whose response to the patient is experienced as determining their well-being. Within a mentalizing framework, this would be understood as *alien parts of the self* (see Chapter 2)—critical, denigrating, humiliating parts—which are externalized into the attachment figure, otherwise they would become a vehicle for aspects of the self-structure that give rise to even more painful and distressing internal persecution from within. In support of this view, Beeney et al. found that self/other boundaries (e.g., difficulties with emotion contagion, feeling separate from others) mediated the relationship between attachment anxiety and AvPD [15]. Because of the externalization of the critical alien part of the self, the possibility of turning to others for protection and support when in distress may rarely seem to be a viable option. The interpersonal world becomes filled with hostile and critical voices.

Mentalizing Difficulties in AvPD

The dimensions of mentalizing are used clinically to capture the limitations that are typically encountered in particular clinical groups. Of course, just as there is an overlap in symptoms between different clinical groups, there is some overlap in mentalizing difficulties across diagnoses, particularly because when a patient is stuck at one end of a dimension of mentalizing this affects mentalizing in other dimensions (for a discussion of the mentalizing dimensions, see Chapter 2). However, thinking about a patient's dimensional profile does provide a useful structure for understanding the clinical picture as it emerges in the course of assessment and treatment. The evidence of mentalizing problems in AvPD is summarized in Box 8.2.

Box 8.2 Mentalizing problems in AvPD.

Automatic/Controlled

- More automatic than controlled.
- Low implicit/explicit reflective functioning on childhood attachment narratives.
- Automatic filling-in of self-experience based on the assumption that the other's experience is negative.
- Hypermentalizing or hypomentalizing, depending on the style of AvPD.

Box 8.2 *(cont.)*

Cognitive/Affective

- More cognitive than affective.
- Low reflectivity on emotional states of self.
- Reduced mentalized affectivity.
- Failure to share emotions with others, and suppression of emotional expression.

External/Internal

- Overuse of external cues and reduced ability to identify internal states.
- Disconnection between internal bodily sensations and relevant external stimuli.
- Misclassification of emotion from facial expression.

Self/Other

- Low scores on monitoring the mental states of self and others.
- Excess focus on others' thoughts about self.
- Excessively self-focused during social interaction, with limited consideration of the other's state of mind.
- Powerful negative characterization of self and other.

Automatic (Implicit)/Controlled (Reflective, Explicit) Mentalizing

Interestingly, of the relatively small amount of empirical research on AvPD that has been reported, a significant proportion is concerned with ways in which mentalizing is limited in this disorder. A study that operationalized mentalizing as *reflective functioning* on narratives of childhood attachment experiences in the Adult Attachment Interview reported an association between AvPD and difficulties with reflective functioning, which loaded highly on to the controlled (reflective, explicit) pole of the automatic/controlled dimension [16]. Another study compared the ability to understand mental states in patients with AvPD and in individuals with social phobia, and reported that patients with AvPD had the lowest scores [17]. Similarly, individuals with AvPD in particular appeared to experience difficulties in monitoring mental states [18]. These difficulties would be expected to leave them uncertain and confused in the course of explicit reflection about their own feelings or thoughts about something. This may be a defensive avoidance of explicit mentalizing because of the profoundly negative characterization of both self and other in their interpersonal representational world. Why would anyone wish to spend cognitive effort on thinking about their sense of shame or worthlessness? Of course, if the automatic assumptions of these self-characterizations are to be addressed, precisely such a focus may be what is most helpful. Without it, automatic assumptions (implicit mentalizing) will ensure the maintenance of this mode of self-experience. The clinician is required to focus their effort on activating and reinforcing explicit mentalizing and, if necessary, challenging this self-perpetuating cycle. They need to approach this process with sufficient empathy to enable the patient to mentalize distressing self-representations, and they should sensitively soften their approach, slow their progress, and become more supportive when explicit mentalizing becomes too painful.

As we mentioned earlier in this chapter, people with AvPD are often characterized by *hypermentalizing* (e.g., intellectualizing, ruminating), which can be seen as the overuse of the controlled pole of the automatic/controlled dimension of mentalizing. Hypermentalizing can occur because the reflective capacity is disconnected from reality—that is, it is in pretend mode. However, low reflective capacity can also manifest as *hypomentalizing* (e.g., blanking out). The intuitive knowing of reality embodied in fast thinking/automatic/implicit mentalizing no longer functions as a brake on ideas, and imagination becomes untethered from external reality. Individuals with AvPD can thus end up using thoughts and reflection as a way of distancing themselves from whatever emotions are evoked by particular situations. Again this is a form of pretend mode. As a reminder, pretend mode (for a more detailed discussion, see Chapter 2) is so named because it resembles mentalizing but lacks emotional authenticity; it can be excessively intellectual, analytical, or just improbable [19,20]. Because pretend mode is disconnected from reality, engaging with it clinically (i.e., discussing it with the patient) is unlikely to be productive. Because it is unconstrained by reality, nothing stops it from being entirely self-serving, which compromises the chances of generating a constructive shift of perspective in other mentalizing dimensions (self to other, cognitive to affective). A particular challenge for the clinician is that the patient, unsurprisingly, experiences highlighting of the limitations of their contributions as criticism, as they are unaware of what the clinician regards as the limitations in their mentalizing. This results in a considerable threat to the therapeutic relationship, which can become mired in repetition and a lack of progress.

Cognitive/Affective Mentalizing

Patients with AvPD tend to be more cognitive than affective in their mentalizing stance. The capacity to perceive, reflect on, tolerate, and express emotional experiences appears limited in AvPD [21]. Affect consciousness and conceptual expressivity are lower in patients with AvPD than in those with BPD [22]. Mentalized affectivity may be more or less absent, generating a notable shift away from balanced cognitive/affective mentalizing toward the cognitive pole. Anxiety and shame often dominate, but mentalizing strategies are configured to avoid these emotional experiences—for instance, engaging in hypomentalizing (e.g., not thinking about feelings at all) or hypermentalizing in relation to them. A functional magnetic resonance imaging (fMRI) study that compared AvPD patients with controls who had not been diagnosed with a mental health problem found amygdala hyper-reactivity in anticipation of an explicit emotion-regulation task in patients with AvPD [23]. Thus we assume that the sequence may commonly be hypermentalizing triggered by heightened amygdala responses, leading to dysregulation, followed by avoidance and hypomentalizing.

The cognitive capacity to perceive and make sense of emotions may also be impaired in people with AvPD, as suggested by studies that examined alexithymia (difficulty in recognizing one's own feelings) in this population [24], although more recent studies have shown this to be a substantial problem in only a proportion (perhaps 50–60%) of individuals with AvPD [25]. Supporting the key role of problematic mentalizing in these patients, this latter study of "non-comorbid" AvPD patients showed that alexithymia scores were powerful independent predictors of personality dysfunction. People with AvPD have marked problems in sharing their feelings with others. This creates potential problems not only for clinicians but also for the individual's family, who may be unaware of the pain that the person experiences [26]. In mentalizing terms, this may be viewed as gross communication problems with both the congruency of affective mirroring and the marking of emotions.

Internal/External Mentalizing

Clinical experience and some systematic studies suggest that patients with AvPD have difficulty tapping into the harder-to-judge internal sources of information about mental states, leading them to place undue emphasis on external cues. In an investigation of specific subcomponents of metacognitive abilities, patients with AvPD were found to have difficulty monitoring both their own internal states and the internal states of others ("decentration," described in more detail later; see this chapter: Self/Other Mentalizing) [18]. This finding is all the more interesting because the comparison groups were individuals with other personality disorders, which indicates that there is a specific difficulty in people with AvPD. The findings of an fMRI study may point to the cause of this difficulty. When shown pictures with strong negative affective content, AvPD patients exhibited less insula–ventral anterior cingulate functional connectivity compared with either BPD patients or non-clinical controls [27]. This points to a potential failure of full understanding of internal states rooted in an anomaly of interoceptive awareness. The process of making connections between internal bodily sensations and relevant external stimuli may be disrupted in patients with AvPD. Significantly, a dysfunction of this kind has also been identified in patients with SAD [28].

One study suggested that there was some impairment of judgment of external indicators of emotion, where AvPD patients were shown to misclassify full facial expressions of fear [29]. As Simonsen and Euler have pointed out, this may not be a misreading of emotional expression but rather the manifestation of an attentional strategy by these individuals to avoid focusing on intense emotion altogether, as a way of managing their vulnerable affect regulation [14].

We know less about emotional expression in AvPD, although it is likely to be significantly impaired. From clinical experience we know that people with AvPD may not express their emotions externally, which makes it harder for them to be understood by others and generates a communication challenge for those close to them, as well as for the clinician. Appropriate and marked contingent expression of affect is essential for both empathy and communication, and is likely to be vital for both learning and affiliation [30]. The blunted expression that we see in AvPD may be an important but little-studied cause of the social isolation of these individuals [31] and the epistemic vigilance that they generate in those close to them.

Self/Other Mentalizing

The challenge for AvPD patients in organizing their mentalizing appears to be related to a bias toward self-mentalizing and decentration (discussed later in this section). As we have seen, the configuration of attachment strategies in AvPD is predominantly fearful. Both self and other are seen in a negative light. Benign representations of others (good internal objects) are fragile and insufficiently developed, so are not able to provide a background of safety for exploration. Therefore free and unconstrained delving into the mental states of others is avoided, resulting in both psychological and behavioral inhibition.

The default mentalizing position of people with AvPD is the self rather than the other [32,33]. The mental state of the other may be the apparent focus for individuals with this diagnosis, but *the other's thoughts and feelings about the self* are the primary area of concern. Individuals with AvPD have more severe metacognitive difficulties with both alexithymia and the capacity for decentration—that is, dealing with the fact that others have a different perspective from their own [18,24]. This understanding of AvPD helps to elaborate detail about the way the self/other dimension of mentalizing—and MBT—is organized, distinguishing between self and other functions in social interaction and psychopathology. Maresh and Andrews-Hanna suggest that three mentalizing foci for the self require elaboration in the complex process of differentiating self from other: (a) the self as the target of inferences about mental states; (b) the self-experience as the source of information about mentalizing inferences; and (c) the image of the self as seen by the other, which is constructed from interaction with the other [34]; in Chapter 6 we described this as "self-as-object" mentalizing or the "me-mode."

Inferring one's own mental states—or, as William James termed it, "introspection" [35]—is mentalizing when the self is the target. This is the "I." Although this seems straightforward and unambiguous, in normal social interactions we do not know the extent to which individuals actually consider themselves as targets of mentalizing [36]. As we discussed in Chapter 2, the available sources of information for self-focused mentalizing are physiological and emotional reactions—internal experiences that are not normally accessible when the target of mentalizing is the other. In addition, the pervasiveness of self-perception biases shows that there are substantial limits to self-knowledge, and that much of the information that should intuitively be available to reflective, explicit mentalizing actually occurs outside conscious awareness, making it impossible to use during social interaction. In MBT, the concern with effective mentalizing leads to a focus on the balance and appropriateness of mentalizing along the self/other dimension.

Self-focused (self-as-target) mentalizing uses the same, or similar, mechanisms for inference as other-focused mentalizing. It may, for example, involve one's observation of one's own behavior as the basis of introspection to make accurate inferences about mental states [34]. We begin to know what we feel and what we think by what we do. We begin to know someone else by understanding ourselves. There has been suggestion that specific neural structures operating in self-focused versus other-focused mentalizing may point to qualitatively distinct processes, but they are substantially the same. Evidence from neuroscience studies suggests that there is a significant overlap in the activation patterns of the ventral and dorsal regions of the medial prefrontal cortex (mPFC) of the brain in both cases. It is likely that this brain structure constitutes the "agent-independent" location for processing person-relevant information. It is not specific to either the self or the other, but to both. Evidence for a distinct location in the mPFC for self versus other mentalizing is more likely to be attributable to differences in the level of abstraction for which the ventral and dorsal regions of the mPFC are specialized. It seems that the dorsal mPFC subsystem has a primary role in both self-focused and other-focused mentalizing when these involve abstract and reflective mental processes [37].

In AvPD, mentalizing is excessively self-focused during social interactions. This is at the expense of processing information from the social environment. Individuals with AvPD focus excessively on monitoring thoughts, feelings, and internal sensations. Given the complementary nature of the self/other poles of mentalizing, we can expect that an excessive focus on the self occurs at the expense of accurate mentalizing of the other. The apparent "zero-sum game" of self or other mentalizing occurs because self-as-target mentalizing inevitably diverts attention from the other toward the self. As individuals with AvPD avoid genuine consideration of the other's mental state, the excessive activation of self-mentalizing may simultaneously bias inferences about the other's thoughts and feelings so that they are more like the internal state of the self. In other words, the experience is that "*others see me as I see myself.*"

The bias that prioritizes content relevant to the self also colors inferences about the mental state of the other. As seen in studies of categorizing faces depicting fear expressions [38], the bias away from the other may cause impairments of judgment that reduce the accuracy of other-focused mentalizing. Inadequate allocation of cognitive resources to the other may also contribute to more serious dysfunctions. The lack of resources may lead to a disconnection of physical reality from other-focused mentalizing, which comes to be characterized by hypermentalizing in individuals with AvPD. Thus the inaccuracy does not only involve difficulty in the recognition of internal and external signals of mental states. More seriously, the lack of attention paid to such signals, caused by a negative, hypermentalizing focus on the self, means that the individual does not receive valuable social information that might counter the spiral of negative self-mentalizing. Consistent with these assumptions, brain imaging studies have shown increased ventral mPFC activation in socially anxious individuals, reflecting the greater salience of self-related stimuli [39].

When describing the self/other dimension of mentalizing in Chapter 2 we discussed biases that can arise when the source of information for mentalizing is not the external world, but is inappropriately drawn from either the point of view of the self or the perspective of the other. The former is commonly referred to as *egocentric bias* [40], whereas the latter is known as *altercentric bias* [41,42]. Although the inevitable pull to take the other's perspective into consideration may cause problems in some contexts (e.g., excessive vulnerability to mimicry in BPD), altercentric bias is not a prominent problem in AvPD. Disorders associated with avoidance are good examples of the substantial problems involved in mentalizing another person ("other-as-target" mentalizing) when the source of information for this actually comes from the self. To overcome egocentric bias it is necessary to contrast the information available to the self with the information available about the mental state of the other [43]. In situations of pressure (e.g., negative self-appraisal in an interpersonal context), this will be beyond the capacity of someone with AvPD.

Clinical experience confirms that mentalizing in which the self is the source of information about the mental state of the other is common in AvPD; this has also been noted to commonly occur in individuals with social anxiety [44]. We assume that individuals with AvPD generate images of themselves in social situations that are supposed to reflect the perception of others. However, these images are deeply affected by egocentric bias and reflect negative internal self-perspectives. This tendency is self-sustaining because it precludes acquiring information that is inconsistent with the egocentric understanding. In the absence of new information, the progression is restricted to ever more detailed analysis of the sparse data accessible to the individual. The hypermentalizing typical of AvPD reflects the limitation of egocentricity ("self-as-source" mentalizing), and may be a part of the general picture of ruminative hypermentalizing in people with a predisposition toward avoidance [45,46].

As we have seen, the subjective experience of AvPD entails the construction of memories and mental images that reflect the individual's interpersonal interactions with their social world. In principle, these images can be constructed from a first-person perspective (i.e., seen through the eyes of the self) or a third-person perspective (i.e., where a visual image of the self is constructed and is perceived as an object of the mental image) [47]. It has been suggested that the difference between the two forms of imagery reflects a level of abstraction [48]. The first-person perspective reflects experiential and concrete aspects of the event, whereas the third-person or observer perspective reflects the overarching personal meaning of the experience that is remembered [48,49].

This differentiation may also be true of mental-state attributions, where first-person imagery corresponds to concrete interpretations of action whereas third-person imagery reflects abstract interpretations [34]. People who are socially anxious form images of themselves as social objects. They imagine themselves from a third-person perspective that depicts how others might be thinking of them. The dominance of the self pole in mentalizing means that this image is based on their own feelings and experiences. Use of the third-person perspective to depict social situations in memory, thus eliciting a more abstract level of processing, may be one of the underlying causes of the highly embedded negative self-mentalizing that is characteristic of a high level of social avoidance. Avoidance may be a consequence of generalizing the thinking where the self is perceived as an object; it is re-experienced from the third-person perspective, giving it a semblance of reality that is not in fact based on any real social information. However, the abstraction involved in this third-person perspective solidifies the negative self-image in a generalized structure of "me as I am seen." The third-person (self-as-object) perspective "bakes in" negative content into self-imagery that is already negative. Seeing oneself in one's mind's eye as inadequate, embarrassing, laughed at, or awkward becomes an inescapable image that is ready to return whenever the "me-mode" of how the individual is seen is activated. Furthermore, when anxious individuals use such images, they may be readily generalized across contexts and settings because of their abstract nature, invading situations that are historical but in which the image is now irrelevant, or infiltrating anticipated future events that serve to justify avoidance in all similar situations.

Summary of the Mentalizing Formulation for AvPD

Avoidance is an extreme form of psychic equivalence. The outcomes imagined by the patient with AvPD are in all respects *reality* and must, at all costs, be avoided. Psychic equivalence exaggerates consequences, and in the imagination of the patient the possible outcomes of action are often catastrophic. Reflection and explicit mentalizing are not available to counter these imagined outcomes, and the fear becomes untethered. The ultimate frightening consequence is the complete loss of agency (control) and consequent humiliation, denigration, or ridicule. The agency denied to the self is attributed to the other, who acquires unusual power and an almost oppressive destructive influence over the self. The escape from the oppression of this "inevitable" feared imagined consequence is a pervasive adoption of pretend mode—the separation of subjective from physical reality through an escape into meaningless detail that serves to enable avoidance. The extreme psychic equivalence entails the bodily self and physical reactions. Thus the person with AvPD can imagine bodily reactions consistent with their subjective state, such as blushing, and be convinced that anyone observing them will notice their emotional response.

We have noted the absence of reflective explicit mentalizing and the dominance of cognition over emotion (with some indications of alexithymia) in people with AvPD. We also suspect that anomalies in the interoceptive experience associated with linking emotional arousal to external circumstance may underpin the alexithymic experience of those with AvPD. Three aspects of the self/other dimension may be relevant to therapy with patients with AvPD:

1. the inappropriate dominance of the self as a target of mentalizing
2. the source of information for mentalizing being the self
3. the mental representation, principally in imagery, of past and future experience being dominated by a third-person rather than first-person perspective.

These and similar biases in relation to other disorders covered in the different chapters of this book have been noted. The preference for inferring one's own mental states rather than focusing on those of others may be characteristic of depression, post-traumatic stress disorder, and NPD. It may in fact be the kind of transdiagnostic indicator of psychopathology that the notion of the "p factor" (discussed in Chapter 2) logically demands [39]. Similarly, the egocentricity bias, which may be better interpreted as difficulty in inhibiting a self-perspective, may be dominant in AvPD because processing of the self demands fewer cognitive resources than directing attention to the other. Again, this is unlikely to be specific to AvPD. Finally, the predisposition to view the self from outside—to take the perspective of an observer who is imagined to be objective but of course is not—may be something that AvPD shares with all or most other personality disorders. If it were to be demonstrated that the third-person perspective in representing memories and creating images of a potential future is favored in all personality disorders, this might help to explain why these disorders have traditionally been considered to be more stable and less likely to change with the passage of time. The argument in relation to the observer perspective is that seeing oneself from the outside is likely to give the event an overarching personal meaning combined with a paralyzing sense that this perspective must be shared by everyone and so must be objectively true [48,49]. The sense of certainty and significance that such a perspective creates makes it difficult to shift, even if circumstances change.

Treatment Approach

In general, the treatment approach to AvPD requires patience and detailed scrutiny of the often sparse material that the patient brings. Engaging with this in a sensitive way that reflects interest, genuine curiosity, and compassion in relation to the pain and distress just below the surface of the ideas being presented is an important and significant therapeutic challenge. In contrast to the issues that emerge with the "dramatic" cluster of personality disorders, here the technical challenge is to prevent total avoidance and eschew the acceptance of easy solutions, and to achieve this without generating a level of anxiety that a person with AvPD is unlikely to be able to manage effectively.

If we consider the establishment of epistemic trust as being the core feature of the MBT approach to treating personality disorders, we can see the combination of anxiety and fearful attachment as initiating and maintaining the persistence of epistemic hypervigilance and as a barrier to the re-establishment of epistemic trust. The goal of MBT in AvPD, as in all other disorders, is to regain the patient's mentalizing. Given the formulation described in the previous section, the reason why the anomaly characterized as AvPD can occur and be maintained is the failure of appropriate balanced mentalizing of self and other. Therefore, in individuals in whom AvPD is a significant feature, the clinician has to:

- reduce the influence of the "inner eye"
- discourage the self from being "lent to" the other
- minimize the obsessive turning on the self, negatively appraising and scrutinizing its activities.

In addition, the clinician needs to consider:

- psychic equivalence bundled as the whole way of experiencing the self in a social world; the clinician must help the patient to calibrate internal experience against external reality, using explicit mentalizing to bring uncertainty and perspective
- hypermentalizing pretend mode as a dominant non-mentalizing mode, with avoidant hypomentalizing as a way of managing overly painful dysregulated internal states within social contexts, including therapeutic encounters.

The first step is to enshrine the work within the MBT formulation.

Formulation

From the perspective of an MBT treatment protocol, the clinical formulation translates fairly simply into clinical priorities that guide practice in relation to AvPD. A clear priority is to address the imbalance between self and other mentalizing, and treatment of AvPD calls for a specific shift in self/other mentalizing. The clinician needs to pay special attention to instances where the self is inappropriately or overly readily used as the target of mentalizing. The specific problems resulting from overuse of the self as the main focus for all mentalizing need to be identified, agreed with the patient as problem areas, and then illustrated with examples from the patient's life. MBT asks clinicians to routinely assist the shift from self to other, and from other to self, with the aim of increasing the flexibility of mentalizing—that is, to use contrary moves (see Chapter 4). This remains a priority, and should be explicitly identified as a process that the clinician will insist on working on.

Supporting patients in the task of inferring mental states in all of the protagonists in a particular setting is perhaps the highest priority for intervention. The clinician and the patient need to become alert to mental states of the self being offered as explanations for the outcome of social situations without appropriate consideration of the role that others may have had. Using standard MBT techniques, the clinician should express curiosity and concern about the accuracy of judgments in relation to the other when these judgments appear to be based on inadequate attention being given to the subjective experience of the other. Failure to free up the mentalizing process through the use of a not-knowing stance in this situation indicates that the use of role plays or a game centered on an aspect of the social narrative might be helpful.

Clinical Example: The Formulation Discussed with Jane

Here is a summary covering a few things we have talked about.

1. We have noted that you spend a lot of time thinking about yourself and trying to work out why you are like you are. You mentioned that you have tried to put things down in writing and tell stories about yourself. While you have been doing that, you always come

back to how negative you are about yourself and how you think you are "weird," just like your brother told you. It is really difficult for you to see yourself in any other way.

Focus for treatment: How you see yourself. (*Self representation—mentalizing I-mode.*)

2. When you are with others you always find yourself looking at them as if you are not really with them. There is a distance between you and them, and you think that you don't understand something about being with other people that they do seem to. You imagine all the time that they see you like you see yourself—as "weird" again, perhaps.

 Focus for treatment: What happens between you and other people, and how do you work out what is in their minds and what they actually think about you? (*Other second-order representation system and other-to-self mentalizing—me-mode and personalized me-mode.*)

3. You want to hide a lot of the time, and this helps on the one hand but on the other it increases the pain of your isolation, which is something you want to change.

 Focus for treatment: Consider times when you know you are melting into the background and what makes you have to do that. What might happen if you don't? (*Using narrative of events to focus on experience and avoidance processes in real time.*)

4. You have lots of understanding about your story and have been over it many times. We should respect that and of course refer to it, but it might help if we avoid too much going over and over it, as you have already done that.

 Focus for treatment: Let's look out for when we both start explaining things more and more only to find that things don't change. (*Attempt to sensitize both the clinician and the patient to hypermentalizing as a block to progress.*)

5. You and I seem to come to a full stop when we are thinking about things sometimes. Can we agree to notice those times and for both of us to search in ourselves to explore what has happened? I think it might be important to go back to see what is happening, as it tends to make it seem like there is a disconnect.

 Focus for treatment: Any disconnection as we try to open up a discussion. (*This is an affect focus, locating a relational interference in treatment that might be part of Jane's ingrained avoidance pattern.*)

6. Let's look at the relationships that you have. You mentioned how you long for connection with other people and to stop feeling you are "looking in." You want relationships but you also dread people being close and asking you to be with them. In the end you think it is better to be alone, but you don't want that either.

 Focus for treatment: Perhaps we will call it "Fear and Longing" so that we can start to work out when it is really strong in you and what is bringing it to the foreground. (*A shorthand phrase summarizing the content for discussion in the subsequent sessions.*)

This is enough to be going on with. We can change all this as we go along if it does not seem to be relevant.

Side Effects of the Intervention to Be Noted in the Formulation

The main risk in the treatment of AvPD is that of encouraging pseudomentalizing, so this is highlighted in the formulation—for example, "*We can easily get into an over-*

detailed discussion and not see the wood for the trees. Perhaps we can both be aware of when this is happening and stop to consider what we night be missing." In the formulation discussed with Jane (see previous box) this is noted in point 4 as something for both parties to look out for—also referred to in MBT as something to "Notice and Name" (see Chapter 4).

How can this risk be mitigated when it happens, as it surely will? By stopping and exploring! Stopping the patient in order to take time to acquire information relevant to judging the mental state of another actor, closely following the inferences drawn, and mildly challenging the patient when necessary become a staple part of the intervention with AvPD.

Reducing the Influence of the "Inner Eye": Tackling Excessive Focus on Self to Understand Others

A further priority is to look out for content that suggests egocentricity bias. These are instances when self/other distinctions are blurred and the self is focused on excessively as the most appropriate source of information about others. Such instances are likely to be very common, and must be repeatedly identified and questioned. We assume that the mental state of the other is avoided systematically in part because of the anticipation of mental pain. This may be true, but we also know that egocentricity bias for an individual with a profoundly negative self-image generates just as much or perhaps even more mental pain in relation to the social environment as the inaccurate judgment of the mental state of the other might do. Therefore the counteracting of avoidance is just part of what is necessary. The move away from egocentricity bias has two separate requirements.

1. **It should enable the emergence of a genuine other** through the usual steps of empathic validation, clarification, and presenting an alternative perspective. The clinician sensitively asks the patient to consider all of the participants in any narrative. The other person has to emerge from the narrative gradually and be experienced from a range of perspectives:

   (a) the protagonist's own perspective (what they thought and might have felt); can the patient consider this?

Clinical Example: The Other Person Experienced from Jane's Perspective

JANE: *They looked at me in a funny way. They were seeing me as weird as usual.*

CLINICIAN (EXAMPLE QUESTIONS): *How do you get to that? What were you picking up there? Was this an external focus of mentalizing, based on their facial expression or their tone of voice?*

   (b) the patient's perspective—what they knew for certain and what their imagination adds to complete the picture (as everyone's imagination does): "*How come you are so certain? What effect did it have on you that you read it like this?*" Does the patient describe the experience as if it is objectively real truth that would be shared by the world in general, or can they describe it as an idiosyncratic, personal point of view? If they describe a more generalized understanding of the protagonist, this needs to be sensitively challenged.

(c) the perspective of a genuine observer—for example, what the clinician would have made of it independent of the subjectivities of all those involved: *"If I was there, I would have thought this, given what you are saying."*

(d) the vicarious perspectives of other protagonists if they are part of the picture (i.e., if there are at least two protagonists in addition to the patient): *"How did John see Fiona, do you think? What did that tell you about Fiona? Was he right? How does that compare with what you thought?"*

This should not be mechanistically performed with each related episode, but dynamically explored across many such situations. But multiple perspectives should be encouraged as appropriate in relation to each incident. It is essential that Jane reflects on the difference between what she sees others were thinking and how they were reacting, and what this tells her about the "third" person (observer) perspective that she failed to recognize.

2. **It should support the inhibition of egocentricity.** If egocentricity is not inhibited, concern about a real other, even if it gradually emerges, will never flourish. The predisposition to egocentricity is strongly established and has a powerful defensive function, reducing severe mental pain. The challenge is to create an attractive and non-anxiety-generating alternative. Perhaps this is best achieved not by confrontation but by a persistent request to "move beyond egocentricity." The inhibition of egocentricity is not achieved by demolishing it but by enrichment of the mentalizing alternative. Identifying positive cognitions (admiration, affection, concern, empathy, interest, or even love) in the other, to replace the self-generated negative mentalizing, may in itself create intrinsic value that overrides avoidance. Of course, progress will be slower if the patient's social environment is negative and so they are genuinely surrounded by hostile attitudes, but this does not mean that the clinician should be deflected from the task.

Calibrating Internal Experience and External Reality: Affect Focus and Relational Mentalizing

Psychic equivalence, when bundled into the whole structure of AvPD, needs more diversion than is commonly used in the MBT intervention for psychic equivalence (see Chapter 4). One way to begin to generate less certainty and dysregulation and to reduce anxiety—all of which create such distress in a patient who is functioning in psychic equivalence—is to introduce games. Games can be used as a way into an underlying affect focus, the "elephant in the room." The clinician explores the barriers and limits of the patient's experience in role play to generate a modestly uncomfortable but more bearable state than would be generated by working directly on the therapeutic relational process, which is so heavily intruded upon by self-bias. Relational mentalizing interventions directed toward the detail of the patient–clinician interaction are likely to engender too much anxiety and lead either to pretend-mode hypermentalizing or to behavioral and mental avoidance with hypomentalizing.

An inverted role play to explore a problematic interaction between the clinician and patient can be started by the clinician stating: "*Imagine that I am you and you are me . . . I am telling you how I feel, and you, as the therapist, will have to respond to what I am saying.*" Less problematic in terms of anxiety for the patient is role play based on an interaction the patient reports as having been difficult.

Clinical Example: Jane (continued)

CLINICIAN: Let's take that example of you being at work with your colleague. They were asking you about what you had done with a specific tax form and whether you had assessed it as requiring investigation. I am going to be you and you can be your colleague.

(beginning the role play)

CLINICIAN AS JANE: *(taking her immediate negative self-experience)* Why are you asking me? Do you think I did the wrong thing?

JANE AS COLLEAGUE: Oh. I don't know. I didn't mean that, I don't think.

CLINICIAN AS JANE: Well, what did you mean?

JANE AS COLLEAGUE: I wanted to know what you thought.

CLINICIAN AS JANE: Oh well, I thought it did mean you thought I'd done the wrong thing. I suppose that was just my assumption.

The role play is highlighting the negative self and is now beginning to expose Jane's personal sense of shame within the negative self-experience that she applies to others. This can then be explored further in different contexts of her interactions. Jane and the clinician focus on what happened, while maintaining a mentalizing stance: "*What do you think about my reactions? How close are they to yours? What do you think about how accurate my understanding of your motives was?* The clinician will also say what their experience was.

Role play is one type of game that is designated as "play" or "pretend," and is therefore acceptable to the person whose primary mode of coping is via this mechanism. They can *appear* to be in something rather than being in it in reality. They can approach others' mental states without infusing them solely with their own. Yet although the patient's habitual motive for pretending is avoidance, in the context of therapeutic games it becomes its polar opposite and in MBT terminology would be called a compassionate *challenge*. However, as with other modes of challenge in MBT, the aim is not merely experiential but is keenly focused on the recovery of mentalizing.

Games that are focused on what is going on in minds can be organized. For example, the "mind–brain scans" that are used in family work (see Chapter 15) can be used.

Clinical Example: Mind–Brain Scan Used with Jane

The clinician gives Jane a drawing of an outline of a brain showing the ventricles and surrounding areas. The outline is modified with a number of blank spaces to be filled in—"me," "them," "them about me," and "me about them."

CLINICIAN: Jane, here is an outline of a brain and its structure. But it has some blank spaces, so that we can work out what the brain is up to and treat it as if it was a person's mind. The spaces are there for us to write in what people think. Imagine that this is your colleague. You write in what was going on in his mind and I will write in what I was hearing, too.

What makes this and other games therapeutic is not just that they encourage the elaboration of mental states. The main benefit is that they bring about communication about mental states between people. Therefore games like this must be undertaken in an atmosphere of fun—for example, the clinician can write things that Jane might feel are ridiculous, even though they may have some validity.

Games in themselves are not considered to be an end point in MBT. They are important stimuli that start from clinician-directed explicit exposition of mental states and move gradually toward more patient-owned and implicit reflection. Importantly, they can also be used to generate a trusting relationship between the patient and the clinician. The joint experience of "having fun" while playing can create a "we-mode" in the consulting room, triggering epistemic trust, which paves the way for credible reassurance and acceptable advice giving.

Counter-Relational Responsiveness

Perhaps a less obvious aspect of the engagement in play is its function in modifying the clinician's counter-response to the patient. As we pointed out earlier in this chapter, the pervasive avoidance of AvPD patients may lead to frustration and ultimately loss of agency in the clinician. Hitting one's head against a brick wall is rarely an edifying and liberating process. Games can help the clinician to regain agency in a relational context where an avoidant person's configuration of the therapeutic dialogue deprives them of a significant part. Games can be helpful in countering not only avoidance in the patient but also the secondary avoidance of the clinician. "*It is quite difficult for me when you are unable to say more* (avoidance has been triggered) *as eventually my mind dries up and I am not sure what to ask or what to suggest. I am not sure what has happened at the moment but my mind has gone blank, as if I am giving up a chase. Maybe I need a bit of therapy from you to free my mind up* (playfulness), *as I know this happens to you a lot. How do you get your mind back?*"

Like patients with BPD, many individuals with AvPD fear abandonment [50], but often they also have a sense of being controlled, criticized, and ridiculed, without being able to mentalize explicitly that this is what is going on inside them. Therefore the humor within a counter-relational intervention such as the example just given has to be used carefully and with compassion both toward oneself as a clinician and toward the patient. Sometimes the patient's fear of abandonment can manifest as passive-aggressive behavior, but most commonly it is apparent as a feeling in the clinician of not "being on the same wavelength" as the patient. The clinician needs to be aware that such reactions from the patient are not necessarily about discomfort with affiliation, but may equally have been triggered by the patient feeling that their autonomy is being threatened.

Hypermentalizing in Pretend Mode

The primary mode of mentalizing that causes clinical difficulty in AvPD is hypermentalizing. This is also seen in BPD, where challenge (see Chapter 4) is more feasible than it is in AvPD, and it is especially common among adolescents (see Chapter 14), who hypermentalize to reduce confusion, and in doing so become isolated from their peers. In people with AvPD the motivation is more likely to be the avoidance of anticipated criticism and also the need for approval and acceptance—particularly in the therapeutic setting, in which patients talk about things in a way that initially appears relevant and salient to their problems. However, patients with AvPD focus on micro aspects of a mentalizing interchange or interpersonal event and consider it from so many perspectives, with an endless array of unlikely implications, that the meaning of the encounter is impossible to re-create.

The clinician (like all of those communicating with the patient) tends to lose the thread of the patient's exploration, which may be focused on seemingly insignificant aspects. The result is another experience in which, from the patient's perspective, mentalizing leads to abandonment and rejection, and they feel isolated, exhausted, and unsupported. There is a massive communication gap, with the patient and the clinician each in their own "silos." The patient's cognitive pseudomentalizing, focusing on ineffectively understood internal indicators of thought and superficially appreciated emotions, feels deeply unsatisfactory to the clinician, who will struggle to find common ground with the patient. In therapy with AvPD patients, the aim should be to reverse this process and judiciously balance gentle exploration with maintaining safety as they move attention consistently to the outside and to the emotional, away from the soulless focus on the internal, fearful, hypermentalizing position (about being liked or disliked) in which the patient is trapped.

Playfulness in MBT

The embedded nature of ineffective mentalizing in AvPD and the severity of the relational and counter-relational problems encountered in treatment suggest that additions to the MBT model are required. Playfulness is a key part of the MBT core model, but is used more explicitly as an intervention for mental avoidance. It has been noted that patients with AvPD have marked difficulty in accessing feelings of play and curiosity [51]. In MBT work with couples and families (see Chapters 15 and 16) the judicious use of structured role plays and of video feedback helps to create an atmosphere that is conducive to mentalizing, even in families where the avoidance of mentalizing is dominant. Structured "mentalizing games" challenge avoidance and generate an experience of a safe (playful) non-consequential alternative. As described earlier in this chapter, very simple role plays, which involve simple implementations such as switching roles ("stepping into someone else's shoes"), are widely used. When working with individuals with high levels of alexithymia, games such as the "feeling finder game," in which emotions written on cards drawn from a deck have to be enacted, and others playing the game have to role play the emotion in the same way as the original protagonist if they draw the same card, can be useful. More complex but quite effective role-playing games involve planning challenging interpersonal encounters and "preparing" for these with the clinician adopting (sometimes in challenging ways) the role of the patient's protagonist. On occasion the clinician may provide a coping model to support the patient coping with challenging situations. The content of such extensions to the MBT protocol matters less than the general attitude of inconsequentiality (playfulness) that is created in the consulting room by their use. These games serve to shatter the tyranny of psychic equivalence for the patient.

Memory Elaboration and Imagery

A further technical initiative that is suggested by the mentalizing formulation involves supporting the elaboration of memory and even the fantasy imagery of the patient. The patient's bias toward presenting a self-as-object view can be addressed by asking them to provide less abstract and more concrete imagery. This forces the patient to create and present a self-as-subject perspective. The patient may be all too ready to present such detail in terms of a self-perception (another example of egocentricity), but the clinician needs to gently decline and sideline this in favor of requesting a view of others in relation to the particular event that is being discussed. Whereas excessive detail should be a warning sign of hypermentalizing in relation to the dominance of the self on the self/other dimension, in this instance detail close to physical reality, such as perceptual detail, images, and sound, strengthened by guided imagery in relation to the physical context of the event, is a legitimate way of ensuring that "me-mode" is avoided.

In the authors' experience, dramatic interventions such as mischievous or "wacky" challenges, which are sometimes used in MBT for BPD, are rarely effective in AvPD. It is relatively easy to cause intense emotion in the consulting room, but quite hard to contain it once it has become part of the interpersonal reality between the patient and the clinician. Increasing emotional arousal deliberately when it is chronically low is part of MBT's toolbox. However, implementation of this tool requires sensitivity and some skill. Confronting a patient who has a tendency to overlook alternative explanations for a reaction of, for example, disappointment from someone else that they themselves immediately (but erroneously) attribute to themselves as the cause may not bring with it the desired consequence of increased concern with and interest in the other—"*What makes you so disappointed?*" is substituted in the patient's mind with "*I am so disappointing and you know it.*" In fact, making the other's mental state a more concrete part of therapeutic shared reality may be a counterproductive move. We recommend the use of traditional MBT techniques of puzzlement, surprise, and the not-knowing/inquisitive stance accompanied by empathy in relation to the reaction of disappointment before the context of the event is explored in too much detail. Once there is a solid platform of shared understanding this might indeed increase the potential for alternative explanations. Using a collaborative (democratic) approach will ultimately pay dividends where, as often as possible, discovery is left to the patient rather than to the impatient clinician.

Supervision

Supervision by senior practitioners and peer discussion of one's work is a central part of MBT (see also Chapter 4). It is important that clinicians working with patients with AvPD are able to discuss their patients and receive regular supervision, to avoid them colluding with the patient's avoidance or acting out feelings of boredom. Above all, clinicians need help in order to stay emotionally alive. The tendency for the clinician to join in with hypermentalizing modes is a constant pitfall and may only become apparent in discussion with others. Finally, the repetitiveness and circularity of the conversation and the poverty of the content can have a crushing effect on the mentalizing of the clinician, who becomes unable to think clearly in sessions. Supervision can support the clinician in maintaining their own mentalizing and retaining the ability to take a curated and coherent approach that is linked directly to the mentalizing formulation, rather than becoming lost in a labyrinthine and over-detailed exploration of the patient's world.

MBT-Compatible Evidence-Based Approaches to AvPD

There is limited clinical empirical evidence to support a mentalization-based approach to treating AvPD [14]. To our knowledge there have been no trials of MBT for AvPD, so we reach to techniques and evidence from interventions that are compatible with MBT. By "compatible," we mean techniques that explicitly address mentalizing capacity in a manner that respects the limitations of social cognition and does not appear to undermine the individual capacity for processing change. Both schema-focused therapy (SFT) and metacognitive interpersonal therapy (MIT) follow some of the principles—adopted in this book—of focusing on a formulation of the patient's core difficulties that then dictates specifically tailored approaches to therapy.

By and large, integrative third-wave cognitive therapies fit into this pattern, as they draw on ideas and techniques from various theoretical orientations. SFT, in common with MBT, builds on attachment theory, as well as on elements of psychodynamic and experiential therapies [52]. SFT focuses on the various maladaptive coping modes that an individual internalized in childhood and continues to use in adult life. In AvPD, the "detached protector" mode, defined as disengaging from inner emotions, experiences, thoughts, and feelings, and from people, provides a formulation not dissimilar to the one outlined here for use in MBT. The motivational processes are also analogous to those in MBT, specifying that protection of the individual from feelings of loneliness and inferiority is at the core of the conceptualization. In parallel with the central place that MBT gives to epistemic trust, SFT considers fears of others' evaluations to be the source of the pervasive suspiciousness that characterizes the attitude of patients with AvPD. As with MBT, therapeutic techniques are personalized and directive, with the therapeutic relationship providing corrective interpersonal experiences to address issues of mistrust and the detachment from internal experience in self and other. Some limited empirical support for SFT comes from observational studies [53], generally for patients with cluster C (avoidant, dependent, and obsessive) personality disorders, who show lower dropout rates and better recovery with SFT compared with treatment as usual or clarification-oriented therapy [54].

MIT is influenced by narrative and relational approaches to personality disorders, as well as ideas from psychodynamic therapies, including MBT [55]. It assumes that anomalies in metacognitive abilities—mental operations aimed at decoding and understanding the mental states of self and others—and related dysfunctions, such as alexithymia, play a role in the phenomenology and experience of personality disorder [56]. In the formulation of AvPD, MIT also emphasizes the over-regulation of emotion (i.e., a controlled/reflectiveness bias on the automatic/controlled dimension) together with inhibition of affect (i.e., a cognitive bias on the cognitive/affective dimension) and avoidance of social interactions (teleological mode—assuming that physical avoidance can circumvent the confrontation of internal states), as well as relational avoidance (MBT would see this as the culmination of ineffective mentalizing). MIT, like MBT, focuses on interpersonal episodes to create awareness and to develop formulations, which inevitably address failures of mentalizing, to help to change patients' interpersonal schemas. MIT uses MBT-like interventions to reduce general distress; these interventions aim to improve metacognitive functioning, including a focus on narrative integrative capabilities, generating a sense of agency and self- and interpersonal functioning, and addressing affect dysregulation [55,56]. The current evidence base in relation to MIT for AvPD consists largely of uncontrolled case (or case series) studies [56–58].

Other psychotherapeutic orientations that are less compatible with MBT have also reported relevant work with patients with AvPD, including acceptance and commitment therapy combined with dialectical behavior therapy [59], radically open dialectical behavior therapy [60], and interpersonal psychotherapy [61].

Concluding Remarks

MBT-AvPD follows all the principles of the mentalizing approach, with the clear aim of establishing more effective and stable mentalizing that is more adaptive and flexible in relation to the patient's social world. The initial phase of formulation and agreement of aims is the basis of treatment. The not-knowing stance is crucial to prevent the clinician from filling in for the patient's poverty of mental-state understanding. Importantly, a mentalizing profile, most often centered around hypermentalizing and hypomentalizing modes and self/other dimensional problems, is established and shared between the patient and the clinician, and its use and misuse as the patient engages with their social world is then systematically explored. Focused work on the imbalance of mentalizing dimensions, especially minimizing the overuse of the self, is central to the treatment of patients with AvPD, as is the discovery of the other's mental states from the perspective of the other, rather than being based on self-biases. To this end, additional techniques for triggering the self/other mentalizing process without engendering excessive anxiety, including games and playfulness, are used by the clinician. Eventually, exploration of the momentary relational processes in the session, with careful marking and contingent responsiveness from the clinician, can be harnessed to generate in the patient a more genuine experience of others' mental states.

References

1. American Psychiatric Association. *Diagnostic and Statistical Manual of Mental Disorders*, 5th ed. Washington, DC: American Psychiatric Association, 2013.
2. World Health Organization. *ICD-11: International Classification of Diseases 11th Revision*. 2019. https://icd.who.int/.
3. American Psychiatric Association. *Diagnostic and Statistical Manual of Mental Disorders*. 4th ed., text rev. Washington, DC: American Psychiatric Association, 2000.
4. Millon T. *Disorders of Personality: Introducing a DSM/ICD Spectrum from Normal Styles to Abnormal Types*, 3rd ed. Hoboken, NJ: John Wiley & Sons, 2011.
5. Alden LE, Laposa JM, Taylor CT, Ryder AG. Avoidant personality disorder: current status and future directions. *J Pers Disord* 2002; **16**: 1–29.
6. Winarick DJ, Bornstein RF. Toward resolution of a longstanding controversy in personality disorder diagnosis: contrasting correlates of schizoid and avoidant traits. *Pers Indiv Diff* 2015; **79**: 25–9.
7. Lampe L, Malhi GS. Avoidant personality disorder: current insights. *Psychol Res Behav Manag* 2018; **11**: 55–66.
8. Wright AG, Pincus AL, Conroy DE, Elliot AJ. The pathoplastic relationship between interpersonal problems and fear of failure. *J Pers* 2009; **77**: 997–1024.
9. Marques L, Porter E, Keshaviah A et al. Avoidant personality disorder in individuals with generalized social anxiety disorder: what does it add? *J Anxiety Disord* 2012; **26**: 665–72.
10. Eikenaes I, Hummelen B, Abrahamsen G et al. Personality functioning in patients with avoidant personality disorder and social phobia. *J Pers Disord* 2013; **27**: 746–63.
11. Carr SN, Francis AJP. Do early maladaptive schemas mediate the relationship between childhood experiences and avoidant personality disorder features? A preliminary investigation in a non-clinical sample. *Cogn Ther Res* 2010; **34**: 343–58.
12. Eikenaes I, Pedersen G, Wilberg T. Attachment styles in patients with avoidant personality disorder compared with social phobia. *Psychol Psychother* 2016; **89**: 245–60.
13. Riggs SA, Paulson A, Tunnell E et al. Attachment, personality, and psychopathology among adult inpatients: self-reported romantic attachment style versus Adult Attachment Interview states

of mind. *Dev Psychopathol* 2007; **19**: 263–91.

14. Simonsen S, Euler S. Avoidant and narcissistic personality disorder. In: Bateman AW, Fonagy P, eds. *Handbook of Mentalizing in Mental Health Practice*, 2nd ed. Washington, DC: American Psychiatric Association Publishing, 2019; 351–68.
15. Beeney JE, Stepp SD, Hallquist MN et al. Attachment and social cognition in borderline personality disorder: specificity in relation to antisocial and avoidant personality disorders. *Personal Disord* 2015; **6**: 207–15.
16. Antonsen BT, Johansen MS, Ro FG et al. Is reflective functioning associated with clinical symptoms and long-term course in patients with personality disorders? *Compr Psychiatry* 2016; **64**: 46–58.
17. Pellecchia G, Moroni F, Colle L et al. Avoidant personality disorder and social phobia: does mindreading make the difference? *Compr Psychiatry* 2018; **80**: 163–9.
18. Moroni F, Procacci M, Pellecchia G et al. Mindreading dysfunction in avoidant personality disorder compared with other personality disorders. *J Nerv Ment Dis* 2016; **204**: 752–7.
19. Fonagy P, Target M. Playing with reality: I. Theory of mind and the normal development of psychic reality. *Int J Psychoanal* 1996; **77**: 217–33.
20. Target M, Fonagy P. Playing with reality: II. The development of psychic reality from a theoretical perspective. *Int J Psychoanal* 1996; **77**: 459–79.
21. Normann-Eide E, Johansen MS, Normann-Eide T et al. Personality disorder and changes in affect consciousness: a 3-year follow-up study of patients with avoidant and borderline personality disorder. *PLoS One* 2015; **10**: e0145625.
22. Johansen MS, Normann-Eide E, Normann-Eide T, Wilberg T. Emotional dysfunction in avoidant compared to borderline personality disorder: a study of affect consciousness. *Scand J Psychol* 2013; **54**: 515–21.
23. Denny BT, Fan J, Liu X et al. Elevated amygdala activity during reappraisal anticipation predicts anxiety in avoidant personality disorder. *J Affect Disord* 2015; **172**: 1–7.
24. Nicolo G, Semerari A, Lysaker PH et al. Alexithymia in personality disorders: correlations with symptoms and interpersonal functioning. *Psychiatry Res* 2011; **190**: 37–42.
25. Simonsen S, Eikenaes IU, Bach B et al. Level of alexithymia as a measure of personality dysfunction in avoidant personality disorder. *Nord J Psychiatry* 2021; **75**: 266–74.
26. Carlson EN, Vazire S, Oltmanns TF. Self-other knowledge asymmetries in personality pathology. *J Pers* 2013; **81**: 155–70.
27. Koenigsberg HW, Denny BT, Fan J et al. The neural correlates of anomalous habituation to negative emotional pictures in borderline and avoidant personality disorder patients. *Am J Psychiatry* 2014; **171**: 82–90.
28. Klumpp H, Angstadt M, Phan KL. Insula reactivity and connectivity to anterior cingulate cortex when processing threat in generalized social anxiety disorder. *Biol Psychol* 2012; **89**: 273–6.
29. Rosenthal MZ, Kim K, Herr NR et al. Speed and accuracy of facial expression classification in avoidant personality disorder: a preliminary study. *Personal Disord* 2011; **2**: 327–34.
30. Kavanagh LC, Winkielman P. The functionality of spontaneous mimicry and its influences on affiliation: an implicit socialization account. *Front Psychol* 2016; **7**: 458.
31. Kongerslev M, Simonsen S, Bo S. The quest for tailored treatments: a meta-discussion of six social cognitive therapies. *J Clin Psychol* 2015; **71**: 188–98.
32. Dimaggio G, Lysaker PH, Carcione A et al. Know yourself and you shall know the other… to a certain extent: multiple paths of influence of self-reflection on

mindreading. *Conscious Cogn* 2008; **17**: 778–89.

33. Dimaggio G, Procacci M, Nicolò G et al. Poor metacognition in narcissistic and avoidant personality disorders: four psychotherapy patients analysed using the Metacognition Assessment Scale. *Clin Psychol Psychother* 2007; **14**: 386–401.
34. Maresh EL, Andrews-Hanna JR. Putting the "Me" in "Mentalizing": multiple constructs describing *Self* versus *Other* during mentalizing and implications for social anxiety disorder. In: Gilead M, Ochsner K, eds. *The Neural Basis of Mentalizing*. Cham, Switzerland: Springer, 2021; 629–58.
35. James W. *Principles of Psychology*. New York, NY: Henry Holt, 1890.
36. Bryant L, Coffey A, Povinelli DJ, Pruett JR, Jr. Theory of Mind experience sampling in typical adults. *Conscious Cogn* 2013; **22**: 697–707.
37. Raffaelli Q, Wilcox R, Andrews-Hanna JR. The neuroscience of imaginative thought: an integrative framework. In: Abraham A, ed. *The Cambridge Handbook of the Imagination*. Cambridge, UK: Cambridge University Press, 2020; 332–53.
38. Marsh AA, Blair RJ. Deficits in facial affect recognition among antisocial populations: a meta-analysis. *Neurosci Biobehav Rev* 2008; **32**: 454–65.
39. Andrews-Hanna JR, Christoff K, O'Connor M. Dynamic regulation of internal experience: mechanisms of therapeutic change. In: Lane RD, Nadel L, eds. *The Neuroscience of Enduring Change: Implications for Psychotherapy*. Oxford, UK: Oxford University Press, 2020; 89–131.
40. Peters U. Human thinking, shared intentionality, and egocentric biases. *Biol Philos* 2016; **31**: 299–312.
41. Kampis D, Southgate V. Altercentric cognition: how others influence our cognitive processing. *Trends Cogn Sci* 2020; **24**: 945–59.
42. Marshall J, Gollwitzer A, Santos LR. Does altercentric interference rely on mentalizing?: Results from two level-1 perspective-taking tasks. *PLoS One* 2018; **13**: e0194101.
43. Tamir DI, Mitchell JP. Anchoring and adjustment during social inferences. *J Exp Psychol Gen* 2013; **142**: 151–62.
44. Clark DM. A cognitive model. In: Clark DM, Wells A, eds. *Social Phobia: Diagnosis, Assessment, and Treatment*. New York, NY: The Guilford Press, 1995; 69–73.
45. Hezel DM, McNally RJ. Theory of mind impairments in social anxiety disorder. *Behav Ther* 2014; **45**: 530–40.
46. Washburn D, Wilson G, Roes M et al. Theory of mind in social anxiety disorder, depression, and comorbid conditions. *J Anxiety Disord* 2016; **37**: 71–7.
47. Libby LK, Shaeffer EM, Eibach RP. Seeing meaning in action: a bidirectional link between visual perspective and action identification level. *J Exp Psychol Gen* 2009; **138**: 503–16.
48. Libby LK, Eibach RP. Visual perspective in mental imagery: a representational tool that functions in judgment, emotion, and self-insight. In: Olson JM, Zanna MP, eds. *Advances in Experimental Social Psychology*, Vol. 44. New York, NY: Academic Press, 2011; 185–245.
49. Libby LK, Eibach RP. The role of visual imagery in social cognition. In: Carlston DE, ed. *The Oxford Handbook of Social Cognition*. Oxford, UK: Oxford University Press, 2013; 147–66.
50. Pedersen G, Eikenaes I, Urnes O et al. Experiences in close relationships – psychometric properties among patients with personality disorders. *Personal Ment Health* 2015; **9**: 208–19.
51. Karterud S, Pedersen G, Johansen M et al. Primary emotional traits in patients with personality disorders. *Personal Ment Health* 2016; **10**: 261–73.
52. Fassbinder E, Arntz A. Schema therapy with emotionally inhibited and fearful patients. *J Contemp Psychother* 2019; **49**: 7–14.
53. Skewes SA, Samson RA, Simpson SG, van Vreeswijk M. Short-term group schema

therapy for mixed personality disorders: a pilot study. *Front Psychol* 2014; **5**: 1592.

54. Bamelis LL, Renner F, Heidkamp D, Arntz A. Extended Schema Mode conceptualizations for specific personality disorders: an empirical study. *J Pers Disord* 2011; **25**: 41–58.
55. Dimaggio G, Montano A, Popolo R, Salvatore G. *Metacognitive Interpersonal Therapy for Personality Disorders: A Treatment Manual.* New York, NY: Routledge, 2015.
56. Gordon-King K, Schweitzer RD, Dimaggio G. Metacognitive interpersonal therapy for personality disorders featuring emotional inhibition: a multiple baseline case series. *J Nerv Ment Dis* 2018; **206**: 263–9.
57. Dimaggio G, Salvatore G, MacBeth A et al. Metacognitive interpersonal therapy for personality disorders: a case study series. *J Contemp Psychother* 2017; **47**: 11–21.
58. Popolo R, MacBeth A, Canfora F et al. Metacognitive interpersonal therapy in groups for over-regulated personality disorders: a single case study. *J Contemp Psychother* 2019; **49**: 49–59.
59. Chan CC, Bach PA, Bedwell JS. An integrative approach using third-generation cognitive-behavioral therapies for avoidant personality disorder. *Clin Case Stud* 2015; **14**: 466–81.
60. Lynch TR, Hempel RJ, Dunkley C. Radically open-dialectical behavior therapy for disorders of over-control: signaling matters. *Am J Psychother* 2015; **69**: 141-62.
61. Gilbert SE, Gordon KC. Interpersonal psychotherapy informed treatment for avoidant personality disorder with subsequent depression. *Clin Case Stud* 2013; **12**: 111–27.

Part III

Application and Adaptations for Mental Health Presentations

Chapter 9

Depression

Introduction

Recent reviews and meta-analyses, including more than 500 clinical trials examining the effects of pharmacotherapy and more than 600 trials of different psychotherapies, suggest that all bona fide treatments for depression are about as effective as each other [1,2]. Typically, only around 50% of patients with depression show substantial improvement after treatment. This means that there is a great deal of room for improvement, particularly in more complex cases [3–5]. Mentalizing approaches may be of particular value here, as mentalization-based treatment (MBT) has been specifically developed to address temporary or long-term impairments in mentalizing that, as will be described in more detail in this chapter, are typical of patients with depression across the spectrum of severity, including patients with substantial features of personality disorder [4]. From a mentalizing perspective, patients who present with depression are on a continuum of severity based on four related features:

1. the nature of their depressive experiences
2. the extent of mentalizing impairments
3. their dominant attachment style (i.e., organized versus disorganized attachment strategies)
4. the severity of impairments in epistemic trust (see Table 9.1).

Clinical Example: Patients at Different Points on the Spectrum of Severity of Depression

Mark: Mild to Moderate

Mark has been feeling depressed for a few months, ever since he broke up with his girlfriend, Jenny. Although they still love each other, they realized that they had very different interests in life. Mark always valued his closeness with Jenny, but she increasingly distanced herself from him; she felt that he "suffocated" her. After a painful separation, Mark had difficulty concentrating at work and spent most of his leisure time at home, watching television. His parents are quite concerned about him. They have always had a loving relationship with their son and they are desperate to help him, but they do not know how to do this. They have always felt somewhat emotionally disconnected from him. Mark realizes that something has to change, and has sought help from a mental health professional. Fairly quickly he becomes able to reflect on his own role in his relationship break-up, and can work collaboratively with the clinician to explore his pattern of emotional distancing.

Lucy: Moderate to Severe

Lucy has a history of emotional abuse and neglect. Her parents say that they did their best to raise her, but they were often not there for her and could also be very critical of her. As a teenager, Lucy began to rebel, and she became involved in often chaotic romantic relationships characterized by idealization and denigration. She also began to consume alcohol excessively and engage in self-harming behavior. Although she struggled at university, she managed to graduate and to find a good job. However, at work she often gets into conflicts with colleagues and has felt "underwhelmed" in recent months. She feels empty, lonely, and an "emotional wreck."

Angela: Severe to Very Severe

Angela was rather an outcast as a child. She had very different interests from other children and often retreated into her own fantasy world. As a teenager, she experienced little or no connection with her peers. Around the age of 18, she began to develop delusional ideas about herself. She felt completely alone in the world, and developed the belief that something was physically wrong with her—that she was the ugliest woman in the world. At the intake interview with a clinician she is very agitated; she says she feels completely exhausted and that she almost constantly thinks about killing herself.

Patients whose depression is at the less severe end of the spectrum benefit most from a combined mental-process and mental-representation focus in therapy [6,7]—that is, an approach that focuses on distortions in the content of mental representations (cognitive-affective schemas or internal working models of self and others) alongside a focus on improving mentalizing (see Table 9.2). Dynamic interpersonal therapy (DIT) [8], for instance, is a brief manualized treatment that has been developed for patients with mild to moderate depression, and which combines a mentalizing (process) focus with a mental representation focus [9]. In patients with marked features of personality disorder, a mental-representation approach might be iatrogenic, particularly in the early phases of treatment. Because these patients often have severe impairments in mentalizing and high levels of epistemic mistrust, they are likely to lack the mentalizing capacities that are typically required for such a focus, and they may even lack the capacity to establish a therapeutic alliance because of their profound distrust of others [6,7]. Longitudinal studies of patients with co-occurring major depressive disorder and borderline personality disorder have suggested that unless the personality disorder is treated there will be only a limited response to treatment of the depression [10]. These patients are at great risk of self-harm and suicide, particularly when they are functioning in teleological mode (see Chapter 2). For these patients, dynamic interpersonal therapy for complex care (DITCC) [11], or, with increasing severity, MBT for personality disorder are indicated. Both of these treatments have shown good results in patients with depression and substantial personality problems [12].

The mental-process focus that is characteristic of "traditional" MBT may be most appropriate for patients whose depression is at the more severe end of the spectrum. For the most severely depressed patients, MBT for psychosis may be indicated (see Chapter 10). Of course, the distinction between a mental-process focus and a mental-representation focus is not absolute, and work with depressed patients typically includes both approaches. For instance, as the patient's mentalizing becomes increasingly robust, the focus in traditional MBT shifts toward relational mentalizing (including mentalizing

Table 9.1 The spectrum of severity of depression

Distinguishing features	Mild to moderate	Moderate to severe	Severe to very severe
Nature of depressive experiences	Mild to moderate depressed mood and some somatic symptoms of depression	Greater affective instability, more profound feelings of emptiness and diffuse negative affectivity, higher levels of self-criticism and fears of abandonment, shame, and self-destructive behavior	Psychotic symptoms, such as delusions of guilt, greater psychomotor agitation (excessive purposeless movements and restlessness) or psychomotor retardation (slowing of mental and physical activities)
Mentalizing impairments	Typically mild; mentalizing is relatively easily recovered after it is lost	More severe impairments in mentalizing	Severe impairments in mentalizing
Nature of attachment problems	Relatively securely attached; use of secondary attachment strategies is often in response to stress and mood problems	Over-reliance on secondary attachment strategies is typically present before the onset of depression and is exacerbated by depressed mood; disorganization of the attachment system may be present	Disorganization of the attachment system
Impairments in epistemic trust	Impairments are often secondary to depressed mood	More severe problems with epistemic trust	Severe problems with epistemic trust

Table 9.2 Mental-process and mental-representation approaches to the treatment of depression

	Mental-process approach	Mental-representation approach
Main aim	Improve the process of mentalizing	Improve insight
Main therapeutic techniques	Spectrum of mentalization-based techniques, with an emphasis on fostering basic mentalizing	Spectrum of insight-oriented techniques, with an emphasis on insight (i.e., the identification and working through of a repetitive pattern of self in relation to others that is related to the onset and course of mood problems)

Table 9.3 Major adaptations of the MBT model for the treatment of patients with depression

Adaptations of the MBT approach	Implications for intervention
Address mentalizing impairments typical of depressed states of mind	Supportive interventions, and validation and normalizing interventions in particular, are important to counter depressive pessimism that may hinder the patient's engagement in the therapeutic process
Tailor treatment to the patient's use of secondary attachment styles and associated mentalizing impairments	The clinician moves flexibly along the spectrum of interventions, placing greater emphasis on relational mentalizing in patients with higher-level functioning
Address problems with embodied mentalizing	Use of interventions that foster embodied mentalizing

about the therapeutic relationship), and thus to mentalizing about the relationships between the patient's representations of self and others and their depressive symptoms, typical of the mental-representation focus. Likewise, even with less severe depression, a mentalizing focus is typically required, particularly in the early stages of treatment, as depressed mood is associated with non-mentalizing modes of experiencing the self and others. For instance, depressed mood often gives rise to psychic equivalence (see Chapter 2) in which the patient feels beyond help. However, the difference in emphasis is important when considering the focus and aims of treatment.

This chapter will first provide an outline of the mentalizing approach to depression. It will focus on three key adaptations of the MBT approach to tailor it to the treatment of depression, based on our evolving understanding of depressive states of mind (see Table 9.3):

- the importance of supportive, validating, and normalizing interventions to counter the impact of depressed states of mind on mentalizing; these states of mind may hinder not only mentalizing but also engagement in the therapeutic process
- the MBT clinician's capacity to move flexibly along the spectrum from interventions aimed at fostering the process of mentalizing to interventions that focus on increasing insight into repetitive interpersonal patterns (advanced relational mentalizing), tailored to the patient's attachment style and associated specific mentalizing impairments
- the role of interventions aimed at increasing embodied mentalizing in depressed patients, as most if not all of these patients have problems in this area.

This chapter will end with a brief description of the spectrum of mentalizing approaches, which will also illustrate how to tailor MBT to the needs and capacities of depressed patients.

The Mentalizing Approach to Depression

Mood and Mentalizing

From a mentalizing perspective, depression is an evolutionarily determined response to threats to attachment relationships and thus threats to the self (e.g., separation, rejection, loss, failure), which impairs and distorts mentalizing [8,13]. This results in a vicious cycle

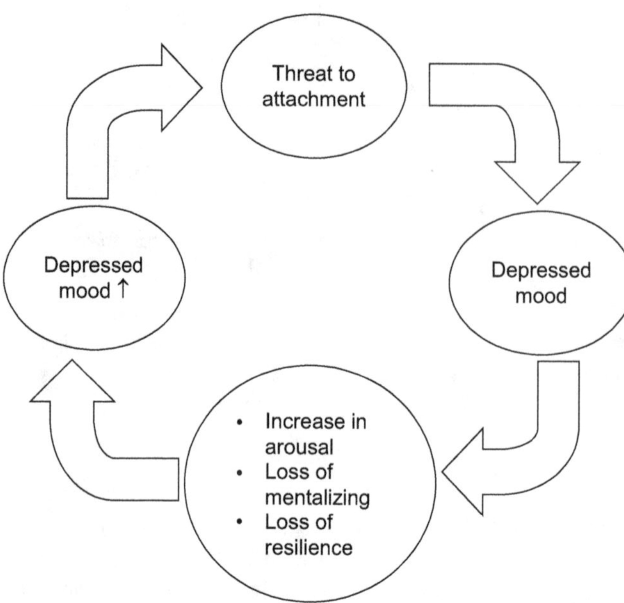

Fig. 9.1 The relationship between threats to attachment, mood, mentalizing, and resilience in the face of adversity.

as depressed mood further increases stress and arousal, leading to further impairments and distortions in mentalizing (i.e., psychic equivalence, teleological, and pretend-mode functioning, which are described in Chapter 2), resulting in a loss of resilience in the face of stress, thereby increasing vulnerability to depression (see Figure 9.1). Individuals with depression typically do not want to reflect on what is happening to them, and when they attempt to do so, their mentalizing is likely to be distorted by their depressed mood.

This is why a process focus aimed at restoring the patient's mentalizing capacity is indicated, particularly in the early phases of treatment and in patients with more severe depression. A more insight-oriented approach is likely to exceed depressed patients' ability to mentalize (other than in milder cases), leading to their experiencing more self-criticism, rumination, helplessness, and even thoughts of suicide. The identification of the non-mentalizing modes of functioning that are typical of depressed patients is a good starting point for MBT interventions for depression (see Table 9.4).

In depressed patients, *psychic equivalence* functioning, expressed as a lack of desire and/or inability to explore their inner mental states, is very common. In psychic equivalence, thoughts are experienced as reality—the depressed patient *is* beyond help, *is* worthless, there *is* no future, and things *are* what they are. In addition, in psychic equivalence, psychological pain feels like physical pain, and emotional and physical exhaustion are equated, which in part explains the high comorbidity between depression and conditions characterized by chronic pain and fatigue [14]. This equivalence between emotions, feelings, and physical states is primarily expressed in impairments in embodied mentalizing—worries feel like a painful weight on one's shoulders, criticism by others really hurts, depressive thoughts literally "press down on" the self, and emotional conflicts seem to "paralyze" the patient. Hyperembodiment is typical in many depressed patients, as subjective experiences are experienced as "too real" and are felt in terms of bodily experiences. However, as will be discussed in more detail later in this

Table 9.4 Individual differences in attachment styles, typical clinical features, and associated mentalizing profiles

	Attachment hyperactivating	Attachment deactivating
Associated personality dimensions	Dependency/sociotropy	Self-criticism/autonomy
Experiential mode	Affective, figurative, visual	Logical, focused on overt behavior, clear cause–effect relationships
Cognitive style	Simultaneous processing, synthesis of discrete elements into a cohesive whole	Manifest form, analytic, detailed
Interpersonal relatedness	Seeks relatedness, harmony; and fusion; more field dependent	Influenced by internal disposition instead of social environment; more field independent
Stress-regulation strategies (defensive style)	Recruitment of the support of others	Isolation, non-interpersonal regulation
Typical mentalizing profile	Hypersensitivity to mental states of others, imbalance between cognitive and affective mentalizing: affect-driven hypermentalizing accounts concerning love, rejection, and enmeshment with attachment figures	Often shows "mind blindness"; imbalance between cognitive and affective mentalizing: cognitive hypomentalizing or hypermentalizing, disconnection from emotions, derogation of mental life as such

chapter, the patient is often barely aware of the connection between these embodied states of mind and their presenting problems. Neuroscience studies have shown impairments in neural circuits that are implicated in mentalizing in patients with depression, including the medial prefrontal cortex, amygdala, hippocampus, and ventromedial parts of the basal ganglia, reflecting an imbalance between cognitive and affective mentalizing [15–17].

As depressive symptoms reflect responses to threats to attachment relationships, their interpersonal nature should be kept in mind. For instance, rumination and self-criticism clearly have an interpersonal function, as a "pull" for attention and help, and thus reflect attempts to co-regulate arousal and stress. Hence interventions that involve empathic marked mirroring of feelings of helplessness, hopelessness, or worthlessness can be particularly helpful in the early stages of treatment, as they may lead to recovery of patients' mentalizing by restoring their feelings of agency and selfhood (as well as fostering epistemic trust; see Chapter 3). These "holding" and "containing" interventions signal to the patient that even unbearable emotions can be discussed and reflected upon. Communicating the tolerability of affect is essential in therapeutic work with depressed patients, as many of these patients are convinced that they should be able to bear painful feelings and/or are ashamed to admit to and talk about them. In this context, psychoeducational interventions concerning the influence of mood on mentalizing may also be helpful, just as psychopharmacological treatment, exercise, and restoring sleep and a healthier lifestyle in general may be helpful in the recovery of mentalizing.

Psychic equivalence functioning may also increase the risk for suicide as an attempt to silence psychological pain. Again, careful marked mirroring of unbearable feelings of psychological pain typically leads the patient to open up about opposite feelings—that is, the wish to live—which decreases the risk of suicide, as such interventions restore the patient's mentalizing and counteract the "tunnel vision" that is typical of suicidal states of mind.

Teleological mode functioning in depressed patients is often related to the origins of depressed states, consistent with the assumption in the mentalizing approach that depression is interpersonal in nature. For example, patients with depression may make often frantic attempts to get attachment figures (including their therapist) to show that they care for or love them. Patients may demand to have longer or more sessions, or ask their therapist to touch, hug, or caress them. However, some depressed patients who are functioning in teleological mode may deny any relationship between their depressed mood and relational issues, or may try to limit the interpersonal origin of their problems to simplistic cause–effect relationships: "*Depression runs in the family, it must be genetic,*" "*I have been abused, I can't help it.*"

Extreme *pretend mode* or *hypermentalizing* functioning in depressed patients is also extremely common. This can lead to hypomentalizing–hypermentalizing cycles, which can confuse the patient and the clinician alike, leaving them both with feelings of emptiness and helplessness. Hypermentalizing in depressed patients typically takes the form of elaborate narratives involving the self and others. These narratives may at first come across as fairly accurate narrative accounts that reflect genuine mentalizing, particularly in higher-functioning patients. However, a number of features of these narratives indicate their roots in hypermentalizing.

1. They are typically overly analytical, repetitive, and lengthy in nature, and are distorted by depressive themes such as self-criticism, guilt, and shame (excessive rumination).
2. They may be self-serving (e.g., to control or coerce others, or to portray the patient as the victim of neglectful others), often leading to counter-responsive feelings of aggression or boredom in the clinician.
3. They have an imbalance between cognition and affect that is characteristic of hypermentalizing (i.e., they are either overly cognitive in nature or affectively overwhelming).
4. The patient shows an inability to switch perspectives from self to other or vice versa, or from cognition to affect, even when the clinician tries to foster this switch by using contrary moves (see Chapter 4).

In this context, it is also important to discuss the nature of *depressive realism*, which refers to the fact that depressed patients may look at the world without "rose-tinted spectacles," and thus their perception may be more accurate than that of people who are not depressed. Although this can sometimes be the case, depressive realism is not always more "realistic," as it may reflect either hypomentalizing or hypermentalizing. Studies suggest that having a positive bias is normative and conducive to healthy functioning

[18]; the loss of this positive bias seems to be implicated in vulnerability to depression. Hence there may be a flipside to the capacity for mentalizing and increased self-awareness and self-consciousness, as they enable self-conscious emotions such as shame and guilt. Although these emotions serve important adaptive interpersonal functions, when they are too intense or chronic they may give rise to excessive feelings of depression and anxiety. In addition, the capacity for self-consciousness also brings the awareness that there may be a difference between one's current self-state and one's wished-for self-state [19]. Particularly at specific developmental stages and transitions (e.g., adolescence, midlife, old age), coming to realize that there is a discrepancy between one's wished-for and actual self-states may lead to feelings of despondency, depression, and even despair. Findings that neural circuits involved in mentalizing undergo major structural and functional changes at crucial developmental stages (e.g., adolescence, old age) may further help to explain the increased risk for depression associated with these developmental stages, particularly as mentalizing capacities are challenged during these crucial transitional periods. The emergence of sexuality and new forms of aggression in adolescence provides an important test for the young person's mentalizing capacities, as does the loss of loved ones and health in old age. This may result in either excessive mentalizing (pretend-mode functioning or hypermentalizing: "*What if I had made other choices in life?*") or the defensive avoidance of mentalizing (hypomentalizing: "*Everything has been meaningless*").

The Role of Attachment in the Co-Regulation of Stress in Depression

It is clear that feelings of depression are not intrinsically maladaptive or pathological. As we mentioned earlier, depression is a response to threats to attachment relationships, and even severely depressive states of mind should be seen as attempts to minimize the distress associated with separation and loss, and thus as attempts to (co-)regulate distress [20–22]. From this perspective, depression can be seen as a reward-depletion disorder as much as a stress-related disorder—everything seems hopeless and meaningless, nothing appears to bring joy, pleasure, or satisfaction any more, and the individual enters into a state of protest [23,24].

However, in the situation where others who might have provided care and support to the depressed person are either no longer available or perceived as unavailable, the person's primary attachment strategy—to attempt to down-regulate distress by finding relief and support in others—fails. As a result, the individual begins to rely on secondary attachment strategies. Attachment-hyperactivating strategies are typically used by anxiously attached individuals (e.g., those with a preoccupied attachment style), and involve frantic efforts to find support, love, and relief, often expressed in demanding and clinging behavior. Attachment-deactivating strategies are typical of avoidant individuals (e.g., those with fearful-avoidant and dismissive attachment styles), and involve denying attachment needs and asserting one's own autonomy, independence, and strength. Many patients with depression show an organized attachment style, and thus tend to rely primarily on attachment-hyperactivating or attachment-deactivating strategies. However, patients with disorganized attachment show more severe dysfunctions of the attachment system, typically manifested as marked oscillations between attachment-hyperactivating and attachment-deactivating strategies. Patients with disorganized attachment have more pronounced mentalizing impairments and may also have more severe problems with epistemic trust. These assumptions are well supported by research findings that show marked heterogeneity in the attachment styles of people with depression [19,25], and by evidence for a prospective relationship between attachment insecurity and depression, which suggests that attachment experiences play a causal role in vulnerability to depression [26–28]. Consistent with the assumptions outlined in this chapter, disorganized attachment is associated with more severe depression than organized attachment. Attachment disorganization is also more prevalent in depressed individuals with borderline-level functioning, characterized by more severe depression and feelings of emptiness, anger, shame, and identity diffusion [4,29]. Attachment-deactivating strategies, in particular dismissive attachment styles, appear to be associated with greater vulnerability to a hostile/aggressive subtype of depression [30].

The role of mentalizing impairments in depression has been well established [19,31,32]. Similarly, it is known that a subgroup of individuals with depression has profound difficulties in seeking and accepting help—indicative of high levels of epistemic mistrust [31]. Furthermore, longitudinal studies have shown that individual differences in attachment styles mediate the relationship between early adversity and later vulnerability to depression through their effects on affect regulation, stress responsivity, and impairments in social problem-solving skills [25,33–35]. Four decades of research on psychodynamic and cognitive–behavioral approaches to depression have provided evidence for prospective relationships between the personality dimensions of dependency/sociotropy and self-criticism/autonomy (which overlap theoretically and empirically with attachment anxiety and attachment avoidance, respectively) and vulnerability to depression [36–39] (see Table 9.4 and Figure 9.2).

For the MBT clinician, two major clinical findings have emerged from this body of research in relation to both the mental-representation focus and the mental-process/mentalizing focus in the treatment of individuals with depression. First, with regard to the mental-representation focus, studies have shown that both individuals with high levels of attachment anxiety/dependency/sociotropy and those with high levels of attachment avoidance/self-criticism/autonomy are characterized by distinct dysfunctional interpersonal transactional cycles or "self-fulfilling prophecies" [40]. Individuals with high levels of attachment anxiety may elicit annoyance, resentment, and eventually rejection and abandonment by others as a result of a clinging relational style that arises from underlying fears of rejection and abandonment. Individuals who have high levels of attachment avoidance, meanwhile, may be more aloof and critical of others; this causes them to be perceived as cold, distant, and unlikable, and others' reactions to them confirm their beliefs that others are unavailable and critical of them. Moreover, whereas individuals with high levels of attachment anxiety are often able to maintain a few positive supportive relationships with others because of their strong relational orientation, those with high levels of attachment avoidance are more often isolated and have fewer positive relationships. These self-fulfilling prophecies also influence the relationship that patients have with their clinician, so that their initial perceptions and experiences of the clinician will match their beliefs and expectations (either idealizing their clinician, or perceiving them as critical and aloof). This is especially important when focusing on relational mentalizing, and when mentalizing the therapeutic relationship in particular.

With regard to the mentalizing focus when treating depressed patients, patients who rely primarily on attachment-deactivating strategies tend to inhibit mentalizing defensively. As a result, teleological mode and psychic equivalence tend to dominate in these

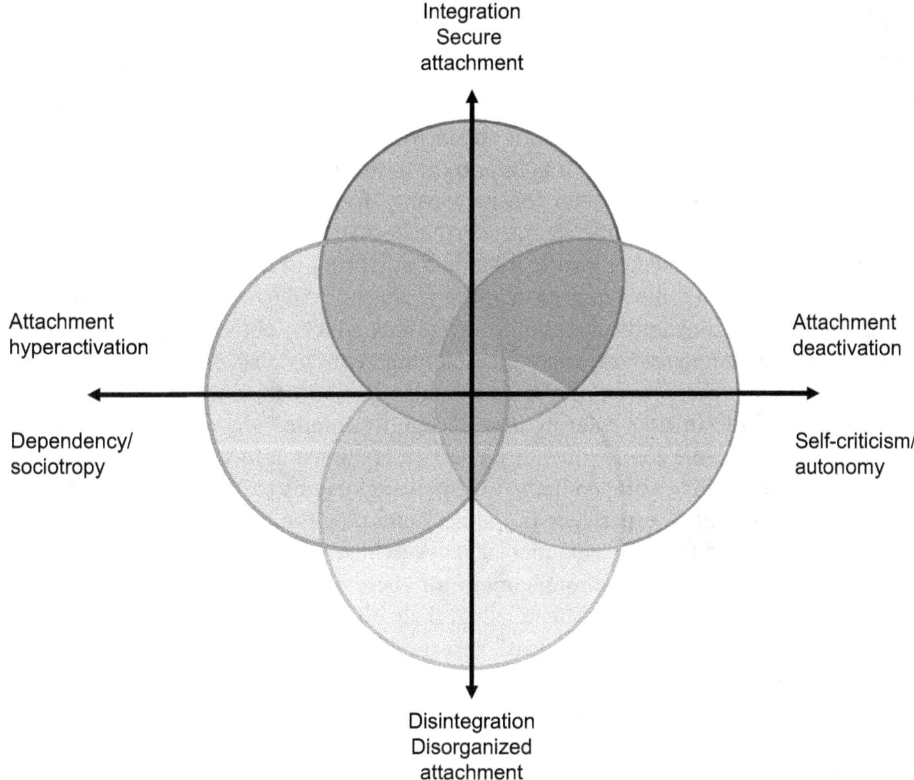

Fig. 9.2 The relationship between attachment dimensions and personality features in depressed patients.

patients. For example, activity and work are used to defensively inhibit painful feelings of depression, anxiety, and loneliness, and to "prove" self-worth. As we shall describe in more detail later in this chapter, these individuals also often show profound impairments in their capacity for embodied mentalizing, as they seem to be "disconnected" from their emotions and their body. Particularly when depressed, many of these patients show a derogation of mental life as such, leading to "mind blindness" about the role of internal mental states. Things are what they are ("*Nobody likes me, I just know,*" reflecting psychic equivalence), and they only believe in "objective" causes ("*My depression is the result of imbalances in my brain chemistry,*" reflecting teleological thinking). There is an imbalance in mentalizing, with an emphasis on cognitive mentalizing and little if any affective grounding of experiences. Sometimes such cognitive accounts may be misidentified by the clinician as genuine mentalizing, but their self-serving, highly cognitive nature, which leads only to increasing feelings of helplessness and hopelessness, helps to identify them as pseudomentalizing/pretend mode. Extremely dismissive accounts (e.g., denying that one has a problem) or extremely idealizing accounts of one's attachment history (e.g., "*I had a perfectly normal childhood,*" in combination with an inability to provide examples to support such accounts) are easier to identify as pseudomentalizing/pretend mode.

Balancing the Intervention to Support Effective Mentalizing Process and Attachment Strategies

With depressed patients the first task is to foster a mentalizing stance, before addressing the underlying psychological issues; this entails focusing on mentalizing as a process and capacity, rather than on content. It is important to focus in the early stages of treatment on issues that are congruent with the personality functioning of these patients (e.g., autonomy, identity, power, guilt, shame, worthlessness), to try to reduce the risk of these individuals feeling attacked or shamed. Marked mirroring of these experiences typically opens up the path to exploring more painful feelings of vulnerability and loneliness in particular. Normalizing and validating interventions are key, but at the same time there needs to be an emphasis on affect-focused interventions that increase arousal. As depressed patients characteristically have considerable difficulties with verbalizing their emotions, the clinician risks entering into a "cognitive mode," too, and the arousal level in sessions can become too low for any effective mentalizing to emerge. Interventions that are focused on increasing embodied mentalizing may be particularly useful here, as these help the patient to experience in the here and now the relationship between their depressed mood and their internal mental states (which will be discussed in more detail later). On the other hand, although many of these patients are very restricted and constricted in their capacity for mentalizing, their often marked cognitive abilities may lead them to enjoy "playing with ideas" and the kind of exploratory work that results from increased basic mentalizing skills. This may be a turning point in treatment as it leads to increased curiosity about the therapeutic process and the clinician's mind, and to more lasting changes in the interaction between the patient and their interpersonal environment (i.e., opening up to salutogenesis [12]; see also Chapter 11 and later in this chapter).

Patients who rely primarily on attachment-hyperactivating strategies in response to threats to attachment relationships show a paradoxical pattern of hypersensitivity to the mental states of others in combination with a tendency to be overwhelmed by fear of rejection and abandonment on the one hand, and fear of their own aggression and rage on the other. As a result, these patients tend to have a low threshold for decoupling of mentalizing, and they may have considerable difficulty in recovering from mentalizing impairments. Therefore they may want to please the clinician, which can make it difficult to identify mentalizing lapses. Patients with borderline features may be prone to confusion with or contagion by others' mental states [41]. Although mentalizing is typically overly cognitive in depressed patients who rely primarily on attachment-deactivating strategies, mentalizing in depressed patients who rely on attachment-hyperactivating strategies is typically strongly affect driven, often leading to hypermentalized accounts of interpersonal relationships and a defensive decoupling of mentalizing because they are easily overwhelmed by the emotions linked to these experiences. In psychic equivalence mode, these individuals interpret even slight signs of separation or rejection as meaning that others are bored or want to get rid of them. This then leads to teleological functioning, in which the patient desperately wants to prove their love, or wants the other to provide proof of their love and care. It can also lead to pretend-mode functioning, in which there are often seemingly endless ruminative accounts of social interactions characterized by thoughts about perfect or unrequited love, or attachment narratives marked by enmeshment with attachment figures (e.g., parents), leading to further self–other confusion. In patients with higher-level functioning with histrionic features, pretend-mode functioning gives rise to fantasies in which the self is depicted as the victim of the bad intentions of others. This hypersensitivity to mental states, and its propensity to lead to psychic equivalence, teleological, and pretend-mode functioning, is often also present in relation to the clinician. For instance, when the clinician announces that they will be taking a break for a holiday, the patient feels rejected, wants to prove that they are worthy of the clinician's attention, and cannot stop thinking about the incident between sessions.

Thus, although these patients typically like to talk about relationships, their hypersensitivity to the mental states of others in combination with their low threshold for the decoupling of mentalizing means that fostering a better balance between cognitive and affective features of mentalizing may be difficult, particularly as many of these patients are convinced that they are good "mind readers" ("*I know people. All of my friends come to me for advice about their relationships*"). As a result, clinicians may struggle to find an optimal balance between the activation of the attachment system, which increases arousal, and the decoupling of mentalizing, particularly with interventions that attempt to clarify links between symptoms of depression and interpersonal conflict and ambivalence (i.e., a mental-representation focus). Careful marked mirroring of feelings of loss and separation based on micro-slicing of recent interpersonal events may improve the patient's capacity for basic mentalizing and improve their ability to mentalize more difficult feelings of aggression, anger, and autonomy. Anxiously attached individuals typically have difficulty considering these feelings, which they experience as threatening to their relationships. Mentalizing the therapeutic relationship—that is, identifying the patient's responses to the clinician in the here and now of the therapeutic situation—plays an important role in fostering relational mentalizing in these individuals, although, as we mentioned earlier in this chapter (see also Chapter 4), this has to wait until stable mentalizing is better established. Moreover, as treatment progresses, encouraging the patient to experiment with new ways of relating to others outside the "interpersonal laboratory" of the therapy sessions is important, as it provides new opportunities to examine the re-emergence of non-mentalizing modes of functioning and to monitor progress in the emergence of more robust mentalizing.

Embodied Mentalizing

Research findings from different theoretical traditions have shown that a significant proportion of depressed patients have difficulties with several components of embodied mentalizing, either because of pre-existing problems with embodied mentalizing, or as a result of their depressed mood, or both [42–46]. These problems can be summarized as follows:

1. **problems with recognizing emotions**—many depressed patients seem to be unable to relate bodily experiences to inner mental states ("*I don't know what I feel, I feel bad, tense, that's it*"), and some patients even argue that they do not feel anything at all ("*I used to feel something, but I no longer seem to have feelings*")
2. **problems recognizing emotions as their own**—they are easily "infected" by others' emotions or deny that they feel depressed or sad
3. **problems reflecting on and modulating emotions**—they are easily overwhelmed by emotions or are readily triggered to respond in teleological mode, leading to enactments

Table 9.5 Interventions aimed at increasing embodied mentalizing: the RADLE sequence

Intervention	Method
Recognizing emotions	Focus on physical sensations (somatic markers of emotions) and explore their emotional context, using the not-knowing, inquisitive stance to generate possible hypotheses about underlying emotional states, which are shared with the patient in order to arrive at a joint understanding
Amplifying emotions	Amplify the emotional experience: *"So you felt anxious"*
Differentiating emotions	Explore the different emotional experiences one at a time; amplify and explore the causal relationships between them
Linking of emotions to the patient's typical patterns of feeling and thinking	If possible and appropriate, link emotions to the patient's prototypical ways of feeling, thinking, and relating
Marking the **E**motional (and often physical) cost of problems with embodied mentalizing	Validate and normalize problems with embodied mentalizing as understandable responses to stress, but also discuss the high emotional (and often physical) cost associated with these problems

4. **problems sharing emotions appropriately**—depressed patients often believe that it is a sign of weakness to share their emotions with others, or, conversely, they immediately begin to talk about their difficult emotions as if they have known their clinician for many years, often assuming that the clinician is completely familiar with the details of their life.

When working with depressed patients, it is therefore important for the clinician to carefully explore, using the not-knowing, inquisitive stance, the relationship between bodily experiences (so-called somatic markers of emotions) and unmentalized states of mind. This is also particularly important in patients who present with somatoform features [14].

To achieve this the clinician uses the well-known basic mentalizing techniques of *stop and explore* and *stop and rewind* (see Chapter 4) to micro-slice embodied experiences in the here and now of the therapeutic situation. A typical sequence of interventions aimed at promoting embodied mentalizing focuses on *recognizing*, *amplifying*, and *differentiating* between emotions, *linking* these emotions to the interpersonal dynamics associated with the onset and persistence of symptoms, and marking the *emotional cost* of problems with embodied mentalizing. This is known as the "RADLE" sequence (see Table 9.5).

Recognizing Emotions

Initially patients often describe only physical sensations linked to their depressive state (e.g., "*I always feel tense,*" "*I feel so tired*"). This points to unmentalized emotions, and so the first task is to recognize such apparently undifferentiated bodily experiences as emotions. The clinician must often use their own mind to generate hypotheses about these unmentalized bodily experiences, and test these against the patient's experience. For example, a patient relates how he got into an argument with his wife and then "shut down." When the clinician asks how the patient felt during the argument, he responds: "*I don't know, nothing, I think,*" but he clearly feels tense, begins to blush, and clenches his hands. In response, the clinician says that he can't imagine that the patient felt nothing at all, and adds: "*When you just said you didn't feel anything, I saw you become all tense over your body; you turned your face away from me, began to blush, and clenched your hands tightly together. Do you feel anxious or ashamed?*" Again, the not-knowing stance implies humility and the clinician must model misunderstanding: "*Ah, you didn't feel anxious, I am glad you corrected me. So you felt angry and then ashamed.*"

Amplifying Emotions

Because the patient is usually largely unaware of these unmentalized bodily experiences, the clinician needs to amplify the underlying emotions one by one, using marked mirroring: "*Ah, so you felt anger in the first place. How did that feel?*"

Differentiating Emotions

Unmentalized bodily experiences typically involve several emotions that are also causally related. In the example that has just been described, in addition to anger the patient felt ashamed and anxious as a result of his anger. Therefore the clinician actively explores each of these feelings together with the patient, identifies them, and attempts to arrive at a coherent narrative that ties all of these feelings together.

Linking Emotions

The next step in the sequence entails linking emotions to prototypical ways of relating to the self and others and their connection with presenting symptoms. Micro-slicing of previously unmentalized bodily experiences leads the patient to experience, in the here and now of the session, the relationship between typical patterns of thinking and feeling and their presenting symptoms. This process plays an important role in fostering mentalizing in the patient and allowing them to increasingly make these links in their everyday life.

Emotional Cost

Finally, a focus on improving embodied mentalizing includes the clinician highlighting the emotional cost of problems with (embodied) mentalizing. For instance, to continue with the clinical example outlined earlier, the clinician may link the patient's various problems with embodied mentalizing to their depressive symptoms: "*If I am correct, we have seen how, when someone criticizes you, you tend to respond with anger, quickly followed by anxiety and shame because of your feelings of anger, followed by you 'shutting yourself down,' leaving you feeling empty and drained. Is that about right?*" If the patient recognizes this sequence as typical of their way of responding, the clinician could then go on to add: "*However understandable this response may be, it also has clear disadvantages, as you do not seem to be aware of what is happening to you in such circumstances and you are left with a lot of feelings that you can't seem to digest.*"

In this way the patient is able to shift from experiencing the self in terms of a *physical self* to experiencing it in terms of a *psychological self*, developing second-order representations of the self and mentalized affectivity—the capacity to reflect and modulate embodied emotional experiences.

Epistemic Trust

A mental-representation focus relies heavily on mentalizing capacities that a considerable subgroup of patients who present with depression does not possess. Using this focus too early in treatment, before the patient has strengthened their capacity to mentalize, is therefore likely to be associated with iatrogenic effects. In these patients, mentalizing capacities are easily lost, leading to increasing pressure to externalize non-mentalized aspects of the self (e.g., aspects related to traumatic experiences), and this can trigger the emergence of the alien self (see Chapter 2). These patients also often show pronounced epistemic mistrust, either related to their attachment history or resulting from unhelpful treatments in the past, or a combination of both. Insight-oriented interventions (in particular, brief insight-oriented interventions) for depression which assume that the patient has sufficient mentalizing capacities and epistemic trust to establish a working alliance are not indicated for such patients (see Tables 9.1 and 9.2).

A mental-process focus is more appropriate for these patients. Particularly when working with individuals with high levels of epistemic mistrust, marked mirroring of often profound feelings of depression and despair is needed to restore (or, in the most severely affected patients, to develop) epistemic trust. In line with our hypothesis that effective treatments rely on three communication systems [12,47] (see also Chapter 2), the clinician first needs to communicate to the patient in an empathic and supportive way that the clinician's mind is available and is able to tolerate, contain, and reflect upon mental states that the patient finds unbearable, through careful and progressive marked mirroring of such mental states in the here and now (communication system 1). Only when the patient feels truly understood will their epistemic vigilance be relaxed, and at the same time their sense of agency and selfhood will be restored, leading to more robust mentalizing capacities and an increased curiosity about the mind of the clinician. In the majority of cases this is a slow and painstaking process characterized by trial and error, and it is imperative that the clinician models humility, imperfection, and misunderstanding as inevitable features of human communication, while at the same time unwaveringly modeling the not-knowing, inquisitive stance. The not-knowing stance is particularly important because many of these patients will have encountered others in their environment, including health professionals, who "knew" what was wrong with them and provided them with advice that they did not feel was helpful.

If all goes well with this early stage of treatment, the marked mirroring of unbearable experiences gives rise to a sense of "we-ness" in the treatment, and an increase in the patient's mentalizing capacities (communication system 2). If the patient's mentalizing capacities are robust enough at this stage, a mental-representation focus might now be indicated. However, many of these patients will continue to struggle with a mental-representation focus, particularly those with marked borderline or psychotic symptoms. Next, the patient needs to be actively supported to increasingly create and open up to a more benign social environment (the basis of communication system 3).

The Spectrum of Mentalization-Based Interventions

This section will briefly summarize some aspects of MBT that are pertinent to the treatment of depression, and the basic principles of DIT [8], a brief manualized treatment for depression that combines a mentalizing (i.e., mental-process) and a mental-representation focus, which has been shown to be effective in the treatment of mild to moderate depression [9]. In patients with more marked personality disorder symptoms this approach might be iatrogenic, particularly if it is used as a first-line treatment, because these patients often have severe impairments in mentalizing and profound epistemic mistrust [6,7]. For these patients, development of a trusting and collaborative relationship as a basis for treatment is needed first—something that is taken for granted in many models of treatment for depression. For work with these patients, an extended version of the DIT model for patients with more complex problems, DITCC [11], or MBT for personality disorder (as outlined in Chapter 4) seem to be more appropriate [12]. There is research evidence for the effectiveness of MBT in the treatment of depression, including self-harm and suicidality, in both adults [48,49] and adolescents [50,51] with personality disorders. MBT for psychosis (see Chapter 10) may be considered as an option for depressed patients with psychotic symptoms, although at the time of writing no studies have investigated the effectiveness of MBT in these patients. Similarly, the effectiveness of MBT in patients with bipolar disorder awaits investigation.

Mentalization-Based Treatment for Patients with Moderate to Severe Depression

The MBT approach to depression is based on the view, common to all types of MBT, that vulnerability to a loss of mentalizing in combination with epistemic mistrust characterizes severe forms of psychopathology, including depressive states of mind. In patients at the more severe end of the spectrum of depression there is therefore a focus on improving mentalizing in the context of an enduring attachment relationship with the clinician. For these patients, a focus on "insight," particularly concerning the potential relationship between events in the past and current functioning, is typically unhelpful and often even harmful. In MBT for depression the focus is therefore on improving the patient's reflective functioning with regard to their *current* mental states, while avoiding the emergence of non-mentalizing models of experiencing subjectivity, which readily emerge in patients with severe depression, as we outlined earlier in this chapter. Thus the MBT approach de-emphasizes "deep" interpretations in favor of a focus on near-conscious experiences in the here and now or the recent past, with an emphasis on emotional and relational experiencing (the affect focus) (e.g., "*Your wife called you just before the session; how did that make you feel?*"). This approach also includes the avoidance of extensive discussions of past events, in particular traumatic events, except when these discussions are helpful for understanding the patient's current mental states. Instead, MBT for depression aims at the recovery of mentalizing ("*I can see that she hurt you, but can we pause and talk about what just happened between the two of you?*").

The key task of the MBT clinician is therefore—using the not-knowing, inquisitive stance—to promote curiosity in the patient about their mental states, even in depressed states of mind. This leads the clinician and the patient to jointly realize that there is meaning and coherence where no meaning or coherence is felt or expected. This leads to the restoration of feelings of agency, autonomy, and self-coherence in the patient, and, because the patient feels mirrored in a marked way by the clinician ("*Here is someone who does not run away from the awful feelings and who seems to understand me*"), increasing epistemic trust and the (re-)emergence of mentalizing (leading to changes in communication systems 1 and 2). By "staying with the patient" even when the patient feels completely helpless or hopeless, the clinician communicates concern, agency, and the tolerability of affect, however difficult it may be. It is important to realize that this inquisitive yet not-knowing stance is exactly the opposite of the psychic equivalence that is typical of the depressed patient's state of mind, as psychic equivalence is characterized by either a lack of curiosity about mental states (hypomentalizing) or excessive certainty about the mental states of the self and others. Pseudomentalizing/pretend mode and other "fillers" that reflect non-mentalizing need to be explored in depressed patients, along with the lack of practical success that comes with using these modes ("*Well, I can now see that you seem to have the feeling that you are beyond help, but this feeling is not really helping you, me, and us today, as you yourself just said that this feeling is so discouraging that you can hardly think or feel any more*").

The typical starting point for MBT interventions with depressed patients, as in MBT more generally, therefore entails the following sequence.

1. Interventions typically start when the clinician identifies a break in mentalizing (i.e., psychic equivalence, pretend mode, or teleological mode of thought) as a result of the patient's depressed mood ("*This is useless, I cannot see where this is leading us*").
2. The patient and the clinician then "rewind" to the moment before the break in mentalizing, with the clinician opening up the possibility that they contributed to this lapse in mentalizing ("*What happened so that you feel like that—is it related to something that I said?*").
3. The clinician and the patient then explore the current emotion, with a focus on identifying the momentary affective state between patient and clinician (affect focus) ("*We were talking about your wife, and then I asked you how you felt when she called you, and then you became very sad and extremely self-critical—is that what happened?*").
4. The potential contribution of the clinician to the lapse in mentalizing is identified and acknowledged ("*Oh, I see, you were so hurt when she called you, and then you had to talk about these feelings*").
5. If possible and appropriate, the clinician and patient then try to understand the mental states implicit in the current state of the patient–clinician relationship (i.e., to mentalize the therapeutic relationship) ("*And then I asked you how it made you feel, which just increased your feelings of sadness and worthlessness—is that what happened? Oh, I understand now, and I must confess I started to feel sad and helpless as well!*").

When treating depressed patients, it is also crucially important for the clinician to adopt the following principles.

- Model humility, consistent with the not-knowing stance ("*Well, I am glad you told me, because I didn't realize how much she hurt you the other day. I thought she made you angry, so you see how important it is that you tell me what you are feeling, and how easily I can misunderstand you*").
- Continue to identify differences in perspectives, particularly as depressed states of mind may easily lead to self–other confusion and thus similar feelings in the patient and the clinician ("*Well, you may feel that life is meaningless, but I tend to differ, as I can see that you do enjoy certain aspects of life, like playing with your grandchildren*").

- Continue active questioning, asking for detailed descriptions of experience ("what" questions) rather than explanations ("why" questions) ("*So, what did you feel when she didn't turn up?*").
- Avoid the need to understand everything that the patient relates; this is particularly important when the patient is functioning in pretend mode. When this happens, the clinician should stop and rewind to a point when the patient's mentalizing was stronger ("*Sorry, but you lost me there, can we return to what you said earlier?*").

Thus, in work with depressed patients, it is imperative for the clinician to be aware that they are constantly at risk of losing their capacity to mentalize when faced with the patient's depressed states of mind. Loss of mentalizing in this context is typically experienced by the clinician as experiences of "running round in circles" or "being sucked into a black hole." This may lead to psychic equivalence functioning in the clinician ("*I am lost, this patient is beyond help, I no longer know what to do or say*") or teleological mode, in which the clinician may intervene in a concrete way (e.g., by having the patient hospitalized). Of course, such lapses of mentalizing are inevitable in the treatment of depressed patients, and require the clinician and the patient to jointly explore the (interpersonal) experiences that lead up to such events.

Finally, in the case of severely depressed patients, both pre-existing personality-related vulnerability and a history of depression may have left significant "scars" on their interpersonal environment. More often than not, severely depressed patients have become socially isolated or are entangled in long-lasting interpersonal conflicts. Hence, in MBT for depression, there is a strong emphasis on helping these patients to experiment with new ways of relating to the self and others, and fostering the capacity for salutogenesis (communication system 3). Particularly in patients with substantial personality problems, a broader systemic approach—for example, involving the patient's GP and, where appropriate, social services—is indicated to help the individual to bring about the necessary changes in their social environment.

Dynamic Interpersonal Therapy for Depression

DIT is an integrative treatment that incorporates mental representation and mentalizing approaches [8,52]. It thus combines treatment principles and interventions that are central to MBT with a mental-representation focus, in that an interpersonal affective focus (IPAF) is formulated jointly with the patient in the initial sessions and is then used as the focus of the treatment. The IPAF can be seen as an extension of the traditional case formulation in MBT (described in Chapter 4). The difference is that in DIT the focus is much more on the *content* of the case formulation in the treatment, whereas in MBT the focus is on the *mental processes* that generate the content. DIT thus also incorporates more traditional psychodynamic insight-oriented or expressive techniques to develop the IPAF in interaction with the patient, and to work through it during treatment. However, the mentalizing focus, together with more directive interventions that foster change in patients, allows tailoring of the treatment to the individual patient's needs and capacities. As in MBT, transference interpretations ("mentalizing the therapeutic relationship") are de-emphasized and are mainly used to clarify the IPAF in the here and now, particularly in patients with strong relational sensitivity, in order to prevent premature ending of the treatment by the patient. This view is based on studies that have shown a negative relationship between a high frequency of transference interpretations and both the therapeutic relationship and the outcome of treatment, even in patients with high levels of functioning [53,54]. Similarly, the main focus in DIT is on the patient's current (interpersonal) functioning as it relates to their depressive symptoms, and DIT therefore has less of a focus on past experiences compared with traditional psychodynamic approaches (although past experiences are, of course, explored in relation to the patient's current functioning).

The original DIT model is a 16-session time-limited intervention. Subsequently, DITCC, an extended 28-session model consisting of 20 weekly sessions followed by six fortnightly sessions and two monthly follow-ups, was developed, with a greater focus on addressing problems with epistemic trust and mentalizing in patients with more marked personality problems.

The original DIT model consists of three phases (initial, middle, and ending), each with its own specific aims and therapeutic strategies. The primary task of the initial phase (sessions 1–4) is to identify and jointly formulate with the patient the IPAF, a core recurring unconscious interpersonal pattern (or attachment style) related to the onset and/or maintenance of the patient's depressive symptoms. This pattern consists of four components, which show the roots of the DIT model in mental-representation approaches: (a) a particular representation of self (e.g., "*I am worthless*"); (b) a typical representation of others ("*Others always criticize me*") that characterizes the patient's typical interpersonal style and is linked to the onset of depressive symptoms; (c) particular affect(s) linked to these self-in-relation-to-other representations (e.g., depression, sadness, and anxiety); and (d) the defensive constellation of the IPAF (e.g., to defend against underlying feelings of aggression). In treatment, this repetitive pattern, its relationship to depressive symptoms, and its high (interpersonal) costs are explored. As the patient develops increased insight and greater mentalizing capacities, they are then encouraged to explore and experiment with new ways of relating to others, which leads them to relinquish their "old" pattern. This typically occurs in the middle phase of DIT, which involves maintaining a focus on the agreed IPAF and helping the patient to identify the interpersonal "costs" of the IPAF (mental-representation focus), while also fostering the patient's capacity to reflect on thoughts and feelings (the mentalizing focus). When the patient and clinician struggle to formulate an IPAF, or when the patient seems to have two opposite IPAFs (e.g., the patient is the victim of others, but at the same time also appears to be hypercritical of others), it is likely that the patient has a disorganized attachment style. In this case, DIT is not indicated, as neither the patient nor the clinician can be sure what exactly they are trying to address from a mental-representation perspective, particularly as the patient may lack the mentalizing capacity to reflect on the two opposing patterns and their interrelationship. Again this emphasizes the importance of the distinction between a mental-representation and a mental-process focus.

The final phase in DIT is devoted to empowering the patient to consolidate changes and, consistent with the focus on change in communication system 3, to foster their capacity for salutogenesis. This is initiated by the clinician writing the patient a "goodbye letter," which sets out the initial agreed formulation, the progress that has been made during treatment, and the work that remains to be done in the ending phase and after the treatment has finished. Again, extreme responses from the patient toward the end of treatment may be indicative of more severe underlying problems, as the approaching end of treatment may generate strong anxieties about abandonment or feelings of aggression in them. Therefore the ending phase plays an important role in gauging therapeutic progress. For this reason, this phase is extended in DITCC to enable the patient to experiment with new ways of relating to the self and others, while at the same time having a "safe haven" in which to work through potential problems with the ending of the treatment.

Concluding Remarks

The mentalizing approach to the conceptualization and treatment of depression starts from the assumption that symptoms of depression arise from reactions to threats to attachment relationships—and thus threats to the self—and associated impairments in mentalizing that may be present before the onset of depressive symptoms and/or are exacerbated by depressed mood. Based on these assumptions, depressed patients can be viewed as being on a spectrum of severity based on differences in the nature of their depressive experiences, their typical mentalizing impairments, their dominant attachment styles, and the nature of their impairments in epistemic trust. This chapter has summarized the basic principles of a range of mentalization-based approaches to the treatment of depression and how those principles can be tailored to the individual patient, depending on their position on the spectrum of severity as defined by their mentalizing capacities.

References

1. Cuijpers P, Stringaris A, Wolpert M. Treatment outcomes for depression: challenges and opportunities. *Lancet Psychiatry* 2020; **7**: 925–27.
2. Cuijpers P, Karyotaki E, de Wit L, Ebert DD. The effects of fifteen evidence-supported therapies for adult depression: a meta-analytic review. *Psychother Res* 2020; **30**: 279–93.
3. Rost F, Luyten P, Fearon P, Fonagy P. Personality and outcome in individuals with treatment-resistant depression: exploring differential treatment effects in the Tavistock Adult Depression Study (TADS). *J Consult Clin Psychol* 2019; **87**: 433–45.
4. Luyten P, Fonagy P. Psychodynamic treatment for borderline personality disorder and mood disorders: a mentalizing perspective. In: Choi-Kain L, Gunderson J, eds. *Borderline Personality Disorder and Mood Disorders: Controversies and Consensus*. New York, NY: Springer, 2014; 223–51.
5. Cuijpers P, van Straten A, Bohlmeijer E et al. The effects of psychotherapy for adult depression are overestimated: a meta-analysis of study quality and effect size. *Psychol Med* 2010; **40**: 211–23.
6. Fonagy P, Edgcumbe R, Moran GS et al. The roles of mental representations and mental processes in therapeutic action. *Psychoanal Study Child* 1993; **48**: 9–48.
7. Luyten P, Blatt SJ, Fonagy P. Impairments in self structures in depression and suicide in psychodynamic and cognitive behavioral approaches: implications for clinical practice and research. *Int J Cogn Ther* 2013; **6**: 265–79.
8. Lemma A, Target M, Fonagy P. *Brief Dynamic Interpersonal Therapy: A Clinician's Guide*. Oxford, UK: Oxford University Press, 2011.
9. Fonagy P, Lemma A, Target M et al. Dynamic interpersonal therapy for moderate to severe depression: a pilot randomized controlled and feasibility trial. *Psychol Med* 2020; **50**: 1010–19.
10. Gunderson JG, Morey LC, Stout RL et al. Major depressive disorder and borderline personality disorder revisited: longitudinal interactions. *J Clin Psychiatry* 2004; **65**: 1049–56.

11. Rao AS, Lemma A, Fonagy P et al. Development of dynamic interpersonal therapy in complex care (DITCC): a pilot study. *Psychoanal Psychother* 2019; **33**: 77–98.

12. Luyten P, Campbell C, Allison E, Fonagy P. The mentalizing approach to psychopathology: state of the art and future directions. *Annu Rev Clin Psychol* 2020; **16**: 297–325.

13. Luyten P, Fonagy P. An integrative developmental psychopathology approach to depression. In: Jiménez JP, Botto A, Fonagy P, eds. *Etiopathogenic Theories and Models in Depression.* Cham, Switzerland: Springer, 2022; 245–63.

14. Luyten P, Fonagy P. Psychodynamic psychotherapy for patients with functional somatic disorders and the road to recovery. *Am J Psychother* 2020; **73**: 125–30.

15. Drevets WC, Price JL, Furey ML. Brain structural and functional abnormalities in mood disorders: implications for neurocircuitry models of depression. *Brain Struct Funct* 2008; **213**: 93–118.

16. Savitz J, Drevets WC. Bipolar and major depressive disorder: neuroimaging the developmental-degenerative divide. *Neurosci Biobehav Rev* 2009; **33**: 699–771.

17. Johnson MK, Nolen-Hoeksema S, Mitchell KJ, Levin Y. Medial cortex activity, self-reflection and depression. *Soc Cogn Affect Neurosci* 2009; **4**: 313–27.

18. Moore MT, Fresco DM. Depressive realism: a meta-analytic review. *Clin Psychol Rev* 2012; **32**: 496–509.

19. Luyten P, Fonagy P, Lemma A, Target M. Depression. In: Bateman A, Fonagy P, eds. *Handbook of Mentalizing in Mental Health Practice.* Washington, DC: American Psychiatric Publishing, Inc., 2012; 385–417.

20. Panksepp J, Watt D. Why does depression hurt? Ancestral primary-process separation-distress (PANIC/GRIEF) and diminished brain reward (SEEKING) processes in the genesis of depressive affect. *Psychiatry* 2011; **74**: 5–13.

21. Gilbert P. Evolution and depression: issues and implications. *Psychol Med* 2006; **36**: 287–97.

22. Davey CG, Yucel M, Allen NB. The emergence of depression in adolescence: development of the prefrontal cortex and the representation of reward. *Neurosci Biobehav Rev* 2008; **32**: 1–19.

23. Bowlby J. *Attachment and Loss: Separation.* New York, NY: Basic Books, 1973.

24. Spitz RA. Hospitalism: an inquiry into the genesis of psychiatric conditions in early childhood. *Psychoanal Study Child* 1945; **1**: 53–74.

25. Brown GW, Harris TO, Craig TKJ. Exploration of the influence of insecure attachment and parental maltreatment on the incidence and course of adult clinical depression. *Psychol Med* 2019; **49**: 1025–32.

26. Dagan O, Facompre CR, Bernard K. Adult attachment representations and depressive symptoms: a meta-analysis. *J Affect Disord* 2018; **236**: 274–90.

27. Spruit A, Goos L, Weenink N et al. The relation between attachment and depression in children and adolescents: a multilevel meta-analysis. *Clin Child Fam Psychol Rev* 2020; **23**: 54–69.

28. Khan F, Fraley RC, Young JF, Hankin BL. Developmental trajectories of attachment and depressive symptoms in children and adolescents. *Attach Hum Dev* 2020; **22**: 392–408.

29. Lecompte V, Moss E, Cyr C, Pascuzzo K. Preschool attachment, self-esteem and the development of preadolescent anxiety and depressive symptoms. *Attach Hum Dev* 2014; **16**: 242–60.

30. MacGregor EK, Grunebaum MF, Galfalvy HC et al. Depressed parents' attachment: effects on offspring suicidal behavior in a longitudinal family study. *J Clin Psychiatry* 2014; **75**: 879–85.

31. Luyten P, Fonagy P. The stress–reward–mentalizing model of depression: an integrative developmental cascade approach to child and adolescent depressive disorder based on the Research

Domain Criteria (RDoC) approach. *Clin Psychol Rev* 2018; **64**: 87–98.

32. Fischer-Kern M, Tmej A. Mentalization and depression: theoretical concepts, treatment approaches and empirical studies – an overview. *Z Psychosom Med Psychother* 2019; **65**: 162–77.
33. Bifulco A, Kwon J, Jacobs C et al. Adult attachment style as mediator between childhood neglect/abuse and adult depression and anxiety. *Soc Psychiatry Psychiatr Epidemiol* 2006; **41**: 796–805.
34. Styron T, Janoff-Bulman R. Childhood attachment and abuse: long-term effects on adult attachment, depression, and conflict resolution. *Child Abuse Negl* 1997; **21**: 1015–23.
35. Widom CS, Czaja SJ, Kozakowski SS, Chauhan P. Does adult attachment style mediate the relationship between childhood maltreatment and mental and physical health outcomes? *Child Abuse Negl* 2018; **76**: 533–45.
36. Blatt SJ. *Experiences of Depression: Theoretical, Clinical, and Research Perspectives.* Washington, DC: American Psychological Association, 2004.
37. Beck AT. Cognitive therapy of depression: new perspectives. In: Clayton PJ, Barrett JE, eds. *Treatment of Depression: Old Controversies and New Approaches.* New York, NY: Raven Press, 1983; 265–90.
38. Blatt SJ, Luyten P. A structural-developmental psychodynamic approach to psychopathology: two polarities of experience across the life span. *Dev Psychopathol* 2009; **21**: 793–814.
39. Luyten P, Blatt SJ. Interpersonal relatedness and self-definition in normal and disrupted personality development: retrospect and prospect. *Am Psychol* 2013; **68**: 172–83.
40. Luyten P, Blatt SJ, Van Houdenhove B, Corveleyn J. Depression research and treatment: are we skating to where the puck is going to be? *Clin Psychol Rev* 2006; **26**: 985–99.
41. Fonagy P, Luyten P. A developmental, mentalization-based approach to the understanding and treatment of borderline personality disorder. *Dev Psychopathol* 2009; **21**: 1355–81.
42. Jurist EL. Mentalized affectivity. *Psychoanal Psychol* 2005; **22**: 426–44.
43. Lane RD, Quinlan DM, Schwartz GE, Walker PA. The Levels of Emotional Awareness Scale: a cognitive-developmental measure of emotion. *J Pers Assess* 1990; **55**: 124–34.
44. Taylor GJ, Bagby RM. Psychoanalysis and empirical research: the example of alexithymia. *J Am Psychoanal Assoc* 2013; **61**: 99–133.
45. Lumley MA, Schubiner H, Lockhart NA et al. Emotional awareness and expression therapy, cognitive behavioral therapy, and education for fibromyalgia: a cluster-randomized controlled trial. *Pain* 2017; **158**: 2354–63.
46. Luyten P, De Meulemeester C, Fonagy P. Psychodynamic therapy in patients with somatic symptom disorder. In: Kealy D, Ogrodniczuk JS, eds. *Contemporary Psychodynamic Psychotherapy: Evolving Clinical Practice.* Philadelphia, PA: Academic Press, 2019; 191–206.
47. Bateman A, Campbell C, Luyten P, Fonagy P. A mentalization-based approach to common factors in the treatment of borderline personality disorder. *Curr Opin Psychol* 2018; **21**: 44–9.
48. Bateman A, Fonagy P. 8-year follow-up of patients treated for borderline personality disorder: mentalization-based treatment versus treatment as usual. *Am J Psychiatry* 2008; **165**: 631–8.
49. Smits ML, Feenstra DJ, Bales DL et al. Day hospital versus intensive outpatient mentalization-based treatment: 3-year follow-up of patients treated for borderline personality disorder in a multicentre randomized clinical trial. *Psychol Med* 2022; **52**: 485–95.
50. Rossouw TI, Fonagy P. Mentalization-based treatment for self-harm in adolescents: a randomized controlled trial. *J Am Acad Child Adolesc Psychiatry* 2012; **51**: 1304–13.

51. Feenstra DJ, Hutsebaut J, Laurenssen EM et al. The burden of disease among adolescents with personality pathology: quality of life and costs. *J Personal Disord* 2012; **26**: 593–604.

52. Lemma A, Target M, Fonagy P. The development of a brief psychodynamic protocol for depression: Dynamic Interpersonal Therapy (DIT). *Psychoanal Psychother* 2010; **24**: 329–46.

53. Høglend P. Analysis of transference in psychodynamic psychotherapy: a review of empirical research. *Can J Psychoanal* 2004; **12**: 279–300.

54. Høglend P, Bøgwald K-P, Amlo S et al. Transference interpretations in dynamic psychotherapy: do they really yield sustained effects? *Am J Psychiatry* 2008; **165**: 763–71.

Part III

Application and Adaptations for Mental Health Presentations

Chapter 10

Psychosis

Introduction

During the past 15 years, clinicians have attempted to employ the clinical framework of mentalization-based treatment (MBT) to inform the psychotherapeutic treatment of patients with schizophrenia-spectrum disorders and other psychosis disorders* [1–5]. Clinicians in a number of different countries have tailored their methods to include elements of MBT, and have proposed different ways to provide their patients with MBT-informed therapy for psychosis [5–7]. These pioneering strides have been extremely useful in:

1. providing preliminary evidence of the feasibility and acceptability of MBT-informed therapy in patients with psychosis
2. identifying the needs of this patient population, specifically with regard to their clinical profiles and severity of illness
3. promoting the creativity of MBT-trained clinicians in their attempts to alleviate the suffering and alienation that individuals with psychosis experience.

Along with conceptual developments [8,9], these clinical developments have contributed to identifying the core components of the MBT approach to psychosis. To date, however, a comprehensive framework outlining the core components of the MBT approach to psychosis has been only partially proposed [10,11]. In this chapter we shall attempt to collate the available empirical and clinical knowledge gained from early adaptations of MBT for psychosis, and articulate them with recent developments in the core MBT model (see Chapter 4). The overarching aim of this chapter is to present and illustrate the core principles of application of the MBT model to psychotic disorders.

The MBT Clinical Approach to Psychosis

Not unlike other adaptations of MBT to various clinical presentations of psychopathology, the MBT approach to psychotic disorders considers the age and history of the individual in relation to the onset of their psychological problems, and requires an assessment of the severity of the disorder in terms of both a staging approach [12] and the severity of its functional impact [10]. Both of these domains will influence the structure and aims of treatment, which are discussed in more detail in the next section.

In keeping with MBT's developmental approach, and in line with contemporary clinical research on the schizophrenia spectrum [13], psychotic disorders are understood

* This chapter will use the terms "psychosis" and "psychotic disorders" interchangeably to refer to the DSM-V category Schizophrenia Spectrum and Other Psychotic Disorders [1].

as (neuro)developmental disorders. Importantly, the etiology of psychotic disorders most probably builds on a strong and significant genetic basis [14]. This does not mean that early environmental adversity does not come into play—on the contrary, many developmental studies are uncovering what Paul E. Meehl referred to as interactions between psychosocial stress and polygenetic potentiators [15,16]. There are at least five neurobiological routes by which early adversity, developmental trauma, and attachment insecurity may each contribute to increase the risk for onset of a psychotic disorder (for a review, see Debbané et al. [9]). Therefore a careful history of the patient's relationship patterns, stressful life events, and developmental trauma, as is required in the initial/formulation phase of MBT, assists in framing the context in which psychosis has emerged (see later in this chapter) and how it has affected different functional areas in the individual's life.

From a clinical standpoint, such a developmental model informing MBT requires three main clinical actions:

1. assessing the developmental stage of the patient's illness
2. identifying the patient's social resources as factors that will contribute to the intervention
3. formulating treatment objectives and obstacles in order to begin treatment with co-constructed representations of the clinical problem, integrating the viewpoints of the patient and of the clinical team and care network.

We start with a formulation that models how mentalizing can be used as a tool for communicating about needs and emotions, and work through a collaboration that aims to secure safe and meaningful relationships, as well as ties to social and professional environments. In the following sections we shall examine each of these three clinical reference points separately, using the clinical example of Robert.

Clinical Example: Robert

Robert is a 39-year-old man who is seeking treatment to enable him to *"be able to talk to potential clients who show interest in my artwork."* Robert was first diagnosed with schizophrenia at the age of 23. He suffered relapses/hospitalizations twice in his twenties and once in his thirties, all in the context of failed attempts to initiate romantic relationships, which each time led to delusional syndromes, visual and auditory hallucinations, and eventually hospitalization. The first hospitalization lasted almost a year, the second and third hospitalizations were shorter in duration (3 months), and the most recent one, when he was 33 years old, lasted approximately 1 month. Robert recalls his childhood as having been entrenched in the fear of being separated from his family, especially his mother, a housewife whom Robert describes as *"a very critical and solitary woman."* He describes his relationship with his father, a military engineer, as distant. He recalls himself as a slightly overweight boy who always felt there was something wrong with him inside. His body always felt like a strange, vulnerable, and unpredictable place, and as a young adult he suffered from severe anxiety about contracting life-ending diseases through any kind of contact with women. Robert's first psychotic breakdown happened approximately 18 months after he moved to a university campus to start a Master's degree in sociology. By that time, his social use of cannabis had increased to daily solitary use in his new university surroundings. During the first year he felt very lonely, and eventually opened up about his romantic feelings to a long-time female friend, only to be rejected. During the following months, his natural suspiciousness toward people gave way to paranoid ideation about the intentions of classmates and teaching staff. He became delusional to the point of retreating to his hall of residence, and taking day-long baths because *"I only felt safe when immersed in water."* He was hospitalized after he attempted to fill his entire bedroom with water. At that point he experienced hostile voices and command hallucinations, which were commenting on his behavior and ordering him to perform bizarre actions. At present Robert spends most of his time at a local pub, where he can meet with familiar faces, all of whom are unemployed people. He receives a small benefit payment because of his incapacity to work due to psychiatric illness. He has been training in a variety of painting techniques, and this has attracted the attention of his pub mates. A friend of a friend offered him a couple of square meters of space for him to display his paintings at a weekly, highly popular open-air market. Although his paintings attract much interest, he is incapable of talking to the potential clients.

Assessing the Developmental Stage of the Illness

In the following section, we shall consider the different stages of the progression of Robert's illness, keeping in mind that MBT for psychosis may be helpful at any stage of illness. First, we shall distinguish four distinct periods along the developmental and clinical continuum of Robert's psychotic illness [17]:

1. premorbid stage
2. clinical high-risk stage
3. first episode of psychosis
4. psychosis trajectory stage.

The premorbid stage encompasses the period from conception to adolescence, during which distal risk factors such as genetic and perinatal risk, childhood and adolescent environmental risk factors (e.g., bullying, cannabis use), and personality factors (e.g., schizotypy; see Lenzenweger [18]) interact. In Robert's case, the premorbid signs include a family history of schizophrenia (affecting his grandfather and uncle on the paternal side) and perhaps subtle schizotypal signs such as uneasiness with his own body, feeling that something is not right with himself, and some shyness and social withdrawal during adolescence. Of course these signs would require a proper evaluation, as they could also be the result of internalizing problems. Interestingly, recent research has found that the most common premorbid psychopathological manifestations that precede psychosis onset include mood disorders, drug misuse, and anxiety disorders [19].

Next, during the clinical high-risk stage, subsyndromal symptoms such as perceptual, cognitive, or behavioral abnormalities often occur, but their frequency and functional impact are below the diagnostic threshold for psychosis spectrum disorders (for further information, see Schultze-Lutter et al. [20]). This stage may be an important opportunity for prevention, because some individuals might ask for professional help, although they do not always explicitly report pre-psychotic symptoms [12]. For Robert, the signs included subtle thought blockages, ideas of reference (having the impression that people, particularly strangers, paid extra attention to him), and psychotic-like experiences such as hearing music playing when he was alone in the family home or in the university hall of residence (for clinical interviews evaluating clinical high risk, see Schultze-Lutter et al. [21]). Robert did not seek help for these phenomena—although they started approximately 1 year before he increased his cannabis use, he would write them off, thinking that they were best explained by his new cannabis habits.

Robert's first psychotic episode probably lasted for 1–2 months before it was detected by his best friend. At that point he was spending entire weeks cloistered in his room, and held the secret belief that a specific breed of aliens would come to make the world a better place; he was responsible for greeting them and showing them around so that they could accomplish their mission. This gave him both a sense of a meaningful existence, and an immense fear that he might not be able to deal with such a great responsibility. He recalls bizarre phenomena, such as feeling that rain came from the ground, not the sky, or that entire football matches that he watched on television would proceed without the ball ever going out of bounds. This last impression alerted his best friend, who questioned him and only then realized the extent of the delusional state that Robert was experiencing. The friend alerted Robert's family and the university's mental health network, which promptly intervened after the episode in which Robert flooded his room. He was hospitalized shortly thereafter.

Further along the developmental continuum, trajectories following the first diagnosis of psychosis can, schematically speaking, follow three different routes. Almost one-third of patients receive a first diagnosis, and treatment leads to remission without relapse [22]. Another one-third to half of patients who receive a first diagnosis go on to develop a lifelong pattern of treatment, recovery, and relapse [22]. The prognosis appears to partly depend on premorbid factors, such as cognitive and interpersonal functioning and negative symptoms, as well as the duration of untreated psychosis [23]. Finally, the remainder (up to one-third) of patients develop a chronic state of psychosis, which is often resistant to treatment and accompanied by severe functional deficits; these can also be accompanied by cognitive deficits, as well as significant impairments in autonomous daily functioning.

Depending on the stage at which Robert would hypothetically have encountered a service that delivered an MBT-informed approach to psychosis, the treatment interventions would initially need to be tailored to the clinical needs of that stage (for a full description, see Armando et al. [12]) and modified for any subsequent stage. The principle is that in the first two stages, MBT-informed psychosocial and psychoeducational treatment is provided to reinforce the protective factors, using a group approach (either within the family or with young adults), as well as providing some psychoeducation on the nature of subclinical signs of psychosis (e.g., delusional thinking, perceptual abnormalities). Importantly, at this stage, the patient's stress factors, triggers of anxiety, depressive ruminations, and social withdrawal must be made explicit and shared with the care network. If individual psychotherapy is accessible and feasible, this can also be useful [3]. If existing risk then transitions to full-blown psychosis, the patient will require referral to services that can provide specialized care for psychosis. As with the treatment of patients with eating disorders (see Chapter 12) or antisocial personality disorder (see Chapter 7), MBT is not an all-encompassing approach that can address the full set of patients' clinical needs. Usually, multidisciplinary teams trained in specialized care *and* mentalization-based approaches will adapt their multidimensional treatment plan to foster mentalizing with the patient, the family, and the nursing/educational teams in order to maximize the potential success of the intervention. Similar to AMBIT (Adaptive Mentalization-Based Integrative Treatment) (see Chapter 17 and [24]), an adaptive clinical approach can stimulate mentalizing as an active ingredient that ideally permeates the multilevel interventions that are necessary during the third and fourth stages of psychosis progression. In terms of clinical staging and tools, group psychoeducation, family sessions, and psychotherapy sessions will involve MBT techniques, for which the key adaptations of the clinical principles of MBT are described later in this chapter.

Identifying the Social Resources within the Treatment

Although patients with psychosis typically have fewer significant interpersonal relationships and relatively reduced social activities compared with individuals with other mental health diagnoses, clinicians can often underestimate the importance of attachment relationships in the patient's life, especially if the patient suffers from strong negative symptoms of withdrawal. Yet interpersonal relationships are central to the quality of life of patients living with psychosis [25,26]. Therefore a careful analysis of the key interpersonal and attachment figures available to the patient will significantly contribute to the success of the treatment. These figures typically include family members, other service users, keyworkers in the community, or other significant individuals in the patient's life. Supporting and empowering the key interpersonal and attachment figures may constitute the single most important factor for increasing the quality of life of patients with psychosis.

Clinical Example: Robert (continued)

Robert's testimony is compelling with regard to the centrality of interpersonal relationships in his trajectory with psychosis. When questioned on what helped to get him out of the difficult periods, he promptly indicated two people:

Robert: The first time I got out of hospital, I was almost mute. My dad, who by then had retired, insisted that we take a 1-hour walk almost every other day. We took these regular walks for at least a couple of years. I did not speak a word for the first few months; I was convinced he hated me. I was in really bad shape; he was always waiting for me to catch up. I noticed that he seemed to insist that I show up for these walks, and somehow I discovered he could be patient with me. I started perceiving that he was actually enjoying spending time with me. That made me feel normal.

After all my hospitalizations, I had lost all my friends except one. He's the one who initially alerted everyone back at the university, and he stuck with me through all the mess that followed. I don't know why really. But I am grateful. I feel he's always treated me like Robert, not like some lunatic who'd lost it, like all the doctors would treat me. He was just with me, and I remained a friend to him. In a world where everyone seems to want to put you in the loony bin, to avoid you or not trust you, it was extremely precious to have him maintain a friendship with me. We still have coffee together, and sometimes I feel I can help him to sort things out.

Often, significant individuals in the patient's life will experience bouts of compassion fatigue; they may also be discouraged when the psychosis leads to fluctuations in symptoms or a need for (re-)hospitalization. Significant individuals may give up trying to help in the face of strong avoidance, lack of reciprocity, and low energy on the part of the patient. The care team's support in keeping mentalizing active in the interpersonal network of the patient is critical to the journey with psychosis. When these relationships are explicitly integrated into the case formulation and treatment plan, they are usually more readily included in network meetings during difficult periods. A key point is to address the needs of the caregiving environment in order to sustain positive trajectories during psychosis [27].

Furthermore, friendships with other service users are likely to develop and significantly contribute to the patient's quality of life and well-being. Often, attending psychosocial and therapeutic activities in the service may be the only regular and reliable social activity for patients. In this framework, monitoring of friendships and levels of interpersonal trust will act as a barometer of well-being for many service users. Associations between regular contact with friends and decreased negative symptoms have been reported [28]. Guided peer groups have been shown to increase quality of life [29]. Work on building a mentalizing culture contributes to both trust and feelings of belonging, which protect against not only the exacerbation of psychotic symptoms but also internalizing symptoms that may lead to depression and suicidal ideation [30].

Formulating Concrete Treatment Goals in Keeping with Mentalizing Abilities

Formulation is a key aspect of any clinical intervention in MBT. When these interventions are used with patients whose capacity for mentalizing is either underdeveloped or severely compromised, clinicians will find it useful to think of the formulation as a two-sided coin. On one side of the coin is the full and complex formulation of the clinician; on the other side is the formulation tool—that is, the actual explicit formulation used in MBT, which is usually in writing (or sometimes other forms, such as drawing) and agreed upon by both the patient and the clinician. The full and complex formulation represents an exercise in making the case formulation in the therapist's mind, on the basis of what is shared by the patient during the assessment sessions. The formulation usually includes a number of sections, and benefits from being made explicit (for details, see Chapter 4). However, it is often the case that these complex descriptions of assessments can be read by the patient as if they are written in a foreign language, and this experience can be alienating for the patient. When working with individuals who are seeking treatment related to psychosis, clinicians must be aware that cognitive complexity can actually cause breakdowns in mentalizing. Therefore careful attention should be given to the process of formulating, jointly with the patient, treatment goals that include the essential elements of an MBT formulation. Let us consider a small part of a formulation that was jointly created with Robert.

Clinical Example: Formulation Sheet (Reusable Tool) Used with Robert during the Formulation Process

My Treatment Objectives: What I Want from Treatment

- I would like to **(doing):** *Be able to talk to clients who are interested in my artwork.*
- I would like to **(feeling):** *Control my anxiety better when I'm with people.*
- I would like to **(thinking):** *Stop aggressive thoughts taking over in my head.*

Obstacles to My Objectives: What Might Get in the Way

- I can **(doing):** *Start smoking cannabis heavily and then retreat.*
- I can **(feeling):** *Get anxious, and then keep away from people.*
- I can **(thinking):** *Feel like people don't want to talk to me, so I stay silent.*

When engaging in the formulation process with Robert, the first key point is to start off from his main interpersonal motive—talking to clients about his artwork. Specifically, the clinician initiates a conversation with Robert about treatment goals and obstacles to treatment. Using a sheet of paper divided into two sections ("My Treatment Objectives" and "Obstacles to My Objectives"), each with three subsections ("Doing," "Feeling," and "Thinking"), the clinician asks Robert to summarize or write down what they talk about, using the headings.

The shape that the formulation takes, in Robert's mind, is a rather teleological structure. What he writes on the sheet involves an action taken as proof of an underlying mental state. Therefore the clinician encourages him to make explicit his feelings and thoughts, which at the time of evaluation appear noteworthy as treatment goals or obstacles. During the assessment, Robert indicates that he can recognize some kind of anxiety when he is with people generally, especially strangers, but does not really connect this with his experience at the market where he displays his work. When asked what kind of thoughts he would like help with, he switches to aggressive thoughts taking over in his head. In Robert's mind, and in his experience, these are not linked to the episode at the market, but they are what he would like some help with. Therefore this is written down, and any potential links with the interpersonal and affective domains are noted as treatment progresses.

The clinician then encourages Robert to write down some possible obstacles to treatment, while carefully maintaining a collaborative process and avoiding overstimulating him. Indeed, as will be discussed later in this chapter, patients with psychosis often promptly interpret criticism or hostile intentions when others formulate thoughts that may involve some kind of expectation. Therefore, during the formulation process, a key point is to engage with the obstacles that the patient can recognize and about which they feel that they have at least a minimal level of agency. As can be noted from Robert's formulation, asking him about the obstacles to treatment impairs his mentalizing. His descriptions of feelings and thoughts are generic ("*I get anxious*") and are primarily described in teleological form, linked to behaviors. This indicates the starting point from which to work with Robert. His teleological functioning needs to be addressed before it is possible to move on to the next step for him, which is to experience some agency over his anxiety and notice whether he is able to attenuate his impulse to withdraw socially and limit the length of time for which he has to withdraw from others.

In a similar way to other types of MBT, the initial phase will also include a crisis plan (for details, see Chapter 4). In MBT for psychosis, the specialized team will usually have established protocols for dealing with episodes of psychotic decompensation. It is useful to go over past hospitalizations to identify the types of triggers which may lead to the re-emergence of clinical needs that can only be addressed by hospitalization. The clinician will attempt to establish a crisis plan with the patient focused on identifying triggers and planning stages of intervention that would precede actual hospitalization. It is also worthwhile considering the advantages and disadvantages of hospitalization, in order to sketch out the mental landscape of how the patient thinks about past episodes and when they could envisage that this option is reasonable.

To summarize, an approach to clinical intervention in patients with psychosis will explicitly outline three clinical reference points at the initiation of treatment:

1. the stage of development of psychosis
2. the social and interpersonal resources available to the patient, including their important attachment relationships
3. a shared collaborative formulation of treatment aims and obstacles.

The staging approach orients the treatment team to treatment targets adapted to the progression of illness, and indeed this may be important in order to avoid the use of multiple interventions that address specific symptoms but fail to integrate the overall clinical needs of the patient and their family. To date there is no research evidence of benefit from psychoeducation for families with a member affected by psychosis, but such an intervention is likely to contribute to a positive prognosis (for a description of mentalization-informed family work, see Chapter 15). In the treatment strategy, specific attention is then given to identifying and harnessing the interpersonal and social resources available to the patient, as this will help to reduce their social alienation and focus the necessary clinical resources to allow developmentally adapted social integration. Finally, building MBT for a patient with psychosis involves engaging in a formulation process that can be adapted to the patient's level of mentalizing, while fostering a collaborative and agentive process that is oriented toward meaningful treatment goals and an awareness of obstacles that are likely to arise. Of course, further mentalizing strengths and weaknesses are outlined within the formulation and treatment plan. The next section will cover some of our basic assumptions about psychosis as understood from an MBT-informed perspective.

Understanding Psychosis from an MBT-Informed Perspective

Changes in mentalizing are likely to account for part of the therapeutic effect of any treatment for patients whose condition lies on the continuum of clinical manifestations of psychosis. Indeed, the three points enumerated in the previous section—staging the development of psychosis, assessing the patient's attachment relationships, and co-creating a mentalizing formulation—involve the mentalizing of others and self and an ability to regulate the processes involved in social interactions, namely attention, emotion, and thinking about intentions, behaviors, and group dynamics. Relationships to self and others will therefore potentially stimulate mentalizing, but may also overwhelm the patient's capacity to mentalize. This leads us to the main point of the MBT approach to psychosis. Critically, if we are to inform our interventions using an MBT framework, we need to conceptualize the nature of the relationship between mentalizing and core self-disturbances experienced by individuals with psychosis as the central issue.

This section will begin with a review of conceptual developments that link psychosis to mentalizing, followed by a summary of contemporary neuroscientific and clinical conceptions of psychosis as a condition stemming from disturbances in core self-experience—the way the patient integrates (or fails to integrate) such experiences in their life ties into clinical presentations of psychosis. The section ends with a discussion of the links between core self-disturbances and non-mentalizing modes and the cycles of ineffective mentalizing that are encountered in the clinical treatment of individuals with psychosis, as they are of considerable importance for treatment.

Psychosis and Mentalizing: Historical Links

The relevance of mentalizing in the field of psychotherapy for schizophrenia dates back to both Eugene Bleuler and Sigmund Freud [31–34]. Bleuler coined the term "schizophrenias" to signify clinical states characterized by a splitting of the mind [31]. He did not subscribe to the biologically grounded view proposing a direct link between biology and schizophrenic functional deficits. Although early psychoanalysts did not specifically use the term "mentalizing," they observed the troubling disconnect between affect and mind in their patients with psychosis, who experienced the activities of feeling and thinking with a reduced sense of agency, and appeared to suffer severe mental pain when experiencing such a disconnect within themselves.

These characterizations from the field of psychoanalysis resonate with phenomenological accounts of psychosis [35], and with recent developments in metacognitive reflection and insight therapy. Contemporary phenomenological accounts suggest that an instability in experiencing minimal selfhood acts as the basis for schizophrenia. This instability can manifest as diminished self-integration (e.g., going through one's day with the feeling that "*I am not totally me*," and that somehow "*a part of I is missing from my experience*"). It can also manifest as hyper-reflectivity, evident as states of hyperawareness of stimuli that are usually trivial or tacit. This instability signals what phenomenologists call a *core self-disturbance*—that is, a fundamental disturbance in experiencing oneself as the subject of one's experience, which results in one experiencing reduced agency in relation to one's life. Interestingly, the psychoanalysts John Auerbach and Sidney Blatt hypothesized that "Schizophrenic hyper-reflexivity may follow from failure to establish or find a bodily sense of self" ([36], p. 306). The potential disintegration of links between bodily signals and mental processing is a common leitmotif across most theories of psychosis. From a psychotherapeutic perspective, Paul Lysaker and colleagues have developed a model of psychotherapy that is focused on metacognitive reflection, where metacognition constitutes a key psychological process sustaining the binding or integration of thoughts and feelings [37]. Their view is similar to the approach in MBT, where the disturbing and threatening nature of self-experiences in psychosis is emphasized, and the psychotic symptoms are seen to provide ultimate protection against loss of agency, affect, meaning, and self-coherence. In this framework, working on mentalizing, metacognition, and other higher-order processes may help to alleviate some of the pain engendered by experiences with oneself and others. However, mentalizing dysfunction is not the cause of psychosis. Following contemporary neuroscientific models, which are reviewed in the next section, and in line with psychoanalytic descriptions of schizophrenia, psychotic experiences are conceptualized as "disturbances in core self," and psychotic symptoms are viewed as attempts to regulate and give shape to such disturbances.

From Neuroscience to the Consulting Room

The mentalizing account of core self-disturbances is consistent with a contemporary neuroscience perspective which hypothesizes that psychotic experiences entail a disconnect between feeling and thinking (sensory and cognitive priors), and critically, that this disconnect temporarily disables the individual from integrating their senses and thoughts into a coherent self-experience [38]. Readers who have never experienced psychosis can try to imagine a rising sense of panic stimulated by intense arousal; this panic can lead to experiencing oneself as "out of control" and subject to potential annihilation—an existential panic. This example could be conceived of as a momentary psychotic experience where bodily arousal (the sensory system) cannot connect with and be regulated by one's mind (the cognitive system), which momentarily threatens one's self-integrity. Similarly, but at the cognitive edge of the experience, persecutory thoughts can lead to intense reflective activity (hyper-reflectivity), leading one to experience a momentary loss of bodily sensations and to experience oneself as split from one's body. Recognizing this sensory–cognitive disconnect helps clinicians to imagine and empathize with the kind of process that underlies the patient's psychotic experience, while preventing them from applying meaning to the psychotic symptoms, which in the experiential moment may be harmful as it adds to the split cognitive experience and intensifies the disconnect. Imagining this whole process may help the clinician to maintain their own mentalizing, which is necessary for them to be able to "ground" the patient and pull them away from their symptoms.

Let us take an example from an individual session, during which a patient signals the experience of a sensory–cognitive disconnect. This segment takes place during an exchange in which the clinician was exploring, somewhat cognitively, the patient's lack of motivation to look for a job.

Clinical Example: Signaling a Sensory–Cognitive Disconnect

Patient: Don't know really, I just can't get myself to look for a job, even thinking about it is …

Clinician: … Is …? What is it like not thinking about it?

Patient: I'm feeling myself coming out of my body …

Clinician: Oh! I'm sorry, indeed, I am noticing that you are struggling …

Patient: I can't think … just … no, don't say anything …

Clinician: OK … (*The clinician is actively regulating self to maintain a psychological presence to the patient.*)

Patient: I can feel myself drifting away from my body … Aargh … I can't take it any more … (*The patient screws up his face and stares blankly, indicating the rising dreadful experience.*)

Clinician: It's OK, I'm here with you (*The clinician is slowly moving in the patient's line of sight to stimulate the patient's sensory system in a non-threatening way.*)

Patient: (*After 15 seconds of silence during which the patient moves his body in apparent attempts to cope with the experience, he looks at the therapist, blinks twice, and adjusts his body posture slightly.*)

Clinician: It's OK, let's just slow down … (*The clinician is actively trying to stay in the moment and provide non-threatening and relaxed mirroring from his own bodily gestures.*)

Patient: (*The patient looks at the therapist again, and more readily adjusts his body posture; gradually his eyes unlock from the blank frightened stare, and he glances briefly at the clinician.*)

Clinician: (*on seeing the patient's bodily cues of regulation*) It seems it can feel unsafe for you in here. Just to let you know my only intention right now is to help make this feel safer for you. (*The clinician gradually reintegrates the sensory–cognitive connection.*) It seems you were quite frightened for a moment there. Is it OK if we talk about it, or should we leave it for another time?

Patient: It's OK, sometimes it's too much, it's like you are getting inside my head.

From this temporary breakdown, the individual with psychosis is prone to experience thoughts as sensations ("*I can feel my internal voice being broadcast*") or to experience sensations as overwhelming ("*My racing heart is going to burst, and I can feel blood coming out of my eyes*"). Current neuroscientific accounts suggest that individuals appraise the world using sensory and cognitive *priors* (i.e., minute "in-the-moment" predictions of how the world is), and then employ incoming information to update and align these priors into "refreshed" priors, which hopefully come close to reality [39]. Neuroscientists are confirming a long-standing clinical observation, namely that we *create* perception. In other words, our perceptions are much more the process of our own doing than that of "reality." Reality as we know it is built upon the sensory and cognitive priors, which successively build our sense that the world is a continuous and predictable place through a complex hierarchical structure of representations. Indeed, when brain function is stable, that works well for us, and we create the sense that we are continuous beings in a continuous and perceivable reality.

A key point here is that we "self-evidence"—that is, we *need* to act on the world in order to maintain our feeling of existing and being in relationship to the world. When locked in isolation or sensory deprivation, any brain is likely to start hallucinating [40]. An internal feedback loop between intention and action is key to perceiving that one's own intentionality can have an impact on:

- one's own behaviors
- others' perception and behaviors
- the physical environment.

For individuals who are experiencing psychosis, it appears that feedback loops, or self-monitoring mechanisms [41], can unexpectedly disconnect. The patient with psychosis, and often the clinician as well, will have difficulty in tracing the triggers of temporary disconnects. They can be affective in nature, but their temporality is often less clear than, for example, in borderline personality disorder (BPD). To summarize, contemporary neuroscience suggests that temporary disconnects between sensory and cognitive integration are linked to impaired self and other monitoring and loss of the experience of agency, and result in the different manifestations of psychotic symptoms.

Subjectively, this process plunges patients with psychosis into core self-disturbances of varying duration, in which they experience themselves as being alienated from sensory and mental function, as well as having a profoundly disturbed sense of agency in the domains of thinking, feeling, or behaving. These mechanisms can be placed on a continuum of severity. For example, when access to a stimulating environment is interrupted (as during the COVID-19 pandemic) or more severely thwarted (as in psychotic states), the cognitive and sensory systems decalibrate, leading to atypical states in thinking (e.g., more or less delusional beliefs) and feeling (e.g., feeling that one's actions can be more or less controlled by an external agent). We hypothesize that atypical connectivity between sensory and cognitive signaling alters self-experience—that is, the experience of oneself as a coherent body–mind unit that is in a relatively predictable relationship to other people and things in the world [3].

Such an account has clinical implications when working in accordance with the mentalization-based model. Indeed, an MBT clinician, during a session, will—as usual—maintain the balance between the cognitive and affective poles of mentalizing (see Chapters 2 and 4). Importantly, the clinician needs to pay attention to the patient's experience in the room, in particular how they experience reflectivity, and how they may experience concrete material that might be used in the room (e.g., paper, chair, flip chart, pencils). The clinician will seek to help to regulate this felt experience by mapping it against the experience that comes from reflective activity. Given that mental functioning in psychosis tends to disconnect, the sensory–cognitive balance will be a focus of constant monitoring during the session. Mentalizing work can be potentially over-activating for patients. To guide clinical work further, we find it useful to distinguish clinical presentations that indicate when mentalizing work can be pursued, as outlined in the next section.

Psychosis in the Patient's Life: Clinical Presentations

To build a mentalizing framework within a specialized clinical practice when treating psychotic disorders, it is necessary to embed the phenomenology of psychosis within the MBT framework. As we mentioned earlier in this chapter, a variety of psychotic phenomena can be represented as severe disturbances to the experience of oneself as a coherent unit—the experience itself threatens the individual's self-integrity. Schematically, there are three different clinical presentations, which reflect different degrees of integration or disintegration of the psychotic experiences in the patient's life. A patient may move from one presentation to another in relation to developmental stages, life events and challenges, and access to medical care and psychosocial resources.

1. **Decompensation occurs**. This presentation marks the failure of psychotic symptoms to hold the disturbing self-experience. Within this clinical state, the decompensated patient relies on the external environment to contain and stabilize profoundly disturbing experiences to such an extent that psychotic decompensations often lead to hospitalization, and may require lengthy inpatient care.
2. **There is significant functional impairment, but decompensation is avoided**. This state prevents the individual from having a fully autonomous and participative life. The clinical presentation usually builds upon a delusional narrative, in which the patient is experiencing a relationship to the world and others that is anchored in targeted or generalized fear and suspicion of others, as well as profound distrust in their own capacities to deal with the regular challenges of relationships, professional activities, and other activities that entail personal responsibility and accountability. The clinical presentation involves varying levels of psychotic symptoms (positive, negative, or disorganized symptoms) of a magnitude that can be managed in outpatient and community care. In this clinical presentation, the individual experiences regular disturbances in the core self, structured within a delusional narrative that offers an explanatory model of the phenomena (e.g., experiencing that one is under investigation by the highest government authorities). Within the course of psychosis, the patient is prone to decompensation following overwhelming core self-disturbances.
3. **There is integration and gradual deactivation of the intensity of psychotic clinical states** through a number of different contexts—psychosocial activities, group psychoeducation, significant relationships, vocational training, and psychotherapy, to name a few. Ideally, the social context will offer a variety of opportunities and adaptations to allow social stimulation at a level that can be withstood by the patient. Integration of the vulnerable part of self-experience is the hallmark of this clinical presentation, and places the individual on the path toward recovery.

It is evident that mentalizing work can assist in the second and third of these clinical presentations. In fully decompensated states, by contrast, mentalizing work with the patient will only cause more disorganization. However, it is important that carers and clinicians who are helping these patients maintain their own mentalizing during these times, and do not treat patients as dehumanized beings who require only pharmaceutical interventions. Indeed, patients retain some memories of their crises, particularly of the people who managed to be kind to them even when their psychological distress was intense.

Linking Core Self-Disturbances to Non-Mentalizing Modes and Cycles of Non-Mentalizing

In MBT jargon, experiencing "disturbances in core self" means that patients are experiencing themselves and the world by using non-mentalizing modes. These modes result from an attempt by the patient with psychosis to manage self-disturbances by embedding them in non-mentalizing (for clinical examples, see Figure 10.1). At their most extreme, non-mentalizing modes are fully embedded within or take the form of psychotic symptoms. For example, paranoid thinking may initially take the form of a delusional mood in which psychic equivalence is transitory, but gradually a fixed delusion forms in which psychic equivalence of thought is dominant and fixed. Hyper-reflectivity represents an extreme form of pretend mode; sudden delusional beliefs based on actions and behaviors ("*The traffic lights changed to red and the car that stopped had a number plate with my initials in it so I knew the aliens had arrived*") may represent extreme forms of teleological functioning, and other ordinary events are interpreted in the same way (e.g., a patient walks into his therapist's office, and later says "*The chairs were rearranged when I walked in; you clearly aren't interested in listening*").

During the first stage of evaluation and case formulation, discussed earlier, the clinician and the patient attempt to map out the strengths and weaknesses in mentalizing

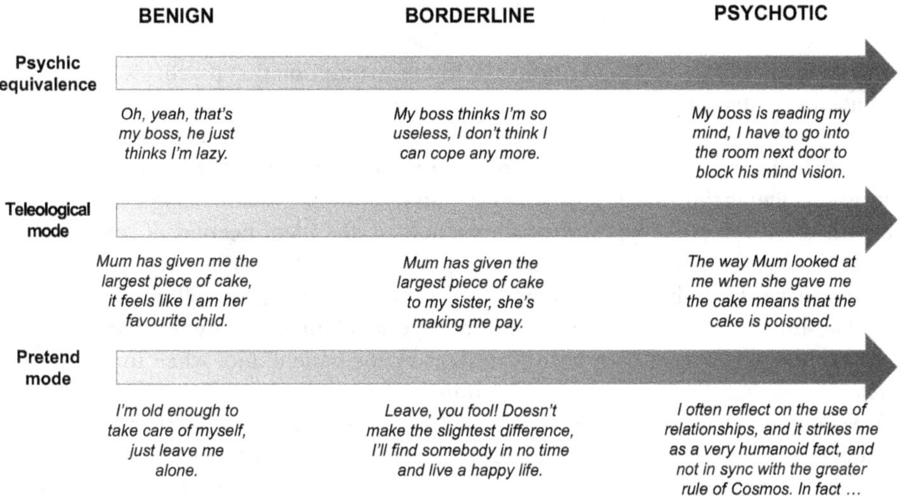

Fig. 10.1 Non-mentalizing modes along the clinical continuum, with illustrative examples.

to this level of detail, and, as we shall see, one important aspect is to identify idiosyncratic triggers that tend to be followed by impaired psychotic mentalizing. Figure 10.1 shows the continuum of non-mentalizing modes with examples of psychotic manifestations in psychic equivalence, teleological, and pretend modes.

The temporary sensory–cognitive disconnect, and the impossibility of integrating incoming sensory or cognitive information to reconnect, provides a clinical framework for thinking about different symptoms of psychosis in mentalizing terms. During instances of disturbances in the core self, sensory and cognitive psychological processes are active but imprecise (decalibrated or disconnected), leading to experiences of various forms of loss in personal agency, which may be related to bodily, cognitive, and/or affective control. Part(s) of selfhood, experienced in the here and now, are alienated. In other types of psychopathology, such self-experience is rescued by *alien self*-representations (see Chapter 2). For example, individuals with BPD will experience intense psychological saliency when experiencing themselves as, for example, "bad," "ugly," or "worthless." In a sense, alien self-representations can help these individuals to cope with self-disturbances; however, such representations can be quite threatening to their psychological integrity because of their intense affective burden, and can often lead to aggressive behaviors (violence, self-harm, and suicide attempts) linked to the affective pressure emanating from the alien self-experience. Importantly, psychological contact with alien self-representations may also lead to dissociation, which is a hallmark of a psychotic process activated as an attempt to protect psychological self-integrity. For patients with psychosis, this disconnect can be sudden and will not necessarily be accompanied by manifest changes in affective arousal. It is more likely that shifts in body posture, gaze, and speech are better indicators of disturbing self-experiences.

For the patient, the atypical cerebral activity that is sustaining psychotic states will then reorganize in unusual ways of experiencing one's body–mind unit in relation to the world. One key assumption in MBT for psychosis is that disturbances in the core self are accompanied by a cycle of impaired mentalizing, which can be momentary or, in occurrences of psychotic breakdown, more sustained. Figure 10.2 attempts to map out some of the subjective consequences and ensuing effects on mentalizing in individuals who are experiencing disturbances in the core self.

As shown in Figure 10.2, and starting from the assumption that psychosis is intrinsically linked to instability in core self-experience, the ensuing vulnerability in self-integrity and agency has a negative effect on the individual's capacity to mentalize (point 1 in Figure 10.2). This is not surprising given that, for any individual, threats to self-integrity shut down mentalizing. With regard to the initiation of non-mentalizing cycles, and in line with MBT for other types of psychopathology, the identification of idiosyncratic triggers of disturbances in the core self will provide key information for the treatment. Research suggests that in addition to attachment stress, triggers can fall into three broad domains—intense affective experiences, social evaluation, and cognitive complexity. Additional triggers might have been identified by the patient and, when included, will enrich the collaboratively created formulation.

Psychosis is further associated with information-processing biases, such as jumping to conclusions, which impair the individual's capacity to consider contrary evidence or alternative perspectives (point 2 in Figure 10.2); this means that subjective apprehension of reality can become very rigid and impermeable. Non-mentalized ways of understanding self and other in psychic equivalence, pretend, or teleological modes will not be counterbalanced by a mentalizing part of the patient's mind, and these modes are likely

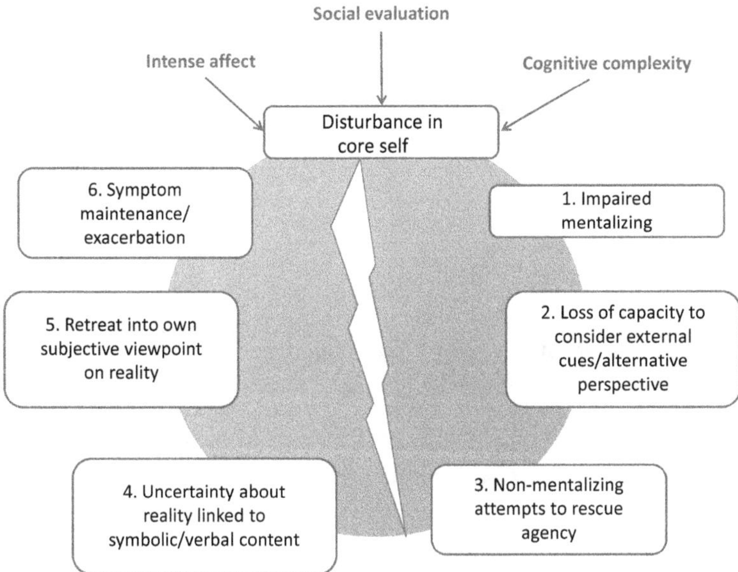

Fig. 10.2 Characterizing the cycle of non-mentalizing following core self-disturbance.

to temporarily take over the patient's subjectivity as a way to maintain minimal agency over selfhood (point 3 in Figure 10.2). In such instances, verbal/symbolic content such as cognitive challenges or interpretations are likely to widen the disconnect between feeling and knowing (point 4 in Figure 10.2). A common protective strategy adopted by patients is to retreat into their own subjective viewpoint as a way to diminish external stimulation and maintain a degree of internal coherence with themselves (point 5 in Figure 10.2). Unfortunately, over time this cycle of non-mentalizing reinforces reliance on symptoms and strengthens delusional narratives as ways of understanding and interpreting self, others, and the world (point 6 in Figure 10.2). Working with patients who are prone to cycles of non-mentalizing that sustain psychotic psychological processing will entail some adjustments in our approach to delivering MBT.

MBT for Psychosis: Key Elements of Practice

In this final section of the chapter, some of the key clinical implications for each domain of intervention in MBT (as explained in Chapters 4 and 5) are outlined as they relate to working with patients with psychosis.

Treatment and Session Structure

As we discussed in the introduction to this chapter, MBT can offer a valuable clinical tool for specialized services that are providing treatment for patients with psychosis. The structure of the treatment will be adapted to the service's culture and competencies. From the standpoint of MBT, the three clinical reference points mentioned earlier in the chapter will be established at the beginning of treatment:

- determining the clinical stage of psychosis
- identifying the patient's social resources
- formulating treatment objectives.

Depending on the clinical stage of the illness and the jointly agreed treatment objectives, a combination of psychoeducation and group and individual therapy is employed. As is usual in MBT, the formulation and treatment plan will be adapted to the level of mentalizing of the patient, and will take into account the sensitivity and capacities of the individual for self-regulation and attentional control in the context of individual and group settings. As a complement to a clinical evaluation, an assessment of mentalizing identifies:

- strengths in mentalizing
- triggers of disturbances in the core self
- patterns of use of non-mentalizing modes.

The objectives of establishing a treatment structure are to foster agency, to engage the patient, and to harness affective, motivational, and cognitive resources in planning treatment and imagining the next feasible steps for enabling the patient to live a more fulfilling and meaningful life.

In terms of session format, psychoeducational groups for psychosis have been adapted in different services and tailored to educate participants and their families and significant others about:

- psychosis
- the nature of psychotic symptoms
- different ways to integrate the life trajectory with psychosis into a personal development narrative
- engaging with oneself and threats to self
- attachment relationships.

During these sessions, mentalizing is presented as a generic capacity to construct a mental representation of oneself and others as thinking and feeling beings; these mental representations help to regulate hyper-reflective thinking and can also sustain the individual's sense of personal agency, temporal awareness, and, perhaps most importantly, their ability to genuinely relate to and be affected by others [42]. Group MBT sessions have also been adapted for patients with psychosis. These weekly groups follow a structured format, with a maximum of eight participants, and with a duration that can be reduced to 60 minutes depending on the clinical presentations—that is, the symptoms and neuropsychological functioning—of the patients.

As in group work with other patient groups with important impairments in mentalizing, the group interventions may include mediation material, such as that used in groups with severely troubled parents (e.g., the Lighthouse Project [43]). The use of mediation techniques such as playfulness, games, or drawing are linked to the formulation and treatment objectives, while making explicit the path that links the types of in-session activities to the actual objectives in the personal and interpersonal domains outside the consultation room. The idea of mediation tools is to adapt them creatively to foster a process of mentalizing self and others in explicit ways, and charting the regulatory effect on the participants. Lastly, individual therapy is used when the patient's clinical presentation and treatment objectives suggest that it might be useful, and in services that have the capacity to provide long-term (18 months minimum) individual sessions. Formulation and structure are key elements for safeguarding against pretend-mode functioning and for focusing on objectives that can explicitly help to augment the patient's ability to genuinely relate to self and others, and to increasingly engage in active and participatory roles within the social domain of functioning.

A summary of key points about the structuring of treatment is given in Box 10.1.

Box 10.1 Key points about the structuring of treatment.

- Define clinical reference points.
- Jointly establish a formulation as a collaborative process.
- Plan treatment settings.
- Anticipate and use mediation tools creatively.

The Not-Knowing Stance

For any clinician it can be quite challenging to sustain a not-knowing stance and genuine curiosity about mental states in the face of blatantly delusional beliefs or other confusing psychotic manifestations. As in any other clinical situation, the key to effective MBT intervention is the clinician's self-regulation. Although this may appear simplistic, it can become quite challenging when psychotic manifestations erupt. These manifestations can induce fear, confusion, and thought blockages in the clinician, and also tiredness, apathy, and a sense of meaninglessness. It is crucial for the clinician to monitor their own arousal and their ability and disposition to mentalize in order to maintain the not-knowing stance or reactivate it when it has been lost.

The epistemic trust framework is particularly valuable for clinicians in such circumstances. The clinician can tune into the patient's experience through reflective curiosity: "*What is it like for the patient to experience such persecution, such disorganization in thinking? What is it like for them, specifically? What is the actual effect on functioning? How is the effect experienced by the patient?* " These questions need to be "translated" when they are asked of the patient, to put them into words that model curiosity about mental states and make curiosity about those mental states relevant to the patient.

The not-knowing stance involves curiosity, respect for the patient's experience, and observation of the *effects* that disturbances of the core self can exert on the patient, both in the therapy session and in the patient's life. This stance will provide the opportunity to engage in a mentalizing process in which the clinician will be able to observe the specific dynamics that lead the patient to lose mentalizing, to experience perturbations in core self-experience, and eventually to retrieve mentalizing or manage the more difficult moments. The clinician will also be able to assess the different resources used by the patient to regulate their distress in the various therapeutic settings (e.g., individual and group therapy sessions). A summary of key points about the not-knowing stance is given in Box 10.2.

Box 10.2 Key points about the not-knowing stance.

- Monitor the clinician's level of arousal and capacity to mentalize.
- Tune into curiosity about the patient's experience with psychosis.
- Find the words to make curiosity about mental states relevant for the patient.
- Notice the dynamics of loss of mentalizing and regaining mentalizing, as well as the resources used by the patient.
- Dedicate clinical observation to the *effects* of the patient's psychotic narrative.
- Do not seek to explain the unexplainable, either to yourself or to the patient.

The Mentalizing Process

The following four elements of practice require the clinician who is delivering MBT to carefully scaffold interventions, working from "safe" to more activating components. The clinician establishes a basis for intervention by first securing a minimal degree of joint attention. This is usually done through meta-communication, which is more effective when it is marked as coming from the clinician. We provide a few examples here to illustrate marking the clinician's intention to foster joint attention.

Clinical Example: Robert (continued)

Individual Setting

CLINICIAN: Robert, something came to my mind that I'd like to share, if that's OK? You were just talking about your dad, and then somehow I lost what you wanted to say about your relationship with him.

CLINICIAN: Robert, I'm noticing you are very quiet and not looking at me today. That's fine with me, no worries. I just wanted to check in whether everything was OK for you today, being here?

Psychoeducational Setting

CLINICIAN: Can I just ask for your attention? We are about to transition to the next topic for today, is that all right for everybody? Robert? Johanna? Everyone? Do you have anything to add? OK, so now I'll ask you to think about one person to whom you feel attached—can you write down that person's name?

Group Setting

CLINICIAN: Robert, thanks for sharing your feelings on how we ended last week. I feel I now understand your point of view much better. I hope that is similar for all of us? Can I propose we try to all think about last week's emotions at the end of the group, from a personal point of view, and maybe from the point of view of one other group member?

In all of these examples the clinician attempts to affectively mark their own perspective as a starting point for questions pertaining to the mental states in the patients' minds. As patients can experience mentalizing questions as literal intrusions, marking is a key starting point for most interventions in MBT for psychosis. It also has the benefit of repeatedly offering some modeling to distinguish self and other perspectives.

In many circumstances, clinicians will use mediation tools to foster a mentalizing process. There is no validated set of mediation tools for MBT with psychosis, so the idea is to follow some basic principles. First, *playfulness* is probably the most underrated and underused dimension of clinical interventions with patients with psychosis. This is probably due to the influence both of negative symptoms, which can affect the clinician's own creativity and playfulness, and of uncertainty in the clinician's mind as to how well the patient will tolerate humor and emotionally arousing positive affects. Although these concerns are valid, playfulness is a very safe practice, especially when it is used in the MBT framework. It sustains the clinician's engagement, and an MBT-informed clinician will constantly monitor the effect of interventions on the patient's level of arousal. Therefore the calibrated use of playfulness is key to the mentalizing process; playfulness can be obstructed by the climate of negativity which can permeate the treatment of long-term psychosis, particularly when there are persistent symptoms such as withdrawal.

A critical intervention to stimulate the interpersonal mentalizing process is for the clinician to make their own thought process explicit, genuine, and simple. As with any other group of patients who experience mental states as potentially threatening, the clinician needs to normalize the mental-state process through explicit divulging of clear and simple mental processing leading to mentalizing questions. The clinician can also use summaries to convey mental-state processing linked to external, perceivable aspects of behavior, to connect perception and mental-state thinking, and to help the patient to decode the links between non-verbal communication and mental-state processing.

Clinical Example: Connecting Mental State and Physical Expression

CLINICIAN: *(pointing to his own face and head)* Robert, I can't see what type of face I'm making, but here I am wondering how I can interrupt you to ask a question?

CLINICIAN: *(leaning in)* Johanna, I'm leaning in here because I'm wondering whether we've said something that has made you go silent. Would you like to comment on that, or do you wish to keep silent for now?

A summary of key points about the mentalizing process is given in Box 10.3.

Box 10.3 Key points about the mentalizing process.

- Use mediation tools and playfulness.
- Make the clinician's own thought process explicit.
- Make the clinician's own thought process genuine and simple.
- Model the links between non-verbal communication and thought process.

Non-Mentalizing Modes

In order to address non-mentalizing modes in patients with psychosis, it is useful to go back to the conceptualization of the non-mentalizing cycle in psychosis (described earlier in this chapter), which provides the framework for intervention with psychotic manifestations in non-mentalizing modes. The MBT clinician is striving to keep a constant dialectic between the formulation co-constructed with the patient and the additional information gradually acquired through the clinical process, which provides evidence for confirmation and also updating of the formulation. Starting from the idiosyncratic triggers of core self-disturbances that were initially identified (see Figure 10.3), as well as the mentalizing impairments that were characterized at the beginning of the treatment (point 1 in Figure 10.3), the clinician will detect non-mentalizing modes when the patient is increasingly unable to appreciate alternative perspectives. These breakdowns in mentalizing are met by the clinician, who will—in line with the MBT principle of openness of mind states—strive to make their own thought process explicit when this is relevant to the therapy process, and validate the patient's experience while marking the existence of alternative perspectives (points 2 and 3 in Figure 10.3).

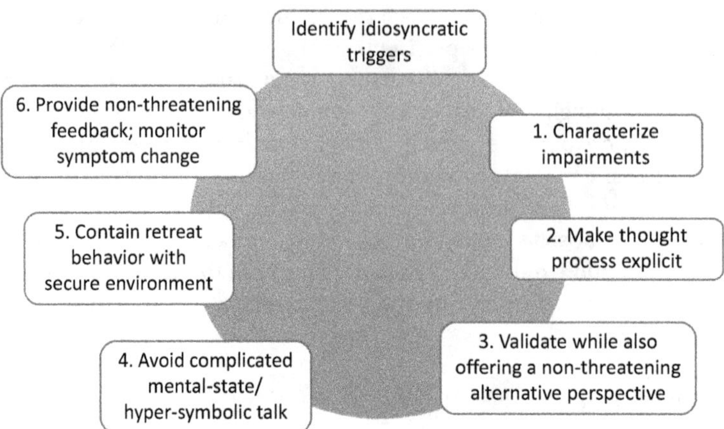

Fig. 10.3 Framework and guiding principles for clinical intervention in non-mentalizing following core self-disturbance.

Clinical Example: Johanna

JOHANNA: Everyone on the bus was looking at me as if I was crazy. I had to get off and walk here.

CLINICIAN: That sounds like a terrible experience, to feel everyone looking at you like that. Did walking here help with that feeling?

JOHANNA: Kind of . . .

CLINICIAN: I see. Is it possible that you think we have these same thoughts here?

JOHANNA: Yes . . .

CLINICIAN: Well, thanks for sharing this, Johanna, I realize that must not be easy for you at the moment. I just want to tell you that as far as I can tell what I'm thinking, I'm currently focused on understanding how that feels for you, and I'm not really thinking—again, as far as I can tell from my thoughts . . . I mean . . . thinking that you are crazy is not a thought that crossed my mind.

JOHANNA: It feels like you are . . . it's just that I would like these thoughts to stop burdening me.

CLINICIAN: And we are very motivated to try to help you with this burden . . .

In gradually shifting the focus from the *content* of delusional thoughts to their *effects,* the clinician tries to avoid complicated or hyper-symbolic thought (point 4 in Figure 10.3), as this can lead the patient to increasingly experience verbal content as unreal. At times, non-mentalizing may be so unbearable for patients that they retreat into their own subjective perspective and demonstrate maintenance or exacerbation of their symptom manifestation. This will signal to the clinician that they need to intervene by providing non-threatening feedback, explore the options for containing potentially disruptive behaviors in safe environments, and chart symptom development as agreed in the formulation and crisis plan (points 5 and 6 in Figure 10.3).

A summary of key points about the clinical approach to non-mentalizing modes is given in Box 10.4.

Box 10.4 Key points for non-mentalizing modes.

- Track idiosyncratic triggers for the emergence of non-mentalizing modes.
- Validate and empathize with the patient's experience, while maintaining a mentalizing stance.
- Avoid complicated mentalizing.
- If psychosis takes over, follow the crisis plan.

Affective Narrative

In MBT for psychosis, intervening in the affective narrative carries the risk of hyper-reflectivity. To safeguard against this risk, the clinician is advised to have a clear focus in the formulation to provide a framework for working in the affective narrative. Furthermore, the level of mentalizing of the patient, as understood in the initial assessments, points the clinician toward the use of interventions that are likely to support the integration of previously disintegrative experiences. In other words, employing mentalizing functional analysis (see Chapter 4) and proceeding with frame-by-frame descriptions of episodes may be particularly useful in helping the patient to integrate the different extremes of experience in their daily life.

Generally speaking, the "elephant in the room" (see Chapter 4) for patients with psychosis concerns both self and others. As a reminder, the elephant in the room is the subdominant affective narrative that tends to interfere with the interaction between patient and clinician. Patients often experience a profound distrust in their own capacity to tolerate stress, limit their expectations within relationships, fail to rely on reciprocity, and, most importantly, fail to recognize inconsistency in their relationship with themselves. This is based on their own experience of themselves, their diminished self-affection and lack of self-compassion, and their hyper-reflectivity, all of which they understand others find difficult to tolerate. Both patient and clinician begin to "live" this agreed narrative implicitly without verbalizing the effects that it may be having on therapy and the patient's life. In this sense, narrative work about the patient's life seeks to increase felt agency both in therapy and in their daily life; the evidence suggests that improvements can be achieved when working on narratives [44]. The other "elephant in the room" is oriented toward the reliability of others and also the nature of their intentions, which tend to be perceived as hostile. In contrast to patients with BPD, in patients with psychosis the nature of distrust in others is related not to abandonment, but rather to perceived intentions of others to alienate the patient. This theme often pervades the patient's relationship with their psychiatrist regarding medication, or with their keyworker regarding housing and occupational issues. The self/other and cognitive/affective dimensions of mentalizing are thus central to the kind of integrative work that can be done in MBT for psychosis.

A summary of key points about the affective narrative is given in Box 10.5.

Box 10.5 Key points about working with the affective narrative.

- Embed work on narrative in the formulation.
- Target integration between the dimensions of mentalizing.
- Maintain awareness of the patient's distrust of self.
- Maintain awareness of the patient's distrust of others.

Mentalizing the Relationship

Similar to work in the affective narrative domain, working on the relationship in MBT for psychosis risks triggering disturbances in the patient's core self. To safeguard against this risk, the clinician offers psychoeducation on using relationships to foster self and other awareness, and links feelings and mental states from the lived experience within the relationships between patients in the groups and the relationship(s) to the clinician(s).

The safest way to intervene is to work *in* the relationship, rather than on *representations of* the relationship. Again, embedding interventions in the relationship by marking and modeling explicit mentalizing of the clinician's own thought processes is useful for maintaining the individual therapy as a safe place in the context of group work. Interventions in the relationship between the clinician and the patient may be necessary in order to address issues of trust and safety, as well as when impasses in treatment are encountered. Again, self-regulation of the clinician is key in such interventions, as patients with psychosis—contrary to popular belief—can be exquisitely sensitive to changes in arousal in other people [45].

Concluding Remarks

This chapter has combined empirical and clinical knowledge gained from contemporary psychotherapy for psychosis as informed by MBT, and has delineated a framework encompassing a clinical rationale, key reference points for treatment, and the domains of intervention in MBT for psychosis. The available evidence suggests that further research on psychotherapy process and technical adaptations, along with better articulation of interventions within multidisciplinary settings, is required in order to sustain growth and meaningful recovery for patients with psychosis. The mentalizing theoretical framework and MBT clinical framework add to the conceptualization and interventions that can address general psychopathology in psychosis, and can also help the patient and the clinician to maintain mentalizing in the face of unpredictable and often frightening psychotic experiences. The domains of MBT intervention are followed in the treatment for psychosis, with key adaptations being made to the mentalizing process and treatment structure.

References

1. American Psychiatric Association. *Diagnostic and Statistical Manual of Mental Disorders*, 5th ed. Washington, DC: American Psychiatric Association, 2013.
2. Brent B. Mentalization-based psychodynamic psychotherapy for psychosis. *J Clin Psychol* 2009; **65**: 803–14.
3. Debbané M, Benmiloud J, Salaminios G et al. Mentalization-based treatment in clinical high-risk for psychosis: a rationale and clinical illustration. *J Contemp Psychother* 2016; **46**: 217–25.
4. Lana F, Marcos S, Mollà L et al. Mentalization based group psychotherapy for psychosis: a pilot study to assess safety, acceptance and subjective efficacy. *Int J Psychol Psychoanal* 2015; **1**: 1–6.
5. Weijers J, Ten Kate C, Eurelings-Bontekoe E et al. Mentalization-based treatment for psychotic disorder: protocol of a randomized controlled trial. *BMC Psychiatry* 2016; **16**: 191.
6. Lana F, Marti-Bonany J, Sanz-Correcher P et al. Brief day hospital mentalization based group psychotherapy for schizophrenia spectrum disorders: a

feasibility study. *Actas Esp Psiquiatr* 2020; **48**: 64–74.

7. Riddel K, Clouse M. Program development meets theory development: MBGT-I for schizophrenia spectrum and other psychotic disorders. *Clin Schizophr Relat Psychoses* 2020; **14**: 39–44.
8. Brent B, Fonagy P. A mentalization-based treatment approach to disturbances of social understanding in schizophrenia. In: Lysaker PH, Dimaggio G, Brüne M, eds. *Social Cognition and Metacognition in Schizophrenia*. San Diego, CA: Elsevier, 2014; 245–57.
9. Debbané M, Salaminios G, Luyten P et al. Attachment, neurobiology, and mentalizing along the psychosis continuum. *Front Hum Neurosci* 2016; **10**: 406.
10. Weijers JG, ten Kate C, Debbane M et al. Mentalization and psychosis: a rationale for the use of mentalization theory to understand and treat non-affective psychotic disorder. *J Contemp Psychother* 2020; **50**: 223–32.
11. Debbané M, Bateman A. Psychosis. In: Bateman A, Fonagy P, eds. *Handbook of Mentalizing in Mental Health Practice*, 2nd ed. Washington, DC: American Psychiatric Association Publishing, 2019; 443–58.
12. Armando M, Hutsebaut J, Debbane M. A mentalization-informed staging approach to clinical high risk for psychosis. *Front Psychiatry* 2019; **10**: 385.
13. Rapoport JL, Addington AM, Frangou S, Psych MR. The neurodevelopmental model of schizophrenia: update 2005. *Mol Psychiatry* 2005; **10**: 434–49.
14. Lichtenstein P, Yip BH, Bjork C et al. Common genetic determinants of schizophrenia and bipolar disorder in Swedish families: a population-based study. *Lancet* 2009; **373**: 234–9.
15. Meehl PE. Toward an integrated theory of schizotaxia, schizotypy, and schizophrenia. *J Pers Disord* 1990; **4**: 1–99.
16. Debbané M, Barrantes-Vidal N. Schizotypy from a developmental perspective. *Schizophr Bull* 2015; **41** (Suppl. 2): S386–95.
17. Debbané M. Schizotypy: a developmental perspective. In: Mason O, Claridge G, eds. *Schizotypy: New Dimensions*. Abingdon, UK: Routledge, 2015; 83–98.
18. Lenzenweger MF. Schizotypy: an organizing framework for schizophrenia research. *Curr Dir Psychol Sci* 2016; **15**: 162–6.
19. Guloksuz S, Pries LK, Ten Have M et al. Association of preceding psychosis risk states and non-psychotic mental disorders with incidence of clinical psychosis in the general population: a prospective study in the NEMESIS-2 cohort. *World Psychiatry* 2020; **19**: 199–205.
20. Schultze-Lutter F, Michel C, Schmidt SJ et al. EPA guidance on the early detection of clinical high risk states of psychoses. *Eur Psychiatry* 2015; **30**: 405–16.
21. Schultze-Lutter F, Ruhrmann S, Berning J et al. Basic symptoms and ultrahigh risk criteria: symptom development in the initial prodromal state. *Schizophr Bull* 2010; **36**: 182–91.
22. Alvarez-Jimenez M, Gleeson JF, Henry LP et al. Road to full recovery: longitudinal relationship between symptomatic remission and psychosocial recovery in first-episode psychosis over 7.5 years. *Psychol Med* 2012; **42**: 595–606.
23. AlAqeel B, Margolese HC. Remission in schizophrenia: critical and systematic review. *Harv Rev Psychiatry* 2012; **20**: 281–97.
24. Bevington D, Fuggle P, Cracknell L, Fonagy P. *Adaptive Mentalization-Based Integrative Treatment: A Guide for Teams to Develop Systems of Care*. Oxford, UK: Oxford University Press, 2017.
25. Boyette LL, Korver-Nieberg N, Meijer C et al. Quality of life in patients with psychotic disorders: impact of symptoms, personality, and attachment. *J Nerv Ment Dis* 2014; **202**: 64–9.
26. Nevarez-Flores AG, Sanderson K, Breslin M et al. Systematic review of global functioning and quality of life in people

with psychotic disorders. *Epidemiol Psychiatr Sci* 2019; **28**: 31–44.

27. Jones K. Addressing the needs of carers during early psychosis. *Early Interv Psychiatry* 2009; **3** (Suppl. 1): S22–6.

28. Harley EW, Boardman J, Craig T. Friendship in people with schizophrenia: a survey. *Soc Psychiatry Psychiatr Epidemiol* 2012; **47**: 1291–9.

29. Castelein S, Bruggeman R, van Busschbach JT et al. The effectiveness of peer support groups in psychosis: a randomized controlled trial. *Acta Psychiatr Scand* 2008; **118**: 64–72.

30. Weijers J. *Mentalization and Psychosis: Trying to Understand the Un-Understandable.* Maastricht: Ridderprint, 2020.

31. Bleuler E. *Dementia Praecox or the Group of Schizophrenias.* New York: International Universities Press, 1911/1950.

32. Freud S. Three essays on the theory of sexuality. In: Strachey J, ed. *The Standard Edition of the Complete Psychological Works of Sigmund Freud*, Vol. 7. London, UK: Hogarth Press, 1905/1953; 123–230.

33. Freud S. On narcissism. In: Strachey J, ed. *The Standard Edition of the Complete Psychological Works of Sigmund Freud*, Vol. 14. London, UK: Hogarth Press, 1914/1957; 67–102.

34. Freud S. The unconscious. In: Strachey J, ed. *The Standard Edition of the Complete Psychological Works of Sigmund Freud*, Vol. 14. London, UK: Hogarth Press, 1915/1957; 159–216.

35. Sass LA, Parnas J. Schizophrenia, consciousness, and the self. *Schizophr Bull* 2003; **29**: 427–44.

36. Auerbach JS, Blatt SJ. Self-representation in severe psychopathology: the role of reflexive self-awareness. *Psychoanal Psychol* 1996; **13**: 297–341.

37. Lysaker PH, Buck KD, Pattison ML et al. Supervision in the psychotherapy of schizophrenia: awareness of and mutual reflection upon fragmentation. *Am J Psychoanal* 2019; **79**: 284–303.

38. Adams RA, Stephan KE, Brown HR et al. The computational anatomy of psychosis. *Front Psychiatry* 2013; **4**: 47.

39. Friston K. Active inference and free energy. *Behav Brain Sci* 2013; **36**: 212–13.

40. Derome M, Fonseca-Pedrero E, Badoud D et al. Resting-state networks of adolescents experiencing depersonalization-like illusions: cross-sectional and longitudinal findings. *Schizophr Bull* 2018; **44** (Suppl. 2): S501–11.

41. Frith CD. *The Cognitive Neuropsychology of Schizophrenia.* Hove, UK: Psychology Press, 1992.

42. Salaminios G, Debbané M. A mentalization-based treatment framework to support the recovery of the self in emerging psychosis during adolescence. In: Hasson-Ohayion I, Lysaker PH, eds. *The Recovery of the Self in Psychosis.* Abingdon, UK: Routledge, 2021; 12–35.

43. Byrne G, Sleed M, Midgley N et al. Lighthouse Parenting Programme: description and pilot evaluation of mentalization-based treatment to address child maltreatment. *Clin Child Psychol Psychiatry* 2019; **24**: 680–93.

44. Lysaker PH, Klion RE. *Recovery, Meaning-Making, and Severe Mental Illness: A Comprehensive Guide to Metacognitive Reflection and Insight Therapy.* New York, NY: Routledge, 2017.

45. Reininghaus U, Kempton MJ, Valmaggia L et al. Stress sensitivity, aberrant salience, and threat anticipation in early psychosis: an experience sampling study. *Schizophr Bull* 2016; **42**: 712–22.

Part III

Application and Adaptations for Mental Health Presentations

Chapter 11

Trauma

Introduction

Clinical Example: Lydia

Lydia is a 25-year-old nurse. At the start of her intake interview with a clinician she immediately starts to cry, and she says she does not know how to begin to relate what is wrong with her. She says that she always seems to end up in abusive relationships characterized by emotional and often physical abuse. She does not understand why she seems to be attracted to such abusive men, as she herself was emotionally neglected by her parents, and as a result would like nothing more than to be in a loving relationship. She has two young daughters, but child protection services have recently threatened to remove her children because of concerns about neglect and abuse.

Lydia describes her parents as very hard-working but emotionally distant. Although she says she never doubted that they loved her, she cannot remember either her mum or her dad ever telling her that they did so. She has a younger brother who she says is a lot like her; he was also frequently humiliated by their parents, particularly by their mother, and, like Lydia, he came to believe that there was something fundamentally wrong with him. A few years ago, he moved abroad in an attempt to escape from his parents. Lydia also thought about moving away, but she still visits her parents: "*My mum is still my mum, despite everything she has done to me.*" As a teenager, Lydia began to experiment with drugs "*to ease my pain,*" and she also began to self-harm by cutting her arms and wrists, which provided her "*with a sense of importance and excitement.*" She successfully completed her training as a nurse. However, at work she is often involved in conflicts with her co-workers, and it is clear to her that "*they simply cannot stand me, I can tell by the way they look at me that they all think I am a worthless piece of junk who even mistreats her children,*" and although she wanted to become a nurse because she "*has always liked to care for people,*" she says that recently she has felt that she no longer cares about her patients. She says she feels utterly depressed, often anxious, is addicted to alcohol, and still self-harms frequently. In her referral letter, her treating psychiatrist refers her for the treatment of post-traumatic stress disorder, and adds that there is also evidence for borderline personality disorder as well as antisocial features.

Lydia's problems are typical of many patients who present with so-called *attachment trauma* or *complex trauma*. The term "complex trauma" refers to the impact of prolonged early negative life experiences involving neglect and/or abuse, typically within an attachment/caregiving context, in which the caregivers who are supposed to protect and care for the child are at the same time a source of anxiety, threat, neglect, and/or abuse [1,2]. The co-occurrence of mental disorders in patients like Lydia is common—in fact, it is the rule rather than the exception. Research studies have shown that trauma is best considered as a transdiagnostic factor that is implicated in the development of a wide variety of emotional and (functional) somatic disorders. Trauma typically accounts for between 30% and 70% of the population attributable risk for a wide range of mental disorders [3,4]. Furthermore, it can generate an ecophenotype (a group of characteristics that emerge as an adaptation to the environment) that is associated not only with high rates of comorbidity (i.e., the co-occurrence of two or more mental disorders) but also with an earlier age of onset of psychopathology, greater severity of symptoms, an increased risk for suicide, and a poorer response to treatment [3].

This chapter will discuss the mentalizing approach to trauma [5–11], beginning with an outline of how to conceptualize trauma and its impact from a mentalizing perspective, and focusing on the effect of trauma on four basic biobehavioral systems (i.e., interconnected biological and psychological processes) that play a key role in emotion regulation—the *stress*, *attachment*, *mentalizing*, and *epistemic trust* systems [12]. Treatment principles will then be discussed, with a focus on adaptations of the basic mentalization-based treatment (MBT) model to make it more suitable for addressing the problems of people with a history of trauma. Finally, MBT-Trauma Focused (MBT-TF), a specific, modular program of group sessions with some individual sessions for patients with a trauma history, will be described.

Understanding Trauma: A Mentalizing Perspective

There are different types of trauma, which can be thought of as a continuum ranging from *impersonal trauma* (e.g., living through a natural disaster, being involved in a serious car crash) to *interpersonal trauma* (e.g., being abused by a work colleague or a stranger) and on to *attachment trauma* or *complex trauma* (e.g., being abused by a parent or other attachment figure). This continuum is depicted in Figure 11.1.

Clinically, it is important to realize that the typical response of an individual to a single isolated experience of trauma is so-called *minimal impact resilience*. Many people experience only temporary distress after a single incident of (impersonal or interpersonal) trauma and then show a relatively quick improvement back to healthy functioning, although sometimes this can take longer. Research suggests that only a subgroup of individuals develops chronic trauma-related problems as a result of experiencing or witnessing a single incident of trauma [13,14]. From a mentalizing perspective, these findings force us to reverse the traditional perspective on trauma, in that the essence of understanding the impact of trauma lies not in the idea of vulnerability, but in the *absence of resilience*. For example, people who experience a long-term period of distress

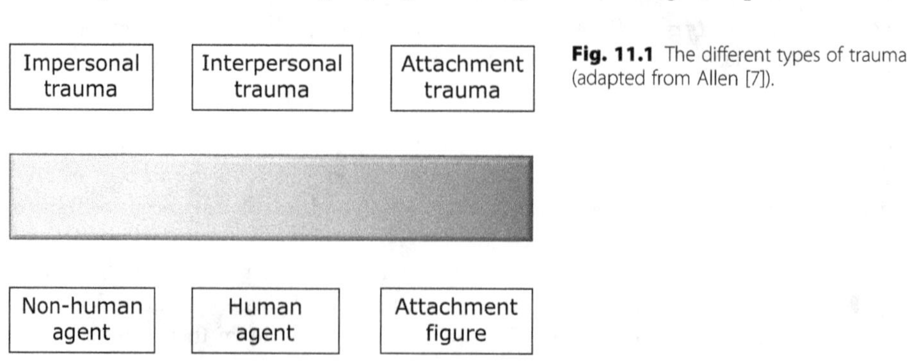

Fig. 11.1 The different types of trauma (adapted from Allen [7]).

Table 11.1 A mentalizing approach to trauma

Biobehavioral system affected by trauma	Effects of disruption of system
Stress system	Temporary or chronic dysregulation of the stress system, leading to hyperarousal
Attachment behavioral system	Increased reliance on secondary attachment strategies; risk of increased dysregulation of the stress response, leading to a sense of isolation, abandonment, and/or neglect
Mentalizing capacity	Non-mentalizing modes tend to dominate subjective experience; this leads to feelings of hopelessness and dread (psychic equivalence), increases the risk of self-harm (teleological mode), and/or results in rumination and dissociation (pretend mode), combined with a pressure to externalize unmentalized experiences ("alien self" states), and re-enactment of traumatic experiences
Capacity for epistemic trust	Epistemic trust is weakened, leading to impaired social communication and salutogenesis. The inability to recalibrate the mind together with a trusted other increases the feelings of isolation and dread

and maladaptation after experiencing a single traumatic event tend to have a history of early childhood trauma and/or poor social support and emotion-regulation strategies [15,16].

To explain these findings from a mentalizing perspective, trauma is thought to disrupt the coordinated functioning of four closely related biobehavioral systems (see Table 11.1). Disruptions in the coordinated functioning of these systems also provide a comprehensive theoretical framework for understanding the main clinical features of patients with a history of trauma, in particular attachment trauma (see Table 11.2 and Figures 11.2 and 11.3).

Trauma—regardless of whether it is single or complex—typically challenges the stress-regulation system. This leads to an often massive activation of the attachment system in an attempt to co-regulate stress and arousal (see Figure 11.3). As will be discussed in more detail later in this chapter, attachment figures play a key role in the co-regulation of stress—when someone is faced with trauma or adversity, they seek help, support, and care from those closest to them. However, when (co-)regulation fails, a state of hyperarousal and associated hypervigilance to threat (which is typical of trauma syndromes) arises. Because of this state of hyperarousal, mentalizing impairments are often inevitable. They give rise to distorted views of self and others, and also increase the risk of intrusions (i.e., re-experiencing of trauma) and the use of avoidance behaviors and dissociation to defend against unbearable feelings of anxiety, anger, shame, guilt, disgust, and dread. For individuals with attachment trauma in particular, these unbearable states of mind also increase the risk of further trauma related to continuing problematic interactions with others triggered by traumatic memories (re-enactments). Many of these individuals have also developed high levels of epistemic mistrust and epistemic hypervigilance (see Chapter 2) as an adaptation strategy to an environment

Table 11.2 Typical features of trauma, their clinical expression, and the underlying biobehavioral systems that are involved

Trauma features	Clinical expression	Underlying biobehavioral system(s)
Hyperarousal and reactivity	• Hypervigilance/anxiety • Heightened startle response • Concentration problems • Sleep problems • Irritability or aggression • Physical symptoms	Stress and attachment systems
Intrusions/re-experiencing and associated avoidance behaviors and dissociative experiences	• Unwanted negative memories • Nightmares • Flashbacks • Emotional distress • Dissociation	Mentalizing system
Negative views of self and others	• Overly negative assumptions about oneself, others, and/or the world in general • Exaggerated blame of self or others/(survivor) guilt • Depressive feelings • Difficulty experiencing positive affect • Feelings of isolation • Feelings of (toxic) shame and/or disgust	Mentalizing and epistemic trust systems
Re-enactments	• Risky or (self-)destructive behavior • Re-enactment of neglect or abuse	Attachment, mentalizing, epistemic trust systems

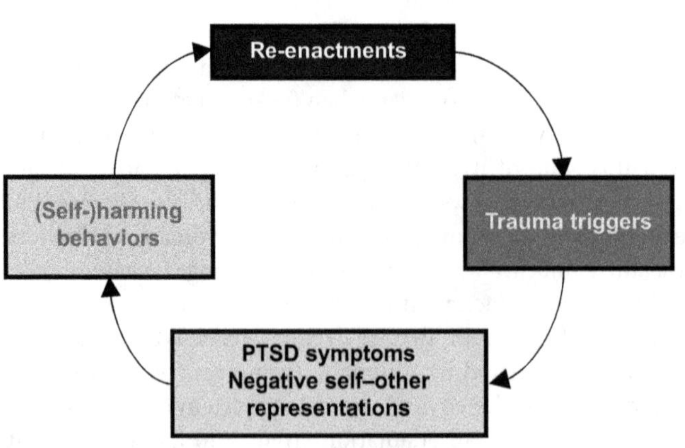

Fig. 11.2 Re-enactment cycles associated with (complex) trauma and post-traumatic stress disorder (PTSD).

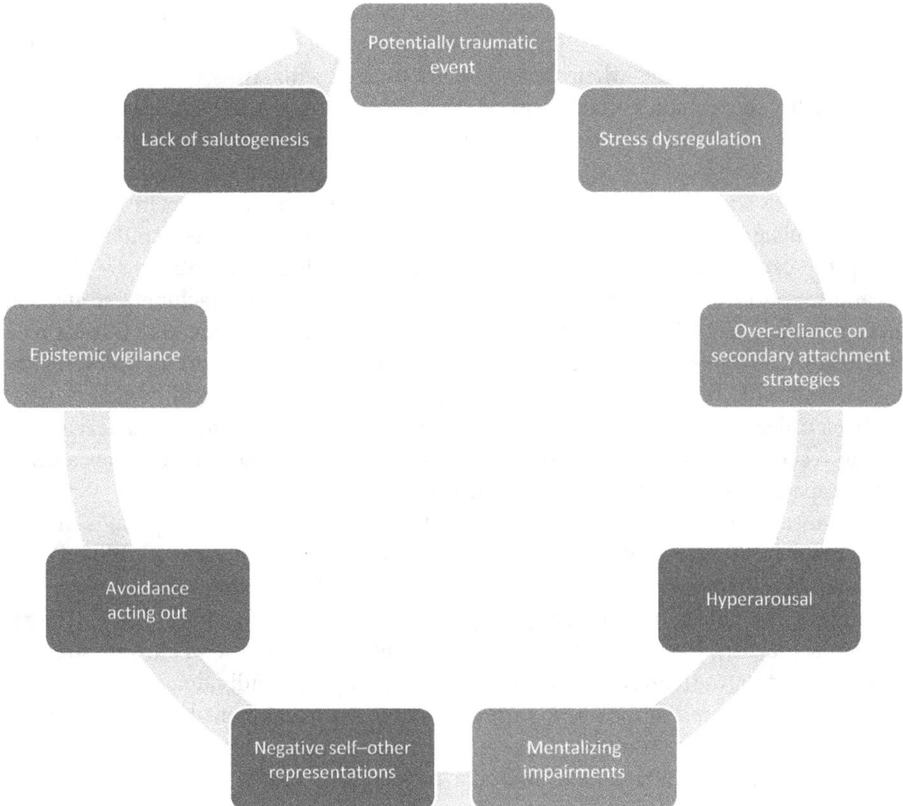

Fig. 11.3 Trauma features and underlying biobehavioral systems.

characterized by abuse and/or neglect. MBT may therefore be particularly appropriate and effective for patients with complex trauma because of its focus both on restoring the process of mentalizing and on the dynamics associated with severe impairments in mentalizing (i.e., the tendency for re-enactments or externalization of unmentalized experiences in relationships, including the therapeutic relationship) and epistemic mistrust. Victims of trauma often show a tendency to unwittingly recreate experiences of neglect and abuse, and tend not to trust other people. These tendencies often seriously compromise the capacity of these individuals to establish a working therapeutic alliance, and as a result there is a high likelihood of dropout from treatment and frequent relapses.

Trauma, Stress, and Attachment

Trauma activates the stress/threat system. In human beings the stress/threat system consists of a distributed set of neural structures—the amygdala, hippocampus, and areas in the prefrontal cortex (PFC), including the medial PFC [17,18]—and a broader set of associated regulatory responses, including responses coordinated by the hypothalamic–pituitary–adrenal (HPA) axis and the autonomic nervous system, the metabolic system, the gut, the kidneys, and the immune system, each of which has relatively distinct biomediators (e.g., cortisol, sympathetic and parasympathetic neurotransmitters, metabolic hormones, cytokines) [17–19]. This coordinated set of responses underlies so-called fight/flight/freeze responses when the individual is faced with stress.

The quality of a person's attachment relationships and their social environment more generally play a pivotal role in the stress response, and continue to play this role throughout development [19,20]. From a developmental perspective, secure attachment is conducive to so-called *adaptive hyporesponsivity* of the stress system in response to adversity. This means that children who grow up in a secure attachment context tend to develop the capacity to cope with adversity because they learn that others are there to help and support them. Hence, for these individuals, the primary attachment strategy in times of need is to seek help, advice, care, and support from others, which leads to a down-regulation of feelings of distress and fear, underpinned by the neurobiological mesocorticolimbic reward system [21]. This sequence of events typically leads to what have been called "broaden-and-build cycles" [22,23], in which the individual learns that they can reach out to others in times of need (i.e., "broaden"), and also develops a belief in their capacity to deal with stress and adversity (i.e., "build").

By contrast, high levels of adversity, particularly during critical periods in the development of the stress system (which in humans extends into early adulthood), are associated with disruption of the stress response, expressed in either overactivity of the HPA axis (i.e., a constant state of fight/flight) or HPA hypo(re)activity (i.e., a "freeze/faint" state; [18,24]). When attachment strategies fail, either because of chronic stress or due to the (perceived) unavailability of attachment figures, individuals begin to rely excessively on *secondary attachment strategies.* These are attachment-hyperactivating or attachment-deactivating strategies, or a combination of both, which is typical of individuals with disorganized attachment and/or a history of complex trauma. Attachment-deactivating strategies are a typical response to the (perceived) unavailability of attachment figures, whereas attachment-hyperactivating strategies develop as an attempt to elicit care and support from attachment figures who are inconsistently available. Individuals with a history of complex trauma often have childhood attachment figures who were a source of security, support, love, and care, but also of abuse and neglect. Children who grow up in this situation are often caught in an approach–avoidance conflict, which is then reactivated and re-enacted when they become involved in similar relationships later in life—that is, relationships characterized by love and care on the one hand, and abuse and/or neglect on the other—because this is the attachment "template" that is familiar to them (see Table 11.3).

Regardless of the type of secondary attachment strategy that is used to deal with increasing stress and adversity, these strategies tend to fail in the longer term, as they are based on an underlying belief that others are ultimately not available to provide care and support. As a result, the effective (co-)regulation of stress fails, leading to a state of hyperarousal characterized by hypervigilance to threat, a heightened startle reaction, cognitive problems (e.g., difficulty concentrating), sleeping problems, and often high levels of irritability and aggression (as listed in Table 11.2). The individual continues to function in a fight/flight state. This also allows us to understand the often long-lasting consequences of attachment trauma for physical health, because of its impact on the neurotransmitter systems, pain-processing systems, and immune system. This is the reason for the high comorbidity between trauma, somatic disorders, and functional somatic disorders, including chronic pain and fatigue conditions [25]. Trauma is

Table 11.3 Types of re-enactment associated with (attachment) trauma

Type of re-enactment	Typical features
Revictimization	The individual unwittingly seeks out relationships characterized by physical, emotional, and/or sexual abuse, often also involving rejection, abandonment and/or perceived neglect. This may lead them to become aggressive
Re-enactment of neglect	The individual is hypersensitive to any signs of neglect, and constantly tends to construe interpersonal situations in terms of neglect; again, this may lead to aggression (out of a sense of righteous indignation) and/or they may become even more convinced that others are neglectful
Re-enactment of attachment trauma/ childhood maltreatment in parenting behavior	Emotional states in the individual's child trigger unmentalized mental states related to the individual's own traumatic history, and these are acted out in relation to the child

associated not only with high "psychological costs" but also with high "metabolic costs," because chronic stress causes wear and tear on the neurobiological systems that are involved in the stress response. In addition, unhealthy behaviors (e.g., excessive drinking, overeating, smoking) are often used as a coping strategy for dealing with traumatic feelings, which further increases the risk of certain physical conditions, such as cardiovascular disease, diabetes, and obesity.

Trauma and Mentalizing

The high levels of arousal that result from a breakdown in normal (co-)regulation of stress also compromise the individual's capacity for controlled mentalizing. Studies have shown an inverse relationship between arousal and the capacity to mentalize [26,27]. With increasing arousal, defensive (fight/flight/freeze) and often biased automatic mentalizing comes online. This switch from more controlled to automatic mentalizing has obvious adaptive value from an evolutionary perspective, as it allows a rapid response to threat ("*I am in danger, I can't trust anyone, and I need to defend myself*"). However, in the longer term, automatic biased mentalizing characteristically leads to overly negative views about the self and others ("*I am worthless,*" "*I am unlovable,*" "*You can never trust others*") (see Table 11.2 and Figure 11.3). Moreover, in psychic equivalence mode (see later in this section, and Chapter 2), trauma triggers lead the individual to re-experience memories of the trauma as if they are real and the traumatic situation is actually re-occurring. This leads to further anxiety, distress, feelings of depression, and defensive avoidance of trauma triggers, often resulting in dissociation and acting-out behaviors in an attempt to down-regulate these highly distressing feelings. Because traumatic experiences are unmentalized, they remain unbearable for the trauma victim, who is thus prone to externalization and acting out, as is shown by the high incidence of (self-)destructive behaviors (discussed in more detail later) and nightmares and flashbacks (see Table 11.2 and Figure 11.3). Trauma impairs the capacity to frame and reframe overwhelming experiences. Individuals with insecure attachment histories in particular have less and sometimes no access to *relational referencing* or the *recalibration of their mind*—the process by which a person can meaningfully reframe traumatic experiences and begin to mentalize what could not be mentalized before. Strong feelings of anger and disgust, and high levels of shame (also called toxic shame), further prevent relational referencing, which means that traumatic memories maintain their original destructive impact on the individual and their attachment and mentalizing capacities.

Therefore, as will be described in more detail later, the importance of relational referencing is particularly emphasized in the MBT approach to trauma. Despite their attempts to avoid traumatic experiences, individuals with a history of trauma still experience a particular need for marked mirroring of these experiences, which involves someone else reflecting back in a marked (i.e., digested and contained) way what is difficult or even impossible for the individual to mentalize. Marked mirroring in this case involves empathic, validating, and normalizing interventions that gradually modulate the traumatic experience of the patient in such a way that they become able to think and feel what they previously were unable to think and feel, leading to *mentalized affectivity*—the capacity to feel and to simultaneously reflect upon one's feelings [28,29].

As in all types of MBT, the starting point of such interventions is often when the trauma patient loses the capacity for mentalizing and begins to rely on non-mentalizing modes of experiencing reality, frequently associated with a tendency to externalize unmentalized experiences, leading to cycles of re-enactment.

In psychic equivalence mode, everything becomes too real, and talking about the trauma leads the person to relive it. The traumatized individual feels stuck in the painful past and present, and for them there is no hope and no way out. These painful feelings, which are often merged with highly "toxic" feelings of shame, often give rise to teleological-mode functioning, in which the person feels that only actions can bring relief. This typically leads to self-harming behaviors (e.g., excessive drinking, self-cutting, overactivity) in an attempt to regulate extremely painful feelings. Pretend-mode functioning in individuals with trauma is often expressed through excessive rumination about past events, in combination with intrusive thoughts, in which the person loses contact with reality. This may lead to dissociative states as an attempt to protect the self against feelings of inner emptiness, badness, or worthlessness.

In these circumstances, re-enactment cycles are particularly likely to occur. Therapeutic work focusing on these cycles is a prominent feature in MBT for trauma (see Table 11.3 and Figure 11.3). Such re-enactments are made all the more likely as the therapist's mind, in interacting with the traumatized individual, tends to freeze as well, which could be thought of as "vicarious traumatization." This only increases the traumatized person's painful feelings of being isolated and beyond help, which leads them to become more prone to acting out unmentalized traumatic experiences.

Attachment experiences provide a template for later relationships, and individuals with a history of complex trauma have often developed strong, albeit destructive, templates for relationships in which love and care are inevitably linked to abuse and/or neglect. The first type of re-enactment cycle shown in Table 11.3 is well known and involves revictimization [30,31]. Being in an abusive relationship as a child not only creates considerable anxiety and distress, but also intensifies attachment needs, as the attachment system is activated as a response to threat. This paradoxically strengthens the child's relationship with an abusive attachment figure, particularly if that abusive figure is also a source of comfort, support, and/or love. This pattern is then repeated in relationships in later life—for example, in romantic relationships with a jealous, possessive, and abusive partner [32]—continuing a disorganized/disoriented attachment pattern [33]. In teleological mode, the individual may engage in self-harm, which may lead to a vicious cycle in which others increasingly feel that they have to distance themselves from the individual (because they feel more and more "traumatized"), confirming the traumatized individual's worst fear—that others are unavailable to them. A state of righteous indignation may arise as the traumatized individual feels that they have every reason to retaliate because of the abusive behavior of others [34]. As aggression typically helps to achieve a sense of coherence, protecting the individual against painful feelings, such vindictive/aggressive states of mind may be very persistent. As a result, as in the case of Lydia described at the beginning of this chapter, these individuals often become "addicted" to others who are (perceived as) abusive, as this allows them to establish and maintain a certain level of stability, however precarious it may be.

The second type of re-enactment cycle (see Table 11.3), namely re-enactment of neglect, may occur in individuals with a history of neglect. Here even minor misunderstandings or disagreements can lead to often extreme dysphoria and/or aggressive or self-harming behavior, and similar re-enactments when the individual is in teleological mode (e.g., accusing a senior colleague, romantic partner, or organization of neglect).

In the third type of re-enactment cycle (see Table 11.3), in the context of parenting, observing emotional distress or happiness in their children may trigger these individuals' own past traumatic experiences of neglect and/or abuse. For instance, Lydia acted out her unmentalized experiences involving envy and anger, repeating the traumatic behavior of her parents in relation to her own children.

Problems with Epistemic Trust

Trauma and adversity are characteristically part of a broader "risky environment" in which individuals grow up [35]. Hence, in trying to understand resilience in the face of adversity, a systemic perspective is essential. Many people who have experienced trauma (especially complex/attachment trauma) often show profound epistemic mistrust and epistemic hypervigilance; this may have arisen either as a chronic trait or as a consequence of unhelpful interactions with healthcare professionals, or a combination of both. Epistemic mistrust/hypervigilance is an understandable adaptation strategy for individuals who have grown up experiencing abuse or neglect. However, in adopting this strategy, they also close themselves off from the possibility of social recalibration of their mind and hence *salutogenesis*—that is, the capacity of an individual to benefit from positive social influences in their environment [12,36].

Attachment trauma in particular leads the patient to feel unrecognized as an independent agent. They often lack experiences of marked mirroring by attachment figures that would typically give rise to a feeling of agency and autonomy, which opens up what we think of as an "epistemic superhighway" that allows the fast communication of knowledge about the self, others, and the world. Hence, as will be discussed in more detail later, a central task in MBT for trauma is to recover (or develop, depending on the severity of epistemic vigilance) the patient's capacity for epistemic trust. For many patients who have a history of attachment trauma, even thinking about the minds of other people and their intentions will lead them to re-experience the trauma, and it is understandable that this might be defensively blocked. This makes these individuals particularly "hard to reach" via therapeutic interventions. In the case of Lydia, for instance, it took a long time before she was willing to even consider the idea that her mother might not have been the good mother that Lydia thought (wished) she was.

Mentalization-Based Treatment for Trauma

People with a history of attachment trauma are often less responsive to psychotherapy than those who have not experienced trauma [3,12]. As a result, a number of treatments specifically focusing on trauma have been developed. MBT has shown considerable effectiveness in treating disorders that are characterized by high levels of (complex) trauma, such as borderline personality disorder [37] and antisocial personality disorder [38]. A recent study also found that trauma had little or no impact on treatment outcome in two types of MBT for borderline personality disorder (intensive outpatient MBT and day-hospitalization MBT) [39]. These findings open up promising perspectives for the treatment of patients with trauma, although we believe, as we shall describe later in this chapter, that more focused trauma work may improve the effectiveness of MBT for trauma even further.

General Principles of MBT for Trauma

The MBT approach to trauma is based on five related general principles that are elements of all types of MBT, but deserve greater attention in the treatment of these patients.

First, a structured treatment approach that is coherent, consistent, and continuous over time is crucially important in the treatment of patients with trauma, particularly those with attachment trauma, as these characteristics of the treatment will help to structure the patients' sense of self and others. An environment that has high levels of predictability and reliability is a key requirement. For the same reason, psychoeducation about trauma and its impact on psychological functioning, as well as about the MBT program itself, is an important component of MBT for trauma, as it not only scaffolds the mentalizing capacities of traumatized individuals but also further increases the predictability of treatment and decreases the patients' feelings of epistemic mistrust, as the MBT clinician (or service) is open and explicit about the treatment and what it involves.

Second, it is essential to provide a physically and psychologically safe and containing holding environment to help the patient to develop a trusting relationship with the clinician. Therefore, particularly in the early phases of treatment, there is an emphasis on developing the "we-mode," taking a collaborative stance from the beginning (see Chapters 2 and 4), and on validating and normalizing feelings, with the clinician adopting an empathic, validating stance. A core feature of MBT for trauma is to work collaboratively with the patient toward formulating specific aims of treatment, as this fosters feelings of agency, communicates realistic hope, and counters epistemic mistrust. This process also includes crisis management and the formulation of goals related to decreasing trauma-related symptoms and features, such as reducing self-harm, avoidance behaviors, and re-enactments.

Third, and related to the previous point, MBT for trauma focuses on helping the patient to manage strong feelings (e.g., anxiety) related to trauma and to actively avoid dissociation, self-harm, and re-enactments before the content of trauma is discussed, based on the identification and discussion of re-enactment cycles (see Figure 11.3).

Fourth, it is crucial to consider not only the "what" but also the "how" of change and social communication in patients with a history of trauma—that is, how they might open up again to the social recalibration of their mind. The communication systems discussed in Chapters 2 and 9 are helpful in this regard. In communication system 1, the clinician communicates that their mind is available and able to tolerate, contain, and reflect upon feelings and thoughts that are unbearable for the patient—essentially, that the patient is "not alone." This not only helps to restore the patient's mentalizing capacities but also decreases their epistemic vigilance, and fosters increased curiosity about the mind of the clinician. As a result, in communication system 2, the patient's mentalizing capacities increase, as does the patient's capacity to manage their emotional states and to navigate interpersonal relationships in more adaptive ways. Next, in communication system 3, the patient is actively supported to increasingly open up to and/or create a more benign social environment. This may involve helping the patient to change their social environment (e.g., by ending specific relationships). Hence, in addition to the content of what is discussed, MBT for trauma has a strong focus on the process of mentalizing and the process of change.

Finally, supervision is an essential component of MBT for trauma, as there is a constant risk of secondary or vicarious traumatization of the clinician, and of subsequent re-enactment in the clinician's relationships with others, including patients and members of the therapeutic team.

Specific Principles of MBT for Trauma

MBT for trauma follows a number of specific principles (summarized in Box 11.1). Of greatest importance, right from the start, are the first two principles—*fostering a trusting relationship* and *developing a formulation* with the patient. These have to be adopted in the context of considerable wariness and distrust shown by the patient. The attitude of the clinician—the not-knowing stance (see Chapter 3)—is key to this process. Although MBT for trauma does not follow a neat linear trajectory, and each intervention based on the principles may be applied throughout treatment, they are listed here in the order in which they are central to the various phases of MBT, from the start of treatment to the ending phase.

1. **Psychoeducation:** Psychoeducational materials about the nature of (complex/attachment) trauma, its impact, and the structure of the MBT program are provided and discussed with the patient. This fosters the patient's mentalizing, increases their sense of agency, and decreases their epistemic vigilance.
2. **Validating and normalizing feelings:** Trauma patients typically feel that what they have experienced is beyond anything that other people have experienced and they dare not speak about it, particularly when they also have strong feelings of shame, guilt, and/or anxiety. Moreover, many trauma patients believe that they have to be able to bear these experiences alone, however traumatic they have been. Therefore normalizing and validating interventions that reframe the patient's experience in terms of understandable responses to trauma not only reinforce a sense of emotional connection, but also spark mutual understanding between the patient and the clinician, leading to the re-emergence of mentalizing and epistemic trust. In this way the clinician also communicates that even supposedly "intolerable" feelings can be tolerated and talked about.
3. **Mentalizing traumatic experiences and their impact**: Once the patient's mentalizing capacities are more robust, specific traumatic events can be "micro-sliced," with

careful monitoring of the patient's anxiety and arousal. Micro-slicing is used to help the patient to mentalize traumatic experiences and their impact on the patient and their relationships. Initially the focus is on fostering the process of mentalizing, rather than on making sense of the content of what the patient is describing. As treatment progresses and the patient's mentalizing becomes more robust, alternative and more adaptive ways of looking at the past and its influence on the present become possible.

4. **Improving emotion regulation strategies:** This is achieved by considering and discussing alternative and more adaptive ways of regulating emotions. As the patient's need to externalize unmentalized traumatic experiences decreases, their need to use maladaptive emotion regulation strategies typically also diminishes.
5. **Salutogenesis and fostering changes in interpersonal relationships**: Improvements in mentalizing, emotion regulation, and epistemic trust allow a greater focus on salutogenesis and fostering changes in interpersonal relationships. As the patient's tendency to re-enact traumatic experiences decreases, they can begin to experiment with new ways of being in relationships, and the clinician needs to actively support these efforts. This may also include supporting the patient to end maladaptive attachment relationships and to bring about other positive changes in their social environment.

Box 11.1 Specific MBT principles in the treatment of trauma.

- Develop a trusting relationship.
- Formulate aims collaboratively.
- Provide psychoeducation about trauma and mentalizing.
- Validate and normalize feelings in relation to trauma.
- Manage anxiety and dissociation.
- Improve emotion regulation.
- Mentalize traumatic experiences ("micro-slice" events) and their personal impact.
- Address interpersonal relationships and salutogenesis.

MBT-TF: A Group-Based Modular Program with Some Individual Sessions

MBT-TF follows a group-based modular approach to trauma that can be offered either as a stand-alone treatment or before a full course of MBT. Individual sessions are offered at the beginning of treatment to develop the formulation (as described in Chapter 4) and to identify core aspects of trauma that will be discussed in the group. In addition, individual sessions may be offered if necessary to support the patient's work in the group. The program follows principles of treatment common to other applications of MBT (see Chapters 4 and 5). MBT-TF is divided into three phases that mirror the three communication systems described in Chapter 2, based on the principle that stability in each phase is necessary for effective communication before moving on to the intervention in the next phase. The first phase focuses on stabilization and the development of emotional and personal safety, the second phase focuses on processing trauma memory, and the third phase focuses on mourning the developmental and relational loss associated with trauma, and looking forward to the future.

Phase 1: Establishing Safety, Group Values, and the Framework of Treatment

The key aims of the initial sessions in the MBT-TF group are to establish safety with others and to outline the framework of treatment. As a result, the focus is on participants meeting each other, agreeing group values, psychoeducation, and practicing anxiety management. The sessions in this phase include:

1. agreeing shared group values
2. psychoeducation:
    - the impact of trauma on the mind and the body
    - the window of tolerance
    - epistemic trust
    - emotion regulation—anxiety, shame, and avoidance
    - dissociation, flashbacks, and nightmares
    - introduction to mentalizing
    - non-mentalizing states
    - mentalizing, me as a person, and relationships (alien self)
3. building relationships in the group
4. learning to recognize and manage anxiety, dissociation, and other emotions (in oneself and in each other).

During phase 1 the clinician asks the patients to refrain from discussing details of their personal trauma history, and does not engage in exposure and exploration of any individual events. One at a time the patients introduce themselves to the other members of the group and are asked to say something about themselves in relation to their decision to ask for referral to MBT, and a little about their personal life (similar to what they would say if they were meeting someone new in a social situation). Establishing group values (discussed in Chapter 5) is essential in MBT groups for trauma if safety is to be maintained throughout the running of the group. Clinicians email the agreed group values to the patients after the session, asking them to reflect on them, and both clinicians and patients refer back to the values whenever the cohesion and "we-ness" of interactions in the group is threatened. Group values that have been discussed and found useful by patients include the following:

- when we feel overwhelmed, letting the group know
- fairness—how we use a shared space together
- tolerance—respecting different opinions and perspectives
- recognizing that we come with good intentions—trusting others
- kindness toward each other
- open communication—saying what we really think on the inside
- checking in with how other people are feeling
- giving each other feedback
- safety and sensitivity when interacting with each other
- confidentiality.

Once safety has been established, and knowledge and understanding of mentalizing as the organizing principle of processing trauma have been embedded, phase 2 can start.

Phase 2: Mentalizing Trauma

The work in the MBT-TF group on mentalizing the trauma has two primary strands:

1. *mentalizing the feelings and thoughts surrounding the trauma* in terms of how they are processed and experienced through different memory systems
2. *mentalizing relationships affected by the trauma* in terms of how they function and are processed and experienced through different memory systems and ultimately impact on the participant's lived experience.

Mentalizing the Feelings and Thoughts Surrounding the Trauma

This process is one of linking and integration. Fragmented experiences and memories that trigger intense anxiety and avoidance because they are experienced in psychic equivalence are mentalized through a carefully and systematically implemented process of gradual elaboration, using the framework outlined in Table 11.4.

As we described earlier, experiences become traumatic through not being shared or experienced in a way that makes the individual feel that they are with someone in the experience ("we-mode"). The group setting is used to focus joint attention on the traumatic event through the following stepwise procedure:

1. recall
2. reflection (implications)
3. reflecting on the reflection (*meta-reflection*, or reflecting on the implications) while maintaining the experience with sufficient vividness to enable everyone in the group to appreciate the feeling(s) that accompanied the experience historically, in the present, and in reflecting on the present.

In practice, this stepwise procedure is not "stepped" in any rigid form. The process has to be undertaken sensitively, so the steps should be implemented dynamically and informed by the patient's level of mentalizing as they engage in the tasks. The clinician constantly monitors the mentalizing capacity of the patient in the moment, and supports the re-establishment of stable mentalizing at any point when it becomes vulnerable to collapse.

The combination of these steps (whether they are taken together or not) will achieve the mentalizing of the traumatic memory. The making of connections between the experience of recall and the memory itself ("remembering remembering") is an important step in mentalizing the trauma, and may need to be repeated often.

Affective Reflection

Fully mentalizing traumatic experiences requires the capacity for *affective reflection*—that is, an integration of feelings and thoughts (which could be referred to as "felt feelings," combining the experience with the reflection on the experience). Affective reflection is achieved by gradually elaborating the trauma narrative, bringing in the evocative detail of feelings that need to be reflected on in the immediate present and also in relation to the group, and ultimately attempting to experience and reflect on the group's feelings in relation to the experience. In short, this is mentalizing within

Table 11.4 Framework for mentalizing affects and memories

Memory	Retrieving and starting to create a narrative of past experience (*What was he wearing at the time?*)	Affective reflection on elaborated elements, elaborating on the narrative, clarifying and enriching it (*What feelings go with that memory? Are there any thoughts that acompany it?*)	Affective reflection on current feelings in terms of past experience, spelling out the implications of the memory (*How does the memory affect you? What feelings do you have at the moment, as you remember it?*), and affective reflection on current feelings while talking in the group	Affective reflection on current feelings in relation to others in the group (*How might others see your experience?*), and initial testing out of expectations about others' experience (*Is what she thinks what you really thought?*)
Autobiographical: What happened?	X			
Emotional/ implicit: What emotions are linked to it?	X	X	X	X
Procedural: What actions do you take to deal with it/cope/?			X	X
Semantic: What does it mean about you as a person?		X	X	

self-experience ("I-mode"), mentalizing others and their mind states ("me-mode"), and mentalizing others about self ("personalized me-mode") (for further discussion of these modes, see Chapters 6 and 7). All of these processes represent different levels of complexity of mentalizing.

The patient is asked to talk openly about their trauma narrative while the rest of the group listens attentively with minimal interruptions. Once the patient has finished speaking, the group participants are encouraged to help the patient to elaborate on the feelings related to the trauma at the time, along with their current feelings about the trauma. Importantly, the group participants and the clinician do this as *conversational partners*, asking questions and making comments that are "with" the patient (i.e., empathic validation of their experience) rather than "to" the patient (i.e., avoiding giving excessive reassurance, making suggestions, or offering solutions). The aim is to accompany the patient and to prevent them from avoiding over-elaboration of the trauma narrative. This process activates the autobiographical and implicit emotional memory, the "there and then," and it can be painful and frightening.

During the processing sessions, it is important for the clinician to be curious about the narrative, with an explicit focus on opening up the story rather than trying to make links or meaning. The clinician will need to remind the group that there is no right or wrong way to do this task, and that the aim is to create connections between the memories in the past and the present, as trauma memories are fragmented.

Clinical Example: Lydia (continued)

CLINICIAN: Lydia, tell us in your own words what happened and what pieces keep coming back into your mind that trouble you, and we will listen and try to accompany you as you talk.

CLINICIAN: Get your mind back to then. What does it feel like as an innocent girl experiencing that?

CLINICIAN: Can you describe your immediate feeling and then how you felt as a person later?

CLINICIAN: What was it like at school with friends at that time?

CLINICIAN: Was there anyone you could talk to?

As we explained earlier, this process is not a stepwise experience but flows relatively smoothly and serves the purpose of embedding the memory as mentalized and reflected-upon experience. The nature of embedding entails activating different types of memory at selected points. The initial memory experience and description are autobiographical and implicit/emotional. However, the affective reflection should also aim to explore ways in which the memory is retained not simply as the autobiographical memory of the event but also as it affects the patient's behavior—that is, the way the patient has come to act in order to manage or cope with what they have experienced is also reflected on.

Clinical Example: Lydia (continued)

CLINICIAN: Taking that feeling, can you say something about when you have the same feeling now and how you cope with it?

CLINICIAN: Does it make you go into "doing mode"? If so, what happens?

CLINICIAN: How is it affecting your life now? Thinking about that, what sort of judgment do you have on yourself? Are you forgiving or punishing, for example, in how you treat yourself?

A further, more complex part of this process involves exploring how the traumatic experience continues to affect the patient more generally—that is, how the experience has shaped their self-perception—and to address how, for example, aspects of a traumatic event may have led patients to see themselves as bad or guilty.

Clinical Example: Lydia (continued)

CLINICIAN: So let's have a discussion about how you see yourself when you feel like that.

CLINICIAN: Perhaps the group can say afterwards whether they pick up that feeling you have about yourself, so we can think about it together.

The clinician diverts the other group members from saying "*I don't see you like that,*" as they will naturally do this and also offer reassurances such as "*You are not like that*" or "*You shouldn't feel like that. It was not your fault.*" Instead, the clinician tries to steer the group members to consider what aspects of the patient come across to them as showing the feeling they are describing. For example, if the patient is discussing shame, the group members can say what they observe and experience about the patient that reveals the patient's underlying personal sense of shame, and even what they experience about the patient that communicates that they are trying to cope with it or hide it—that is, how does it come across to others? The aim is to encourage the patient to begin to reflect on the expression of their shame in the context of interacting with others: "*How do I see myself and how do they see me when I am like this? What effect does this have on my relationship with others in the group?*"

There will naturally be reluctance to engage in this exercise, which may be expressed as thought avoidance in the following ways:

- slipping into generalities rather than contemplating memories of the specific traumatic episode
- refusal to contemplate the experience
- destruction of thought (dissociation).

The clinician needs to tackle these responses as they arise. Moving between memory systems may be one way in which the group members engage in avoidance, particularly moving into the level of meanings before the specific experience has been explored. A rapid closure of working with implicit emotional memory and moving on to the activation of semantic memory will usher in pretend mode; this will lead to a severing of affect and thought, and to ever-increasing generality and discussion that is detached and devoid of meaningful content. The clinician who is working with the group should try to keep these sudden mental shifts to a minimum while managing the participants' anxiety by using the positive support that the group can offer the patient in this process, modeling encouragement, elaboration, and support.

Mentalizing Relationships Affected by the Trauma

We assume that if communication is opened up within the participant's social network, achievements within the group are more likely to generalize to all of the domains of that individual's social experience. Ideally the exploration of relationships would happen alongside the exploration of traumatic experiences, but in reality it often follows it. However, the exploration of relationships should follow the same structure of affective reflection as that outlined earlier, moving from reflection on immediate relationship experience to reflecting on the implications. Again, the clinician keeps in mind the range of mentalizing components:

1. the experience of past relationships along with the trauma experience and how they played out together

2. reflection on the relationships of the past self from the perspective of the current self looking back
3. experience of the self in the exploration now
4. current relationships as they are experienced in the patient's life and in the group.

Each participant's social network is usually naturally explored by the group. This is facilitated by using a relational map, which can initially be done in the formulation with the individual patients but is now actively used in the group to formalize the exploratory work.

Phase 3: Review, Reappraisal, and Looking to the Future

Care should be taken when planning the MBT-TF group to ensure that there are 4–6 weeks remaining after completion of the sessions that constitute phase 2. The sessions in the final phase are structured in a similar way to those of MBT-G (see Chapter 5), with an initial go-around and check-in with the participants, followed by agreeing a focus for the session, sharing the time between participants so that all of them have space to talk about the issues that they have raised, and integrating topics raised in the session with previous discussions about the processing of trauma that took place during earlier sessions. Patients are asked to explore different perceptions of themselves, looking back on themselves in the light of their new understanding of themselves in the present. This supports the start of a process of reflection on the impact that their negative perception of themselves has had on their lives. If treatment has gone well, trauma reactions are reflected on as understandable but avoidable—going into fight/flight or "shutdown" mode is no longer necessary, and secondary attachment strategies are muted, so that the patients feel less anxious in their relationships.

The focus in phase 3 is also on what has been achieved, thinking about the ending of the group and what this brings up for group members in terms of previous loss, as well as revisiting and reviewing their initial hopes and expectations about treatment. The sessions focus on what the patients have noticed about themselves and each other since the start of the treatment, and involve reflecting on the experience of talking about their traumatic memories. Are they more compassionate toward themselves and forgiving of their problems in their current relationships? Can they accept their past as being "there and then," rather than experiencing it in the "here and now"? Have they built a more coherent life narrative of themselves, and do they no longer need to avoid memories? Do past memories no longer trigger low-mentalizing modes, so that they are less painful and less destabilizing of the present self? Are the patients able to think about themselves coherently across time and be present with others in their current life, rather than being an outsider looking in?

The final sessions provide an opportunity to reflect on what the patients have found useful from the group and what they want to keep hold of in the future. It is helpful at this stage to revisit the initial values of the group and to ask the participants to reflect on those values and decide whether they are relevant to how they will continue to interact with others in their lives.

Concluding Remarks

This chapter describes the mentalizing approach to the conceptualization and treatment of patients with trauma. From a mentalizing perspective, trauma is thought to disrupt the coordinated functioning of a number of key biobehavioral systems, including the stress, attachment, mentalizing, and epistemic trust systems. Complex trauma (or attachment trauma) in particular leads to a cascade of disruptions in these systems, leaving the affected individual prone to closing themselves off from the social environment and at risk of re-enacting traumatic experiences. This often leads them to be perceived as difficult to treat or "hard to reach." MBT provides a systematic approach to the management and treatment of individuals who have experienced trauma. This approach may be particularly helpful in patients with a history of more complex attachment trauma, as it provides a comprehensive and coherent approach to addressing the major features of these patients.

References

1. Luyten P, Campbell C, Fonagy P. Borderline personality disorder, complex trauma, and problems with self and identity: a social-communicative approach. *J Pers* 2020; **88**: 88–105.
2. Asnes AG, Leventhal JM. Connecting the dots in childhood and adolescent trauma. *Arch Pediatr Adolesc Med* 2011; **165**: 87–9.
3. Teicher MH, Samson JA. Childhood maltreatment and psychopathology: a case for ecophenotypic variants as clinically and neurobiologically distinct subtypes. *Am J Psychiatry* 2013; **170**: 1114–33.
4. Anda RF, Felitti VJ, Bremner JD et al. The enduring effects of abuse and related adverse experiences in childhood: a convergence of evidence from neurobiology and epidemiology. *Eur Arch Psychiatry Clin Neurosci* 2006; **256**: 174–86.
5. Fonagy P, Luyten P, Allison E, Campbell C. What we have changed our minds about: Part 1. Borderline personality disorder as a limitation of resilience. *Borderline Personal Disord Emot Dysregul* 2017; **4**: 11.
6. Fonagy P, Luyten P, Allison E, Campbell C. What we have changed our minds about: Part 2. Borderline personality disorder, epistemic trust and the developmental significance of social communication. *Borderline Personal Disord Emot Dysregul* 2017; **4**: 9.
7. Allen JG. *Coping with Trauma: Hope Through Understanding*, 2nd ed. Washington, DC: American Psychiatric Association Publishing, 2005.
8. Fonagy P, Steele M, Steele H et al. The Emanuel Miller Memorial Lecture 1992. The theory and practice of resilience. *J Child Psychol Psychiatry* 1994; 35: 231–57.
9. Fonagy P, Target M. Attachment, trauma, and psychoanalysis: where psychoanalysis meets neuroscience. In: Jurist EJ, Slade A, Bergner S, eds. *Mind to Mind: Infant Research, Neuroscience, and Psychoanalysis*. New York: Other Press, 2008; 15–49.
10. Allen JG, Lemma A, Fonagy P. Trauma. In: Bateman AW, Fonagy P, eds. *Handbook of Mentalizing in Mental Health Practice*. Washington, DC: American Psychiatric Association, 2012; 419–44.
11. Allen JG. *Mentalizing in the Development and Treatment of Attachment Trauma*. London, UK: Karnac Books Ltd, 2013.
12. Fonagy P, Luyten P, Allison E. Epistemic petrification and the restoration of epistemic trust: a new conceptualization of borderline personality disorder and its psychosocial treatment. *J Pers Disord* 2015; **29**: 575–609.
13. Bonanno GA, Diminich ED. Annual Research Review: Positive adjustment to adversity—trajectories of minimal-impact resilience and emergent resilience. *J Child Psychol Psychiatry* 2013; **54**: 378–401.
14. Southwick SM, Bonanno GA, Masten AS et al. Resilience definitions, theory, and challenges: interdisciplinary perspectives.

Eur J Psychotraumatol 2014; **5**. https://doi.org/10.3402/ejpt.v5.25338.

15. Denckla CA, Mancini AD, Consedine NS et al. Distinguishing postpartum and antepartum depressive trajectories in a large population-based cohort: the impact of exposure to adversity and offspring gender. *Psychol Med* 2018: 48: 1139–47.
16. Orcutt HK, Bonanno GA, Hannan SM, Miron LR. Prospective trajectories of posttraumatic stress in college women following a campus mass shooting. *J Traum Stress* 2014; **27**: 249–56.
17. Pervanidou P, Chrousos GP. Metabolic consequences of stress during childhood and adolescence. *Metabolism* 2012; **61**: 611–19.
18. McEwen BS. Physiology and neurobiology of stress and adaptation: central role of the brain. *Physiol Rev* 2007; **87**: 873–904.
19. Gunnar M, Quevedo K. The neurobiology of stress and development. *Annu Rev Psychol* 2007; **58**: 145–73.
20. Gunnar MR, Quevedo K, De Kloet RE et al. Early care experiences and HPA axis regulation in children: a mechanism for later trauma vulnerability. *Prog Brain Res* 2007; **167**: 137–49.
21. Feldman R. The neurobiology of human attachments. *Trends Cogn Sci* 2017; **21**: 80–99.
22. Fredrickson BL. The role of positive emotions in positive psychology: the broaden-and-build theory of positive emotions. *Am Psychol* 2001; **56**: 218–26.
23. Mikulincer M, Shaver PR. Enhancing the "broaden and build" cycle of attachment security in adulthood: from the laboratory to relational contexts and societal systems. *Int J Environ Res Public Health* 2020; **17**: 2054.
24. Miller GE, Chen E, Zhou ES. If it goes up, must it come down? Chronic stress and the hypothalamic-pituitary-adrenocortical axis in humans. *Psychol Bull* 2007; **133**: 25–45.
25. Luyten P, Fonagy P. An integrative, attachment-based approach to the management and treatment of patients with persistent somatic complaints. In: Hunter J, Maunder R, eds. *Improving Patient Treatment with Attachment Theory: A Guide for Primary Care Practitioners and Specialists*. New York, NY: Springer, 2016; 127–44.
26. Arnsten AFT. The biology of being frazzled. *Science* 1998; **280**: 1711–12.
27. Mayes LC. A developmental perspective on the regulation of arousal states. *Semin Perinatol* 2000; **24**: 267–79.
28. Fonagy P, Gergely G, Jurist EL, Target M. Developmental issues in normal adolescence and adolescent breakdown. In: *Affect Regulation, Mentalization, and the Development of the Self*. New York: Other Press, 2002; 317–40.
29. Jurist EL. Mentalized affectivity. *Psychoanal Psychol* 2005; **22**: 426–44.
30. Widom CS. Posttraumatic stress disorder in abused and neglected children grown up. *Am J Psychiatry* 1999; **156**: 1223–9.
31. Cloitre M, Scarvalone P, Difede J. Posttraumatic stress disorder, self- and interpersonal dysfunction among sexually retraumatized women. *J Traum Stress* 1997; **10**: 437–52.
32. Allen JG. *Traumatic Relationships and Serious Mental Disorders*. Chichester UK: John Wiley & Sons Ltd, 2001.
33. Main M, Hesse E. Parents' unresolved traumatic experiences are related to infant disorganized attachment status: is frightened and/or frightening parental behavior the linking mechanism? In: Greenberg MT, Cicchetti D, Cummings EM, eds. *Attachment in the Preschool Years: Theory, Research, and Intervention*. Chicago, IL: University of Chicago Press, 1990; 161–81.
34. Clarkin JF, Kernberg OF, Yeomans F. *Transference-Focused Psychotherapy for Borderline Personality Disorder Patients*. New York, NY: The Guilford Press, 1999.
35. Cicchetti D, Toth SL. Child maltreatment. *Annu Rev Clin Psychol* 2005; **1**: 409–38.
36. Antonovsky A. *Unraveling the Mystery of Health: How People Manage Stress and Stay Well*. San Francisco, CA: Jossey-Bass, 1987.

37. Storebo OJ, Stoffers-Winterling JM, Vollm BA et al. Psychological therapies for people with borderline personality disorder. *Cochrane Database Syst Rev* 2020; **5**: CD012955.

38. Bateman A, Motz A, Yakeley J. Antisocial personality disorder in community and prison settings. In: Bateman A, Fonagy P, eds. *Handbook of Mentalizing in Mental Health Practice*, 2nd ed. Washington, DC: American Psychiatric Association Publishing, 2019; 335–49.

39. Smits ML, Luyten P, Feenstra DJ et al. Trauma and outcomes of mentalization-based therapy for individuals with borderline personality disorder. *Am J Psychother* 2022; **75**: 12–20.

Part III

Application and Adaptations for Mental Health Presentations

Chapter 12

Eating Disorders

Introduction

The model of mentalizing is highly relevant to furthering both our understanding of and clinical practice relating to eating disorders [1]. Severely impaired mentalizing in patients with eating disorders may account for the severe emotional and cognitive fluctuations that contribute to symptom maintenance, compromise the response to therapeutic intervention, affect the capacity of the patient to engage with psychosocial treatment, and destabilize the clinician's mentalizing, with the consequent risk of enactments or iatrogenic effects.

Mentalization-based treatment for eating disorders (MBT-ED) is not an evidence-based therapy at the time of writing, and should be offered as part of, or supplementary to, a better-established therapy such as the Maudsley Model of Anorexia Nervosa Treatment for Adults (MANTRA)—a manualized individual treatment for young adult patients with anorexia nervosa (AN) that was developed by Schmidt et al. [2]. MANTRA is the first-line psychological intervention for adults with AN [3]. This intervention is centered around a patient's workbook that combines elements of cognitive–behavioral therapy (e.g., a diagrammatic case formulation that focuses on maintaining factors) and writing tasks, supporting emotion expression and regulation, based on the seminal ideas of James Pennebaker [4]; it shares elements with an MBT approach (e.g., motivational interviewing techniques) [5]. If an eating disorder presents with co-occurring borderline personality disorder (BPD), MBT-ED can be recommended as a reasonable approach. A randomized controlled trial found MBT-ED to be superior to a control treatment, although it should be noted that there was a very high level of participant dropout in this trial [6]. However, MBT-ED is supported by considerable evidence of specific shortcomings in mentalizing in individuals with eating disorders. This suggests that clinicians working with patients with eating disorders might find it helpful to be aware of these patients' mentalizing anomalies, and that further development and validation of MBT-ED may be warranted. Establishing the evidence base for MBT-ED remains at an early stage.

Mentalizing in Eating Disorders

Embodied Mentalizing

Hilda Bruch, a pioneer of the modern psychodynamic treatment of eating disorders, should be credited with being the first to draw attention to mentalizing anomalies that are characteristic of eating disorders, particularly AN. She noted that her patients commonly lacked awareness of inner experiences and failed to rely on their subjectivity, feelings, thoughts, and bodily sensations to control their behavior; this contributed to a frequent sense of lack of control, which they compensated for by extraordinary demonstrations of determination to assert their identity, competence, and effectiveness through physical or bodily experience [7,8]. We would now consider experiencing the mind via the body—*embodied mentalizing*—to be a key and foundational aspect of ordinary mentalizing [9,10], and view Bruch's clinical observations as a recognition of distortions in the developmental processes related to embodied mentalizing (for further discussion of embodied mentalizing, see Chapter 9). The infant's first experiences of the self being recognized are through bodily contact with a caregiver who accurately perceives momentary changes in the infant's self-states. A caregiver's bodily (i.e., non-verbal) responsiveness to the infant's physical cues of feelings and wishes predicts the infant's socioemotional experience in early childhood, including attachment security at 15 and 36 months of age, and language abilities, academic skills, behavior problems, and social competence at 54 months of age [11–13]. Furthermore, caregiver responsiveness is reduced by parenting stress [14] and postpartum depression [15], highlighting it as a potential mediator of these risk factors for typical development.

The Ineffective/Non-Mentalizing Modes

In the early years of the twenty-first century, Fonagy et al. [16] proposed a mentalizing model of disordered eating. This model suggested that eating disorders might involve an inappropriately persistent emphasis on embodied mentalizing into adolescence, and difficulty in representing mental states as ideas or feelings rather than as bodily experiences: "Physical attributes such as weight come to reflect states such as internal well-being, control, sense of self-worth, and so on, far beyond the normal tendency for this to happen in adolescence" [16, p. 405]. They described the experience of individuals with eating disorders in terms of the three hallmarks of ineffective mentalizing (for a detailed description of the non-mentalizing modes, see Chapter 2):

- "Inside-Out" thinking, or the excessive certainty of psychic equivalence
- "elephant in the room" thinking, or the excessive uncertainty of pretend mode
- the "quick fix" or "Outside-In" thinking of teleological mode.

Psychic Equivalence

In psychic equivalence, bodily metaphors do not function mainly as *representations*, which are capable of containing an experience, but as *presentations*, which are experienced as concrete facts or parts of reality that are impossible to negotiate or compromise. In psychic equivalence, "as if" turns into "is." There is no possibility of alternative constructions of reality beyond the harsh corporeality of immediate experience. Normal weight-related thoughts become oppressive.

Clinical Example: Psychic Equivalence Thinking

"I just knew that thin was attractive, desirable. It was everything that was good. I had always known it, but it somehow became like an edict."

The mere thought of food can be experienced as actually eating it and potentially causing weight gain: *"I would have a 'bad thought' about a cake in a shop window. Then I would think that I had eaten it and then I would have to exercise the corresponding amount to lose the weight."*

Negative beliefs about the self feel real: "*I had no right to exist. I was a fraud. I felt like a cuckoo in the nest, alien, too big, too obtrusive, unwanted. Not fitting in.*"

These examples from the narratives of patients who had recovered from AN offer indications that a mental event (a thought, belief, or wish), although recognized as internal, has the same status for the patient as physical reality. The impression of the body and its appearance becomes equated with the self.

Pretend Mode

The emergence of the non-mentalizing pretend mode also suggests that subjectivity is separated from physical reality. This may be most apparent in the pervasiveness of the self-deception that can dominate the mental states of patients with eating disorders: "*I was cheating, eating things that had no calories in them—cabbage, carrots, celery. But while I was doing it I kind of believed it was nutritious.*" Decoupling of thoughts and feelings from reality (*pseudomentalizing* or *hypermentalizing*) leads to feelings of emptiness, meaninglessness, and even dissociation, which are sometimes dealt with by overeating, bingeing and purging. The pretend reality is protected by the consistent rejection of alternative realities that threaten the pretend mode, which may drive the secretive and isolated nature of eating disorders.

Clinical Example: Pretend Mode Thinking

"*I spent a lot of time trying to hide from people. I was more conscious of how they would see me rather than how I would see myself. They might interfere if they noticed I was anorexic. I wore lots of baggy clothes, ate minimal-calorie meals, and I would try to hide it from people because I thought they would not understand why I was doing it. I did not have the thought that I was anorexic, rather the thought that other people might think I was and would not understand. Occasionally, people would comment and I would get angry and feel intruded on—anxious that they would try to stop me.*"

The protection of this imagined version of reality also manifests as an exaggerated pursuit of self-control to avoid the threat presented by seeing oneself through the eyes of others (social perception): "*I often needed to re-assert myself, which I did* (by purging, bingeing, self-harm). *When I didn't eat for a while, I was in control—so much better than the feeling that nothing meant anything, which I dreaded.*"

In therapy, pretend mode generates endless inconsequential narratives about thoughts, feelings, and interpersonal scenarios that are disconnected from the patient's experienced reality and are felt as meaningless: "*After my first session I knew what I had to say. I said it. I just talked about 'what food meant to me,' I talked about feeling rejected by everyone. It meant nothing. She* [the therapist] *lapped it up. After the sessions I felt quite pleased. 'I could be good at this,' I thought.*"

Teleological Mode

The prominence of teleological mode in patients with eating disorders is suggested by indications that physical action is seen as the only way to alter or manage their mental states. The over-valuing of physical appearance is of course itself teleological, and motivates the patient to engage in behaviors that constitute symptoms of AN and bulimia nervosa (BN). Bodily modifications (e.g., change in body weight, self-harm) occur in the physical domain and are observable, and therefore directly affect mental states. The illusion that the mind can be controlled through controlling the body is a core belief in AN.

Clinical Example: Teleological Mode Thinking

"If I triumphed over my body I triumphed over my mind."

"Being thin keeps me protected."

"Being physically at risk gives me control over the people around me."

"I hope to arrive at something indescribable and good inside that will make others behave differently toward me."

The view that risk and danger, often of social exclusion, are reduced by teleological thinking is implicit in these beliefs. If the external state and appearance of one's body are believed to provide the solution to the problem of achieving a sense of social value, then confusion about what "feeling valued" might actually involve is inevitable. Critically, external markers of self-worth are the only ones that feel real or true: *"I just knew that the perfect body shape would make me wanted, irresistible. It was just that I came to have a crazy idea about what that shape looked like. But I knew that if I achieved it I would be in my perfect place."*

The Wish for a Non-Mentalizing Space

The emergence of the non-mentalizing modes can be seen as part of an active wish to stop thinking and feeling because this generates anxiety and confusion—or, to put it bluntly, to stop mentalizing.

Clinical Example: Closing Down Mentalizing

Clinician *(addressing a patient who had recovered from AN):* What was it like for you being anorexic? Do you remember what thoughts and feelings you had at the time?

Patient: Just being very focused on what I had to do during the day and not having to think about the things that I would have to think about normally. I had been quite introspective before. I had to drive out any mental experience and just focus on what had to be done. Not question things. My experience of everything was rather flat and empty.

Another patient who had also recovered from an eating disorder gave a very similar account:

Patient: Especially anything to do with eating, or getting food ready, or actually eating it, I would do in a very, very mechanical state in which I was not thinking or feeling anything. I was going through the motions in a very ritualized way. I did things like buying stuff from the same place so I wouldn't have to think about it. I remember feeling physical hunger and the satisfaction that I was not giving in to it was the only important thing.

Typically, these retrospective reports capture the experience of an existence marked by a rigid separation of mental and bodily experience. As we described in Chapters 2 and 10, mentalizing has an integrative function—it helps us to draw together our sensory experiences and thoughts to support our sense of self. The shutting down of the possibility of this mentalized self-integration can create a disjointed experience of selfhood.

Clinical Example: Disjointed Experience of Selfhood

Patient: I felt mechanical. I felt my emotions controlled my secret behavior. My mind, my official mind, controlled my public behavior and there was no connection between them. That was something that I had not felt before. There were whole periods of time where I felt like [I was] a spectator, I did not feel I was in my head or in control of what I was doing. This is what I meant by mechanical. I was watching it and managing it.

The pervasive failure of mentalizing and the accompanying loss of its integrative function can reveal pre-existing disorganization of the self-structure caused by social experiences that are known to increase the risk of development of eating disorders. Fonagy and Target suggested that the disengagement of mentalizing tends to reveal pre-existing discontinuities in the self-structure [17,18], and they proposed that disorganized early attachment can segue into discontinuities within the self, which can be amplified by trauma. When mentalizing has broken down, part of the self can be experienced as clusters of persecutory ideas that are felt to be coming from within the self but at the same time are alien to it—untouchable and separated from the self, with little opportunity for moderation or modification. We have referred to these internally tormenting parts of the self as the *alien self* (see also Chapters 2 and 10).

Clinical Example: The Alien Self

Patient: I felt like somebody outside myself was bullying me and not taking any notice of what I thought or felt. It was like being tortured by someone else.

Clinician: Tell me about this person . . .

Patient: Like a bully at school. Someone who did not care, who would just push and push. Totally unsympathetic, with no patience for any feebleness, who wanted to see if I was tough on myself and not at all self-indulgent.

Self-harm can be experienced as relief—a concrete act against these persecutory parts of the self that cannot be reached or regulated through cognition and can only be warded off through physical actions.

Stress and Mentalizing

Stress undermines mentalizing and occurs at toxic levels in individuals who are predisposed to it for various reasons or combinations of reasons, such as constitutionally heightened reactivity, the impact of adverse social experiences, or the physical stress generated by loss of body weight [19].

In our early thinking about the relationship between mentalizing and mental health disorders, we suggested that individual attachment histories and maltreatment may weaken or undermine the mentalizing capacities of individuals in adolescence, and impair their ability to manage everyday stressors as well as attachment stress [16]. Adolescence is a developmentally vulnerable stage even in the normal development of social cognition, but this does not in itself cause eating disorders. We suggested that eating disorders are the consequence of a relatively limited capacity to mentalize ordinary social experiences (e.g., excessive demand for excellence, difficulties going through puberty, or peer rejection), which makes current life experience feel like an insurmountable challenge. Difficulties in mentalizing may be associated with a history of trauma, childhood sexual abuse, early adversity, or neglect; the mentalizing difficulties result in the emergence of non-mentalizing modes when the individual is faced with the challenges of the social world. The disorganization of the psychological or mental self is a manifestation of the dominance of psychic equivalence, pretend mode, and teleological mode that is thought to be responsible for distorted cognitions, dysregulated affect, and a disorganized self-structure, which underpin the eating disorder.

Persistence of Anorexia Nervosa and Other Eating Disorders

Only around half of all patients who receive treatment for AN or BN achieve full recovery after 4–10 years [20], and the proportion does not increase much even after longer time periods [21]. Individuals with persistent AN frequently state that they wish to change but cannot do so [22]. Current models of AN do not distinguish stages of the disorder in which vulnerability and treatment interact to establish significant persistence. The current framework for the MBT model of eating disorders aims to separate several components that unfold across time, from first presentation of preoccupation with body weight and shape to the clinical threshold for weight loss, and finally to a chronic state characteristic of enduring disordered eating. Chronic starvation has an effect on mentalizing. According to mentalizing theory, anomalies of social cognition are seen as adaptations to the ordinary developmental challenges of adolescence in individuals who are vulnerable to eating disorders as a result of personality traits, early experience (including attachment history), and genetic predisposition. Mentalizing theory also views psychic equivalence, pretend mode, and teleological mode as the outcomes of imbalances between the poles of the dimensions of mentalizing (described in detail in Chapter 2). More recent theoretical and clinical discussions about applications of the MBT model have emphasized the role of the social group around an individual in helping them to recover the ability to mentalize [23]. Some individuals might lack a mentalizing social group around them, or they might withdraw from an already existing mentalizing social network for emotional reasons. In individuals with AN, the process of normal recovery of mentalizing may be compromised by the reactions of others to the eating disorder, which are often characterized by anxiety, fear, and frustration; this creates a disconnect because the individual with AN feels that their weight loss is desirable and therefore, feeling misunderstood and perhaps ashamed, they withdraw from the social environment that would normally support their mentalizing [24,25]. The combined impact of social withdrawal and the persistent struggle with mentalizing (again in the context of the known vulnerability factors for AN) generates powerful feelings of epistemic mistrust and epistemic hypervigilance (see Chapter 2 and also [23]). As the person's beliefs about weight, eating, and body shape are not understood by those in their community, they voluntarily abandon the community and their mentalizing is not recovered; this in turn deepens their mistrust and leads to further social withdrawal, making the recovery of mentalizing even more unlikely. Moreover, the traumatic aspects of medical interventions, such as feeding experiences in inpatient or outpatient settings, can further increase mistrust and closing of the patient's mind to information from their social environment, as well as reinforcing their aversive cognitions about food. An additional process that drives persistence of eating disorders relates to chronic stress, which may relate to an overactivation of the fight/flight response that is incompatible with the recovery of mentalizing [19].

Conceptualizing the Complexity of Eating Disorders

The mentalizing model views the symptoms of eating disorders as attempted solutions to underlying problems of social (self-)regulation. We assume that at the core of eating disorders is a social dysfunction consequent to exposure to adverse social interactions, compounded by emotion dysregulation undermined by biological factors and heightened levels of stress, and the disorganization of attachment relationships.

We propose that the social dysfunction that arises from the interaction of these risk factors causes the loss of balanced mentalizing, which—as we have noted throughout this book—is key to engagement in social communication (see Figure 12.1). The individual's loss of interest in social communication interferes with their social learning and the potential for social and self-correction that make change, remission, and recovery possible. The processes of ostension (the self-recognition that is key to accepting communications from others as relevant to the self, generalizable outside the specific and current context, and suitable for integration into a stable self-representation) are ineffective, leading to epistemic dysfunction—that is, epistemic hypervigilance and mistrust or, conversely, inappropriate credulity. The individual's social network is further compromised by external and internal shame, which reinforces social withdrawal and undermines the potential for the recovery of mentalizing that social support can

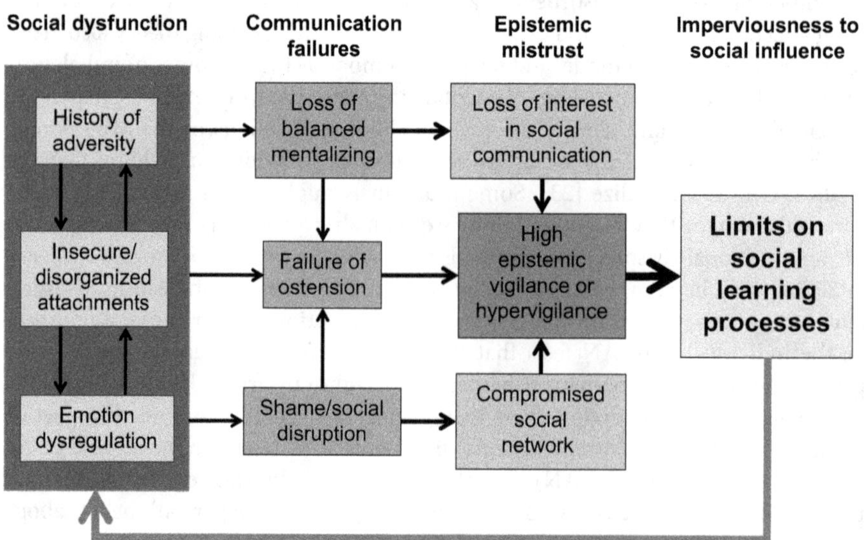

Fig. 12.1 Pathway to the limitations to social learning that lead to eating disorders.

provide. The overall result is imperviousness to social communication, and the persistence of beliefs (e.g., distorted beliefs about body shape) and strategies for emotional self-organization (e.g., control of eating, excessive exercise) that often make the patient inaccessible to change through psychological therapy.

This model is consistent with some early findings from studies of social cognition in eating disorders. There is evidence to suggest that social functioning is substantially impaired in AN, particularly as part of the cognitive interpersonal model first outlined by Schmidt and Treasure [26], with later work summarizing the cognitive and emotional traits and the perpetuating aspects underpinning the model [22,27,28]. The model proposed by Schmidt and Treasure has a great deal in common with MBT theory and its focus on the intrapersonal consequences of isolation, depression, and chronic stress that accumulate in the severe and enduring stage of the illness in a singular causal and maintenance framework. Most individuals with AN show interpersonal difficulties, with, for example, problems with intimacy [29]. Good social functioning is an important predictor of favorable outcomes in AN, whereas premorbid poor social relating, empathy deficits, and social interaction problems have been linked to poor outcomes [30]. Individuals with AN exhibit features of alexithymia [31] and social anhedonia [32] characterized by difficulties in describing subjective feeling states and distinguishing between feelings and bodily sensations, and an impoverished imagination, all of which point to difficulties in social functioning. Converging evidence for this assumption comes from a range of sources, including research on attachment, theory of mind (ToM) and mentalizing, and research on the cognitive and emotional capacities necessary for social self-regulation.

Attachment and Eating Disorders

The MBT theoretical model links vulnerability to eating disorders with insecure attachment, as it sees attachment relationships as the prototypical context within which interpersonal understanding naturally evolves in infancy and thrives in adult relationships [23]. A comprehensive review of the relationship between attachment and mentalizing and their association with child and adolescent eating pathology found 14 studies that demonstrated a positive correlation between attachment insecurity and eating disorders in childhood and adolescence [33]. Attachment insecurity in infancy was a weak predictor of eating pathology in childhood or adolescence, whereas attachment insecurity in the pre-adolescent period predicted the development of eating pathology 1 year later much more robustly. Significantly, attachment to peers, but not to parents, predicted eating pathology in mid-adolescence. Imbalances in mentalizing (i.e., ineffective mentalizing) mirror the association of attachment with eating disorders. Seven studies identified a correlation between problems with mentalizing and eating pathology. Strong associations were found between difficulties in emotion recognition and eating disorders in adolescents, and these associations were particularly strong in relation to AN. For adults, meta-analyses have provided mixed evidence, with some studies showing strong associations [34] and others reporting weaker associations [35] between attachment and eating disorders, mediated by emotion regulation and depressive symptoms [36]. More recently, a meta-analysis of 35 studies found higher rates of insecure attachment in clinical groups of individuals with eating disorders compared with community controls, with a large effect size, across measurement methods and different attachment dimensions [37]. Alongside insecure attachment, identity development is likely to be disrupted by other adverse childhood social experiences, such as childhood maltreatment, teasing, bullying, or social exclusion [38].

Theory of Mind and Social Cognition

Problems related to understanding self and others have long been observed in patients with AN and other eating disorders. There is evidence of a link between eating disorders and specific problems in mentalizing. In a meta-analysis, both BN and AN were found to be associated with significant deficits in ToM, which were more pronounced in the acute phase of illness but also observable in individuals who had recovered from AN [39]. The findings for AN were confirmed by further research [40]. It seems that both cognitive perspective taking and decoding of mental states may be impaired in patients with eating disorders [39]. Although in the acute phase of illness these impairments may be attributable to the direct effects of starvation on the brain, there is evidence that individuals with AN experience social difficulties premorbidly [41,42], and that these difficulties persist after recovery from the eating disorder [43]. Measures of drive for thinness, attachment, and quality of relationships suggest a substantial role for mentalizing and social cognition in eating disorders, even in individuals who are of normal weight [44]. In a study designed to evaluate the interactions between objective measures of mentalizing, empathy, and eating disorder symptomatology using a network analytic approach, inference of cognitive mental states and shape concern were the nodes with the highest centrality in the network [45]. A network analysis comprises a graphic representation of potential contributing factors for a disorder or social process. As an analogy, consider a stage with actors or groups of actors ("nodes") on it, who are contributing to a play—who or which group is center stage and contributing most to the theme of the play, who do they relate to, and what is the strength of that relationship? In this study, inference of emotional mental states was the node with the highest bridge strength in the cluster of social cognition functions, highlighting the importance of mentalizing abilities in that they contribute to the maintenance of eating disorder-related psychopathology and to capacity for empathy. Using computer-administered measures of mentalizing, empathy, and imitation (the degree to which observation of another's actions prompts the performance of those actions by the observer), people with eating disorders showed both hypermentalizing and hypomentalizing, and reduced accuracy of emotional and cognitive mental-state inference, compared with a matched control group of people without an eating disorder [46]. There was no difference in empathy between the groups, but the group of individuals with eating disorders showed less imitation of observed actions than the control group. Imitation is likely to be a distinct process that reflects implicit rather than explicit mentalizing, although it is likely that the two interact in determining everyday social competence [47,48]. As controlling for anxiety and depressive symptoms did not remove these significant effects [46], the study suggests that eating disorders may be directly linked to difficulties in mentalizing and social imitation. Taken together, these emerging findings with objective measures provide a reasonable indication that an intervention to strengthen mentalizing might help to improve the social symptoms exhibited by patients with eating disorders.

In restrictive eating disorders, starvation may contribute to an apparent deficit in social cognition via stress or other mechanisms [34]. This can serve as a motivation for maintaining low weight, because the avoidance or suppression of emotions helps to avoid conflict [43]. As is observed clinically, patients with AN show fear and avoidance of intense emotions, and it is possible that they may maintain a low body weight in order to avoid these emotions. The observation of avoidance of emotion and poor ToM in patients with eating disorders has led to the identification of features that are shared by autism and eating disorders [49], although the common ground is an overlap of problems in social cognition, and may not implicate many of those with eating disorders [50]. The predisposition to social withdrawal may be driven both by problems in social cognition and by the adverse emotional experience that these problems create, which is addressed through eating disorder symptomatology.

Social Self-Regulation in Eating Disorders

Hundreds of studies have measured constructs such as attachment, social communication, perception and understanding of self and others, and social dominance in people with eating disorders (for a review, see [34]). The findings, which are summarized in Box 12.1, are consistent with the hypothesis that a core dysfunction in eating disorders is related to the regulation and management of a social and emotional self.

Box 12.1 Summary of findings which suggest that regulation of the social self or the emotional self is a core component of eating disorders.

Social Self

- Negative self-evaluation.
- Self-absorbing rumination.
- Misalignment in social reciprocity.
- Interpersonal distrust and conflictual interaction.
- Low spontaneous social narrative.
- Problems in identifying the social salience of stimuli.
- Heightened sensitivity to threat in social situations (e.g., social comparison, social-rank cues).

Emotional Self

- Difficulties in recognizing complex emotions.
- Poor expression and regulation of emotion.
- Difficulties in identifying and describing one's own emotions.
- Problems with mentalizing others' emotions.
- Low capacity to manage negative emotions.
- Low trait emotional intelligence.

Of course, these limitations of social self-regulation, especially the deficit in emotional expression and lack of reciprocation of warmth, have an impact on others, who are likely to respond aversively and thus reinforce the pressure on social cognition and the desire for social isolation. Difficulties in emotional mentalizing in individuals with eating disorders have been shown to be associated with increased loneliness [46]. This supports the contribution of socio-cognitive impairment to the perceived poor quality of relationships that people with eating disorders have with their friends and relatives, and can lead to social exclusion and isolation, which is a defining facet of these disorders.

The Epistemic Mistrust Model of Eating Disorders: A Summary

Our developmental hypothesis about eating disorders starts with expectations based on normal development. To summarize briefly, being mentalized in the context of an attachment relationship generates epistemic trust, which in turn drives the ability to form and learn from social connections. Epistemic trust is key to social living, as it underpins the ability to reappraise oneself and adapt to one's social context via mentalizing and, where necessary, to repair, preserve, develop, and increase social connections, interpersonal understanding, and cooperation throughout life. Such openness to the (social) environment is usually adaptive, but in the context of adversity, epistemic hypervigilance may be equally adaptive. We assume that although epistemic hypervigilance is not a mental health issue, it is a potential source of vulnerability, as it reduces opportunities to benefit from social learning and diminishes the quality of social exchange that normally enhances mentalizing. This matters, as mentalizing helps individuals to step beyond the micro-trauma that accompanies all social existence. In other words, whereas epistemic trust generates resilience, epistemic mistrust may reduce an individual's ability to mentalize and to absorb the random shocks of social living by creating epistemic distance between them and their (benign) social context. The primary task of adolescence is the creation of a social network that can take advantage of the input of trusted others—both peers and elders. When the capacity to form bonds of trust is impaired, due to either predisposition (insecure attachment, social deprivation, social constraints, or other structural or individual reasons) or acute pressures on maintaining social connectedness (stress, shame, and social withdrawal), or both, the social network becomes weakened and may collapse catastrophically, leaving the individual in social isolation, with limited opportunity to recover mentalizing. In this non-mentalizing state there is an increased likelihood that they will experience the internal and external world with the exaggerated intensity of psychic equivalence and its counterpart—the meaninglessness and emptiness of pretend mode with the tendency to dissociation. To gain control and social self-regulation, teleological/action/"Outside-In" strategies may represent the only realistic response. However, these strategies—such as restricting, bingeing, or obsessively avoiding certain types of foods—generate their own problems.

We suggest that the range of different symptoms associated with eating disorders may share the common function of being attempts at social self-regulation. Genetic predisposition, early attachment history, adversity in childhood and adolescence (e.g., rejection, physical or verbal abuse), and social messages regarding body weight and shape all contribute to the intense experiences of shame associated with eating disorders, which can not only serve to intensify competitive attitudes and striving for perfection, but also increase the desire to avoid social participation. Shame leads to psychological social withdrawal or disengagement from a mentalizing community. When mentalizing is disavowed, psychic equivalence intensifies the experience of shame, which comes to be experienced as destructive to the self. In individuals with restricting eating disorders such as AN, the experience of excessive shame may drive a focus on greater internalization of beauty ideals (as a standard for defining the self), body image, and weight control. This is a teleological attempt to prevent (in line with cultural messaging) the envisioned negative social outcomes that are non-consciously conceptualized as catastrophic and permanent social exclusion. When this teleological manipulation is successful, the individual may experience pride (which again is intensified by psychic equivalence), which reinforces the beliefs and feelings that initiated the actions (e.g., restricted eating), because it avoids the negative experience of shame. When the self-control fails and the observable outcome is unsuccessful, the shame is intensified, along with the social withdrawal. Shame builds a wall of social exclusion, which undermines the potential for social learning and cognitive change that could modify the social experience of the self. In compassion-focused therapy this is often referred to as a "shame–pride cycle" [51].

Social self-regulation has similar effects in binge eating disorder, where non-mentalized experiences of shame generate emotional instability in interpersonal contexts. Bingeing is the teleological/action/"Outside-In" response which provides the emotion regulation that the individual's mentalizing capacity is unable to provide. It reduces the experience of shame and creates a pretend state (a "mental bubble") that psychologically distances the individual from the intense negative emotional experiences through (ultimately) dissociation. However, binge eating is not an effective way of managing shame, as bingeing itself has the potential to generate shame, creating the same epistemic distance between the individual and their social context that eating disorders characterized by restricted eating can generate. The psychological social withdrawal will then create the same persistent pattern of behavior that is inaccessible to change because social learning is closed down by epistemic mistrust.

The mentalizing model suggests that people with eating disorders may be able to achieve remarkable feats of self-regulation (e.g., self-starvation) but are still at a loss when attempting to regulate their social (presentational) self. This is where the vicious cycle that we have just described may explain the persistence of difficulties in eating disorders. A mentalizing (social-cognitive) vulnerability triggers epistemic mistrust, which in turn triggers social withdrawal and will create a further mentalizing problem, ultimately generating epistemic hypervigilance and making the patient inaccessible to cognitive change. The non-mentalizing, teleological world created by the patient inevitably leads to distress in others who are close to the patient. These close others become critical figures outside demanding that the patient changes their behavior, not realizing that these demands paradoxically serve only to enhance and maintain the patient's social self-regulation and experience of self-stabilization.

The MBT-ED Treatment Model

The General MBT-ED Approach

The MBT approach recognizes that vulnerability factors for eating disorders (e.g., attachment insecurity, adversity, dysfunctional personality traits such as perfectionism) are not appropriate targets for intervention, which instead needs to focus on interpersonal factors that maintain eating disorders, as discussed earlier (see also [27]). Among these, as in the case of other severe mental health problems, we consider dysfunction of relationships and of the self to be the most important. We do not know for sure whether problems with mentalizing are associated with attachment disorganization and precede the development of eating disorders, or whether mentalizing difficulties emerge as part of the complex and cyclical relational issues that lead to the symptoms of eating disorders. It is improbable that the behaviors associated with eating disorders (e.g., self-starvation, frequent binge eating and vomiting) would not compromise a higher cognitive function such as mentalizing. Regardless of its role in the etiology of eating disorders, ineffective mentalizing is, from our perspective, the key factor in the maintenance of these disorders. MBT-ED focuses on facilitating improvements in mentalizing while also addressing—as in all of the implementations of MBT described in this book—the physical constraints of the patient's life, such as housing, employment, physical risk, mental health risk, and symptoms of the disorder interfering with the process of treatment.

To summarize, MBT interventions for patients with eating disorders focus on:

- supporting the mentalizing of emotions
- improving the mentalizing capacities needed for social processing while avoiding pretend mode
- using MBT techniques to address psychic equivalence, which generates the characteristic inflexible "black-and-white" thinking style of exaggerated certainty
- addressing the rewarding experiences associated with the outcomes of teleological thinking leading to self-reinforcing behaviors (e.g., positive beliefs about the value of dysfunctional eating)
- working to reduce the epistemic hypervigilance and extreme epistemic mistrust in relation to family members and other people who are assumed to be personally close to the patient, to improve the patient's communication style with these individuals.

In contrast to both family therapy and cognitive–behavioral therapy, weight and shape concerns are not the target of intervention in MBT-ED. MBT assumes that unmentalized content is poorly addressed by direct attempts to mentalize it (e.g., searching for the meaning of thinness, addressing distorted cognitions). The fundamental deficit is assumed to be relational—that is, the disruption of the social connection between the person with an eating disorder and their social environment, which is both the consequence and the cause of their mentalizing difficulties.

Part of the reason for poor outcomes in patients with eating disorders is the *ego-syntonicity* of the presentation—it includes ideas and features that are comfortable for the patient but create distress in those who are close to them. The mentalizing model of BPD is relevant here. We assume that one aspect of the self-dysfunction that is characteristic of eating disorders can be described as the disorganization created by an alien self [17] (see earlier in this chapter, and also Chapters 2 and 10). This construct, which owes much to the psychoanalytic origins of MBT, suggests that self-hatred and ego-destructive shame can arise through a process similar to identification with the aggressor, where the individual identifies with an external persecutor to the point of experiencing the criticism and shame as coming from within the self, thus threatening the integrity of the self. This is dealt with by externalizing the "alien" part of the self, and generating experiences in which the feeling of being criticized and attacked seems to come from outside rather than from within. In this way the self is protected. A dynamic is created that stabilizes the self and in which, paradoxically, reducing external criticism would expose the self to a far more painful and uncontrollable internal attack. Thus there is minimal intrinsic motivation for recovery, as that would remove the illusion that the destructive parts of the self are not within but outside, as evidenced by the external critical voices around the patient. In MBT-ED, the clinician has to tread a fine line between accepting how things are and insisting on change. Their empathic, respectful, and accepting tone is essential to avoid collusion with the critical voices, which are a creation of the patient and serve to stabilize the patient's dysfunctional self. Sometimes this may be quite an effort, as the patient's teleological mode of triggering actions in others may leave the clinician vulnerable to becoming hypercritical and demanding, and so reinforcing the patient's resistance to recovery.

MBT-ED is a relatively flexible treatment, which is adapted to the needs of the individual patient with the aim of enhancing their agency by directly involving them in determining the focus of the therapy. In the introductory phase of the intervention (MBT-I, described later in this chapter; for a description of MBT-I in general, see also Chapter 4), patients can choose items from the manual that they consider most relevant to them, or add items that they think would make the process more pertinent to their thinking about mental states. In MBT-ED, every opportunity is taken to encourage patients to make choices, create personal routes, and engage in active problem solving and decision making in relation to their own care, and also to give the patient a sense of efficacy and reduce the likelihood of them disengaging and dropping out of treatment.

At the core of all forms of MBT is the mentalizing of thoughts and feelings. In child and adolescent implementations of MBT, practical tasks are often used to enhance mentalizing (outlined in Chapters 13–15; see also [52–55]). MBT-ED also includes drawing and writing to support the enhancement of mentalizing. Drawing, writing, and other practical interventions may be considered "epistemic workarounds." In contexts of epistemic hypervigilance and mistrust in communication, the use of playful and concrete non-verbal approaches fosters thinking in mental-state terms. They offer the potential to make unaccustomed links and connections and perceive new perspectives, and can trigger cognitive (re-)structuring and reduce habitual defensiveness. Importantly, they can bypass the wish to avoid emotions, and they can engage creativity and contribute to the generation of fresh relational solutions.

MBT-ED is, by necessity, an identity-building approach. As we outlined earlier in this chapter, social self-regulation is a core problem in patients with eating disorders because, with limited mentalizing capacity, the patient's identity is too weak to support a stable sense of self that is capable of resisting the pressures of diverse social influences, and the patient has achieved stability by social withdrawal, at the cost of further limitations of mentalizing. In MBT-ED, a focus on creating an identity independent of the highly valued ego-syntonic nature of the current identity, which integrates valued aspects of the illness (e.g., teleological beliefs about body weight and shape), is a priority throughout treatment. The clinician generates role models with the patient so that they can create identifications with thoughts and feelings that are free from illness-driven beliefs and values.

The structure of MBT-ED has been described in detail by Robinson and Skårderud [1,56]. In keeping with the core model of MBT, they emphasize the importance of a good formulation of the disorder in mentalizing terms. They suggest that MBT-ED should be designed as a long-term program combining individual therapy, group therapy, group psychoeducation, and the active use of written case formulations. Medical management is a necessary part of the program, especially when it is offered as part of an inpatient, day-hospital, or intensive outpatient treatment, as patients with eating disorders can require regular physical assessment. The mentalizing principles used in organizing the multidisciplinary intervention AMBIT ([57]; see also Chapter 17) should be used when working with doctors, dietitians, nurses, and psychologists as part of running the treatment program. This mentalizing approach to systems of care considers how to divide responsibility among professionals, and how to support mentalized communication between them, to try to prevent the fragmentation of a helping system that works best when it is integrated, holding together a therapeutic process in the face of frequently encountered medical or mental health crises (e.g., suicide attempts, increased frequency of self-harm).

Formulation in MBT-ED

The MBT model in all its clinical contexts requires a formulation of the patient's current problems, using the patient's impaired mentalizing as a touchstone for the understanding of their current experience. The formulation should include the patient's history and current situation, key factors relevant to the clinical picture, a presentation of hypotheses about critical challenges, and a proposal of a plan for treatment, including anticipated obstacles and challenges in therapy (for a more detailed description of the development of a formulation, see Chapter 4). Specific to the context of eating disorders, the formulation should include the following information about the patient:

- their understanding of their situation
- their beliefs about their eating disorder and the value it has for them
- the attitude of key others in relation to their presentation
- their physical (embodied mentalizing) experiences
- the interpersonal conflicts of which they are aware, and their attitudes to these conflicts
- their strengths and weaknesses in mentalizing, and how these could relate to the issues described in the preceding points.

The formulation should draw attention to the difficulties in social self-regulation that are experienced by the patient, and their ways of coping with life's ordinary interpersonal challenges, which create thoughts and feelings that they struggle to manage. It should also include the contextualization of the eating disorder and the way it is seen by the patient as a solution to these challenges. The formulation ends with the clinician's highlighting of expected challenges in both individual and group MBT.

The formulation in MBT is constructed by the clinician with the patient. It is written (or drawn) by the clinician and then given to the patient for them to check and correct. This process can go through a number of cycles of amendment until the formulation becomes a jointly constructed document. The formulation should be neither too long nor too superficial. Initially, one written page may be enough, and even a single diagram outlining the pathway to low mentalizing and eating problems can be sufficient to orient treatment. Attention should be paid to making sure that patients can recognize themselves in the description. It should be prepared during the first phase of therapy (usually the first month of treatment). The formulation should be optimistic in the sense that it gives equal weight to understanding the patient's difficulties and highlighting their strengths, as well as ways in which MBT-ED could help to address problems that are particularly painful for the patient. The patient's general mentalizing in the past and the present, and how the experience of their eating disorder can make mentalizing difficult, are outlined. Aspects of the disorder (e.g., concern about low body weight and/or shape) that impede the patient's mentalizing and have effects on the symptoms themselves and on the patient's interpersonal relationships need to be set out in the formulation.

Many important aspects of the patient's history, including their relationships with family members and romantic/sexual relationships, are unlikely to be included in the initial formulation, although they may turn out to be critical to the therapy. The formulation is a "live" document and should be returned to and modified during the course of the treatment.

Individual Therapy

The mainstay of MBT-ED is individual therapy. This is delivered according to the general model of MBT (as outlined in Chapters 3 and 4), with attention given to the specific objectives of MBT-ED. If individual therapy and group therapy (described later in this chapter) are both offered, particular emphasis is placed on openness between the different treatment contexts. For example, the secretiveness that is typically associated with eating disorders makes it necessary for the individual clinician to be informed about the patient's ways of functioning in the group. Given the emphasis on social self-regulation in the MBT-ED model, the individual sessions offer an opportunity to provide one-to-one support for the emergence (in the social context of the group sessions) of identity, understanding of emotions, social presentation, perspective taking, and epistemic trust. In this way, individual therapy takes some of its key materials from the patient's experience in group therapy.

Clinical Example: Increasing Reflection on Self and Other Experience within Relationships, Identifying Affect, and Avoiding Pretend Mode

Clinician: You were saying your friends are worried about you. How does that affect you?

Mary: I just see them as saying that. It does not mean much to me. There is nothing to worry about. I tell them that.

Clinician: Hmm ... but I was wondering about how it affects your relationship with them, rather than that they do not need to worry.

Mary: I don't really understand why they worry. I feel fine and they don't have to look after me.

Clinician: So, describe how you feel with them when they are worrying about you.

Mary: I think they do not know who I am. I am on my own at that point.

Clinician: Ah, so you are with them in person but they don't see you as you see yourself? *(The clinician is trying to focus on the mismatch between self-experience and others' experience of Mary, and her consequent social and relational loneliness.)*

Mary: I am OK, but I am on my own I suppose. *(The clinician needs to be alert for pretend mode here, as Mary perhaps agrees too readily.)*

Clinician: You suppose? *(A mild challenge is given.)*

Mary: I am with them but we are not close generally, and I do watch from the sidelines and try to fit in.

Clinician: Something passed across your eyes as you said that. Can you say what it was? *(The clinician is establishing an affect state if possible.)*

Mary: I suddenly felt upset about something.

Clinician: Can you say what it was?

Mary: A shiver that there was no one else in the world and that people were just worrying about me when there is nothing to worry about.

CLINICIAN: I wonder what it would be like if they stopped worrying? *(This counterfactual question is offered as a mild challenge.)*

MARY: It would never happen.

CLINICIAN: Do the people in the group worry about you?

The clinician now tries to work on this central dynamic of Mary's relationships, and begins to explore whether the same dynamic is activated in the group psychotherapy sessions.

Some patients are reluctant to expose themselves socially in groups, whereas others embrace the group experience not as a social challenge but rather as a way of maintaining their "secret identity," and use the group as a shield behind which they are able to hide in plain sight, staying silent and contributing little or nothing beyond superficial support to other group members, thereby hiding their social withdrawal and general passivity. Paradoxically, they experience individual therapy as providing fewer places to hide because of its focus on their identity, which creates more anxiety for them.

Group Therapy

Unsurprisingly, group therapy can be the most stressful part of MBT-ED for the majority of patients. The vulnerability of the self is greatest when it is exposed to potential social scrutiny, and these patients carefully craft their identity to avoid social exposure in which their thoughts, feelings, and true ambitions could be exposed and catastrophic humiliation could follow. Their preoccupation with others' ideas about their physical appearance and mental states makes them feel vulnerable, and they can experience deep mental pain in relation to persecutory patterns of interaction with others who may themselves use group interactions to stabilize their own unstable self through aggressive interactions with group members. The group context inevitably has the potential to activate the core pathology of eating disorders, which highlights our assumption that ultimately these disorders are disorders of self-function. We do not know whether group sessions are either a necessary or a sufficient element of MBT-ED, but it is certain that they do carry a risk of iatrogenic harm. They may set up dynamics that can, on the surface, appear mutually supportive but in fact consist of all the group members hiding from each other in pretend mode; alternatively, the group can become a gathering of people who are all stabilizing themselves through mutual criticism of each other. The MBT group treatment for BPD (see Chapter 5) therefore needs to be adapted to the context of eating disorders, with clinicians being particularly vigilant about the patients' characteristic styles of interaction.

Psychoeducational Groups

Psychoeducational groups, as in the MBT-I groups for BPD patients (see Chapter 4), serve as an introduction to the mentalizing perspective on eating disorders. MBT-I for eating disorders (MBT-I-ED) orients the patients to the MBT treatment model and facilitates their understanding of the clinical process. Eight to ten sessions are devoted to this introduction. These group sessions are focused on individual topics relevant to the model, which are presented by a clinician. The subjects include the nature of mentalizing, with perhaps a greater emphasis on communication than in MBT-I for BPD, in view of the avoidant tendencies of many patients with eating disorders. Misunderstandings, difficulties in "reading" other people, and difficulties in knowing oneself are considered at length. The strategy for engaging patients includes a didactic style that requires contributions from the patients, who provide examples and present alternative perspectives on issues from their personal history to illustrate particular points. Discussion deliberately often remains at quite a high level as the topics themselves can be stressful, as is the experience of being in the group (as outlined earlier). The language used in the sessions is simple, and the examples brought by the clinician should be from other patients with eating disorders from their own clinical experience. These can trigger emotional reactions in the participants. For this reason, the clinician tries to maintain a light-hearted attitude throughout the MBT-I-ED course. In-depth explorations of personal experience are discouraged during these sessions. The aim is not to allow discussions to become too "hot" or emotionally intense, and also to ensure that these group encounters are quite different from the weekly group therapy.

In a randomized controlled trial of MBT-ED compared with specialist supportive clinical management [6], MBT-I-ED (five sessions) took place before the main part of MBT-ED, which constituted weekly individual and group sessions over 12 months. Patients with co-occurring BPD and eating disorders were difficult to retain in this program, so it is possible that the "dosage" of MBT-I-ED sessions followed by both group and individual sessions is not ideal. In patients with eating disorders and co-occurring personality disorders, it is likely that attendance at both individual and group sessions may be possible only in a day-hospital context. It is also likely that 12 months is insufficient time for the combined treatment of BPD and eating disorders. On this basis, it may be advisable to follow the lead of the MBT program for BPD and offer 18 months of MBT-ED, the first 3 months of which consists of psychoeducational MBT-I-ED.

Concluding Remarks

There is considerable evidence of mentalizing problems in patients with eating disorders. Psychic equivalence thinking, teleological mode, and pretend mode dominate, especially in relation to the individual's body weight and shape. The mentalizing model assumes the existence of developmental vulnerabilities, especially during adolescence, and that the range of different symptoms associated with eating disorders may have the common function of being attempts at social self-regulation. A combined program of individual and group psychotherapy is offered in MBT-ED to address social anxieties while due attention is paid to any physical problems resulting from the eating disorder. The core foci of MBT-ED are social and relational adaptation, improving low mentalizing triggered as part of a retreat from social interaction, and supporting resilience.

References

1. Robinson P, Skårderud F. Eating disorders. In: Bateman A, Fonagy P, eds. *Handbook of Mentalizing in Mental Health Practice*, 2nd ed. Washington, DC: American Psychiatric Publishing, 2019; 369–86.
2. Schmidt U, Wade TD, Treasure J. The Maudsley Model of Anorexia Nervosa Treatment for Adults (MANTRA): development, key features, and preliminary evidence. *J Cogn Psychother* 2014; **28**: 48–71.

3. National Institute for Health and Care Excellence. *Eating Disorders: Recognition and Treatment.* London, UK: National Institute for Health and Care Excellence; 2017. www.nice.org.uk/guidance/ng69.

4. Esterling BA, L'Abate L, Murray EJ, Pennebaker JW. Empirical foundations for writing in prevention and psychotherapy: mental and physical health outcomes. *Clin Psychol Rev* 1999; **19**: 79–96.

5. Miller WR, Rollnick S. *Motivational Interviewing: Helping People Change*, 3rd ed. New York, NY: The Guilford Press, 2012.

6. Robinson P, Hellier J, Barrett B et al. The NOURISHED randomised controlled trial comparing mentalisation-based treatment for eating disorders (MBT-ED) with specialist supportive clinical management (SSCM-ED) for patients with eating disorders and symptoms of borderline personality disorder. *Trials* 2016; **17**: 549.

7. Bruch H. *Eating Disorders. Obesity, Anorexia Nervosa, and the Person Within.* New York, NY: Basic Books, 1973.

8. Bruch H. Four decades of eating disorders. In: Garner DM, Garfinkel PE, eds. *Handbook of Psychotherapy for Anorexia Nervosa and Bulimia.* New York, NY: The Guilford Press, 1985; 7–18.

9. Shai D, Belsky J. When words just won't do: introducing parental embodied mentalizing. *Child Dev Perspect* 2011; **5**: 173–80.

10. Shai D, Fonagy P. Beyond words: parental embodied mentalizing and the parent-infant dance. In: *Mechanisms of Social Connection: From Brain to Group.* Washington, DC: American Psychological Association, 2014; 185–203.

11. Shai D, Dollberg D, Szepsenwol O. The importance of parental verbal and embodied mentalizing in shaping parental experiences of stress and coparenting. *Infant Behav Dev* 2017; **49**: 87–96.

12. Afek E, Lev-Wiesel R, Federman D, Shai D. The mediating role of parental embodied mentalizing in the longitudinal association between prenatal spousal support and toddler emotion recognition. *Infancy* 2022; **27**: 609–29.

13. Vaever MS, Cordes K, Stuart AC et al. Associations of maternal sensitivity and embodied mentalizing with infant-mother attachment security at one year in depressed and non-depressed dyads. *Attach Hum Dev* 2022; **24**: 115–32.

14. Shai D, Belsky J. Parental embodied mentalizing: how the nonverbal dance between parents and infants predicts children's socio-emotional functioning. *Attach Hum Dev* 2017; **19**: 191–219.

15. Garset-Zamani S, Cordes K, Shai D et al. Does postpartum depression affect parental embodied mentalizing in mothers with 4-months old infants? *Infant Behav Dev* 2020; **61**: 101486.

16. Fonagy P, Gergely G, Jurist E, Target M. *Affect Regulation, Mentalization, and the Development of the Self.* New York, NY: Other Press, 2002.

17. Fonagy P, Target M. Attachment and reflective function: their role in self-organization. *Dev Psychopathol* 1997; **9**: 679–700.

18. Fonagy P, Target M. Playing with reality: III. The persistence of dual psychic reality in borderline patients. *Int J Psychoanal* 2000; **81**: 853–73.

19. Arnsten AF. Stress signalling pathways that impair prefrontal cortex structure and function. *Nat Rev Neurosci* 2009; **10**: 410–22.

20. Steinhausen HC. The outcome of anorexia nervosa in the 20th century. *Am J Psychiatry* 2002; **159**: 1284–93.

21. Eddy KT, Tabri N, Thomas JJ et al. Recovery from anorexia nervosa and bulimia nervosa at 22-year follow-up. *J Clin Psychiatry* 2017; **78**: 184–9.

22. Treasure J, Willmott D, Ambwani S et al. Cognitive interpersonal model for anorexia nervosa revisited: the perpetuating factors that contribute to the development of the severe and enduring illness. *J Clin Med* 2020; **9**: 630.

23. Luyten P, Campbell C, Allison E, Fonagy P. The mentalizing approach to

psychopathology: state of the art and future directions. *Annu Rev Clin Psychol* 2020; **16**: 297–325.

24. Sekowski M, Gambin M, Cudo A et al. The relations between childhood maltreatment, shame, guilt, depression and suicidal ideation in inpatient adolescents. *J Affect Disord* 2020; **276**: 667–77.

25. Fonagy P. The feeling that destroys the self: the role of mentalizing in the catastrophic sequelae of shame. In: *The Problem of Shame: The 2019 John M. Oldham National Mental Health Symposium*. Houston, TX: Menninger, 2019. www.menningerclinic.org/Assets/2019-menninger-symposium-emailwebsite-version.pdf.

26. Schmidt U, Treasure J. Anorexia nervosa: valued and visible. A cognitive-interpersonal maintenance model and its implications for research and practice. *Br J Clin Psychol* 2006; **45**: 343–66.

27. Treasure J, Schmidt U. The cognitive-interpersonal maintenance model of anorexia nervosa revisited: a summary of the evidence for cognitive, socio-emotional and interpersonal predisposing and perpetuating factors. *J Eat Disord* 2013; **1**: 13.

28. Tchanturia K, Hambrook D, Curtis H et al. Work and social adjustment in patients with anorexia nervosa. *Compr Psychiatry* 2013; **54**: 41–5.

29. Castellini G, Rossi E, Ricca V. The relationship between eating disorder psychopathology and sexuality: etiological factors and implications for treatment. *Curr Opin Psychiatry* 2020; **33**: 554–61.

30. Schulte-Ruther M, Mainz V, Fink GR et al. Theory of mind and the brain in anorexia nervosa: relation to treatment outcome. *J Am Acad Child Adolesc Psychiatry* 2012; **51**: 832–41.e11.

31. Westwood H, Kerr-Gaffney J, Stahl D, Tchanturia K. Alexithymia in eating disorders: systematic review and meta-analyses of studies using the Toronto Alexithymia Scale. *J Psychosom Res* 2017; **99**: 66–81.

32. Dolan SC, Khindri R, Franko DL et al. Anhedonia in eating disorders: a meta-analysis and systematic review. *Int J Eat Disord* 2022; **55**: 161–75.

33. Jewell T, Collyer H, Gardner T et al. Attachment and mentalization and their association with child and adolescent eating pathology: a systematic review. *Int J Eat Disord* 2016; **49**: 354–73.

34. Caglar-Nazali HP, Corfield F, Cardi V et al. A systematic review and meta-analysis of 'Systems for Social Processes' in eating disorders. *Neurosci Biobehav Rev* 2014; **42**: 55–92.

35. Faber A, Dube L, Knauper B. Attachment and eating: a meta-analytic review of the relevance of attachment for unhealthy and healthy eating behaviors in the general population. *Appetite* 2018; **123**: 410–38.

36. Cortes-Garcia L, Takkouche B, Seoane G, Senra C. Mediators linking insecure attachment to eating symptoms: a systematic review and meta-analysis. *PLoS ONE* 2019; **14**: e0213099.

37. Jewell T, Apostolidou E, Sadikovic K, et al. Attachment in individuals with eating disorders compared to community controls: a systematic review and meta-analysis. *Int J Eat Disord* 2023. https://doi.org/10.1002/eat.23922

38. Vartanian LR, Hayward LE, Smyth JM et al. Risk and resiliency factors related to body dissatisfaction and disordered eating: the identity disruption model. *Int J Eat Disord* 2018; **51**: 322–30.

39. Bora E, Kose S. Meta-analysis of theory of mind in anorexia nervosa and bulimia nervosa: a specific impairment of cognitive perspective taking in anorexia nervosa? *Int J Eat Disord* 2016; **49**: 739–40.

40. Leppanen J, Sedgewick F, Treasure J, Tchanturia K. Differences in the Theory of Mind profiles of patients with anorexia nervosa and individuals on the autism spectrum: a meta-analytic review. *Neurosci Biobehav Rev* 2018; **90**: 146–63.

41. Cardi V, Tchanturia K, Treasure J. Premorbid and illness-related social

difficulties in eating disorders: an overview of the literature and treatment developments. *Curr Neuropharmacol* 2018; **16**: 1122–30.

42. Troop NA, Bifulco A. Childhood social arena and cognitive sets in eating disorders. *Br J Clin Psychol* 2002; **41**: 205–11.
43. Oldershaw A, Lavender T, Sallis H et al. Emotion generation and regulation in anorexia nervosa: a systematic review and meta-analysis of self-report data. *Clin Psychol Rev* 2015; **39**: 83–95.
44. Rothschild-Yakar L, Levy-Shiff R, Fridman-Balaban R et al. Mentalization and relationships with parents as predictors of eating disordered behavior. *J Nerv Ment Dis* 2010; **198**: 501–7.
45. Monteleone AM, Corsi E, Cascino G et al. The interaction between mentalizing, empathy and symptoms in people with eating disorders: a network analysis integrating experimentally induced and self-report measures. *Cognit Ther Res* 2020; **44**: 1140–49.
46. Corsi E, Cardi V, Sowden S et al. Socio-cognitive processing in people with eating disorders: computerized tests of mentalizing, empathy and imitation skills. *Int J Eat Disord* 2021; **54**: 1509–18.
47. Bird G, Viding E. The self to other model of empathy: providing a new framework for understanding empathy impairments in psychopathy, autism, and alexithymia. *Neurosci Biobehav Rev* 2014; **47**: 520–32.
48. Happe F, Frith U. Annual research review: towards a developmental neuroscience of atypical social cognition. *J Child Psychol Psychiatry* 2014; **55**: 553–7.
49. Saure E, Laasonen M, Lepisto-Paisley T et al. Characteristics of autism spectrum disorders are associated with longer duration of anorexia nervosa: a systematic review and meta-analysis. *Int J Eat Disord* 2020; **53**: 1056–79.
50. Kinnaird E, Norton C, Stewart C, Tchanturia K. Same behaviours, different reasons: what do patients with co-occurring anorexia and autism want from treatment? *Int Rev Psychiatry* 2019; **31**: 308–17.
51. Goss K, Gilbert P. Eating disorders, shame and pride: a cognitive-behavioural functional analysis. In: Gilbert P, Miles J, eds. *Body Shame: Conceptualisation, Research and Treatment.* Hove, UK: Routledge, 2014; 233–69.
52. Asen E, Fonagy P. *Mentalization-Based Treatment with Families.* New York, NY: The Guilford Press, 2021.
53. Midgley N, Ensink K, Lindqvist K et al. *Mentalization-Based Treatment for Children: A Time-Limited Approach.* Washington, DC: American Psychological Association, 2017.
54. Rossouw T, Wiwe M, Vrouva I, eds. *Mentalization-Based Treatment for Adolescents: A Practical Treatment Guide.* Abingdon, UK: Routledge, 2021.
55. Midgley N, Vrouva I, eds. *Minding the Child: Mentalization-Based Interventions with Children, Young People and Their Families.* Hove, UK: Routledge, 2013.
56. Robinson P, Skårderud F, Sommerfeldt B. *Hunger: Mentalisation Based Treatments for Eating Disorders.* Cham, Switzerland: Springer, 2019.
57. Bevington D, Fuggle P, Cracknell L, Fonagy P. *Adaptive Mentalization-Based Integrative Treatment: A Guide for Teams to Develop Systems of Care.* Oxford, UK: Oxford University Press, 2017.

Chapter 13

Working with Children

Introduction

An important way in which mentalization-based treatment (MBT) has been adapted for children has been in the development of MBT-C by Nick Midgley and his colleagues [1]. Although there is good evidence for cognitive–behavioral interventions for children, many children may not be able to make full use of cognitive–behavioral strategies if they do not have the necessary self-regulatory or cognitive strengths. Midgley and his colleagues realized that a model that integrated mentalizing, attachment, and a psychodynamic approach might provide a valuable additional treatment option for children and families. MBT-C is a time-limited program (usually 12 weeks) for children between the ages of about 5 and 10 years, which has an emphasis on supporting the development of mentalizing. It is considered an appropriate approach for many mental health difficulties, including conduct and behavioral problems and low mood and anxiety.

MBT-C does not seek to resolve all of the difficulties that a child might be experiencing, but aims to strengthen the child's emerging mentalizing—and the parents' capacity to scaffold their child's mentalizing—so that a process of change is initiated. In doing this, MBT-C aims to increase the child's capacity for emotional regulation and to support their parents to best meet the emotional needs of their children. This means providing opportunities for parents and children to practice good mentalizing, and it also involves paying attention to the situations in which mentalizing breaks down, and working on areas where there are deficits in the capacity to mentalize. Midgley and his colleagues suggest that this emphasis on mentalizing is supported by research which shows that mentalizing abilities are associated with a "positive sense of self, healthy relationships, and better emotional regulation" (Midgley et al. [1], p. 6).

MBT-C involves working with parents to support their capacity to take a mentalizing stance toward their children. The approach seeks to help parents to view their child as a separate person with their own mind and experiences, and to enable the parents to become more open to thinking about the mental states that might drive their child's behavior. The parents are also encouraged to think about their own mental states and, crucially, to think about how their own mental states and behaviors are seen by, and affect, their child.

The standard format for MBT-C is 12 individual sessions that take place weekly with the child, with separate sessions held with the parent(s). However, this format is flexible, as it may need to be adjusted according to the setting or the needs of the children and parents: "What is important is that the therapeutic contract is clear and coherent from the beginning—for the parents, as well as for the child. This is a way of creating a sense of safety and collaboration, and avoiding a scenario in which the therapist makes decisions that the family is unaware of.

This transparency is part of the mentalizing stance, and contributes to a sense of shared ownership of the therapeutic process" (Midgley et al. [1], p. 252).

The Mentalizing Stance in MBT-C

In terms of technique, MBT-C is fundamentally informed by the mentalizing stance, which is viewed throughout this book as core to all mentalizing-informed work. As with any MBT approach, the experience of the richly mentalizing relationship, characterized by empathic attunement, openness, and curiosity about mental states, is at the heart of the intervention, rather than any specific techniques. The following extract is from a clinical vignette described by Midgley and his colleagues in their book on MBT-C [1]. It is an account of a therapist's first meeting with Belinda, a 7-year-old girl who is withdrawn, anxious, and struggling to make friends.

> When the therapist first meets Belinda, he is struck by how little eye contact she makes. At their first individual meeting, Belinda follows the therapist to the playroom but sits rather listlessly, drawing circles on a piece of paper. When the therapist invites her to play a game of catch, Belinda looks surprised, but accepts. She throws the ball a few times, but her coordination is poor, and one of her throws knocks a plastic cup off the table on to the floor. Belinda glances quickly at the therapist and appears scared. The therapist smiles at Belinda and gets down to floor level, picking up the cup. "*Don't worry—not broken,*" he says, and shows Belinda the cup. Then he goes on: "*I don't know what you're like, but when I go somewhere new, I'm always a bit nervous about what people are going to think of me. I don't know if they're going to like me or not.*"
>
> Belinda looks at the therapist with a bit of curiosity. "*Know the feeling*?" he asks, but Belinda doesn't reply. Instead, she picks up the ball, and they carry on playing catch. The therapist starts adding in different tricks, and soon they are laughing. "*Good catch!*" he says, when Belinda reaches a ball that is quite high. And when he misses one and the soft ball bounces off Belinda's nose, the therapist says, "*Ouch!*" in a playful, somewhat exaggerated manner. "*Did that hurt?*" he asks, but Belinda shakes her head no.
>
> (Midgley et al. [1], p. 85)

What is so well conveyed in this vignette is how lightly the therapist's stance is held, yet it consistently involves empathy, authenticity, interest, positivity, and a non-judgmental openness: "Belinda's therapist presents himself as an interested, well-disposed adult, who engages with Belinda in a reciprocal way and shows interest in understanding how Belinda is feeling. He is not a 'blank screen' but speaks about feelings and discloses a little of his own personal experience and what goes on in his own mind" (Midgley et al. [1], p. 86).

The therapist is warm and supportive rather than inscrutable or detached, but at the same time he is not overly emotional or elaborate in his attempts at mentalizing, which could be over-arousing for Belinda. Rather, the approach that the therapist uses is to create a safe environment in which two minds can meet together in the room in a regulated way, and can begin to think together about what is in those minds and how they respond to each other.

Another clinical example captures how heightened affect and misunderstandings are managed. This case involves Mohammed, a 7-year-old boy who is attending a session after he got into trouble at school for physically attacking a classmate.

> The therapist begins the session with Mohammed, who at first makes no reference to what had happened that day but begins a game in which a doll is being picked on by all the other dolls. At one point the doll kicks back and tells the others to go away. The therapist says, with some

> feeling: "*It seems like she wants them all to get out of her face!*" Mohammed turns round, abruptly, and throws the doll toward the therapist's face, at the same time screaming at her, "*I hate you! I hate you!*" The therapist has not expected this and immediately moves backward, away from Mohammed, breaking eye contact. As she does so, she says, "*Mohammed, I'm really sorry. I'm not quite sure what I've done, but I can see that I've really upset you. I'm so sorry.*" At that point, Mohammed bursts into tears.
>
> (Midgley et al. [1], pp. 98–9)

The therapist was genuinely surprised by Mohammed's reaction, but her first response was to apologize for having behaved in a way that was so upsetting to him. This response was to help to regulate Mohammed and acknowledge that something had gone wrong between them. The therapist did not try to come up with a theory about Mohammed's mental state at the time, but simply modeled a stance in which the difficulty of understanding mental states (in this case the therapist's difficulty in relation to Mohammed) was acknowledged, but not catastrophized.

MBT as a Play-Centered Approach

Play is at the heart of the MBT-C model. Fonagy and Target have suggested that play is an antecedent of mentalizing [2–4]. There is evidence from research which indicates that the capacity for pretend play is associated with improved reflective functioning (i.e., mentalizing); a study of children with a history of being sexually abused found that play mediates the relationship between having experienced abuse and children's later mentalizing capacity [5]. While a child is playing, the therapist can use various approaches to improve the child's awareness of mental states. At its simplest, this can take the form of describing the play process [6]. This is a process in which the therapist describes, summarizes, and integrates the child's feelings, behaviors, and thoughts during their play. A further step is for the therapist to then describe the child's behavior in terms of their mental states, allowing them to touch on difficult thoughts or aspects of the child's play that might feel too overwhelming to talk about. Midgley and his colleagues describe various ways in which mentalizing and play can come together, and we shall summarize these approaches in this section.

Stimulating the Play Narrative

For a child who is anxious, inhibited, or withdrawn in relation to their play, it may be helpful for the therapist to ask questions, to help them to understand the story of the play. "This technique is the first step to understanding the play context that the child is presenting during the session and helps the therapist make sense of what is going on. Additionally, this technique encourages the child to elaborate the stories presented during the play through gentle inquiry about the material presented and by asking for more details and descriptions" (Midgley et al. [1], p. 136).

Midgley and his colleagues draw a parallel between this technique and the clarification and exploration that are used in MBT for adults (described in Chapter 4).

Mentalizing the Play

With a child who is able to engage in symbolic play, the therapist can take the step of *mentalizing the narrative of the play*. This means verbalizing the story of the play, and supporting greater exploration of the thoughts and ideas behind it. The therapist remains cautious and wondering (not-knowing) about their description of the narrative, and allows the child to elaborate or correct the therapist's account. The aim of this approach is to stimulate mentalizing in a playful and undogmatic manner, allowing the introduction of different perspectives in a way that is respectful of both the play itself and the child's own possible thoughts and feelings about it. A keen message that is conveyed in this process is that the child's play is valued; their sense of agency and what they are doing are treated as interesting, and the therapist engages with the play in a playful way themselves.

Problems with Symbolic Play

Some children may not engage in symbolic play. Older children might feel that they have grown out of pretend play and will be more interested in using drawing, painting, or clay than engaging in symbolic play; board games can be another option for some children. Younger children who cannot or will not engage in pretend play can be asked to join in activities that are more body based—for example, throwing and catching a ball, sword fighting, or playing music. Using clay or a sand box can be a valuable way into being playful for children who are inhibited or unwilling to engage in symbolic play. All of these games involve interaction, rhythm, and ritual, and allow experimentation with different sensations and activities.

Pitching the Right Intervention for the Child, at the Right Moment

An often repeated idea in this book is that when someone's mentalizing has gone "offline," it is not helpful to seek to use an explicitly mentalizing response at that moment. Instead, it is more helpful to reduce the patient's arousal, to show empathy, and to validate the patient's experience. This applies in just the same way when working with children. Almost inevitably there will be times when the therapist gets this wrong—for example, they might introduce an intervention that is too demanding or explicitly mentalizing at a moment that feels overwhelming or makes the child feel misunderstood. The task of the therapist at such moments is to be honest and apologetic about their misattunement, as we saw in the clinical example of Mohammed earlier in this chapter.

Mirroring and Contingent Responding

Children who are chaotic and who seem disorganized in their responses and unregulated in their actions are often referred for behavioral difficulties. These children seem to lack the foundations for self-mentalizing; their actions can appear unpredictable, even to themselves. When working with these children, the challenge of trying to make sure that the room is safe for the child and the therapist, and that objects in the room do not get damaged, can take over. Midgley and his colleagues suggest that in such cases it can be important for the therapist to express "contingent coordination with the child, drawing on nonverbal modalities such as making a soothing sound with a soft tone of voice or a facial expression full of compassion. . . . Such interventions can help these children to attend to and process information and modulate their emotions, before opening the door to developing other mentalizing abilities" (Midgley et al. [1], pp. 145–6).

For such children, creating a sense of joint attention, being together, and predictable responsiveness may be particularly important. Meanwhile, providing some feedback on the child's physical actions can provide greater awareness of the self and how it is experienced by others—"*That's a big loud noise, you hit so hard!*" This is a form of marked mirroring—that is, reflecting back to the child a sense of what they are doing, but in a regulated way. To return to our developmental theory, it is through the regulatory marked mirroring of the other that children learn to understand and regulate their feelings. Children who behave in an out-of-control, unregulated way are often (in, say, a school environment) met with a rejecting or punitive response that does not allow them to feel recognized or responded to in a way that helps them make sense of their experience.

Clarifying and Naming Feelings

Once the MBT-C therapist has established their contingent coordination with the child, they can start to attempt to make links between behaviors and feelings, elucidating and labeling feeling states. Feeling states can be named with the assistance of various tools—for example, picture books or drawings; sometimes it may be useful to ask the child to make up a little story about what might be going on for a character in the book or drawing.

Responding to Breakdowns in Mentalizing

MBT-C suggests that the therapist should respond to breakdowns in a child's capacity to mentalize by using techniques described for MBT for adults (see Chapter 4), which are adapted to be appropriate to the age of the child—for example, offering empathy and support, using "stop and rewind," identifying and validating mental states, improving perspective taking and differentiation between self and other, and creating mentalizing narratives around difficult experiences or traumatic events (Midgley et al. [1], p. 152).

The use of *empathy and support* is particularly indicated during moments of heightened affect and dysregulation. The aim here is to help to reduce the child's arousal and distress in a supportive and non-judgmental way.

Stop and rewind may be used after some mentalizing has been restored (through the use of empathy and support) following a moment of dysregulation. Stop and rewind can be used to explore and address a collapse in mentalizing of this kind, and to think about what happened—again, crucially, in a non-judgmental and curious spirit. It may then be possible to explore other examples of when the child has experienced similar incidents in different situations.

Mentalizing the relationship is something that can be used in MBT-C to bring the child's attention to the therapist's mind, and to use that attention to allow the child to see other perspectives and to become aware of differences between how the child feels they are seen by others and how they are thought about. As with MBT in general, mentalizing the relationship in MBT-C is not about providing transference interpretation, but rather it is used as a way of bringing in thinking about other minds, and using this to support the child's mentalizing. As with other more demanding mentalizing tasks, mentalizing the relationship in this way is better introduced when the child's affect is reasonably well regulated. An example might be after a rupture in therapy, in which the child expresses anger and frustration with the therapist. Only after the moment of rupture has been repaired, through the use of empathy and support, and the child is feeling calmer and more relaxed, might it be appropriate for the therapist to introduce—gently and in a non-dogmatic way—their own perspective on the incident and how they experienced it. Such an intervention should be used carefully and with a clear sense that the purpose of it is *not* to provide transference-informed insight into relational patterns. The point of such an exchange is to help to show the child the value of accessing other minds, and to generate an experience of the improved interpersonal connection that can arise from thinking together in this way.

Time and the Use of a Calendar

The time-limited nature of MBT-C is actively addressed throughout the program. It is also emphasized in MBT-C that the purpose of the work is to support the parents' and child's mentalizing capacities so that they are more able to respond to challenges and emotional difficulties in an ongoing way. Being transparent about endings and the finite nature of the work can be particularly important for children who have been exposed to multiple separations and who may not have previously felt supported or prepared for these.

One of the ways in which MBT-C manages the issue of timing is by using a calendar. The calendar is normally a large piece of paper with the sessions marked on it as circles or rectangles. The therapist introduces the calendar during the first session, and they explain that at the end of each session the child will draw something in the shape for that session, and that by doing this, the child and the therapist can keep track of the sessions that they have had and look ahead to how many empty shapes remain. The child is also allowed to decorate and draw on the calendar as they like, to make it feel as if it belongs to them. When the child is asked to fill in the shape for that day's session (normally about 5–10 minutes before the end of the session), they are encouraged to draw whatever they like. The therapist should not try to direct or suggest what goes in the shapes, but simply let the child do as they wish—although the therapist may need to intervene if the child seeks to spoil the calendar. The calendar creates a shared narrative of the child's work with the therapist, and allows them both to keep track of how many sessions are left.

Structure of MBT-C

Assessment Phase (Three or Four Meetings)

The assessment stage of working with children involves gaining some understanding of the difficulties that the child is presenting with, and developing a formulation. MBT-C has developed an innovative emphasis on a focus formulation, which is informed by the ideas of developmentally directed time-limited psychotherapy for children [7,8]. The focus formulation can be quite short—for example, a phrase or a story that captures the child's problems in a way that makes sense to them. The important thing is that it is easy to understand and that the child can see themselves in it.

Midgley and his colleagues give the following example of a focus formulation for a 10-year-boy struggling with behavior at school, attentional difficulties, and bed wetting. He and his mother were having problems in their relationship following a difficult period 4 years earlier in which the mother (who was herself struggling with her mental health) had hit the boy. The boy wanted to be a soldier when he grew up, so the formulation was developed in the following way.

> His mother had worked really hard on her own problems and could regulate her emotions much better. The boy, however, kept trying to please his mother, not speaking his mind, and being tense in the relationship. As the assessment period came to an end, the therapist and family decided to formulate a focus connected to this relational problem and the boy's love for computer games and soldiers. The therapist asked him what kind of soldier he wanted to be: A soldier who could not feel what was going on inside himself, who could not sense fear or anger, and simply tried to obey others? Or a soldier who could be firm and decisive and true to himself and others, who could feel his emotions and bodily signals to help him to stay safe, even when the going got tough? The boy loved this focus formulation, and once in therapy he worked really hard to become more connected with his body and emotions, as well as understanding himself better. At the end of the 12 sessions, the boy could talk about what had happened between him and his mother, he hardly wet his bed any more, and he felt better attuned to peers at his school.
>
> (Midgley et al. [6], p. 257)

This is a great example of how a focus formulation speaks to the child's view of their world, and their strengths, hopes, and motivation to develop in an engaged and positive way.

Sessions 1–3: Initial Phase

The main objective of the initial sessions of MBT-C is to start to develop a therapeutic alliance with both the child and the parent(s). The therapist adopts a stance of empathy, attunement, interest, and engagement with the child and how the child sees the world. Play is used to introduce the child to being in therapy; a box of play materials is used during the sessions, and the idea of using the focus formulation as a theme of the play is introduced.

Sessions 4–8: Middle Phase

The central part of the therapeutic activity, in which there is a focus on supporting the child's mentalizing with regard to the focus formulation, takes place during the middle phase of MBT-C. It is during this stage, too, that work in relation to the parents and supporting their reflective parenting takes place. If there are frequent breakdowns in mentalizing during this stage, resulting from unregulated affect, the approach will involve considering these situations when they arise and attempting to draw attention to what had happened to cause the process of escalating mentalizing breakdown. When the therapeutic process is less punctuated by moments of mentalizing difficulty, the work with the child and parent(s) involves developing perspective taking and, more explicitly, mentalizing. Again, this work is undertaken under the umbrella of the mentalizing stance, in which there is an emphasis on empathic attunement, openness, and curiosity about mental states, rather than the therapist seeking to laboriously "mentalize at" the parent or the child.

Review Meeting

A review meeting is offered around two-thirds of the way through the program. This meeting is for both the parent(s) and the child, and it provides an opportunity to review the initial focus and treatment goal. It may be agreed that the first eight sessions have been enough and that it is now possible to think about drawing the therapy to an end, or a decision may be made to continue with the sessions. In cases where it is felt that more ongoing treatment would be useful, another program of 12 sessions can be offered, up to a maximum of 36 sessions in total. This may be indicated in cases where the child's needs are more complex—for example, if the child has experienced trauma. The focus formulation will be reconsidered during the review meeting, in order to assess whether it still feels relevant and accurate, whether it has changed, or whether it appears to have a different significance or meaning.

Sessions 9–12: Ending Phase

During the last few sessions, when the end of the therapeutic process is in sight, there needs to be an additional focus on getting the child ready for the ending. As part of this focus, thought needs to be given to how the gains made in therapy can be supported in the longer term. As MBT-C is a time-limited treatment, keeping the ending in mind is important; as part of this, the calendar is actively used throughout the process to allow the child to have a sense of how many sessions they have completed, and how many are still left.

Concluding Remarks

When working with children, it is important to bear in mind that learning to mentalize is something that gradually develops throughout childhood and adolescence, and the emerging capacity to mentalize is scaffolded by the social environment around the child. Although mentalizing is an evolutionarily prewired capacity, in that normatively developing children typically show joint attention and shared intentionality—capacities that reflect mentalizing—from early infancy [9,10], considerable environmental input is needed for the child to develop a fully balanced capacity for mentalizing. Beginning in infancy, when mentalizing is very basic, the job of the parent is to make sense of the infant's mental state and reflect it back to the infant in a regulated way, through the process of *marked mirroring* [11]. This reading of the baby's state and modeling of it for them, while also making it clear that the parent is not overwhelmed by whatever feeling the baby is experiencing, is quite demanding for a parent's mentalizing. This is not helped by the fact that the experience of caring for children—especially young children, or older children whose mentalizing capacities are less well developed for whatever reason—might require the parent to operate in an intensely non-mentalizing social system. In this situation the parent cannot draw on the child's mentalizing to recalibrate their own mentalizing, while the intensity of the child's needs can put a lot of pressure on the parent's ability to maintain balanced mentalizing. This is one of the reasons why a network of support around children and parents is so essential. Although children's undeveloped capacity for understanding mental states is understood and expected by most parents, this understanding can be hard to hold on to under the pressure of heightened distress, exhaustion, and so on. For some parents with more vulnerable pre-existing mentalizing capacities, holding on to the ability to think about mental states in a regulated way while looking after a child can be a real challenge. The purpose of MBT-C is to provide an additional space in which the mentalizing of children and their families can be supported and encouraged to grow.

References

1. Midgley N, Ensink K, Lindqvist K et al. *Mentalization-Based Treatment for Children: A Time-Limited Approach.* Washington, DC: American Psychological Association, 2017.
2. Fonagy P, Target M. Playing with reality: I. Theory of mind and the normal development of psychic reality. *Int J Psychoanal* 1996; **77**: 217–33.
3. Target M, Fonagy P. Playing with reality: II. The development of psychic reality from a theoretical perspective. *Int J Psychoanal* 1996; **77**: 459–79.
4. Fonagy P, Target M. Playing with reality: III. The persistence of dual psychic reality in borderline patients. *Int J Psychoanal* 2000; **81**: 853–74.
5. Tessier VP, Normandin L, Ensink K, Fonagy P. Fact or fiction? A longitudinal study of play and the development of reflective functioning. *Bull Menninger Clin* 2016; **80**: 60–79.
6. Midgley N, Muller N, Malberg N et al. Children. In: Bateman A, Fonagy P, eds. *Handbook of Mentalizing in Mental Health Practice*, 2nd ed. Washington, DC: American Psychiatric Association Publishing, 2019; 247–63.
7. Hansen BR. *I Dialog med Barnet: Intersubjektivitet i Utvikling og i Psykoterapi* [*In Dialogue with the Child: Intersubjectivity in Development and in Psychotherapy*]. Oslo: Gyldendal, 2012.
8. Haugvik M, Johns U. Facets of structure and adaptation: a qualitative study of time-limited psychotherapy with children experiencing difficult family situations. *Clin Child Psychol Psychiatry* 2008; **13**: 235–52.
9. Csibra G, Gergely G. Natural pedagogy. *Trends Cogn Sci* 2009; **13**: 148–53.
10. Tomasello M, Vaish A. Origins of human cooperation and morality. *Annu Rev Psychol* 2013; **64**: 231–55.
11. Gergely G, Watson JS. The social biofeedback theory of parental affect-mirroring: the development of emotional self-awareness and self-control in infancy. *Int J Psychoanal* 1996; **77**: 1181–212.

Chapter 14

Working with Adolescents

Introduction

Mentalization-based treatment for adolescents (MBT-A) was originally developed to treat adolescents who self-harm. MBT-A has subsequently been developed more broadly into an approach to help young people to improve their capacity to represent their own and others' feelings more accurately, particularly in the context of emotional challenges and interpersonal stressors; it has a strong focus on impulsivity and affect regulation. The rationale behind MBT-A is that mentalizing problems underlie most of the difficulties that adolescents experience in the arena of impulsivity and self-regulation, and often drive relationship challenges and conflicts. The MBT approach as a whole is primarily concerned with mental states in the here and now rather than with the unconscious processes that drive these states, or with cognitive–behavioral management strategies for behavioral symptoms; this emphasis can be particularly salient when working with adolescents who find moments of their day-to-day experiences overwhelming. As with MBT-C (outlined in Chapter 13), MBT-A seeks to help young people to regain a more helpful place on the developmental trajectory, which has the specific task of achieving self-identity and agency.

Adolescence brings with it particular challenges to the young person's capacity to maintain balanced mentalizing. Research indicates that the previously accepted idea that social-cognitive development is largely achieved by the beginning of adolescence is inaccurate, and that the brain is still undergoing significant neurobiological change during adolescence, particularly in relation to social cognition [1–3]. For example, Mills et al. [2] have found that the gray matter volume in regions of the brain that are associated with mentalizing—the temporoparietal junction, posterior superior temporal sulcus, and medial prefrontal cortex—decreases from childhood into the early twenties. Meanwhile, the gray matter volume of the anterior temporal cortex, another part of the "social brain" network, increases until early adolescence, and cortical thickness increases into early adulthood. More research into the developmental neurobiology of mentalizing is needed, but there are suggestions that "while brain regions involved in social perception develop early in life, the fine-tuning or functional specialization of other regions of the social brain network may continue during adolescence" (Moor et al. [4], p. 50). This is reflected in findings of a slight decline in performance on the Reading the Mind in the Eyes task in 14- to 16-year-olds compared with adults [4].

The clinical implication of such research is that individuals who enter adolescence with a predisposition to weakness in their capacity for mentalizing (which may arise for many different reasons, such as genetic or environmental factors, or an interaction of the two) may be particularly vulnerable when faced with the considerable developmental demands of this life stage. Given the challenges that adolescents experience in relation to maintaining the capacity for mentalizing, wider systems around them that support the social-cognitive processes that underpin affect regulation in the face of challenges and stresses have an important role to play. For example, an experimental study indicated that a brief intervention to encourage empathic discipline reduced school suspension rates by 50% among adolescents [5] (for a discussion of mentalization-based interventions in schools and other settings, see also Chapter 17). When working with children, adolescents, and families, the interactive and mutually reinforcing nature of mentalizing is particularly evident, as is the value of supporting a mentalizing environment around adolescents across different settings and forms of working (e.g., pastoral care in school, youth work, psychotherapy). Regardless of the cause of an adolescent's difficulties, supporting their capacity to mentalize can be helpful because mentalizing supports affect regulation. Moreover, being able to recognize mental states and think about them can help a young person to identify that, for example, they might need help. Being able to think in a more complex way about other people may enable a young person who tends to be aggressively reactive to pause when they feel provoked by someone else, rather than immediately retaliating.

A clear sense of the mentalizing profile of the young person (and, where relevant, the mentalizing profiles of their parents or carers) will provide the clinician with valuable insights. Just as all interventions need to be age appropriate, it is also essential that they are appropriate to the adolescent's mentalizing capacity. Understanding an adolescent's mentalizing profile requires knowledge of what might be approximately normative for an adolescent at that age, and how the individual's profile differs from what might be typically expected. Examples of this may be seen in the kinds of problems that a school counselor or mental health worker might encounter in the course of their work at a secondary school. Here we provide two clinical examples of adolescents with different presenting problems and different underlying mentalizing profiles.

Clinical Example: Eddie

Eddie, who was 15 years of age, was referred for panic attacks and high levels of social anxiety, which were causing low mood, school refusal, and considerable distress. Eddie was an intelligent and thoughtful adolescent who was interested in other people's minds and attempting to make sense of his own mental states. In fact, this may have been part of the problem for Eddie—when he was bullied both in person and on social media (the seriousness of the bullying was not initially adequately addressed by his school) he became highly preoccupied and distressed by what he experienced as coming from the minds of his peers. At times, Eddie would feel so overwhelmed by his thoughts and fears about his peers and their behavior that he would become angry and aggressive, and on occasion the alien self (see Chapter 2) would become active. In a non-mentalizing state of mind, Eddie would become hostile and even threatening to his peers, which created a vicious cycle of difficult and problematic social relations. From a mentalizing perspective, Eddie's situation could be understood in terms of his naturally high capacity for mentalizing becoming overactivated and unbalanced in response to the quite considerable social stressors he was facing. As a result, therapeutic work with Eddie could be approached in terms of thinking about overthinking and the sudden emergence of underthinking when he was feeling stressed. Eddie found it useful and interesting to be introduced to thinking reflectively about mental states, his process of hypermentalizing other people, and understanding his non-mentalizing in moments of stress and distress. An additional factor that was essential in helping Eddie was initiating discussions with some of his schoolteachers about the level of hostility from his peers to which he had been exposed, which led to certain teachers (his form teacher and some significant subject teachers) acknowledging what he was experiencing and expressing their support. This caused a major shift in how frightening and non-mentalizing he found the social climate at school, leading him to be able to access help and reduce his sense of panic and the escalating presence of the alien self when he was exposed to difficult interactions.

Clinical Example: Maya

Maya, who was 15 years old, was experiencing depression, anxiety, and chaotic eating patterns. She found it quite difficult to think about her state of mind in any way at all. In discussions about how she was feeling and her thoughts about her difficulties, she was only able to describe a very general sense of stress and physical symptoms, such as having a headache or feeling sick. Although Maya was the same age and at the same level of academic competence as Eddie, she really struggled to think in mental-state terms about her experiences and about other people's motivations—her teachers were seen as simply wanting to stress her out, and a friend with whom she had fallen out was described as just wanting to annoy her. As we mentioned in Chapters 3 and 4, it is not helpful to respond to someone's non-mentalizing with mentalizing. Rather, in Maya's case, it was more helpful for the clinician to begin by validating Maya's experiences and for the two of them to talk together about these, even as Maya discussed them in quite concrete terms, in order to begin the process of showing an interest in Maya's experience and reflecting back to her something of her experience and its reception by someone else's mind. Only after generating this initial experience with her was it appropriate to start to explore her mental states a little more, in the first instance via the clinician's expressions of curiosity and interest and simply raising the possibility of there being more complex thoughts behind Maya's responses, which could then be explored by Maya as well. In Maya's case, a warm but rather light-hearted and tentative, even self-deprecating approach by the clinician seemed to help to introduce this way of thinking. For example, the clinician made comments such as *"You know I'm always very interested in what things are like for you, Maya, and I'd be so keen to understand more about how you are feeling—but I know I probably get things wrong most of the time* (the clinician rolls her eyes at herself) *so tell me if I'm being totally clueless here, but I wonder if . . ."*

Key Concepts Involved in Working with Adolescents

Many of the major ideas that inform MBT theory and practice and which were covered in Part II of this book are relevant to working with adolescents—for example, the role of the non-mentalizing modes and careful consideration of the interpersonal situations that are likely to stimulate the emergence of these modes. When working with adolescents, this will usually involve careful additional consideration of the young person's family and educational environment. Often non-mentalizing behavior by parents or caregivers can be a part of established spirals of reactive non-mentalizing. Understanding the perceived hostile, rejecting, or punitive stance that can trigger these cycles is frequently an important aspect of making sense of non-mentalizing behavior, and it is for this reason that family MBT is normally recommended alongside individual MBT-A.

Similarly, the mentalizing stance is core to MBT-A. The therapist's open curiosity, compassion, and warmth are at the heart of MBT-A. Trudie Rossouw has beautifully captured the significance of the mentalizing stance in relation to working with adolescents: "So often young people are caught in a frightening inner world of self-hatred which renders them vulnerable to expect similar feelings of disdain from the world around them . . . these youngsters often relate to themselves in a dehumanising way. We need to embody humanity in our interactions with young people in therapy. We show authentic interest and curiosity about the young person's life and mind, and we explore the richness of all possibilities in a non-judgmental way" (Rossouw [6], p. 45).

As Rossouw and her colleagues have described, within the framework of the mentalizing stance there are four key forms of therapeutic technique in MBT-A practice [7]:

1. support and empathy
2. clarification and elaboration
3. challenge
4. mentalizing the patient–therapist relationship.

This group of techniques forms the basis of the original MBT approach developed for the treatment of adults with personality disorders [8]. Rossouw and her colleagues have applied and developed these techniques in relation to working with young people, and readers who are interested in learning more about MBT-A are encouraged to read their indispensable practical guide to this approach [7]. For the purpose of providing an introduction to how MBT-A has been developed, we shall offer a brief overview here.

Support and Empathy

The provision of support and empathy by the therapist is the most continuously applied technique in MBT-A; it is particularly important at the start of treatment and whenever patients are overwhelmed and dysregulated. As we mentioned in Chapter 4, when a patient is distressed and their mentalizing abilities are under siege by overwhelming emotions, the therapist makes no immediate attempt to introduce a mentalizing intervention designed to re-stimulate the patient's mentalizing. Instead it is recommended that they provide some support, empathy, and validation and recognition of the patient's experience—a form of emotional marked mirroring. This may involve statements such as "*Wow, hearing you describe that, I can really see how difficult it must have felt.*"

Clarification, Elaboration, and Challenge

The techniques of clarification, elaboration, and challenge are used alongside support and empathy. For example, if a young person describes an incident in which they self-harmed, the therapist seeks clarification about what was happening during the build-up to the incident. The therapist might then work to engage the patient in thinking about the steps from the (social) trigger that stimulated such feelings of hurt and upset in them.

Clinical Example: Holly

Holly reported having had a terrible day at school that week; once she got home, she binged on junk food and then self-harmed. On being asked to say a little about what had gone on at school, she said: *"I hate school. I just hate it, that's all—I just spend the whole day thinking 'I hate this and I don't want to be here.'"*

The task for the clinician is to find the correct balance between validating and empathizing with the young person's experience, and avoiding feeding the affect by completely accepting the young person's account.

> **Clinician:** I can tell you had a really awful day and how horrible and upsetting school was that day. And I know you feel you hate school all the time, but can we just think back to that particular day at school? Tell me about your day, if you can remember. I'd be interested to know whether there was anything that made things worse.

As Holly walked the clinician through her school day, it became clear that she had felt exposed to what she perceived as the humiliating scrutiny of the group of "popular mean girls" in her sports lesson, sparking intense feelings of shame and rejection. She had spent the whole morning in anxious anticipation of the experience, and although in fact nothing in particular happened during that lesson, she spent the day in a state of extreme anxiety and discomfort. By going through the detail of the day, the story of heightening affect became clear, increasing her anxious arousal and leading to a vicious circle of hypermentalizing about what the girls in the group were thinking. By the time she got home from school, Holly was so overwhelmed that she felt she could only manage her state by an act of self-harm. Through careful exploration of the day and the escalating affect that characterized it, Holly could start to understand her feelings better.

It is important to note that the clinician's initial response to Holly's upset was supportive and validating. Only once Holly felt understood and less alone in how she felt was it appropriate for the clinician to explore and clarify in more detail, and only when Holly was clearly more in touch with her mentalizing capacities would it be appropriate to lightly challenge her perspective, by introducing a less catastrophic view about the other girls in the class on whom her hypermentalizing stance had become fixed. If such a challenge had been introduced too early or too dogmatically, it might have left Holly feeling misunderstood or criticized.

At the heart of this work of clarification, elaboration, and challenge is careful attention to affect and affect identification. This emphasis on affect is vital for preventing the work of mentalizing from slipping into a pseudomentalizing stance in which what may be going on for someone might be discussed almost as an intellectual exercise (i.e., pretend mode; see Chapter 2), without sufficient appreciation of the emotional meaning, which gives whatever is going on its real meaning, nuance, or salience. In elaborating affect, the clinician seeks to explore the feeling states of the patient empathically.

Basic Mentalizing

Clinical Example: Empathic Exploration

> **Patient:** My friend said she was out on the high street and saw my boyfriend talking to another girl. She said the girl looked really flirty, and I know what a slag she is.

> **Clinician:** So do you know the girl your friend said he was talking to?

Patient: No, but I can bet she was a slag. You don't have a clue, of course she was or she wouldn't be talking to him. She just wants to ruin it all for me, by taking him off me.

Clinician: I can see that your friend telling you this about your boyfriend talking to another girl would make you jealous, especially as you've often thought that about some other girls who you *do* know (*the clinician is normalizing*). But what makes you so sure about him wanting to go off with her?

Patient: Because I know, that's what girls like that do, just to get at me. They just think they can walk over me as if I don't exist and I'm just not worth anything. It makes me feel like they know how shit I am and they're just showing it to the world.

Clinician: It is really difficult to know how to cope with the feeling of jealousy when someone tells you something like that, and then it makes you feel so terrible so fast (*the clinician is trying to identify the effect of the initial emotion*). Let's look at how it jumped so far so quickly.

In this moment, the patient has jumped from the feeling of discomfort when she heard her friend's provocative report, to certainty about her boyfriend's infidelity, to intense feelings of low self-worth, with the risk that she will respond to these feelings with an act of self-harm. The process is one of psychic equivalence (see Chapter 2), in which what the patient believes and fears—about her boyfriend and then about other people's perception of her as worthless—becomes a terrifying truth. Rather than arguing with the patient about her beliefs, the therapist should empathize without escalating, work to identify and normalize the affect, and then identify its impact on the patient's state of mind.

The central focus of MBT-A is to restore basic mentalizing in young people. Sometimes young people may find it difficult to pinpoint any clear emotion and how it relates to their mood. A profile of hopelessness and joylessness can be highly characteristic of distressed young people, and the task of thinking about those feelings, in order to challenge them, can be an active part of restoring basic mentalizing. This indicates the way in which mentalizing is not in itself the final objective of MBT. Rather, the purpose of supporting mentalizing is to make other ways of experiencing oneself and others possible—in this case, in a way that makes pleasure possible.

Let us return to the case of Maya, who found it difficult to think about her own or other people's mental states. When Maya returned home from school, she shut herself in her room and attempted to sleep all afternoon and evening. This caused her to fall behind with her schoolwork, leaving her more stressed, and she would be unable to sleep at night, so would end up lying in bed scrolling through social media.

Clinical Example: Mentalizing the Relationship

Clinician: When you have these feelings of being very tired and just wanting to sleep when you get stressed out about school, I wonder if that's about trying to escape from how you're feeling (*not-knowing exploration*).

Maya: I don't know. I just get tired and stressed out and it's the only way to get a break from the stress.

Clinician: It must be exhausting, feeling that tired and worn out by everything that's been going on (*initial empathy*).

MAYA: Yes. Well, I know I need to change my routine but it's so hard when I just want a break and to sleep. There's nothing else that I can do when I'm so tired.

CLINICIAN: I can see that, it makes me tired, too, just thinking about it. Which makes me wonder if there's something about being tired and wanting to sleep that both of us are doing because we don't know what to do! (*The clinician is beginning to mentalize the relationship.*)

Mentalizing the Relationship

In the previous clinical example, we see that the clinician introduces something of how they are feeling—a sense of their response to the feelings of tiredness and the interaction between Maya and the clinician at that moment, and how it may impact on what is happening in their work. This is an example of mentalizing the relationship.

Hypermentalizing

One of the areas of research developed by Carla Sharp and her colleagues is the significance of the phenomenon of hypermentalizing in adolescence [9,10]. Hypermentalizing involves the young person being in a state where they develop an idea about the mental states of others, or frantically seek to elaborate a theory about what someone else might be thinking or feeling (often in a way that manifests as quite a persecuted view about the other person's hostility, contempt, or rejection), but this is based on distorted or mistaken beliefs. In hypermentalizing, there may be excessive certainty about what the other person is thinking (i.e., psychic equivalence). It can also manifest as a form of pseudomentalizing (or pretend mode) in which the mental states of others are speculated upon, often with great intensity, but without sufficient grounding either in the real world or in an awareness of the truth that an individual simply cannot know what other people are thinking with complete accuracy or certainty. Sharp and her colleagues found that hypermentalizing may be a characteristic of young people with borderline personality disorder (BPD) or those who develop BPD later in life [9,11,12]. Hypermentalizing may also occur in more moderate forms in adolescents who are experiencing social anxiety—as in the clinical example of Eddie, who would find himself unhelpfully speculating about the states of mind of his peers or teachers. Hypermentalizing is not seen exclusively in adolescents, but it can be particularly pronounced in adolescents as they encounter a wider and more challenging social world. Helping adolescents to reduce their intense but unsuccessful attempts to "get inside" the minds of others can be an important contribution to lessening some of the painfulness and instability of their social relationships. It is made harder at times because hypermentalizing is to some extent adaptive, protecting the individual from impulsive action such as self-harm or violence resulting from a collapse into teleological mode (see Chapter 2).

The Alien Self

A key concept that we use to understand the impulse toward self-harm and suicidality is that of the *alien self* (see also Chapter 2). When an individual's capacity to mentalize collapses, in addition to the emergence of the non-mentalizing modes of functioning, they are also vulnerable to the overwhelming intrusion of the alien self. To return to our developmental model of mentalizing, a young child develops an appreciation of their own mind, and then other people's, through experiences—beginning in infancy—of having their subjective state accurately recognized, mirrored, and responded to by their caregiver. The infant's experience of having these "secondary representations" of their mind being reflected back to them helps their construction of their self-representation and agency. Constitutional (i.e., genetic or biological) vulnerabilities, or exposure to caregiving in which the caregiver is consistently inaccurate or unmirroring in their responses, can leave the child with a weakened representation of their own state, which is incompatible with coherent self-representation. For example, if the caregiver fails to respond to the infant, or if the infant's frustration is met by the caregiver expressing their own anger *at* the child (rather than mirroring the *infant's* frustration back to them), a mismatched or inaccurate secondary representation of the infant is generated for them to internalize. The child's sense of anger is experienced as a generalized sense of the world being angry with and at the child, producing an experience of psychic equivalence. The internalization of this non-contingent representation of the infant's state creates what we describe as the alien self. The representation of the child's mind by the caregiver is necessarily internalized by the infant to forge their sense of self, but the representation is not properly congruent with the infant's self-state, invoking a discontinuity in the self-structure. Such discontinuity is an aversive experience—it involves the uncomfortable sense of holding a feeling, belief, or wish that does not really feel like one's own.

In cases where the alien self has become the vessel for the self-representations arising from caregiver abuse or neglect, it can be a particularly persecuting presence, and the need to get rid of it and externalize it may be intensely felt. This need can be manifested by, for example, provocatively irritating someone else if one is angry, or by generating uncertainty in someone else if the alien affect is associated with vulnerability. It can also be externalized in relation to one's own body—in the need for punishment or relief in the form of self-harm or suicidality. Clinical work in adolescence has frequently revealed the presence of a malignant alien self which leads to severe internal attacks and generates terrifying internal states in which the young person feels overwhelmingly useless, like a failure, unlovable, hopeless, and so on. The ferocity of the internal attack is such that it is unbearable, and what makes it particularly unbearable is that due to the young person's lack of capacity to mentalize their experience, the experience is felt not as a feeling, but as a fact. Therefore the flight into action is necessary. To return to the clinical example of Eddie, he occasionally found that his hypermentalizing thought processes around a problematic or hostile peer would create such heightened affect (anxiety, fear, and feelings of rejection and hostility) that when a difficult or potentially difficult encounter with that peer loomed, his capacity to think about what was going on completely dissolved, and he would lash out with quite extreme verbal attacks or threats.

Structure of MBT-A

MBT-A is usually delivered as individual MBT sessions combined with either mentalization-based family therapy (MBT-F; described in Chapter 15) or group MBT (MBT-G; described in Chapter 5). Usually, individual MBT is combined with both MBT-G and MBT-F when a more intensive program is indicated. Typically, the individual MBT-A sessions take place at least weekly, whereas the MBT-F sessions occur less frequently, perhaps once a month. Treatment normally continues for 12 months.

Assessment

The assessment phase involves the use of diagnostic, cognitive, and mentalizing measures such as the Reflective Functioning Questionnaire for Youth [13]. It also considers family functioning, and the stressors that may disrupt the parents' mentalizing are identified. The assessment phase typically lasts for 2 weeks and involves one or two sessions with individual therapists and one or two sessions with the family therapist. Ideally, the family therapist and the individual therapist are different individuals.

Initial Phase

Formulation

The initial phase of treatment begins with the patient receiving a written formulation, followed by a discussion between the patient and the clinician about the formulation. The same process of providing and discussing a formulation takes place with the parents in the family component of treatment. Creating the family formulation frequently highlights—and requires thought about—the fact that different family members may well have quite different perspectives on the nature of the difficulties the family is facing. The development of the formulation itself is, as always in MBT, a collaborative effort that requires acknowledgement and consideration of differences in views.

Crisis Plan

When working with young people who are at higher risk of harming themselves or others, it is essential to have a very clear crisis plan. As Rossouw [6] has pointed out, a concrete crisis plan is important for two reasons—it helps to provide a way to manage the risk presented when working with young people, and it provides a supportive and mentalizing network to scaffold the young people as they seek to manage their emotions and encounter challenges.

A detailed crisis plan is included in the formulation for the young person. This plan seeks to highlight factors that might trigger emotional dysregulation and impulsive behavior, and suggests ways to reinstate mentalizing and, if that fails, sets out alternative immediate courses of action rather than the dangerous ways forward that the young person may otherwise use when they are dysregulated and distressed. An example of a crisis plan (based on Rossouw [14], p. 63) is given here.

Clinical Example: Crisis Plan

Trigger factors that you and I identified are times when you feel rejected, humiliated, or bad about yourself. As we have discussed, these feelings do not just arrive out of the blue—they are likely to have been triggered in a close relationship. When you have those feelings you tend to rush into an action to take the feelings away.

When you feel like that again, I would like you to try and stop the action by trying to delay it for 10 minutes. Then use the 10 minutes to try and reflect on what was happening a few moments before you had the bad feeling. That might help you to understand more clearly what it is that you feel as well as what might have happened in a close relationship which may have contributed to the feeling.

Once you have this understanding more clearly, it may be easier to think about a solution or to see things from a different perspective. Once that has happened you may not feel as if you need to rush into action any more.

If that fails and you still feel at risk of harming yourself, try to explore alternatives to self-harm—do something physical and strenuous like going for a run, try to distract yourself, talk to a friend or someone you trust, or try to think about a person you know who loves you and imagine what that person would feel and say to you if you were to talk to them.

Sometimes you harm yourself in order to numb yourself emotionally. When you get into such a state of mind, try to remember that it is not a good state of mind for you to be in and it is harmful to you.

Try to bring yourself back to reality—do something to occupy yourself, like talking to someone, playing a game, writing a poem, painting, or watching something that can hold your attention on television. Don't just sit and stare into space with your mind full of negative thoughts about yourself.

If all else fails, call the clinic and ask to speak to me and I will call you back when I can.

Another crisis plan is presented to the parents. This plan includes some basic education about self-harm, and advice on how to respond to self-harming behaviors. It includes some basic safety advice, such as keeping medication locked away or, if relevant, keeping access to razors or knives restricted. The parents are encouraged to listen, understand, and communicate to the young person that they are supportive and that they are there for them. They are encouraged not to panic, blame, or punish the young person.

Contract

The contract is an agreement about the treatment plan, including the duration of treatment and the commitment required of all participants in the treatment, including the parents.

Psychoeducation

The formulation session with the family is usually followed by a psychoeducational session. The purpose of this session is to introduce the underpinning principles of MBT—that behavior has meaning, that feelings arise in a relational context, and that people have a powerful emotional impact on one another.

The format of this session can be either a multi-family group or an individual family session. It is generally approached as a discussion with the family or families using examples from everyday life to illustrate the main principles. Particularly in a multi-family group context, it may be helpful to use games, role play, and video materials to assist the discussion.

Middle Phase

The middle phase of MBT-A usually lasts for 9–10 months. The overall purpose of this stage of treatment is to improve the mentalizing skills of the patient and their family. MBT-A sessions are largely unstructured; this is necessary because the focus of each session is generally on the young person's current or recent interpersonal experiences and the mental states evoked by these experiences. A key component of the process involves helping both the young person and their family to achieve better impulse control. Specific interventions are used to manage suicidal, parasuicidal, and other harmful or impulsive behaviors such as substance use, threatening behavior, or bingeing and purging.

Final Phase

The aim of the final phase of MBT-A, as with all psychotherapeutic treatments, is to develop the patient's independence. A crucial aspect of achieving this goal is building up relational stability and supporting the patient's sense of agency and autonomy within their relational networks. A coping plan is also created so that the patient and their family know what to do if difficulties recur. The final phase usually lasts for about 2 months, with the appointments becoming more widely spaced toward the end.

Concluding Remarks

The socially responsive nature of the development of mentalizing informs the theory and practice of MBT-A in three different ways. First, the nature of the work must be appropriate to the developmental stage—it is essential that the work is informed by an understanding of the nature of the mentalizing strengths and weaknesses that are typical of adolescents, and that it is sensitive to the fact that even into late adolescence and young adulthood the capacity to retain balanced mentalizing remains vulnerable. Second, developmental processes can lend a certain urgency—an intervention that can support the adolescent's growing capacity to think about mental states may support their development in different and valuable ways. Third, the emergent mentalizing should be regarded as a therapeutic opportunity—adolescents are often extremely curious about other people's mental states, and thrive on the opportunity to stimulate those ideas in a regulated way. The experience of having a secure and robustly mentalizing therapeutic intervention that explicitly signals an interest in the adolescent's mind in a regulated and non-intrusive way, while also respecting its separateness and agency, can provide a boost to the adolescent's developmental trajectory.

References

1. Dumontheil I, Apperly IA, Blakemore SJ. Online usage of theory of mind continues to develop in late adolescence. *Dev Sci* 2010; **13**: 331–8.
2. Mills KL, Lalonde F, Clasen LS et al. Developmental changes in the structure of the social brain in late childhood and adolescence. *Soc Cogn Affect Neurosci* 2014; **9**: 123–31.
3. Crone EA, Dahl RE. Understanding adolescence as a period of social-affective engagement and goal flexibility. *Nat Rev Neurosci* 2012; **13**: 636–50.
4. Moor BG, Macks ZA, Guroglu B et al. Neurodevelopmental changes of reading the mind in the eyes. *Soc Cogn Affect Neurosci* 2012; **7**: 44–52.
5. Okonofua JA, Paunesku D, Walton GM. Brief intervention to encourage empathic discipline cuts suspension rates in half among adolescents. *Proc Natl Acad Sci U S A* 2016; **113**: 5221–6.
6. Rossouw T. MBT technique when working with young people. In: Rossouw T, Wiwe M, Vrouva I, eds. *Mentalization-Based Treatment for Adolescents: A Practical Treatment Guide*. Abingdon, UK: Routledge, 2021; 43–56.
7. Rossouw T, Wiwe M, Vrouva I, eds. *Mentalization-Based Treatment for Adolescents: A Practical Treatment Guide*. Abingdon, UK: Routledge, 2021.
8. Bateman A, Fonagy P. *Mentalization-Based Treatment for Personality Disorders: A Practical Guide*, 2nd ed. Oxford, UK: Oxford University Press, 2016.
9. Sharp C, Vanwoerden S. Hypermentalizing in borderline personality disorder: a model and data. *J Infant Child Adolesc Psychother* 2015; **14**: 33–45.
10. Bo S, Sharp C, Fonagy P, Kongerslev M. Hypermentalizing, attachment, and epistemic trust in adolescent BPD: clinical illustrations. *Personal Disord* 2017; **8**: 172–82.

11. Sharp C, Ha C, Carbone C et al. Hypermentalizing in adolescent inpatients: treatment effects and association with borderline traits. *J Personal Disord* 2013; **27**: 3–18.
12. Sharp C. The social-cognitive basis of BPD: a theory of hypermentalizing. In: Sharp C, Tackett JL, eds. *Handbook of Borderline Personality Disorder in Children and Adolescents*. New York, NY: Springer, 2014; 211–26.
13. Sharp C, Steinberg L, McLaren V et al. Refinement of the Reflective Function Questionnaire for Youth (RFQY) Scale B using item response theory. *Assessment* 2022; 29: 1204–15.
14. Rossouw T. The structure of therapy. In: Rossouw T, Wiwe M, Vrouva I, eds. *Mentalization-Based Treatment for Adolescents: A Practical Treatment Guide*. Abingdon, UK: Routledge, 2021; 57–73.

Chapter 15 Working with Families

Introduction

Mentalization-based treatment for families (MBT-F) has been developed as a way of integrating the mentalizing approach into existing models of family therapy—a therapist can use MBT-F either as a stand-alone intervention or as an additional tool to draw on and to help to shape their thinking. Applying a mentalizing approach to working with families involves a focus on interactions where mentalizing breaks down and the non-mentalizing modes come to the fore. Children who are frequently exposed to such collapses in mentalizing will miss out on the helpful developmental experience of being exposed to thinking about mental states that drive people's behavior in regulated ways. Typically, a family system suffers a collective crash in mentalizing at times of conflict, and the emergence of non-mentalizing generates a breakdown in affect regulation, so the possibility of thinking about what is going on in the minds of fellow family members becomes overwhelmed.

A mentalization-based family approach often seeks to engage the family in conversation about typically difficult scenarios in their family life, noticing and drawing attention to changes in affect and how they influence other family members. The purpose of the work is to mentalize family behavior, and to draw connections between the mental states and behavior of the self and others. Many of the techniques used in MBT-F are in fact well-known, pre-existing systemic practices. However, MBT-F differs from other family interventions in its explicit focus on mentalizing. A key objective of MBT-F is to develop the understanding that family members are able to experience in relation to one another (taking into account the developmental capacities of children and adolescents). Because MBT-F is not a structured program, we shall describe here some of the key ideas and techniques used in MBT-F.

The Mentalizing Stance in MBT-F

We have referred to the mentalizing stance throughout this book, and the facets of the mentalizing stance described in previous chapters apply just as much to MBT-F. As a reminder for the reader, the mentalizing stance involves the following qualities and behaviors. It is inquisitive, constantly affirming the value of mentalizing by means of a respectful, curious, and tentative inquiring attitude. The therapist shows interest but not certainty in relation to mental states, and openly models their own mentalizing, which includes an openness about admitting to mentalizing mistakes and breakdowns. Indeed, these moments of rupture can be useful for restoring co-mentalizing and demonstrating the lack of certainty with which any of us can know mental states. The stance involves responding in a non-judgmental way to patients' non-mentalizing, in the first instance through the use of empathy and validation. As the therapeutic process develops, the stance evolves to start introducing clarification, affect focus, and elaboration to encourage the exploration of mental states. A further process is then introduced, involving gentle challenge, interruptions of non-mentalizing, and drawing connections.

The task of the MBT-F clinician in maintaining the mentalizing stance is to *keep a balance* between observing natural interactions and intervening to promote change by helping family members to make sense of the feelings that are experienced by each family member; this also involves highlighting the ways in which miscommunication or misunderstanding (or lack of understanding) of these feelings leads to interactions that maintain family problems. Furthermore, the therapist works to *interrupt non-mentalizing* interactions and create a context that can help to generate new and different perspectives. Another important task of the therapist is that of *marking and supporting effective mentalizing*, to help to develop the family members' ability to connect feelings, thoughts, and intentions positively; this is done by highlighting and discussing examples of effective mentalizing.

The MBT Loop

One frequently used technique that is available for creating a framework in which mentalizing can be practiced by a family is the MBT Loop (which is described in more detail in Chapter 4). In the context of family therapy, the "loop" is extended to bring the family members together so as to create a sense of collectively mentalizing the moment, while also holding on to the idea that each family member has a different perspective [1].

The MBT Loop is initiated by the therapist making an observation about a family interaction: "*I saw that when Josh described how he doesn't care when Dad gets angry when he thinks Josh is being disrespectful both Mum and Dad started to look quite cross, but Lucy looked a little upset.*" The therapist is drawing attention to the observable emotional responses of the family—external mentalizing—but at this point also needs to check in on the internal mentalizing of the family members: "*Does what I just described seem right to you, or is it not quite the right description of what's going on?*" In switching to this internal focus, the therapist is modeling a mentalizing stance (not overly definite, but curious and wanting to explore mental states). By bringing in the therapist's perspective, the interaction is now opened up as something for the family to consider together.

Assuming that there is some engagement among the family members with what the therapist has said in initiating the loop, the therapist can expand on the process by seeking to further "mentalize the moment." This involves focusing more closely on the interaction in the here and now, in order to draw closer attention to thinking about the mental states behind it. For example, the therapist might say: "*If we try to imagine being in Lucy's place at that moment, can we try to imagine what she was feeling or what thoughts went through her mind when she was looking so sad?*" By wondering what it is like to be in Lucy's shoes, the therapist is deliberately encouraging the parents to mentalize their child—by looping out of their low mentalizing and focusing on the mind of another person. On the whole it is better to begin by asking the parents to think about their child's mental states, before asking them to mentalize themselves. Only after the parents have given some thought to the here-and-now experience of the child might the therapist encourage each parent to explore their own mentalizing in response to the child—for example, by asking: "*Seeing Lucy looking tearful like that, what feelings does that make you have?*"

After hearing one parent's perspective on what was going on for Lucy, the therapist then expands the MBT Loop to another family member: "*So Mum says she thinks Lucy is relieved that the family is trying to understand each other a bit more instead of shouting at each other. Dad, what do you think about what was happening for Lucy at that moment?*" The therapist would ask all the family members for their thoughts on this in a similar way: "*Josh, if Lucy had cartoon thought bubbles coming out of her head, what do you think they would say?*" The process of the therapist trying to get the whole family to "brainstorm" the interaction—being careful to check in with all the family members and to encourage them to say how they see things, similarly or differently—produces the loop: "what has been noticed is named and what has been named is questioned, and perceptions are checked all round. When family members are encouraged to rewind and review a specific sequence in this way, a meta-perspective is generated, which can reignite an effective mentalizing stance"(Asen and Fonagy [1], pp. 28–9).

In addition to focusing on what is happening in the room, the therapist may ask a family member to connect the here-and-now mental states with similar situations that may have arisen in the family, and to connect the interactions that are taking place in the session with family patterns of behavior. The loop is therefore extended to encompass wider family patterns and typical scenarios. This encourages family discussions of typical difficulties, with the therapist working to help to keep the focus on tracing the meanings and feelings behind these typical behaviors for all of the family members involved. A simple question from the therapist can help to achieve this: "*Have you noticed that things like this are also happening at home? . . . And how might you manage this differently next time something like this happens?*" (Asen and Fonagy [1], p. 29). It is this shift to *generalizing and considering change* that aims to stimulate the family members' own ideas and solutions. If it leads to proposals by one family member, then this is *noticed and named* by the therapist: "*I can see that Dad thinks if this happens, Mum should take him calmly aside and not talk in front of your daughter—have I got that right?*", and the "checking" loop starts again (Asen and Fonagy[1], p. 29).

The therapist attempts to slow down the interactions between the family members by asking questions or highlighting their curiosity about what is going on for each individual in the interaction. The purpose of introducing this pause into the flow of family relationships is that it allows more scope for reflective mentalizing. The overall objective is for the family members to shift their perspective so that they become less caught up in the specifics of what took place in the session, and develop a more generalized understanding of how problematic interactions unfold.

Exercises in MBT-F

MBT-F has developed a range of techniques and borrowed others from systemic family therapy in order to find ways to restore individual mentalizing and to encourage the family's attention and interest in mental states to be distributed between and across all of the family members. Exercises in MBT-F are designed to be fun, and they are a further example of the use of play in MBT. The use of play has been outlined as being particularly important in work with individuals with avoidant personality disorder (see

Chapter 8) and also with children (see Chapter 13), although playfulness is an essential component of all forms of MBT. The exercises do not always require explicit reflection, but rather the implicit, intuitive understanding of internal states that supports the creation of a mentalizing culture within a family. MBT-F incorporates this implicit learning principle by articulating that the main task of the therapist is to construct a mentalizing culture by facilitating shared reflection on the family members' lived experiences.

The exercise known as "stepping into someone else's shoes" was developed to encourage family members to think about things from each other's perspective. It begins with each family member being asked to take a piece of paper, put it under their feet, and draw the outline of their shoes. The family is then asked to talk about a recent difficult interaction or misunderstanding, spending about 5 minutes on this. Each family member then gets up and moves to the seat of the person on their left, putting their feet on to the outline of the shoes of the person who had been sitting next to them [2]. The therapist asks questions: "*What does it feel like to sit there in these shoes? Are they too big or too small? Is it a good feeling or a bit uncomfortable? Just imagine you are now that person and you have to continue the discussion you just had, but from that person's standpoint.*" In occupying the "shoes" of each other, the family members are being encouraged to think about the issue from each other's perspective. This has two benefits. First, the person who is occupying another person's shoes is exercising their capacity to mentalize that other person, and second, this can generate in the person whose shoes are being occupied the experience of being recognized, and of their perspective being acknowledged and understood. The communication of understanding that such an exercise provides will ideally stimulate openness to further co-mentalizing and reduce epistemic vigilance.

The "body–feeling scan" is an exercise in which each family member is asked to lie on a large piece of paper while another family member draws their silhouette around them [2]. Each family member then draws or paints their feelings into their respective body outline, using whatever colors, shapes, or images come to mind, and they are asked to label these feelings. Finally, they show their "scan" to the rest of the family, while explaining the feelings. The family members might compare where different feelings, such as worry or anger, are placed in their bodies, and in explaining their scans they convey exactly how these feelings feel—how some feelings are hard to express, how some are difficult to control—as well as describing happy or fun feelings that are more accessible and can be shared with the family. When jealous or angry feelings are described, this can be an opportunity to talk about how the family member can recognize them and share them with others, to help to manage these feelings before they become too intense. Sharing these experiences of feelings and bodily states introduces the idea that mental states can drive physical states. Behaviors can be mentalized, and furthermore they can be co-mentalized with other family members to help self-regulation and reduce the sense of isolation and being stuck or overwhelmed in a separated, withdrawn physical state.

A variation of this exercise is the "mind–brain scan" [3], in which each family member is given a simple line drawing of a cross-section of the human brain. Instead of the anatomically correct depiction of four brain ventricles, this picture of the brain contains 10 larger and smaller spaces. The family members are asked to imagine what "goes on in the head" of another family member and to fill in the spaces with the feelings, wishes, beliefs, or thoughts they imagine that person has in their mind. In a family of four, it would be possible to get three mind–brain scans of each member, allowing thoughtful comparisons to be made about how different perceptions can be formed [1]. In this exercise, the contents of the "spaces" in the brain are important primarily because they aid communication between the family members. What makes this and the other games that can be used in MBT-F therapeutic is not just the elaboration of mental states that they involve—it is also that they allow implicit understanding to be made explicit through reflection.

Another method for exploring how family members mentalize one another involves the use of sculptures made with modeling clay. Family members are asked to work together on a joint sculpture or, alternatively, children and parents can each create their own sculptures in parallel. The therapist starts the exercise by explaining it to the family members: "*I'd like you to make a sculpture of how you each [or all] see your family now. It doesn't need to be a piece of art, but just a quick way of describing who is in the family, where everybody is in relation to everyone else, who is seen as being right in the middle of the family, or most on the outside, or who is in charge and who is not.*" When the sculptures are finished, the sculptor(s) can explain how and why they captured the family in the particular way that they did. Before or after the sculptor explains their work, the other family members can be asked how they see the sculpture and what it conveys about the thoughts and feelings of its maker. The focus can be moved backward and forward from what was on the mind of the artist when making their sculpture, to speculating on what is on their mind when they are listening to the other family members' descriptions of their work. There is a special value in the activity accompanying the sharing of perspectives. There is nothing "magical" about family sculptures showing how a family member views the family structure, or what an individual's experience in the family might be—it is the active engagement with the knowledge that is presented by all of the family members that generates progress.

Role play, based on psychodrama techniques [4,5], is another activity that can encourage perspective taking. Role plays can be developed based on current or past problematic interactions, with family members being invited to enact these, and then the therapist can introduce some thinking about how the situation might have been handled differently. For example, when parents are invited to attend a session without their child(ren), they can be asked to think about a typical conflictual scenario and then "enact" it [6]. If the situation becomes difficult and heated, the therapist asks the parents to pause and to consider each other's thoughts and feelings. This often proves to be challenging, in which case the therapist suggests that they "replay" the argument, but with their roles swapped—they are asked to swap seats and the mother has to pretend to be the father, and vice versa, with each having to use the exact lines the other had delivered previously. An empty chair, possibly with a photo of the child(ren) placed on it, can represent the child(ren) who are absent from the session. Each parent can then be asked, still in the role of the other, to come up with some different lines about the same problematic scenario, with the aim of having a constructive outcome, rather than the typically stuck one. They can also be asked to imagine themselves in 3 months' time, when hopefully the issue is less heated and the relationship has improved, and to role play how a discussion about a similar problematic scenario might develop then. They are also asked to think about the imaginary child(ren) sitting on the chair and what they might make of the conversation. Finally, each parent is asked to adopt the new lines created by the other and make these their own in a repeat staging of the previously problematic scenario. When doing little role plays of this nature, the parents will usually come up with more than one version; this should stimulate mutual curiosity and entails exploring reasons for the differences in the envisioned possible future scenarios.

When employed by a mentalizing-oriented therapist, the "mind-reading stethoscope" can be used to elicit comments on one's own thoughts and feelings, as well as those of others. In a family session, the therapist encourages a child or a teenager (or even an adult) to see whether they can "hear" something through the stethoscope, placing the earpieces into their ears and the sensor on the head of another member of the family. Although the stethoscope is normally used to identify respiratory and cardiovascular problems (e.g., heart murmurs or lung congestion) rather than to listen to someone's thoughts, it can be surprisingly effective as a prop to enable family members to suspend their general reluctance to mentalize explicitly about each other and in relation to delicate issues.

Clinical Example: The Mind-Reading Stethoscope

Therapist: (*putting the stethoscope on Mum's head*): What do you think goes on in there, in your mum's head? Imagine that you could hear what goes on in her brain . . . What sort of thoughts or wishes might she have? Let us just put the stethoscope on that part of her head . . . right at the back of your mum's mind? Sometimes people put their secret thoughts or feelings right at the back of their head . . . what do you imagine could those be? And what might she feel there? Or maybe she feels things somewhere in a different part of her body . . . this stethoscope can also listen to hearts and tummies. Do you think her heart is big enough for more than one child . . . just listen to the part that is there for you . . . what is it feeling?

Listening to oneself can be done in a similar way, with the person placing the stethoscope on their own heart, brain, or abdomen:

Therapist: . . . and listen to yourself for a moment now . . . that heart of yours, if it could speak, what might it say?

With a bit of encouragement, children generally tend to find it easier to make use of such playful techniques than their parents do—although the parents, encouraged by their child's example, may eventually feel able to use the "mind-reading" stethoscope themselves. Placing the sensor of the stethoscope on the organ that needs to be "listened to" is a simple device for making the link between the physical and mental worlds, the integration of which probably developmentally underpins effective mentalizing. But the playfulness also separates the person from embedded ways of thinking, and light-heartedness reduces anxiety. What seems like a simple device actually turns out to be quite complicated.

Parents and children can build together their own "parent-o-scopes" and "child-o-scopes," using cardboard tubes and other materials. The therapist can observe family processes while the family members construct these pretend instruments together—how they interact and communicate, who leads and who follows, whether there is any give and take, and so on. If parents are unwilling or unable to take part in this exercise, the therapist can supply their own "scopes" from a stock and allow each family member to choose one of them. The *physical structure* of the device concretizes the "viewing" process and thus allows effective mentalizing to be kick-started, particularly in situations where each family member is preoccupied with their own perspective.

There are obvious variations on this playful activity—for example, the construction of "teacher-o-scopes," "police-o-scopes," "best-friend-o-scopes," and so on, further enhancing family members' ability to view a dilemma, a problem, or a person through a number of very different lenses. The essence remains the same—the creation or enhancement of a mentalizing stance in the family by developing increased willingness to break the mold of psychic equivalence and to question and reflect on assumptions and enrich the complexity with which others' perspectives are represented.

Concluding Remarks

In MBT-F, as in all other forms of MBT, mentalizing is the target for treatment. Families are given psychoeducation about mentalizing during the assessment phase, and are then asked to apply what they have learned about mentalizing to their problems. Techniques for encouraging and stabilizing mentalizing within the family follow the MBT model, with the perspective of each family member being validated and explored. The clinician then helps the family members to see things from each other's perspective. Importantly, the family are helped to take charge of their difficulties and discuss how they will address them together while being alert to the dangers of low-mentalizing interactions.

References

1. Asen E, Fonagy P. Mentalizing Family Violence Part 2: techniques and interventions. *Fam Process* 2017; **56**: 22–44.
2. Asen E, Fonagy P. *Mentalization-Based Treatment with Families*. New York, NY: The Guilford Press, 2021.
3. Asen E, Fonagy P. Mentalization-based therapeutic interventions for families. *J Fam Ther* 2012; **34**: 347–70.
4. Moreno JL, Moreno ZT, Moreno J. *The First Psychodramatic Family*. Beacon, NY: Beacon House, 1964.
5. Yablonsky L. *Psychodrama: Resolving Emotional Problems through Role-Playing*. New York, NY: Gardner, 1981.
6. Minuchin S. *Families and Family Therapy*. Cambridge, MA: Harvard University Press, 1974.

Chapter 16

Working with Couples

Introduction

A couple relationship forms one of the most constant co-mentalizing systems for many people, one in which familiarity particularly lends itself to automatic mentalizing in day-to-day functioning. As we mentioned in Chapter 2, intimate relationships, which by their very nature activate attachment systems, tend to cut out mentalizing processes. This can generate scenarios in which mentalizing imbalances can become entrenched, and familiar triggers for the emergence of non-mentalizing modes can be readily enacted. However, a couple relationship can also form an environment in which the potential for salutogenic (resilience- and wellbeing-enhancing) co-mentalizing is rich. Mentalization-based treatment (MBT), with its focus on modeling, supporting, and restoring mentalizing and epistemic trust and the associated capacity to learn socially and emotionally in close relationships, is particularly well suited to thinking about and working with couples. In this chapter, we shall outline the structure and techniques of MBT for couples (MBT-CO), a form of working that has been developed primarily by Efrain Bleiberg and Ellen Safier with Peter Fonagy [1].

Structure of MBT-CO

MBT-CO starts with an initial assessment of the couple's history, functioning, and the extent to which they are able to maintain—and recover—a mentalizing position within the relationship, which involves:

- each partner having a sense of being recognized and understood by their partner
- a common feeling of safety and trust, characterized by the idea that each partner can assume that their partner is "on their side"
- finding in each other an "epistemic partner," who shares their knowledge about the world and about what is going on for the couple in relation to each other and the outside world
- the relationship working both as a "secure base" that invites exploration, playful interactions, and new learning and discovery, and as a "safe haven"
- the relationship being able to maintain a balance between closeness and the erotically charged "otherness" that generates sexual intimacy and pleasure [2].

The initial assessment phase involves exploring how the partners in a couple relate to each other, and identifying to what extent the five qualities listed are present in the relationship, what kind of interactions undermine them, and the moments when non-mentalizing modes of functioning emerge. Specific patterns of interaction—those moments or scenarios in which mentalizing and trust are more likely to break down—are asked about and considered.

Clinical Example: Breakdown of Mentalizing and Trust

Taking the example of a couple who have a young child, the refusal of the child to eat the meal that one parent has prepared might lead to a stand-off between the parent and the child, with the parent feeling increasingly irritable and frustrated. The other parent may appear on the scene and attempt to break the impasse by soothing the increasingly upset child, leaving the first parent feeling unsupported and rejected by both their partner and the child, not helped by the second parent's irritation about the situation and protectiveness toward the child. A cycle of defensiveness is created, in which *teleological mode* (the child must eat and the second parent must get the child to eat, in order to show affection and support for the first parent) and *psychic equivalence* (the first parent feels hurt and frustrated by the child's refusal to eat, so the child is hostile, stubborn, and rejecting—and their partner is, too, in their "complicity" with the child) emerge. What began as a difficult interaction between one parent and the child becomes a crisis between the couple, underpinned by a lack of trust in the other's intentions—the intervention of the second parent is not thought about by the first parent as an attempt to break up a difficult moment, but rather as an attack.

The assessment comprises one or two sessions with the couple, followed by one or two separate sessions with each of them individually. In these sessions, the therapist tries to develop a clear understanding of the difficulties that brought the couple to treatment, their individual history (particularly their attachment history), the couple's history, and their mentalizing strengths and vulnerabilities.

In the individual sessions, the therapist explores each partner's family of origin, relationship history, and views of current strengths (i.e., what they value in their partner and in the relationship and would not want to change) and difficulties, as well as their commitment to the relationship and to the process of therapy, which seeks to address challenges and repair problems. The individual sessions also offer an opportunity to assess each partner's personality, attachment style, level of functioning (i.e., their rigidity, flexibility, coping strategies, cognitive style, and patterns of communication), and their compatibility with their partner. In addition, the individual sessions are used to raise any matters that would be difficult to discuss in the presence of the partner (e.g., physical and/or mental health problems, substance abuse, worries about safety or violence, infidelity, trauma), which both exacerbate and are exacerbated by difficulties in mentalizing. The raising of such issues demands careful thought from the therapist about how to approach supporting the couple in relation to the things that they may be keeping secret from each other, safety and the possibility of creating a safe therapeutic environment, and the appropriateness and readiness of the couple for therapy.

After completion of these joint and individual assessment sessions, a joint session is held in which the therapist presents a formulation for consideration. The formulation explains the therapist's perception of the couple's strengths and weaknesses, and draws particular attention to their mentalizing strengths and vulnerabilities, and their difficulties in trusting and learning. The formulation also suggests a possible path to recovery in terms of couple functioning. As with other types of MBT, the formulation can be presented verbally or in writing; if the formulation is written, it will provide a useful document to refer to and for reviewing progress in the therapy. Remember that the formulation is always very much a "work in progress" rather than a final document.

The assessment and formulation-sharing stage can also be used to introduce and define some ideas about mentalizing and epistemic trust, and to explain the process of MBT. This educational process usually involves an explanation of how mentalizing develops in the context of attachment relationships, and how mentalizing tends to break down when people are defensive or when their attachment systems are highly activated. The consequences of breakdowns in mentalizing in terms of closing the channel for epistemic trust and social communication within the couple are also described, in an attempt to convey the idea that mentalizing is not an end in itself but part of an ongoing cyclical process of communication and openness to communication. Some educational material, such as reading matter and video clips, can also be provided.

As part of the discussion of the formulation, the therapist proposes a treatment structure, which typically involves a weekly session with the couple, and the option of further individual sessions. In addition, one or both of the partners may be referred to individual psychotherapy, medication management, or alcohol and substance use treatment. These options will be suggested as indicated when one or both partners present with significant mental health problems or when breaches of trust, such as infidelity, are apparent.

The Mentalizing Stance in MBT-CO

MBT-CO is built around two key features:

1. the therapist's mentalizing stance ("how to be")
2. the spectrum of interventions available to the therapist ("what to do").

We have described the mentalizing stance in detail in Chapters 3 and 4, and we have referred to it throughout this book. It is a therapeutic stance characterized by a "not-knowing" approach that is open, curious, and non-judgmental in relation to mental states, and it is a fundamental practice on which any MBT work is based. Certain aspects of the mentalizing stance deserve particular attention in work with couples, and we shall briefly focus on these here.

Holding the Balance

Effective mentalizing involves maintaining a flexible balance between the four dimensions of mentalizing (see also Chapter 2)—between attending to self and paying attention to the other, between affect and cognition, between automatic and controlled mentalizing (which is more available when stress and arousal are reduced), and between mentalizing based on internal and external features and experiences as played out by the different people in the room. The clinician gauges the state of mentalizing and arousal of both partners and how an interaction is affecting them, and allows each partner to communicate their experience and feel heard and understood by their partner and the therapist.

Interrupting Non-Mentalizing

A central tenet of MBT-CO is that non-mentalizing tends to emerge as a defensive mechanism during a difficult interaction. This can then cause a negative spiral as the non-mentalizing behavior causes further difficulties and is liable in turn to trigger non-mentalizing in the partner. Therefore, when non-mentalizing functioning becomes apparent during a session, an intervention by the therapist is indicated. The first requirement is for the therapist to recognize that there has been a breakdown in mentalizing, either in one or both of the partners or in the therapist. Non-mentalizing by the clinician is indicated by them arguing with one or both partners, becoming excessively definite about what is happening for the couple, or finding it difficult to hold on to the different points of view of the people in the room. Once the breakdown in mentalizing has been identified, the clinician needs to interrupt the process. One method of doing this is to take a momentary break to allow the therapist to step back and think about what is going on—for both the therapist and the couple.

Highlighting and Marking Mentalizing

Another way in which the therapist displays attentiveness to what is going on in terms of mentalizing is by identifying and marking moments of effective mentalizing on the part of one or both partners. Effective mentalizing can be found in moments when a partner shows evidence of being curious, respectful, and interested in understanding the other's perspective, or of being aware of the impact that they are having on the other. It can also be found when an individual is able to express feelings of vulnerability without becoming defensive or excessively dysregulated, or can accept responsibility for mistakes or the pain they may have caused.

The Spectrum of Interventions in MBT-CO

The interventions described here provide the MBT-CO therapist with suggestions on ways to respond to the couple's current levels of mentalizing. These techniques have been described in more detail elsewhere in this book, as they are used in different MBT programs. Here we describe these interventions in the context of working with couples and the particular considerations and extensions to therapeutic working that the couple environment requires.

Empathy, Support, and Validation

In MBT-CO, the task is not only for the therapist to support and validate the partners in the sessions, but also to help each partner to cease invalidating the other and to develop a more empathic stance toward them. The therapist is treating the relationship itself rather than the individuals, and so they also work to support and validate the couple's attempts to develop a more mentalizing relationship, empathizing with the challenges and effort that this may involve for the couple. One approach to scaffolding a mentalizing stance in a couple is for the therapist to hold a supportive and empathic conversation with each partner in the presence of the other, who is asked to listen and try to understand.

Clarification, Affect Focus, and Elaboration

Once the partners in the couple are beginning to show some reflective curiosity and more compassionate openness toward each other, the therapist can start to develop their mentalizing capacity further by introducing the technique of clarification and elaboration. This process seeks to reconsider what was going on in an interaction that culminated in a breakdown in mentalizing, by asking for the details of the feelings and thoughts that each partner had as the difficult interaction was unfolding. Developing this account of an interaction can involve the use of "rewind and reflect"—a technique in which the therapist asks the couple to trace back and pinpoint the last moment at which they felt as if they were able to think clearly and respond to each other more freely. The therapist then starts a mentalizing functional analysis (see Chapter 4), which involves elaborating in detail how each person's mental states changed in response to what they saw as the meaning behind each moment in the interaction. In this process, the therapist works to draw out and open up the hidden feelings of anxiety and vulnerability that often drive what manifests as defensive distancing activity—this is an intervention that some individuals might experience as quite challenging. The exploration of meanings may lead the partners to consider their earlier experiences, whether as a couple, in previous relationships, or in their families of origin.

Challenge and the Therapeutic Bargain

When the partners in the couple have reached a point at which they are able to work cooperatively with each other and with the therapist, the use of challenge can be introduced. This technique can be particularly useful in couples where there is an element of pretend mode going on in the cooperation, particularly if this involves ignoring or downplaying significant or worrying/damaging behavior, such as substance abuse or other addictive behavior, infidelity, or undisclosed financial decisions or secrets that could put the partnership at risk.

Challenge may typically involve looking at the potential downsides of changing a behavior, even one that appears problematic. The therapist may be quite explicit about the fact that they are moving into difficult territory—for example, they might say "*I hope you will bear with me but I think this is really important.*" Facing an uncomfortable experience of sharing vulnerability is difficult and requires skill. The dilemma is whether to retain defensive, non-mentalizing approaches that provide a semblance of control, safety, and protection, or whether to take the risk involved in giving up those protections to allow a more honest and supportive relationship of trust and co-mentalizing.

Repairing Mentalizing and Epistemic Trust in the Here and Now

The greatest mentalizing demand for the partners in a couple is to expose their vulnerabilities to each other and to maintain trust and mentalizing in the face of intense emotions. The greatest likelihood of generating a virtuous cycle of social learning in a relationship is built on the development of a safe haven and a secure base for each other. This capacity to repair offers each partner the best chance of acquiring a set of tools that can be generalized to other relationships outside the couple and to other contexts outside the treatment relationship, reinstating the resilience-enhancing possibilities of social learning.

The therapist's readiness to take responsibility for their own mistakes and misattunements, and the pain that these cause, sets the stage for a different kind of interaction. Here the therapist is holding themselves accountable in the relationship in a way that parallels what they hope for with the couple they are treating. Apologizing to the couple when these situations arise, and encouraging them to initiate this crucial step within their relationship, opens the door to greater intimacy. When each member of the couple can own their mistakes and genuinely appreciate the impact that they have on their partner, they then become able to express with humility and conviction a desire to earn their partner's trust. It is often helpful to educate couples about the rules of effective apology [3]. In encouraging apologies, the therapist highlights the fact that repairing ruptures in the relationship requires first the capacity to take responsibility—not for the other person's feelings, but for our own hurtful actions. In order to take responsibility, we must first be interested in and then willing to learn about our partner's perspective, and we have to tolerate the fact that we inevitably fall short of our partner's needs and wishes and are likely to disappoint our partner sometimes, no matter how hard we try.

Concluding Remarks

MBT-CO follows clear principles of intervention to promote mentalizing in the couple relationship. As we have emphasized throughout this book, non-mentalizing leads to more non-mentalizing, and nowhere is this better exemplified than in couples who are struggling to relate to each other constructively.

References

1. Bleiberg E, Safier E. Couples therapy. In: Bateman A, Fonagy P, eds. *Handbook of Mentalizing in Mental Health Practice*, 2nd ed. Washington, DC: American Psychiatric Association Publishing, 2019; 151–68.
2. Perel E. *Mating in Captivity: Unlocking Erotic Intelligence*. New York, NY: HarperCollins, 2006.
3. Lerner H. *Why Won't You Apologize? Healing Everyday Hurts and Big Betrayals*. New York, NY: Gallery Books, 2017.

Part IV

Application of Mentalization-Based Treatment in Different Populations and in Different Settings

Chapter 17

Mentalizing in Other Settings

Introduction

A mentalizing individual will reflect, empathize with the self and others, modulate affect fluctuations, set boundaries, and have a strong sense of agency. The same principles can be applied to social groups. Dysfunctional social systems cause the collapse of mentalizing and result in highly reactive, tense, and defensive interactions. In Chapter 2 we discussed the relationship between mentalizing, epistemic trust, and the generation of a "we-mode" of social cognition. We set out how breakdowns in mentalizing might be so detrimental to social function because they trigger the closure of epistemic trust in social communication and preclude the formation of the we-mode with others; joining together in thinking with others becomes aversive or simply inaccessible because of the impossibility of an accurate "epistemic match." We have recently thought about this issue in relation to culture and psychopathology, and have argued that exposure to a non-mentalizing social environment —for example, in the form of socioeconomic alienation and inequality—is linked to a higher risk of psychopathology because such experiences disrupt the loosely coupled systems of mentalizing, epistemic trust, and joint attention [1]. A non-mentalizing social system creates vulnerability in that it reduces mentalizing; furthermore, it undermines access to the protection and support that are provided by social communication and joint attention, with the sense of social inclusion that they bring. In this chapter we shall discuss areas in which mentalizing work has been applied to thinking about wider social systems, developing mentalizing-informed approaches that do not involve a standard MBT clinical program.

AMBIT: Mentalizing the Professional Community

AMBIT (Adaptive Mentalization-Based Integrative Treatment) is a relatively new approach to creating a mentalizing treatment community in teams working with individuals who have mental health and social problems that are often complex and interacting [2]. The AMBIT model was developed for use when working with young people with complex histories of drug abuse, criminality, severe mental health problems, experience of social care and a history of failed placements, and, most characteristically, the simultaneous involvement of a large number of helping professionals (e.g., therapists, outreach workers, youth workers) and services (e.g., education, social care, criminal justice system). Those working with such young people have frequently experienced loss of courage and motivation as their offers of help have been rejected or, even when they have been accepted, generally found to be inadequate. AMBIT has adopted a mentalizing framework as a common language that offers the potential for a shared perspective on the challenges that young people with multiple problems present to the helping systems around them. The approach is well documented and has its own website and "wiki manual" (https://manuals.annafreud.org/ambit/), which can be dynamically updated by teams who have been trained in AMBIT as they develop and record (manualize) their practice. It has been enthusiastically adopted by combinations of services, and several thousand workers in teams in the UK and a growing number of other countries in Europe have been trained in the approach.

AMBIT starts with the assumption that the young person/client has probably rejected help for a good reason, that their mistrust is justified, and that their attitude has adaptive value. Similarly, a mentalizing stance is adopted in relation to the workers involved in such cases. Anxiety about the case is in most instances justified, but feeling ashamed about inadequate progress can be counterproductive because it reduces the likelihood of the worker seeking help from other sources. AMBIT focuses on the lack of integration (termed "dis-integration" in AMBIT terminology) of helping services around the young person, and accepts that this is the natural resting state of complex networks, rather than the consequence of individual acts that could be interpreted as resulting from laziness, incompetence, or even malice. The approach proposes that what needs to be reversed is the dis-integration and simultaneous demoralization of the system, which reflects the breakdown of trust between the professionals and services that make up the helping system. When the system contains little or no epistemic trust, change is impossible.

The commonly advocated model for complex cases is "the team around the client." In these instances, often, each of the committed professionals involved in helping a young person feels that they are making an essential and unique contribution to supporting the young person. Yet, for the young person themselves or their family, the involvement of multiple professionals and services is seen as confusing and sometimes intrusive. It would be challenging for anyone to have to integrate the multiple perspectives and disparate philosophies of specialized agencies working in domains such as education, social care, and mental health—but for individuals who have great difficulty in understanding even one perspective that is distinct from their own, the task of reconciling and genuinely grasping several understandings is mind-boggling.

Based on the principle of epistemic trust and its roots in attachment theory, AMBIT favors the use of an individual keyworker—the person whose relationship with the client is strong and who is most likely to be trusted by them. What often requires attention and adjustment is the connection of this keyworker to the other professionals and teams involved in the case. The keyworker with such privileged access to the young client deserves the respect and comprehensive support of all the other workers and teams. In this model, all professionals—for example, the therapist, psychiatrist, social worker, and youth justice worker—work through the keyworker. All of them can make systemic inputs through this much simpler—and for the young person far less confusing—route. Thus, although working in multiple domains remains possible, the keyworker retains responsibility for integrating these domains.

The AMBIT model is structured by four core areas of practice, known as the quadrants of the AMBIT wheel [2], all of which need to be attended to for the work of helping clients to be safe and effective. These are:

1. working with your client
2. working with your team

3. working with networks
4. learning at work.

Only one of these quadrants deals directly with the client; the radical aspect of AMBIT is that it assumes that the mentalizing capacity of individual workers, teams, and their wider professional networks is just as critical to providing effective help as working to support the clients.

AMBIT has the virtue of simplifying great complexities. Rather than presenting approaches that are the product of high-level thinking in neuroscience, learning theory, cognitive–behavioral therapy, social ecology, systems theory, attachment theory, and psychoanalysis, among others, AMBIT draws on mentalizing theory, which offers a common language and models the integration that AMBIT strives to achieve. In an analogous way, the role of the keyworker represents a single pathway between the young person and their family and the professional systems, managed by the most trusted individual, regardless of their original location in the professional network. Whereas in the "team around the client" approach the emphasis tends to be on rules and skills, the "team around the worker" approach proposed by AMBIT emphasizes relationships.

CAPSLE: A Mentalizing Program for Schools

The mentalizing approach for schools discussed here is Creating a Peaceful School Learning Environment (CAPSLE), a mentalization-based program for dealing with aggression and bullying in troubled school environments. CAPSLE is a whole-school approach that attempts to develop a mentalizing climate in which individual acts of violence or bullying are recognized and challenged, so that when such incidents do occur they do not escalate and gain social currency [3,4]. CAPSLE has four components.

1. A **"positive climate" campaign** uses reflective discussions of incidents immediately after these have occurred; the discussions take place in the classroom and are led by counselors.
2. A **classroom management plan** enhances the teachers' discipline skills by focusing on understanding and correcting problems at their root, rather than punishing and criticizing only the behaviors that are apparent. For example, problem behavior in a single child is conceptualized as a problem for all of the pupils in the class, who—often unwittingly—engage in bully, victim, or bystander roles. This approach reduces scapegoating, and it also means that insight into the meaning of the behavior becomes paramount.
3. A **physical education program**, derived from a combination of role playing, relaxation, and self-defense techniques, teaches children skills for dealing with victimization and bystanding behavior. This component of the program helps children to protect themselves and others by using non-aggressive physical and cognitive strategies. For example, enacting bully–victim–bystander roles in role plays provides pupils with the opportunity to work out alternative actions to fighting. Learning ways to react (e.g., when grabbed, pushed, or punched), coupled with classroom discussion, teaches personal self-control as well as respect for and helpfulness toward others.
4. Schools may put in place **a peer mentorship and/or an adult mentorship program**. The mentoring relationships that develop in these programs provide additional

containment and modeling to assist children in mastering the skills and language to deal with power struggles. For example, mentors might teach children how to referee games or resolve playground disputes, as well as the importance of helping others.

School is usually the main and most important social environment that children and young people encounter as they begin to experience the world beyond their family system. It can provide a crucial lesson in reinforcing their perceptions of the world as safe and reliable—or as dangerous and unpredictable. Although secure early parent–child attachment increases the likelihood of a positive developmental outcome [5], peer—not parental—support and acceptance turns out to be the best predictor of resilience in adolescence [6]. However, the mechanisms that we have identified in the context of studying early development [1] may well apply to understanding how the social environment of adolescents can generate risk. Epistemic trust can be understood as expressing a generalized trust in one's social community. Shared intentionality ("we-mode") may be experienced by the individual at a group level as well as an inter-individual level, and is related to the expectation that the social environment will protect, care for, and help to realize their aims and ambitions. Non-mentalizing social systems present a powerful cue that the individual is in an environment where social relationships are not operating on the principle of shared goals, cooperation, and interdependence. The school environment is a powerful tool for shaping the stance of children and adolescents in relation to social communication.

CAPSLE focuses on the power dynamics in the relationship between bullies, victims, and bystanders, and emphasizes the role of bystanders in restoring mentalizing. Bystanders are trained to act to encourage bullies, victims, and other bystanders to recognize, and move away from, their respective "pathological" roles. In a non-mentalizing environment, the witness to a power struggle or an act of violence—the bystander—may experience sadistic feelings of pleasure in seeing another's difficulty or suffering. According to our thinking, this is only possible when the witnesses feel distanced from the internal world of the other person, and are able to use the victim to contain the unwanted (usually frightened) part of themselves. The enjoyment and excitement that bystanding groups often show when witnessing fights or aggression in violent schools—for example, the crowding around fights and stirring up of grudges that often take place—do not involve complete mentalizing failure, because some level of empathy is necessary for this projective identification with the victim's suffering. However, the mentalizing that does take place is highly limited by the social setting, such that the victim's suffering is not fully represented as a mental state in the bystander's own consciousness—that is, it is *recognized* but not *felt* by the bystander. It is not surprising that such a dynamic unfolds in schools, as mentalizing is a fragile capacity until early adulthood (or even later in life), and it requires a social environment that can scaffold it and ensure that the mental states of self and other can be reflected upon. CAPSLE constitutes a deliberate attempt to scaffold the imbalanced, fluctuating, and incompletely emerging mentalizing capacities of children and young people (and the school staff who react to them) by creating a social environment in which more balanced mentalizing can be practiced and reinforced, and its benefits experienced.

Working with Parents, Carers, and Families in Wider Settings

The next group of interventions—Reflective Parenting, Reflective Fostering, and Minding the Baby—are all highly creative ways in which mentalizing theory has been applied to supporting families and carers outside a mainstream clinical setting. They are forms of work that can take place in community settings, and often seek to develop a community of support among the individuals who are being supported. The work that we describe here is not a typical program of more formal mentalization-based treatments, but rather it involves forms of working with families that use the idea of mentalizing and a focus on the value of mentalizing in supporting functioning.

Reflective Parenting

Reflective Parenting is a form of help for families in which a focus on mentalizing is central [7]. It places a strong emphasis on putting into effect the reflective self to help parents to develop a more attuned and connected relationship with their child(ren). Self-mentalizing plays a key role in the Reflective Parenting model and is the first step for parents in this work. The program centers around a highly pragmatic approach that takes full account of the stresses and strains of family life and how these inevitably lead to moments of mentalizing difficulty.

The Reflective Parenting program has adopted an innovative approach to helping families to develop healthy relationships and respond to family difficulties, and helping parents to support children and young people with emotional and behavioral problems [7]. The parent's ability to understand their child's state of mind is often referred to as *parental reflective functioning*. This construct emerged from the well-known London Parent–Child Project study, in which ground-breaking findings showed that there was a high level of concordance between a parent's patterns of attachment and those of their child [8]. It was suggested that this relationship was shaped by the parent's capacity to see the child as a separate psychological entity with a mental experience of their own [9]. In addition to this, the parent's ability to not only perceive but then also reflect back the mental state of the child and respond through their own behavior was seen to be strongly linked to attachment security. This led to the development of the Reflective Self-Function Scale and the subsequent development of the Reflective Functioning Scale [10], a significant measure of parents' capacity to understand their own mental states. This ability to have a "reflective self" is a careful interplay between reflecting on the self (parental) state of mind and turning this reflective capacity to the state of mind of the developing child. This balance is key to work that aims to increase a parent's capacity to mentalize, as parental mentalizing (reflective functioning) is not simply about the parent's capacity to reflect on their child, but also about their capacity to reflect on their *own* mental activity.

Two key tools have been developed for use in the Reflective Parenting model (and also, in modified form, in the Reflective Fostering program, which is described later in this chapter). The first of these is the Parent Map. Based on the idea that the capacity to self-mentalize is critical for affect regulation, particularly during an affect-laden experience, the Parent Map helps parents to recognize their current state of mind and the different experiences that play into this—both immediate experiences, and their family history and their own early experiences. In particular, it aims to help them to identify experiences that may spark intense emotions and risk a loss of mentalizing and affect regulation. Parents are helped to build a map of how they want to parent and when they parent at their best. To support the parent's capacity to mentalize their child, the second tool, known as the Parenting APP, has been developed. The name of this tool is based on the initials of three key aspects of a mentalizing stance toward others: Attention and curiosity, Perspective taking, and Providing empathy. The Parenting APP is used to draw the parent's attention toward what their child is experiencing that may be shaping their behavior [11].

Reflective Parenting is a model for parents of children of all ages, abilities, and levels of difficulty. The model aims to:

1. encourage professionals who are working with parents to take a mentalizing stance toward the parents; as a result, the parents feel understood, which helps them to begin to mentalize
2. increase the parents' awareness of their own mind, particularly in relation to parenting
3. provide psychoeducation to enable parents to develop their knowledge of how understanding feelings (both their own and those of their child) links to managing feelings and behavior
4. help parents to become aware that understanding the "back story" that lies behind why their child behaves in a particular way will lead to a better connection between the parents and the child
5. increase the parents' ability to help their child to understand how they are feeling and why.

One of the ways in which Reflective Parenting help is offered is in a program of group sessions. The core objective of the program is to promote parents' ability to understand their own and their children's thoughts, feelings, and needs—or, put more simply, to improve their capacity to mentalize. The group follows an 8-week program. The first week introduces Reflective Parenting, including the research behind it, and explains how it can be helpful and the impact that it can have. In this session, the group members have a chance to get to know each other and to hear about each other's children. In weeks 2 and 3, the impact of the parents' own states of mind on parenting is explored with the help of the Parent Map. In week 4, the parents think about the "back story" to their child's behavior and explore different perspectives and ways to understand the meaning behind it. This helps parents to take a developmental perspective (understanding what behaviors are common and to be expected) and to examine their own assumptions about their child's intentions. In this session, the reflective or mentalizing stance to parenting is introduced, which can enable the parents to understand their child in a different way, and in turn help the child to manage their feelings and behavior with the parents' help. In week 5, the emphasis is on helping the parents to manage both their own and their child's "emotional temperature" in order to achieve a better relationship. In weeks 6 and 7, issues around discipline and authority within the parent–child relationship are considered. The final session, in week 8, focuses on how parents can keep Reflective Parenting going, looking to the future, and helping parents to consider how they can enjoy better times with their child.

Reflective Fostering

Another area of recent interest for mentalizing approaches is the application of mentalizing thinking to the needs of looked-after children. This is an area of considerable need. In March 2021, the number of children being looked after by local authorities in England was 80,850, a figure that has risen year on year [12], and an increasing number of looked-after children are being fostered rather than placed in residential homes [13]. This movement toward fostering has been undertaken in recognition of the fact that children's development is best served by stable, predictable relationships provided by present and available caregivers [14]. The Reflective Fostering Programme (RFP) was developed in response to the fact that despite the clear potential advantages of fostering as an intervention for looked-after children, the emotional work and the emotional demands of fostering have traditionally been given insufficient attention [13,15]. Children in foster care are more than five times as likely to have a diagnosable mental health disorder as children in the general population, with a reported prevalence of 72% [16].

Further vulnerability and instability are generated when foster placements break down; placement instability is estimated to be 22–56%. Breakdown in placements is associated with poorer outcomes for the children—multiple disruptions are associated with increased physical, emotional, and behavioral problems. Therefore fostering as an intervention has a considerable amount riding on it—it has the potential to be a highly valuable form of help for some of the most vulnerable children, and placement stability is of considerable importance. But at the same time, foster carers are often not provided with sufficient training and support for the important work that they undertake. The existing interventions and training program for foster carers have tended to focus on managing children's challenging behavior. Given that attachment and relational difficulties tend to be more prevalent among looked-after children, the RFP was designed with these needs in mind. The RFP builds on research which indicates that improving a parent's capacity to mentalize both their own and their child's behavior may help them to respond better to worrying or difficult behavior, and to more effectively support the emotional well-being of the child. When a child feels that they are being mentalized, they feel more recognized and understood, and this creates in them a stronger sense of agency and personal value. Research has shown that good parental mentalizing is associated with better socio-emotional and cognitive outcomes in children, and reduces the risk of poor mental health outcomes later in life [17]. The RFP builds on the Reflective Parenting model that we discussed earlier, which promotes both self-focused and child-focused reflective functioning in the context of managing stress and heightened emotional states.

The RFP uses a set of tools that represent the principles of Reflective Parenting in a brief, highly engaging form, for foster carers to use on themselves and on the children in their care. Unlike other mentalization-based interventions for fostered and adopted children, which were designed to be delivered by mental health professionals, the RFP was designed to be easily learned by social care professionals so that it could be implemented and tailored to fit the needs of a wide range of foster carers. The evaluation of a pilot program showed that it was feasible to train National Society for the Prevention of Cruelty to Children (NSPCC) staff—social workers experienced in working in children's social care settings—to deliver the program, that foster carers were eager to attend the course, and that most of them stayed for the entire program. The program was also found to have a real impact on reducing stress levels for foster carers and improving relationships between carers and the children they were looking after [18].

The RFP is a group-based program to support foster carers of children, initially between 4 and 11 years of age; it has subsequently been extended to children up to the age of 13 years. The RFP is psychoeducational in focus and teaches the practical application of the principles of reflective caregiving. The program consists of 10 sessions, each 2–3 hours in duration, held over a period of 12–14 weeks, in groups consisting of 6–10 foster carers. The RFP seeks to provide practical and realistic ways for carers to develop and maintain supportive relationships with the children they are caring for. Two key tools that are used in the RFP are the Carer Map and the Carer APP, which are analogous to the Parent Map and Parenting APP described in the section on Reflective Parenting earlier in this chapter. The Carer Map seeks to support the foster carer's capacity for self-mentalizing, and the Carer APP aims to improve the foster carer's ability to mentalize the child by elucidating a mentalizing stance characterized by attention and curiosity, perspective taking, and providing empathy.

Each of the 10 sessions has a specific focus [19]:

1. introduction to the RFP
2. reflecting on yourself as a foster carer—the Carer Map
3. seeing and thinking about your foster child in different ways
4. understanding and helping your foster child who has experienced developmental or other trauma
5. trust, relationships, and helping your foster child to get on better with other people
6. responding to problematic behavior in a reflective way
7. understanding misunderstandings—putting your Carer Map and APP together
8. getting the help and support you need as a foster carer—from family, friends, and the team around you
9. moving on—getting ready for the end of the RFP
10. review and ending session—how to keep the model in mind and stay feeling supported.

The sessions are delivered by pairs of trained facilitators (one registered social care worker and one experienced foster carer), who are provided with a weekly consultation with specialists at the Anna Freud Centre in London. The co-delivery approach can build competence and capability within the system, and it expands the holding of "expertise" within the system's network. After the program has ended, foster carers are provided with access to materials about Reflective Fostering online, and are encouraged to form an online support group.

At the time of writing, a definitive, superiority, two-armed, parallel, pragmatic, randomized controlled trial, with embedded process evaluation and economic evaluation, and an internal pilot, to evaluate the effectiveness and cost-effectiveness of the RFP, is being run in local authorities across England [19]; this follows on from two development and preliminary projects [13,15,18], which showed high recruitment, retention, relevance, and acceptability for foster carers, and improvements in foster carers' stress and carer-reported measures of foster children's mental health.

Minding the Baby

Minding the Baby (MTB) is a home-visiting program for vulnerable first-time mothers, which aims to support these mothers in developing their reflective functioning skills in the context of their relationship with their baby [20–22]. It begins toward the end of the second trimester of pregnancy and continues until the baby is 2 years old. Mothers are visited weekly through the pregnancy and after birth until the child is 1 year old, and once a fortnight for the second year of infancy. The frequency of visits is also adjusted according to need, with more frequent visits arranged at times of crisis. Although the mother and baby are the primary focus of MTB, fathers are also encouraged to become involved, as are any other important figures for the mother and child, such as siblings, grandparents, or close friends.

MTB focuses help on young mothers who are emotionally vulnerable and lack the psychological resilience and support to deal with the considerable challenges of parenting. The program operates in deprived areas, and the women who are recruited to join the program are often struggling with the combined disadvantages of poverty, social isolation, poor education, and complex mental health needs. Many of them have a history of trauma, abuse, or neglect in their own childhood or adolescence.

MTB takes an interdisciplinary approach. The team is made up of a nurse and a social worker who alternate visits and provide a range of help that is carefully tailored to match each mother's needs. High levels of practical parenting support are an important part of the work, and involve individual and family health assessments, as well as nutritional and family planning advice. The provision of this intensive parenting support reflects the fact that the women in the program are often under-supported and under-resourced in every sense when it comes to the care of their child. The program also addresses physical safety and access to necessities such as nappies and food. The nurse's role is focused on health promotion and mental health screening. The social worker provides support with issues that may arise in relation to housing, schooling, and navigating challenging social care systems, as well as using psychotherapeutic approaches to support the mother's mental health, family functioning, or issues relating to trauma [22]. To give parents the mental space that they need to enable them to focus on their relationship with their baby, they often require support in dealing with severe stressors that would otherwise get in the way. Working with the mother to assist her in providing better care in this way also strengthens the links between the mother and the team; building the relationship between the mother and the MTB practitioners is crucial to the success of the program, and the personalized nature of the help that is provided and the consistency of the relationship with known and trusted practitioners all work toward this goal.

The emphasis on engagement and fostering ongoing relationships with these at-risk, first-time young mothers, as well as ensuring that the team has the professional expertise appropriate to meeting the mothers' complex health, social, and mental health needs, builds trust and reduces dropout from the program. The integrative model of MBT, which combines practical and mental health support, is considered to be crucial for optimizing both parental and child outcomes across a range of domains. In combining multimodal support to tackle social adversity with a close focus on the mother–child relationship, particularly the sensitivity of parental care and parental reflective functioning, MTB aims to combine best clinical practice in early prevention with scientific evidence relating to the developmental processes that promote optimal child outcomes. A randomized controlled trial of young mothers who took part in MTB for 27 months (from pregnancy to the child's second birthday) found that the women in the MTB group were more likely to show improved reflective functioning, and their infants were significantly more likely to show secure attachment and less likely to show disorganized attachment, compared with mother–child pairs who had not participated in the program [22].

Concluding Remarks

The models of practice described in this chapter all show how mentalizing can be applied in different settings, often in the community, and by a range of practitioners, such as social workers, experienced foster carers, and teachers—or, as is particularly the case with AMBIT, the whole network around a client and the key helping figure whom the client identifies as having the strongest relationship with them. All of these forms of practice seek to build the capacity to mentalize within existing relationships and in communities, without the application of a clinical MBT program for a particular mental health disorder.

In Chapter 2 we described the three communication systems that we have proposed to underpin effective forms of psychotherapy. All of the forms of work described in this chapter are particularly attentive to the third communication system—that is, *applying social learning in the wider environment*. They are informed by the knowledge that focusing on an individual's capacity to mentalize while failing to attend to the wider social system around that person is less likely to result in meaningful help, particularly for individuals with multiple or complex needs and/or those who would benefit from the experience of a mentalizing community around them, in which it is possible to think together in the "we-mode." Whether the work is with parents struggling to regulate and manage family life, foster children and carers working to form and sustain a positive caring relationship, a young socially vulnerable mother, a child in an intimidating school environment, or an individual with complex and/or multiple needs, it is hoped that—by providing a space for individuals to think together, to experience a "we-mode" and reduce isolation—it may become possible to improve social functioning and connectedness.

References

1. Fonagy P, Campbell C, Constantinou M et al. Culture and psychopathology: an attempt at reconsidering the role of social learning. *Dev Psychopathol* 2022; **34**: 1205–20.
2. Bevington D, Fuggle P, Cracknell L, Fonagy P. *Adaptive Mentalization-Based Integrative Treatment: A Guide for Teams to Develop Systems of Care*. Oxford, UK: Oxford University Press, 2017.
3. Twemlow SW, Fonagy P, Sacco FC. A developmental approach to mentalizing communities: I. A model for social change. *Bull Menninger Clin* 2005; **69**: 265–81.
4. Twemlow SW, Fonagy P, Sacco FC. A developmental approach to mentalizing communities: II. The Peaceful Schools experiment. *Bull Menninger Clin* 2005; **69**: 282–304.
5. Simpson JA, Collins WA, Tran S, Haydon KC. Attachment and the experience and expression of emotions in romantic relationships: a developmental perspective. *J Pers Soc Psychol* 2007; **92**: 355–67.
6. van Harmelen AL, Kievit RA, Ioannidis K et al. Adolescent friendships predict later resilient functioning across psychosocial domains in a healthy community cohort. *Psychol Med* 2017; **47**: 2312–22.
7. Cooper A, Redfern S. *Reflective Parenting: A Guide to Understanding What's Going On in Your Child's Mind*. Abingdon, UK: Routledge, 2016.
8. Fonagy P, Steele H, Steele M. Maternal representations of attachment during pregnancy predict the organization of infant-mother attachment at one year of age. *Child Dev* 1991; **62**: 891–905.
9. Fonagy P, Steele M, Steele H et al. The capacity for understanding mental states: the reflective self in parent and child and its significance for security of attachment. *Infant Ment Health J* 1991; **12**: 201–18.
10. Taubner S, Horz S, Fischer-Kern M et al. Internal structure of the Reflective Functioning Scale. *Psychol Assess* 2013; **25**: 127–35.

11. Redfern S. Parenting and foster care. In: Bateman A, Fonagy P, eds. *Handbook of Mentalizing in Mental Health Practice*, 2nd ed. Washington, DC: American Psychiatric Association Publishing, 2019; 265–79.

12. National Statistics. *Children Looked After in England Including Adoptions: Reporting Year 2021*. 2022. https://explore-education-statistics.service.gov.uk/find-statistics/children-looked-after-in-england-including-adoptions/2021.

13. Redfern S, Wood S, Lassri D et al. The Reflective Fostering Programme: background and development of a new approach. *Adopt Foster* 2018; **42**: 234–48.

14. National Institute for Health and Care Excellence. *Looked-After Children and Young People*. London, UK: National Institute for Health and Care Excellence, 2013. www.nice.org.uk/guidance/qs31.

15. Midgley N, Sprecher EA, Cirasola A et al. The reflective fostering programme: evaluating the intervention co-delivered by social work professionals and foster carers. *J Child Serv* 2021; **16**: 159–74.

16. Sempik J, Ward H, Darker I. Emotional and behavioural difficulties of children and young people at entry into care. *Clin Child Psychol Psychiatry* 2008; **13**: 221–33.

17. Ensink K, Begin M, Normandin L, Fonagy P. Parental reflective functioning as a moderator of child internalizing difficulties in the context of child sexual abuse. *Psychiatry Res* 2017; **257**: 361–6.

18. Midgley N, Cirasola A, Austerberry C et al. Supporting foster carers to meet the needs of looked after children: a feasibility and pilot evaluation of the Reflective Fostering Programme. *Dev Child Welfare* 2019; **1**: 41–60.

19. Midgley N, Irvine K, Rider B et al. The Reflective Fostering Programme-improving the wellbeing of children in care through a group intervention for foster carers: a randomised controlled trial. *Trials* 2021; **22**: 841.

20. Sadler LS, Slade A, Mayes LC. Minding the Baby: a mentalization-based parenting program. In: Allen JG, Fonagy P, eds. *The Handbook of Mentalization-Based Treatment*. Chichester, UK: John Wiley & Sons, 2006; 271–88.

21. Sadler LS, Slade A, Close N et al. Minding the Baby: enhancing reflectiveness to improve early health and relationship outcomes in an interdisciplinary home visiting program. *Infant Ment Health J* 2013; **34**: 391–405.

22. Slade A, Holland ML, Ordway MR et al. *Minding the Baby*®: enhancing parental reflective functioning and infant attachment in an attachment-based, interdisciplinary home visiting program. *Dev Psychopathol* 2020; 32: 123–37.

Chapter 18

Mentalizing and Emergency Care

Introduction

The risk of severe crises is high in individuals with personality disorders. In every clinician's mind, their patient's suicidal risk requires constant monitoring. As we discussed in Chapter 4, the mentalization-based treatment (MBT) program integrates risk evaluation as a continuous assessment process that is linked to a carefully crafted and personalized crisis plan for each patient. Notwithstanding these significant precautions, patients may need to be hospitalized during treatment. On average, approximately 20% of patients will be admitted for psychiatric hospitalization during treatment [1]. Therefore, for a significant proportion of patients who are being treated with a specialized therapy, psychiatric emergency care represents a key area of work in the patient's treatment trajectory. In this chapter we shall describe how MBT can inform emergency care when a crisis is handled by the multidisciplinary team of mental health practitioners in psychiatric emergency settings. Indeed, an increasing number of psychiatric emergency practitioners have engaged in specialized training in, for example, MBT, dialectical behavior therapy (DBT), or other forms of specialized treatment for personality disorders. This training provides clinical principles of intervention that are usually implemented over a timescale of around 12–18 months. However, hospital emergency care practitioners and mental health crisis units intervene on a very different timescale, usually a 1- to 3-day brief hospitalization format, with a mission to contain dangerous behaviors related to the crisis, and to safely discharge the patient with a plan to reconnect with their outpatient treatment plan, or to initiate outpatient treatment when the crisis represents the entry point to treatment.

The clinical framework of MBT can significantly inform emergency hospital care practice [2–4]. In order to specify how MBT can be employed in emergency care, the notion of psychological crisis will be defined, and the key elements of crisis intervention will be reviewed, bearing in mind the timescale over which crises unfold. This narrows down the objectives of very short-term emergency care hospitalizations. Taking these restrictions into account, a four-step model of MBT-informed emergency care has been developed:

1. intake and admission into emergency care
2. uncovering the crisis
3. integration and formulation of the crisis area
4. preparation for discharge.

Throughout this chapter the model will be illustrated with a clinical example of an emergency crisis.

What Is a Crisis?

The way that professionals define a crisis affects the way in which they engage with the mental states of a patient who is presenting with acute emotional and behavioral disturbances. It is important to first define the nature of a crisis, and then relate that definition to mentalizing theory, in particular the concept of the alien self (see Chapter 2). Building on this conceptual framework, it becomes clear that the patient's sense of agency is at the center of recovery from a crisis episode. Furthermore, in the context of psychiatric emergency care, which is provided in a hospital or crisis assessment center setting, time is of the essence. In other words, there is a limitation on the length of hospitalizations if these are required, and a specificity to clinical presentations that are deemed appropriate for assessment in these contexts. In this discussion, patients with personality disorders or first-time hospitalizations, who represent about 25% of all psychiatric emergency hospitalizations, will be considered. For patients with personality disorder who are experiencing a suicidal crisis, and probably for others, too, psychiatric emergency care can be informed by mentalizing. Among these patients, approximately 20–30% will meet the criteria for borderline personality disorder (BPD). Psychological work with these patients will build upon first defining and understanding the nature of their crisis.

Crisis: A Working Definition

Patients may experience crises during treatment, but how are these defined and delineated for an individual? James [5] offers a useful starting point for answering this question: "an individual crisis is the perception or experiencing of the event by the person as an intolerable difficulty that exceeds the individual's resources and coping abilities. Unless the individual obtains some relief from the situation, the crisis has the potential to create severe affective, behavioral, and cognitive malfunctioning to the point of becoming life threatening or injurious to oneself or others" (p. 387).

In keeping with the MBT approach, a crisis is defined first from the patient's perspective—it both overwhelms the individual's regulatory mechanisms and exceeds the resources (notably at the individual, interpersonal, therapeutic, and social levels) available to address acute dysregulation. Furthermore, a crisis has life-threatening potential. Crises that entail hospitalization in psychiatric emergency care represent a kind of prototype of how a crisis is represented from an MBT perspective. However, crises can unfold in the absence of emergency hospitalizations, through a variety of episodes that involve acute dysregulation leading to life-threatening behaviors. But a crisis is rooted in an individual's *experience*—from the standpoint of MBT the patient's subjectivity directly connects with how the self, others, and the world are combined in lived experience. As we have already mentioned, the patient's perspective is a key area of inquiry for any MBT therapist who wishes to foster epistemic trust (see Chapter 2).

A key element of the patient's experience is its unfolding, or temporality; in James's definition [5], cited earlier, these can be unpacked from the warning issued: "*Unless the individual obtains some relief from the situation* . . . ." The notion of relief as an end point to a crisis trajectory stimulates several central questions relating to the key characteristics of a crisis—not only the temporality of the crisis, but also the form of the crisis, the nature of the crisis, and additional characteristics of the crisis such as its length and potential lethality (see Table 18.1). All of these characteristics will contribute to evaluation of both

Table 18.1 Key characteristics that contribute to delineating the field of a crisis

	Crisis characteristics	Examples
Time point	Pre-crisis	Increased arousal, risk behaviors
	Crisis	Hospitalization, fugue
	Post-crisis	Reintegration into the household, therapy
Form	Internalized/avoidance	Isolation, disengagement, etc., leading to adverse consequences
	Externalized on self	Suicide attempt, self-harm
	Externalized on others	Violent assault, verbal abuse
Nature	Personal	Personal failures, mistakes, fraud
	Interpersonal	Separation, conflict, loss
	Loss of resources	Loss of employment, household, social network
Other	Duration	Hours, days, or weeks of enduring crisis
	Lethality	Degree of threat to life
	Threat	Threats concerning life and death (of the self and/or others), planning illegal activities, gambling

the severity of the crisis and the nature of what may indeed relieve the patient from the intolerable experience that acutely exceeds their resources and capacity to cope with it.

Emergency hospital care typically comes into play during the acute phase of the crisis, which often takes the form of self-destructive behaviors such as suicidal ideation and/or suicide attempts. The nature of the crisis may combine different levels of functioning, from personal to social, yet it is often the case that from the subjective point of view of patients, specific elements or triggers such as a sense of failure (personal), shame (interpersonal), or exclusion (social) have contributed to making a difficult situation unbearable to experience.

In this chapter, a prototypical patient, Jill, will be used to illustrate an emergency crisis, showing how difficult situations can evolve into crisis-level episodes.

Clinical Example: Jill

Jill is describing an episode that led up to her suicide attempt by swallowing the contents of a whole packet of paracetamol tablets:

> *"I had been feeling unloved by Jeremy, and I thought we would make our holiday a moment to reconnect. I reserved an apartment in a resort. He spent the entire first two days working, leaving me feeling unimportant to him, and I got very depressed. On the second evening, I managed to prepare a special dinner, which he ate very quickly and barely said thanks. Later on, when I asked him if we could talk, he said he had enough problems already and was not interested in my 'mood swings.' I started crying, and cried for at least an hour, non-stop. As I saw him going to bed, I told him, 'Jeremy, I can't go on living like this!' and he answered that I could just go back to the city if I wasn't happy. I started*

screaming that I would kill myself and he replied 'Honestly, I don't give a shit.' I was shocked. I vaguely remember heading to the bathroom, and eventually I swallowed all the meds I could find."

This example resonates with the description of psychological crises given by Nizum et al. [6]: "Crises are subjective experiences that threaten and overwhelm a person's ability to deal with the situation using their normal problem-solving abilities, coping mechanisms, or current resources. . . . The overwhelming experience can have detrimental effects on mental health, including intense feelings of personal distress, implications on physical health, inability to meet basic needs, unusual behavior" (p. 349). From an MBT perspective, such intense subjective experiences have been characterized using the term *alien self* (see Chapter 2), which, to paraphrase, consists of alienating self-experiences that take hold of the patient's mind during a crisis. These experiences relate to episodes in which the individual's self is under a type of threat that involves a significant loss of personal agency—desperate and violent actions are engaged in an attempt to regain agency in the face of such a threat. The alien self theory and how it applies to emergency care will be discussed in the next section. For now, it is possible to hypothesize that in the clinical example that has just been described, Jill alerted her boyfriend to the intensity of her experience ("*I can't go on like this*"), which was met by Jeremy's contingent but insensitively non-congruent mirroring response ("*go back to the city if you are unhappy*"). The lack of emotional congruency arises from the mismatch between the despair and fear expressed by Jill and Jeremy's mirroring back to her of her emotions as being unjustifiable feelings of being unhappy and unsatisfied. This fails to resonate with her emotional state and so is affectively disqualifying. This increases Jill's arousal to a level of suicidal threat ("*I will kill myself*"), and Jeremy further mirrors to Jill that she is not worth any attention even when she is in such a state. The ensuing psychological shock transports Jill into a form of alienating self-experience in which, paradoxically, overdosing on medication is perceived as the only viable option for relieving the psychological pain that she is experiencing. The alienating self-experience that we can imagine taking hold of Jill's mind may resemble a self-representation such as "*My life is not worthy of any attention.*" The affective consequence here is such that it threatens the integrity of Jill's sense of agency. In the face of such a threat, recourse to violence and/or paradoxical action can kick in, because they represent the last resource available to stop the pain, even if this leads to death.

Later on in her crisis episode, Jill was driven to a nearby psychiatric clinic where, fortunately, emergency care was provided. Ideally, the staff in an emergency service should embody a safe and trustworthy environment that can provide the appropriate care to allow de-escalation of the crisis. Yet Johnson et al. note that a psychological crisis is a "challenge for mental health services aiming to focus on supporting recovery," and they further highlight the fact that "relapse after an acute crisis episode is common" ([7], p. 409).

The focus of interventions in emergency care can be summarized in terms of three objectives [5]:

1. stabilization
2. reduction of the risk of possible escalation to suicide
3. prevention of repetition.

These objectives entail a number of clinical challenges for the emergency team during the period of assessment and hospitalization (which will be time-limited), and also depend on their ability to connect with the patient's mental health network in the community. Crisis work integrates de-escalating interventions with mentalizing work to formulate the crisis episode and plan the necessary elements for securing the patient's reintegration into their usual environment. Indeed it is known that discharge from hospital has the potential to trigger discontinuation of care, which itself may lead to an increased risk of suicide [8]. Recent research has investigated how to improve the efficiency and outcomes of emergency hospitalization periods [8,9]. In MBT, the initial focus is on how emergency care can be integrated with elements of the patient's ongoing psychotherapy, especially the formulation process around crises that occur during treatment (see Chapter 4).

In summary, a mental health crisis is defined as the subjective experience of an intolerable state (alienating self-experience), which typically takes hold of the patient's mind following an event or situation that exceeds their resources and impairs their coping skills and autonomy, to the extent that they need external help to recover safe functioning and avoid a damaging and possibly lethal escalation. Psychologically speaking, a crisis entails a central alienating self-experience (or a set of such experiences) tied to potentially lethal teleological solutions. In the next section we shall describe in some detail the theoretical basis of the clinical model of MBT during emergency care.

When the Alien Self Rears Its Ugly Head

In this section the psychological parameters underlying the concept of the alien self proposed by Peter Fonagy and his colleagues [10] (see also Chapter 2) are discussed within a framework of *alienating self-experiences.* These experiences are key to understanding MBT's clinical approach in psychiatric emergency care. The fundamental question when dealing with suicidality is *how an individual's mind can be co-opted to unite the means of, and proceed with the attempt at, eliminating itself.*

In suicidal states, the individual experiences the "I" as the source of intolerable suffering (see Chapter 6). This can take a variety of forms: "*I am bad,*" "*I am disgusting,*" "*I am worthless,*" "*I am not worthy of love,*" "*I am sick,*" "*I am void,*" "*I am meaningless,*" and so on. As long as these ways of perceiving oneself can be partially mentalized as "me" representations and not the whole of "I" experience (i.e., only a part of me is "bad," "disgusting," or "worthless"), partial mentalizing usually prevents recourse to action to harm or eliminate oneself. However, when mental states collapse into psychic equivalence and take over the momentary "I" experience of oneself, then representations such as "*nobody loves me*" become strong, and rigid feelings of "*I am unlovable*" dominate the "I" experience, hijacking the "me" representational space. In such instances, the psychic pain is fully embodied and threatens the agency of the self, because it is nothing other than "bad," "unlovable," and so on. Recourse to self-harm and suicidal actions represents the self's last recourse to agency—self-directed aggression [11]. Aggression is then used against the self to try to eliminate the pain that is robbing the person of agency. This is possible only because the human mind has the capacity to "objectify" itself—a capacity that seems to step in during crises, fueled by a wish to survive and overcome the mental pain, and indeed to regain agency. This can lead the individual to assemble the necessary means of eliminating the alienating self-experience, possibly at the cost of their life. Most often, when a suicide attempt does not result in death, the individual is relieved that this battle with the alienating self-experience, which is now contained in a "me" representation ("*part of me wanted out so badly!*") did not succeed in eliminating the self. This suggests that in the great majority of cases, the alienating self-experience is momentary, and is then reintegrated into a more complex experience of the self that integrates the multiplicity of "me" representations that make up our self-models.

How can we link this back to mentalizing? Peter Fonagy and his colleagues have outlined a developmental model that links the alien self to poorly mirrored interactions during early childhood [10,12]. Of course, poor parental mirroring is not the only trigger of alienating self-experiences. Indeed, all situations that cause individuals to experience themselves as having no agency carry the potential for alienation; these situations range from abusive experiences to physical illness, through catastrophic interpersonal events (e.g., infidelity), social phenomena (e.g., being caught in a dangerously swarming crowd), or environmental events (e.g., facing a tsunami). Similarly to early clinical insights [13], we believe that the nature of trauma lies in its alienating potential—its capacity to cause a powerful loss of agency, subjecting the individual to a degree of helplessness that threatens their integrity (see Chapter 11).

Coming back to mentalizing theory, the marked mirroring response of the parent is a rich and useful model for illustrating the dynamics of agency and alienation [10]. Poor mirroring will induce an alienating subjective experience because of its effect on agency; in fact, the experience of alienation can be conceptualized as being on the opposite pole of the continuum that it forms with agency. In MBT terms, we conceive of an agency–alienation continuum translating this key feature of subjective experience, and link it to how mirroring can foster or deplete individual agency, depending on the degree of sensitivity of the caregiver's mirroring response (see Figure 18.1).

The three main characteristics of affective mirroring by the caregiver—contingency, congruency, and markedness—all contribute to activating the sense of agency in the child [14]. Although affective mirroring plays a central role in the development of the self, recent work by Fotopoulou and Tsakiris has led to increased interest in the centrality of *embodied* experience in the constitution of the self [15]. Neuroscientific evidence provides support for

AGENCY | **ALIENATION**

Sensitive affective mirroring	**Insensitive affective mirroring**
A **contingent** response generates in the baby a sense of "having an effect" on the caregiver (based in teleology)	A **non-contingent** response generates a sense of "having no effect" on the caregiver, generating panic and intensifying dysregulated affective arousal
A **congruent** response generates a sense of "feeling together"—a similar emotion, a base for belongingness	An **incongruent** response generates a sense of being "alien," "too different," or "not right," which can lead to solitude, or to over-adaptation ("false self")
A **marked** response generates in the baby a sense of recognition and legitimacy of being a worthy social agent in the mind of the caregiver	A lack of **marking** generates a sense that one's affect is dangerously contagious and threatens the stability and availability of the caregiver

Fig. 18.1 The agency–alienation continuum.

the view that skin-to-skin and body-to-body contact in the attachment relationship with infants strengthens their early self-regulation capacities by fostering multisensory integration. Furthermore, mentalizing is first and foremost communicated through holding, handling, and presenting, as anticipated by D. W. Winnicott (as discussed by Fonagy and Campbell [16]). In other words, the vehicle for the transmission of affective mirroring is initially the parent's body and their way of physically attending to the infant's needs. According to this developmental perspective, teleology is not so much a "non-mentalizing" mode as a foundation of mentalized interactions. In fact, the developmental theory of mentalizing suggests that pre-mentalizing modes constitute building blocks of the fully matured capacity for mentalizing. This is relevant because both early attachment and emergency care environments are settings that operate in a way that is based on teleology—the baby's brain is mainly wired to apprehend reality on the basis of perception, and similarly, a patient in an acute crisis is very much engaged in "perception-as-proof" mode, not to mention the hospital environment, which largely functions in terms of "doing mode," simply because life-and-death matters require *action*. Therefore both the mentalizing parent and the mentalizing mental health professional will find it useful to keep in mind that neither the baby, nor the patient, nor the hospital will suddenly be transformed into a sophisticated mentalizing agent. However, injecting mentalizing into such contexts represents an investment in mid- to long-term outcomes, both for the staff and for the patient and their family. The key task for the parent and the mental health professional alike is to meet the needs of the vulnerable individual (the infant or patient) through empathic validation of the recourse to action (for a description of working with teleological mode, see Chapter 4), while keeping their own mentalizing online. This starting point is essential for MBT work, which seeks to build or increase the mentalizing process from "ground zero," where it shut down. The principle can be encapsulated in four steps, which are necessary to enable the patient to pursue their life following hospitalization:

1. Clinically assist in de-escalating the crisis.
2. Prevent worsening of suicidality.
3. Block relapses of suicidal behavior.
4. Build a mentalizing narrative of the crisis.

It may be useful to note that alienating self-experiences have an additional adverse effect—they disconnect the individual from the idea that others can help them. Momentarily, others cease to exist as potential resources that can provide help and support. When the patient makes their way to emergency psychiatric care, the relational rupture effect of alienating self-experiences is often still active. This suggests that the first step for mental health professionals is to engage with the patient on a human level, in order to reopen a place in the patient's mind where they can feel that others represent a resource for them, both in the present moment and in the future. This links to MBT's clinical approach, and especially to epistemic trust as a gateway to building a mentalizing process. We shall now focus on the application of the MBT approach to the context of emergency care.

Clinical Approach: From Epistemic Trust to Mentalizing the Crisis

Engaging with the patient in emergency care represents the first and perhaps most important area for successful emergency care. Indications for short psychiatric hospitalization emergency programs can be informed by MBT. The rest of this chapter will provide an outline of the criteria for emergency psychiatric intervention, followed by a summary of the clinical steps necessary to build a mentalizing process to inform the formulation of the crisis and post-discharge prevention and treatment plan. Finally, each element of the four-step model (see this chapter: Introduction) will be described, and will be illustrated using the clinical example of Jill's hospitalization.

Approximately 70% of psychiatric emergency consultations represent the first contact an individual has with the mental healthcare system [17]. Suicidal behavior, self-injury, and internalizing symptoms of anxiety and depression are the most common reasons for contact with psychiatric emergency services [18]. Criteria for admission for brief inpatient care can vary between different hospitals. Box 18.1 lists the most common criteria for admission for MBT-informed emergency care.

Box 18.1 Admission or referral criteria for MBT-informed emergency care.

Criteria for Admission

- Patient in crisis, suicidal threats, or self-harm requiring immediate care.
- First contact with the psychiatric system and requiring hospital care.
- Any patient presenting an indication for a crisis intervention, which is brief and sustained, cannot be carried out on an outpatient basis, and may avoid a longer hospital stay.
- By extension, the presence of suicidal ideation or a suicide attempt, acute anxious-depressive symptomatology, severe adjustment disorders, or borderline personality disorder.
- No immediate medico-surgical needs.

Criteria for Other Types of Psychiatric Care

Strong Criteria

- Somatic comorbidity requiring treatment not offered in emergency psychiatric unit.
- Psychotic breakdown.
- Mania or hypomania.
- Psychomotor agitation or violence.
- Drug addiction with focus on treatment for withdrawal and rehabilitation.

Relative Criteria

- Patients in late adolescence*
- Patients with decompensating mental disorder requiring hospitalization for more than 7 days (e.g., severe depression).

* Note that patients between 16 and 18 years of age can be hospitalized if the unit can provide the necessary setting (individual room, competences in adolescent psychiatry, etc.).

In terms of the stages of a crisis, it is helpful to visualize an overall sequence of an unfolding crisis intervention in emergency psychiatry. The evaluation and admission for emergency hospitalization usually take place during the first stage of the crisis (see Figure 18.2). The evaluation is handled by the emergency ward staff, who evaluate and triage the patient.

Elements of the context in which the crisis arose begin to emerge from the referring clinician's discussions with the emergency ward staff and from the first contact with the

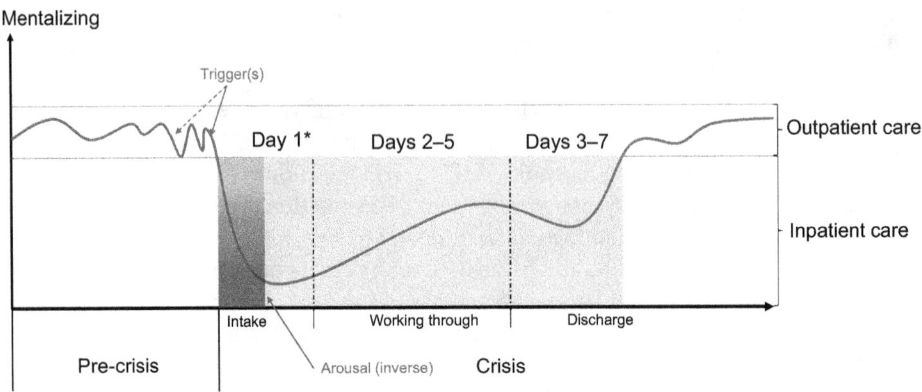

* Days are indicated as approximate time intervals, which can vary between services.

Fig. 18.2 Overview of emergency hospitalization from admission to discharge.

patient. Like any storyline that is shared in a real-life setting, the elements that emerge typically lack narrative structure, and they do not necessarily respect the sequence of events or the order of importance with regard to the triggers and key alienating self-states that led to the hospitalization. These will be uncovered gradually as the patient and the staff gather the relevant information about the crisis episode and its context. The patient and staff will work through these elements to co-create a crisis narrative, with the intention of working out how a teleological solution (in Jill's case, taking a whole packet of paracetamol tablets) came to be seen as the only possible way to handle psychological suffering at the culmination of the crisis. Working around the narrative before, during, and after the crisis, as well as imagining what could have been done differently, and what will be done the next time similar factors converge to create difficult mental states in the patient, will provide the necessary elements to begin to develop a post-hospitalization crisis and treatment plan, and to work on the contextual elements accompanying the patient's discharge from the hospital and safe return home.

Summary

Mentalizing can be particularly helpful to clinicians working in emergency care where first-time hospitalizations and hospitalizations related to personality disorders are treated separately from the other, "revolving-door"-type emergency consultations, which often imply substance dependence, bipolar disorders, or psychotic disorders. In a service that is dedicated to first-time users and users with personality disorders, approximately 20–30% of cases will be related to a diagnosis of BPD or other personality disorders. Importantly, for many individuals this will be the entry point to mental health treatment [3]. The MBT framework is well suited to the heterogeneity of the clinical presentations of patients with suicidal risk and behaviors. Broadly speaking, mental health professionals trained in MBT will be equipped with the skills to:

1. engage with the patient
2. develop a shared understanding of the problem

3. co-create a crisis formulation, together with a prevention and treatment plan
4. prepare the patient for discharge.

The benefits of such an emergency intervention lie in directing the patient toward the most appropriate treatment, reactivating the resources that could provide help within the network around the patient, and reducing the risk of a relapse into suicidality.

The Four Steps of MBT-Informed Emergency Care

In this section we shall outline the four interdependent steps for delivering MBT-informed psychological care in the context of short-term psychiatric emergency hospitalizations. We shall follow the timeline of a typical hospitalization, describing several principles for each step, and illustrating them by referring to the clinical example of Jill's presentation to services. In many services, "hospitalization" is in fact now provided in the community by intensive support from a crisis service. Therefore, although "brief hospitalization" is outlined here, it is possible for the whole process to take place within a safe community setting if crisis support and 24-hour team intervention are available.

Intake and Admission into Emergency Care

The intake process consists of three stages:

1. receiving the request for hospitalization
2. the initial meeting with the patient
3. the team debriefing after the patient's admission.

Receiving the Request for Hospitalization

A request for hospitalization commonly follows an assessment by general medical or nursing staff who may themselves have become anxious about the patient's level of risk. Their evaluation determines whether the crisis level meets the criteria for hospitalization for a longer evaluation. The purpose of this initial contact is to reach an initial formulation of the patient's problem as requiring hospitalization, and to foster enough agency to allow every individual involved in the request for hospitalization, including the patient and their family members and/or significant others, to be explicit about the kind of care they are seeking for the problem that requires inpatient emergency care. In essence, the idea is to jointly formulate a therapeutic plan that fits with the role of the crisis team and the patient's needs. This usually takes a simpler form than a clinical case formulation, and is formulated as a consensus statement: "*What we will be treating during hospitalization or work with the crisis team, and why.*" This therapeutic plan is usually written down and shared with all of the staff who are involved with the patient's care.

We shall now give some examples of open-ended questions that will help everyone to gather the information needed to formulate the consensus statement. These questions are designed to help the referring psychiatrist, the patient, and the family members to begin to focus on affects and representations of self and others, as well as the actual teleological/factual elements of the situation.

- In your current understanding, how has the situation become unbearable?
- In your/the patient's mind, what do you think is different from other situations that is now precipitating the need for hospitalization?
- What do you think you/the patient expect from the hospitalization?

- Do you have the same expectations as the patient?
- What information has the patient communicated to their relatives about the situation?
- Are there any current difficulties being experienced with the medical and nursing staff?

At this stage, teleology is often entrenched: "*She needs hospitalization because she has attempted to kill herself!*" While validating the need for a teleological solution to provide safety and de-escalation of the crisis, the mental health professionals informed by MBT also try to orient thinking around affect and representations of self and others, which may reveal information about the nature of alienating self-experiences and interpersonal triggers involved in the crisis: "*Yes, I understand she tried to kill herself and we will try to better understand what happened. I was asking whether you had any sense of how she is feeling about herself, and what she might seek in terms of help from us?*"

Clinical Example: Jill's Admission

As Jill left the living room after Jeremy told her he "didn't give a shit" about her suicide threat, he went to the bedroom to fetch his mobile phone and call her mother: "*Hello? Yeah, this is Jeremy, I think your daughter's gonna do something stupid again, and this time don't count on me.*" Jill's mother immediately called her daughter, who fortunately answered her mobile: "*Mum, I've just swallowed a box of paracetamol, I'm feeling dizzy and . . . I'm scared.*" Jill's mother, who lived 15 miles away from the holiday resort, decided to check up on her daughter, as she was unsure about the severity of the situation; Jill was consistently portrayed by the family as vulnerable and needy. When Jill's mother arrived, she found her daughter semi-conscious on the ground outside the apartment, alone. She drove Jill to the nearest hospital emergency department.

During the intake process, the evaluating team took the time to medically assess the situation to ensure safety with regard to the dose of paracetamol that Jill had taken. Fortunately, she was out of harm's way, medically speaking. Jill had consulted the same psychiatric emergency team about 4 months previously, accompanied by Jeremy and her mother, following a self-harm episode in which she had superficially slashed her wrists after an argument. She was discharged the same day, and contact between her and the hospital's psychotherapy outpatient service was facilitated, but she had attended only a few sessions.

Upon evaluation, the emergency team thought that this time Jill met the criteria for hospitalization. The meeting with the emergency team is briefly illustrated by the following excerpts.

Clinical Example: Questions from the Emergency Team

***Question:* In your current understanding, how has the situation become unbearable?**

Psychiatrist: She's gone from self-harm to suicide attempt in a few months, there is an escalation of risk that needs a proper evaluation.

Mother: Her boyfriend, he is even more of an [expletive] than I thought. This has to stop.

***Question:* What does the patient expect from the hospitalization?**

Psychiatrist: I think she hopes the boyfriend will come and see her to mend things. Hopefully you [the emergency team] will get her to stick to therapy; she's on a slippery slope.

Mother: Her therapist was useless, obviously. I have borderline personality disorder myself, I know what it's like. My daughter needs to figure out how toxic he is, this guy is ruining her life.

***Question:* Are there any current difficulties being experienced with the medical and nursing staff?**

Psychiatrist: It is like she's not really there, I don't know what you'll be able to get out of her, it feels like she is "saying yes" to please but that she wants to see this relationship through no matter what the cost, which is a cause of worry for us.

Mother: I'm happy they decided on hospitalization this time . . . They should have done so last time around.

It is clear that the questions do not always get straight, informative answers, but the answers do give an idea of the kind of low-mentalizing modes that are operating, as well as glimpses of possible mentalizing. Follow-up questions will be necessary to assess how much mentalizing can already assist in identifying affects and representations involved in a crisis. We can see how the teleological mode structures everyone's thinking, along with some powerful psychic equivalence blended with some possibly attuned mentalizing. In this situation, there is in addition a sense of the dependency and volatility of the patient, indicated both by her mother's answers and by those of the psychiatrist. The mother appears to be an ally who senses that her daughter is caught in a difficult romantic relationship. The mother's own experience can represent both a resource and an obstacle for everyone's mentalizing, and her need to affirm her own experience may sometimes get in the way of mentalizing her daughter.

On the basis of these exchanges, an initial formulation of a consensus statement and therapeutic plan was sketched around the idea of helping Jill to lower the intensity of her thoughts about not being able to be a lovable girlfriend to Jeremy, which seem to trigger strong feelings that compel her to harm herself, although in her mind this is not intentional as she is trying to escape from mental pain. She also talks about a sense of losing control at one point, which needs further understanding if a cycle of repeated episodes of harming herself is to be disrupted. There needs to be discussion with Jill and her mother about the advantages and disadvantages of involving Jeremy in this process, as well as perhaps other significant interpersonal supports.

Jill's First Meeting and the Emergency Team's Admission Debrief

Following an induction to explain how the ward functions, and agreement on a safety plan (e.g., surrendering any medication that could be used for a further overdose), an initial meeting is scheduled involving Jill and two keyworkers. The purpose of this meeting is to engage with Jill and begin to explore the crisis episode. One way to orient the staff during this interview is to roughly follow five themes of interviewing:

1. introductions
2. exploration of the crisis
3. contextualizing

4. in-session experience
5. planning the hospital stay and two-level contract.

Introductions

The staff members present themselves, using a typically warm and humanistic approach while maintaining a professional role, and they ask the patient to briefly present themselves, while attentively maintaining a balance between the staff and patient presentations. The idea is to "break the ice" and explain the context for this first meeting. With the aim of transparency, the staff will share all of the patient information that was sent through from the emergency department to the team, so that the patient can begin to perceive the nature of explicit communication and be encouraged to take the opportunity to correct any of the information that has been received. Furthermore, the "not-knowing" stance is used right from the start to model interest in mental states as the staff divulge what they have understood and what they are trying to further understand, using language tailored to the patient's mentalizing capacities. The patient might correct or add information, which provides an opportunity for the staff members to demonstrate that they will take this into account and further mark their interest in the patient's point of view. The agenda for the meeting is agreed upon, especially that the crisis will be explored at a pace that is acceptable to the patient, and the patient is encouraged to alert the staff if they feel that the interview is going too fast or does not feel right for them. The beginning of the exploration of the crisis is sensitively marked. Importantly, the staff members' overall attitude seeks to foster agency in the patient. It is important to relate to the patient as an individual who wishes to engage with the service to find the help that they feel they need. It needs to be clear in the minds of both the staff and the patient that this is not a long-term therapeutic relationship, nor is it a magical short-term intervention that will "solve" everything. It is more of a starting point to the patient being accompanied through a therapeutic journey with the aim of enhancing their capacity to manage their own thoughts and emotions and to be able to engage in relationships while preventing risky behaviors.

Exploration of the Crisis

The exploration of the crisis typically takes the form of a mentalizing functional analysis (see Chapter 4) in which information on the narrative of the crisis is obtained, attempting to get a sense of the affective narrative, the mental states involved, and the attachment triggers that may have primed themes such as loss, rupture, shame, rejection, and so on. Self and other representations along the narrative can be sensitively prompted without going into a full not-knowing mode. Careful observation of changes in arousal and/or possible dissociative phenomena will guide the clinician's investigation of the crisis. Under- or over-empathizing with the patient at this stage will increase their vigilance or credulity, respectively. The epistemic trust that is generated through the clinician's humane interest can only be activated if the patient feels that they are an object of respect, with their own experience as an area of joint attention. Interventions in the "mentalizing process" domain, such as contrary moves, clarification, reformulation, and brief summaries, as well as empathic validation, are typically used by MBT-informed clinicians (see Chapter 4).

At this stage, similar questions to those formulated with the referring psychiatrist may be asked.

Clinical Example: Exploration of the Crisis

***Question:* In your current understanding, how has the situation become unbearable?**

JILL: It seems I can never please my boyfriend, I don't know, I just lost it when he said he doesn't care, I need him, I can't live without him!

***Question*: What do you expect from the hospitalization?**

JILL: I want to show my boyfriend I'm not crazy, I can do better this time. I'm scared I won't succeed . . . Why doesn't he love me?

***Question*: Are there any current difficulties being experienced with the medical and nursing staff?**

JILL: No, thank you, people here have been really nice. I don't know if they can help, they must think I'm just looking for attention.

Contextualizing

As the session continues, the staff usually move in and out of the crisis exploration, notably because contextual and biographical information about current and past significant relationships, their history, and other factors assist in going beyond a superficial comprehension of the current situation. Much like the case formulation procedure (described in Chapter 4), the staff will prompt the patient for information on their relationship patterns, and will try to assess the interpersonal landscape that inevitably includes factors relating to both risk and resilience. The assessment of mentalizing function in the patient continues during this phase with regard to their capacity to formulate a narrative, to structure timelines, and to identify mental state and emotions in both the past and the present, as well as areas of low-mentalizing functioning.

In-Session Experience

In-session experience is the object of observation for everyone involved in the session. What types of feelings and thoughts are provoked in the staff during the session? What kinds of emotions, changes in arousal, experiences of feeling recognized, or experiences of feeling discounted seem to be apparent in the patient? In getting to know the patient's arousal and mentalizing systems, the staff try to pay attention to the patient's reactions to their interventions and to how their stated intentions are received by the patient. On many occasions, although the intentions of the staff are to try to better understand the patient's affect in order to help the patient to regulate it, during this process the patient may feel judged, misunderstood, or discounted. Conversely, the patient may feel that one of the staff members understands "exactly" what they are going through, or a staff member might feel that they have a particularly good understanding of the situation because of who they are or because of how the patient relates to them specifically. Any increase in *certainty* such as this is a marker of decreased mentalizing. All of these elements require careful attention, as they may alter the quality of mentalizing in communication with the patient as well as between staff members.

In the first session, the clinical staff dynamically maintain the balance between helping the patient to feel accepted for who they are and what they are going through, and seeking to understand the mental states involved in the crisis. Keeping the interventions around the structure, not-knowing stance, and process domains while sensitively attending to the patient's low-mentalizing modes is key. Although the affective narrative and relational mentalizing can be present, they occupy less space within the session. For example, "soundbites" of relational mentalizing may be useful for navigating through moments of the session without getting into an extensive relational mentalizing intervention. Again, the clinicians strive to work toward an acknowledgment of the patient's experience in order to ignite a spark of epistemic trust, however small it may be.

Case Example: Excerpt from the First Meeting between Jill and the Staff

During the first meeting, Jill appears to engage with the staff only briefly, and repeatedly switches between talking about what she should do (call Jeremy or send him a text message) and her mother's incomprehension of her life. She is not responsive to the initial validation attempts in relation to these two topics, and the psychiatric nurse increasingly feels that it is as if Jill is having a conversation with herself.

Nurse: Jill, may I just interrupt you for a minute?

Jill: Euh . . . yes, of course!

Nurse: I can hear that you are preoccupied with what to do with Jeremy now—to call, to text, or to wait, right?

Jill: Yeah.

Nurse: . . . and that you are also feeling like your mum is not understanding the current situation . . .

Jill: . . . and my whole life for that matter (*preparing to continue speaking on this topic*)

Nurse: Right, just a minute! Before you continue I want you to know that *I am getting* that this is what is in your thoughts at the moment. Can I just ask—how can *we* help?

Jill: Well, you could tell me what to do. Should I call Jeremy?

Nurse: Can we leave that for later in your hospital stay?

Jill: I need to know if he still loves me!

Nurse: I am hearing you, indeed it sounds like *that* is the emergency for you!

Jill: Yes!

Nurse: As you are saying this, Jill, are you feeling that your life depends on it?

Jill: *YES!*

Nurse: OK, we are hearing you, and we can imagine that being here without knowing where he stands is leaving you with doubts that seem really unbearable for you.

In this example, the soundbite of relational mentalizing ("How can *we* help?") realigned the therapeutic exchange, and led to an additional empathic validation that could be somewhat better contextualized from the patient's perspective. In the aftermath of the first meeting, the clinical staff will keep an eye on how the patient actually engages with thinking about the crisis rather than thinking of immediate solutions. Indeed, as the environment around the patient will typically involve a reduction in their usual social, family, and other triggers, the patient's mind will engage more in thinking about the current situation, where they are, and the degree of severity of the crisis episode—all of which can create emotional turmoil that requires some support as the patient starts the hospitalization period.

Planning the Hospital Stay and Two-Level Contract

Toward the end of the initial session, structural and psychoeducational elements are introduced for the patient to continue developing a representation of the hospitalization. Among the psychoeducational elements, attention can be drawn to the variation in the degree to which self-experience is bearable, in relation to life before the crisis, within the crisis episode, and during the hospital stay. Psychoeducation about the identification of triggers and episodes that can switch self-experience from bearable to increasingly unbearable helps to educate the patient about their vulnerabilities to different self-experiences, and to increase their awareness of how self-harming mental states can come to take up the whole of their mental space. This brings us back to the relationship between mentalizing and affective arousal, and specifically how intense affect will reduce an individual's capacity to use a variety of ways to cope with a given situation. The more intense the affect becomes, the fewer the options that are available, and the greater the risk that self-harm will come to seem like the only available option for dealing with the unbearable feelings.

At this stage, the patient will find it useful to have a more concrete sense of what any hospital stay will actually involve. A two-level contract is introduced—one level is valid for the next 24 hours, and the second level relates to the remainder of the stay. The idea is that the patient will engage themselves in working for at least 24 hours on reducing the level of affect that led to the crisis episode. Once the intensity of affect has been lowered, thinking about the rest of the stay becomes more feasible. This way of working helps the patient—during the first 24 hours—to notice any changes in mental-state function and the opening up of the possibility of mentalizing during periods when affect is less intense. As a rule of thumb, the first 24 hours are devoted to settling into the unit (room and facilities), to thinking of activities that might assist in reducing the affect, to planning to contact the people who need to know where the patient is currently, and to prospectively imagining how the patient is going to actively involve themself in the treatment—a task that involves both the treatment team and the patient.

Post Meeting and Transmission of Information within the Unit

After admission to the unit and the first session, the information gathered needs to be collated and transmitted to the team. Of particular interest is the integration of the different points of view and counter-relationship experiences of the different members of staff who have interacted with the patient—they all represent sources of information about the patient and the nature of the crisis. The structure of team functioning allows time to create a provisional common understanding of what the patient is presenting in terms of unbearable mental states and to map out the areas that require further investigation and what kinds of affects may, for team members, facilitate or impede the work with the patient. It also facilitates a common understanding of what has been agreed upon in terms of activities during the time at the unit, and the people who will be informed about the patient's hospitalization. The patient's use of their mobile phone and communication with attachment figures and other people outside the unit requires planning and agreement. As we have highlighted in earlier chapters of this book, attachment stress challenges mentalizing, and when the patient is in a vulnerable state this can quickly trigger a worsening of their condition. This means that reducing contact with attachment figures for a short time might be beneficial.

Uncovering the Crisis

Following the first step of the hospitalization, the second step consists of working through the psychological complexity of the crisis to co-create with the patient a working hypothesis of how the crisis came about. This usually takes place from the second or third day to the fourth or fifth day of hospitalization (or work with the crisis team if the process is being completed in a community setting), and it involves four to six sessions, each lasting 45 minutes. As the sessions follow one another, there is a progression, guided by the clinicians, from consideration of external trigger factors to consideration of internal affective-representational factors. The clinicians seek to gather the most pertinent information that will constitute the building blocks for the upcoming third step—the formulation. Therefore these sessions are still very much in mentalizing process mode, to give everyone an opportunity to assess as accurately as possible the emotional and relational landscapes that increase the risk of alienating self-states taking over the patient's mind and leading to serious self-harm.

The staff will take the time to make explicit that the brief and focused hospitalization period is entering this phase, usually when they review the 24-hour contract. The purpose of this phase is to extend the investigation from the actual crisis to the following seven contextual domains:

1. obtaining a reliable developmental timeline of the patient, noting all of the risk factors along the way, the patient's previous contact(s) with mental health services, if any, and investigating previous crises and how they were resolved
2. obtaining a satisfactory description of the history of the patient's key relationships, and, more specifically, their more recent evolution and the possible challenges and conflicts encountered
3. obtaining a good representation of role functioning for the patient, specifically professionally (or in terms of training/education, if appropriate to the patient)
4. investigating the affective domain of functioning in close relationships in order to assess satisfaction and possible concerns (this can include the sexual life of the patient)
5. prompting and looking for areas of creativity, as well as strengths and domains that contribute as protective factors
6. charting the resources available to the patient (e.g., personal, interpersonal, social, community)
7. throughout the process, collecting information to establish a profile of the mentalizing capacities of the patient.

The clinical techniques employed during the sessions are in keeping with the domains of intervention of MBT—mentalizing process, managing ineffective mentalizing modes, exploration of affective narrative, and relational mentalizing (see Chapter 4)—and the patient will have been informed that these domains will be considered systematically during the sessions. The clinician therefore orients the sessions in a semi-structured fashion, maintaining a balance between guided exploration and letting the patient "think out loud." The aim is to maintain the level of arousal in the sessions at an optimal degree of activation to foster some segments of the patient's mentalizing while keeping the clinicians' mentalizing online. The clinicians employ the context domains template, summarized in the 7-point list of contextual domains, to update the work done after each session and to plan further investigation of areas that require this.

The main goal of this phase, which is made explicit to the patient, is to build a working hypothesis of the crisis that links both external and internal factors to alienating self-experiences that trigger self-harming behavior. In this sense, there is a clear psycho-educational component that guides the support provided to the patient in making their formulation about the crisis. As we mentioned earlier, the clinical staff will make it a priority to enable agency in the patient, and sometimes this can conflict with the staff wanting to provide support and relief to the patient who is experiencing difficult emotions. However, as this work is very short term, it is of key importance that the clinicians work with affect, but maintain a balance between affect identification and elaboration, and activation of the patient's coping resources.

From a systemic point of view, the patient's crisis is embedded in a network of relationships (a system) in which they tend to bear the responsibility for problems or dysfunctions. Yet, as they are working on understanding the crisis, they are offered an opportunity to appreciate the overall picture and the scope of the problem(s) within their relational system. This perspective is fundamental to reappraising the situation as a system in which everyone involved contributes to engaging in helpful and regulating interactions, or in unhelpful and coercive interactions where roles and responsibilities become confused and trigger attempts to regain domination or control. The staff may find it useful to employ tools to map out the interpersonal and social network surrounding the patient—for example, by drawing concentric circles on a piece of paper, placing the patient at the center (by writing their name inside the innermost circle), and asking them to plot their family members and friends according to their level of emotional closeness or distance. The different types of support that may be available to the patient can then be charted, as well as the gaps that need to be filled in order to promote salutogenic (health-promoting and health-sustaining) relational dynamics.

One aspect that has not yet been mentioned in this chapter is the profound persuasive power that alienating self-states hold over the patient's mind. How can it be that individuals can feel so bad about themselves and appear to hold on to this vision of being worthless in the face of either contrary evidence or a positive and supporting environment that does not see them in that way? We believe that this issue is intimately linked to identity and personality [19]. Indeed, the way that individuals define themselves plays a role in the expression of how they experience mental pain, because individuals experience crises as "who they are" rather than "what they have." To put it plainly, the alien self is *part of* any individual—in a crisis, it comes to be not part but the totality of being, a kind of defining hypothesis of one's identity: "*My life is like this because I am such a useless person.*" Now, coming back to the emergency intervention process, it can perhaps be more easily perceived that what we are trying to do is to re-establish balance so that the alien self is not alone but surrounded by other functional parts of the self and others. It is important that clinicians do not try to persuade these patients that they are "wrong" about their alien experience of themselves—no clinician can be more persuasive than an alien self.

Working through the contextual domains will provide an opportunity to co-create a formulation as the hospitalization period enters its third and fourth steps. By this time the patient's acute distress will have decreased to a tolerable level, and the staff should have almost finished investigating all of the contextual domains that require integration with the nature of self-alienating experiences that have emerged within the subjective experience of the patient. More concretely, the staff will have met the patient's family and other individuals who are susceptible to impact, and who can help with the resolution of the crisis. Contact is also initiated with the outpatient treatment team or therapist to assist in collecting the contextual information and to assess the feasibility and organization of pursuing treatment after the hospitalization period has ended.

Integration and Formulation of the Crisis Area

Hospitalization is likely to stir up a variety of experiences, memories, and feelings for patients. Although staff members strive to offer a clear understanding of all the elements that the patient brings up, this task is ultimately impossible. The staff are more likely to be helpful if they give the patient their sensitive and attuned attention while striving to expand on the essential lines of tension that have brought the patient to the point of crisis. Therefore the formulation in the hospital emergency setting, which is elaborated by the staff and the patient together in the final days of the hospitalization period, attempts to collate the main points that have been discussed and learned about the crisis during the stay, and it eschews the impulse to want to understand everything and offer all-encompassing explanations. To help to achieve this, the emergency care formulation is structured by the following main headings:

1. emergence of a crisis
2. activating resources
3. do's and don'ts (crisis plan)
4. anticipating future treatment.

Emergence of a Crisis

In the first section of the formulation, the patient is encouraged to note down what they have learned from the emergence of crises in the past through to the present episode, and how they might notice a crisis emerging in the future. With regard to attachment, the patient will be encouraged to reflect on what they can control in their relationships, as well as what they have to gain and what they might lose if they do not employ their usual relational strategies. With regard to mentalizing, the staff and patient will attempt to identify the main triggers that reduce the patient's mentalizing, as well as what makes it difficult for them to recover mentalizing. With regard to alienating self-experience, some thought will be given to the parts of the self that the patient wished to avoid or destroy by self-harming or ending their life, and how thoughts about self-harm may indeed signal specific ways of experiencing the self. Discussions about ways to prevent such self-alienating experiences from overwhelming the patient take place at this time. Figure 18.3 shows an example of this section of the formulation.

Activating Resources

In the second section of the formulation (e.g., see Figure 18.4), the staff and the patient consider agency, in particular the identification of resources that can be activated

1. Noticing crisis emergence

- Relationship(s) pattern(s)
- Benefits from/cost of these patterns
- Mentalizing stoppers
- Attitudes and emotions making things worse
- Unbearable state(s) that may lead to serious self-harm
- What did I wish to avoid/destroy by my serious self-harm?

1. Noticing crisis emergence

- Relationship(s) pattern(s):
With Jeremy: I become needy and he becomes disrespectful

- Benefits from/cost of these patterns:
When he responds he makes me feel like he's the only one who sees who I really am. Without this I would need to find other ways of feeling appreciated by him.

- Mentalizing stoppers:
Him ignoring me

- Attitudes and emotions making things worse:
People not taking me seriously
Feeling alone
Feeling stupid

- Unbearable state(s) that may lead to serious self-harm:
Thinking I'll never be loved, I'll be alone forever

- What did I wish to avoid/destroy by my serious self-harm?
Being a failure

Fig. 18.3 Example of Section 1 of the crisis formulation, with headings on the left-hand side and the patient's formulation on the right-hand side.

2. Activating resources

- What are the benefits of mentalizing?
- How would I try to reactivate trust in others?
- How would I try to reactivate trust in myself?

2. Activating resources

- What are the benefits of mentalizing?

Taking a step back, or seeing things from above -> Calms me down and de-dramatizes

Speaking to friends -> Thinking that I may be exaggerating, and they normalize situations

Just taking a step back

- How would I try to reactivate trust in others?
I don't know, maybe asking them if I am burdening them?

- How would I try to reactivate trust in myself?
Do an activity I'm good at
Try to meet new people
Start playing football again, or another sport

Fig. 18.4 Example of Section 2 of the crisis formulation, with headings on the left-hand side and the patient's formulation on the right-hand side.

when the patient identifies a new crisis emerging. Some psychoeducation on the benefits of mentalizing, together with personalized examples during the hospitalization period and in the patient's general life, may help the patient to formulate how mentalizing might be helpful in the future. The issue of trust in oneself and others is discussed from the perspective of thinking about ways to activate trust in situations where it seems to be challenged.

Do's and Don'ts (Crisis Plan)

The crisis plan (e.g., see Figure 18.5) maps out "do's and don'ts" to help to manage crisis situations. The "who, when, what, where" of helpful and unhelpful elements of a crisis are spelled out for the patient to make explicit some of the processes that tend

3. Do's and Don'ts (Crisis plan)

- Signals of crisis:
- Do's:
  Who:
  Where:
  What has worked in the past:
- Don'ts:
  What:
  Who:
  Where:
  What has failed in the past:

3. Do's and Don'ts (Crisis plan)

- Signals of crisis:
Feeling needy, desperate to make things magically better again, losing control over self-harming thoughts

- Do's:
Who: 1) Jenny; 2) Tom or Michael; 3) Mum
Where: outside generally, park, maybe gym
What has worked in the past:
Calling people
Getting busy with work
Shutting off phone and social media profiles

- Don'ts:
What: Ruminate and harass my boyfriend
Who: I guess my boyfriend, sometimes
Where: I should avoid going to parties with him, I get jealous
What has failed in the past:
Self-harming (wrists)
Yelling at people
Believing everything can change quickly

Fig. 18.5 Example of Section 3 of the crisis formulation, with headings on the left-hand side and the patient's formulation on the right-hand side.

4. Anticipation of future treatment

- What are the elements that are likely to make treatment useful?
- What are the elements that are likely to make treatment not useful?
- Agenda: What is my therapeutic agenda in the next two months?
- What do I think I need to work on?

4. Anticipation of future treatment

- What are the elements that are likely to make treatment useful?
Someone who will be active in therapy and give me good advice

- What are the elements that are likely to make treatment not useful?
Making me feel judged, like I am not understanding or being the right way

- Agenda: What is my therapeutic agenda in the next two months?
Before I leave the hospital, I'd like to set at least one date per week for therapy or meeting with a nurse. Right now, I've got a date for next week only

- What do I think I need to work on?
Why I despise myself so much and let other people walk all over me

Fig. 18.6 Example of Section 4 of the crisis formulation, with headings on the left-hand side and the patient's formulation on the right-hand side.

to repeat themselves, leading to negative spirals, as well as the elements of coping that seem to work or that could be enriched.

Anticipating Future Treatment

The fourth section of the formulation (e.g., see Figure 18.6) is devoted to projecting oneself into the future, specifically within a therapeutic framework. The staff engage the patient in thinking about the elements that are likely to make treatment useful and also those that might be unhelpful. In addition, the staff strive to set an agenda of meetings with professionals from the mental health network. Research shows that around 50% of rehospitalizations usually occur within the first 6 months [20], and that access to care is a key variable contributing to positive outcomes. The staff also encourage the patient to imagine some of the areas of work for future therapy.

Preparation for Discharge

Discharge is a part of the process that in almost all cases will activate anxiety and therefore a potential relapse in mentalizing. As the patient prepares to face their world again, it is not surprising that they may show a noticeable reduction in their mental functioning, or their mind organizes in a pseudomentalizing mode to "keep it together." It is important that the staff carry on their work in the same way and avoid providing anxious mirroring in the face of the return of the patient's symptoms.

An important aspect of preparation for discharge is to concretely plan the week ahead and make sure that appropriate contact has been made with the outpatient therapist, team, or clinic. There is a risk of treatment dropout after hospitalization, and this is associated with a significantly increased risk of relapse with suicidal crises. Therefore everything that can be put in place during the intensive assessment phase can contribute to reducing the risk of a crisis recurring. For example, the clinician who is offering follow-up may visit the patient, contact with the outpatient team is organized, or other arrangements are made to facilitate the transition from one team to the next.

The identification of resources, the formulation, and the crisis plan all contribute to the safe discharge of the patient. Social and interpersonal resources are key to fostering a sense of belongingness and to ensuring that human contact is available in times of need. Self-stigma is another problem, because individuals who have been hospitalized can ruminate on themselves as being "weak" because they have needed psychiatric hospitalization. Others may feel a sense of disconnection, or even be afraid of such levels of distress returning. As the hospitalization ends, it is important for the staff to check these risk factors and attempt to provide some support in dealing with the challenges that the patient faces. Crises are recognized by the staff as moments of distress, but also as moments of plasticity and change. In every crisis lies an opportunity to effect change and increase agency in one's life. Maintaining a positive outlook on this period is important for the staff, as this helps patients to maintain a balance between shame, self-criticism, and engaging with themselves to increase agency and connectedness with their social and interpersonal resources.

When human contact and epistemic trust have been rekindled during the assessment and stabilization phase, they can powerfully and favorably orient the life trajectory of the patient toward increased self-care, thereby directly contributing to a positive outcome. If the emergency service staff can be remembered by the patient as people who really cared and tried to be helpful to them, much of the work has been accomplished.

Concluding Remarks

MBT can be applied to inform emergency care in psychiatry. Indeed, many professionals who are working in the setting of emergency care have completed training in specialized therapeutic methods such as MBT or DBT to increase their skills in working with individuals who meet the diagnostic criteria for BPD. This chapter goes a step further in proposing a model of structured care—using a mentalizing framework for short-term hospitalization or crisis intervention in emergency care—that may be beneficial for individuals who are struggling with an acute crisis. Alienating self-experiences require de-escalation, empathic validation, and work toward a formulation of the crisis for the patient to be able to meaningfully (re-)connect with an outpatient therapeutic program and prevent further instances of self-harm. Research is under way to investigate whether such mentalization-informed care helps to reduce episodes of rehospitalization, increase adherence to treatment recommendations, and support resilience in mental health professionals who are working in the emotionally challenging environment of psychiatric emergency care services.

References

1. Bateman A, Fonagy P. Randomized controlled trial of outpatient mentalization-based treatment versus structured clinical management for borderline personality disorder. *Am J Psychiatry* 2009; **166**: 1355–64.
2. Besch V, Greiner C, Magnin C et al. Clinical characteristics of suicidal youths and adults: a one-year retrospective study. *Int J Environ Res Public Health* 2020; **17**: 8733.
3. Besch V, Debbané M, Greiner C et al. Emergency psychiatric management of borderline personality disorder: towards an articulation of modalities for personalised integrative care. *Encephale* 2020; **46**: 463–70.
4. Prada P, Cole P, Bondolfi G et al. Mentaliser en psychiatrie de liaison? [Mentalizing in liaison psychiatry?]. *Rev Med Suisse* 2017; **13**: 363–6.
5. James RK. Crisis interventions. In: Norcross JC, VandenBos GR, Freedheim DK, eds. *APA Handbook of Clinical Psychology*, Vol. 3. Washington, DC: American Psychological Association, 2016; 387–407.
6. Nizum N, Yoon R, Ferreira-Legere L et al. Nursing interventions for adults following a mental health crisis: a systematic review guided by trauma-informed principles. *Int J Ment Health Nurs* 2020; **29**: 348–63.
7. Johnson S, Lamb D, Marston L et al. Peer-supported self-management for people discharged from a mental health crisis team: a randomised controlled trial. *Lancet* 2018; **392**: 409–18.
8. Henzen A, Moeglin C, Giannakopoulos P, Sentissi O. Determinants of dropout in a community-based mental health crisis centre. *BMC Psychiatry* 2016; **16**: 111.
9. Heyland M, Johnson M. Evaluating an alternative to the emergency department for adults in mental health crisis. *Issues Ment Health Nurs* 2017; **38**: 557–61.
10. Fonagy P, Gergely G, Jurist E, Target M. *Affect Regulation, Mentalization, and the Development of the Self.* New York, NY: Other Press, 2002.
11. Jeammet P. La violence à l'adolescence: défense identitaire et processus de figuration [Violence in adolescence: identity defense and figuration process]. *Adolescence* 1997; **15**: 305–21.
12. Fonagy P, Target M. The mentalization-focused approach to self pathology. *J Personal Disord* 2006; **20**: 544–76.
13. Ferenczi S. Confusion of tongues between adults and the child (the language of tenderness and of passion). *Int J Psychoanal* 1949; **30**: 225–30.
14. Gergely G, Watson JS. The social biofeedback theory of parental affect-mirroring: the development of emotional self-awareness and self-control in infancy. *Int J Psychoanal* 1996; **77**: 1181–212.
15. Fotopoulou A, Tsakiris M. Mentalizing homeostasis: the social origins of interoceptive inference. *Neuropsychoanalysis* 2017; **19**: 3–28.
16. Fonagy P, Campbell C. What touch can communicate: commentary on "Mentalizing homeostasis: the social origins of interoceptive inference" by Fotopoulou and Tsakiris. *Neuropsychoanalysis* 2017; **19**: 39–42.
17. Walter M, Genest P. Réalités des urgences en psychiatrie [The reality of psychiatric emergencies]. *L'Inform Psychiatr* 2006; **82**: 565–70.

18. Seletti B. Situations psychiatriques dans un service d'urgence [Psychiatric situations in an emergency department]. *Ann Méd Psychol Rev Psychiatr* 2002; **160**: 187–91.

19. Luyten P, Fonagy P. Integrating and differentiating personality and psychopathology: a psychodynamic perspective. *J Pers* 2022; **90**: 75–88.

20. Li X, Srasuebkul P, Reppermund S, Trollor J. Emergency department presentation and readmission after index psychiatric admission: a data linkage study. *BMJ Open* 2018; **8**: e018613.

Index

Numbers: **bold** = box or table, *italics* = figure;

numbers within a span are listed *first* (e.g., **279**, **284**, 278–86);

small words ("and", "as", "at", "for", "from", "in") *are* alphabetized.

action mind, 83, 127
action person, **65–66**
adaptive hyporesponsivity, 282
Adaptive Mentalization-Based Integrative Treatment. *See* AMBIT
adolescence, x, 8, 11, 177, 237, 299, 303, 308
  defining feature, 9
adolescents, xii, 16–18, 29, 222, 305, 328–39, 356
Adult Attachment Interview, 210
adult mentorship (CAPSLE), 355
affect focus, 129–30, 171, 194, 197, 245–46
affect regulation, 19, 43, 119, 212, 328–29
affective mirroring, 369–70
  characteristics, 369
affective narrative
  psychosis patients, 273
affective reflection
  trauma sufferers, 290
affective states, 45, 47
age, 16, 278
agency, 10, 12, 16, 21, 78–79, 84, 198, 215, 235, 259, 261, 263, 266, 268, 385
  children, 322
  recovery from crisis episode, 365
  suicide attempts, 367–68
agency–alienation continuum, *369*
aggression, 15, 184, 190, 193–95, 200, 282, 285
Airaldi C, 11
alexithymia, 213, 216, 223, 225, 305
  definition, 211
alien self, 12–13, 120, 176, 209, 244, 266, 302, 310, **329**, 367, 381
  adolescents, 334
  definition, 12
  psychological crisis, 368–70
alienating self-experiences, 368, 370, 374, 382
  triggers, 369
alienation, 153, 180, 202, 253, 260
altercentric bias, 214
AMBIT, 311, 362
  complex cases, 354
  draws on mentalizing theory, 355
  epistemic trust principle, 354
  keyworker role, 354–55
  mentalizing professional community, 353–55
  model structure, 354
  origins, 353
  starting assumption, 354
AMBIT wheel, 354
amygdala, 211, 235, 281
anger, 164, **168**, 183–84, 188, 190, 198, 335, 343
Anna Freud Centre, xiii, 360
anorexia nervosa (AN), 298, **300–1**, 300, 306–8
  interpersonal difficulties, 305
  persistence, 303–4
  social functioning (impairment), 305
antisocial personality disorder, xi, 28, 45, 54, 69, 116, 143, 174–202
  addressing equality versus hierarchy, 181–83
  Bryan case study, 181, **182**
  formulation, 181–84
  James case study, **200**
  links with BPD and NPF, 174
  primary emphasis of change, 175
antisocial personality disorder (MBT aims), 174–78
  changing identity and achieving desistance, 174
  mentalizing and violence, 175–78
anxiety, 17, **56**, 194–95, 211
  interaction with mentalizing, 45
apologies (effective), 352
arguments, **160**
ASPD. *See* antisocial personality disorder
assessment sessions, 138
at-risk patient, 117–34
  clinical top tips, **118**
  outside-in mind, 119
  self-harm (function), 119
  suicide attempts, self-harm, violence (simplified summary), 118–20
  teleological mode, 119
  useful MBT principles, 129–33
  warning signs, **117**
at-risk patient (clinical intervention process), 120–29
  1. establish shared responsibility, 121
  2. safety planning (risk assessment), 121–23
  3. focus on mental states before event, 123–25
  4. exploration of context of wellness, 125
  5. mentalizing functional analysis, 125–28

6. identification of strategies for managing mental turmoil, 103
attachment, 281–83
and MBT, 13–14
role in co-regulation of stress, 237–39
attachment anxiety, 46, 136, 176, 209, 238
relationship with mentalizing quality, 45
attachment avoidance, 209, 238
attachment behavioral system, **279**
attachment dimensions
relationship with personality features (depressed patients), *239*
attachment insecurity, 308
link with eating disorders, 305
attachment loss, **130**
attachment patterns
anxious-ambivalent, **61–62**
anxious-avoidant, **61**
insecure-ambivalent, 61
insecure-avoidant, 61
attachment problems, **232**
attachment processes, 56, 60–62
attachment relationships, 13, 15, 233, 235, 249, 282, 304, 349
psychosis patients, 257
attachment security, 11, 61, 282, 299, 356–57, 361
attachment strategies, **162**, 212, 240–41
attachment styles, **64**
anxious-ambivalent, **66**
DIT, 248
attachment system, 13–14, 44, 119, 123, 166, 177, 237, 241, 279, 284
attachment theory, 13, 225, 354
attachment trauma, xii, 22, 277–78, 285–86
re-enactment (types), **283**, 284
attachment-deactivating strategies, 238, 240, 282
attachment-hyperactivating strategies, 240, 282
Auerbach JS, 261
autism, 2, 25, 206, 307
autonomy, 245, 285, 338
avoidance, 188, 279
avoidant personality disorder, xi, 55, 116, 203–29
assessment, 206–8
assessment (hypermentalizing form), 207
assessment (hypomentalizing form), 206
characteristic difficulty, 204
characteristics, **203**
clinician boredom and emotional numbness, 224
clinician challenge response "unfair", 207
clinician impatience, 207
clinician's counter-response, 208
diagnosis, 203–4
experience, 204–5
fear of being found out or exposed, 205
formulations (two-fold challenge), 204
humiliation "critical issue", 205
Jane case study, **205**, **207**, **217**, 219–20, **221**
MBT goal, 216
MBT-compatible evidence-based approaches, 224–25
paucity of research, 203
secondary avoidance phenomenon, 208
therapeutic challenge, 216
treatment approach, 216–24
avoidant personality disorder (mentalizing difficulties), 209–16
automatic/controlled, **209**, 210–11, 225
cognitive/affective, **210**, 211, 225
external/internal, **210**
formulation summary, 215–16
internal/external, 212
self/other, **210**, 212–15, 217, 224, 226
self/other (three aspects), 216
avoidant personality disorder (treatment approach), 216–24
affect focus and relational mentalizing, 220–22
calibrating internal experience and external reality, 220–22
compassionate challenge, 221
counter-relational responsiveness, 222
formulation, 217
formulation (side effects of intervention), 218
hypermentalizing in pretend mode, 222
memory elaboration and imagery, 223
playfulness in MBT, 223
reducing influence of inner eye, 219–20
supervision, 224
tackling excess focus on self, 219–20
avoidant personality disorder (treatment phase)
attachment strategies, 209
limitations, 208
mentalizing difficulties, 209–16
AvPD. *See* avoidant personality disorder

basic emotion
driver of existence, 71
Bateman A, 2, 28, 69
Beeney JE, 209
beliefs, 1
Besch V, 364
bifactor modelling
definition, 18
bingeing, 309
biobehavioral systems, 278, **279**, *281*
Blatt SJ, 261
Bleiberg E, 347
Bleuler E, 260
body posture, 58, 151, 199, 266
body–feeling scan (MBT-F exercise), 343
boom brain, 127, 129

borderline personality disorder, 12, 14, 116, 155, 161, **162**, 231, 365, 372, *See also* Sarah case study
  difficulties experienced, 14
  emotional state (interference with decision making), 126
  epistemic mistrust (development), 22–24
  links with BPD and NPF, 174
  and MBT, 14–15
  mentalizing, 15–17, 25
  mistrust (core feature), 21
  online treatment, 149
  push-me-pull-you dynamics, 204
  relational and attachment problems "central", **128**
  symptoms, 15
brain, 13, 18, **59**, 213, 263, 306, 328
  connections between different areas (problems), 18
breakout rooms, 150–52
Brentano FC, 1
broaden-and-build cycles, 282
Bruch H, 298–99
bubble mode, **66**, 83
bulimia nervosa (BN), 300, 303, 306
bullying, 12, 306, **329**, 355–56
Burlingham D, 26

calendar, 324
Cambridge Guide to Mentalization-Based Treatment
  book aim, ix
  book focus, ix
  practicality, 2
Campbell C, 22, 370
CAPSLE
  components, 355
  focus, 356
  mentalizing programme for schools, 355–56
  whole-school approach, 355
caregivers, 9–11, 13, 330, 369
Carer APP, 360
Carer Map, 360
challenge, 197
  MBT for couples, 351
chameleon effect, 170
chat mode, 146, 189
Child in Need, **62**, **81**, 82, **84**
child protection team, **128**, 179, 182, 200
childhood, x, 8–9, 225
childhood adversity, 22, 82, 177
childhood trauma, 23, 25, 279
child-o-scopes (MBT-F exercise), 345
children, xii, 18–19, 319–27, 344–45, *See also* MBT for children
classroom management plan (CAPSLE), 355
clinical process
  MBT step-by-step guide, 52–135
  at-risk patient, 120–29
clinician–patient interaction, 44, 108, 152, 163, 170–71, 246
  sitting "side-by-side" (rather than "opposite"), 107
clinicians
  assessment by patients, 163
  AvPD "special challenge", 203
  counter-responsiveness, 129
  humility demanded, 109
  interpersonal strengths and mentalizing weak spots, 116
  mentalization-based treatment, 43–51
  must quarantine own feelings, 109
  personal psychology, 109
  personal safety, 197
  secondary avoidance, 222
  sensitive spots, 113
Cochrane Reviews
  MBT and BPD (2020), 27
  self-harm in adolescents, 29
cognitive-behavioral therapy, 298, 319
Cohen's *d*, 11
collaboration, 48–49
collaborative clinical agreement, 63, 66, 167
collective mentalizing, 143–44
co-mentalizing, 21
  couples, 347, 351
  families, 340, 343
communication, 57, 304, 349, 376
communication systems, 26–27, 244, 246–48, 287–88, 362
  1. teaching and learning of content, 26
  2. re-emergence of mentalizing, 26
  3. applying social learning in wider environment, 27
compassion, 25, 171
complex trauma, xii, 278, 282, 285–86
  definition, 277
computer games, 22, 148
context, xii, 198
contextual domains template (emergency care), 380
contrary moves, 79
conversational partners, 49–50, 53, 57–58, 68, 170, 291
  patient–clinician versus patient–patient, 141
core self-disturbance, 261, 263–64, 269, 274
  clinical intervention (guiding principles), 272
  definition, 265
  links to non-mentalizing modes and cycles of non-mentalizing, 265–67
  non-mentalizing cycles, *267*
  triggers, 266, 271
counter-relational mentalizing, 108–13, 171
  definition, 109
  Stanley case study, **112**
  suggested four-step procedure, 109
counter-relational responses, 115–16
couples, xii, 347–52
Covid-19 pandemic, 148, 263
Creating A Peaceful School Learning Environment. *See* CAPSLE
criminal justice system, 178, 201
crisis planning, 121, 149
cultural learning, 20
culture, 10, 353
curiosity, 269, **269**, 287, 292, 323, 330–31, 345, 350
cyberball paradigm, 25
  definition, 24

DBT. *See* dialectical behavior therapy
decentration, 212–13
 definition, 212
decompensation
 psychosis patients, 264
default mode network (DMN), 18
delusion, 265, 272
democracy, 48–49, 103, 108
Denmark, 28–29
Dennett D, 2
depression, xii, 17, 216, 230–52
 attachment styles (individual differences), **235**
 attachment, mood, mentalizing, resilience (relationship in face of adversity), *234*
 clinical features (typical), **235**
 clinician contrary moves, 236
 clinician feelings of aggression or boredom, 236
 clinician loss of mentalizing capacity, 247
 comorbidity with chronic pain and fatigue, 234
 dynamic interpersonal therapy, 247–49
 MBT clinician (key task), 245
 mentalizing profiles, **235**
 mild to moderate, 245
 mild to moderate (Mark case study), **230**
 moderate to severe (Lucy case study), **231**
 moderate to severe (mentalization-based treatment), 245–47
 severe to very severe (Angela case study), **231**
 severity continuum, **232**, 249
 severity continuum (features), 230
 spectrum of mentalization-based interventions, 244–49
depression (mentalizing approach), 233–44
 attachment (role in co-regulation of stress), 237–39
 embodied mentalizing, 241–44
 epistemic trust, 244
 intervention to support mentalizing process and attachment strategies, 240–41
 mood and mentalizing, 233–37
depression treatment
 adaptations of MBT model, **233**
 mental-process and mental-representation approaches, **232**
depressive experiences, **232**
desistance, 174–75, 177, 184
 influences, 175
destructive action pathway, 119
detached protector mode
 definition, 225
developmental perspective, 158, 358
developmental stages, x, 338
 depression risk, 237
developmental theory, 323, 370
Developmentally Directed Time-Limited Psychotherapy for Children, 324
dialectical behavior therapy, 15, 27, 225, 364, 385
dis-integration
 AMBIT terminology, 354
dissociation, 14, 279, 293, 308
DIT. *See* dynamic interpersonal therapy
domestic violence, 62
dropouts, 225, 281, 298, 311, 385
drug addiction, 53
DSM, 155, 203, 253
dynamic interpersonal therapy, 231, 244
 depression, 247–49
 original model, 248
 phases, 248
dynamic interpersonal therapy for complex care (DITCC), 231, 245, 249
 extended DIT model, 248
Eating Disorder Examination, 29
eating disorders, xii, 298–318
 core, 304
 emotional self as core component, **307**
 epistemic mistrust model (summary), 308–9
 pathway, *304*
 persistence, 303–4
 social dysfunction, 304
 ultimately disorders of self-function, 314
Ebert A, 23
ecophenotype
 definition, 278
effective mentalizing, 341
 MBT for couples, 350
 underpinning, 345
egocentricity bias, 214, 216, 223
 abandonment requirements, 219
 inhibition, 220
ego-syntonicity, 310–11
Eisenberger NI, 24–25
elephant in room, 152, 171–72, 220, 299
 exploring affect focus, 103
 psychosis patients, 273
 shame, 188
embodied mentalizing, 72, 234, 239–40, 312
 depressed patients, 241–44
 eating disorders, 298
 RADLE sequence, **242**
emergency care, xii, 370, *See also* MBT-informed emergency care
 focus of interventions, 367
 formulation, 373
 mentalizing, 364–87
 psychoeducational elements, 379
 research under way, 386
emergency care (intake process), 373–80
 1. receiving request for hospitalization, 373–75
 2-3. initial meeting with patient and team debrief, 375–80
emergency care formulation, 382
 1. emergence of crisis, *382*, 382
 2. activating resources, 382

emergency care formulation (cont.)
  3. crisis plan, 383, *384*
  4. anticipating future treatment, 384
emergency care interviewing (five themes), 375–79
  1. introductions, 376
  2. exploration of crisis, 376
  3. contextualizing, 377
  4. experience in session, 377
  5. planning hospital stay and two-level contract, 379
emergency hospitalization
  admission to discharge (overview), *372*
emergency psychiatry
  sequence of unfolding crisis intervention, 371
emergency room visits, 28
emotional arousal, 23–24, 119, 216, 224
emotional dysregulation, 14, 19, 55, 127
  domain associated with mental disorder, 19
emotional intelligence, 25, 307
emotional regulation, 12, 84, 305
  strategies, **56**, 279, 288
emotional self, **307**
empathic emotional validation, 47, 83, 169
  components, 71
empathy, 7, 10, 25, 72, 113, 179, 323–24
employment, **193**, **262**
emptiness feelings, 55, 60
environmental factors, 254, 329
epistemic hypervigilance, 303–4, 308–11
epistemic match, 21, 26
epistemic mistrust
  definition, 22
  development, 22–24
  eating disorders, 308–9
epistemic trust, x, 17–21, 49, 103, 115, 153, 170, 172, 175, 216, 222, 225, 235, 238, 245, 248, 287, 343, 356, 376, 378, 385
  biobehavioral system, **279**
  definition, x–xi, 19
  depressed patients, 244
  dimensions, 22
  impairments, **232**
  MBT for couples, 351
  not-knowing stance, 269
  problems (trauma patients), 285
  systemic, 354
equity, 48–49, 129
  importance, 106
Euler S, 209, 212
everyday life, 155, 187
executive function
  definition, 19
  domain associated with mental disorder, 19
experts by experience, 180, 184, 186
  over-involvement, 185
exploring affect focus
  definition, 103
eye movements, 58, 151, 199

Facebook, 194
facial expressions, 7, 16–17, 22, 58, 151, 195, 199, 212, 214, 219, 322
false beliefs, 9–10
false self, 60, 158
families, xii, 340–46, *See also* MBT for families (MBT-F)
  mentalizing theory in wider contexts, 356–62
family communication, 344–45
Faux Pas test, 25
fear, 5, 190, 195
feeling finder game, 223
felt feelings, 290
fight/flight/freeze responses, 45, 282–83
first-order mentalizing, 131
first-person mentalizing, 215–16
Fonagy P, 2, 15, 19, 28, 69, 299, 302, 321, 347, 369–70
formulation, xi–xii, 138
  agreed treatment goals, **64**
  aims, 62
  anticipated treatment difficulties, **64**
  attachment styles, **64**
  central component of MBT, 115
  content, **63**
  definition, 62
  essential to be agreed with patient, 62
  focus on mental processes, 247
  language, 62
  MBT clinical process, 62–69
  mentalizing vulnerabilities and low-mentalizing modes, **64**
  overall, **63**
  resilience, **64**
  vulnerability factors, **63**
Fotopoulou A, 369
Freud A, 25
Freud S, 260
Frith U, 2
functional impairment
  psychosis patients, 264
functional magnetic resonance imaging (fMRI), 22, 211–12

general psychopathology factor (*p factor*), 17–20
genetic approach
  definition, 104
genetic factors, 18, 128
genetic risk, 18, 43
genetics, xii, 18, 254–55, 308, 329, 335
Global Assessment of Functioning, 28
Graham P, xiii
grandiose narcissism, 161, 166, **167**, 173, 192
  addressing interactive style, **160**
  characteristics, **156**
  same as "thick-skinned" narcissism, 156
Greiner C, 364
grey matter volume, 328
group leaders, 70
group therapy, 52, **66**, 268
group values, 150–51
  trauma patients, 289, 294
groups, xii
  aim, xi
  essential part of MBT, xi
groupthink, 197
guilt, 188, 236–37

high persistent psychological distress, 19
hippocampus, 235, 281

Hooley JM, 23
hospitalization, 28, 264, 364–65, 368, 371–72
housing, 179, 191–92
humiliation, 157, **168**, 192–93, 198, 201
humility, 243, 246
humor, 98, 222, 270
hyperactivation, 14, **162**
hyperarousal, 279, 282
hyperembodiment
  depressed patients, 234
hypermentalizing, 48, 90, 165, **209**, 211, 214, 217, 220, 224–25, 300, 306, **330**, **332**
  adolescents, 334–35
  block to progress, 218
  definition, 211
  depressed patients, 236–37
hyper-reflectivity, 261–62, 268, 273
  extreme form of pretend mode, 265
hypersensitivity, 11, 14, 16, 25, 157, 160, 240–41
hypervigilance, 279, 282, 285
hypoactivation, 162, 170
hypomentalizing, **209**, 211, 217, 220, 225, 246, 306
  definition, 211
  depressed patients, 236–37
hypothalamic–pituitary–adrenal (HPA) axis, 281–82

iatrogenic effects, 166, 244, 298, 314
ICD-11, 155, 203
identity, 174–75, 204, 311
identity affect, **313**
I-mode, 106–7, 158, 166–67, 169–70, 173, 183, 186, 218, 291
impersonal trauma, 278
impulsive behavior
  intervention algorithm, *130*
impulsivity, 15, 28, 53–55, 62, **122–23**, 140, 208, 328
individual therapy, 52, 268
ineffective mentalizing, 59, **131**, 159, 208, 225, 305
  eating disorders, 299–301
  hallmarks, 299
  key factor (eating disorders), 309

infancy, 334, 360
infants, 9, 12–13, 20, 101, 106, 370
inside-out mind, 68, 127, 179, 299
  characteristic, 83
intentional stance, 1–2
internet connections, 151
interpersonal affective focus, 247–48
  emphasis on content, 247
interpersonal context, 99–100, 127, 198, 214
interpersonal interactions, 15, 17, 43, 47, 55–56, 61, 123, 133, 215
interpersonal problems, 12, 14, 28, 54
interpersonal relationships, 44, 60, 205, 287
  trauma patients, 278, 288
interpersonal trust, 15, 101
interpretation
  definition, 108
intrapersonal functions, 119
IPAF. *See* interpersonal affective focus
irritation, 171

James RK, 365
James W, 213
jealousy, **333**, 343
Johnson S, 367

know and now mind, 83, 127

Lieb K, 2
Lighthouse project, 268
listening, x, **139**, **141–42**, 162–63, **165**, 172, **182**, 200, 291
London Parent–Child Project, 357
look, 200
  trigger for aggression and violence, 200
low mentalizing, 129, 341
  clinician intervention, 82–97
  pretend mode, 90–97
low mentalizing, 176, 181, 195, 208, 375, 377
Lysaker PH, 261

major depressive disorder, 17, 22, 116, 231
Malle BF, 8
Maresh EL, 213
marked mirroring, 101, 158, 235, 240–41, 243–44, 284–85, 323, 326, 331, 369
Maudsley Model of Anorexia Nervosa Treatment for Adults (MANTRA), 298
MBT. *See* mentalization-based treatment
MBT clinical process
  adaptations of MBT model, 117–34
  final phase, **53**
  formulation, 62–69
  general strategies, **52**
  individual sessions (structure), 71–113
  initial phase, **52**, 54–62
  MBT supervision, 113–17
  psychoeducation (MBT-I), 69–71
  at-risk patient, 117–34
  specific strategies, **53**
  step-by-step guide, 52–135
  treatment phase, **52**, 71–113
MBT clinical process (initial phase), 54–62
  assessment, 54–55
  assessment of mentalizing profile, 55–58
  attachment processes, 60–62
  ineffective mentalizing, 59–60
MBT for adolescents (key concepts), 330–35
  alien self, 334
  basic mentalizing, 333
  clarification, elaboration, challenge, 331
  hypermentalizing, 334
  mentalizing clinician–patient relationship, 334
  support and empathy, 331
MBT for adolescents (MBT-A), 328–39
  central focus, 333
  clinical example (Eddie), **329**, 334–35
  clinical example (Holly), **332**
  clinical example (Maya), 330, 333

MBT for adolescents (MBT-A) (cont.)
core (mentalizing stance), 331
empathic exploration, **332**
more research needed, 328
techniques, 331
MBT for adolescents (structure), 335–38
assessment, 335
final phase, 337
initial phase, 336–37
initial phase (clinical example), **336**
initial phase (contract), 337
initial phase (crisis plan), 336
initial phase (formulation), 336
initial phase (psychoeducation), 337
middle phase, 337
MBT for children (MBT-C), 319–27
aims, 319
Belinda case study, **320**
clarifying and naming feelings, 323
format, 319
mentalizing stance, 320–21
mirroring and contingent responding, 322
Mohammed case study, **320**, 322
responding to breakdowns in mentalizing, 323
right intervention at right moment, 322
therapeutic contract, 319
time and use of a calendar, 324
MBT for children (play-centered approach), 321–22
mentalizing play, 321
problems with symbolic play, 322
stimulating play narrative, 321
MBT for children (structure), 324–26
assessment phase (3–4 meetings), 324
developing a formulation, 325
review meeting, 325
sessions 1–3 (initial phase), 325
sessions 4–8 (middle phase), 325
sessions 9–12 (ending phase), 326
MBT for couples (intervention spectrum), 350–52
challenge and therapeutic bargain, 351
clarification, affect focus, elaboration, 350
empathy, support, validation, 350
repairing mentalizing and epistemic trust, 351
MBT for couples (MBT-CO), 347–52
central tenet, 349
clinical example, **348**
formulation, 348
relationship quality (initial assessment), 347
MBT for couples (structure), 347–50
highlighting and marking mentalizing, 350
holding balance, 349
interrupting non-mentalizing, 349
mentalizing stance, 349
MBT for eating disorders (MBT-ED), 298–318
MBT for eating disorders (treatment model), 309–15
focus, 310
formulation, 312
general approach, 309–11
group therapy, 314
individual therapy, 313–14
Mary case study, **313**
psychoeducational groups, 314
MBT for families (MBT-F), 340–46
clinical example (mind-reading stethoscope exercise), **345**
exercises, 342–46
key objective, 340
MBT loop, 341–42
mentalizing stance, 340
purpose, 340
task of clinician, 341
MBT for trauma, 286–88
core feature, 286
crucial consideration, 287
essential component (supervision), 287
general principles, 286–87
key to process, 287
mentalizing traumatic experiences, 288
specific principles, 287–88
specific principles (summary), **288**
MBT Group, x, 52, 69, 136–53, 294
collaborative and democratic process, 142
macro versus micro culture, 136
mentalizing culture (components), 137
online, 150–52
session trajectory, *137*
structure, 136–37
values, 137
MBT Group (clients with ASPD), 183–201
agreed values, 185
Bryan case study, **180–81**, **186–87**
discussion of values before entry to group, 182
engagement in treatment, 179
format of treatment, 178
MBT-I for MBT-ASPD-G, 183–84
meeting an expert by experience, 185
preparation, 178–81
randomized control trial (in progress), 201
self-agency, 186–90
structure of group, 185–90
treatment process (summary), 179
MBT Group (clients with ASPD) (common clinical problems), 190–201
clinician reponses, 192–93, 195, 197–201
defiance, 193
emotional expression (self), 198
emotion recognition in other (misused), 199

escalating threats (client to client), 194
escalating threats (client to clinician), 196
examples, 191
idealization of themselves as group, 197
moving external mental focus to internal focus (other), 199
paranoid reactions, 200
paranoid reactions (clinician options), 201
recruitment to cause, 191
MBT Group (engaging new patient), 138–41
1. clinician introduces members to new patient, 138
2. personal introductions (prepared week before) delivered, 138–39
3. discussion of group values, 140
MBT Group (members)
Cora, **140**, **143**, **145**, 148
John, **141**, **143**, **145**, 147
Stanley, **145**, **147**, 147, **151**
MBT Group (stimulating interpersonal mentalizing), 141–48
allocation of protagonists of discussion, **142**
closure, 147–48
purpose of group, 142
role play and exercises, 146–47
triangulation leading to four-way (or more) interaction, 143–44
MBT Group online
individual therapy, 152
MBT Introductory Group (MBT-I), x, 26, 69–71, 103, 127, 136, 198
format, 69
goals (important factors), 69
not-knowing stance, **78**
online, 149
purpose, 69
role of group leader, 70
session principles, 70
session structure, 70
topics, 70
MBT Introductory Group for MBT-ASPD-G
attachment module, 184
emotions module, 184
mentalizing modules, 183
violence module, 184
MBT Loop, 83, **125**, 180, 193, 201
families, 341–42
three-step maneuver, 83
MBT online, 148–53
assessment and formulation, 149
MBT-G online, 150–52
MBT-I online, 149
secure links, 149
MBT patient
typical (moderately responsive), xi
MBT principles, 136
equality between patients and clinicians, 153
openness of mind, 271
MBT supervision, 113–17
ensuring mentalizing theory links to clinical practice, 115
essential topics, **114**
implementation and clinical structures, 113
maintaining mentalizing of clinician, 116–17
skill in itself, 117
supervisor materials, 114
supporting refining of clinical skills, 115–16
tasks, **113**
MBT supervisor
role, 113, 115, 117
MBT-ASPD-G. *See* MBT Group (clients with ASPD)
MBT-G. *See* MBT Group
MBT-I. *See* MBT Introductory Group
MBT-informed emergency care
clinical approach, 370–73
criteria for admission, **371**
four-step model, 364
from epistemic trust to mentalizing crisis, 370–73
summary, 372
MBT-informed emergency care (four steps), 373–85
1. intake and admission into emergency care, 373–79
2. uncovering crisis, 380–82
3. integration and formulation of crisis area, 382–84
4. preparation for discharge, 385
MBT-NPD. *See* MBT for narcissistic personality disorder
MBT-Trauma Focused (MBT-TF), xii, 278, 288–94
phase 1 (establishing safety, group values, treatment framework), 289
phase 2 (mentalizing trauma), 290–94
phase 3 (review, reappraisal, looking to future), 294
medial prefrontal cortex (mPFC), 9, 213–14, 235, 281, 328
mediation techniques, 268, 270
Meehl P, 254
me-mode, 159, 166–67, 169, 173, 181, 183, 186, 213, 215, **218**, 224, 291
memory, 16, 18, 84, 186, 223, 292–94
mental disorder, 18
defining feature, 4
mentalizing model, ix
no single cause, x
mental escape procedure, 118
mental health disorders
neuroscience (implication of two domains of functioning), 19
vulnerability (flipside of advantages of mentalizing), 4
mental health professionals, 12, 370, 374
MBT skills, 372
mental states, 1, 3, 5, 10, 48, 50, 109, 166, 192, 210
detailed consideration phase (by clinician), 98
processing, 48
mentalization-based treatment, ix
adaptations for mental health presentations, 155–73
aim, 129

mentalization-based treatment (cont.)
application (settings), 319–27
backbone, 157
central question, 29
clinical principles, x
clinician requirements, xi
Cochrane Review (2020), 27
collaborative discovery, 78, 107
communication systems, 26–27
constellation of interventions, 44
core processes, 208
defining principle, 68
democracy principle, 103
developmental approach, 253
effectiveness (much further to go), ix
empirical research, 27–29
essence, 107
focus on mentalizing process, 48
general versus specific (balance), x
history, 1–3
model overview, 1–3
non-judgmental stance, 157
origins, 2, 14
planning of supervision sessions, 114
play-centered approach, 321–22
practice, 136–53
pragmatism, 2
primary objective, 44
prime idea, 2
psychoanalytic origins, 310
psychotherapy paradox, 44
purpose, ix
RCTs, 27–29
rejects notion of objectivity in therapeutic setting, 109
research trials, 54
safety first (do no harm) approach, 166
starting point for clinician, 175
supporting theory, 4–41
transdiagnostic approach, xii

mentalization-based treatment (principle-driven intervention), 44–50
activate relational process, 46
authenticity and "not-knowing" stance, 50
balance mentalizing, 46
democracy, equity, collaboration, 48–49
empathic validation of impact of experience, 47
manage anxiety, 45
process versus content, 47

mentalization-based treatment (principles)
emotions and mentalizing, **45**
mentalizing focus, **45**
responsiveness of clinician, **45**

mentalized affectivity
definition, 285

mentalizing
arriving at alternative perspective, 107
basic techniques, 242
and BPD, 15–17
center of everything MBT clinician does, xi
clinician required to see things from patient's perspective, xi
clinician–patient relationship, 323
developmental aspects (child, adolescent, adult), 8–10
developmental model, 334
difficulties, 8
emergence (impact of environment), 10–12
emergency care, 364–87
essence, 70
external versus internal (families), 341
fragile capacity, 356
integrative function, 301–2
interpersonal understanding lens, xi
journey, not destination, 78, 104, 127
MBT for couples, 351
openness to different perspectives, 48
origin of term, 2
psychopathology, 17–19
purpose, 333
qualities and behaviors, 340
social learning and epistemic trust, 17–21
social rejection, 24–25
understanding feelings, 2

mentalizing affective narrative, 127
content, *98*

mentalizing capacity, 9, **279**
mentalizing climate, 12, 355
mentalizing dimensions, 6–8, 46, 55, **64**, 209, 349
automatic/controlled mentalizing, 6, 15, 57–58
cognitive/affective mentalizing, 7, **56**, 235, 241, 263, 273
internal/external mentalizing, 7, 16, 57–58
self/other mentalizing, 6, 16, **56**, 68, 79, 103–4, 273

mentalizing foci for self (Maresh and Andrews-Hanna), 213

mentalizing functional analysis, 125–28, **126**, **128**, 131, 351, 376
a. focus on affect and contextualizing emotions, 126
b. management of mind states, 127
c. identification of core domain of problem, 127
d. establishing dominant theme, 128
e. respect for subdominant theme, 128

mentalizing impairments, **232**, 240, 245, 266, 279, 281, 312
role in depression, 238

mentalizing in eating disorders, 298–309
anorexia nervosa (persistence), 303–4
attachment and eating disorders, 305
conceptualizing complexity, 304–5
embodied mentalizing, 298
ineffective mentalizing modes, 299–301
social self-regulation, 307

stress and mentalizing, 302
theory of mind and social cognition, 306–7
wish for non-mentalizing space, 301–2
mentalizing polarities. *See* mentalizing dimensions
mentalizing process management, 77–79
mentalizing profile, 55–58
mentalizing relationship. *See* relational mentalizing
mentalizing theory, 303, 369
origins in psychoanalysis, 6
mentalizing trauma, 290–94
affective reflection, 290
feelings and thoughts surrounding trauma, 290–93
framework, **291**
relationships affected by trauma, 293
mental-process focus, 244, 248
mental-representation focus, 238, 241, 244–45, 248
mentors, 356
meta-analyses, 15–17, 27, 230, 305, 307
metacognition, 99, 131, 158, 261
metacognitive disorganization, **56**
metacognitive interpersonal therapy (MIT), 224–25
meta-reflection
definition, 290
meta-therapeutic
definition, 98
micro-slicing, 241–43, 287–88
Midgley N, 319–22
example of focus formulation, 324
Miller CE, 55
Mills KL, 328
mind, 1–2
mind recalibration, 284–85, 287
mind states, 46, 53
mind-brain scans, 221, 343
Minding the Baby, 356, 360–62
emphasis, 361
integrative model, 361
interdisciplinary approach, 361
nurse's role, 361
primary focus, 361
RCT, 361
social worker involvement, 361
mind-reading stethoscope (MBT-F exercise), 345
mind-wandering, 16, 18
minimal impact resilience, 278
mood, 54, 236
mother–child relationship, 60
mothers, 12
anxiety level (impact on children), 26
Movie for the Assessment of Social Cognition (MASC), 15
MTB. *See* Minding the Baby

narcissism
aspects, 155
attributes, 155
relational activation, **159**
thick-skinned versus thin-skinned, 156
narcissistic personality disorder, xi, 143, 155–73
assessment and formulation, **166**
dismissive attachment strategies (indicators), **162**
formulation, 164, 169
intervention (I-mode to me-mode to we-mode), **167**
James case study, 167, **168**, **172**
outcome of assessment process, 163–64
outcome of assessment process (James case study formulation), **164**
outcome of assessment process (James case study), **163**
research lacking, 155
narcissistic personality disorder (assessment and formulation), 157–62
grandiose narcissism (interactive style), **160**
narcissism and attachment strategies, **162**
narcissistic activation (context), 159
narcissistic expectation and disappointment, 160
self and other mentalizing, 158
self-expectation, self-devaluation (thin-skinned narcissism), **161**
narcissistic personality disorder (mentalizing)
automatic and controlled processing, **165**
cognitive and affective function, **165**
relationships, **165**
self and other experience, **164**
narcissistic personality disorder (session focus and intervention), 166–73
affect focus and narcissism, 171
counter-relational mentalizing, 171
elephants in room, 171–72
I-mode to me-mode to we-mode, 169–71
relational mentalizing, 169–71
supporting narcissism to establish alliance, 167
narcissistic personality functioning, 155, 158, 160, 163
links with ASPD and BPD, 174
session focus and intervention, 166–73
natural selection, 4, 20
Netherlands, 28
network analysis, 306
neural circuits, 7, 235, 237
neuroscience, 4, 10, 19, 213, 235, 369
disconnects between sensory and cognitive integration, 263
psychosis patients, 261
neurotransmitter systems, 282
Nizum N, 367
non-judgmentalism, 99, 163, 188–89, 320, 323, 331, 341, 349
non-mentalizing, 129, 131, 174, 184, 245, **330**
couples, 352
eating disorders, 308
interruption, 341, 349

non-mentalizing (cont.)
 quick reference, **59**
 verbal indicators, 132
non-mentalizing modes, 4–5, 59, **71**, 330, 347
 clinical examples, **300–2**
 eating disorders, 301–2
 pretend mode, 5
 psychic equivalence, 5
 psychosis patients, 271–72
 teleological mode, 5
Norway, 28
notice and name, 83, 219
not-knowing, 50, 70–71, **72**, 80, 104, 115, 125, 129, 137, 141, 144, 146, 151, 153, 163, 171, 180, 189, 207–8, 217, 224–25, 242, 244
 aim, 77
 burden on clincian, 269
 emergency care, 376–77
 essence (process of discovery), 79
 identification of strategies for tolerating mental turmoil, 103
 key points, **269**
 MBT for children, 322
 psychosis patients, 269
 purpose, 77
 trauma patients, 287
 treatment phase, 77–79
NPF. *See* narcissistic personality functioning

Orme W, 22
ostension
 definition, 304
outpatient treatment, 28, 364
outside-in mind, **65–66**, 68, 80, 83, 127, 179, 299
 at-risk patient, 119
over-imitation, 20
 definition, 20
Overt Aggression Scale – Modified, 184
oxytocin, 23

p factor, 216, *See* general psychopathology factor
panic, 261, **329**
paranoid thinking, 265
Parent Map, 357–58
Parenting APP, 357
parent-o-scopes (MBT-F exercise), 345
parents, 11–12, 22, 162, 330, 336–37, 341, 344–45
 mentalizing capacities, 13
 mentalizing theory in wider contexts, 356–62
 psychoeducation, 358
passivity, 71, 79
patients
 conversational partners, 53
 mentalization-based treatment, 43–51
 reflection versus reaction (double-edged sword), 77
patients' notes, 152
patterns of mutual regulation, 106
peer acceptance, 356
peer mentorship (CAPSLE), 355
Pennebaker JW, 298
perception, 263
personal narratives, 102
personal second-order mentalizing, 7, 131
Personality Belief Questionnaire, 22
personality disorders, xii, 17, 245
 categorization failure, 174
philosophy, **165**
physical education programme (CAPSLE), 355
physical reality, 5, **58**, 148, 157, 214–15, 224, 300
playfulness, 146, 223, 226, 268, 270, 345
 essential component of MBT, 343
poor urban communities, 12
positive climate campaign (CAPSLE), 355
post-traumatic stress disorder, 25, 54, 178, 216, 277, *280*
power differentials, 48–49
Prada P, 364
prefrontal cortex, 18, 22, 281
pregnancy, 11
pre-mentalizing, 5, 8, 370
pretend mode, 5, 48, **59–60**, 60, 62, **64**, 78, 90–97, 126, **147**, 152, 155–57, 162, 176–77, 183, 189, 191, 197, 207–8, 211, 215, 217, 247, 268, 293
 anxiety (after bubble popped), 97
 clinical example, **300**
 clinician's response, 91
 dangers, 97
 depressed patients, 236, 240
 eating disorders, 300, 303, 308, **313**, 314
 hypermentalizing, 222
 patient's purpose, 91
 result, 91
 trauma patients, 284
pretend we-mode, 170
primates, 9, 20
priors, 263
pseudomentalizing, 5, 239, 246, 300, 332, 334
psychiatric care
 relative criteria, **371**
 strong criteria, **371**
psychiatric disorders, 18
psychiatric emergency care, 364–65, 368, 386
psychic equivalence, 5, 59, **59**, 62, **64**, 68, **72**, 72, 78, 119, 126–27, 130–31, **131–32**, 155–57, 165, **168**, 176, 179, 183, 190, 217, 220, 223, 233, 238, 247, 265, 375
 adolescents, 333–34
 alien self, 368
 AvPD "extreme form", 215
 characteristics, 246
 clinical example, **299**
 couples, **348**
 definition, 5
 depressed patients, 234, 236, 240
 eating disorders, 299, 303, 308, 310
 quick reference, **59**
 trauma patients, 283–84, 290
psychodynamic therapy, 2, 104, 225
psychoeducation, 69–71, 103, 236, 256, 260, 268, 274, 286
 emergency care, 383
 family session, 337
 MBT for trauma, 287
 trauma patients, 289

psychological crisis, 364
  characteristics, **366**
  definition from patient's perspective (MBT approach), 365
  four steps (post-hospitalization), 370
  Jill case study, **366**, 371–73, **374**
  Jill case study (exploration of crisis), **377**
  Jill case study (first meeting with emergency team), 375–80
  narrative, 372
  relief, 365
  triggers, 366
  working definition, 365–68
psychology, 163, **165**, 170
psychopathology, 8, 17–19, 209, 213, 353
  characteristics, 245
  transdiagnostic indicator, 216
psychosis, xii, 17, 231, 245, 253–76
  clinical deactivation, 264
  common leitmotif, 261
  continuum of severity, 263
  first diagnosis, 256
  further research required, 274
  hallmark (dissociation), 266
  hospitalization, 254–55, **257**, 259
  information processing biases, 266
  phenomenological accounts, 261
  premorbid stage, 255
  treatment structuring, **269**
  usage, 253
psychosis (key elements of MBT practice), 267–74
  affective narrative, 273
  Johanna case study, **271–72**
  mentalizing clinician–patient relationship, 274
  mentalizing process, 270–71
  non-mentalizing (framework for clinical intervention), *272*
  non-mentalizing modes, 271–72
  not-knowing stance, 269
  treatment and session structure, 267–68
psychosis (MBT clinical approach), 253–60
  assessing developmental stage of illness, 255
  clinical actions required, 254
  formulating concrete treatment goals, 258–60
  identifying social resources within treatment, 257–58
  key assumption, 266
  main point, 260
  Robert case study, **254**, **257–58**, **270–71**
  staging, 260
psychosis (MBT-informed understanding), 260–67
  clinical example, **262**
  clinical presentations, 264–65
  core self-disturbance (link to non-mentalizing modes), 265–67
  from neuroscience to consulting room, 261–64
  psychosis and mentalizing (historical links), 260–61
psychosis (mentalizing process)
  critical aspect, 271
  group setting, **270**
  individual setting, **270**
  key points, **271**
  psychoeducational setting, **270**
psychosis patients
  elephant in room, 273
  memories of kindness shown, 265
  non-mentalizing modes, *265*, 271
  psychoeducational groups, 268
  sensory-cognitive disconnect, 266
psychotherapy, 15, 115–16, 230, 256
  essence, 103
  generalist approach, x
  inherently relational, 44
  time-honored method, 148
psychotic disorders
  usage, 253
quality of life, 27, 29, 127, 252, 257–58

RADLE sequence, **242**
  1. recognizing emotions, 242
  2. amplifying emotions, 243
  3. differentiating emotions, 243
  4. linking emotions, 243
  5. emotional cost, 243
randomized control trials, 27, 298, 315
  mentalization-based treatment, 27–29
Reading the Mind in the Eyes, 17, 328
real world, 5, **142**, 148
reciprocal adjustments, 106
Reflective Fostering, 356, 358–60
Reflective Fostering Programme, 359
  design, 359
  facilitators, 360
  focus, 359
  group-based, 359
  pilot programme, 359
  RCT (in progress), 360
  sessions, 360
  tools, 359–60
reflective functioning, 1, 11, 15, 209–10, 245, 321, 357
  identical to "mentalizing", 357
Reflective Functioning Questionnaire for Youth, 335
Reflective Functioning Scale, 357
Reflective Parenting, 356
  aims, 358
  definition, 357
  emphasis, 357
  group sessions (core objective), 358
  innovative approach, 357
  key role of self-mentalizing, 357
  tools, 357
Reflective Self-Function Scale, 357
rejection, 204, 206, 240
rejection sensitivity, 17, 23, 25, 53, **57**, **123**
relational activation, **159**

relational mentalizing, 100, 103–8, 152, 169, 220–22, 231, 241
  components, 103
  depressed patients, 238
  quintessential intervention to activate we-mode, 103
  series of steps, 104
  shorthand term, 108
relational passport, 139, **139**, 150
relational referencing, 284
resilience, **64**, 98, 129, 234, 308, 351, 356, 361, 377
  absence, 278
respect, **140**, 141, 164, 170, **182**, 185
revictimization, 284
rewind and reflect technique, 351
RFP. *See* Reflective Fostering Programme
ridicule, 215, 222
risk, 55, 121, 364
  clinical intervention process (summary), **117**
  mentalizing understanding, *117*
Risk-Taking and Self-Harm Inventory, 29
Robinson EA, 160
Robinson P, 311
role play, 115, 217, 220–21, 223, 355
  MBT-F exercise, 344
romantic relationships, 285
  interpersonal trust (BPD individuals versus control group), 23
Rossouw T, 331, 336
Rubber Hand Illusion, 16
rumination, 235–36, 284

SAD. *See* social anxiety disorder
safety learning, 26
safety planning, 121
Safier E, 347
Sahi RS, 24
salutogenesis, 240, 247–48, 381
  definition, 285
  trauma patients, 288
Sarah case study, x–xi, 53
  action person and outside-in mind, **65**
  assessment of mentalizing profile, **55–58**
  attachment processes, **62**
  basic information, **53**
  contrary moves, 79
  counter-relational mentalizing, **109**
  cycle of problems, *67*
  elephant in room, **102**
  formulation, **65**
  group learning, xi
  know and now mind, 65
  MBT, **66**
  MBT Loop, **84**
  mentalizing affective narrative, **98–100**
  non-mentalizing modes/ineffective mentalizing, **59–60**
  not-knowing and managing mentalizing process, 78–79
  pretend mode, **96–97**
  problems, **65**
  relational mentalizing, **104**, **107**
  relationship with son (Jack), **81**
  relationships, **66**
  at-risk patient (clinical intervention process), **120**, **122**, **124**, 126, **128**, **130–31**
  strengths, **65**
  treatment aims, **66**
  treatment phase (empathic validation, clarification, elaboration of experience), **71**
  wellness (context), 125
Sarah case study (MBT Group), 137, **147**
  allocation of protagonists of discussion, **143**
  first session, **139**
  group purpose, **142**
  group values, **140**
  online, **151**
  preparation of group for entry of new patient, **139**
  triangulation, **145**
schema-focused therapy (SFT), 224–25
schizophrenia, 25, 253
  basis, 261
schizotypy, 255
Schmidt U, 298, 305
school environment, 356
sculptures (MBT-F exercise), 344
secondary attachment strategies, 282, 294
secondary representations, 10, 335
self and other, 9, 209
self representation, **218**
self-agency, 186–90
  1. I-mode to me-mode, 186
  2. recognition of others' emotional states, 187
  3. working with shame as problematic emotion, 188–89
  4. future self, 189
  5. pretend mode, 189
  6. working with anger as problematic emotion, 190
self-awareness, 9, 237
self-compassion, 129, 189, 273
self-criticism, 71, 131, 189, 235–36
self-devaluation, **161**
self-esteem, 155, 157–58, **159**, 160–61, **166**, 181, 183, 190, 193, 204
  threats, 176
self-expectation, **159**, **161**
self-experience, **56**, 57, 59, **72**, 158, **159**, **164**, 188, 210, 213, 221, **313**
self-harm, 12, 14, 29, 52, 116–17, 127, **131**, **133**, 190, 231, 245, 266, **277**, 285, 328, **332**, 335
  adolescents (clinical example), **336**
  can be experienced as relief, 302
  function, 119
  patient's unwillingness to discuss, 129
  simplified summary, 118–20
self-harm enquiries
  before event, **121**
  clinical top tip, **122**
  event itself, **118**
  fact-finding, **121–22**, 123
  following event, **122**
self-identity, 328
  threats, 176
self-image, **166**

self-injury, 17, 28, 121, 129
self-perception, 24, 213, 223
self-regulation, 9, 19, 305, 309, 328
self-representations, 10, 166, 210
sense of self, 10, 13, 21, 73, 119, 126, **128**
sexual abuse, 11, 73, 321
shame, 131, 157, **168**, 178, 184, 192–93, 198, 201, 210–11, 221, 236–37, 284
 activation, 176–77
 clients with ASPD, 188
 eating disorders, 304, 308
 elephant in room, 188
 multifaceted emotion, 188
 prototypical events, 189
 trauma patients, 293
shame–pride cycle, 309
Sharp C, 334
siding, 196, 199
Simonsen S, 209, 212
Skårderud F, 311
sleep, 282
social anxiety disorder, 17, 24, 204, 212, 214–15, **329**, 334
social cognition, x, 6, 10, 15–16, 21, 34–35, 303, 305, 328
 definition, 18
 eating disorders, 306–7
social context, ix, 12, 175, 208, 264, 308–9
 neuro-economic tasks, 22
social environment, 178, 282, 310, 326, 356
social exclusion, 15–17, 38, 53, 179, **301**, 306, 308
social interaction, 22, 115, 213
social learning, 17–21, 26–27, 52, 179
 application in wider environment, 27
social media, **329**
social mentalizing
 foundations, 173
social network, 12, 175, 294, 304, 381
social perception, **300**
social rejection, 24–25, 188
 implicated in psychiatric disorders, 24
social self, **307**
social self-regulation, xii, 311–12
 eating disorders, 307
 emotional self as core component of eating disorders, **307**
social sensitivity, 9, 47
social withdrawal, 188, 205, 303–4, 308–9, 314
social world, x, 3–4, 20, 29, 55, 174, 176, 202, 215, 217, 334
somatic disorders, 282
somatic markers of emotions, 242
stabbings, 191–92
stepping into someone else's shoes (MBT-F exercise), 343
Stone MH, 2
stop and rewind, 242, 247, 323
Strange Stories task, 25
stress, 12, 68, 129, 174, 234, 237–39, 281–83
 eating disorders, 302
stress system, **279**, 281
subdominant narratives, 102–3
substance abuse, 15, 54
subtle challenges, 194
suicidal ideation, 117, 121, 129, 258, 366
suicidality, 12, 52, 129, 149, 171, 245, 334–35, 368
suicide, 14, 231, 234, 236
suicide attempts, 13, 28, 116–17, 121, 127, 266, 369
 clinical example (Jill), **366**
 generic MBT intervention process applies, 118
 patient's unwillingness to discuss, 129
 simplified summary, 118–20
suicide risk, 278, 364, 368, 385
supervision. *See also* MBT supervision
 central part of MBT, 224
supervisors, 126
support, 323–24

Target M, 302, 321
TAU. *See* treatment as usual
teasing, 10, 306
telehealth, 148
teleological mode, 5, **59**, 60, 62, **64**, 68, **72**, 80, 123, 126–27, 155, 157, 176, 179, 183, 192, 225, 231, 238, 247, 375
 adolescents, 334
 at-risk patient, 119
 clinical example, **301**
 couples, **348**
 depressed patients, 236, 240
 eating disorders, 300, 303
 trauma patients, 284–85
Theory of Mind, 1–2, 4, 9–10, 228, 305
 eating disorders, 306–7
therapeutic alliance, 44, 69, 97, 149, 163, 166–67, 173, 180, 196, 231, 281, 325
therapeutic games, 220–23, 226, 268
 benefits for clinician, 222
therapeutic relationship, 211, 225, 233, 241, 246
 depressed patients, 238
 mentalizing, 247
thick-skinned narcissism, 163
thin-skinned narcissism, 163
 self-expectation and self-devaluation, **161**
third-person perspective, 215–16, 220
threats to self, 233
time, 324, 365, 368
toddlers, 8, 10
tone of voice, 58, 159, 177, 195, 219, 322
trait inference, 9
transdiagnostic approach, ix–x
transference tracers
 definition, 103
trauma, 11, 13, 277–97, 326, 369
 best considered as transdiagnostic factor, 277
 developmental approach, 26
 high rates of comorbidity, 278
 Lydia case study, **277**, 285–86, **292**
 mentalization-based treatment, 286–88
 mentalizing, xii, 25–26, **279**
 re-enactment cycles, *280*
 thought avoidance, 293
 types, *278*

trauma (cont.)
typical features (clinical expression), **280**
underlying biobehavioral systems, *281*
trauma (mentalizing perspective), 278–86
epistemic trust (problems), 285
stress and attachment, 281–83
trauma and mentalizing, 283–85
trauma continuum, 278
trauma memories, 83, 283
Treasure J, 305
treatment as usual, 27–29
treatment phase (MBT clinical process), 71–113
contrary moves, 79–82
counter-relational mentalizing, 108–13
creating compassionate story, 97–101
elephant in room, **120**, **126**, 128, 130
elephant in room (exploring affect focus), 102–3
empathic validation, clarification, elaboration of experience, 71–73
low mentalizing (clinician intervention), 82–97
mentalizing affective narrative, 97–101
not-knowing and managing the mentalizing process, 77–79
relational mentalizing, 103–8
tree of social cognition, 8–9
triangulation, 146–48
clinical example, **144**
trust, 29, 115, 183, 189
BPD, 21–25
trust game, 23
Trust Scenario Questionnaire, 22
trusted friend, 101
Tsakiris M, 369
twins, 18

United States, 2
University College London, xiii

validation of feelings
MBT for trauma, 287
values sheet, 141, 148
video, 115, 223
violence, 12, 117, 175, 178–79, **180**, 183–84, 190, 200
mentalizing, 175–78
simplified summary, 118–20
virtual and digital health (online MBT), 148–53
vulnerable narcissism, 157, **159**, 166, **167**, 172
same as thin-skinned narcissism, 156
vulnerable self, 148

we-mode, 46, 50, 66, 98, 100, 102–4, 106, 108, **120**, 136, 142–43, 148, 152, 166–67, 169–70, 173, 178, 183, 185, 189, 222, 286, 290, 356
definition, 21, 107
entry point, not end of process, 107
WhatsApp, 194
Winnicott DW, 60, 370
working formulation, 67–68, 71
worthlessness, 210

young adulthood, 9, 16

Zeegers MAJ, 11

Printed in the USA
CPSIA information can be obtained
at www.ICGtesting.com
CBHW061455240924
14861CB00003B/143